# The Pit

*Transcend Money, Heal the World*

Travis Ruhland

FIRST ASCENSION BOOKS EDITION, MAY 2021


Published in the United States by Ascension Books, Wisconsin.

Library of Congress Cataloging-in-Publication Data

Travis Ruhland.
The pit : transcend money, heal the world / Travis Ruhland.
LCCN: 2021908396 (print) | ISBN: 978-1-7371328-2-0

*The Pit* web address: https://www.bookthepit.com/

Printed in the United States of America.

1 2 3 4 5 6 24 23 22 21

# DEDICATION

To Kaitlyn Julia Zolper, of course!

# TABLE OF CONTENTS


| | | |
|---|---|---|
| 1 | SEEDS OF DELUSION (PREFACE) | 1 |
| 2 | THE APPETIZER (INTRODUCTION) | 12 |
| 3 | MONEY'S PURPOSE | 19 |
| 4 | BIRD'S-EYE VIEW OF THE PIT | 28 |
| 4.1 | THOUGHT EXPERIMENT | 35 |
| 4.2 | COMPANY TOWNS | 54 |
| 4.3 | LIES AND WAR | 58 |
| 4.4 | COMPETITION BE DAMNED | 63 |
| 4.5 | DEMOCRACY? | 65 |
| 5 | GRAND MAESTER: THE "FEDERAL" RESERVE | 74 |
| 5.1 | A BRIEF HISTORY OF THE FED'S RISE TO POWER | 87 |
| 5.2 | CHAPTER CONCLUSION | 105 |
| 6 | MONEY: THE ULTIMATE PRECONDITION FOR NEGATIVE OUTCOMES | 107 |
| 6.1 | CHILDHOOD POVERTY: THE GREATEST TRAGEDY ON EARTH | 110 |
| 6.2 | ECOLOGICAL DEGRADATION | 122 |
| 6.3 | EXPLOITING POOR PEOPLE DOMESTICALLY AND INTERNATIONALLY | 136 |
| 6.4 | WAR: TRADING RED FOR GREEN | 147 |
| 6.4B | BULLYING THE LITTLE KIDS ON THE PLAYGROUND | 159 |
| 6.5 | CRIME | 163 |
| 6.6 | TRUST: THERE'S A PILL FOR THAT | 175 |
| 6.7 | CHAPTER CONCLUSION | 205 |
| 7 | EFFICIENCY: A MONETARY SYSTEM'S GREATEST ENEMY | 210 |
| 7.1 | SNAKE HOLES ON THE CLIMB | 228 |
| 7.2 | TECHNOLOGICAL UNEMPLOYMENT: BEWARE, BEWARE, BEWAAAARE | 235 |
| 8 | LAISSEZ-FAIRE CAPITALISM: A GAME WITHOUT REFS | 245 |

| | | |
|---|---|---|
| 8.1 | INVENTIONS AND INNOVATIONS | 264 |
| 8.2 | PRIVATE SCHOOLS: PUNISHING POOR CHILDREN | 269 |
| 8.3 | PRIVATIZING MILITARY: INCENTIVIZING CONFLICT | 273 |
| 8.4 | NATIONAL PARKS, POWER COMPANIES, ROADS, POLICE | 276 |
| 8.5 | CHAPTER CONCLUSION | 283 |
| 9 | HUMAN MOTIVATION: WHAT THE HECK WOULD WE DO ALL DAY WITHOUT MONEY | 285 |
| 10 | THE ANSWER | 323 |
| 10.1 | BASIC DESIGN | 341 |
| 10.2 | RESOURCE MANAGEMENT | 344 |
| 10.3 | FOOD | 346 |
| 10.4 | WATER | 351 |
| 10.5 | ENERGY | 352 |
| 10.5A | GEOTHERMAL | 354 |
| 10.5B | SOLAR | 355 |
| 10.5C | WIND | 357 |
| 10.5D | WATER | 359 |
| 10.5E | NUCLEAR POWER | 359 |
| 10.6 | TRANSPORTATION | 362 |
| 10.7 | HOME & BUILDING CONSTRUCTION | 367 |
| 10.8 | EDUCATION | 371 |
| 10.9 | HEALTHCARE | 377 |
| 10.10 | ADDITIONAL FEATURES | 384 |
| 10.11 | ADDRESSING RATIONAL CONCERNS | 387 |
| 10.11A | CONCERN #1 – TECHNOLOGY = CONTROL | 387 |
| 10.11B | CONCERN #2 – SOCIALISM/COMMUNISM/ MARXISM | 389 |
| 10.11C | CONCERN #3 – NEW WORLD ORDER | 393 |
| 10.11D | CONCERN #4 – THE BIBLE/REVELATIONS | 394 |
| 10.11E | CONCERN #5 – CULT | 394 |
| 10.11F | CONCERN #6 – TRAVIS MAKING MONEY | 396 |
| 10.12 | THE TRANSITION | 396 |
| 11 | B-YUP, B-YUP, THAT'S ALL FOLKS | 402 |
| | APPENDIX A – WAR | 405 |
| | APPENDIX B – MASLOW'S HIERARCHY OF NEEDS | 410 |

# 1 SEEDS OF DELUSION (PREFACE)

"A dead thing can go with the stream, but only a living thing can go against it."[1] – G.K. Chesterton

It all started with an itch. An idea.

I slothed into my 9 AM Macroeconomics class with heavy eyes, a red face, and watery snot threatening to escape my nose. It was February 2008 in Wisconsin after all, which meant testicle-shrinking cold and, in that particular winter, a relentless pummeling of snow. The walk from my dorm to the business hall was not a long one; nevertheless, I could not evade the effects of the sub-zero temperatures.

Professor Harper walked through the classroom door as I shoved a wad of Kleenex up my left nostril to dam the flow of mucus. "Good morning, everybody," the professor said.

As he set his things on his desk, I opened my Macroeconomics book to the chapter about the Law of Supply and Demand, as indicated by our syllabus. The first thing I saw on the first page was a rudimentary Supply/Demand graph. In an attempt to seem somewhat knowledgeable just in case I was called upon during lecture, I quickly skimmed the material. *Ok, ok, when Demand increases, Supply decreases. Got it! But wait…if Demand increases, wouldn't manufacturers increase their Supply to meet Demand? Oh I see, within a vacuum of fixed Supply, higher Demand would deplete that fixed Supply.* I was ready!

"Did anyone happen to watch Ben Bernanke's talk yesterday about the state of the economy?" the professor asked.

Oh, yeah, and then there was that little thing everyone was talking about – The Economic Recession. It was in full force and had our nation bent over a barrel. People's small businesses were turning belly up left and right. People were starting to lose their jobs. Home foreclosures were becoming uncomfortably common. Whores of the liberal media were blaming Bush and his cronies. Prostitutes of conservative media were placing blame on ludicrous policies left in Clinton's wake. It was the Banks! It was the Fed! It was sub-prime mortgages! It was Wall Street losing sight of hard-to-understand derivatives! Heck, people were even blaming it on the exorbitant salaries of teachers.

It was really the first time as an adult that I got to witness other adults being truly ugly to one another, with constant finger pointing, name calling, and endless debates where it was obvious each participant was merely championing the tribe they chose to side with, blindly accepting and repeating narrow talking points of only a few media bobbleheads they looked up to. Gee whiz it was nauseating! Of course, I had seen human ugliness in the obvious places growing up such as the news, movies, or even between squabbling family members. But this was different. It was almost as if all of these grownups who I looked up to in reverence, who I used to place on a pedestal simply because they were older than me suddenly took off their disguises to reveal that they were merely children dressed up as and playing adult this whole time. It was shocking! It quickly dawned on me that just because someone turns 18 years old doesn't mean they are magically imbued with wisdom from the ether or an ability to effectively manage their emotional responses. Though knowledge and life experiences help build upon the foundation of our being, the same core traits that existed for us as 12-year-olds remain generally intact throughout our life; at least that is what I observed. I guess you could say that was an important revelation for me as it put everyone on a level plane in my mind. Nobody was special, and nobody stood on a pedestal anymore.

As a Finance Major with no income and little to no voice, all I could really do was sit and observe and absorb as much as I could. But, it was during those times of observation that I would often find myself staring off into the middle distance, in deep thought, trying to understand everything my mind was consciously and subconsciously soaking in throughout every day. Whether I was walking to class or staring at the ceiling while lying in my bed at night, I was constantly cerebrating over the dilemma that had befallen our nation and its people and what possible solutions were lurking in the shadows. I was convinced that there must have been something we just weren't seeing – a silver bullet that could quickly fix the woes of America.

And then, one day in the weeks leading up to that morning of class, it hit! I had an idea, I thought, but it was an idea that seemed so crazy I wouldn't dare talk about it to anyone, especially not to my professor or peers, for risk of being ridiculed or even banished from the herd. So I shelved it for future consideration. I needed to work out the kinks.

"Who here watched Bernanke's talk? Anyone?" Professor Harper asked once more.

He scanned the class, likely assuming nobody had tuned in to watch the former Chairman of the Federal Reserve speak, and he would have been mostly right. Only a few students raised their hands. And of those few, I assumed 2 of the 3 were probably lying.

"What did you guys think of it? Who's to blame, Jeff?"

"China?"

"Mmm…I wouldn't think China's the reason for the mess we are in, though we have been borrowing an excessive amount of money from them to keep interest rates low, keep inflation down, and yada, yada, yada. What about you, Bro? What do you think?"

We all sat in our wooden seats wide-eyed and in awkward silence. Bro was the term he used when calling on Greg – the lone black student in our class. I always wondered what was going through Greg's head in those moments. Did he feel singled out? Did it make him feel uncomfortable? Did it further any sort of disdain he might already have toward white folk?

"Uh…I don't know…the banks?"

"What about the banks?"

"Um, they were super careless in giving out sub-prime mortgages to people who barely qualified. It should have been obvious that they would eventually default," Greg said.

The professor nodded, "Yeah, carelessness by the banks is certainly a common talking point out there. So where do we go from here? What can we do to solve this crisis?"

I remained as still as possible in my seat in hopes of becoming completely invisible. I even moved my head so that the kid in front of me was blocking the professor's path of vision to my eyes.

"How about….you, Ryan? Where do we go from here?" the professor asked.

"Uhhh….I…I really don't know," Ryan said.

"Yeah, it's a tough question. People getting paid a lot of money in Washington have the same answer."

As the professor paced to the left side of the room, I slowly tried moving my head to stay behind the kid in front of me. Just then, I made the critical mistake of looking up. Professor Harper's eyes instantaneously connected with mine, and I knew I was caught. *Crap!* I froze in my hunched position as he looked at me with a subtle "I gotcha" smirk. It was all over. I was exposed. I was about to look like a fool to the world because the answer I did have would sound ludicrous to the masses.

"What say you, uh…," he couldn't even remember my name.

"Travis," I said.

"What say you, Travis?"

I suddenly felt a restlessness in my bowels, a condition I'm almost certain was passed down by my father's side of the family. Any time my dad or his brothers were about to engage in any sort of competitive activity, the event was almost always delayed right before the start by a sudden exclamation of, "Oop, I gotta take a shit!" And the man would rush to the bathroom, cheeks clenched, putting everyone else on hold for an extra five to thirty minutes.

So there I was, pants around my ankles, Kleenex still shoved up my nose, and the spotlight shining bright on me. I didn't know what to say, but everyone was waiting with bated breath, so I had to say something. And just like when Ralphie accidentally blurted out his yearning for a Red Rider BB Gun to the mall Santa in *A Christmas Story*, I blurted out the only thing that came to my mind.

"Couldn't we just erase the debt…everyone's debt, and start over?"

My sheepish response received a chuckle from a couple kids in the class. Professor Harper's smirk intensified.

"Erase all of the debt, huh? Well, this certainly isn't a new concept. But what makes you think that would be possible?"

"I don't know. I guess I figured since money is artificial, we could just easily erase the debt and nothing would change in the physical world.

Everyone would still be able to go about their business, doing the exact same thing they were doing the day before. Nothing would change except for the imaginary number hanging above everyone's head."

The professor paused for a moment. I could tell the red on my face was darkening as beads of sweat formed above my upper lip. I pursed my lips and moved only my eyes to the ceiling in an attempt to make it seem like I was just being facetious – a court jester entertaining the crowd. I also didn't realize it in the moment, but my foot was rapidly tapping the floor.

"Hmm….I wonder what the people who America owes money to would have to say about that. The ramifications worldwide would be disastrous, and the value of the dollar would be all but dead. I can assure you things would absolutely change in the physical world if you were to erase the debt. Thank you for playing, though. Next!"

Some of the students laughed as the professor gave me a cocky wink of assurance that I'll be okay while pointing his finger toward the rest of the class to call on his next victim. I smiled along with everyone else to seem unfazed, but my innards were swirling. I felt pretty stupid, as I expected I would. Professor Harper pointed out just a couple of the many flaws in my unoriginal, "lightning-in-a-bottle" idea. It was not feasible, and I had no counter for it in my head. I left class feeling a little defeated, but failure can be a good teacher.

The more I thought about it, I understood that the professor was right, to an extent. Within the worldwide game of money and trade, the US alone would not be able to just erase their debt and start over on a blank canvas. An act this extreme would most definitely incite some sort of retaliatory measure by other countries, and the US Dollar would no longer be taken seriously in the world market. The only way my idea would work is if every country agreed to wipe the slate clean – an idea that was completely and utterly preposterous.

But for some reason, even though I understood this idea was not feasible, I couldn't get the thought out of my head. It was like an annoying itch. No matter how much I scratched the damn thing, it was there, constantly, and it seemed to be quickly evolving and infecting every sulcus and gyrus of my brain. Somewhere, deep down in the recesses of my mind, I knew I was on to something. But what? I had this sudden, intuitive sense of *knowing* that something was fatally flawed not only with our system, but with all of the monetary systems around the world. But why? I knew it had something to do with money and its artificial nature. But how? As a cute little sapling in a giant forest, it was simply too much for me to fully or even partially comprehend. The thoughts needed time to grow and mature.

Following college graduation, life seemed to be going relatively well for me. I was earning money at my first big boy job as an accountant for the State, I began paying off my massive college debt with a gulp and a smile, and I became engaged to my college sweetheart, Kaitlyn. Though the economy was still struggling a bit, things were getting predictably better, at least on the surface. We measure the health of our country based on economic measures such as GDP, GNP, the stock market, job growth, etc. All of these were on the ups, so I figured it was safe to assume the health of the people within our borders was also on the ups – right?

With things improving, it no longer seemed necessary to concern myself with solving the economic puzzle I had burdened myself with. So I buried it. I buried it somewhere deep within my brain where it remained dormant for a couple years as I just lived my life like everyone else. Plus, with work and bills and a wedding to plan for, I didn't really have the time or energy to pay attention to the questions and curiosities bubbling beneath the surface.

The only thing that didn't seem to be improving was the ugliness of the adults in my general periphery. They were still arguing, still bickering, and still name calling on behalf of the tribe they associated with over anything and everything. This all came to a head in early-2011 in Wisconsin as the spotlight was shining on the newly-elected Republican governor, Scott Walker, and school teachers from around the state. Money, as is the case with most disputes, was at the heart of it all. It was in short supply in Wisconsin, and the governor and his team wanted to find a way to get some of the money sitting in the bucket of the public sector redistributed to those in the private sector who they believed were best fit to invest it in a way that could increase jobs and bolster the economy. To kick the tires on that plan, Mr. Walker rolled out his Wisconsin Budget Repair bill, which included a plan to limit collective bargaining between teachers and unions.

And boy oh boy, if I thought people were divided before the newly elected governor took office, I ain't seen nothin', yet. Teachers and their unions were furious! Teachers, in particular, felt like their very livelihoods were being threatened, which inspired them and their supporters to take to the streets. They protested for weeks at the state capitol and in other areas of the state in hopes of persuading their governor to change his mind on passing the legislation, while counterprotests of teams on the other side of the coin sprung up in other areas of Wisconsin. Democratic leaders fled the state in order to delay voting on the bill, death threats were being issued, Governor Walker was caught on tape talking about a "divide-and-conquer" strategy on *the people*, teachers and their "lucrative" salaries were being dragged through the mud, prank calls were being successfully levied, chants of "shame" were being showered upon Republican leaders. It was sheer pandemonium!

The sense of urgency and panic on both sides was at an all-time high.

"There just has to be a better way," my coworker, Roger, a registered Republican, said.

"But, Roger, we're out of money," Dan, my other coworker, replied in a frantic tone.

And that sentiment prevailed. The governor and his team had done their analysis, made their decisions, and they weren't going to compromise. The Wisconsin Supreme Court agreed as they voted to uphold the bill that summer.

But the craziness was far from over. Efforts had begun to recall the governor and a number of state senators from their positions, which kicked off another slate of cringe-worthy commercials and pointless debates (I say pointless because they're usually filled with empty talking points and buzzwords), which then capped off another round of voting. In the end, though two Republican senators were ousted, Scott Walker beat the recall and maintained his position as Wisconsin's Governor.

Phew! Are you out of breath? I know I am. And that's just a very quick recap. Since the office I worked at was right next to the state capitol, I basically had balcony seats to the whole show, a show I had no interest in attending. Unfortunately, the exit doors were barricaded and there was no intermission. I was left to endure the entire annoying episode. Give this guy a tissue, am I right?

After the dust had settled, I found myself reflecting on the messy situation. What was the impetus of it all? The wheels in my brain started spinning, albeit slowly. *Hmm…let's see. I guess it would be too simple of an answer to just blame money,* I thought to myself. *Money is not inherently good or evil. There is something else coupled with money that summoned the rage of the masses. What were people most worried about? Let's see. The governor and his team wanted funds to be channeled to private businesses, but the other side in the spotlight – teachers – wanted money to stay in education. So it seems to me that the whole argument was based around how to best distribute what little money Wisconsin had, because money was scarce. Ah ha…*

*Scarcity! Money is scarce! Money is limited! People are forced to compete for what little money is in circulation. And, a competition for that which grants access to the means of survival is bound to get ugly.*

*But what about when the economy grows and money is added to the pile? It doesn't always have to be scarce, right? Hmm…good questions, self.* I continued to follow my train of thought. *Let's see once more – when money is added to the economy, that means the American consumer theoretically has more money and more ability to buy things – Purchasing Power. If people have more purchasing power, companies see an opportunity to generate more revenue, so they increase prices in an attempt to capture a piece of the growing economic pie.*

*Ok, so what does that mean?*

*Well, it would seem that even when the economy grows and more money is added, prices grow with it, which means the money supply and prices remain proportional to what they were before, which essentially means Purchasing Power naturally falls into a sort of equilibrium (not accounting for employee income).*

*So then, what that essentially means is no matter how much money is added to an existing supply, money always remains Scarce.*

*Huh…well isn't that just interesting. But it has to be that way, because resources are scarce, and money represents available resources, right?*
*Um…uhh….owwwch…*

The processing capacity of my brain was not powerful enough to handle the deluge of information pouring in. The pressure between my ears became too intense, as I needed to give it more time. So again, I deposited my thoughts and questions deep within my brain for my subconscious mind to work through while I simply enjoyed life.

Well, not too long after the political debacle in Wisconsin, things took a pretty dark turn in my world.

Kaitlyn and I were trying to live a normal American life like everyone else. I was still working my 9-to-5 job while also dabbling in Stock Options and website development during my free time. And she had recently graduated college and was in the beginning of her career as an elementary school teacher in Madison. Things were going seemingly great as our wedding day drew near.

However, in late-2011, Kaitlyn was diagnosed with the most dangerous and aggressive form of skin cancer – melanoma. For a year and a half, our days were filled with doctor appointments, cancer treatments, emergency hospital visits, stress, fear, and worry. Kait battled the beast as hard and as courageously as she could with her head always held high during that short stretch which felt like an eternity. Devastatingly, in the end, we ran out of time and options. And on the day we bumped up our wedding and were scheduled to marry, Kaitlyn was instead laid to rest. She was only 24.

Uhh…that hurt. Boy did it ever hurt. The whole episode was, needless to say, the worst time of my life. The pain from head to heart was intense. I will spare everyone the entire story in this writing since I already wrote a whole book about it, but from the initial Stage 4 diagnosis to well beyond her passing, it was dreadful in every way – a nightmare from which I could not awaken. The weeks and months following her death consisted of a lot of soul searching, a lot of tears, and a lot of questions. I spent many days and nights alone, staring off into the void of nothingness, reflecting, pondering. Why am I here? Why are we here? What's our purpose? What's my purpose? What's the point of life? Is there an afterlife? Is there not an afterlife? Does Kait still exist? Or is life on earth the one and final frontier? Is God real? Are ghosts real? The questions were abundant.

I began tirelessly exploring every avenue in hopes of discovering answers to all of those questions. Information couldn't come fast enough as I started reading books, attending seminars, watching lectures, watching documentaries, and even doing thought experiments in an attempt to whet my appetite. Call it confirmation bias, but the conclusions I was able to draw based on the information I stumbled upon did bring me a certain level of comfort. And if nothing else, it at least served as a temporary distraction from the constant reruns in my head of Kait's suffering and the pain that followed.

Well, eventually I reached a point where my soul felt satisfied with what I had learned, and though it was all incredibly interesting, it served its purpose and I was ready to explore other areas of intrigue. I was slowly working through my stages of grief – the denial, the anger, the depression – and I was coming upon acceptance. With acceptance came the realization that I still needed to live my life. Moving on from Kaitlyn was not an option, but I knew I had to get on with living. I mean, I still had another 50 or 60 years to fill up, and sitting around feeling sorry for her or myself would be a gross disservice to Kait.

Like many people who suffer through a major life event, I felt like a changed person. I felt inspired. And how couldn't I after witnessing Kait and her indomitable strength while she faced the prospect of having her life and dreams cut short. So, to honor Kait and everything she had to endure, I wanted to try and be a better person, one stronger in his moral convictions and always aspiring to do "right." And I understand that the notion of what is right and what is wrong differs from human being to human being and depends on so many different factors in life, including cultural norms. However, I contend there are universal rights and universal wrongs. How are we able to distinguish between these two? Empathy.* Empathy allows us to put ourselves in someone else's shoes and feel what they feel to an extent. Through empathy, if we do something to someone else that we know would cause us physical or emotional harm should that person do the same thing to us, then we are able to determine that it is wrong. This does not necessarily stop us from performing said action, but it does allow us to discern and understand in our heart when something just ain't right.

Tangent and moral high-horse aside, I wanted to take on something that would make Kait proud.

With that in mind, I subsequently took my figurative map and shovel, traveled through the suppressed regions of my brain, and dug up the treasure chest of those pernicious questions regarding money and economy. I had a gaping hole to fill in my life and a lot of free time in which I needed a meaningful distraction from, so I figured why not revisit the topic that has at once brought me great intrigue as well as great strife. It felt purposeful. So, with that, I set sail on what would become a long and arduous journey spanning many years and costing me the majority of my hair follicles. I began devoting much of my free time to educating myself

***Mirror Neurons**

on our economy and the economies around the world. I spent hours upon hours of feverishly exploring, learning, and branching off into various related subjects, and slowly, but surely, answers to all of my questions began to manifest. Each little piece of information found its place within the greater puzzle of my mind, and the overall picture was becoming clearer and clearer every day, until – I feel like I've reached a point of almost complete clarity regarding the matter, at least in my mind, and I now feel confident enough to share my perspectives with you.

In the end, though the wheels were set in motion a few years earlier, Kaitlyn has ultimately been the catapult that has launched my pursuit of what will likely be a materially fruitless endeavor. Through her, I have reoriented my priorities and acquired new perspectives, which has ultimately led me to who I am and where I am today, writing this book. So, if I am tasked with finding some positives amongst the plethora of negatives during our situation, I am at least grateful for that.

Now that my life story is out of the way, let's slip into our mud boots and prepare to slop around in what I have deemed, "The Pit"!

# 2 THE APPETIZER (INTRODUCTION)

When people first migrate to a new land, one of their first priorities of business is to design a system that ensures the group's survival needs are met – that is, its people receive adequate food, shelter, clothing, etc. Because, what is a system's purpose if not to serve the people it was designed to serve? So, when planning for food production, for instance, the challenge lies in how to develop a process that can feed 100% of the community. Not 95%. Not 70%. 100%! Any idea or process that falls short of this mark would be considered unacceptable and would require the think-tank to go back to the drawing board and come up with a better process. This is what I define as a *sane* society – one that doesn't accept the idea that suffering, starvation, poverty, and homelessness are natural and unavoidable elements within an economy.

What I define as an *insane* society is the one we reside in now where 14-18% of American children live in poverty,[1,2] yet 30-40% of food is thrown away.[3] And where, on a global scale, although enough food is currently produced to feed the entire population of the world, approximately 3.1 million children die of hunger each year, while over 150 million children under the age of 5 experience stunted growth and over 50 million suffer from wasting due to malnutrition.[4] This to me is absurd.

So where in the schematics of our economic design does our process fall apart? Food production is clearly not the problem as we produce an abundant supply and have the technological capability of producing much more. Supply exists. Demand exists. But only a portion of the supply is reaching just a portion of those in demand. So then where's the kink in the line? Where is the process failing? Well, it appears where the system begins to stumble is in the mechanism we use to distribute this supply. And what is that mechanism of distribution? What is the primary tool used to facilitate the transfer of goods to households in need?

Money.

Money, or the lack thereof, is the major impediment in our ability to efficiently deliver the abundance of food to those in need, to those suffering from poverty and starvation. The way we currently have global society organized is you can usually only acquire food by first obtaining money and then exchanging it for food. If you fail in obtaining requisite funds, then you don't get food, even if it is readily available. The excess food produced but not distributed due to lack of money then goes to waste.

One does not need a Ph.D. in Economics to recognize the glaring inefficiencies here. And that's just within the sphere of food and hunger. In my explorations I have found that all industries and institutions are affected by those same defects inherent to the money-for-goods system, though to varying degrees. Such revelations have led me to conclude that…

Money is OBSOLETE!

It is no longer necessary to employ money as our main tool for distributing goods within the global community, and it is no longer fit to manage society. In addition to being an inadequate means for allocating resources, money can also be traced as a root precondition underlying just about every negative sociological and ecological issue on the planet, and it is my contention that if we want to reverse the trends threatening all life systems, then it is in our best interest to start considering a transition away from this outdated tool.

In this text, I have done my best to illustrate why I have arrived at such a seemingly radical conclusion. To properly support my thesis, I spend the first few chapters discussing money and the monetary game from my perspective using a relatively simple approach, which includes a chapter about America's central banking system – the Federal Reserve. After easing into, maybe too slowly, and establishing the foundations of the monetary game in an attempt to get us on the same page, I delve deeper into the most glaring issues across the globe and try to explain how the existence of money serves as a core contaminant to such issues. I attempt to point out how our infinite growth and infinite consumption model is unsustainable, and how the established economic setup is not only destructive to the health of society's inhabitants, but how it threatens to destroy the very thing that provides us with life (Earth), and much more. Main topics here include Childhood Poverty, Ecological Degradation, Exploitation, War, Crime, and Trust. From there, I go on to talk about Laissez-Faire Economics, Human Motivation, Technological Unemployment, and the idea that efficiency is a monetary system's greatest foe. And lastly, I finish this writing by presenting what I feel is a plausible replacement to the global economic system.

Now, before we jump into the meat of this thing, I do feel compelled to address a few housekeeping items first. I understand you might feel the urge to skip this introductory portion, as I often do when reading texts. Though I would like you to read this entire intro, if you do decide to flip forward, I ask that you at least read the final paragraph of this chapter involving a specific "request" – number 17 on the list below.

1. I understand most people are sick and tired of hearing about all the problems in the world as we are bombarded with negative stories all day, every day. I share in this exhaustion. However, before presenting what I feel are feasible solutions, I unfortunately believe it is important to first address the problems and analyze what's causing them so that it becomes undeniable that major change is necessary. If it ain't broke, don't fix it. If I can't prove our global monetary system is broken beyond repair, then all subsequent solutions I present will be muted.

2. For better or worse, I will be picking on the United States more often than other territories when addressing national and global issues. I do this for multiple reasons, none of which include my being "anti-American" or anything silly like that. I love where I live and the surrounding culture (well, some of it), but at the same time I am not averse to facing flaws. We cannot improve, as individuals or groups, if we are too afraid to confront our faults and work toward remedying them. Also, I am not anti- any country or group of people, as I don't necessarily recognize countries as entities separate from each other, which I will clarify later. As for the reasons I more often chose to pick on the United States in this book? First of all, I grew up in the US; therefore, I understand the US better than other nations and cultures. Second of all, I tend to subscribe to the philosophy

that goes something like: "Make sure your house is clean before you start pointing out the dirt on other peoples' houses." Or, as is written in Matthew 7:1-5 in the Bible: "Before I start pointing out the speck in my neighbor's eye, I first try to deal with the log in my own eye." Though I'm guilty of it, and though I do it in this book, I typically don't feel comfortable criticizing, insulting, or demeaning other individuals, groups, or cultures, because I recognize I myself am flawed to the bone. On top of that, I feel as though insulting other individuals or groups is largely a sign of insecurities – it indicates inner weakness rather than strength. As humans, it is not unusual for us to question our self-worth, especially on a subconscious level. Many of us need consistent reminders to reassure ourselves that we are in fact worth a damn in this world, that we are not worthless failures. Demeaning other individuals or groups is but one method we use to calm such human insecurities. When we knock down an individual, it is often to elevate ourselves above said individual. "I might be worthless, but at least I'm not as worthless as that guy." By moving up on the social hierarchy ladder, we are reassured, however falsely, that we are better than those we demean, and therefore more worthy of respect, acceptance, and love in spite of our flaws. For a moment we feel safe in our skin. However, deep down, what we are really saying is we fear we might be weak and unworthy, so we attempt to dominate others to prove otherwise.

It seems to me a man secure enough in his own skin has no need to dominate or knock down others to pick himself up; he does not need an elevated position in the pecking order to validate his life or reinforce his value, and he does not cower from personal criticism; he has courage enough to confront his flaws. Of course, I am not that man; I teem with insecurities, though I do my best not to feed into them. All that being said, I identify as American; therefore, I feel more comfortable pointing out the dirt on "myself" before pointing out the dirt on others, hence my justification for predominantly using the United States as my focal point in this writing. Plus, much of the issues I do speak of can be applied to regions all over the world, anyway.

3. This book is not meant to read as a textbook or a scholarly work; however, its primary purpose is to inform.

4. I have chosen a simple, informal, conversational tone for accessibility and ease-of-understanding. Though I try to properly follow

rules on grammar, I sometimes sacrifice grammatical accuracy so the sentence reads as I speak it, which, for instance, might include omission or inclusion of commas where omission or inclusion goes against orthodoxy.

5. I feel like the subject matter in this book is inherently boring, so I wanted to find a way to make it at least slightly entertaining. However, halfway through writing I realized I am not talented or creative enough to make economic theories and information fun; so, my tone eventually shifts. My first version actually contained a talking pug, a harangue comparing economics to religion, and a bit where my head bursts and splatters blood and brain matter all over the wall. Needless to say, I changed course and eventually killed those darlings.

6. I wrote most of this book in 2019. Though I did update a few passages to account for the insanity that was 2020, most of what I wrote consists of pre-pandemic data.

7. It seems nowadays an overwhelming percentage of us believe we are "right" and that we know the "truth" based on the limited and biased information we've been exposed to, and that others expressing differing thoughts and opinions are wrong and misled. With that in mind, I have tried taking the approach here that I might be wrong or I might be right – I don't know. I have simply developed an opinion/thesis, and I have gathered existing information to support said thesis in a way that best suits my style and limited skillset. It is up to you whether you want to take it or leave it, or take some of it and leave some of it.

8. This is not a conspiracy theory book; however, I do spend a few paragraphs on topics that might be construed as "conspiracy theory."

9. I apologize for redundancies. I do repeat myself at times while completing various thoughts for purposes of clarity.

10. I typically prefer not to explain too much in my writings, but in this one I admit I am often guilty of just that. The topic and hypothesis I am presenting typically elicits heavy scrutiny, and sometimes even pedantry (as it should). So, to ensure or increase understanding and to reduce questions and misinterpretations, I do overexplain in many instances. Unfortunately, pacing is sacrificed for clarity, which I do not like, but feel is necessary. Adequately supporting my position is most important here.

11. If you are tempted to put this book down permanently before finishing, I would recommend reading Chapters 9, 6.6, and 6.1 (in that order) at least. Those are my favorite.

12. Curse words. If curse words offend you or diminish my credibility, I apologize. There are roughly 25 instances of curse words out of 165,000 total words in this text.

13. So that we are on the same page, when I use the term "money" I am referring to any medium of exchange that helps facilitate the transfer of goods and services. This includes fiat currency (paper money, coins), cryptocurrency (Bitcoin), commodity money (gold, silver), money of account, etc.

14. What I promote in this book in regards to removing money is entirely different from the "cashless" society being promoted in mainstream society, and it has zero affiliation with the "Great Reset" discussed at the World Economic Forum amongst the world's most powerful individuals, which I briefly address much later in this book. I don't support either.

15. When I use the term "man" in this text, I am usually not referring specifically to hose-bearing males. I am referring to humans, in general. In the context of this book, I don't really differentiate between males and females of the human species.

16. Before I end this chapter with my "request," I want to quickly address my political affiliations.

I don't subscribe to the whole notion of Left/Right, Republican/Democrat politics. I contend that labels have a tendency to pigeonhole us and limit our vision. That once we brand ourselves, we as humans tend to seek conclusions that adhere to that label and adhere to the group mind. Aligning with our inherent need for social belonging, we humans like feeling as though we are part of a team. We like feeling included. It validates us and makes us feel important, as though we matter. That said, once we've chosen a herd to affiliate with, fear of exclusion pressures us into saying or doing things we might not otherwise say or do. Eventually, with enough exposure and repetition, our brains start to mold into the Group Mind brain, and we fully adopt its way of thinking. A Group Mind bias then develops. So, in an attempt to better understand and evaluate the subject of economy and life in general, I have consciously tried to pull myself out of the game of left/right politics and merely observe human interaction from a point of neutrality – almost like a bird perched atop a tree branch. I don't mean to sound too self-righteous, but I do try my best to simply assess various situations independently, and I try to judge rightness or wrongness based on my own moral code rather than succumbing to the pressures or influences of a Liberal or Conservative mindset. I try not to concern myself with being part of a team, nor do I let the fear of social exclusion steer my thoughts. "Insanity in individuals is something rare – but in groups, parties, nations, and epochs it is the rule," or so said Friedrich Nietzsche.[5]

17. The previous housekeeping item segues neatly into this last item here. I have a request of you. As you are reading this text, I ask that you quiet the outside "noise" – news, social media, marketing, and family and friends largely influenced by news, media, and marketing. I ask that you try your best to tune out all of the external chatter trying hard to get you to think a certain way and feel a certain way and simply listen to YOURSELF. Forget what everyone wants you to believe or feel, and trust and listen to your own inner voice. That inner voice, your own individual wisdom is smarter than you might think. I ask that you judge what I have written based on *your* own beliefs and what *feels* right to *you*!

Alright. This introduction has gone on long enough. Let's move on to the meat of this thing and plunge into "The Pit." I hope you enjoy.

# 3 MONEY'S PURPOSE

What is the purpose of money? Well, it has a number of functions. Primarily, however, it serves as a Resource Allocation tool; an intermediary or medium of exchange helping to facilitate the distribution of goods. But on a secondary level, money is used as a crude method of calculating supply and demand, a rough representation of available resources, a loose measure of the value of goods relative to other goods, and a store of wealth. There is a large faction of people who think money is an effective tool for motivating humans to produce and achieve. However, though there are partial truths to that assumption, I will explain in Chapter 9 how this is an incomplete and mostly false belief system. Lastly, though money's primary purpose is supposed to be as a tool to equitably and efficiently distribute resources, it has naturally been used throughout history as a means to control populations for the purpose of maintaining a competitive advantage in the monetary game.

Money has come in many shapes and forms throughout human history, from shells and cigarettes to paper and metal coins, and has been used to make trade more efficient for thousands of years and across many cultures, from the ancient Mesopotamians, Egyptians, and Romans to our modern-day, globally interconnected civilizations.

However, the thing about money is, it's artificial; it's an idea. Sure, the paper and the coin are real, but the numerical value slapped on those physical mediums is theoretical, existing solely in our minds. Through a collective faith, when the US Treasury prints a piece of green paper and stamps the number '5' on it, we accept that it has a value of $5. When they print that exact same piece of green paper, but this time stamp the number '20' on it, then we collectively accept that this piece of paper of same weight and size now has a value of $20. In actuality, the paper has very little intrinsic value.

The other thing about money is, no matter what type of system employs it, it is finite. At any given *snapshot* in time, the amount of money that exists within any economy is fixed. If I dump a pile of $100 on an island of 20 people, then that $100 is the only amount they have to compete for. And I understand we've created phony mechanisms of "growing" money, like through Fractional Reserve Banking or through the government simply issuing bonds and getting more money printed out of thin air, or now through the phenomenon of "mining" money out of nothing with computer algorithms, but as I alluded to earlier, through inflation, prices and existing money remain relatively proportional. When more money is added to the economy, Purchasing Power is increased for a brief moment, which drives the prices of goods up, which consequently devalues the dollar. Once market equilibrium is achieved again, Purchasing Power essentially falls back to where it was before the money was added. Plus, if I dump an extra $20 on that same island of 20 people in the example above, now the people simply have $120 to fight over. Within that snapshot of time, that $120 is the set amount in that society. And, if this island is like America, tactics and legislation have been put in place so that the excess amount that is dumped onto the island rapidly filters up to the people with the most influence, those with the most financial leverage.

Money within any economy is a *Zero-Sum Game*. That is, since the amount at any given time is fixed, if a person wants to gain more money, then that means some other person within the economy has to lose money. Think of a teeter-totter – if one person goes up, another must come down (financially speaking). If we divvied up the roughly $20 trillion available to compete for in the US economy amongst the 330 million Americans, that would give everyone about $60,000. But, if I wanted $100,000, then that means someone else somewhere would have to dip below $60,000 for me to achieve that. I liken the whole process to a game of Poker.

In a Poker tournament, a group of participants sits down at a table to compete against each other. Each participant is given an equal amount of chips before the game begins. For this example, let's say that 10 people sit down at this poker table, and they are each given 100 chips, meaning there are 1,000 chips in circulation. If one of the competitors wants to acquire more chips, he has to acquire them from one of the other competitors. As the game goes on, poker chips are transferred back and forth from player to player. Some people gradually gain more chips, while others gradually lose chips. And, chips are neither added to the game nor are they ever removed. All the players have to compete with is the 1,000 chips originally poured into the game.

Well, eventually, through a combination of skill and luck, one man acquires all of the chips at the table, leaving the other competitors without any. This is when the game ends. The only difference between a poker game and real life is that in real life those poker chips are used to access the means of survival. If one person acquires all of the poker chips in the economy and the game ends, then people start to suffer and die and the economy collapses. Some systems have it set up so that when someone acquires most of the chips, they have to give some chips back in order for the game to continue. Other systems have it set up so that more chips are simply thrown into the economy from some chip overlord. In our American economy, both mechanisms exist in the form of taxes and the Federal Reserve and banks. However, when more chips are thrown into the pile, into the system, the person who has the majority of chips at the time has much, much more leverage over the other competitors. The odds of this person siphoning the small amount of chips added to the game from the other competitors are almost 100%.

So, again, the practice of using money to trade goods is a Zero-Sum Game. The money within a group of people is neither created nor destroyed; it simply transfers back and forth from one person's hand to another. Whoever plays the game best will eventually acquire a larger share of the money pie, whether his methods are fair or not, or whether through hard work or sneaky trickery. However, when it comes to wealth, food, and other regenerative resources, it doesn't have to be a zero-sum game. If two people want an apple, we have the ability to grow two apples. If two people want a shirt, we have the ability to produce two shirts. In the game of life, one's gain doesn't have to be another's loss, unlike the game of money. As an aside, I understand in the game of money the idea that if I want an apple and give $2 to another person for that apple, then we have both gained since we both received what we wanted. However, though some transactions result in a perceived equal gain, this is not the case for many transactions. We often part with our money out of necessity and have very little bargaining power over goods we purchase. And in the most extreme examples, people, bent over a barrel and with little choice, are coerced into giving up a lot more for the sake of survival. Also, if most transactions were a 1-to-1 trade off, we wouldn't see such tremendous wealth disparity in our country, and we wouldn't see such massive amounts of hunger and homelessness. As of 2019, the combined wealth of the world's nine richest men is roughly equal to the poorest 4 billion.[1]

No matter how much money exists within an economy, the amount is always limited, which means it is always scarce. And to make matters worse, people can hoard money. When people like me hoard (save) their money, as many are advised to do, that money is taken out of the game, which decreases the amount in circulation and the amount available to acquire, making it even more scarce. However, the silly thing here is, resources like food are actually quite abundant, and through technological advancements and improved cultivation techniques can be made ever more abundant without further straining the planet. So, in that vein, we are actually competing for something that is scarce (money) in order to obtain something that is abundant (food). The supply of food is plentiful. The supply of money is not.

Imagine if you lived on an island that consisted of you and only one other person (Derek), and all around both of you are trees filled with bananas. But now imagine you have set up rules with each other so that the only way you can acquire any bananas is by exchanging money. Now imagine in this abstraction you've somehow lost all of your money. Derek will deny you access to the plentiful bananas, because you don't have money. You now go hungry, and while you lie on the sand dying of starvation, bananas fall from the trees and land right in front of your face, bananas that neither you, nor Derek will eat. The limited amount of money and arbitrary rules you and Derek created on your island acts as a barrier to that which is abundant. You are competing against each other to obtain intrinsically meaningless paper in order to access real, life-sustaining goods. In our American society, bananas (food, housing, etc.) are all around us, but we don't let people access them unless they obtain scarce money first. As a result, famished people look on as a large percentage of bananas die and are thrown away on a daily basis.

Back to hoarding. Unlike money, food cannot be hoarded in the same way. If someone hoards food, then people can just grow more food. But when someone hoards money, people are unable to buy food, and then the food just grows and dies, grow and dies, grows and dies.

And when it comes to consumption, people can consume an infinite amount of money. However, with food, nature has built-in mechanisms within our bodies so that we are limited in the amount we can consume at one time. Even with water, the very essence of life, if we consume too much at one time, we can die from water intoxication. This safe guard ensures one person can't consume too much, which makes sure there is enough food for everyone and that Earth is not put under too much stress. In the game of money, which has been superimposed over the game of life, people can consume an infinite quantity of things – acquire as many cars as you can, collect as many houses as you can, or shoes. In fact, the game of money promotes and encourages unlimited consumption, because that is how it flourishes. More product turnover means more money exchanging hands. The game of money, detached from nature, runs in complete opposition to nature, a nature which promotes efficiency and careful consumption.

Because the supply of money is always limited, we are always handcuffed and limited by the amount of money in circulation or at our disposal to solve problems. Even if all of the resources and labor are available and ready to be put to use, projects cannot proceed without money. When Kaitlyn was in her fight against cancer, we tried looking up various clinical trials to enter her into. We found a clinical trial in Seattle using a new technique that made sense to us and sounded rather promising. However, as the date approached for the clinical trial to open up to candidates, the project had to be temporarily shut down because the administrators weren't able to secure the amount of money needed to run the trial. Again, the equipment was available, the labor was ready, and the necessary resources were waiting to be used, but lack of this paper medium halted all operations. Another relevant and more extreme example of money's limiting effect came during the Great Depression. Businesses were shutting down production and going bankrupt at an alarming rate, causing a massive spike in joblessness. Because people were no longer earning income, they were unable to pay for the necessities of life, resulting in an influx of homelessness, starvation, and suffering across America. However, although millions were enduring this hardship, nothing changed in the physical world. Factories were still intact. Food was still able to grow. Plows could still plow. Electricity could still electrify. Everything that was being done before the Great Depression to sustain life could still be accomplished. The only thing that was different was that money was less available to the consumer. We allowed the lack of this artificial resource to stop us from managing real resources and society. Children and adults were suffering and dying even though all of the necessary resources for life were still available. Again, money's scarce nature limits us from efficiently managing society.

To some extent, money's scarcity is supposed to be a rough reflection of available resources – the premise being that resources are also scarce. For a time, this might have been true. It was more difficult to cultivate and harvest food decades and centuries ago. It was more difficult to produce clothing in mass quantities. Due to scarcity and the notion that there wasn't enough to go around, people were encouraged to simply fend for themselves, to get "theirs" and not worry about the wellbeing of others. The notion of "survival of the fittest" became the prevailing belief system, and competing amongst each other for survival was simply a harsh reality of life. However, with improved technology and an increased ability to produce more goods with less effort, scarcity of physical goods is no longer an issue, making this primitive competition for survival amongst ourselves unnecessary and barbaric. When you have 15 bananas in a society of 10 people, yet you still make people fight for bananas, there is no other way to describe it but as barbaric. Well, actually there are plenty of adjectives that can be used to describe it: archaic, primitive, animalistic, idiotic, insane.

Earth is a pretty incredible machine. Many of the goods we need to survive can be recycled and regenerated over and over again. Through intelligent design and careful management, we can regrow cotton, we can regrow wood through trees, and we can regrow food without harming Earth. It was built for that. It was created with the intent of providing for all of its passengers enjoying this galactic trip through space. Now more than ever, we can produce an abundance of all of life's necessities, meaning money is no longer an effective representation of available resources. And as for the resources that are finite and may not possess this regenerative property, again through careful management, we can use these finite and rare resources to their optimal capacity to ensure they do not go to waste. Silver has many practical uses, especially in electronics, but as a coin, silver is useless.

Now I want to go back and talk about the utility of money – money's purpose. I want to talk about money's function as a resource distribution and supply/demand calculation mechanism. First, by using money, resources are distributed to where they are needed. If a family household needs or is in "demand" of a loaf of bread, they exchange money with a supplier (grocery store) to acquire it. Built into this process is a crude way to manage supply and demand. When that family buys a loaf of bread from the grocery store, that store knows it now has one less "supply" of bread in its inventory. When the store's inventory of bread reaches a certain minimum threshold, the store manager, now in *demand* of bread, contacts his distributor. The distributor replenishes the grocery store's bread *supply*, but now the distributor's inventory or *supply* of bread has been reduced. The distributor then reaches out to the manufacturer and lets him know how many loaves of bread he is in *demand* of. Oversimplifying, the manufacturer then calculates how many pounds of wheat he needs to make more bread. He then might contact a local wheat farmer and demand some wheat. Using money, the wheat is then distributed to the manufacturer. Now, the farmer's *supply* of wheat has been reduced, so he calculates how many seeds he might need to harvest more. And the cycle goes on and on.

Second, the price of any good is supposed to be a reflection of a good's value in society. A lower price might indicate a product is not actively sought after or that too much of the product exists in the marketplace, signaling to the producer that he should produce less. Conversely, a high price indicates the good is highly valued and in demand in society and signals to the producer he should produce more. However, in this crude method, the process quickly becomes distorted and convoluted once marketing enters the game, plays tricks on our small brains, and manufactures a sort of false demand, like with De Beers and diamonds, or when price-fixing and collusion become a strategic tool in an attempt to drive up the price of certain products, or when measures are taken to restrict the supply of certain goods to make them more scarce and hence more valuable, like when dairy producers began slaughtering cows in the 2000s in an attempt to inflate prices of dairy products.[2,3] When any number of these methods enters the fray and prices are tampered with, the pricing system and money quickly lose their credibility to accurately reflect supply and demand in a society.

For the most part, the process of using money to distribute goods and manage supply and demand seems to work well on the surface. However, once you start taking a closer look and analyze it on a deeper level, you see that using this intermediary as a distribution tool does not work. Going back to an earlier statistic, 14-18% of American children live in poverty,[4,5] yet 30-40% of food is thrown away.[6] Food is in demand by these children, and the supply is more than abundant. However, this excess in supply is not distributed to the children in need. In terms of housing, in 2018 the estimated number of homeless in America was around 550,000, while the number of empty houses was measured at over 17 million.[7] Again, the supply of homes clearly is not the problem. The mechanism for distributing this need to people is where the problem lies. Just looking at these two pieces of data alone indicates that money has failed miserably as a tool to effectively distribute goods to its people.

That leads me to my next question. Do we really need this intermediary, this ancient tool of exchange to efficiently distribute goods or to calculate supply and demand? The technology and computers of today can easily manage this task, putting less strain on Earth and less strain on the people the system was designed to serve. Technology like that used in a warehouse to automatically calculate inventory and demand could easily be expanded and rolled out into society. If a household is in demand of bread and the supply of bread exists, do we really need money to facilitate this exchange? No. Money is an unnecessary step in the process. Computers can calculate how much bread a distribution center needs based on the population in its general area. When its inventory is reduced, the proper contacts can be made to manufacture more. Further detail is provided in Chapter 10.

Money is a manmade tool, like a hammer. Why do we create tools? To make life easier for humans. Tools are invented to alleviate us from boring, dangerous, difficult, or monotonous tasks. As humans have progressed over the last many centuries, just about every single tool of antiquity has become obsolete as we've developed better, more efficient tools for completing similar tasks. The car has made the horse and buggy obsolete. Google Maps coupled with cell phones has made atlases all but obsolete. Computers have replaced typewriters. Just about every tool you can think of has been vastly improved upon or completely removed from society due to its inefficiency when compared to newer, competing technologies. However, the one tool – money – that has existed for thousands of years to help distribute goods is still used today for that same purpose. Sure, the tool itself is a bit more efficient as paper and coin money have made way for electronic money, but the same mechanism of exchanging this intermediary in order to distribute goods is still at its foundation. However, advancements in technological capabilities have rendered money obsolete (Chapter 10).

Now I want to talk about money's not-so-secret ability to control and manipulate others, and how it incentivizes abhorrent behavior.

# 4 BIRD'S-EYE VIEW OF THE PIT

"Whosoever controls the volume of money in our country is absolute master of all industry and commerce."[1] – James Garfield (20th President of the United States. Assassinated.)

"The real truth of the matter is, as you and I know, that a financial element in the larger centers has owned the Government ever since the days of Andrew Jackson."[2] – Franklin D. Roosevelt (32nd President of the United States)

Even men who hold the most prestigious titles in our society understand that those who possess the majority of the money supply wield immense power and control over the rest of the population. And it's not difficult to observe that money controls everything in the modern world, from the government, politics, and the justice system, to the media, education, healthcare, and the food industry. In many cases throughout history, especially over the last few decades, though presidents may have had more money than the average citizen, they usually are not part of the group that has enough to influence society. Presidents have masters they must dance for, and it's certainly not *the people.*

But how does the monetary game work exactly, and what is it about the lifeless tool of money that so easily grants individual men and groups such tremendous power over other individual men and groups? What is it about this artificial medium of exchange that is at the heart of history's wars, poverty, ecological degradation, exploitation, crime, structural violence, American racism, and just about every negative externality we face on this planet? I mean, if an asteroid hit Earth tomorrow and wiped out our entire food supply, it is not like we could eat a nickel or a twenty-dollar bill. So why then do men fight with such ferocity to acquire it?

Well, it's simple; it's because we "need" money to access the goods we consume to stay alive. But, in this zero-sum game, money is always scarce. In referring back to my Poker analogy, if one man acquires most of the finite poker chips in the game and becomes Chip Leader, that leaves very few left for the other players to compete for. But the other players can't survive solely off of what few chips they have; they will need more (at least the way society is arranged). The only way they can obtain more chips, however, is by somehow acquiring them from the Chip Leader with the overwhelming majority. But the Chip Leader is unlikely to hand his chips over for nothing. In exchange for pittance, he is going to demand a service from one of the lesser players, of which the lesser players would be hard-pressed to decline; they need his chips if they want to purchase food to stay alive, meaning they have little other choice than to comply. So, simply by having the majority of what every other man needs in society to survive, the Chip Leaders, in a nutshell, can get other players to essentially do what they want them to do. In effect, lesser players of society are and always have been at the mercy of those who have the majority of poker chips in circulation.

Within this monetary game we've unleashed to facilitate the flow and distribution of goods, people strategize and compete against one another to capture as much money (poker chips) as they can so they can continually access life necessities and ensure survival. The number one goal in this game is to not run out of chips, because that risks suffering and death. The secondary goal is to game your way toward becoming Chip Leader, because the more money one acquires, the longer he is able to secure his ability to live and live comfortably. Unfortunately, one's having more money than the average player comes at a cost as that means other players in the game have less, which means those other players might find it difficult to access the means to survive. Imbalance in the distribution of money can result in hardship and even death for players on the wrong end of the wealth continuum.

Now, in this monetary game masquerading as an economy, there are an infinite number of methods in which participants can acquire money from other participants; we are limited only by our imagination. Some players are able to obtain money by producing goods or providing services valued in society, like from cultivating food or serving as a doctor, while other players obtain money by producing nothing of value at all, like Wall Street traders or actual poker players. Of course, it doesn't really matter how one "wins" money in the game; it is his right to compete and sustain life as he sees fit. We in our national and global culture reasonably prefer that people do it within an arbitrary set of rules and without causing harm or discomfort to anyone else.

However, we are playing a game of survival at its core where the tool we need to access that survival is finite, so the expectation of fair play quickly flies out the window as the game progresses, money becomes scarcer and scarcer for many, and peoples' ability to survive is threatened. And most humans don't want to be faced with the idea of struggle, starvation, suffering, or death; most people don't want their lives threatened; so, with the understanding that more money correlates with more security and less struggle, it is not hard to fathom that a number of players would be willing to break the rules or behave ruthlessly if it means getting ahead in the game, gaining a competitive advantage over others, and ensuring survival for "x" amount of days longer. In any game we've ever played, we know that playing outside the lines or cheating can garner one significant advantage toward reaching the finish line before everyone else; so, players within this monetary game will and have used innumerable cheating techniques to advance themselves ahead of other players – like by using violence, bribery, tax evasion, lying, money laundering, etc. Such undesired behavior, you might say, is incentivized in the monetary game as it can provide players with a nice boost and help them reach the top and climb out of The Pit; it can better help them survive and survive comfortably.

Of course, we have referees (government) installed to prevent players from cheating; however, as will be discussed in Chapter 8, the referees happen to be playing the game and officiating at the same time, so they are also trying to obtain as much money as they can to ensure their survival; therefore, it is quite common for the game's officials to accept bribes and bend or even create rules that benefit a few players at the expense of everyone else. What many refer to as "Crony Capitalism" is simply an inevitable outcome of a game-like economic system, as few players in the competition amass a large share of a nation's money and then use their incredible financial power to manipulate the "neutral" governing body to their favor, to protect their winning positions. After all, the last thing the "winners" want is to be pulled back down into the mud where they have to scratch and claw for entrails amongst all the other players. Though it can be fun to compete and strategize within the depths of The Pit, the game grows tiresome after a while. That being said, a number of players believe that removing the refs will prevent "crony" gaming; however, I say it is a damned if you do, damned if you don't situation. Without refs officiating the game, the competition simply opens up to bullies, snakes, and the most ruthless to take advantage of players with stronger principles and virtues, while having refs allows the wealthiest to essentially create rules that benefit them and hinder everyone else.

Like "crony" gaming, a governing body is a natural and inevitable outgrowth of a monetary system that needs rules to reduce foul play and suffering. Whether they take the shape of traditional governments or whether they resemble organized, hierarchical groups like those found within gangs or the mafia (traditional government and mafia are not overly dissimilar), governing institutions inevitably form. Unfortunately, at this stage in the monetary game those snakes and bullies I mentioned above have found a way to infiltrate government, and they've placed their constituents, their dogs, in key influential positions; the greater populace is playing against loaded dice.

On a very basic level, that is how the game works. And, woven into the fabric of the game as some players capture a majority share of the money supply is loss of control, autonomy, and volition for the "losers." The game's "winners" know this, so to divert the attention of the losers and make sure they never catch on to the idea that they are being used and controlled, the winners use intense media and marketing campaigns to convince people that they are free, and that they are in absolute control of their lives. They utilize advanced techniques in social engineering to convince the rest of the population that not only are they not enslaved, but to happily shackle themselves to life-wasting, meaningless chores and then hide the key. Even more, they hypnotize the masses into being grateful for their metaphorical restraints.

To clarify, humans generally want responsibility in life (Chapter 9);

they want to participate in tasks and projects that add purpose and self-esteem to their short existence here on Earth – prolonged idleness and boredom can be torture. However, what most humans don't want is to be made to feel like they *have* to do something; as though they have little other choice than to dig coal, build houses, or manipulate spreadsheets for the majority of their waking hours until they retire or find reprieve in a casket. Unfortunately, those are the circumstances a large sector of national and global society have found themselves in; engaged in work activity they perceivably had or have little choice in, are bound to, and feel like they must participate in every single day else lose their ability to survive.

To puppeteer society and get the greater populace to emulate mindless cattle and submit to lifelong tasks they might not otherwise choose to perform, the majority money-holders, the masters of our global monetary system use the instrument of FEAR; most commonly, the *fear of survival.* As I will continue to reiterate, in the global game of money, we "need" money to access the means of survival. But, when a small handful of players have a significant share of the money supply, that means the rest of the players have much less to compete for, acquire, and then use to buy food, water, and shelter. And when people's wallets start to grow thin, feelings of stress and insecurity propagate, and our irrational minds become impregnated with visions of suffering and even death; for some, those thoughts turn rational when they actually do suffer or die after failing to acquire a sufficient amount of the limited supply of money to access life necessities. So, to avoid the threat of struggle and death altogether, people lower on the socioeconomic totem pole "willingly" submit to unattractive jobs that those higher on the totem pole want completed, but don't have the time, means, or desire to complete themselves. The majority money-holders have the unique ability to essentially enslave lesser players by exploiting their innate fears of survival; after all, the majority money-holders have what the lesser players need to stay alive, meaning they can perpetually manipulate and extort those lesser players into submission.

Fear of survival in concert with using a finite intermediary as a barrier to life necessities makes population control easily attainable, and it is part of the reason why we have more slaves now in the world than at any other time in history.[3,4] Unfortunately, generation after generation have been born into the economic model of having to submit to a master to earn life, and it has become as normal and necessary as the air we breathe.

Again, in the present-day monetary system, we are competing amongst each other to acquire what is scarce (money) to gain access to that which is and can be made ever more abundant (food, water, clothing, energy, etc.), which has often led to suffering and death amongst the participants who become "losers" and their children. One might use the term Structural Violence to describe such a circumstance, where suffering and death are direct or indirect results of inefficiencies in an economic system; by all accounts, structural violence is responsible for more death and hardship than all modern wars combined. That is why I have branded the environment harboring this insane, maybe even psychopathic, game of acquisition as The Pit. And it is this game, this competition of survival that has extracted from us our worst human characteristics. It is this global system of gaming one another, as I will do my best to prove throughout this book, that has produced such unwanted behavior such as greed, desperation, and violence. Though we inherently seek positive social interaction, when peoples' lives are threatened, like when they are unsure day in and day out how they will acquire enough money to access food and shelter, they can be driven to terrible actions. And no one is immune to the pressures of this game – both rich and poor partake in deplorable behavior to secure comfort and survival and to avoid struggle, suffering, and even shame. Feelings of inferiority and shame inherent to the monetary game are at the heart of many violent crimes, according to criminal psychiatrist James Gilligan and other experts (Chapter 6.5).

Now, as you've been reading this chapter, you might be thinking that I am purposely using careful language to conceal the economic system I am actually intending to criticize to avoid vitriol from devout followers. You might be thinking that I am secretly expressing dismay for…Capitalism. However, I assure you, I am not. First of all, the American version of Capitalism is not pure, Laissez-Faire, "Free" Market Capitalism (see Chapter 8 for a deeper analysis on Laissez-Faire Capitalism). It is a hybrid system. Second of all, as I will point out again later, I don't differentiate Capitalism from Socialism (as understood in modern terms) all that much. Though I understand the aspects and ideologies that distinguish one from the other, they, along with most economic systems across the globe are mere monetary *subsystems*; they are all variants of the overarching money game. In both Capitalism and Socialism alike, the core concept of humans having to acquire money from other humans in order to access the necessities of life is present; the central theme of obtaining as much money as one can to ensure survival and healthy living links all systems; they just adhere to slightly different rulebooks. Both seemingly adversarial systems are playing a game of poker – only, in Capitalism, the chip leaders get to keep most of their chips, and in Socialism, the chip leaders must give some back. In total, the whole world is intertwined within one giant, interconnected monetary market system. Separation is merely an illusion, as all the world's citizens compete and strategize against each other to acquire money to access life sustaining goods.

Of course, survival is the ultimate driver within the inner core of the game; but, as we move to the outer layers, secondary elements like social status, ego, self-esteem, respect, and dopaminergic activity play prominent roles in driving us to game each other for cash and material rewards. Historically, those with more material wealth are held in higher regard than those with less material wealth; those with more crap are generally considered more successful, while those with less crap might be perceived as failures, which adds stress and damages health. If one must aggressively compete to avoid being perceived as a failure and receive adulation or acceptance from peers, one will aggressively compete.

Anyway, no, in my critiques throughout this book, I am not referring to daughter systems like Capitalism or Socialism; I am referring solely to the parent Monetary System, the overarching game of money where the ultimate goal is to acquire as much paper as one can to secure survival and make it out of The Pit.

In order to illustrate the fundamental mechanics of the monetary game and how easy it is for individuals to gain power and control over a population once they've acquired the majority of a nation's money, I have performed a rudimentary Austrian-School-of-Economics-style Thought Experiment in the next section, followed by real life examples attempting to support the presented content at the end of this chapter. Bear with me; for some this thought exercise will resonate and paint a clearer picture of the game, while for others it will seem overly simplistic, redundant, and unreflective of our national and global monetary system as a whole. Simplicity *is* the purpose here though. Economists have historically made the subjects of finance and economics much more complex and complicated than they actually are; they have made the subject inaccessible to a general audience, which results in feelings of disempowerment and, thus, dependence, as the widely-read economist John Kenneth Galbraith once said:

> "The study of money, above all other fields in economics, is one in which complexity is used to disguise truth or to evade truth, not to reveal it."[5]

At its core, however, economy, prices, supply & demand, it's all just simple arithmetic. As we delve deeper into various topics, my analyses and descriptions will become less vague and much more detailed. Again, this is merely foundational.

## 4.1 THOUGHT EXPERIMENT

Okay, now let's take a step back and follow that basic train of thought using a simple fictional anecdote (based on a true-ish story) to help illustrate how our globally connected game of money can quickly grow out of hand and afford few individuals massive control over the vast majority of society and its resources. And just to clarify, though my tone might seem like it at various points throughout this book, I don't condemn or label a man wrong or immoral for amassing great sums of financial wealth at the expense of others. As will be repeated throughout this text, the "winners" of the game are simply doing what the game allows and encourages them to do; they are simply doing what they feel they need to do to mitigate the risk of survival and "win." Don't hate the player, hate the game.

Let's begin.

To set the scene of this abstract Thought Experiment, let's imagine we have a very small, isolated community of five individuals – John, Samson, Isaac, Nathan, and Bill (the names are mostly irrelevant). Let's also imagine that $100 is dumped onto this small community and each person is given $20 to conduct business. With the finite money supply equally distributed, each member then erects his quaint little shop, and the game of commerce and acquisition commences. In the beginning, life is good for everyone. Players wheel and deal, wine and dine, produce and seduce. Goods exchange. Money circulates. Individual bank accounts fluctuate slightly above and slightly below $20, but balance is maintained overall. And for the most part, the players seem happy in the broad field of economic battle; they go home feeling gratified; fulfilled. They perch their feet up each night with a sense of importance, as though they are contributing members of society.

Unfortunately, change is the only constant in life, and as we fast forward six months to the relevant part of this exercise, we find that one member – John – has grown tired and bored of the tedious game. He's been performing the same tasks every day of every week since the competition began; his daily routine has become so monotonous, as he wakes up each morning, drinks coffee, goes to work, comes home, makes dinner, watches TV, goes to bed, and then wash, rinse, repeat the following morning, that he wants out. He wants the freedom to take on different challenges and do the things he actually enjoys in life. "No more," John says to himself.

So, one night, John wracks his brain in an attempt to discover ways to liberate himself from his repetitive and suffocating lifestyle. Eventually, a light bulb flickers on in his brain. "Ah ha!" John realizes that if he can somehow manage to acquire most of the money from the other four members of society, then the other members would have no alternative option but to go through him if they want money to eat. Such incredible leverage would give him the power to coerce the other players into doing whatever he wants them to do. Brilliant! So, feeling inspired and with renewed vigor, John maps an elaborate plan on the walls of his dingy garage; he develops innovative marketing schemes and begins cleverly gaming his colleagues to convince them to hand over a slightly higher proportion of their money with each exchange. The transactions can't diverge too far from the 1:1 ratio that had been standard since the game's inception however, lest the other players catch on too soon and foil his ingenious plot. In addition to innovative marketing and clever gaming, John decides to cut a few corners with his wine business to reduce costs and increase profit margins; he fills his wine bottles with a half portion of wine and a half portion of water. Whatever it takes to win and get ahead, right? And I mean, hey, if you ain't cheatin', you ain't tryin'!

With time's unraveling of the game, John finds himself gaining a larger and larger share of the community's money supply. And it matters not which methods of acquisition were most effective – whether his gains came through ethical means, clever marketing, cunning manipulation, or outright thievery – what matters in this hypothetical is that John has amassed a tremendous portion of the financial wealth within this micro-society – let's say $95 – and has placed himself in prime position to achieve his goals of freedom and control. Since there is only $100 in circulation within society, if John has $95 then that means only $5 remain for the other four members to survive off of. By all measures, John has won the game! This is bad news for the four losers, however, because goods are not cheap, and they need money to access those goods if they plan on staying alive.

Well, at this juncture in the game, John is virtually the only person the losers can obtain money from because there is no magical, nanny-state entity creating cash out of thin air and dumping it onto their system. The initial $100 is all that exists. Consequently, the other members will have no other choice, at least that's what they believe, than to submit to John if they want to acquire money. It's at this moment that John has seized control over the others and can get an empire built around him without lifting a finger.

Now, for this exercise I'm going to conveniently expand our population to 10,000 people, because it would take a long time for John to build an empire with only four slaves. He needs more. The circumstances are still the same, however; John still has the lion's share of the monetary wealth, leaving the rest of society with very little to compete for, acquire, and use to purchase the means of survival.

Shifting character perspectives, one evening Samson's daughter says, "Daddy, I'm hungry…" With a pit in his stomach, Samson opens his kitchen cupboard to find a lone can of soup hiding between cobwebs and shadows. He sighs; at least his daughter can eat for tonight. Behind the intermittent slurps of chicken noodles, Samson pulls the cushions off his couch and plunges his hands into its dusty cracks. *There must be a fallen quarter or at least a nickel somewhere in this house.*

"What're you doing, Daddy?" His daughter catches Samson scrounging for scraps.

Concealing his shame, he replies, "Just building a fort, sweetie."

*What'll I do*, Samson thinks to himself. Bank account depleted, tummy rumblin', and desperation growing, Samson sees no other alternative than to turn to John for help. Again, John is the majority money holder and virtually the only person Samson can acquire money from. So, the next day he takes a deep breath and enters John's domain. "Samson, my friend, what brings you to these parts?"

"Hey John… I, feel ashamed to admit, but we've run out of food at home, and I've no more money to buy more. Is there any chance you could spare a few dollars? How's Peggy by the way?"

"Sharon's good, thank you for asking," replies John.

Samson's hard swallow echoes through the dreary corridor.

John continues, "For such a loyal friend, I have a few dollars to spare."

Samson lights up, "Oh thank God!"

"But you'll have to do something for me."

"Name it! I'll do anything!"

John thinks for a moment. "Hmmm… we have been running a little low on coal. How about this, go into the mine over there and dig up some coal, and you will be fairly compensated."

"Absolutely! Anything you say, sir! Thank you, thank you, thank you!"

With that, Samson grabs a pickaxe and shovel and runs to the mine where he spends his entire day extracting coal. The dangerous and dirty work isn't necessarily his life goal, but he is excited to feed his family, so he'll endure it. His research into curing cancer hasn't necessarily been paying the bills, anyway, since he hasn't quite found a cure, yet. Sure he's made progress, and sure it's important and valuable to society, but research and testing doesn't sell in the free market; only a final, marketable product does. And there is no government entity to subsidize basic R&D; John is the nanny, and he has no interest in cancer treatments right now. I mean, why would he? Neither he, nor his closest family and friends are suffering from it. So, Samson sets aside his noble research and submits to work that can actually get him paid.

Well, at day's end Samson runs back to John with a bucket of coal and a proud smile. "Here you are, sir!"

"Good, Samson, good…" John digs into his right pocket as Samson anxiously awaits. "Here you go."

John opens his clenched fist and drops four quarters into the coal miner's palm. Samson's smile evaporates. *$1? What the hell can this buy me? A loaf of bread and some milk? Wtf?*

John, that sly fox. See, he knows that if he pays Samson only enough to purchase a few necessities, it ensures Samson will be back the next day to complete other undesirable chores. And John also knows that

Samson understands how foolish it would be to bitch or ask for more compensation considering the long line of people experiencing similar financial circumstances who would be willing to perform the work for less if it means acquiring money to feed their families – it's amazing what people will do for full bellies. So, with zero bargaining power and seeking to remain in John's good graces, Samson quickly puts his smile back on and says, "Thank you, John!"

"Say, there's more where that came from. Just come back tomorrow."

"Um, s-sure… No problem." What other choice does Samson have?

The next day, Samson returns – reluctant on the inside, eager on the outside. "What can I do for you today, sir?"

"Hmm, you know I'm getting too old to swim across that river to get to my vegetable garden. It would be great if you could build a bridge for me."

Samson's jaw drops. "A whaaa…?"

"Just a bridge. Should be easy, right? Or maybe you've got all the groceries you'll need at home?"

"Oh, you said 'bridge.' Right, yeah, no problem at all," Samson says with a gulp and a grin.

"You'll need some help, though. See that sorry group of men standing in line outside? Just pluck two of them and have a gay old time."

Samson nods his head, "On it." He then grabs two eager men, and they get to work. Like Samson, building a bridge isn't a task the other two men want to perform, but they've also run out of money and feel like they have little other choice than to serve John for a nominal allowance. And what's great for John is that a number of society's inhabitants have become homeless due to being unable to obtain money and afford house payments. Why's that great? Because the homeless essentially act as scarecrows – heads on a stake – for Samson and the rest of society; those destitute souls set a wonderful example of what awaits should they refuse John's polite requests. So, Samson and his crew keep their heads down, asses up, and build away.

At sun down, John pays each of the men just enough money so they can go to the grocery store and buy a few necessities. But again, they will have to return the following day if they seek to continue stocking their households with food. And what's also great for John? He owns the grocery store in town, so all of the money that these men spend on food filters right back up to him, allowing him to maintain a tighter grasp over the money supply, and thus the community (see *Company Towns* section).

Samson and the other losers of society essentially become trapped in a life of servitude to John – one might even be so bold as to call them "slaves." Their fear of survival keeps them docile and obedient; after all, they need John's money to live. If they fail to acquire John's money, they can't buy food. If they can't buy food, they can't eat. If they can't eat, they starve and suffer. If they starve long enough, they die. At least, that is the scenario presented in their heads. The instinctual survival mechanism in their brain paralyzes them with fear and perpetual worry, and by exploiting that fear, John can watch his empire flourish whilst enjoying Brandy Old Fashioned Sweets on the beach surrounded by his harem – he can even pay people to recruit and procure vulnerable men and/or women to join his harem.

And as for *the people*, constantly worrying about money and having to submit to undignified labor for chicken feed leaves them stressed, sick, and unhappy. They feel powerless. They feel voiceless, because again, there is a cavalcade of desperate people who also need John's money to survive and would be willing to take on chores at a lower rate (even though food around everyone is abundant).

Now, other players within the game have made attempts to dethrone John and yank him from his luxurious castle and back into The Pit, but with John controlling such a magnificent stake of the money supply, all have failed. He just has way too much financial leverage that he can swiftly stamp out all competitors. For instance, Nathan tried entering the oil market when he discovered a black gold deposit beneath his basement, to which he jumped in the air and kicked his heels together, but his bid for market supremacy didn't last long before he was found with his tail tucked between his legs, trudging back to the tomato fields. He never stood a chance. See, after Nathan refused John's initial offer to buy the oil, the competition quickly escalated as John employed a bevy of ethical and unethical tactics to utterly destroy Nathan. He paid goons to intimidate Nathan at his house; he brokered favorable distribution deals using his savvy business acumen; he even paid a man to set fire to one of Nathan's storage facilities. With his steadfast resolve, however, Nathan could endure those relentless attacks on his budding enterprise; but, what he could not endure was John's move to engage in a series of price wars (see section on *Standard Oil and Mr. Rockefeller*).

When Nathan opened up his first few Gas Stations, he set the price of gasoline at $3.00 per gallon, slightly below John's price and just enough to turn a profit. But John wasn't about to let a child defeat him at his own game, so he immediately undercut Nathan and charged $2.50 per gallon, even though it meant taking a temporary loss. John could afford it, though. Nathan could not. He tried lowering his prices several times to compete with John, but with each attempt John simply lowered his prices even more without batting an eye; again, he had the financial means to do so. Since the rest of the community was strapped for cash, of course they were going to purchase their fuel from the gas station offering the lowest prices. Though they understood John wasn't the most upstanding human being and would've liked to see his empire crumble, they needed every extra penny they could get to stave off suffering. Consequently for Nathan, people stopped giving him their business, and the only activity at his gas stations became the tumbleweeds bouncing past his pumps and the whining buzzards flying overhead waiting to pick at his haggard corpse; he wasn't dead, yet, but they sensed his demise was near. With all of the gas money filtering into John's pockets, Nathan eventually had to close up shop. And shortly after Nathan barricaded his doors, John swooped in and acquired Nathan's assets for a fraction of his initial offer. Thus, Nathan lived the rest of his days in despair pickin' maters for 12 hours a day, 6 days a week. John was a religious man, thankfully, and at least gave his servants Sunday off so they could pray to their Lord – John.

With John's overwhelming financial clout, he had no trouble annihilating competitors and maintaining a stronghold over the controlling share of society's money, and thus, over *the people. The people* were all trapped with little other choice if they wanted to avoid becoming worm food. Of course, that isn't to say the citizens didn't have choices. Though they virtually had no choice but to be a servant in John's empire, they could at least choose in what capacity they served. For instance, one could choose if he wanted to build bridges, dig coal, or pick produce – as long as there were vacancies of course. If there were no vacancies, then one submitted his talents to whatever was available. And once a person was plucked out of a sea of candidates to fill a specific role, his family rejoiced.

"Yayyy, you get to live!!!"

[I could stop this thought exercise here, but I feel compelled to continue for a few more beats]

Several weeks into John's reign, he has an epiphany. He realizes that he is merely one man. If the majority of the population found out they didn't necessarily *have* to be John's slave, they could band together and overthrow him with little effort. To reduce the risk of mass insurrection, John takes a number of measures.

First, he wants to divert attention away from himself and onto a faceless entity. That way if the people do become enraged, all of their anger and all of the blame will be focused on that institution, keeping the spotlight off of him and allowing him to retain his ability to weave webs in the shadows. To accomplish this first task, John hires a group of individuals and anoints them as stewards of the game; their job is to maintain the rulebook and make sure everybody plays within the lines; it is up to this group to essentially manage the affairs of his kingdom. And, if John feels like a competing player is becoming too strong and threatens to pull the rug beneath John's feet, he can also order his governing body to create new rules that hinder that competing player and ensure John's cushy position is safe.

Next, John hires a second set of individuals to act as his muscle. It is this group's duty to enforce the rules and protect the overall infrastructure of the community – and John. Now, of course the rules that are created and enforced do not apply to John. Why would they? He is the one paying these bodies of management and enforcement. Should any of them threaten John with punishment, he could easily kick them out of the coveted "in-group" – removing their ability to purchase life necessities – and find replacements; after all, he is paying them slightly more than his other subordinates, meaning people on the outside looking in would love to attain a role within John's cabinet if it means more money, respect, and further alleviation from financial worries. So, it is in the best interest of John's managers and muscle to lick, rather than bite, the hand that feeds them, to obey and pledge loyalty. They would be risking their high-profile positions and wellbeing if they don't.

With his referees and enforcement arm secured, John's next move is to hire a "head official" to not only oversee and manage these authoritative branches of society, but also to serve as the face of the community. In this way, if restless citizens want a specific individual to point the finger at rather than a faceless organization, they will have this executive officer to do that with. It will also further separate John from the bubble of society and allow him to operate outside of the game's jurisdiction. Thus, John hires Bill and gives him a fancy title. He brands him…President!

With a smirk on his face, Bill puffs out his chest. *I'm the man now. People will have to answer to me!*

"Damn you, Bill! Gloat outside, not in here," yelled John.

"Oh, right. Sorry sir…"

President Bill immediately withdrew into himself and scurried out of John's chambers after being castigated. Although Bill has a neat label, a slightly higher salary, and a greater perceived importance within society, he still answers to the Money, obviously, since he relies on the money for subsistence. John is still Bill's master.

So now that John has a team to manage his vast estate, provide protection, and jiggle keys in front of the faces of the public, he realizes he needs to make one final crucial move before retiring from the game and vanishing behind its emerald curtains. John understands that if he can slowly mold people's thoughts using an onslaught of psychological techniques, he can manipulate them into accepting their figurative chains as normal, as though subservience is a necessary part of their short, transitory existence, which makes them less likely to revolt against John or his managing subordinates. Sure the first generation or two are always resistant to change, but by about the third generation, as more and more servants are born into their shackles, it simply becomes a standard way of life – the beforetimes are nearly forgotten. The idea loosely aligns with the popular "frog-in-boiling-water" analogy, where a frog is placed in a pot of water, and if the water's temperature rises too quickly, he will jump out. But, if the heat of the water increases only gradually over time, the frog will continually acclimate his body to the rising temperatures and won't jump out; even as the heat becomes oppressive and life threatening, the frog remains in the water, oblivious to his detrimental environment.

To properly manipulate the public and achieve social conformity, John acquires control over the media tendril of society and sets up multiple news outlets that air slightly different programs and broadcasts. On a microlevel, John orders each outlet to take opposing positions on various topics to give the people a sense of choice and free will, while also keeping them distracted as they form tightknit gangs based on similar opinions and then fight with other gangs that hold opposing opinions. He learned from studying prison environments that if you divide prisoners into groups and then pit them against each other, that it takes attention away from the guards, and the prison population becomes much easier to manage. So, "divide-and-conquer" is his preferred method on a microlevel for maintaining order; however, on a macrolevel, John instructs all of his media puppets to push the same general overarching narratives and ideologies to make sure the population is on the same page in regard to the most important topics – namely anything related to national loyalty. He wants the masses conditioned to believe that they are the best, that they are part of the golden "in-group," and that their life circumstances are better than all other "out-groups" living on the opposite side of the imaginary fence – even though the majority of the population is stressed, tired, and unhappy, and even though they have high levels of murder, crime, depression, suicide, cancer, heart disease, and a lower life expectancy than similar civilizations. John understands if he can get his livestock to buy into an "us-vs.-them" mentality, he can create a sort of group pride, a herd mentality that will further divert their attention, ensure loyalty, and prevent recalcitrant behavior, which will further insulate John from civil agitation. So, with the knowledge that verbal repetition and visual and auditory cues are effective in embedding information into the subconscious mind – knowledge he acquired from studying prior empires – John orders the talking bobble heads of his media tendril to constantly use positive buzzwords like "freedom" and "liberty" when talking about his kingdom and negative buzzwords to describe neighboring kingdoms.

By repeating the same general messages over and over and over and over again, not only do his people start to believe what he wants them to believe, but they start reciting and conveying the messages themselves, like programmed machines. And the best part of it all is the lowly peasants have no clue their thoughts are being engineered and artificially implanted; their inflated egos actually have them thinking their beliefs come from their own "superb" intellect and free will. John laughs. "Baha! Bahaha!"

However, John understands, also, that there will be a small percentage stubbornly resistant to the social hypnosis. To combat these self-righteous deviants, he has his media arm employ methods of shaming those who question John's established order. Because humans have such a strong aversion to social alienation, if the media can convince most of the population to attack and reprimand those with opposing perspectives that threaten to expose John to the light, which could erode his empire, that small minority can easily be silenced or driven to conformity. And for the ones that create too much noise, for the ones that repeatedly refuse their muzzles, well, extreme measures can be taken to "neutralize" those rabble-rousers outside of the public's awareness.

Lastly, as it pertains to John's media arm? Under no circumstances does he want them to mention his name. It is his intent to disappear from society, after all, as power structures prefer to remain hidden, because the more he is exposed, the more he makes eye contact with the snake-headed mob, the greater the chances are he, along with his empire, will turn to stone. President Bill was anointed as the face of society for a reason. All complaints and hate are to be directed at him, even though he has little to do with any negative externalities in society, as they are largely caused by the inevitable inequities of the monetary game itself.

With his primary pillars of control now established, John could close in for checkmate, but he sees a secondary threat that could topple his empire if he plays too carelessly, and that threat is the progressive intellect of the people. An educated populace is important for material growth, John realizes, but a mob that can think critically might start to unearth the core preconditions behind poverty, resource depletion, planned obsolescence, desperation, and overall societal distress. If too many people come to understand that much of the community's problems are caused by monetary scarcity and imbalance in this zero-sum game of survival, they might consider putting the game back in the closet and constructing a real economy actually equipped to serve the population; and if that happens, John fears he could lose his kingdom and his cozy position of dominance. *Oh no! My harem!* John thinks to himself. *Without the need for my money, they will flee.*

So, to further clamp down on society and prevent his ship from sinking, John also seizes control of the educational tentacle. Again, he wants the people to be smart, but not too smart. He'd rather his citizens pat themselves on the back for reciting baseball statistics or memorizing names of actors and movies. And if they are interested in learning how the game works, he'd rather "economists" add layers and fatty rules to the system and encourage folks to master the complexities of those added layers rather than strip the game down to its knickers and understand its deeper, simpler mechanics.

John strategically restructures education to groom up-and-coming members of society specifically for the "workforce" and to happily accept servitude within his kingdom. He has history books updated to paint a cleaner picture of his kingdom's past and present, which serves to instill his subjects with pride and positivity, further buffering him from any sort of future rebellion. And since one-track minded individuals are easier to manage, he has his educational constituents encourage students to choose a focused vocational path and to not venture too far off of that path once they've chosen it. Most importantly within his educational arm, John wants students conditioned to believe that there is no alternative for subsistence outside of the game they were nurtured into. He wants them carefully bred to take a number and fall into place. Such a setup accomplishes two goals. It ensures that budding adults see a lifetime of daily servitude and attachment to a superior as normal, which keeps them from asking dumb questions, like "why." Second, it serves to keep the people out of John's hair, as once they enter the workforce, most of their free time will be tied up in the required activity they were conditioned to believe they *must* accept, and they will be too distracted and too exhausted to notice John's maneuvers.

One night, as John stared up at the glow-in-the-dark star and planet stickers on the ceiling above his bed, he began talking to himself. "Illusion of choice seems to be the theme here. The people seem more content when they feel like they have volition," he said. "So how can I find a way to make everyone feel like they have a say in matters concerning 'their' nation, and give them a greater sense of ownership and responsibility, which would further instill them with pride and keep their attention off of me? How can I give them the feeling of agency and empowerment without giving them any power at all?" *Hmmm.* John fell asleep counting dancing dollar bills in his head.

That night, an angel in the form of John appeared to him in his dreams and delivered a cryptic clue to his perplexing question. "My dear John," the angel said. "The throne is faux. The throneeee isssss fauxxxxxx......"

John's eyes burst open as he thrust his body forward in bed.

Breathing heavily and oozing cold sweat, he swiveled his head around the room before eventually resting his gaze upon President Bill curled up, sound asleep in his kennel at the end of John's bed. At that moment, John was struck with a sudden, almost divine revelation. "The throne is faux. President Bill! That's it!!! It matters not who sits on the throne. All that matters is who controls the money. And I control the money! So what I will do is I will let the people choose which puppet sits on the artificial throne every few years. It'll give them the illusion of choice and control, and make them think their opinion matters in society even though it doesn't. It'll be like owning a car; it's mine and I get to choose where it's driven, but to get the kids in the backseat to shut up because they don't like where the car is headed, I will give them a decoy responsibility. I will tell them that they have the privilege, no no, the honor of getting to choose the 'all-important' paint job of my car. I will convince them how vital it is that they participate in the process of electing whether or not my car gets a red or blue exterior. They get to choose the meaningless paint job; I get to choose where and how the car is driven. And if they don't like where the car is going, I will tell them to choose a different color next time, and the process will repeat over and over again." John smirks. *What a brilliant ruse!* (see section called *Democracy?*)

So, the following day John picks two citizens who he is familiar enough with to know that they will remain submissive to him, and who he is confident will not venture too far from status quo. He then turns around and tells the people that it is up to them to choose which one "manages" society. Galvanized by the newfound sense of control and empowerment, the people spend two years bickering amongst each other with puffed chests and furrowed eyebrows over which color everyone should vote for – red or blue. They've all become convinced that the health of their society rests on their broad, collective shoulders, unaware that the money structure is the one that chose both candidates, that both puppets are ultimately controlled by the money structure, and that the money structure still gets to choose how the country operates. John, arms crossed on his kingdom's mountaintop, hovers over the ants and enjoys the amusing theater of it all. "Should I feel bad for taking advantage of such gullibility, of such primitive and malleable brains?"

John ponders his question for a moment as he looks back at the servants watering his ornate flower gardens that cast a beautiful reflection off the koi pond tracing a path to his castle. He returns his gaze to the quarreling ants. Then back again to his tranquil abode.

"Fuck'm." John turns and saunters into the setting sun.

Well, months later, after the population elected Manny as President, wait no, Isaac? Was it Isaac or Manny they elected? Ah, who gives a shit; it doesn't matter. Months later, after the people voted for society's new wallpaper and with the economic apparatus chugging along without a hitch, John began directing his attention to territories outside of his arbitrary borders. As he peered over the fence at one of the neighboring countries – Pluto – he recognized they had a surplus of a resource that his people and the rest of the world coveted. The asset had nicknames like "golden oil," "John Blood," and "nectar of the Gods," but its official name was Sun Drop, and it also happened to be John's favorite beverage. Being the savvy businessman that John was, he understood that if he could acquire control over the foreign Sun Drop deposits, not only would it increase his wealth and the wealth of his kingdom, but it would also earn him a considerable amount of leverage in the world game.

So, the following week, John hatches a brilliant scheme and instructs his media tendril to run a disparaging, though false, story involving Pluto's ruler, King Tyrannus, to get his citizens angry enough that they wouldn't demur when he decided to send his muscle over to rough up Tyrannus and seize control over his sweet, sweet Sun Drop. And by all reports, Tyrannus wasn't a nice guy to begin with, so drumming up support for an invasion wouldn't be overly difficult in the first place. Thus, the myrmidons of John's media arm subsequently reported that Pluto's tyrannical king was caught taking litters of puppies and catapulting them off of mountains. An organization tied to John even hired an actor – a man who looked and sounded like a Plutonian – to divulge his "eye witness account" of King Tyrannus' atrocities. That night, John watched with a bowl of popcorn as the actor stood at a podium in front of reporters and flashing bulbs and delivered his confession while trying desperately to force tears. John cringed, "Who hired this chump? I could do a better job of acting than him."

The man's sincerity mattered little, however. The following day, John's citizens were enraged. High on emotions, low on pragmatism, the mob wanted nothing more than to see King Tyrannus come to justice for his reprehensible actions; they wanted him skinned alive. So, with the nation's unwavering support, John, through his governmental fixture, ordered his muscle to enter Pluto and track and seize the vile king. The operation was a success, which came as a surprise to no one since Pluto was considerably smaller than John's kingdom. King Tyrannus was captured, and John secretly acquired control over Pluto's Sun Drop stash. And though a large number of John's troops were killed, went home with injuries and psychological damage, began committing suicide at a disturbing rate, struggled financially and even wound up homeless after the fighting had ceased, John's propaganda campaign was effective enough to convince them that the war was for a noble and righteous cause. John was incredibly charming after all, and nobody believed he was capable of lying to them for his own personal benefit. And on the Plutonian side, not only did thousands suffer and die, but they lost control of their most lucrative resource, and thus their ability to earn money and pay off foreign debts; it wouldn't take long for their economy to collapse. With King Tyrannus erased from the global canvas, John swiftly installed a new leader of his choosing, one he knew would obey his demands. The citizens didn't know it, but the new king of Pluto was on John's payroll; John was his master. (see section on *Lies and War* and Chapter 6.4)

"Boy was that easy," John said to himself. "I bet I could do that with all of those small territories down there. All I have to do is loosely convince my servants that they pose a credible threat to our safety, and they won't even bat an ethical eye. I imagine stealing candy from a baby wouldn't be this easy." Beaming with confidence and inspiration, John aligned his crosshairs with another neighboring territory – Caeliferia. The small, yet belligerent, nation was overflowing with exotic grasshopper skins – an intrinsically useless commodity that had become synonymous with elevated social status and success amongst John's people; for some odd reason, the skins had become a luxury. So, to rile up his citizens once more, John concocts another false story to make Caeliferia seem uncivil and dangerous. In his simple fabrication, John has his media arm report to the empire that Caeliferian ships had attacked John's ships unprovoked, to which John's people responded once again with outrage – as they did with the puppies. They wanted revenge! And to top it all off, John appealed to the humanitarians of his kingdom by informing them that Caeliferia was operating under an inhumane economic system, and that their natives were suffering and enslaved because of it. Even though John couldn't have cared less about the Caeliferian people or what system they used, he was perceived as a sympathetic and caring leader for taking such a bold stance against injustice.

With the full support of his pawns, John once again ordered his muscle to enter the small country; they successfully rooted out the Caeliferian leadership, and John acquired control of their grasshopper skins and installed a new puppet leader of his choosing. John's loyal team of supporters couldn't have been more proud that they were dependents beneath a leader willing to risk the lives of strangers to do the "right" thing. What a man!

*But wait,* John thinks to himself. *What if the herd somehow exposes the truth? What if they find out I was somewhat "liberal" with the facts and that I sacrificed human lives for my own personal gain? Oh I can't have that.*

To hedge his lucrative investments, John calls up Rupert at Chupacabra News and Jeff at BNN (Bullshit News Network) in a subdued panic. "You guys! I'm gonna need you to double down on division and deception! Got it?!"

"But sir, haven't we already gone far enough with misleading the public," replied Rupert.

"Yeah, this is starting to feel immoral," said Jeff.

"Hmmm, it sounds to me like you guys don't want money anymore. You both must be tired of buying food. Is that what I'm hearing? Here, why don't you two leave your suits and leashes at my doorstep and I'll find a couple replacements."

"NO NO NO!!!" They both replied in unison.

"Ramping up domestic division won't be a problem," said Rupert.

"I thought so." John abruptly ended the call.

That night BNN ran stories about how the conservative factions of society were vicars of the devil, and that their collective intellect made Kevin Malone look like Walter White. Conversely, Chupacabra reported that cross-eyed, brain-dead liberal tribes wanted to see society burned to the ground, and that they were the biggest threat to peace and stability that the nation had ever encountered. And boy oh boy did that divisive rhetoric prove ever successful; what had previously been a controlled, calculated burn had suddenly exploded into a raging wildfire, as competing tribes began incessantly hurling vitriolic flames at one another. Tempers were flarin'. Blood was bubblin'. And the pair of media bellows kept pumpin' hot air into the cauldron to keep the fires alive and cracklin'. And through the thick plumes of smoke billowing into the air from the in-house friction, beneath the hazy shroud, John was able to slither in and around the polarized masses, completely undetected. He was able to add new rules to the game and take nefarious actions outside of the nation's imaginary walls, and the public was none the wiser. All they knew and all they cared about was what BNN and CN told them to care about; as far as the public was concerned, nothing else existed outside of what their television or computer screens displayed, at least nothing relevant. It was a perfectly contrived disaster for John. With his inmates thoroughly distracted, he could do anything and everything he wanted while maintaining his competitive advantage and continuing to build his empire.

And it all started, it was all made easy once John acquired majority control of the money supply and subsequently began exploiting the population's fear of survival. The game's other players needed money to access the necessities of life, but with John having it all, they could only obtain it by going through him. Thus, with the financial upper hand, John could dangle the carrots of survival in front of the faces of the competing players – but just out of reach – and coerce them into submitting to undesired labor if only for food and shelter. Again, in capitalizing on their fear of survival, he could sit and watch his empire grow at an impressive rate. And by extending and wrapping his tentacles around all other institutions of society, he could maintain a tight grasp over the oblivious, divided masses, allowing him to rest secured atop his perch outside of The Pit forever and ever…or at least until he dies and his kin take up the mantle.

The End.

Phew! That was a long, seemingly exaggerated hypothetical, wasn't it? However, as I will continue to point out throughout the rest of this text, much of what I laid out in the exercise above reflects many elements of our current national and global arrangement. And whom exactly does John represent in the thought experiment above? Well, he doesn't necessarily represent one man, per se; he embodies various power structures throughout the world that possess an overwhelming amount of financial resources, that then use those financial resources to keep the game tilted in their favor and to maintain a dominant and controlling position over the majority of the human population. You might say he represents central banks, powerful corporations, the current plutocratic configuration, corporate oligopolies, wealthy individuals and families, etc.

Whether Communism or Capitalism, the logical end result is roughly similar when a small group of individuals have seized monetary control and have captured an overwhelming share of a society's valuables. What's the difference if one controls most of a country's physical resources or if one controls most of the artificial medium that represents a country's physical resources? The end game in each scenario usually leaves a community with a dictatorship, oligarchy, or plutocracy of some sort where the opulent minority use their clout to rule the majority. Those who control the money supply control the nation. Those who control the money supply of the most powerful nation in the world, control the world. The most effective controllers are the ones who are able to manipulate and convince their people they are not being controlled.

Throughout history, whenever civilizations have experienced rapid material growth and expansion within their infrastructure, whether it be Egypt, Rome, or America, it has almost always been on the backs of slaves or indentured servants. The only difference between America and the civilizations of old is that the John's of our society have perfected what I call "covert" slavery – whips and chains are no longer needed. In this new paradigm, the inhabitants are provided with an illusion of choice; and, rather than having shackles blatantly forced upon them, they willingly shackle themselves.

Every man wants to have a purpose. Every man wants to fulfill a contributive role in society. It gives him a sense of worth in the community and in his life. Working hard to accomplish a goal or task feels great, especially when that accomplishment benefits others. However, virtually no man wants to spend the majority of his days, every day, for most of his short and capable life taking orders from a master and doing tasks that are physically or mentally demanding, dangerous, or just plain boring. Few men, if any, want to spend their entire lives pouring concrete, mining resources, picking strawberries, or balancing financial statements. That's a waste of the most amazing and complex development in the history of mankind – consciousness. For a man to commit his life to drudgery, it stands to reason that he must be made to feel like he *has* to, as though few other choices exist if he wants to live. So, when those who "have" dangle the carrot of survival in front of the faces of those who "have not," they can coerce men into spending their lives breaking their backs for them. Withholding survival pressures a man into walking into the coal mines – he is made to feel like he has no alternative if he wants to eat. Though the word slavery might seem a little extreme, since that word invokes images of Africans being brought over on boats and physically forced to work in chattel slavery, I see no better word for this form of coercion and servitude – withholding survival from someone unless he does a task for you is a form of enslavement.

I call it "covert" slavery; however, Republicans and laborers of the $19^{th}$ and early-$20^{th}$ centuries had a different term for a similar circumstance – "wage" slavery – and they even campaigned against it.[6] Unfortunately, what was seen as an injustice over 100 years ago is now largely considered normal as generation after generation have been born into it. Frederick Douglass, an African American who experienced and escaped chattel slavery, once said of "wage" slavery that it is "a little less galling and crushing in its effects than chattel slavery…," but that "…this slavery of wages must go down with the other."[7]

Because the tool that grants us access to the items we need to survive – money – is limited and finite, it is also used as a means to control resources, effectively game participants, and gain a competitive advantage over others. It is used to deprive people of the things they need to live, which makes it easy for the ruling class of society to exploit the lower classes, which for the lower classes adds an unnecessary layer of fear, pressure, shame, and stress to their lives. The necessities of life are abundant and can be made ever more so in this world. By getting rid of the tool of money and making survival resources accessible to all, the incentive to control, manipulate, and exploit others quickly fades. There is no need to covet that which is abundant and accessible.

The following sections consist of only a few real-life examples that I picked out of a sea of many that serve to support my previous Thought Experiment involving "John." In the spirit of not tying up too much of your time, I have kept these examples relatively short; they are merely quick summaries in lieu of in-depth analyses.

## 4.2 COMPANY TOWNS

In the 1947 Merle Travis song *Sixteen Tons*, made ever popular in 1955 by Tennessee Ernie Ford, the main character in this old ditty tells Saint Peter that he can't go to heaven because, "I owe my soul to the company store." And what was Travis referring to in his song? Why, Company Towns of the Industrial Revolution, of course. More specifically, the simple melody references the depressed life of a coal miner trapped in a cycle of debt and servitude to the owner of the Company Town he resided in.

Love'em, hate'em, or couldn't care less about'em, Company Towns of the Industrial Revolution were a shining example of how easy it is for one or a few individuals to control and exploit a large population once they have amassed the overwhelming majority of a society's money and wealth. And as a disclaimer before I progress any further, I have no interest in entering a debate of why they were so wonderful or why they were so awful. I've heard the arguments on both ends, that they either helped bolster communities and provide dignified livelihoods along with a currency free from government influence, or that they were the pinnacle of worker oppression and abuse – one's position is relative. My sole purpose of dragging Company Towns of old into this book is to illustrate how a man with a substantial portion of a community's wealth can coerce other men into subordination by withholding survival just out of their reach and how fear of survival keeps men submissive to their ruler.

So, what were Company Towns exactly?[1] Well, they consisted of a scenario in America, primarily throughout the 1800s and early-1900s, where a single private entity would set up his business within a relatively small community, and then employ just about every person in that community. It was common for company owners to own all of the stores in a Company Town, and they would often even issue their own currency – referred to as Scrip – that was detached from the US Dollar. All orders of business in Company Towns, including one's right to live, essentially went through its owner. With the controlling stake of the town's wealth, the owner had the power to create his own laws and regulations, and he would hire his own law enforcement agency, sometimes consisting of brute thugs, to handle rule breakers and keep the local population in line. The entire town was at the mercy of the company owner, as they needed what he had – money – to access the means of survival. He was essentially their Daddy.

Paternalism, or dad (owner) knows best for his children (the people), was the prevailing theme within the Company Towns scattered throughout the States. And like in all families, some Company Town "daddies" were nice to their children, while others could be mean and abusive. If a man were lucky, he would be born into a town where the parent company cared about its subordinates and the owner would genuinely try to raise a healthy and happy community, as seems to be the case within Hershey, Pennsylvania. However, if one were unlucky, he would wind up in Company Towns infamous for worker oppression and striking that spawned violence and death, like in Ludlow, Colorado or Matewan, West Virginia, or Homestead, Pennsylvania.

Again, because individual owners possessed the majority share of a Company Town's wealth pie, the rest of the community was essentially at his mercy. The townspeople had to submit their daily efforts to the company owner if they wanted to acquire money from him to access the necessities of life. Like in my Thought Experiment with John, even though most of the men of a town didn't want to submit to physically demanding and boring labor, like with coal mining, they felt like they had little other choice. The company owner had control over the means of survival, and in order to gain access to those means, men had to do the owner's "chores." Oftentimes the chores involved very long hours, poor and dangerous working conditions, and low pay. And if local citizens didn't like their life situations and refused to work or broke the company-created laws, they were often met with physical force by the owner's privately purchased law enforcement agents. The laws across Company Towns were certainly not uniform, either. Some towns enforced strict curfews on their residents, while others forbade booze. Some towns had dress codes, while others required their residents to attend church every Sunday. And of course, the arbitrary rules of the towns did not apply to the owners, just the lowly peasants.

Personal and observed accounts describe widespread misery in a large number of the "bad" Company Towns. Not only did citizens lack autonomy and have to endure dangerous drudgery, but as I said, they were also paid low wages – just enough so they could purchase life necessities, but that's it, which ensured they would come back the next day. And when citizens received their paychecks, when they received their company-issued Scrip, it was typically only exchangeable at the local stores: and since company owners often owned the food stores, clothing stores, housing units, and all other places of business, all of the money that was exchanged for goods filtered right back up into the owners' pockets, allowing them to secure a perpetual controlling stake in the community. To make matters worse, owners oftentimes inflated the prices of goods in order to squeeze as much money out of their subordinates as possible, driving many residents into debt. As Merle Travis wrote in his song: "You load sixteen tons and what do you get? Another day older and deeper in debt."

And in some instances, if workers were caught trying to use their money at stores in neighboring communities in search of better prices, they risked punishment from the owner's personal law enforcement. Now, Scrip could be exchanged for US Dollars; however, since Scrip was valued less than the US Dollar, workers would lose money in the exchange, leaving them even poorer outside of the community than they were inside of it, which further deterred them from trying to escape to greener pastures. They were all but trapped.

Workers, as I mentioned, were often subjected to dangerous working conditions in a number of Company Towns, since they lacked regulations, and as a result, injuries and death were a common feature of the workday. Installing safety protocols in factories or mines simply didn't pay; actually, it cost. For instance, in, say, the coal mining industry, workers were usually only paid by the "tonnage" – the amount of coal they accumulated. They were not paid for tasks that made the mines safer to work in, like fixing roofs or laying track, because building safe mines didn't turn a profit in the marketplace, only coal did. And since workers were already paid so little, they didn't want to waste any amount of time performing tasks that wouldn't earn them money, so they often sacrificed their health and safety if it meant obtaining just a bit more Scrip and an improved ability to feed their families. Unfortunately, if negligence resulted in a father's death, his family was left with nothing, and they would struggle to survive in turn.

And one would logically think if working conditions were so abysmal and the pay so low that workers could just band together and speak up; however, they didn't for the most part. They were afraid to, for if disgruntled employees did express concern or threaten unionization they were fired and swiftly replaced by other eager workers just waiting to earn some money and a chance to survive. In many ways, the "bad" Company Towns were not too dissimilar from oppressive Communist economies we've been taught to despise and fear. The town owners controlled the local resources and all aspects of production, and some dictated how citizens lived their lives. They were basically mini-dictatorships buried not too deeply within a supposed democratic, capitalist country. Additionally, the conditions of many workers didn't deviate too far from chattel slavery in colonial-America, either. Residents basically had no choice but to work for their "John," and some were met with punishment should they disobey their masters.

The almost non-existent worker rights and unjust environments ultimately culminated with strikes and violent clashes in some Company Towns, like the one that occurred in Ludlow, Colorado in 1914, infamously known as the "Ludlow Massacre."[2,3] As anger amongst workers peaked, miners throughout Colorado demanded better working conditions from their various companies, like the Colorado Fuel & Iron Company owned by John D. Rockefeller and later by John D. Rockefeller, Jr. But, owners weren't having it; they repeatedly refused worker demands. And to send a message, they began evicting dissenting and striking workers from their company-owned homes, sometimes forcefully behind their hired muscle, pushing those miners to relocate to tent colonies set up by their union. And of course, to fill the void left behind by the evicted residents, company owners simply brought in new labor. Piece of cake!

However, as attempts to quell disgruntled Colorado workers continuously failed, strikes intensified and violence became the eventual course of action. As tensions boiled, owners hired private security and detective companies, like the renowned Baldwin-Felts Detective Agency, to break up worker demonstrations in tented strike camps. Some of the patrolling agents of the Baldwin-Felts organization actually fired bullets into the strike camps to disrupt and disburse protesting miners, but when stray bullets ended up injuring and even killing some people, tensions escalated beyond a point of control between both parties.

On April 20th, 1914, guards hired by Rockefeller, agents of Baldwin-Felts, and Colorado National Guardsmen began spraying a striking tent community just outside of Ludlow with intermittent machine gun fire.

While women and children took cover – some hid underground where they risked burning or suffocating, some ran – many strikers fought back, igniting a fierce battle. The violent clash between the two sides ended up lasting the entire day, but the tent colony could not withstand the overwhelming barrage of bullets and explosions administered by company-backed opposition. And when strikers finally fled the encampment at sundown, company militia moved in and began looting and setting fire to the tents; one of the strike's leaders who remained with the camp was found executed.

Tempers flared for days following the "Ludlow Massacre," and fighting only ceased once the US Government intervened with federal troops, as they moved in and disarmed both sides. Once the dust settled, many lives had been lost, including women and children, and the striking workers didn't even receive what they had demanded; they were actually worse off after the incident, as they no longer had jobs nor the ability to support their families. Company owners simply had too much power. However, as a side note, one could say the strike did help pave the way for improvements to worker rights years later.

To conclude, Company Towns during America's Gilded Age are one of many examples throughout history of the immense power an individual can wield over a population once he has amassed a substantial share of a society's monetary wealth. By having the ability to withhold survival from the people, a man can exploit an entire community, or even an entire country, and coerce the people into performing whatever tasks he wants completed. Games are meant to be won, and when a man wins in the game of money, he can then use the weapon of fear to keep people docile like livestock and maintain his winning position in perpetuity.

## 4.3 LIES AND WAR

"The urge to save humanity is almost always only a false-face for the urge to rule it."[1] – H.L. Mencken

War is most certainly a racket (see Chapter 6.4 for more on war). When it comes to making money, there is no business like war business. For millennia, rich and powerful men have had few qualms with sending thousands of domestic strangers to kill thousands of foreign strangers in the name of a big payday, arriving in the form of lucrative contracts or resource acquisition. And for millennia, leaders across countless nations have woven incredible tales to foment local outrage toward neighboring countries and to gain public support for entering into deadly conflicts.

See, the men who have stood to benefit most from fighting know that the majority of the human population generally prefers peace over stress-inducing, health-damaging violence. They understand that empathy – our ability to feel another's pain – compels us to reject war in the absence of just cause. Unfortunately for global rulers, acts of aggression, of sending sons and daughters to kill and be killed, are often difficult to justify. So, concocting grand stories that appeal to our fears and emotions becomes vital in winning support from moral and empathetic civilians; it allows countries to maintain the façade of honor and righteousness that keeps populations loyal.

Exhibit A.

The United States supported Saddam Hussein during the Iran-Iraq War in the 1980s and provided him with weapons, advanced technology, and other aid[2] (Saddam and CIA had a working relationship long before the conflict).[3,4] Because the US opposed Iran, Western leaders turned their cheeks the other way to Saddam's brutal tactics during the fighting. However, following the war between the two Middle Eastern countries, Saddam and his oil rich nation quickly grew out of favor with US officials. And when the Iraqi president chose to invade Kuwait in 1990,[5] western leaders were eager to step in and oust their rabid dog; however, they knew the American public would not be too keen on sacrificing its sons and daughters to fight a foreign, Arab-Arab war.

Enter Nayirah Al-Sabah and the American propaganda machine. In October of 1990, a teen who went only by the name of Nayirah stood before the Congressional Human Rights Caucus and tearfully claimed that Iraqi soldiers had entered a Kuwaiti hospital, pulled babies out of incubators, and left them to die.[6] After Nayirah's story was aired on television sets across America, George H.W. Bush and a number of Senators used her testimony to drum up support from their initially reluctant citizens. And it worked. Once the people heard of these atrocities, temperamental men became red in the face, and they wanted justice brought to the vicious leader.

However, as was later discovered, Nayirah's story was a lie.[7] Not only was it later revealed that Nayirah was the daughter of Kuwait's ambassador to the US, Saud Nasir al-Sabah,[8] but it was also found that she had been working with Hill & Knowlton, an American PR firm whose president and COO worked under Bush when he was Vice President, and the Citizens for a Free Kuwait leading up to her fabricated testimony. To help come up with a PR campaign to gain the support of the American public, Hill & Knowlton was paid a reported $10.7 million.[9]

As we all know, with the support of his people, Bush sent military personnel to the Middle East, and Iraq was quickly defeated. Whether right or wrong, and whether the motives were altruistic or otherwise (oil, central bank, etc.), American leaders relied on public gullibility and had no problem feeding them a gross lie if it meant gaining their support.

Two decades before the Nayirah incident, tensions had been escalating between America and North Vietnam, and military pressure had been mounting. In August of 1964 it was reported to Congress and the American population that North Vietnamese boats had launched attacks against US destroyers in the Gulf of Tonkin.[10] Using this information along with the support of American media and the public, President Lyndon Johnson ordered a "retaliatory" attack against the Communist country.

Well, just like with the Gulf War, one of the precursors to the Vietnam War, which is now known as the Gulf of Tonkin Incident, was later confirmed to be a lie.[11] North Vietnamese boats did not attack American ships. Lyndon Johnson even stated later that, "For all I know, our Navy was shooting at whales…"[12] And, James Stockdale, one of the Navy pilots flying overhead claimed he was, "…chasing some imaginary PT boat…," and that there were, "No boats, no boat wakes, no ricochets off boats, no boat gunfire, no torpedo wakes – nothing but black sea and American firepower."[13]

A lie was vomited down the throats of the American public, and though this wasn't the *only* reason America entered into a war with the small country, it certainly played a role. 50,000-plus dead American soldiers and millions more dead Vietnamese later, this one becomes difficult to justify as the years go by.

It seems there is no limit to the lies individual men might be willing to sew for independent gains and the lengths they would be willing to go for a chance at winning the monetary game. Leading up to the Bay of Pigs and the conflict with Fidel Castro, American officials were deliberating on how best to deal with the Communist Cuban leader. One day, in 1962, a document from the US Department of Defense, as part of its Operation Northwoods plans (released in 1997 by the John F. Kennedy Assassination Records Review Board), came across the desk of high-ranking US government officials.[14] The document contained a list of "ethically questionable" and, one might even say, "sinister" proposals aimed at ousting Fidel:

> "The suggested courses of action…are based on the premise that US military intervention will result from a period of heightened US-Cuban tensions **which place the United States in the position of suffering justifiable grievances**. World opinion, and the United Nations forum should be favorably affected by **developing the international image of the Cuban government as rash and irresponsible** and as an alarming and unpredictable threat to the peace of the Western Hemisphere."[15]

Among the many ideas considered, one involved the CIA or other government agencies carrying out staged hijackings on US soil, while another involved staging riots. Other proposals suggested painting an F-86 to look like a Cuban MIG, while Proposal #3 suggested: "A 'Remember the Maine' incident could be arranged in several forms…We could blow up a US ship in Guantanamo Bay and blame Cuba."[16]

However, the worst of the proposals included plans to orchestrate attacks on American civilians, US military compounds, and civilian structures, and again, blame them on the Communist leader and the Cuban government to make them look like dangerous aggressors, which could have provided US leaders with necessary justification to take action against the island nation:

> "We could develop a Communist Cuban terror campaign in the Miami area, in other Florida cities and even in Washington… We could sink a boatload of Cubans enroute to Florida (real or simulated)."[17]

Although some of the plans were almost implemented and carried out, Kennedy ended up rejecting the unsettling proposals.

The three examples above are some of just a few verifiable cases of deception used by those in power to gain an advantage for a multitude of reasons. Who knows how many more lies have been told that have not been officially confirmed? And, who knows how often these tactics are used nowadays to keep the public sufficiently angry to justify a continued presence in the Middle East? Or to keep people hating communism? Or to keep American whites and blacks at each other's throats? If it's so easy for them to lie about big things, one has to wonder how easy it would be to tell small lies on a daily basis, to keep the venom flowing in our veins and make sure we don't come to our senses?

Of course, American leaders (individual men, nothing more, nothing less) are not alone in their willingness to lie in order to justify invading other countries or passing legislation. Deception and lies have been practiced throughout history by many countries and civilizations. For example…

In the 1931 "Mukden Incident," Japan blamed China for a series of explosions on a train track owned by a Japanese company, which led to Japanese invasion and occupation of Manchuria. As was later discovered by the Lytton Commission in 1932, it was Japanese troops who set off the explosions.[18,19]

In 1939, a group of Polish-dressed people attacked a radio station in Gleiwitz, Germany. Hitler and the Nazis blamed Poland for the incident and used it, as well as a number of similar incidents, to manufacture national outrage and justify invasion of Poland. However, as was later revealed in the Nuremberg Trials, it was a group of Germans posing as Polish nationals who stormed the radio station in an operation orchestrated by the Gestapo and Nazi Germany. They were trying to falsely paint Poland as dangerous.[20,21]

In 1955, Turkish officials wanted to incite disgust and violence toward Greece, so they devised an attack on their own Turkish consulate in

Greece and blamed it on the Greeks.[22]

The list goes on and on. Even going back to the days of the Roman Empire, historical claims have been made that the Great Fire of Rome in 64 AD was initiated by Emperor Nero and his supporters. His motives? Among many, reasons included growing disdain for local Christians, a desire to rebuild Rome in his image, and that he allegedly wanted a large chunk of the city dedicated to constructing a massive complex – Domus Aurea – which would include a statue of himself.[23,24,25]

Those who have attained financial power and control rely on ignorance, emotions, fear, and the malleability of the human mind to carry out plans that usually seek to benefit only a few. For centuries, these leaders have been creating false narratives to drive their cattle into whatever pastures they desire, and yet we continue to buy into just about every story they tell us. Fool me once, shame on you. Fool me twice, shame on me. Fool me every single day? Shit, you deserve the keys to the empire. As I will state a few pages from now, our Founding Fathers never really believed in Democracy. They felt the general population was not intelligent enough to make wise decisions. Well, I can't say I fault their logic; by us so easily believing every false narrative drilled into our brains, we continuously prove our fathers right.

## 4.4 COMPETITION BE DAMNED: ROCKEFELLER & STANDARD OIL

"We will either get them or starve them."[1] – J.N. Camden to John D. Rockefeller

To draw a real life parallel with how "thought-experiment John" so easily stamped out competition, I turn the spotlight to John D. Rockefeller, one of the most successful "gamers" and wealthiest businessmen in American history. In the 1800s, the oil industry was booming in America, and like thousands of American men, Mr. Rockefeller sought to ride the "Earth Blood" gravy train to fortune and prominence. And that's just what he did. With his strong work ethic, savvy business acumen, and innovative ambitions, Rockefeller quickly emerged from the scuffle and became an oil giant after establishing his company, Standard Oil, in 1870. In a relatively short period of time, he was able to accumulate enormous wealth. He absorbed refineries all across eastern America – New York, Cleveland, Pittsburgh, Philadelphia, West Virginia, Baltimore, and beyond – allowing him to control 90 percent of the oil industry at his company's peak.[2]

Once Mr. Rockefeller had acquired an overwhelming controlling stake in the industry, small competitors didn't stand a chance if he thought they could be a threat to his business, as is evidenced by his comments to an associate in regards to upstart refineries in Pittsburgh: "At this particular moment it is especially important that outside Pittsburgh refineries should have no chance whatever in any market for local trade oil."[3]

Like a wrecking crew, Rockefeller used his pendulous balls to demolish anyone who dared invade on his share of the market. If a competitor didn't simply sell his company to Rockefeller, the oil magnate had a wide range of strategies up his sleeve and would take measures to cripple the competing business, like buying all of the oil barrels to cause a supply shortage, "running arrangements," or cutting deals with train companies to refuse to transport competing oil. And, if he felt it was necessary, Rockefeller had the financial leverage to undercut his competitors' prices and remove their ability to turn a profit and survive. If a competing business didn't sell his company to the oil mogul, its failure was almost inevitable.[4]

As the saying went, "Run, children, or Rockefeller'll get you!"[5]

Another example of a company using its financial prowess to weed out competitors and monopolize its respective market was and has been De Beers in the diamond business (though in recent years they have been losing ground to other companies). Because of their massive controlling stake in the industry in the late-1800s and throughout a large portion of the 1900s, the diamond company was able to control the supply of diamonds. For the most part, they would use this control to withhold diamonds from the public, making them more rare, which drove prices up. However, if they needed to eliminate competition, they could flood the market with the shiny stones and drive prices to a point so low as to destroy competing businesses.[6,7]

Using one's financial strength to uproot competition and "win" the game isn't earth-shattering information. However, this helps illustrate how once a man does win by capturing a large share of the market, it gives him a significant advantage over competing businesses; dominating and destroying other players becomes much simpler. Microsoft, Google, and Amazon are modern examples out of many.

## 4.5 DEMOCRACY?

"The wealth lords of America are already busily engaged in attempts to insure their control of the nominees of the Republican and Democratic Parties... They will endeavor…to place in nomination at both conventions candidates whom they can control. If this can be accomplished, the election will be of small interest to them, for the people will have to elect one or the other of their candidates."[1] – John F. Hylan (Mayor of New York City – 1918-1925)

"You suggest danger to our elections – I could tell you very curious anecdotes of elections carried by these banks and elections lost."[2] – John Adams (2nd President of the United States)

Though originally founded as and considered to be a Constitutional Republic or a Democratic Republic, America is widely thought of as operating under the ideals of a Democracy. Literally translating from Greek to mean "power of the people" or "rule by the people," the outward intention of our founding fathers was to give some responsibility of day-to-day decisions to the people of the nation. By adding the voting feature for choosing political candidates, American citizens were meant to feel like they had a say over which direction their country was headed.

However, I say "outward intention," because many of our founding fathers, including men like James Madison and Alexander Hamilton, didn't actually believe that the citizens in the lower and middle classes were capable or smart enough to carry such an important and heavy burden of deciding what actions their nation should take. Hamilton once said:

"All communities divide themselves into the few and the many.

> The first are the rich and the well born, the others the mass of the people… The people are turbulent and changing; they seldom judge and determine right. Give therefore to the first class a distinct, permanent share of government. They will check the unsteadiness of the second."[3]

Philosophers and political leaders throughout recorded history reasoned that in a pure democracy, a disenfranchised poor could band together and vote away the rights and property of the rich. Aristotle, who thought of democracy as "rule of the poor,"[4] insinuated that the poor were less educated, less virtuous, "slavish," and, "incapable of ruling."[5]

And James Madison echoed those fears, that a Democratic society could fall victim to mob rule, and suggested safeguards be put in place to "protect the minority of the opulent against the majority."[5]

The act of voting is predicated on the assumption and collective trust that each voter has done his due diligence and has fully educated himself on pertinent topics before developing his conclusions. Unfortunately, we need only make a quick observation of our modern American culture to intuitively know that this isn't the case, as the general public is typically not fully informed before punching their ballots and are often easily swayed by media, their group affiliations, and emotions; and like dogs, when one person in a pack starts barking about something, others start barking, too, even if they have no idea what they're barking at.

It's for this reason (well, and for the purpose of protecting the opulent minority from having their rights voted away by the mob) that the system has been set up whereby we don't typically vote for specific actions or policies, rather we vote for and elect officials to represent our interests. These special men and women are then tasked with educating themselves on socioeconomic matters and listening to *the people*. On the surface, such an arrangement seems reasonable, as it removes the decision-making burden off of the working man's shoulders. However, where the process starts to fall apart and becomes unreasonable is in the interference and seductive powers of money. Everything in our culture has a price tag on it. And for the right price, anyone and anything can be bribed for or bought, including the decisions made by the individuals we elect to represent us. And that's where the lucrative industry of lobbying comes into prominence.

Bigger wallets have bigger voices. Armed with the knowledge that money is more persuasive than actions or words, corporations (big oil, big tech, big pharma, big food), labor unions, and other entities invest, as of 2019, over $3.4 billion in lobbying efforts per year in an attempt to seduce "unbiased" government powers into passing legislation that can give them a competitive advantage, help bolster revenue, ensure rights aren't taken away, provide tax breaks or rebates, or help them achieve a number of other measures.[7] With enough money, a single corporation or entity can indirectly or directly "buy" a congressman and convince him or his office to pass a bill or sneak obscure language into a bill that the general public doesn't necessarily support or is completely unaware of.

Now, is the lobbying industry as insidious as the general public perceives it to be? No. Not necessarily. It can be and certainly has been, e.g., Jack Abramoff. But the way the monetary game is set up, even if an organization supports benevolent causes like child abuse or labor rights, that organization will have an incredibly difficult time reaching Congress and affecting rules and regulations without first hiring a connected individual to go to bat for him. Though the public is generally in gross disfavor of what is often described as legal bribery, one might also consider lobbying as a "necessary evil" in today's political and economic landscape.

Obviously, if citizens want legislation passed or regulations added or changed, they first need to get the attention of someone in Congress. However, elected officials are merely individual human beings with one brain and one set of ears working within a short 24-hour day, so, although *the people* have the ability to reach out to Congress with requests or complaints, it is unrealistic to believe that everyone's unique concerns will be heard. So then how does an individual or organization get the attention of a congressman? How does one hurdle over others on the priority list and rise to the top? Well, by ponying up and hiring a lobbying firm connected with key players on Capitol Hill.

Lobbyists, many of who have spent years working in government positions and developing relationships, have the ability to enter the gates of Washington and speak face-to-face with relevant politicians in a way the average Joe cannot. They have the ability to persistently badger representatives for weeks or months without being escorted out by security; sometimes congressmen even enjoy the schmoozing because cutting deals can come with dinners, vacations, box seat tickets to sporting events, and even under-the-table "cash prizes" (as restrictions tightened, lobbyists and congressmen have discovered "workarounds").[8] Now, soliciting the services of a lobbying firm to advocate for one's cause certainly is not cheap. And logically, the more a congressman is exposed to an organization's cause through its lobbying conduit, the better the chances are of that congressman taking that cause to the House and pushing it through. However, more exposure means more money. Thus, the ones most capable of reaching the ears of a congressman are the ones most capable of spending money, e.g., corporations, labor unions, special interest groups, wealthy individuals, etc. The implication here is that the highly-sought-after attention of elected officials essentially goes to the highest bidders, meaning it is those with the most financial resources that are best able to "win" the services of the most connected lobbying firms to influence Congress and get rules and regulations added or changed. What this also means is, in an indirect way, it is the money structure that creates the rules in our grand monetary game, not the average Joe and certainly not those in the lower classes of society. Those positioned on the lower rungs of the socioeconomic ladder basically have no voice in our world.

So, without the ability to purchase a lobbyist to occupy the ears of Capitol Hill, it is commonly known that one is likely to be left in the dust when it comes to legislation. The cold truth is that money has a much greater influence on decisions made in this country than any average citizen casting her biennially votes. Money speaks, not *the people*. And that should come as a shock to very few. As will be a recurring theme throughout this book, reform has done and will do little to get money's seductive powers out of Washington and politics.

Continuing with the idea that money talks, though we live in a supposed democratic society, one needs only to do a quick scan to discover just how often decisions are made not only without knowledge or approval from the population, but many times in the face of a disapproving public. When it comes to American involvement in the Middle East, marijuana, bailouts to private banks, or how money is appropriated across government agencies, the opinion of the people is generally irrelevant. In 2014, researchers out of Princeton University and Northwestern University released a report analyzing 1,800 policy issues, and what they discovered was that wealthy interests, using their vast financial resources, have "far more independent impact upon policy change" compared to the average

American who has almost no say.[9] In their conclusion, they state:

> "When the preferences of economic elites and the stands of organized interest groups are controlled for, the preferences of the average American appear to have only a miniscule, near-zero, statistically non-significant impact upon public policy."[10]

Overall, "policymaking is dominated by powerful business organizations and a small number of affluent Americans."[11]

So, given the knowledge that the average American has very little say in state and national policies, that brings us to the final segment I want to pick on; and that is, the pièce de résistance, the crown jewel resting upon the mantle of our American democratic system – the quadrennial Prom King & Queen elections. Every four years in this beautiful country, US citizens have the great honor of participating in the most grandiose, most expensive popularity contest in the entire world. In this political pageant, aspiring Royalty submit their names to be on Prom Court, whereby they then polish their veneers, practice their disingenuous smiles, work on posture, cadence, and gait, develop a fake laugh, and put on their shiniest tiaras before parading around the country like show ponies in an attempt to appeal to *the people* and win their support. For roughly two excruciating years leading up to "the big event," budding candidates cringe beneath their spray-tanned faces as they force themselves to pretend to actually like an unlikeable public; they do little turns on various catwalks, shaking germy hands and kissing powdered cheeks; they sing sweet nothings into the ears of captivated audiences across the nation; and if they aren't spouting callow lies to smear competing Court members, they are shouting meaningless platitudes and empty slogans like "Yes We Can!" or "Make America Great Again!" or "Build Back Better!"

And the public absolutely feasts upon the superficial courtship. But why shouldn't we? After all, this is *our* moment! This is our rare chance to voice our opinions, or so we are reminded over and over again, by casting our 1 vote out of 150,000,000 participants.[12] And even though the money structure largely decides which direction the "country car" is headed; and even though the public has almost no say in important policies; even though the President has little influence on economic booms and busts or even the ebb and flow of commerce as the "health" of the economy is attributed to many other factors, including actions taken by the Federal Reserve which, one could argue, has more power than the President as it controls the money supply and operates largely outside of the President's and government's oversight; even though Congress, influenced by Lobbyists who are influenced by money powers, has the power to override a President's veto and push a bill through; and even though we question every election whether or not fraud impacted the final vote count; we have it drilled into our heads how ever important it is that we participate in choosing this one human being to steer the ship. We have embedded into every fiber of our mind this fantastical faith that if only we pick the right person out of two choices that the nation will be saved from potential ruin and that our wants and needs will be met.

And each election is approached with the same escalated level of urgency, as we are repeatedly told, "THIS! THIS is THEE most important election the country has ever faced!" Thus, imbued with this deep sense that the fate of the nation rests upon our shoulders, we clench our fists, furrow our brows, purse our lips, and stick our chins in the air. *I'm a proper adult and I have a responsibility to my fellow American.* And the way we are told we can fulfill that responsibility? Not by being respectful to one another and helping each other out, but by participating in an election circus that largely tears us apart. Because, as we all know, division is how we flourish, not through unification.

So finally, after the Tiara Boys and Girls have been whittled down to two sets, often through having the most media exposure and securing the most money from special interest groups, corporations, and other wealthy donors, it comes time for our ever-important vote, to choose between what is often perceived as the lesser of two evils within what is also often perceived as a broken two-party system. We must choose which unhealthy option we want representing our country. Do we want McDonald's or do we want the "vastly different" Burger King on our nation's billboards? Do we want the red or blue paint job? And once the line is drawn, individuals stand firmly on the side of the candidate they want chosen to wear the happy-meal crown, leading the American population to descend into its most insufferable state of petty tribalism. For months, rational thinking is suspended as competing factions, when their members are not lounging inside opinion-reinforcing echo chambers, catapult insults at one another. The blue team is convinced the red team is dangerous and stupid, while the red team is convinced the blue team is dangerous and stupid; cookouts become fraught with tension. And politicians and the media (heavily controlled by the money structure) – by constantly arguing with, insulting, interrupting, and demeaning one another, set a clear and mature example that civil conversation and interactions that threaten to build unity and understanding are not to be tolerated. Consequently, like the children in Albert Bandura's "Bobo Doll"[13] experiment who began beating the crap out of a doll because they observed an adult, whom they looked up to, doing the same thing, the public also observes "intelligent," well dressed, trustworthy-looking politicians and media figures arguing with one another, and because we subconsciously look up to them, we think that that behavior is normal and okay, too. We are thus trained to attack and dismiss first, inquire and understand later (if ever).

In the end, after the two sets of candidates take their final laps around the arena for the population to judge, the public submits their ballots, votes are tallied, and a Prom King & Queen duo is elected and crowned. The multibillion-dollar popularity contest concludes as the champions stand behind a podium with beaming smiles; half of the population hoots and hollers, while the other half walks away in agonizing defeat. And the money structure? They linger patiently beyond the haze with a leash in hand, waiting to wrangle their new whipping boy. "We paid for you. We own you!"

Days later, once the charade has ended and the wool removed from our eyes, our cortisol levels drop as the dust settles and life returns to normal. People stand in their front yards, take a breath of fresh air, look around and realize, "Hmm, nothing really feels different." As we come to our senses some personal relationships are mended, while others remain permanently fractured – some people even delete former friends from their social media accounts. Oh, the humanity!

Then, on January 20th of the following year, the new president is sworn into office and takes his first seat upon the throne of fool's gold, while the government returns to business as usual. For the inaugurated leader, it's time to return favors in a quid quo pro agreement to those who pledged significant dollars to him and to those who govern the money supply; whatever affluence wants, affluence generally gets, even if it means breaking promises to the general public or even going against popular opinion. Although the president might have the power to make verbal promises to audiences on his campaign trail, he doesn't really have the power to follow through on them once in office. The "leader of the free world" has his masters. Whether he has the mark of Democrat or Republican seared into his skin, he ultimately answers to those actually driving the "country car," rendering the grand spectacle that is the presidential election a joke at best, ranging from hilarious to offensive depending on one's level of humor; it's a magnificent ruse to keep the children distracted and out of the patriarchy's hair for a couple years.

Additionally, a president's actions, influenced by financial interests, oftentimes do not differ much from the actions taken by previous administrations, whether Democrat or Republican, and many times even contradict the virtues their party stands on. For instance, George W. Bush, whether pressured by the left or not, provided socialistic bailouts to the tune of trillions to private banks during the recession, even though the political right he was affiliated with is generally in gross disapproval of big government intervening in private affairs. Conversely, Barack Obama consistently provided tax cuts to the wealthy throughout his presidency, even though the political left is usually opposed to actions that cater to those living in excess.

The election circus seemingly never ends in America; the keys never stop jiggling above our faces. Following the chaotic, madness-inducing presidential election, an exhausted public receives necessary respite for but a few months before preparation begins for the Homecoming elections (midterm elections) that seek to grab our attention all over again. What's going on outside of the American borders? What's happening in Congress? That information is buried in hard-to-reach caverns deep beneath an ocean of stories and advertisements regarding the elections and other irrelevant topics, like, "Did you see what that 'idiot' Kanye West did?" And as a benefit of keeping us consistently distracted and divided, the elevated positions of the virtuous minority are permanently protected from the "bewildered herd," as James Madison and other founding fathers intended; the money controllers get to continue on playing their own, separate game unencumbered, while the masses bicker amongst each other in the murky depths of The Pit.

Once you analyze American democracy on a deeper level, you realize the term is merely a sugar pill served to give the general public a sense of ownership and relevance in their country's actions. But real democracy doesn't exist, and it was never intended to. Real decisions have been and always will be made by those with the majority share of the finite money supply. The word used to describe such a scenario, a society ruled by the wealthy, is "Plutocracy," a term I used earlier that much more accurately reflects the current state of American society, and just about any global society for that matter. The opulent minority rule, and that shouldn't be any real surprise.

Alright. I've spent more time than I intended this chapter in discussing money's not-so-secret ability to control institutions and people, so let's move on. Now I want to talk about this country's greatest power structure, the Grand Maester perched atop America's pyramid of subordination, the institution responsible for overseeing and regulating the nation's money supply – the Federal Reserve.

# 5 GRAND MAESTER: THE "FEDERAL" RESERVE

"The Federal Reserve is an independent agency, and that means, basically, that there is no other agency of government which can overrule actions that we take."[1] – Alan Greenspan (Former Federal Reserve Chairman)

"Some people…think that the Federal Reserve Banks [are] United States Government institutions. They are private monopolies which prey upon the people of these United States for the benefit of themselves and their foreign customers."[2] – Louis McFadden (served in Congress from 1915 to 1935)

"It is perhaps well enough that the people of the Nation do not know or understand our banking and monetary system, for if they did I believe there would be a revolution before tomorrow morning."[3] – attributed to Henry Ford by Charles Binderup in a 1937 Congressional Record

What is the Federal Reserve, you might ask? Commonly referred to as the Fed, it is the Central Banking system of the United States.[4] The system is comprised of 12 Federal Reserve Banks located in separate regions across the country.[5] The Federal Reserve also has a bank vault located 86 feet underground in Manhattan.[6] To supervise the 12 regional branches, the president appoints seven men or women to the Federal

Reserve Board of Governors, which is located in Washington, D.C.[7] It should be noted, board members can make financial decisions without the president's approval.[8] In addition to supervising and supporting the regional Federal Reserve banks and other member banks, the Board of Governors, as part of the Federal Open Market Committee, is also responsible for implementing monetary policy, including setting interest rates, across America with the goal of maintaining a stable economy and stable prices, promoting continued economic growth, and achieving full employment.[9] Essentially, America's central bank acts as the gatekeeper and key master of its money supply.

So you might be wondering why I put quotations around the word Federal in the title of this chapter. Well, the reason is because the word Federal indicates government entity; however, though the Board of Governors "reports" to Congress, the Federal Reserve is not an institution of the government, as stated by the Federal Reserve Bank of St. Louis: "The Federal Reserve Banks are not a part of the federal government," and they, "are set up like private corporations."[10] Federal Reserve banks issue stock to nationally chartered banks all over the country, which include up to a 6% annual dividend.[11] However, even though the Federal Reserve is not a government agency, the government derives great benefit from the Fed.

Another misdirection in the name Federal Reserve is that, unlike commercial banks that must maintain a set percentage of reserves, the central bank holds no reserves of its own.[12] If it needs more money, it prints more money. Though, it should also be noted, the Federal Reserve doesn't actually print physical currency. It authorizes the Treasury to print paper money at the Bureau of Engraving and Printing and coin money at the US Mint.[13,14] However, the Fed does issue credit to banks, which is as easy as authorizing a bank to add an electronic number to their ledger.

Now let's circle back and discuss the Federal Reserve's role in controlling America's money supply. There are two main ways by which money is created in our country: through the Fed conducting activity in Open Market Operations and through Fractional Reserve Banking.[15,16] I'm going to do my best to simplify these methods so they are easy to understand, but it is even difficult for me to fully comprehend at times because the process can be so convoluted and involves multiple steps. If you happen to find yourself confused, don't fret. Our money-creation process almost seems intentionally confusing, as John Maynard Keynes once said, "The process engages all the hidden forces of economic law on the side of destruction, and does it in a manner which not one man in a million is able to diagnose."[17]

The first method used in creating money in this country is through Open Market Operations. In the simplified version of this process, the US Treasury holds an auction for and sells US Treasury Bonds. Banks from around the world bid on and buy these bonds. After the auction is over, the banks give cash to the US Government, and the US Government issues its Treasuries* to the purchasing banks. The US Government now has extra cash from selling its Treasuries, and the banks hold onto the bonds and earn money from the interest. So far, however, no money has been created.

Next, the Federal Reserve can choose to buy Treasury Bonds from the various banks. When a bank sells a bond to the Federal Reserve, the Federal Reserve essentially writes a check to the bank for that amount. However, here's where things get funny. The Fed doesn't have any money in its checking account. It has a zero balance. So, when the Fed writes a check to the banks to purchase their bonds, it simply creates money out of thin air, from nothing, and gives that money to the banks. This money that the Federal Reserve hands to the banks is new money. See, when you or I write a check to purchase something, we must have that amount in our checking account, otherwise we get penalized. Not the Fed. They make purchases with no money in their account, and they never get penalized. But don't take it from me, here it is straight from the horse's mouth, the Federal Reserve Bank of Boston: "When you or I write a check there must be sufficient funds in our account to cover that check, but when the Federal Reserve writes a check there is no bank deposit on which that check is drawn. When the Federal Reserve writes a check, it is creating money."[18]

So, the Federal Reserve gives money to commercial banks, and the banks give their held Treasury Bonds to the Fed. The Federal Reserve then holds onto the Treasury Bonds, while the banks can use their *new* money to invest or loan out. From the Federal Reserve creating money out of thin air and giving it to the banks, the money supply in the US economy has increased, and so has the national debt.

*** the plural of Treasury Bonds is widely accepted as 'Treasurys,' but my brain sounds the alarm every time I see it spelled this way, so I have stuck with the form 'Treasuries'**

Then, the process repeats. The US Treasury creates more Treasury Bonds and later holds another bond auction for banks to bid. The money that the Federal Reserve printed then makes its way to the US Government when banks use that money to purchase more bonds. After the auction ends, the US Government has more cash, and the banks have additional Treasuries. And just like before, the Federal Reserve then creates more new money with the flick of a wrist, and they give that money to the banks in exchange for the new Treasuries they purchased. The money supply in the US, along with the national debt, is increased once more; and the process continues over and over again. New money and more debt are constantly being created through this process. In a roundabout manner, the banks merely serve as middlemen between the Federal Reserve and the US Government. The Fed essentially creates money from nothing, while the US Government creates Treasury Bonds from nothing, and they exchange them. And with its new, virtually free money, the government can then turn around and pay for its various public projects – education, roads, energy, etc. – or war.

However, the money that the Fed prints and gives to the Government has to be paid back, with interest. Who do you think has to pay for that debt? The government? Bankers? No! Don't be ridiculous. The debt gets deflected to the American public. *We* have to pay back the debt. What this means on a basic level is the Fed can print, say, $10,000 and give it to the government. Individual men comprising what we refer to as government can then spend that $10,000 how they wish. Maybe those men whom we entrust to run our country use that money to pay for improved education, OR maybe they use it to pay their buddies at Halliburton for bloated war contracts and make them incredibly wealthy. And then when all is said and done, the average, hard-working American citizen is on the hook for that $10,000 bill. Sounds like a pretty good deal, huh? It's like a stranger using your debit card to have a wild night in Vegas while you were at home watching reruns of *Friends*.

Okay, so that's the money creation process of Open Market Operations in a nutshell. A second way money is created in America is through a method called Fractional Reserve Banking or Fractional Reserve Lending. This method is just as silly as the first, but it is a bit harder to follow.

So, after selling their Treasuries to the Fed, or after the government pays its people and the people deposit their money into their checking accounts, the banks have new money. And with the new money, banks can either invest it into various securities, or they can loan it out. When a bank uses its money to loan to others, it creates new money in the economy through Fractional Reserve Banking. Here's how.

Let's pretend average-citizen Tyler has $1,000. Now let's pretend he deposits that $1,000 into his bank account at City Bank. City Bank now has an extra $1,000 to loan out to other people. However, the Federal Reserve Board sets a Reserve Ratio that banks must abide by. For this example, let's say the Reserve Ratio is 10%, an easy number to follow. That means, of the $1,000 Tyler deposited into the bank, $900 of it can be loaned out to other people, while $100 of it must be kept in reserves.

Now let's say I want to buy a pug puppy. The puppy costs $900, but I don't have that money in my checking account. So, I go to City Bank and ask them to give me a $900 loan. The bank gives me $900, and I sign some paperwork that says I will pay back the $900 plus interest.

After giving me the $900, City Bank now only has $100 left of that original $1,000 deposit. So, if Tyler comes in and wants to withdraw his money in full, the bank won't have it, which could be a problem. So, as a solution to this potential problem, when the bank gave me $900, they replaced that money with $900 worth of *Bank Credit.* On the bank's ledger, that $900 in Bank Credit is treated as money. What this means is, out of that original $1,000 deposited, the bank can give me $900 and still have $1,000 on its books. In effect, City Bank still has $1,000 on their books, and I have $900 to make a purchase; that's a total of $1,900 now in circulation. In the end, $900 of <u>new money</u> was created.

The process doesn't end there. Now, let's say I take my $900, give it to Gilda, and she gives me a pug puppy. I name the pug puppy GusGus, and Gilda takes that $900 and deposits it into her local bank – State Bank. State Bank now has $900 in extra cash to loan out to someone else. Adhering to the 10% Reserve Ratio, Gilda's bank can loan out $810. When they issue an $810 loan to Reginald, the bank replaces that money with $810 in I.O.U.s, in Bank Credit. These I.O.U.s are treated as money, and in this manner, $810 has been added to the economy.

Reginald then takes that money, buys an elephant from Stevie, Stevie deposits the $810 into his local bank, and now that bank has $729 to loan out. When Stevie's bank issues a $729 loan to Jenkins, then the money supply increases by $729.

As this cycle is repeated over and over again, almost ten times that original $1,000 is created as new money.[19] That's right, 10x, meaning almost $10,000 of new money can be added to the American economy from that simple $1,000 seed, by loaning it out to people and then magically replacing that loan with money that never existed. Oftentimes the Reserve Ratio is smaller than 10%, which means even more money can be created from an initial deposit.

Through the process of Fractional Reserve Banking, 92-96% of America's money is created. And just like with Open Market Operations, it is money that is created from nothing and backed by nothing. And with that money created out of thin air, a bank can indirectly "buy" a house or other assets (a bank owns the property purchased through loaned money until it is paid off). They can then, say, "rent" out that house to a citizen and acquire monthly payments from him. And if that citizen experiences hardships and fails too often to make monthly payments, the bank can boot him from his home and reclaim an asset that they originally acquired from money they arguably never had. Normal citizens can't simply create money from nothing and indirectly acquire assets with it; that is called counterfeit. Banks can, though. They do it every day, and all it really takes is typing a few numbers into a computer, leading one to ponder the age-old question, is it a greater crime to rob a bank or to own one?

By using a limitless credit card, individual men at the Fed and within government can essentially print as much money as they want and use it to purchase whatever they want and pay whomever they want. However, such a unique privilege comes at great cost. First, it diminishes the bragging point of, "We have the world's most billionaires and millionaires." When you continuously print money without threat of consequence, then of course high volumes of billionaires and millionaires will inevitably be produced. Second, the national debt continues to soar, where the burden of that debt has the greatest effect on America's lower classes. Third, continuously creating more and more money causes Inflation – $1 in 1960 is equal to $8.55 in 2019, an increase of 755%.[20] With inflation, prices of American goods rise and purchasing power decreases, which again affects America's lower classes most. When prices rise, those in the upper class are somewhat insulated from the increase since they are still able to afford the basic necessities of life quite easily. However, folks in the lower classes of society already feel the pinch of living paycheck to paycheck, so when prices rise, money becomes even tighter in those households. The effects wouldn't be nearly as detrimental if working wages increased with inflation, but that has not been the case for a long time. A 2018 report out of the Pew Research Center shows that over the last 50 years, wages of the average working American have remained roughly the same when adjusted for inflation.[21] In fact, from 1979 to 2013, the Economic Policy Institute calculated that median real hourly wages actually decreased by 5% for lower class citizens, while middle class wages increased by 6%.[22,23] And as for the upper class? Those in the 95th percentile saw their wages increase by a whopping 41% during that span. Money has rapidly siphoned upward in recent decades.

Inflation is really just a hidden tax on the poor and middle classes – a tax that people don't throw a fit about because they are unaware of it. It's a covert means of consolidating wealth from the masses into the hands of a few – "trickle-up economics," if you will – and it creates a larger divide in the wealth gap in America. As more and more of the money pie transfers from lower- and middle-class hands to the small percentage of upper-class hands, more and more people at the bottom end of the economic spectrum get devoured by the poverty monster, as they can't keep up with increased costs brought on by inflation. And, as I will discuss later, poverty has a wide range of negative effects on individuals, and therefore, the population. Among a multitude of issues, it affects a child's physiological and psychological development, it causes stress which leads to diseases, and the pressure of not being able to afford the basic means of survival can push a person to desperation and crime.

Printing endless amounts of money also has the effect of decreasing the value of the US Dollar in the world economy, because like with any product, the more you have of something, the less valuable it becomes. Fortunately for the United States, we are somewhat buffered from default or economic collapse, unlike other countries, as Alan Greenspan once asserted: "The United States can pay any debt it has because we can always print money to do that. So there is zero probability of default."[24] Now, poorer countries don't have those same, seemingly unrestricted capabilities. They face sanctions and other crippling consequences in the world market if they act irresponsibly with their money supply; however, no one is about to sanction or punish the US. Why? I see two main factors:

1. The US Dollar is considered the reserve currency of the world. As of 2019, the US Dollar makes up over 60% of all known central bank foreign exchange reserves.[25] Some countries have adopted the US Dollar as their own currency, while many more nations either peg the value of their currency to the dollar or keep it within a close range. Also, 90% of foreign exchange trades involve the dollar and 40% of the world's debt is issued in US Dollars.[26] The overall reliance across the globe on America's currency keeps it relatively insulated from collapse.

2. As the adage goes, "Might makes right." Simply put, America has the strongest military force in the world. If foreign leaders, like Saddam Hussein of Iraq or Muammar Gaddafi of Libya, want to start accepting different forms of currency for commodities, like oil, such a move could threaten the credibility and the value of the US Dollar in the world market, which would put the local economy and America's powerful world position at risk. So, to squash such potentially devastating threats, the rulers of America have the ability to manufacture justifications and then use their significant influence to involve military forces. In 2000, before the second US invasion of Iraq, Saddam had made it known that he was planning to sell oil using the Euro instead of the US Dollar, which would have dealt a heavy blow to the integrity of the US Dollar and the US economy, and could have encouraged other oil-rich countries to follow suit.[27,28] "Saddam Hussein demanded Euros for his oil. His arrogance was a threat to the dollar; his lack of any military might was never a threat,"[29] said former presidential candidate Ron Paul.

   Similarly, in 2011 Gaddafi made plans to create a gold-backed Libyan currency, and he wanted to use that currency to trade for oil rather than the US Dollar. Again, the ramifications could have been devastating to the world economy and the world financial system, as well as the US Dollar.[30,31]

   Likewise, both of these leaders were quickly sniffed out and "neutralized," allowing the US Dollar to remain on top as the strongest and most used currency in the world.

> Never threaten a man and his money, especially when that man has enough financial leverage to call on the strongest military force on the planet.

All of the money that is created and loaned out in the US is debt; it must be paid back. And like I said, it is the average American citizen who ends up being responsible for that debt. See, once banks loan out and individuals in government use the money willed into existence by the Fed, it eventually "trickles down" into the arena of The Pit. And of the flakes of money that gradually trickle into the economic battlefield, the rest of the population must then labor and compete against each other to obtain it. When an individual obtains little bits of that trickling, they then use some of it to pay for survival, while some of it goes right back up to the Fed through what we as a species have collectively accepted for millennia as "taxes."

Of the money we labor and sweat for, a certain percentage is taken out as an Income Tax. That taxed money then goes to the Internal Revenue Service (IRS). The IRS then gives that money to the Treasury. The Treasury then uses our taxed income to pay the Federal Reserve for the Principle we owe, plus Interest – money they created with a magic wand, money they never had in the first place. Currently, the interest on the principle amount of our national debt has grown so large that much of our income taxes go to paying the interest on the debt, rather than to government funded programs like we expect it to, as was discovered by the Grace Commission delivered to President Reagan:

> "With two-thirds of everyone's personal income taxes wasted or not collected, 100 percent of what is collected is absorbed solely by interest on the Federal debt and by Federal Government contributions to transfer payments. In other words, all individual income tax revenues are gone before one nickel is spent on the services which taxpayers expect from their Government."[32]

Oftentimes, too, we have to take out loans just to make our debt payments, plunging us further into debt.

Ready for the next best part of this whole process, of this whole system? The national debt can never be paid off. That's right. And I'm not just saying that to be cynical due to its overwhelmingly high level. The debt *literally* can never be paid off. Why? Because when the Fed creates new money, when it creates the Principle of a loan it gives out, it comes with Interest. That interest can never be paid back, because the interest doesn't exist in circulation.

Let's say the Fed creates $1,000 and throws it into the economy. Let's then pretend this is the only money that the Fed has ever created, meaning it is the only money the people have to trade with. Now let's say the Fed charges 10% on that $1,000. Now, when it comes time to pay back the loan, we will owe the principle amount of $1,000 plus the amount in interest of $100; we will owe a total of $1,100. But here's the problem, the only amount of currency, of money that exists in this hypothetical economy is $1,000. That's the only money that was ever created and given to us. We can only ever pay back the principle of $1,000. It is impossible to pay off the extra $100 in interest because that $100 does not exist.

But, just for a moment, let's pretend that it was possible to pay off the debt, that interest was never charged on the initial loan. Even in this situation, we still couldn't do it. The national debt *is* the money supply. If we ended up paying off the debt, that would mean we would no longer have any money in the economy to trade with. If we gave all of our money back to the Fed, then that money would no longer be in circulation, and our economy would collapse (unless we replaced it of course, say, with Greenbacks or Bitcoin or any other made up form of money).

For those two reasons, but mainly due to interest, the debt cannot be paid off. In this way, the American worker is permanently indebted to the Federal Reserve, its private controllers, and the banks. It's really a cruel joke. A scam on the people. They create money from nothing, purchase assets and services with it, and then *the people* have to compete against each other to acquire droplets of that money just so they can give it back. With this process, the American economy has been, and always will be, Socialism for the virtuous elite and Capitalism for everyone else.

What's even funnier is that presidential candidate after presidential candidate, the Clintons and the Trumps, has won favor of the American voter by talking about how he or she has a plan to tackle the national debt. Empty statements regarding our debt typically elicit heavy applause from those supporting their candidate. To me it's just another indication that our two-party system and the election process is a complete farce. The presidential candidates know the debt can't be paid off. They aren't dumb. However, they know the general public is ignorant to many of the machinations of our country and its government, so they chant sweet nothings into our ears, even if it includes flat out lying. Whether the Douche or Turd (South Park) is voted into office, it doesn't matter; we bend the knee to our debts, and our debts are ultimately owed to the Fed and the private bankers who have attained substantial wealth from this system.

Lastly, any time Congress is panicking about the debt ceiling and threatens to shut down government, know too this is also a farce. The national debt will inevitably continue to rise, and Congress is well aware.

So, let's do a quick recap here:

- Money is created with the flick of a pen or the tap of a computer keyboard by The Fed and banks through Open Market Operations and Fractional Reserve Banking
- The government gets to use that money as they wish, even though they did absolutely nothing to receive that money, and the banks get to hand out large bonuses
- Banks can use that made-up money to create new loans, which, put another way, means they get to acquire assets and rent them out to average citizens. When you take out a loan for a house, the bank owns your home until you pay off your mortgage.
- When money is created, the American taxpayer goes into debt, not the Fed, even though the Fed is the one who wrote a check without any money in its account
- Even though the government didn't have to work for that money, the American taxpayer has to work to obtain crumbs of what's thrown into The Pit, otherwise she doesn't get to survive.
- The American taxpayer uses his or her hard-earned dollars to pay the debt, to pay for something they didn't purchase
- Because of interest, the debt can never be paid off, keeping us forever shackled to the Fed

The Federal Reserve is the most powerful entity in the United States, because they control the country's money supply. He who controls the money controls the nation. The government cannot overrule actions that it takes. It is an entity ultimately controlled by private interests, whose regional banks operate as corporations and pay out annual dividends to its shareholders. So, who exactly are the prime beneficiaries of the Federal

Reserve system? The answer is, no one really knows. It's a closely guarded secret. See, even though the Fed and Board of Governors are subject to perfunctory financial audits (e.g., balance sheets, financial statements, etc.),[33] its monetary policies and intimate activities are not fully audited.[34] The 1978 Federal Banking Agency Audit Act[35] (an amendment to the Accounting and Auditing Act of 1950) restricts auditing of the Federal Reserve's:

> "(A) transactions conducted on behalf of or with foreign central banks, foreign governments, and nonprivate international financing organizations;
> "(B) deliberations, decisions, and actions on monetary policy matters, including discount window operations, reserves of member banks, securities credit, interest on deposits, and open market operations;
> "(C) transactions made under the direction of the Federal Open Market Committee including transactions of the Federal Reserve System Open Market Account; and
> "(D) those portions of oral, written, telegraphic, or telephonic discussions and communications among or between Member of the Board of Governors, and officers and employees of the Federal Reserve System which deal with topics listed in subparagraphs (A), (B), and (C) of this paragraph."

Attempts to fully audit this private institution have been shut down over and over again under the guise that it could be a "danger to the Fed's independence and traditionally low profile."[36,37]

However, once you explore the complete history of central banks around the world and follow their steamy footprints, you eventually wind up at a few names that I'm sure you've heard of, but aren't mentioned often, and that's by design. If you start with the most powerful banks in Europe, find out who was running those banks over the last couple centuries, and then figure out who were the main players pressuring America into establishing a central bank, you can quickly pinpoint those who would benefit most from the Federal Reserve system. There has been a great deal of speculation and whispers as to who these people are, and many of those whispers chant the same names. But they are the

Voldemorts of the real world. They are not to be named, as former president Woodrow Wilson once declared:

> "Since I entered politics, I have chiefly had men's views confided to me privately. Some of the biggest men in the United States, in the field of commerce and manufacture, are afraid of somebody, are afraid of something. They know that there is a power somewhere so organized, so subtle, so watchful, so interlocked, so complete, so pervasive, that **they had better not speak above their breath when they speak in condemnation of it**."[38]

However, nowadays if you are so bold as to throw out names, prepare yourself for the painful branding of an immensely shameful label indicating irrationality, mental instability, and gross unintelligence. Prepare to be labeled as…Conspiracy Theorist!!! (*The Creature From Jekyll Island* by G. Edward Griffin is a fascinating and entertaining read on the subject if you find yourself curious.)

The process used by the central bank of the United States is not unlike other central banking systems around the world, including the "central bank for central bankers" – the Bank for International Settlements.

Additionally, at the end of 2020, America's national debt approached $28 trillion, while it only had about $19 trillion in its money supply.[39,40] And, at the end of 2019 the world's total debt in US Dollars had ballooned to roughly $255 trillion;[41] however, just over $95 trillion exists in the world economy.[42] The entirety of Earth is in debt, but to who, damn you, who?!?!

So where did the Federal Reserve System get its start? Where did it all begin? How was our government or the population ever duped into approving of such a scam? Well, let's take a peek by exploring a very brief history of central banking in America.

## 5.1 A BRIEF HISTORY OF THE FED'S RISE TO POWER

"Banks have done more injury to the religion, morality, tranquility, prosperity, and even wealth of the nation, than they can have done or ever will do good."[1] – John Adams (2nd President of the United States)

"Behind the ostensible government sits enthroned an invisible government owing no allegiance and acknowledging no responsibility to the people."[2] – Theodore Roosevelt (26th President of the United States)

Snap. Crackle! POP! Jagged bolts of lightning crashed down upon and illuminated the shadowy landscape of Jekyll Island in the fall of 1910, as a small group of some of America's most financially astute men conspired behind the closed doors of an exclusive resort owned by the Jekyll Island Club, a club boasting such elite members as the "Hero of the Panic of 1907" – J.P. Morgan. What was the conclave's primary objective? To lay the foundations of establishing a new Central Banking system in America, one that would be responsible for controlling the country's money supply.

Just days before the meeting commenced, six of the men were instructed by Nelson Aldrich to arrive separately at a New Jersey train station. They were also instructed not to acknowledge each other and to only use first names.[3] The men were well known, and it was feared that if reporters were to spot them, America would go bonkers over the story.

So, who were the seven men handpicked to develop the ground rules of what would become the Federal Reserve System? The list reads like a 1930s New York Yankees roster:

- Nelson Aldrich – Rhode Island Senator. Chairman of the National Monetary Commission (one of the purposes of the Commission was to find ways to break up the stronghold of the 'money trust'). Business associate of J.P. Morgan and father-in-law of John Rockefeller, Jr.
- Paul Warburg – Part of Warburg banking dynasty. Partner at international investment bank Kuhn, Loeb & Company. Maintained close ties with Rothschild banking dynasty after

his father, Moritz, was an apprentice under the family in France and Italy. One of the wealthiest men in the world.

- Abraham Piatt Andrew – Assistant Secretary of the Treasury
- Frank Vanderlip – President of National City Bank of New York (largest bank in America)
- Benjamin Strong – Head of J.P. Morgan's Banker's Trust Company
- Henry Davison – Senior Partner of the J.P. Morgan Company
- Charles Norton – President of the First National Bank of New York

[Cheesy, fictionalized dialogue]

"Did you tell the press we were fishing for red herring like I told you?" asked Nelson.

"I understand the general public is dumb, but even that seemed too obvious. Instead, I just told them we were…on a duck hunt," said Paul with a crooked smile.

"Excellent…"

Claps of thunder and roars of laughter filled the room as the dastardly clan busted out in unison, "Muahaha….MUAH-HA-HA-HA-HAAAA!!!"

The duck hunting diversion was a true and necessary ruse for the group to proceed unimpeded by a wary populace and government, as Paul Warburg would later write: "It is well to remember that the period during which these discussions took place was a time of the struggle of the financial Titans – the period of big combinations [of businesses], with bitter fights for control. All over the country there was a deep feeling of fear and suspicion with regard to Wall Street's power and ambitions."[4]

See, for about 150 years prior to that Jekyll Island meeting in 1910, many of our founding fathers and revered leaders fought tirelessly to keep a central banking system out of America, especially one that kept them tethered to British power structures and gave enormous control to individual financiers, both foreign and local. However, money was a consistent mess in the colonies, and figuring out how to create and maintain a stable economy proved to be problematic. States were constantly battling inflation (2300% inflation in Rhode Island in the 1750s),[5] and whatever forms of currency were circulating throughout the country – whether fiat or commodity-based, or whether it was issued by state banks or private banks – it was unreliable, causing various periods of prosperity followed by depressions. So, it seemed at times that the only way to remedy the young nation's economic volatility was to establish a national bank with a singular, sound currency.

And that's where the "Little Lion," Alexander Hamilton, comes into play. As many are well aware, the busy-minded Hamilton was a banking and financial prodigy. Near the end of the Revolutionary War, he assisted Robert Morris, a man who profited from war contracts, in establishing America's first private national bank – the Bank of North America (BNA) – to help rein in national and state debts. Then, after that bank failed, Hamilton founded the Bank of New York with a group of wealthy financiers before eventually making his way into President George Washington's cabinet. It was during his time as the nation's first Secretary of Treasury, circa 1790, that he began laying the foundations for another attempt at a central bank. And much like the Bank of North America, he modeled the new system after the Bank of England.

However, men like Thomas Jefferson, James Madison, Benjamin Rush, and others said no way! Such an institution would "…lay the foundation for an Aristocracy in our country," said Benjamin Rush;[6] aristocracy and monarchy were exactly what colonialists were trying to escape when they fled Europe for the "new" world in the first place. And Jefferson and Madison worried that a central bank printing volumes of fiat money could be "particularly calamitous" to the nation's economy.[7]

Additionally, they observed the dirty tricks that the money powers pulled shortly after the Revolutionary War, and they didn't want to see the wealth of ordinary, hardworking citizens secretly confiscated and consolidated into the hands of a few.[8] After all, it was those ordinary citizens – the soldiers, the farmers, the wives, etc. – who sacrificed everything to help America win the war and gain her independence. Unfortunately, instead of seeing their loyalty and sacrifices rewarded, many fell victim to "high way robbery,"[9] as Rush described, and were cheated out of basic income owed to them. Here's how:

As the Revolutionary War raged, America struggled to gather funds to support the Continental Army's fight against the Redcoats, and states became unable to pay the soldiers. So, the nation's leaders had to develop creative ways to raise and save cash. One of the methods used was, instead of paying the soldiers and other citizens upfront, they issued army certificates, or IOUs, with a promise that they would pay later – in full and at interest.

However, after the war ended in 1783, though America unshackled itself from British control, it had racked up an incredible amount of debt, much of which was held by foreign financiers. Questions started to raise as to whether or not the government could fulfill its promise to pay those soldiers, farmers, widows, and orphans who held war certificates. This doubt caused the value of the certificates to tumble; in many pockets of America they became close to worthless.

And this is where the dirty tricks came into play, the "high way robbery." When Hamilton became the nation's Secretary of Treasury in 1789, he had a plan to consolidate and settle domestic debts. Included in his proposal was a move to pay for war certificates at their original, face value plus interest – even if their price in the market had plummeted to nothing. Now, as one of the founders of the Bank of New York, Hamilton was well connected with local and foreign investors.[10] Somehow word began to tip-toe around tightknit banking circles that the US government was considering paying for the Revolutionary War certificates in full.

Such insider information prompted financiers to buy up the IOUs all over the country.[11] But the average citizen was unaware of Hamilton's or the government's plans. In their minds, they weren't getting paid, ever. So when speculators showed up at their doorsteps offering cash for what were perceived as "worthless" pieces of paper, many citizens parted with their certificates for fractions of their face value – if they were owed $1, say, they might have given away their IOU for $0.10. Keep in mind, too, that these ordinary citizens agreed to forego payment during the war with the understanding that they would be paid in full later; but, when they weren't paid, many experienced financial hardships and had little other choice but to part with their certificates for whatever cash they could get.

A number of Americans in elevated positions pled on behalf of the voiceless majority; they were outraged by the deceit displayed by those pledged to serve the public. Pelatiah Webster, known by many as the "American Adam Smith," said:

> "...by a strange fatality of events, absurdity of reasoning, and perversion of counsel and right...this money is...to be diverted

> from, and never paid to, them [the worthy and deserving patriots]; but to be given to another class of citizens and foreigners."[12]

Benjamin Rush was clearly flustered when offering his blunt perspective in regard to the Wall Street speculators who hawked America's worthy patriots and acquired their certificates, telling James Madison:

> "I could fill a volume with facts & anecdotes of the characters of those men who now hold the greatest part of the alienated certificates of this state. Many of them are not worthy of the privileges of citizenship of the United States... The whole profits of the war will soon center in the hands of American tories [British loyalists]...while the brave men who deserved them will end their lives in gaols, hospitals, or beg their bread from door to door."[13]

Though Rush, Webster, and many others expended considerable effort in going to bat for the average citizen, it was to no avail. After much deliberation between Hamilton, Jefferson, and Madison, a compromise was struck, and the Funding Act of 1790 was passed – an act that was essentially a precursor to the forthcoming Bank of the United States. Hamilton got what he wanted. The federal government assumed state debts and agreed to pay for war certificates at face value plus interest, and those well-informed Wall Street and foreign speculators who acquired the certificates and Continental currencies for pennies on the dollar secured incredible profits. And as for those who parted with their IOUs, those responsible for America's independence and who had no idea of the government's plans? They became victims of legal pillaging by their own people; they were never compensated for their sacrifices. The flock was fleeced. But it wouldn't be the first time in this story – not even close.

Jefferson criticized the measure, saying: "It was unjust, in itself oppressive to the states... It enabled Hamilton so to strengthen himself by corrupt services to many, that he could afterwards carry his bank scheme..."[14]

After the legislative thieving of America's most deserving citizens, Hamilton's next order of business was to persuade Congress to establish his private central bank. "A national debt, if it is not excessive, will be to us a national blessing," he argued.[15] Jefferson, who seemed to be campaigning for the average American citizen at the time, refuted Hamilton's assertions, saying:

> "[The people], and not the rich, are our dependence for continued freedom. And to preserve their independence, **we must not let our rulers load us with perpetual debt.**"[16]

He worried that a "deluge of bank paper" would ruin the country and shackle its people to the money powers.[17]

Those on Team Jefferson also argued that erecting a central bank was unconstitutional and outside the rights of Congress;[18] but Hamilton, a proponent for big government and blessed with the gift of gab, countered that government can and should impose rules outside the constitution when "necessary and proper"[19] and that such actions would be for the general welfare of *the people.*

Nevertheless, Hamilton's persuasive abilities proved too effective. Though Washington was initially hesitant, he eventually caved, and in 1791 the Bank of the United States (aka First Bank of the United States) was created. It was given a 20-year charter, and though it was a quasi-government institution, many of its shares were owned by private foreign investors. In his book *The Creature from Jekyll Island*, G. Edward Griffin shines a spotlight on some of those European financiers, explaining: "The blunt reality is that the Rothschild banking dynasty in Europe was the dominant force, both financially and politically, in the formation of the Bank of the United States."[20] Griffin's statement is corroborated by a number of historians, including Gustavus Myers, who wrote: "Under the surface, the Rothschilds long had a powerful influence in dictating American financial laws. The law records show that they were the power in the old Bank of the United States."[21] Remember in the previous section I mentioned that the Federal Reserve was protected from having its foreign dealings audited? I wonder what they don't want the public to see.

Anyway, in the beginning of the First Bank of the United States' life in the 1790s, it actually served as a catalyst for economic growth in America. It had borrowed over $6 million to the federal government in the first five years – raising its capital from $2 million to $8 million – and the government turned around and pumped some of that money into the nation's economy.[22] However, as always, with an increase in (or stretching of) the money supply comes inflation. And during that short span of time, prices in America increased by 72%. People were paying more for goods, meaning more money was being filched from their pockets and into the hands of a few – the hidden confiscation of the public's wealth that Jefferson, Madison, John Adams, and many others warned.

Average citizens were being swindled, and they didn't even know it, which was one of the many reasons the aforementioned former presidents never warmed up to the idea of the central banking system, or even banks for that matter. Overall, these men "harbored a deep-seated distrust of banks as sanctuaries for corrupt profiteers, [and] gambling houses where the public trust was systematically put at risk and sold to the highest bidder."[23] It was believed that the profits of bankers were acquired without merit, that they simply manipulated money and interest rates without performing any productive labor themselves, without adding any intrinsic value to society. "There is no honest bank but a bank of deposit," said John Adams. "A bank that issues paper at interest is a pickpocket or a robber."[24]

Throughout his life, both politically and personally, Jefferson continued to make known his contempt for the banking system:

> "I have ever been the enemy of banks, not of those discounting for cash, but of those foisting their own paper into circulation, and thus banishing our cash…I was derided as a maniac by the tribe of bank-mongers, who were seeking to filch from the public their swindling and barren gains… The mania [of the banks] is too strong. It has seized by its delusions and corruptions all the members of our governments."[25]

and more pointedly:

> "I sincerely believe…that banking establishments are more dangerous than standing armies."[26]

Well, those within Team Jefferson's camp would soon get their wish. Opposition toward the Bank had been mounting as its 20-year charter approached expiration, and Congress voted not to renew it. Thus, in 1811, the First Bank of the United States was forced to close up shop.

The international money vultures might have been down, but they were far from out. The War of 1812 commenced shortly after the First Bank was disbanded, and that gave them the perfect opportunity to expand their wealth and push for a new central bank charter. War is a blessing to banking powers. As we know, fighting costs a lot of money, and nations typically have to take out massive loans to fund their forces. Of course, through the mechanisms of interest and fractional-reserve lending, the more money banks can lend, the better. It's no wonder, then, that financiers, both domestic and foreign, became known for funding both sides of conflicts. To the moneyed interests, it didn't matter who won or lost a fight – all that mattered was their wallets grew in size, and with bigger wallets came greater political influence. Money has no loyalties.

Leading up to the senseless War of 1812, the United States had cut its national debt from $83 million down to $45 million in 11 years. However, after nearly three years of fighting, thousands dead, and the nation's capitol burnt to the ground, the national debt had about tripled to $127 million[27] – a victory for banking institutions. The US Congress, backed into a corner and needing a way to tame the country's staggering debt, reluctantly voted to reestablish the charter of the Bank of the United States (aka the Second Bank of the United States) in 1816. The money powers had reassumed control of America's cash supply and were back in business! With one-third of its money held by foreign investors, the Bank was "rooted as deeply in Britain as it was in America."[28]

The monetary masters of the "new" central bank wasted no time in disrupting financial growth in America. In 1818, in the midst of an economic boom, the Bank took measures to contract the money supply.[29] A wave of defaults, bankruptcies, and unemployment followed, and America was thrust into what many consider its first "Great Depression." Whether purposefully contrived or not, property values and other assets plummeted in value, and those in favorable financial positions were able to swoop in and acquire those devalued assets for pennies on the dollar. Subsequently, when the economy returned to its feet in the 1820s, those assets rose in value, which translated into wonderful profits for those money and banking powers. The flock was fleeced once more, and wealth consolidated into the hands of a few.

But, like the First Bank, the life of the Second Bank would prove to be a short one. Andrew Jackson was voted into the White House in 1829, and his tolerance for the central bank was as low as any before him. Like his Jeffersonian predecessors, he saw the Bank as unconstitutional and that it gave individual men, especially European financiers, a disproportionate amount of influence within America. He wrote: "More than eight millions of the stock of this bank are held by foreigners… It is to be regretted that the rich and powerful too often bend the acts of government to their selfish purposes."[30] And later, he would say:

> "It is one of the serious evils of our present system of banking that it enables one class of society – and that by no means a numerous one – by its control over the currency, to act injuriously upon the interests of all the others and to exercise more than its just proportion of influence in political affairs."[31]

Though he was no saint, "Old Hickory" appealed to the "common man" at the time, and he denounced that the Bank allowed a privileged few to oppress the will of the average many. He thus made it one of his chief goals to abolish the Bank of the US.

Standing firm in his path, however, was the head of the Bank – Nicholas Biddle – one of the most powerful men in America at the time as he controlled the nation's credit and used his financial influence to bribe and puppeteer Congress to his liking. In this political chess match, Biddle made the first major move against Jackson. He strategically persuaded Congress to renew the Bank's charter four years early in 1832, right as Jackson was campaigning for reelection. Biddle reckoned that Jackson wouldn't risk his chance at a second term by challenging the early renewal, but he was wrong. Jackson vetoed the bill!

He then went on to win the election, too. But the fight wasn't over.

In 1833, Jackson returned with the next major play. Shortly after his second term began, he removed all federal funds from the central bank and began redistributing the money to state banks across America. Check! The private national bank's demise seemed imminent. Or so Jackson assumed.

Biddle had one last trump card up his sleeve, however, and that was control over the nation's money. Wielding such great power, he figured he could use it to cause a financial panic. He could then blame the panic on President Jackson for removing funds from the bank, and then the House would be left with no other choice but to renew the Bank's charter. "Nothing but widespread suffering will produce any effect on Congress," he penned in a letter to William Appleton. "I have no doubt that such a course will ultimately lead to the restoration of the currency and the recharter of the Bank."[32] And create a panic he did.

With zero concern paid to the lives of the average, unassuming American, Biddle tightened up credit and contracted the money supply, throwing the country into deep economic hardship. Americans battled unemployment and businesses filed bankruptcy across the nation. And as planned, Jackson was indeed blamed for the "widespread suffering" engineered by Biddle, which led to the president being censured in 1834.[33]

Oh, Andrew Jackson was fuming! "You are a den of vipers and thieves," he shouted to the Bank's allies. "I intend to rout you out and by the Eternal God I will rout you out."[34] The president remained steadfast in his resolve. He continued fighting to expose Biddle's and the Bank's deceit. But it wasn't until after Biddle himself bragged in public of his ingenious schemes that the public and the Senate became keen to the truth.[35] They subsequently turned against the Bank.

Advantage once again swayed to Jackson's side, and with the deadline looming to renew the Bank's charter, the ground began shrinking beneath Biddle's feet. He would need a miracle to keep the Bank alive. And well…

It was January 30, 1835. Andrew Jackson exited the House chamber from a funeral when a man named Richard Lawrence approached him. The stranger pulled out a derringer pistol and aimed it at the president. Jackson froze. Lawrence pulled the trigger.

Click.

The gun misfired! A scuffle quickly ensued. But Lawrence managed to pull out a second gun! Amidst the chaos he lifted his arm toward Jackson once more and pulled the trigger.

Click.

Defying astronomical odds – 1 in 125,000 according to Smithsonian researchers – the second gun misfired, too.[36]

Jackson's life was spared! But he was convinced his banking opposition was behind the assassination attempt – "The bank, Mr. Van Buren, is trying to kill me, but I will kill it!"[37] Though it was never proven that the Bank's allies concocted the hit, "loony" Lawrence claimed to be backed by powerful men in Europe.

In the end, Andrew Jackson got the best of Biddle and the Bank. He proceeded to pay off the national debt and then ran up a $35 million surplus, which he disbursed to the states to complete various projects.[38] And then, when the Bank's expiration date arrived in 1836, its charter was not renewed. Thus, the Second Bank of the United States went out with a whimper. And Biddle? He was charged with fraud and died before all litigation was finalized.[39]

Jackson had won!

Celebratory words were delivered during his farewell speech:

> "No nation but the freemen of the United States could have come out victorious from such a contest; yet, if you had not conquered, the government would have passed from the hands of the many to the hands of the few, and this organized money power from its secret conclave would have dictated the choice of your highest officers and compelled you to make peace or war, as best suited their own wishes. The forms of your government might for a time have remained, but its living spirit would have departed from it."[40]

He then proceeded to warn the public to remain diligent:

> "The men who profit by the abuses…will continue to besiege the halls of legislation in the general government as well as in the states, and will seek by every artifice to **mislead and deceive** the public servants… Knowing that the path of freedom is continually beset by **enemies who often assume the disguise of friends**, I have devoted the last hours of my public life to warn you of the dangers."[41]

In reading Jackson's words, it is hard not to reflect on our economic and political landscape today and wonder if we aren't currently being "misled and deceived" by "enemies who assume the disguise of friends."

Nevertheless, though he thought the Bank was trying to kill him, it was Jackson who ultimately killed the Bank.

Next up to take on the overwhelming power of the European financiers was Abraham Lincoln, arguably the most beloved and revered president in American history. Leading up to the Civil War, Lincoln at first sought to borrow money from private banks to finance the North. However, when banks told him they would charge between 24 and 36 percent interest on loans, Lincoln refused as he worried such high rates would cripple the United States.[42] He needed an alternative solution to fund his army.

Confounded by the issue, "Honest Abe" recalled consulting one of the only men he trusted at the time – Colonel E.D. Taylor. "What shall we do?" Lincoln asked.

"Why, issue treasury notes bearing no interest," said Taylor.[43]

And that he did. In heeding the words of the Colonel, Lincoln had a bill passed by Congress allowing America to print its own, interest-free money – green-colored bills that became known as "Greenbacks." From 1862 to 1863 over $400 million worth of greenbacks had been issued, which isn't necessarily a good thing as limitless printing of money leads to inflation and currency devaluation, but it helped Lincoln finance and eventually win the war.[44] He would go on to say, "(we) gave to the people of the Republic the greatest blessing they ever had – their own paper to pay off their debts."[45]

Of course, by turning his back to the European financiers and banking powers, he created more enemies than friends. British and French forces began positioning themselves to assist the Confederate South against Lincoln and the Union, as they wanted to see the powerful United States divided into two nations to make expansion for them easier. So, the British had forces stationed in Canada, while the French had soldiers readied in Mexico.[46] Lincoln was surrounded. With the walls quickly caving in, it seemed almost certain that the Union army would suffer devastating defeat. That is until…

Russia! That's right. Russia came to the aid of the Union army. Like Lincoln, the Russian Tsar, Alexander II, also denied the establishment of a central bank in his country, and he then, coincidentally or resultingly, also found himself the victim of pesky European aggression, as England and France considered declaring war on the Tsar with the intent of breaking up the Russian empire.[47] So, Alexander II joined forces with Lincoln, and he sent his Russian naval fleets to the borders of New York and San

Francisco. And in the event of British or French attacks, Lincoln was prepared to command both the Russian Fleet and the US Navy.[48] Though the ships never fired on the European forces, their mere presence kept the international powers at bay and blocked them from delivering supplies to the Southern armies. The unlikely partnership between the United States and Russia proved instrumental in allowing Lincoln to focus on the Civil War and defeat the Confederacy before he could return his focus to the pressures of the money powers.

Two years before the war ended – 1863 – Congress was persuaded to repeal the Greenback laws and replace them with the National Banking Act – a compromise between Lincoln and the moneyed interests that established a network of nationally-chartered banks – a "half-way house to central banking."[49] Lincoln's position on money and banking is somewhat difficult to nail down. As a member of the Whig Party in the 1830s, he openly supported the charter of the Second Bank of the United States. But, after he became president as a Republican, his position seemed to change slightly. Maybe he was simply the consummate politician, saying what he needed to say to further his position on the political totem pole, or maybe once he got into office, he got to see firsthand the incredible influence of the domestic and foreign banking powers. That being said, during his presidency, he did support the establishment of a federally-regulated national bank, as well as government-issued paper currency, but he opposed a central banking system with interest-bearing debt that was heavily dominated by foreign interests.

Anyway, the pernicious European financiers proved to be real thorns in Lincoln's side throughout his time in office. In 1864 he remarked:

> "I see in the near future a crisis approaching that unnerves me and causes me to tremble for the safety of my country…corporations have been enthroned and an era of corruption in high places will follow, and the money power of the country will endeavor to prolong its reign by working upon the prejudices of the people until all wealth is aggregated in a few hands and the Republic is destroyed. **I feel at this point more anxiety for the safety of my country than ever before, even in the midst of war.**"[50]

With the Civil War coming to a close in 1865, Lincoln battened down the hatches for yet another war, one against those powerful "money powers." Unfortunately, as we are all well aware, five days after Robert E. Lee and the South surrendered, Lincoln was assassinated. He never had the opportunity to take on what he might have considered his greatest foe.

As an aside, Tsar Alexander II was also assassinated – in 1881.[51]

Lincoln's death was followed by rapid changes to the country's financial infrastructure. Changes that perhaps benefited the conniving banking cabal? Hugh McCulloch, the acting US Treasury Secretary, began pushing for legislation to retire the greenback and return to gold-backed, interest-bearing money (not a bad idea, except the transitional plan he was proposing would leave ordinary citizens vulnerable to the expected fleecing). However, Henry C. Carey, Lincoln's chief economic advisor, implored McCulloch not to contract the country's currently-traded currency, as it would decimate domestic manufacturers and damage the economy as a whole.[52] Economist Stephen Colwell agreed that contraction was a "remedy…vastly worse than the disease."[53] Plus, the greenback didn't bear interest and it was detached from foreign control, or so the anti-resumption group argued. Needless to say, McCulloch rebuffed, and Congress voted in favor of the Contraction Act in 1866.[54] The Treasury began withdrawing greenbacks from circulation, while McCulloch authorized the "quiet" funding of interest-bearing legal tenders and other quasi-monetary notes even before the bill passed.[55] Now, I imagine at this point it would come as no surprise to find out that European financiers were heavily invested in America's monetary conversion to interest-bearing money. McCulloch estimated in 1866 that $600,000,000 in US securities were held abroad.[56] It might also come as no surprise to know that McCulloch joined the ranks of international financiers once he left his position as Treasury Secretary in 1869.

Well, following the greenback's contraction came a "tightening" of the money market and limited access to credit in 1872, which helped usher in the next "Great Depression" in 1873 (renamed the "Long Depression" after the Great Depression of the 1930s).[57] During this economic bust thousands of American businesses went bankrupt, riots broke out across the country, and property values hit basement levels. And the opulent minority? As you can probably guess at this point, they were able to swoop in like vultures and gobble up the devalued assets at fractions of their original worth. Wealth adequately confiscated and consolidated!

And over the next 30 years leading up to the surreptitious Jekyll Island meeting, America experienced a few more economic collapses – including the Panic of 1893 and the Panic of 1907 – all of which were preceded by intentional contractions of the money supply.

The deluge of financial crises coupled with an ever-growing wealth gap across the country led to a steady uptick in America's distrust of its fiscal policies and the banking community, in general. Of course, the sentiment of the mass of ants is of little consequence to the rulers of this game. Eventually, the money powers always get their way. They simply must wait for the right moment. And for the architects of the Federal Reserve, that moment came following the Panic of 1907. Whether it was intentionally orchestrated by J.P. Morgan spreading rumors that large banks were insolvent and struggling *or* brought on by a combination of poor policies, failed business schemes, a natural disaster, and an unstable banking system, 1907's economic bust seemed to be the final nail in the coffin in the debate of whether or not a central bank was "necessary and proper."

Charles Lindbergh, a Republican member of the US House of Representatives, seemed to think the panic was manufactured, saying:

> "The King Bankers put in motion, in 1907, a great scheme. They had gambled and speculated on Wall Street until so many watered stocks and bonds had been manufactured… The King Bankers knew the condition and informed the favored of their friends what was to come. There was to be a panic in the fall of 1907 that would be advertised as the result of our bad banking and currency laws."[58]

Still, a great many were convinced that a system needed to be created to better manage America's money. And that's where we rejoin our mischievous cast of bankers during the fall of 1910 – Nelson Aldrich, Henry Davison, Frank Vanderlip, Paul Warburg, Benjamin Strong, Charles Norton, and Abraham Piatt Andrew – as they spent hours and days on Jekyll Island crafting a bill modeled after the central banking systems of Europe.

[Cheesy, fictionalized dialogue]

"Henry, can you explain again the purpose of this bill?" asked Frank.

Henry slapped his own forehead with his palm.

Benjamin started winding up his fists and said, "Why I oughta…"

"What? I'm just asking."

Henry intervened, "How many times do we have to go over this? It's to break up the money trust in America."

"Yeah, but, but, Henry…we ARE the money trust," Frank said.

Steam began spewing out of Henry's ears. "Alright, honestly, who invited Frank? You understand that the public doesn't trust all of their money being controlled by a few ugly men like us, right? If we can set up and operate behind a private institution and make it feel like a government entity, the people will forget that we still control their money."

Frank stares blankly forward. "Uh, oh, oh right. I get it. Totally…" His eyes shift left and right.

"Good. Now can we move on? If we told the people we were on a duck hunt, well by golly I want to go duck hunting."

Charles sat at the end of the round table feverishly scribbling on a long paper canvas. "Done! Can we just quick go over some of the bullet points here before we adjourn?"

"Let's hear it," said Paul still circling the table with his pipe.

"Ok, so first we will call the new central bank the Federal Reserve. However, it will not be fully regulated by the government and it will hold no reserves."

"Yup."

"Second, we will tell the rest of the dotes in America that the aim of this institution is to stabilize the economy by setting interest rates, controlling inflation, and yada, yada, yada, but in the hard-to-read, fine print we will lay out our ability to print all of the money we want, spend it how we want, and then ask those dotes to pay us back?"

Snot bubbles burst out of Paul's nose as he tries to hold in his laughter. "Yeah, that, that sounds about right…"

Smiles fill the room. The amount of light reflecting off of the men's toothy grins nearly blinds Billiam, their evening butler, as he attempts to refill their wine glasses.

"Oh, and last but not least, to honor Andrew Jackson's undying support for our cause," Charles starts giggling, "we will put his face on a piece of legal tender, yet to be determined."

"Brilliant. Absolutely brilliant," said Paul.

"Gosh this is great. J.P. and the Red Shields will be so proud of us," said Benjamin.

With a smile, Henry said, "Boys? Let's go hunting."

And on the 10th day, God, I mean, the key orchestrators of what would become America's current central banking system were allowed to rest. After each member signed the bill, they grabbed their guns and went on a good old-fashioned hunting excursion. It was a joyous Thanksgiving. The men enjoyed a decadent feast of wild turkey with oyster stuffing among many other delicacies.

Covert mission accomplished.

With the foundations laid out by the Jekyll Island crew, the Federal Reserve Act was signed by Woodrow Wilson on December 23, 1913.[59] Some people were happy. Some people were sad. Charles Lindbergh was part of the sad group, as he would go on to say:

> "This Act establishes the most gigantic trust on Earth. When the President signs this bill, the invisible government by the Monetary Power will be legalized… The worst legislative crime of the ages is perpetrated by this banking bill."[60]

Nevertheless, from that day forward, the control of America's money supply was delegated to private interests, and as intended the nation's economy has been stable ever since. Oh wait, how could I forget? For the six years after the Federal Reserve was instituted, the Fed significantly increased the money supply in America. People were better able to access loans and business was booming. However, in 1920, the Fed began restricting credit in the economy. This caused widespread panic, as could be predicted, and America was thrust into another recession. Businesses began to crumble and smaller banks that weren't affiliated with the Fed went bankrupt, allowing wealthy banks that were affiliated with the Fed to swoop in and seize them for prices far below their original value.

Once the recession had ended, the Fed repeated the cycle of expanding the money supply during the 1920s, which resulted in a period where business was flourishing and everyone seemed to be prospering. However, after panic ensued in 1929 followed by a run on a number of banks, the Fed again acted by contracting the money supply. The result? America experienced the worst economic downturn in its history – the Great Depression. Like the Long Depression of the 19th Century, the flock was once again ripe for the fleecing. While Americans were suffering and dying and property values plummeted, the few who were in a favorable financial position were able to acquire small banks and other assets at pennies on the dollar – a tactic used over and over again to consolidate wealth. It would take over a decade for America to get back on her feet again, and led Congressman Louis T. McFadden to write in 1934:

> "...we have, in this country one of the most corrupt institutions the world has ever known. I refer to the Federal Reserve Board and the Federal Reserve Banks. This evil institution has impoverished and ruined the people of the United States...and has practically bankrupted our Government. It has done this through the defects of the law under which it operates...and through the corrupt practices of the moneyed vultures who control it."[61]

During the Great Depression, as measures taken by the Fed seemed to have zero positive effect on the economy, FDR took steps to remove the US Dollar from the Gold Standard in America. Because the dollar was attached to gold, the US was limited by how much currency it could produce, and the idea was that we needed to print more money to pull us out of financial ruin. In order to detach the dollar from gold, the president signed legislation that made it so gold was no longer convertible into dollars, and he ordered all Americans to turn in whatever gold they had. Any citizen who refused to relinquish their gold bullion would be penalized with a 10-year prison sentence. By 1933, the dollar was no longer backed by gold within the US.

Then, as the final step in making the US Dollar completely independent from any commodity, Richard Nixon completely severed the US Dollar from the Gold Standard as it pertained to the world market in 1971. Since then, the US Dollar has been a fiat currency in the global economy, meaning it is just a piece of paper backed by nothing but our faith in its value.

And to this day, the Fed is still going strong, and its role in managing monetary policy has only continued to expand, especially in response to the Great Recession of 2008. One pattern of behavior of the banking masters has remained consistent in the last 250 years. And that pattern goes a little something like this: the printing of fiat currency and then channeling it into the market, followed by economic expansion, followed by inflation, followed by contraction, and then ending at panic and recession. Prices of assets fall, and those seated in favorable economic positions amble in and acquire those devalued assets for pennies on the dollar. The fleecing of the flock, the "culling of the cattle," the "flipping upside down and the shaking of the change out of one's trousers" – it's repeated over and over and over again. Whether through inflation or recession, the "money powers" consistently find ways to vacuum up society's wealth and maintain their dominant positions over the masses.

And now, consider the tremendous amount of money being borrowed by the government to fund activities related to COVID-19. The more loans that are taken out and the more cash dumped into the economy, the more money that is gained by wealthy interests through fractional-reserve banking, interest, and inflation. Now, I might argue that economic relief packages are necessary to stymie domestic suffering, but the banking interests and their allies become the ultimate victors in this game. And the average, hardworking American becomes the victim, not only of COVID, but also of legal theft and having their wealth pilfered through hidden means.

It's truly a sneaky, and sinister, operation…

## 5.2 CHAPTER CONCLUSION

The purpose of the first few chapters of this book has been merely to lay the groundwork for how the monetary game functions and how the ancient tool of money is used to facilitate the flow of a society's goods and its people. So far, however, I have done little in making a case to support why it is so imperative that we evolve from the tool of money and transcend our global economic arrangement. Well, that's about to change. In the next many sections of this text, I expend considerable effort in discussing the inevitable perils of operating within the global monetary system, of functioning within a game where the population is pitted against one another in a competition for something that is finite to gain access to the means of survival. And I discuss why this technically inefficient and, dare I say, deadly competition not only threatens to destabilize the world's population, but also how it continues to facilitate the rapid decay of our planet – the habitat we rely on for life, liberty, and the pursuit of happiness. Here I make my strongest case for why we need to nudge money into retirement.

# *6* MONEY: THE ULTIMATE PRECONDITION FOR NEGATIVE OUTCOMES

"It little matters to me whether you shoot a man or starve him to death by inches." – Ghandi

Money, unbeknownst to itself, is a core precondition behind just about every single negative externality in the physical world. It's been at the heart of death and stunted development in millions of children. It's at the heart of environmental decay, crime, fighting, exploitation of the poor, and so much more. But allow me to take a step back. The existence of money is not literally the direct cause of most detrimental outcomes; it's a core precondition, however; it's the finger that topples the first domino that eventually leads to detrimental outcomes. For example, hundreds of thousands of children die each year from diarrheal diseases, most notably in impoverished regions of the planet. The *direct cause* of death in many of these cases ends up being not from money, but from dehydration due to loss of water and nutrients from the diarrhea. However, if we trace a line along the chain of causality, we see that in a large portion of diarrheal deaths among young children, the diarrhea is caused by dirty drinking water. And the dirty drinking water isn't necessarily caused by money, but it is the lack of money in these poor communities that prevents its leaders from accessing and installing widely available technology and equipment to provide clean drinking water to its population.

Money is not the direct cause of a dairy farmer terminating his own life. But if we follow the short path of dominos, we find in many cases a farmer's despair is fueled by a persistent struggle to obtain enough money to adequately provide life necessities for his family. Money is not the direct cause of rainforests dissolving at a rate greater than at any other point in human history, rather it is machinery operated by humans that pierces the bark and decimates resource-rich habitats. However, again, if we follow the dominos, we find the lack and pursuit of money as the catalyst behind rapid deforestation.

Though money may not be the direct cause of negative externalities, if we do enough digging, we will find that the *lack of it* or the *pursuit of it* is rooted deep within most of the world's most unwanted issues.

And it's not that money is evil, per se. It's not. It's simply a tool, a neutral, lifeless, unfeeling tool. But, it's what it represents that draws out of us our worst human tendencies. It's the underlying implications of this lifeless tool that has us in endless skirmishes, that has us irresponsibly exhausting resources faster than they can be replenished. Money represents life. Survival. And it represents success. And because it is scarce within any civilization that uses it (no matter how much of it exists at any one time), humans are driven to questionable behavior just to obtain it, so as to secure survival and the façade of success.

Unfortunately, the questionable behavior wrung out of us by the monetary game has caused massive destabilization within every natural system on Earth (as all are connected), and it has brought us to a dark precipice unfamiliar to any generation of the past. Now, I'm not much for fear-mongering, again, because I've detached myself in many ways from the fate of our species, mostly as a defense mechanism – I'm just along with my 3D glasses and a bag of Sour Patch Watermelon candies for the transitory ride; and I've accepted that all things, both good and bad, must eventually come to an end, and that notion does not induce fear or panic within me; but, that being said, I still care, and if we look at the modern trends and trajectories in terms of sustainability, resource usage, pollution, wildlife extinction, habitat degradation, food insecurity, water pollution, and so much more, all projections and forecasts are disturbing. And with a population predicted to approach 10 billion by 2050 coupled with a distorted value system of mindless consumption festering like a disease in developed and developing nations, it is easy to see how we as a species could push the planet beyond its boundaries of support. It is easy to see where scientists and thinkers have arrived at such grim forecasts.

Though many of my arguments frolic in territories of morality – for instance, a part of me wants change in our economic setup because I don't like seeing people struggling or in pain, and I believe everyone should have the total freedom to author their own lives – I can't expect people to share my morals. We all have distinct values. We all have different definitions for what is morally right and what is morally wrong – try explaining to the Chambri people of Papua New Guinea that the ritualistic scarification with razor blades of its teen boys is morally wrong. So, I can't expect to convince people of the necessity for monetary adjustment by appealing to our moral and ethical sides. Unfortunately, the call to action, the plea for change now goes beyond morality. It has now become, with a hint of dramatic flair, about the longevity of our species as a whole and the survival of precious life systems around the planet. It seems clear we are engaged in habits incompatible with Earth's larger-order system, and if we don't make adjustments to the way we function, we've chartered a drunken, yet avoidable course to oblivion.

The adjustment I am recommending, of course, is the evolution from the finite tool of money and from the global monetary system. I posit that it is money that is at the root of all negative trends in our world, and only by removing this core contaminant can we even begin to reverse the negative trajectories threatening posterity.

The next few sections within this chapter have thus been devoted to discussing what I believe to be our most pertinent issues and how the existence of the antiquated *money-for-survival* system is the central pollutant giving rise to and nourishing all. There are so many issues I could address and then attempt to draw a link between outcomes and money, but instead I've chosen to limit my focus. Therefore, I have narrowed my discussion points to the relationships between money and childhood poverty, war, crime, ecological degradation, exploitation, and public trust. The decline within each *should* be justification enough to consider exploring alternative economic options, but as I talk about later, the word *should* toils in fantasy; it is close to meaningless in the context of human behavior.

Let's start with impoverished children.

## 6.1 CHILDHOOD POVERTY: THE GREATEST TRAGEDY ON EARTH

Our ultra-competitive system of acquiring money from a limited supply in order to survive naturally breeds winners and losers. For many, this method of organizing society is fine, in fact it's great; it can be fun and exciting trying to strategize and outsmart our human competition; for many it provides incentive and makes each individual accountable for his own actions. From this perspective we are products based solely on the choices we make in life. If a man makes the right choices and works hard, he will theoretically end up a winner. If he makes the wrong choices, he will end up a loser. A loser who winds up homeless and hungry then has no one to blame but himself; he made his bed, he must sleep in it. Though this overly simplistic type of thinking ignores a multitude of other elements that can contribute to an individual's circumstances, I've largely accepted on the outside that society doesn't really care about adults who have fallen on hard times, about adults who have become "losers" within the game, within The Pit. They don't really care to hear the events or understand the preconditions leading up to an individual's hardships, for they must have been "lazy" or they must have made stupid decisions along the way. It's simply easier to draw snap conclusions based on localized perceptions, on the limited superficial information readily available to the five senses, rather than approaching a situation from a broader, structural view. Understanding the seemingly infinite amount of intersecting life variables takes a lot of effort and a lot of digging – and ain't nobody got time for that in this workaday world. Again, I've accepted that.

However, what I have a difficult time accepting and what we often fail to remember in this game of winners and losers is that many of these losers have *children*. Now, I am unsure what takes place in the metaphysical world before a fetus enters his mother's womb, but as far as I understand it, a child does not get to pick his parents. He doesn't get to choose the scrotum he exists in, nor does he get to choose the uterus he is squirted into. Yet, when a child is born into a family of "losers," into a financially broken household, it is he who is ultimately punished, and it is he who pays the greatest price.

I mentioned earlier that 14-18% of America's children live in poverty.[1] Because we are currently (2020) in a "boom" phase of our economic cycle, that number has come down a few percentage points in the last few years and will continue to drop, but we can expect this number to climb again once we inevitably hit another "bust" phase; during the 2008 recession, childhood poverty rates rose to 20%. For a child living in poverty, the laundry list of negative consequences is extensive, ranging from stunted physical and neurological development to childhood abuse, drug addiction, and crime later in life. Poor children have increased infant mortality rates, more frequent and severe chronic diseases like asthma, increased obesity, and less access to healthcare. They are exposed to a wide array of environmental stressors, like unsafe neighborhoods, unclean water, parents under stress, and less access to nutrition. The early stages of human life are the most critical in shaping us into the people we become. When a child is born into a family that consistently lacks the financial means to provide everyday necessities for healthy growth, he is forced to endure a steep uphill climb throughout the entirety of his development, a situation that can put him at a heavy disadvantage when he is prepped to enter adulthood and the workforce. Again, he had no say in his circumstances when he entered this world, but it is he who suffers most in the end from being born to poor parents.

So, let's talk about the laundry list of negative consequences a child could experience while growing up in poverty. What sort of setbacks might he deal with as he grows into an adult and must compete against others who had normal, healthy upbringings?

*POVERTY & BRAIN DEVELOPMENT*

A 2015 study completed out of the University of Wisconsin, Madison, explored the relationship between poverty, brain development, and academic achievement.[2] From 2001 to 2007, researchers took MRI scans of the brain at 24-month intervals of 389 children and adolescents from six different collection sites across the United States. Using the scans, they measured brain tissue volume, including gray matter of the frontal lobe, temporal lobe, and hippocampus – areas vital to higher cognitive function, memory, decision-making, reasoning, personality, and much more. What the researchers discovered was that children who grew up in households under the Federal Poverty Line had gray matter volumes 8 to 10 percentage points below normal development. As could be predicted, the maturational lags in the frontal and temporal lobes of these impoverished children were positively correlated with lower academic test scores – for instance, 50% of low-income fourth graders score below basic level on national literacy tests.[3] These negative affects persist into early adulthood. Dr. Seth Pollak, the lead researcher of the study went on to say about childhood poverty that it is "…a biomedical problem, an environmental condition or toxin that's affecting children."[4]

In a larger study published in 2015, researchers from Columbia University explored the link between family income and parental education in brain development in children and adolescents.[5,6] They examined brain images among a cohort of 1,099 individuals between the ages of 3 and 20. What they discovered was family income and parental education were significantly associated with total surface area of the brain, with the association being predictably steepest at the lower end of the income distribution spectrum. The significant variations in brain matter were observed in multiple areas of the brain, including the frontal, temporal, and parietal lobes, and the hippocampus – again, areas responsible for language, memory, reading, and various executive functions and spatial skills. The children who grew up in families in the lowest income bracket – less than $25,000 annually – had up to 6% less surface area of the brain compared to the children living in families making over $150,000. Among the low-income families, for every dollar increase in income, they found the brain surface area of the children was proportionally greater. Additionally, the researchers found that as family income declined, so did cognitive skills such as memory, reading, and vocabulary.

To support the results from the UW-Madison and Columbia teams, a separate study in 2013 out of the Washington University School of Medicine found that children living in poverty had lower volumes of white and cortical gray matter, and reduced hippocampal and amygdala volumes.[7]

*STRESS & BRAIN DEVELOPMENT*

Stress, as we are continuing to learn, has detrimental effects on a person's body and mind and can be linked to an array of health issues. A child living in conditions of poverty is exposed to multiple negative stressors on a daily basis and for prolonged periods of time, and the effects on his developing body and mind are amplified. Not receiving proper nutrition puts stress on the brain and body. Growing up in a loud, unsafe environment can cause a child to lose sleep, which puts negative stress on a developing brain and body. The negative emotions of parents under distress, of parents fighting or arguing, can trickle down to the child, also putting him under distress. Physical abuse from parents obviously causes a child great stress. Going to school with tattered and torn clothes and being subjected to verbal and physical abuse by classmates adds stress (and diminishes personal confidence).

Whereas the previous studies I listed focus on the relationship between *low-income* and brain structure and function, the following studies focus on the relationship between *stress* and the brain (though low-income environments lead to stress, so this is somewhat derivative).

The first, comprised of a series of experiments done at the University of California, Berkeley, demonstrated the long-term effects of chronic stress on brain structure and function.[8,9] Professor Daniela Kaufer and her team found that exposure to prolonged stress can change the structure of the brain in a number of ways. Chronic stress can essentially alter the way neural stem cells mature. Rather than growing into neurons, stress can reprogram stem cells to mature into oligodendrocytes, or myelin. This decrease in the production of neurons affects learning, memory, and other functions. Myelin is important in that it insulates the axon of a neuron (think of the rubber coating around copper wire in electronics) and helps neurons communicate with each other, but too much can disrupt the brain's ability to communicate. Kaufer hypothesized that the excessive volumes of myelin might have evolved in response to stress in order to strengthen the connection between the hippocampus and the amygdala, which could cause a person to startle easier, or induce a quicker fight-or-flight response (think of a person with PTSD in a sort of perpetual defense mode). The series of studies also found that connectivity between the hippocampus and prefrontal cortex was lower than normal, which would also impede memory and learning. The findings of Professor Kaufer and her team might help explain why young people who are exposed to chronic stress are prone to mental problems and learning difficulties later in life.

Another study done by researchers at Rosalind Franklin University focused on the effects of stress on the hippocampus in rats.[10] What they discovered was that severe stress prevented newer brain cells from surviving, which left fewer neurons for processing emotions, memories, and feelings. A meta-analysis published in 2017 by various researchers in

Europe reviewed cases of over 200,000 participants, and they found that children who grow up experiencing more stressful events have increased risk for substance abuse, mental health, sexual health, physical health, and violence.[11] Stress from poor socioeconomic conditions can even alter a child's DNA and cause progressive shortening of Telomeres (chromosome protectors), exposing him to poor health, depression, faster aging, and more.[12,13]

Research results from various organizations around the world were presented at Neuroscience 2018, an annual meeting for the Society of Neuroscience. Among the information presented, researchers concluded that "childhood stress increases the chance of developing anxiety, depression, or drug addiction later in life by *two to four times*, while stress during pregnancy may increase the child's risk of developing autism spectrum disorder, as well as several other psychiatric illnesses."[14] During pregnancy, excessive stress experienced by the mother can alter her gut bacteria and reduce the amount of critical nutrients received by the growing fetus.

### *STRESS & THE IMMUNE SYSTEM*

Not only does stress alter the brain, it also inhibits the immune system. Stress hormones can cause inflammation and lower the number of white blood cells in the body, thus inhibiting one's ability to fight diseases and infections. During the early stages of a child's life, his immune system is building and learning how to fight against bacteria and viruses. So living in conditions of poverty and being exposed to a steady barrage of stressors can weaken a child's immunity, thus leaving him vulnerable to a number of ailments. And to compound any issues, without access to proper healthcare due to low income, if acquired diseases aren't treated, the affects may persist and cause further damage.

Much data and information has been collected and analyzed over the past few decades regarding the relationship between stress and the immune system. In 2004, researchers from the University of Kentucky and Columbia University performed a meta-analysis on nearly 300 studies related to the topic.[15] When exposed to stress for any duration, they discovered that all aspects of immunity were adversely affected.[16] And when experiencing chronic or long-term stress, the immune system is exposed to severe damage.

In 2013, experts at Ohio State University found a connection between stress and the spread of breast cancer.[17] In a separate study published in 2013, researchers concluded that chronic stress changes gene activity in immune cells before they reach the bloodstream.[18] What this means is, when these cells enter the bloodstream, they are expecting to fight disease, which causes an increase in inflammation. Inflammation is a precursor to a multitude of health problems.[19]

In a 2014 study produced out of Sweden, researchers analyzed stress levels in 5-year-old children who lived in households where stress was prevalent compared to children of the same age living in an environment with less stress.[20] Coming as no surprise, the results showed that the children living in families of elevated stress had higher levels of cortisol (stress markers) in their systems, lower immune activity, and lower levels of C-Peptide (part of insulin production).

Various studies have also linked parental stress and other serious life events during the first 2 years of a child's life to an increased risk of type-1 diabetes.[21,22,23]

Based on the findings of the studies I've referenced so far, one can reasonably conclude that growing up in a low-income, high-stress environment can have devastating effects on a child's developing brain and immune system, which can lead to physical and mental problems that persist into adulthood. A child growing up in conditions of poverty is handicapped from the moment he enters this world, which sets him up for struggle and failure throughout his life; children from low-income families perform more poorly on tests, are more likely to leave school, and are more likely to be poor as adults.[24] Kids deprived of essential resources may begin their school careers 18 months developmentally behind fellow classmates – a hole that becomes increasingly difficult to dig out of as they mature and their circumstances persist.[25]

### *POVERTY & CHILD ABUSE*

Five children die each day due to abuse or neglect.[26] And growing up in conditions of poverty subject a child to higher rates of maltreatment – which includes physical, emotional, and sexual abuse and neglect – and therefore stress. When studying the relationship between poverty and maltreatment in children, researchers with the National Bureau of Economic Research found a positive correlation between families with incomes below 75% of the poverty line and child maltreatment.[27] They also found that child abuse increases in families with two non-working parents, and in families with an absent father and a working mother. Though poverty doesn't literally cause a father to hit his child or a mother to neglect her kid, effects of poverty start a chain reaction that can increase the likelihood of such abusive behavior. For instance, loss of employment and therefore the loss of one's ability to adequately provide for his family are positively correlated to reduced mental health.[28] Mental illness is most common in households with low-incomes.[29] And mental illness – depression, stress, anxiety – is associated with increased incidents of child maltreatment.[30] And to corroborate this connection, research completed by teams within the American Academy of Pediatrics concluded that increases in unemployment are linked to child abuse.[31] Additionally, during the Great Recession in America from 2007 to 2008, investigators at the University of Oxford found a significant uptick in child neglect in relation to the widespread loss of employment among adults.[32]

Neglect, which is the most common form of child maltreatment, can be just as harmful to a child's growth as physical abuse, though in very different ways. It is imperative that a child receives attention and affection from a caregiver during his developmental years. A child consistently neglected can experience stunted physical and mental growth from lack of social and cognitive stimulation. To illustrate how important care and affection are, in the most *extreme* cases, children deprived of physical and emotional care or children in isolation can experience a condition known as Kaspar Hauser Syndrome, or Psychosocial Dwarfism, among other names, where the child fails to grow properly, or at all. For instance, children in the worst orphanages around the world (Bulgaria, Moldova, India, Cambodia), who might receive just minutes of attention each day, who are left to rock alone in their cribs, who may not receive food for days, who might be left to wallow in their own feces, who bang their heads or bite their hands in sad states of madness, show a severe delay in cognitive development and experience delayed physical growth.[33,34] A 15- or 16-year-old child might have the body of a 5-year-old, with twisted and deformed limbs and severe mental impairments. They endure significant growth suppression.[35] Love, attention, care, affection – it cannot be stressed enough how critical it all is for a child to grow up healthy. And sadly, impoverished children are less likely to receive such attention.

Some interesting side facts about children in orphanages? About 80 to 90 percent of orphaned children around the globe actually have living parents; however, most often due to lack of money, parents give up their child. And, as always, the child pays the dearest price. Additionally, institutionalized youth are 500 times more likely to commit suicide.[36]

Incidents of alcohol and drug abuse are also high among adults living in poverty.[37] In 70% of reported cases of child abuse and neglect, substance abuse was involved, and the children of substance-abusing parents face an increased risk of developing substance abuse disorders themselves.[38] A study completed out of Johns Hopkins University concluded that children of alcoholics are more susceptible to alcoholism (as well as altered brain chemistry).[39] And in cases where parents abuse alcohol or other drugs, children are three times more likely to be abused and four times more likely to be neglected. Additionally, the US Department of Health and Human Services reported in 1999 that the two primary preconditions in 80% of abuse and neglect cases were poverty and substance abuse.

The tragic paradox of child abuse is that children who are abused or neglected are significantly more likely to perpetuate violence themselves, whether in the form of neglect or physical or sexual abuse – the abused becomes the abuser.[40] Children who are mistreated may grow up to abuse their own children. And children of abused parents may be more likely to experience sexual abuse and neglect. So what comes first, the chicken or the egg? The abused or the abuser? If a child is abused by a parent who was abused by a parent who was abused by a parent, where does the vicious cycle start and where does it end? Where does the blame lie? It's not as simple as claiming an adult is just a bad egg or an evil person. The preconditions that existed before he became an abuser predictably act to mold and shape a man into such a "monster." When a dog is beaten and mistreated in the early years of its life, and it ends up biting another person, we usually don't blame the dog. We blame the owner. We blame the parent for raising the dog improperly. To what extent is this true for humans?

Simply putting an abusive parent behind bars or removing a child from his family doesn't solve the overall problem – it can exacerbate the damage done to a kid. If a child is removed from his family, the toxic waters of poverty still exist, and the child continues to feel its poisonous effects.

So then what needs to be done to eliminate such harmful behavior, behavior that can end up affecting society as a whole in a number of ways? The only way to alleviate such negative outcomes is by changing the unhealthy environment a child grows up in. The only way to clean up a child's unhealthy environment is by removing the preconditions, the toxins that poison the water, that predictably lead to destructive consequences. And the precondition at the heart of it all, the central element responsible for setting the wheels of negativity in motion, is poverty, or lack of money. Unfortunately, as long as money exists, the preconditions of *lack* will persist, meaning the persistence of poor or unemployed parents, therefore depressed and stressed parents and lack of proper nutrition (among other stressors), therefore mistreated children, therefore stressed children, therefore children with stunted development in various forms, and therefore all of the negative outcomes that branch off from such circumstances that threaten to start the cycle all over again once that child reaches adulthood. It's an unending spiral that won't go away until poverty is removed. And it can be removed if we as a collective unit choose to remove it.

## *POVERTY & CHILD MALNUTRITION*

Lack of money in a household also leads to child malnutrition since parents may struggle to afford food. In America, roughly 12 million kids are uncertain from where or when they will receive their next meal.[41] And due to the high costs of healthy food, when a poverty-stricken child is provided with a meal, the chances that their food is cheap and unhealthy are highly likely. Adequate nutrition is absolutely critical to a child's development. If a child is not receiving proper food on a daily basis, he is left with a severe disadvantage compared to kids raised in households that provide consistent meals – malnourished children exhibit lower academic performance and are 20% more likely to be illiterate. Like stress, malnutrition can have devastating consequences on a child's physical and mental development. When studying children in Africa, researchers from North-West University discovered that malnutrition during pregnancy may not only lead to stunted growth in babies, but it can also leave them predisposed to cardiovascular disease and other diseases (anemia, asthma, diabetes, hypertension) later in life.[42] Underfed children are also more likely to be hospitalized. Another study completed out of multiple institutions in Brazil also found that lack of nutrition leads to increased risk for diseases, reduced capacity for manual work, insulin resistance in adulthood, obesity, lower fat oxidation, and many other impairments.[43] This systemic cycle witnesses malnourished kids grow into adults who may then be unable to adequately provide for their own offspring when it comes time for them to have kids. As in the cases of abuse, the spiral of food insecurity and underdevelopment continues on without end.

Hunger in children is most certainly a problem in America, but on a global scale it has become an epidemic. The United Nations Food and Agriculture Organization estimated that around 870 million people suffered from chronic malnourishment from 2010 to 2012. Of those suffering from lack of nutrition, the youth are most vulnerable, as it is responsible for the highest mortality rate in children across the world coming in at over 3 million deaths in 2011.[44,45] Additionally, roughly 200 million children suffer from stunted growth or wasting in relation to being underfed.[46] And remember, enough food is currently produced to feed the world, and technological capabilities exist to produce even more.

## *POVERTY & CHILD HOMELESSNESS*

Child homelessness is another significant issue among families living in poverty. A report produced by the American Institutes for Research found that about 2.5 million children were homeless at one point in 2013, an all-time high for this country.[47] Living without a home, whether that means living on the streets, in cars, parks, shelters, or temporarily doubling up with a family or friend, is yet another negative stressor that hinders a child's development. And like the other negative stressors I've already mentioned which stem from poverty, homelessness contributes to a wide array of adverse effects among the youth, e.g., poor academic performance, increased risk of diseases, stunted physical and mental growth, and more.[48,49] No state in America is immune to the issue of child homelessness as it has spread like a virus across the country, even in small towns where one may not expect there to be any.

For instance, in 2014 I had a discussion with a local school administrator in my hometown of Sauk Prairie, Wisconsin. This quiet, quaint little village running along the Wisconsin River is home to about 7,000 residents, so you might understand my shock when the administrator informed me there were over 70 children within the school district who were classified as homeless that year. She proceeded to tell me stories about how some young students she had worked with would come to school some mornings with sore bellies because they hadn't eaten the night before, or how many of the underfed had difficulty focusing in class, which was reflected in their poor grades.

*RECAP*

The web of interconnected outcomes sees poverty or lack of money as a central precondition or central factor to a multitude of negative outcomes. Again, poverty may not actually cause maltreatment in various instances, but it's a common precondition that has a domino effect on the rest of a child's life and sets the stage for predictable outcomes and predictably destructive behavior. The chains of events connecting poverty are infinitely complex, while at the same time rather simple if you trace those events to their source. Each branch of negative outcome that grows from poverty produces multiple branches of other negative outcomes. For instance, poverty can lead to malnutrition in children. Malnutrition can lead to stunted mental and physical development. Malnutrition can lead to suppressed immune systems. Malnutrition can lead to difficulty focusing. Each of those consequences stemming from malnutrition then births a number of other adverse consequences. If you trace the branches that extend from poverty, many of them end up connecting to the same outcomes, e.g., *malnutrition* and *lack of healthcare* may both stem from poverty, and both may lead to disease. Each piece of the youth development puzzle plays a crucial role in shaping a child into the adult he becomes, in shaping his actions throughout his entire life. To say that we are products of the choices we make oversimplifies things, especially when you take into account that our choices are largely products of our upbringing. And our upbringing is heavily influenced by family circumstances and income, and in the direst of cases can reduce the spectrum of choices a person has as he develops into an adult. And again, the child never had a choice to be born into destitution to begin with.

So, to recap, childhood poverty or lack of money and essential resources is a precondition for:

- Stunted physical and psychological growth
- Suppressed immune systems, therefore various diseases
- Mental illness
- Maltreatment – physical, emotional, or sexual abuse or neglect
- Lack of proper nutrition
- Lack of adequate health care
- Homelessness
- Poor academic performance
- Difficulty obtaining work later in life
- Difficulty creating social and emotional bonds
- Alcohol and other substance abuse
- Increased risk of perpetuating violence
- ...and more

A child living in poverty is forced to endure years of substantial and undue suffering. At the heart of all of this youth hardship, the dead horse that I keep beating, is lack of money, leading to the lack of essential resources for healthy growth and development. The sad reality is that we produce enough food that a child shouldn't have to go to bed hungry. We produce enough housing so that a child doesn't have to live without a home. We produce enough clothing so that a child doesn't have to go to school with tattered and torn clothes. We produce enough so that the "failed" parents of these children don't need to bear the stress of failing their families, a stress felt by the child in a number of ways. The greatest inhibitor to distributing this abundance to those most in need is the tool we use to distribute these essential resources – money. Because suffering children don't have money, they don't have access to such abundance. And it's not about reallocating our limited financial resources to help children gain access to the necessities of life. Such actions only treat the symptoms and won't solve the underlying sickness. Shifting money to and from various buckets of society is like shifting deck chairs on the Titanic – the ship is still sinking, baby. Bottom line, stress and poverty will persist as long as money continues to be the method by which we distribute the means to survive.

And I accept that adults who have fallen on hard times won't gain much sympathy from their average tribesmen. But, I can't accept children growing up impoverished and living in squalor. It's unnecessary and impossible to justify. When you have the ability as a society to alleviate such suffering, to fully take care of those who need taking care of, but don't, then we have collectively failed as a species. We have failed as the unique, privileged group who has been given the gift of higher functioning brains and a seemingly endless array of capabilities. To quote Mark Hollis from the band Talk Talk – "Such a Shame."

## 6.2 ECOLOGICAL DEGRADATION

Earth does not need us. However, we need it! We are born from Earth, and I don't mean that in a religious, spiritual, or evolutionist sense. What I mean is all of the elements that make up our bodies come from Earth. Everything that sustains our lives from the air we breathe, to the food we consume, to the house we live in, and the TV we watch comes from Earth. Whether you choose to accept it or not, this massive, unique planet of oxygen and water and the perfect amount of gravity to keep our bodies from collapsing or expanding is our *home*. And whether you are a staunch, "tree-hugging" environmentalist or an oil-drilling, rain-forest-cutting tycoon, whether you are rich or poor, black or white, we all need Earth to be in proper working order if we want to live happy, healthy lives. We all need this planet to be in proper working order if we want our species to survive.

For roughly 4.5 billion years, at least according to scientists, this intergalactic spaceship barreling across the galaxy has led a relatively peaceful existence. Unfortunately, many thousand years ago, it developed a condition – a rare malignancy known as Human. Records indicate Earth is the only known planet in the universe to have acquired such a condition. It started out as a slow-growing cancer, and because the human tumors covered such a small area of Earth's body, the effects were minimal – in fact Earth barely noticed it was sick. Only over the last few centuries or so (approximately 0.0000044% of its lifetime), as the human tumors have metastasized and begun to spread more rapidly has Earth become more aware of its existence. And unlike all of Earth's normal cells – the plants, animals, etc. – which function in almost perfect harmony with one another, taking from it only what they need to survive, those damn human tumors seem to operate on their own accord. They consume way more resources than they need to, and they do it at a rate faster than Earth's body can replenish. All of Earth's healthy cells are suffering as a result. Many are even dying off. I suppose that's what cancer does, though – consumes in excess and destroys healthy cells.

So, obviously, the degradation of our ecosystems around the world brought about by human activity is most certainly a cause for attention and concern. Now, there are arguments to support Global Warming, and there are arguments to refute it. Both sides, based on the information they've been exposed to, are likely cemented in their positions, as is the case with most contentious topics in modern times, and no matter what one says to challenge another's position, neither pole is going to budge. That being said, I am not here to debate global warming; frankly, I don't care (within a certain context). It seems whenever competing factions broach the topic of environmental decay, the conversation is eventually reduced to one of trying to prove or disprove the existence of global warming and climate change; the discussion thus mutates into a debate, and the focus becomes about winning and illustrating how the other side is ignorant or misinformed. This antipodal gravitation has the detractive and counterproductive effect of luring our attention away from the original, most important, overarching issue itself, and that is ecological degradation. We lose the forest for the trees.

So, whether global warming specifically can or cannot be proven does not matter, per se. What does matter is the undeniable fact that our consumption and waste habits coupled with a human population nearing 8 billion people has had an ecological impact on Earth, especially over the last century or so, and in largely negative ways. As self-anointed stewards of this planet, our *home*, it shouldn't matter what side of the political spectrum we stake our flags to; a sick planet affects us all, and not for the better. Unfortunately, as humans continue to spread and economic growth is still top priority, resource overshoot, biodiversity loss, loss of drinkable water, loss of arable land, air poisoning, and more will only continue to accelerate if we don't adapt and learn to manage our home intelligently. If you have kids or grandkids or great-grandkids, it'll be they who will be left to deal with the negative effects of the current population's mindless habits.

Just as the negative stressors associated with childhood poverty cannot all be *directly* linked to money, the same is true of environmental degradation. Not all environmental problems can be directly linked to the lack or pursuit of money, but if you trace just about every issue to its origin, you will find money as a common, oftentimes central, precondition. For instance, when a company dumps chemical waste into a river, they do it to save money and increase profit margins – disposing of materials in an environmentally friendly way can be costly (dumping is free, though the environment pays a heavy price). The allure of steady streams of revenue encourages the continued practice of chopping down forests and rainforests at a greater rate than we are replanting. Since constant consumption generates greater monetary profits, and since profits come before all else in our current paradigm, the deforestation machine continues full steam ahead. Men don't chase down an elephant or rhino and cut off its tusks while it's still breathing if not for the monetary benefits of selling ivory. Humans don't pump chemicals into the Earth and risk destroying surrounding rivers, landscapes, and wildlife, if not for the intoxicating allure of the revenue that extracting natural gas brings. Humans don't continue squeezing oil out of Earth at an alarming rate or shedding blood to acquire it if not for the incredible amounts of money oil attracts. Of course, I understand the need to extract oil and natural gas for the purpose of meeting energy demands, however burning nonrenewable hydrocarbons has been unnecessary for a few decades now, but industries make way too much money from it, and rebuilding new infrastructure to support less damaging methods is extremely costly and less profitable. Between renewable sources, like geothermal, solar, hydro, wind, and even nuclear power, enough energy exists to power Earth and its inhabitants many times over (to be discussed further in Chapter 10.5).

Believe it or not, the Earth can support 8 billion people. However, it cannot support 8 billion people if our consumption trends do not change. The global human population currently uses Earth's resources at a rate of 1.7 times faster than it can replenish, and in America and other developed nations, that rate is much higher.[1] The population of the United States comprises a mere 4% of the world's population, yet it consumes 17% of its energy,[2] including over 20% of the world's oil and 21% of its natural gas.[3,4] Compared to developed countries like Great Britain and Japan, American individuals consume 2 and 2.5 times more in fossil fuels, respectively, which is largely driven by Americans driving more and seeming generally averse to public transportation.[5] In other words, American citizens consume a considerable amount more per capita than the rest of the world, even though we make up a small percentage of Earth's population. If the rest of the world consumed as much as the people of America, it has been estimated that we would need *five* Earth's to support humanity.[6]

Most Americans operate unaware of this gross imbalance, unfortunately, and in many ways it's not their fault. I don't mean to make excuses for people's behavior, but we are victims, more or less, of marketing; marketing fueled by business. All day, every single day, Americans are bombarded and hypnotized by advertisements. Our minds and our desires are constantly being hijacked by business in order to convince us we need things we may not actually need. We are convinced to desire material junk we might not otherwise desire and to trash products before their expiration date. We are convinced the secret to happiness is buy, buy, buy – consume, consume, consume. The ideas of business have been so concretely embedded into our psyche that needless consumption has become an almost involuntary reflex, a part of our everyday nature. And this manipulation is all in the name of generating more sales, and therefore more revenue. However, this desire for continued sales and economic growth completely ignores the impact outside of itself, the impact it has on every aspect of the environment and connected ecosystems.

All of the overconsumption in the world driven by market forces and globalization has come at a great cost to the natural world. Let's take a look at deforestation and the Amazon rainforest, for instance. Considered to be the "Lungs of the Planet" because of the high levels of oxygen it produces and atmospheric carbon it absorbs, the Amazon covers roughly 5.5 million square kilometers – 60% of which resides in Brazil – and is home to millions of different species.[7] This rainforest is a significant asset to the human population as it provides, aside from oxygen, ingredients for medicines, fruits, vegetables, coffee, spices, rubber and much more. Unfortunately, just in the last 40 years or so, 20% of the Amazon rainforest has been chopped, bulldozed, and burned away; in fact it has shrunk so much that its decline can be seen from outer space.[8] In Ecuador, rainforests once covered 49% of the country's surface; that number has been reduced to a mere 16% and counting.[9]

Much of the rainforest's destruction is due largely to Latin American countries – mainly Brazil as it is home to most of the Amazon – trying to keep up with commerce and demand from developed countries around the world; in a way, environmental degradation has been outsourced by developed nations to underdeveloped nations. These countries have tried to adopt initiatives and take measures to limit deforestation, but with the pressures of maintaining economic development, paying off international debts, meeting global demand, and earning a living their measures for sustainability have been met with little success. In fact, in 2019 and 2020, the amount of Amazonian deforestation reached its highest levels in over a decade.[10,11] The problem is, the industries (agriculture, mining, forestry, etc.) supported by rainforest activities are major components to financial stability and economic success in countries like Brazil. If, say, Brazilians were to decrease their presence in the Amazon, that would essentially mean less revenue being generated. Less revenue means the country's businesses could fall behind on their financial obligations, and its economic growth would be slowed. Additionally, rainforest laborers rely on the work for a steady paycheck in order to provide life necessities for their loved ones; it's their livelihood; it keeps them and their families from falling into poverty or deeper into poverty. A decrease in revenue brought on by a decrease in deforestation could hinder their ability to put food on the table. So, though limiting our presence in the rainforest would be great for Earth and its inhabitants, it threatens business. Since it is business that ultimately provides access to the means of survival in our current economic structures, it is business that takes precedence over the needs of the environment – even though a degraded environment will eventually hinder business, too.

If our consumption habits are not adjusted, organizations like National Geographic estimate that rainforests could be completely wiped out within 100 years – some organizations have predicted even sooner.[12] According to The Nature Conservancy, rainforests once covered 15 million square kilometers of Earth's surface, but as of 2012 they only covered 6 million square kilometers – that's a 60% reduction, most of which has occurred in just the last 50 years.[13]

It's not just rainforests that are being threatened; all forests around the planet have suffered tremendous loss. The World Resources Institute reports that 30% of global forest cover has been cleared and 20% degraded;

they estimate only 15% is still fully intact.[14] Of all the continents in the world, regions of Africa have been experiencing some of the highest rates of deforestation compared to the rest of the globe, as reports claim West Africa has lost an estimated 90% of its forests; and, according to a study completed by the University of Maryland, between 2000 and 2014, the Congo Basin rainforest lost an area of forest larger than the country of Bangladesh.[15,16] On a positive note, trends toward reforestation have increased in the last many years in some countries, and in terms of replanting and tree cover gain, the United States ranks near the top compared to other countries.

It cannot be stated enough how important trees and plants are to the water cycle and overall health of an ecosystem. Not only do they absorb carbon dioxide and release oxygen, trees also absorb water and clean it by filtering out pollutants and other contaminants before releasing it back into the environment. The leafy canopies of trees within forests help intercept rainfall and slow the rate of its release back into the environment, which reduces runoff and prevents soil from eroding into waterways, while also reducing the risks of landslides and flooding during heavy rainfall. Additionally, the water that trees absorb and release back into the environment, either through the soil or into the air as water vapor, can help cool and maintain temperatures. Trees are vital to an environment's watershed; they essentially act as filters to protect rivers, lakes, and other waterways, and they help keep water clean for consumption. Just in the United States, local forests are the source of drinking water for about 60% of the population.[17]

The destruction of the Amazon and forests throughout the planet threatens to set off a chain of events that could impact all aspects of life. For example, since rainforests essentially create much of their own rainfall due to the humidity released into the atmosphere, fewer trees mean less rain. In a cyclical fashion, less rain means less water for trees to absorb, causing more trees to die of dehydration. A dehydrated forest means more wildfires. Fewer trees also means less carbon dioxide absorption and less oxygen production; and, when trees die, they release into the atmosphere the carbon dioxide they had been storing. Fewer trees means less water vapor released into the atmosphere; just a slight change in water vapor levels can affect weather patterns. Fewer trees and less water absorption means more soil erosion. Soil erosion can disrupt vegetation growth and pollute waterways, leading to poor drinking water. Fewer trees means more rainwater hitting the Earth's surface, which means more runoff and the potential for more floods and landslides. Deforestation means fewer trees and less water in the environment, which can lead to the desertification of certain areas of land. The list seems endless.

On a more obvious level, deforestation causes biodiversity loss, or the extinction of animals, plant life, and other life forms; roughly 80% of all plants and animals live in forests.[18]

Biodiversity loss is another major concern on our planet, since most, if not all, life forms play an important role in Earth's natural regulatory processes – processes that we derive immeasurable benefit from. For instance, insects and other pollinators pollinate roughly 90% of flowering plants and 70% of the world's main crops; losing butterflies or bees would have a significant impact on crop yields and vegetation.[19] Just about every life form is threatened by human activity. The World Wildlife Fund reported that from 1970 to 2014 wild vertebrates experienced a 60% decline – this includes all mammals, birds, reptiles, amphibians, and fish.[20] The group that experienced the steepest reduction was that of fresh water vertebrates, which lost 83% of their population during that span.[21] And according to the IUCN Red List of Threatened Species, out of the 129,000 species they have assessed, over 35,500 are at risk of extinction – 40% of assessed amphibians, 26% of mammals, 34% of conifers, 34% of reptiles, and so on.[22] Maybe it's all doom-and-gloom fear mongering, but due to the careless practices of humans, the UN reports that one million species risk extinction in the world, while the Intergovernmental Science-Policy Platform on Biodiversity and Ecosystem Services says the pace of loss is "tens to hundreds of times higher than it has been over the last 10 million years."[23,] Additionally, many experts predict that we are on the verge or already in the midst of the 6th mass extinction event in Earth's history – the most recent one occurring roughly 66 million years ago, which saw the end of the Cretaceous period.[24,25]

Color me a hippie if you will, though I would think I am about as far from that label as one can be, but I like animals. Aside from their ecological utility, they're fun to observe and interact with. And though I don't get out in the wilderness enough (which my pasty white skin can attest to), I like trees and forests and clean water streams. There is something refreshing, something rejuvenating about being surrounded by the natural world. So, I don't like imagining the complete decimation of rainforests, or the extinction of animals like Gorillas or Rhinos or Blue Whales or Bumble Bees. Even if the estimates coming in from various wildlife organizations are incomplete or overexaggerated, I would hate to take that gamble. It's not worth the risk, especially knowing how simple the alternative is – of changing our consumption habits and reorienting our values.

The last aspect of environmental degradation I want to talk about is in regard to natural water sources around the globe and the impact human activity has had on them over the last few decades. Out of all Earth's resources, the most vital to human health is water, as it makes up roughly 60% of our bodies; it is the very essence of life, or so I've heard people say. Due to our use of non-biodegradable materials (plastic), waste dumping, chemical contamination (pesticides), deforestation, overuse and misuse, and pollution through industrial practices, e.g., logging, mining, drilling, clean water sources are quickly becoming unclean, toxic, and scarce. And I don't want to downplay all of the other negative aspects of environmental degradation, especially since they are all interconnected, but the loss of safe drinking water might be the greatest threat to the population – to all species, actually.

Like the human body, water comprises most of the Earth's surface – roughly 71%; however, only 2.5% of it is fresh water.[26,27] Of that tiny percentage of fresh water on Earth, only about one-fourth of that, and maybe even less, is actually accessible for crop irrigation and human consumption. Some countries turn salt water into drinking water, but as of now, desalination processes are extremely costly. Again though, Earth's natural processes are pretty amazing; like with food and other renewable resources, fresh water is also renewable through the planet's water cycle. However, if we use water at a rate greater than can be replenished, if our activities negatively impact the watershed of a water system (removing trees), or if our actions lead to the contamination of lakes and rivers (deliberately dumping chemical waste, oil spills), the net amount of available water can be reduced and the amount of clean water replenished decreases over time.

All of the negative environmental consequences are complex and interconnected, but much of it can be traced back to human activity, and much of the human activity that leads to environmental degradation can be traced back to a desire for increasing revenue and profit margins, maintaining steady economic growth, and keeping up with supply, demand, and consumption habits largely promoted by business interests. For instance, as I alluded to earlier, when companies dump untreated wastewater into a river, it's ultimately to save money and increase the bottom line. In a report released by Environment America Research and Policy Center, it was calculated that local facilities released 206 million pounds of toxic chemicals into American waterways and watersheds in 2012.[28] The greatest offender was Tyson Foods, which dumped an alarming 18 million pounds of waste all across the nation – a number that accounted for 9% of total waste dumping during that span of time.[29] Other known institutions near the top of the list include the Department of Defense, Koch Industries, and US Steel. Also, according to the Environmental Protection Agency (EPA), over 17,000 miles of rivers and 210,000 acres of lakes, ponds, and estuaries have been polluted by toxic discharge from industrial facilities.[30] In 2009, data from the EPA showed that the drinking water of thousands of schools across the country contained unsafe levels of contaminants, like pesticides and lead; lead can adversely affect the brain, which is particularly disconcerting when it is developing children who are consuming it.[31] Additionally, in 2010 the Environmental Working Group (EWG) tested the tap water in 35 American cities for Chromium-6 – a carcinogenic chemical.[32] The EWG found that the tap water of 31 of the 35 cities contained varying levels of the harmful compound – those 31 cities serve water to over 26 million people. And waste dumping is not unique to the United States, as countries across the planet – China, UK, Italy, etc. – face problems with contaminants being released into the environment by local companies.

Organizations have tried to take measures by passing laws to inhibit companies from dumping waste into freshwater sources, but many corporations adamantly oppose such actions. And of course they would; though protecting freshwater systems makes logical sense, dumping waste is quick, easy, and CHEAP! However, even when measures are passed, like when the Clean Water Act was established due to water becoming so polluted that certain waterways could be set on fire, companies such as Pilgrim Pride continued to discharge toxic waste into waterways like Tankersley Creek in Texas.[33] In the end, it is all about that precious bottom line, increasing shareholder value, and sliding more cash into the pockets of a few. Until money is removed from the economic equation, passing legislation will do very little to stop mammoth companies from pursuing practices that might be environmentally harmful, but remain cost-efficient.

Anyway, when a company continuously releases contaminants into a water system, the sinuous network of interconnected consequences quickly expands and branches into multiple areas of society. If a company pollutes a river with toxic waste, that polluted water can flow downstream into other communities and seep into their water wells. The people within affected communities might then use that toxic water unknowingly through drinking, bathing, swimming, fishing, etc., which can expose them to a number of health issues (cancer, developmental issues, reproductive issues, neurological issues, etc.). If a mother is exposed to contaminated water while she is pregnant, she can pass the chemicals to her fetus, which can cause birth defects or developmental problems. The polluted water might also be used to irrigate crops, which can then be absorbed into the food that eventually enters our bodies. Polluted waters also accumulate within fish inhabiting the waterways. We may then eat that fish, which transfers the toxins into the human body. Animals downstream drink from the contaminated waters, which can end up killing them and the animals that eat them; and, groups of animals dying off can ignite a chain of negative ecological effects. Additionally, we might also consume the animals that consume the toxic waters, providing yet another way for us to acquire the harmful toxins. Polluted waters threaten to kill the fish and plant life within *lentic* bodies of water, like lakes or ponds, which can lead to eutrophication, which can eventually cause lakes to become shallow or completely dry up and turn into grassy fields. I mean, the chain of detrimental effects seems endless. According to the EPA, about 53% of assessed rivers and streams and 67% of lakes, ponds, and reservoirs are too polluted for swimming, fishing, or drinking.[34] Yikes!

Though many companies are required to report their toxic chemical and other waste management activities to the Toxics Release Inventory each year, oil and gas extraction companies are exempt from having to report for some reason – [cough, cough] **lobbying** [cough, cough].[35] Therefore, the chemicals released into the ground by the gas extraction method known as "Fracking" has not been quantified, and much remains unknown about the levels of toxic releases of fracking facilities. Though the companies benefitting from fracking might say otherwise, fracking has shown to have negative effects on air and water quality within communities near gas wells, affecting the local human populations and wildlife. Affected communities have reported being able to set their tap water on fire, incidents of peoples' hair falling out, various illnesses, and animal deaths. To further illustrate how the laws of man and money work in complete opposition to the laws of nature, even though fracking is harmful to the environment in that chemicals and pollutants are released into the ground and atmosphere, millions of tons of water are wasted in the extraction process (2 to 4 million tons for a single well), and the technique has even been known to cause seismic activities in central regions of America, fracking operations do help financially stimulate poor communities, bring in tax revenue, provide jobs, and help farmers pull themselves out of debt and buy new farming equipment by leasing their land to drillers – bad for the environment, good for the economy; inverse relationship. I say fracking and oil drilling is all about making loads of cash, because some men have found ways to turn a profit. Others might say it's about meeting society's energy needs; however, society's energy needs can be satisfied many times over through the utilization of cleaner, renewable energies.

So, not only are local waterways (rivers, lakes, etc.) being threatened by human activity, but ecosystems of the majestic oceans and seas of the world have also been suffering. Throughout the last many decades, especially following the introduction of plastic into our lives, our habits of gross consumption and careless waste have led to the oceans quickly becoming littered with trash. Let's look at the Great Pacific Garbage Patch as an example.[36] While returning by boat via a rarely travelled route between Hawaii and California in 1997, Captain Charles Moore and his small crew became the first to really take notice of the magnitude of debris blanketing the surface of the ocean waters. In an article published by Natural History magazine in 2003, Moore would go on to say about his unsettling discovery:

> "Yet as I gazed from the deck at the surface of what ought to have been a pristine ocean, I was confronted, as far as the eye could see, with the sight of plastic… It seemed unbelievable, but I never found a clear spot. In the week it took to cross the subtropical high, no matter what time of day I looked, plastic debris was

floating everywhere: bottles, bottle caps, wrappers, fragments."[37]

What Moore so aptly described is an area of ocean water that is part of the Great Pacific Garbage Patch – the stretch of water Moore navigated from Hawaii to California is referred to as the Eastern Garbage Patch, while there is another subsection known as the Western Garbage Patch that floats near Japan. Both of these regions of the Great Pacific Garbage Patch are connected by the North Pacific Subtropical Gyre, which is a large system of ocean currents that is also home to the largest ecosystem on Earth. With the help of the gyre's currents, trash travels from one continental shore to the other, where vortexes gradually pull the debris in to focused spots and keep it there.

More generally, the Great Pacific Garbage Patch is an accumulation of marine debris spanning thousands and thousands of miles in the Pacific Ocean (the Indian and Atlantic Ocean, as well as a number of Seas also have garbage patches). Though one might find an array of trash in these patches, like boots, fishing gear, or electronics, most of the debris consists of microplastics; since plastic is not biodegradable, plastic products simply break down into smaller and smaller pieces over time. In 2018, a team of researchers at The Ocean Cleanup Foundation published a report after conducting the widest, most extensive assessment of the ocean debris to date. In their findings, they estimated that the Eastern Garbage Patch (their region of focus) covers 1.6 million square kilometers – twice the size of Texas – and that it's estimated to be holding 1.8 trillion pieces and 79,000 tons of plastic debris.[38] The overwhelming majority of the assessed debris, again, is made up of microplastics, which, rather than forming a massive "trash island" as some might visualize, is more like a filthy garbage soup. Much of it actually sinks to the ocean floor.

Plastic can be great in that it is durable, malleable, and can neutralize Magneto's powers, but most importantly, it is relatively cheap to produce, which is a big reason why more and more consumer products contain plastic nowadays. The greatest issue with these synthetic materials, though, is that they are not biodegradable, and most plastic products are not recycled; they wind up in landfills, on roadsides, forests, bodies of water, etc. Not only is the plastic debris and other trash an eyesore in the ocean, but it also poses a great threat to all marine life.

On a more direct level, some animals mistake it for food and eat it.

For instance, albatrosses perceive some microplastics as fish eggs and feed it to their offspring.[39] Suffering from starvation or damaged organs, the offspring may then die. Sea turtles mistake plastic bags for jellyfish. And in many other cases, marine mammals like seals or dolphins often become entangled in discarded fishing nets – of course simply disposing of fishing nets in the ocean is a cheap and easy alternative to disposing of them in more responsible ways.

On a less obvious level, the debris disrupts the entire marine food chain, extending all the way up to the human species. First, the clouds of microplastics and other trash items block sunlight from reaching organisms like algae and plankton, which inhibits their growth. A decrease in algae and plankton means a decrease in food for smaller fish and turtles, which leads to a decrease in food for whales, sharks, and tuna, which can then cause a reduction in the overall marine population. Second, marine animals, like fish or turtles, consume microplastics and the toxic chemicals that leach from the plastic products into the ocean. When these animals become prey, the plastics and chemicals that they acquired are passed on to the predatory animals. Traveling up the food chain, the toxic chemicals and microplastics can eventually wind up in human food, and therefore the human body, which can lead to a number of health issues. Considering the accumulation of contaminants in our water, soil, and food brought on by human activity, one must wonder how much of it has contributed to the massive spike in cancers and other illnesses over the past many decades.

A majority of the trash that winds up in the ocean comes from land activity, about 80%, with 20% coming from marine activity, like from boaters, oil rigs, and cargo ships.[40] It's estimated that 1 to 2 million tons of plastic enter the ocean each year.[41]

Many organizations have focused efforts on trying to clean the ocean, but unfortunately, there's no money to be made with such endeavors, so not as much attention is directed toward cleaning the Great Pacific Garbage Patch as there probably should be. Others have channeled their efforts toward passing legislation to limit or ban certain plastic products, but such actions hardly make a dent in the overall use of the versatile material; too much money is saved through its production, and finding more ecofriendly ways of disposing of plastics is too expensive and requires extra effort.

The sad reality for many is, just like with childhood poverty and poverty in general, as long as we continue to use the limited tool of money to grant access to life, environmental degradation will persist largely unabated. As long as humans are competing against each other for this scarce intermediary in order to survive, they will continue doing whatever it takes to acquire money so that their survival remains secured – even if that means polluting waters, cutting down trees, exhausting finite resources, or pumping chemicals into the ground.

Oh poor Earth. It's had to deal with so much in so little time, and all it wants to do is nurture the world. But, the human malignancy won't seem to let it as the cancer cells have taken over its body and continue to spread, causing Earth's health to be in a state of rapid decline. From the trees to the seas and everywhere in between, it is in much worse shape than it ought to be. Earth has been patient, but with too much strain, it can and will eventually retaliate – in many ways it already has – and when it does, it can easily chew us up and spit us out if it wants to; we are tiny, inconsequential specks of dust on Earth's grand canvas. It's too bad, really. Whether you believe in God or evolution or whatever else, we have been gifted this pretty amazing, one-of-a-kind planet with which we are allowed to experience this adventure we call life. Earth not only has the capacity to provide for and sustain such life, all life, but it also has the ability to allow us to live abundantly. And it doesn't discriminate. This planet couldn't give two shits about which country's flag you have branded on your brain, the color of your skin, or what reproductive organs you carry on your person; it serves all equally.

Unfortunately, in our mortal arrogance, we thought we could do better. Instead of working in synergy with the natural laws that came built into this planet when it formed, we have instead decided to design a system of our own manmade laws. And in doing so we have created a system detached from the laws of nature. Our manmade system of money, which encourages unlimited consumption in the name of increased monetary gain, operates in complete opposition to Earth's system that encourages true economy, conservation, and careful consumption. Whether we want to accept it or not, it is Earth's laws that ultimately govern us all; it's the laws of nature we are at the true mercy of, so we can either shape up or ship out; or rather, get shipped out because we won't have a choice if we push too far. And if it comes down to a race to see which system of laws win out in the end, it is physics and the natural laws of Earth that will be standing at the finish line long after the laws of man have collapsed.

So, fortunately for Earth, unless the sun explodes or a black hole gobbles it up (there are other ways), it can't really die, per se. If the human cancer cells continue to put stress on it, if they don't adapt into normal, healthy cells like the rest of Earth's body, if they continue endlessly sucking the life out of the planet, the condition known as Human will simply eradicate itself long before Earth perishes. Sure, Earth might feel the negative effects for a while, and it might have to deal with the loss of many of its precious healthy cells, but it will still be here. And though it might be bedridden for a bit, it'll regain its health in time. It will flourish once more. And when it does, it might consider changing its habits to avoid a recurrence of Human.

## 6.3 EXPLOITING POOR PEOPLE DOMESTICALLY AND INTERNATIONALLY

In the 1995 hit comedy, *Billy Madison*, Adam Sandler's character of the same name joked, "You ain't cool, unless you pee your pants." He was trying to stick up for a young student who had accidentally urinated himself, because in reality peeing one's pants is not very cool at all. In fact it's quite embarrassing for most people.

Unfortunately, for many poultry workers around the United States, the worry of accidentally urinating or defecating oneself during a normal 8- or 10-hour shift is a very real one. The repetitive, assembly-line type of work in poultry plants is fast-paced, as a person processes a single chicken every few seconds, and if someone needs to pause to use the facilities, the line slows down; a slowdown in processing results in a potential cut in revenue as demand for chicken continues to rise in America. For this reason, in plants of companies like Tyson Foods, Perdue Farms, and Pilgrim's Pride, workers are routinely discouraged and even denied bathroom breaks throughout each day. To combat the threat of sullying one's trousers, many workers in this industry have resorted to wearing diapers.[1] Talk about stealing a man's dignity.

In a 2016 report issued by the Greater Minnesota Worker Center, a survey found that 86 percent of workers interviewed were allowed fewer than two bathroom breaks per *week*.[2] Additionally, in a survey conducted by the Southern Poverty Law Center, 80% of workers said they were not allowed bathroom breaks when needed.[3] Not only do employees have to worry about bathroom privileges, but the grueling pace and repetitive motion at the processing lines also leaves many with musculoskeletal injuries, chemical burns, respiratory issues, and unbearable pain.[4] Some women report having difficulty holding their babies due to their hands becoming so gnarled and deformed. In 2017 the Bureau of Labor Statistics reported that the injury rate among poultry workers was at 6.1%; to compare, the average injury rate for all American workers in the same year was 3.1%.[5]

The poultry industry is not alone in the exploitation and slave-like treatment of some of its workers. For instance, the brutal conditions endured by many "tomato pickers" in Florida in recent years have received heavy scrutiny.[6] The migrant town of Immokalee, Florida, producer of about one-third of America's tomatoes, was once considered "ground zero" for modern-day slavery.[7,8] This was due to its – mostly Hispanic – tomato workers consistently being forced into labor, not being allowed to leave, being forced into sex, being paid well below minimum wage, being forced to work 10- to 12-hour days, seven days per week, receiving regular beatings, being bound by chains at night, and more – and this is the 20th and 21st century, mind you.[9-13]

Unfortunately, the examples I have provided above are not rare, one-off cases of abuse; rather, they are a microcosm of a larger, nationwide problem that extends into multiple industries; more than 22,000 garment shops in the US were in violation of minimum wage and overtime laws in 1996.[14] And the harsh reality is that the abusers derive great benefit from the cheap labor. Each year, companies around the globe generate roughly $150 billion from forced labor, according to the International Labor Organization (ILO).[15]

So why do these laborers submit themselves to such undignified, dirty, dangerous, and demanding work? Why don't they stand up for themselves and demand humane treatment? Well, the answer is pretty simple. Fear. Fear of losing one's job, which leads to fear of not earning money, which leads to fear of not being able to put food on the table, which ultimately ends at fear of survival. The poultry industry rents approximately 250,000 workers. Of this number, it is estimated that roughly 50% are Latino and more than 25% are undocumented.[16] For this demographic striving to support their families (a characteristic that unites all humans), work in America is not easy to find, so when a man does find a job, he will do whatever he needs to do to keep it, even if that means swallowing his pride and withstanding various abuses from his dictator. Workers interviewed by Oxfam have stated that they and their colleagues have oftentimes been threatened with firing or deportation when they do make silly requests, like needing to use the restrooms. So, if speaking up could cost a man his job, he will almost certainly keep his head down and mouth shut. In Florida, when a man rescued a young female tomato picker from being raped by her supervisor, both he and the female were fired the next day, and their ability to purchase life necessities was thus stolen from them.*[17]

With immigration a common boiling point in more recent times in America, many undocumented workers receive no sympathy from their fellow human brethren. That's fine. Like the abused workers who are too scared to speak up for fear of losing their ability to buy life necessities, those critical of other humans crossing the arbitrary border of the United States also do so out of fear. Fear of jobs being taken away. Fear of crime. Fear of resources being used up. Each of those fears are ultimately rooted in the fear of survival. All of that said, one thing I will say is that if it weren't for undocumented workers accepting pay below the minimum wage out of desperation, we would almost certainly witness a rise in prices at our local grocery markets.

The scarce nature of money in any monetary system opens the door for the destitute and impoverished to be exploited and taken advantage of throughout the world, and, as I've just pointed out, the United States included. I know I alluded to the idea of using money and fear to coerce humans into undignified labor in talking about Company Towns and in my Thought Experiment in Chapter 4, but here I am going to expand upon this topic and apply it to examples across present-day Earth.

***Fortunately for laborers in the Florida tomato industry, working conditions have improved over the last few years thanks to the Coalition of Immokalee Workers and media attention.**

So, the poor are obviously ripe for the exploiting. But why is this? Well, we've already established that their glaring vulnerability is their fear of not being able to survive due to lack of finances, which leads to stress and desperation, which leads to the reluctant acceptance of positions that might compromise their dignity or even endanger their physical and emotional wellbeing.

Again, our global society has been engineered such that we must use money to gain access to the means of life. And as we've discussed, the amount of money at any given point in time is finite; it is fixed. Therefore, in this zero-sum game, when the majority of this artificial, finite resource flows into the hands of a few, money quickly becomes scarce for a large subset of people on the other end of the spectrum. Think of a tub of water. If it is tilted slightly to the left, much of the water will flow left and pool on that side of the tub, leaving very little on the right side. People on the right side of the tub of society are left to compete with what little money remains. As that money is stretched increasingly thin amongst this population, many eventually fall into poverty and destitution, and putting food on the table for their kids and themselves becomes a real struggle. From that struggle, from seeing the hungry looks in the eyes of their children and hearing the grumbles of their empty bellies, desperation grows. They become willing to do whatever they need to do to remedy those hungry eyes. Those desperate many struggling to support their families become vulnerable to exploitation by those in control of a great bulk of the limited money supply. Thus, sweatshops, bondage, and abysmal working conditions are born.

Like with John from my previous Thought Experiment, the money-controllers from the left side of the tub simply have to dangle a few dollars in front of the faces of those most vulnerable, and the vulnerable will willingly accept that money even if it means enduring conditions of slavery and sacrificing their own dignity. Again, with limited available options and families to feed, they are left feeling as though they have no other choice. To those in the position of lack, they see the money dangling in front of their faces as food for their sons and daughters, as education, as a potential path away from crime and poverty. They see a glimmer of hope.

As for the man using a few dollars and the illusion of hope as his lure to attract cheap labor, he sees a people with very little bargaining power. He sees a people with seemingly little choice and very little voice, who need his money if they want to live. Ultimately, he sees an opportunity to reduce costs and maximize profitability – the invisible hand at play. Let's do a quick examination of how those in the most vulnerable position on the "right side" of the world are exploited today.

Driven mostly by the thirst for increased profits and market pressures to offer competitive prices coupled with poverty and desperation, slavery is alive and well in the modern world. In fact, the ILO estimated that at any given point in time in 2016, over 40 million humans were living in slavery across the globe.[18] However, rather than brandishing a whip or holding a gun to one's head like in times of old (though it should be noted guns are still used in some parts of the world), employers nowadays simply withhold the means of survival from prospective slaves. It works all the same; one's life is being threatened in both scenarios. As an example, each year in Spain, some 20,000 Moroccan women travel to the country's isolated strawberry fields in hopes of earning decent money for their impoverished families back home.[19] Once they arrive, however, they find themselves stuck in situations of appalling work conditions, physical, racial, and sexual abuse, and nowhere to run. Financially poor and extremely vulnerable, these women are often denied food, water, and bathroom breaks, may work days without pay, are crammed by the hundreds into relatively small shipping containers, and even face human sex trafficking by their employers to men who wait outside the farms each night.[20] When they do seek recourse from local authorities, their cries for help usually fall upon deaf ears, and the lives of some become even worse. They *need* the money to support their families and survive, so most endure the inhumane treatment.

Likewise, desperate workers in the crop fields of Italy find themselves in similar positions as the Moroccan strawberry workers of Spain and are therefore willing to accept miniscule pay in exchange for the hope of survival. These dirt-cheap laborers, arriving by the thousands mostly from poor African nations, endure backbreaking work while facing torturous treatment; many claim they never feel safe. According to a Nigerian woman interviewed by The Guardian in 2019, "Even when you sleep, you have one eye open."[21] Along with working conditions unfit for animals, physical and sexual abuse are common, and sometimes people are even murdered. The hope they arrived with dissolves like Alka Seltzer in water.

Thousands of examples of gross human mistreatment occur within workplaces around the world, and it's all in the name of trying to eke out a profit in ever-competitive markets. When it comes to the produce trade in reference to the scenarios above, foreign supermarkets hunt for the lowest bidder in hopes of providing their consumers with prices below their competitors, and of course, make a little extra cash. If a supplier wants a realistic shot at winning the business of one of these "auctioning" supermarkets, he must continuously find ways to cut costs and offer lowest possible prices. Unfortunately, in many areas of produce cultivation, like with energy and equipment, prices are set outside of a farmer's control. He can't change those expenses; they are essentially fixed. So, if a foreign farmer wants to cut costs to compete against other farmers, the only real variable expense, the only expense he can easily control and adjust is that of labor; therefore, when it comes to the wages of their slaves, it becomes a race to the bottom. The farmers who can get away with paying their labor the least amount of money are the ones who can offer the lowest prices while still being able to churn out some sort of profit; and in effect, they are the ones who end up being rewarded with business contracts. People on every tier of the supply chain, from the farmers to the supermarkets, feel the pressure of the game, of trying to obtain business in order to pay for life, and are thus willing to turn a blind eye to conditions of slavery when it comes to their own individual safety and comfort. The need for money and the competitive nature of the markets incentivize such behavior. Forced labor and debt bondage are a natural outgrowth of unregulated markets, aided by unknowingly complicit consumers.

Let's travel south a bit and turn our attention to the noble world of diamond mining; we can include other precious minerals, like gold, too.

Diamonds are beautiful, aren't they – how they refract light and sparkle before our eyes? In developed countries everywhere, you will find many people adorned with these shiny rocks around their necks, fingers, wrists, or even in their teeth. Diamonds have become a symbol of wealth and status in the modern world. And, thanks to the innovative and aggressive marketing campaigns by De Beers in the mid-1900s, they have become a "must have" if you want to prove to your significant other and your friends and family that you love her; diamonds and marriage have developed an unbreakable bond – can't have one without the other.

Unfortunately, for those in possession of diamond-encrusted

jewelry or are planning on procuring some, there is a decent chance it was mined by child labor and child slaves; it might be a "blood diamond."[22] Some people find this bit of knowledge or revelation to be rather unsettling. Others couldn't care less. And some even think those young workers should consider themselves fortunate to be provided with wage-earning opportunities they might not otherwise have, which theoretically allows for them a "dignified" living. Either way, when it comes to exploitation and unethical labor practices across the globe, there might not be a more flagrant example than that of the diamond mining and diamond polishing industries – offenders coming mostly from African nations and India.

Though it is difficult to nail down an exact number, the ILO estimates that of the 152 million children between the ages of 5 and 17 who are victims of child labor on this planet, about 31.5 million of them are African children involved in "hazardous work."[23,24] In certain regions like in Angola or Mali, children make up nearly half of their country's diamond mining workforce.[25] And for kids working the mines, life is nothing but hardship. Along with working all day long, six or seven days a week, for a dollar or less per day (sometimes they are not even paid), they must endure dangerous and harmful working conditions. Children are typically smaller than adults, so oftentimes they are called upon to descend or crawl through narrow spaces, exposing them to potential landslides that can claim their lives. And like the coal mines I spoke of in the Company Towns of old, most of the African mines are unregulated and lack safety protocols and stable structures, leaving child workers vulnerable to injury or death from said landslides, collapsing pits, falling rocks, sharp or heavy objects, malaria, and more. The strenuous work also exposes them to mercury poisoning, dusty air, and other toxic chemicals while they shovel and carry heavy bags of gravel for hours upon hours in sweltering heat. It's not a happy or healthy way for a human organism to grow.

And the idea of getting an education is an afterthought for many of these kids, even though many express a strong desire to learn. Rather than enrolling in school, a large number of child laborers work the mines year-round. And, of the children who are enrolled, many struggle to keep up with their studies and often skip class due to their taxing schedules.[26] The result? Deprived of proper education and training and exposed to potential stunted development, it becomes increasingly difficult for these children to escape the mining industry once they grow into adults; child miners are all but condemned to a lifetime of digging and pain.[27]

In India, where the majority of the world's diamonds are imported for cutting and polishing, circumstances are similar for the thousands of youth working in factories. Though child labor is against the law in India, it is still quite common as it is estimated that well over 10 million kids are coerced into the business.[29] And, the country derives great financial benefit from the cheap labor in the form of increased profitability and higher GDP; its diamond industry accounts for $23 billion and growing, and its diamond exports have climbed 70% in the last decade.[30] Not only are children preferred in the diamond business because of their affordability, but they also appear to be better at cutting diamonds since they have steadier hands and keener eyes compared to their adult counterparts.[31] It's for this reason they are targeted, especially those living within impoverished households.

The work itself is labor-intensive and generally unhealthy, as polishing material is made from chromium oxide and diamond powder. Children, some as young as 6 years old, spend hours each day bent over in small, crowded rooms performing repetitive tasks in the precision work of cutting gemstones as they breathe in toxic dust; many come from poor families and are illiterate. For those laboring in the slave-like conditions, pain, injuries, and sickness are almost unavoidable. Like the child laborers in Africa, education becomes secondary for many working in the diamond industry of India, hindering their overall growth and future opportunities.

So what's the driving force? Why are such capable children subjected to the grueling and hazardous work of the mines and factories, when they should be spending their most crucial period for growth playing with friends, developing, and learning skills? The specific reasons may vary for each individual child, but it ultimately funnels down to the need for money. Many kids sweat and bleed for diamonds to pay for food and school fees either for themselves or for younger siblings. In other cases, parents might agree to accept money from employers in advance so they can acquire life necessities for their families; and to pay off the debt, their young children are forced to pick up a shovel and get to work – labor for debt. Unfortunately, many such debts become nearly impossible to pay off due to interest, and it is then passed down to their descendants along with a lifetime of servitude. Due to poverty, some adults might consider selling their children into the mining industry. Lastly, many of the children who are forced into diamond and gold mines are orphans or were simply abandoned by their parents.

And from the point of view of slavers, kids are the cheapest labor available, and they are the most vulnerable and easiest to control; it's as simple as that. Though various initiatives and laws have been enacted by countries and world organizations to eliminate the exploitation of vulnerable children in the diamond mining industry, vulnerable children are still widely exploited, and therefore, robbed of a normal life. Some companies maintain that they only buy diamonds from ethical suppliers, but, unfortunately, tracing the origins of a diamond through the chains of distribution can be a rather daunting and oftentimes impossible task, and in many cases information is purposely withheld to skew statistics.

No matter what measures have been taken in the last two decades, nothing seems to inhibit the use of children in dangerous activities. So if no actions or initiatives seem to be effective, then what needs to be done in order to stop child labor and slavery? Well, obviously, the head of the snake, the incentive to continue such unethical practices is the allure of monetary gain – of money. Cut that head off and suddenly the pressure to make money in order to buy life is lifted, and the need to hire children as cheap labor in order to squeeze out a few extra pennies is no longer necessary. Heck, without monetary incentive, companies like De Beers and Jared would probably stop trying to hijack the minds of consumers with their stupid commercials in an attempt to convince them that diamonds represent love and prestige, which might lead people to snap out of their spell and slowly lose their lust for the sparkly rocks, which would cause demand to quickly diminish. Bottom line, the only way to truly put an end to child exploitation is to eliminate the main driver, the primary reason children are used and abused in the first place – money.

Last of all, I can't talk about the exploitation of the poor without at least dipping a toe in the waters of the traditional sweatshops of Asia and Latin America (though they exist on every continent, except Antarctica). I'll make it brief, however, since I feel like I've rattled on enough in this section. I mean, most of us are already well aware of the existence of sweatshops in countries like Bangladesh, Indonesia, China, India, Malaysia, Cambodia, Vietnam, Guatemala, Argentina, Honduras, El Salvador, etc. And most of us are aware that some of our most well-known and beloved brands – Nike, H&M, Apple, Gap, Adidas, Puma – take advantage of these most vulnerable humans and derive great financial benefit from utilizing their cheap labor within hot, muggy sweatshop walls. I probably don't need to go too far in depth about this topic, because it's hardly a secret that sweatshop workers are usually those stricken with poverty and are desperate for wage-paying employment. We all know laborers in many sweatshops are paid very little while enduring long hours of monotonous, mind-numbing, hazardous, and/or dangerous work, or how a large percentage of these people are absolutely miserable, are confined to dorms away from their families, still struggle to provide for their children, feel an overwhelming sense of hopelessness, and may be driven to suicide. Many of us seem to be aware of the suicide nets protruding from sweatshop buildings that were installed to catch depressed workers who attempt to kill themselves on the job.[32] If we don't know, many of us at least have a suspicion of the multitude of human rights violations committed on a daily basis, like female workers being forced to take birth control (over 80% of sweatshop workers are female), females receiving routine pregnancy tests, physical abuse, and of course, child labor.[33] We all seem to have general knowledge that due to low safety standards and loose regulations, the level of injuries and diseases for these workers is quite high; over 1,000 people were killed when a Bangladesh textile factory building collapsed in 2013;[34] over 720,000 cases of pneumoconiosis, a respiratory illness from dust exposure, were reported in China in 2015 (some estimate that over 5 million cases went unreported).[35] And, many of us seem well aware that we as complicit consumers enjoy the fruits of their labor in the form of lower prices on clothing and other sweatshop-produced goods (guilty am I). Even though cheap labor might equate to lower prices for the average consumer, the markup and profit margins on shoes and other apparel remain rather enormous. Our demand fuels unethical practices. But, our demand is fueled largely by marketing. Marketing is fueled by financial motives.

A spoonful of economists and like-minded individuals postulate that multinational corporations are actually helping these poor countries and people by providing them a dignified living, but I must call bull. Sure, the conditions present in rural areas of impoverished countries might be terrible, leading many citizens to grow desperate and be reduced to lives of crime, prostitution, and misery, but let's call a trough a trough here. To say that the lives of impoverished groups are improved by the introduction of corporations is really just a distortion of reality; it's corporate-sponsored reasoning along with mental tricks we play on ourselves to remain shielded from any sort of guilt or shame, because most humans are not sociopaths, and many would feel uneasy if they really knew the depths of struggle and despair experienced by the exploited. Make no mistake about it, while certain aspects of a sweatshop worker's life might be marginally improved only because his ability to purchase survival is loosely secured, many of the exploited people still endure poverty, crime, misery, and squalor.

Do we praise a pimp when he "rescues" a desperate woman from the streets by providing her "gainful employment" as a prostitute? No. "But she can afford food now and maybe even an apartment. That sounds like an improvement to me." Right. Like pimps, Nike, the Gap, Adidas, H&M, and many other "winning" establishments exploit damaged and vulnerable populations for the purpose of reducing costs, increasing profit margins, and expanding business. Pimps seek out struggling women, while multinational corporations seek out struggling people; people who they recognize to have little to no bargaining power, and who they know would be willing to work for pennies on the dollar if only for survival and the false sense of hope that they might one day save up enough money to escape destitution. However, it is not long after accepting sweatshop employment that they realize they are trapped, and their hopes dull entirely. Eventually, they just become cheap, submissive objects for business that feel like they no longer have any other choice but to just lay there and take it; and, business reaps the grand rewards.

When multinationals enter poor segments of the world, not only do they discover exploitable populations, but they come upon territories with lax labor laws similar to the labor laws of the Industrial Age in America and within old Company Towns where workers had no rights. Unfortunately for businesses in America wanting to dominate the global monetary game, America introduced labor laws years ago to give muted workers at least some sort of voice, so poor working conditions have instead been outsourced to underdeveloped regions whose labor laws heavily favor the game's winners. Cheap labor and minimal worker rights offer a perfect recipe for maximum profits. That's the only goal! All else as a result of business ventures, good or bad, is irrelevant collateral. Some communities might improve. Some communities might wither. It does not matter. The bottom line is all that matters.

In some sections of Asia, working conditions have improved and pay increased. However, the catch-22 is that if workers in these countries continue to demand higher wages and costly improvements to workplace conditions, multinational corporations could threaten to either pack up and leave, or replace their labor with automation – a trend that has already been on the rise. Such are the natural machinations of the free market.

Wash, rinse, repeat – money, money, money. Exploitation, worker abuse, taking advantage of the most desperate, it all stems from money and its scarce existence. Deprived of it, slaves seek it. Wanting more of it, slavers seek it. It certainly doesn't have to be this way with current knowledge and technological capabilities.

## 6.4 WAR: TRADING RED FOR GREEN

> "War is a racket. It always has been. It is possibly the oldest, easily the most profitable, surely the most vicious. It is the only one international in scope. It is the only one in which the profits are reckoned in dollars and the losses in lives."[1] – Smedley D. Butler, US Marine Corps Major General, served nearly 34 years from 1898-1931

*DISCLAIMER: Before I talk about war and the role money plays in it, I first want to say that I have the utmost respect and admiration for those who are willing to sacrifice their lives for what they perceive as protecting the freedoms of their fellow man. Every bit of criticism in this chapter is solely aimed at the few individual men who derive great financial benefit from conflict, who feel indifferent toward sending people off to kill and be killed, and has nothing to do with the courageous individuals who have put their lives on the line for others. I am grateful that such humans exist.*

*Additionally, none of my evaluations or criticisms in regard to American intervention overseas involves American citizens. American citizens don't make the decision for military action toward other countries – a small handful of men do this. And I don't necessarily recognize that small handful as being "American," per se. It is clear their interests are not national in scope, but rather individualistic and driven by personal gain – "Money has no motherland; financiers are without patriotism and without decency; their sole object is gain."[2] As such, the most influential individuals operate almost as their own private entities, whilst hiding behind and using the most powerful force in the world for their own benefit. So, all of my words point to them, not toward the average person trying to live a peaceful and happy life within the national borders of the United States.*

Money is a precondition for and incentivizes war, unbeknownst to itself.

I said it in Chapter 4.3, and I'll repeat Butler's sentiments from my opening quote: war is most certainly a racket. There may not be a more lucrative and more profitable endeavor in the entire world. It is absolutely perfect for business. Product markups are large. Product turnover is high. Companies don't have to wait for goods to slowly degrade or breakdown before making more sales. Instead, products are blown up and completely destroyed, and with high frequency. Every time a bomb sends a town into oblivion, it's cha-ching for construction companies. Every fire of a gun or launch of a missile is cha-ching for weapons manufacturers – when the United States bombed Syria in 2018 and Baghdad in 2020 (to neutralize Qasem Soleimani of Iran), stocks climbed for defense contractors.[3] Every time a country sends men and women into another country to engage in war, it's cha-ching for banks and bankers as countries take out huge loans to finance such actions. War has been used to put countries into debt. War has been used to stimulate economies.

America has been in a perpetual state of conflict since its inception, whether provoked or acting as provocateurs, and it is no wonder once the monetary benefits are revealed. With just about every war over the last 400 hundred years, you will find monetary incentive either at the heart or within arm's length of the heart of it all; though, of course, all wars and conflicts are disguised to the cud-chewing public as some noble effort to fight evil.

But don't take it from me that war is a racket. At the time of his death in 1940, Smedley D. Butler was the most decorated US Marine in the history of America. He served for nearly 34 years as a Marine, and his rank as Major General was the highest authorized during that period. Throughout his career, Butler led military interventions in countries all across the globe, and it was during his tenure that he slowly became exposed to the real motives behind war and the devastating consequences left in its wake.[4] Because of this, Butler became outspoken about his role and the role of America and its business interests in global conflict. In 1933, two years before publishing his popular book titled *War is Racket* (a recommended read that is as relevant today as it was in 1935), the former US Marine Corps Major General gave a speech. It's brief, and cogent, so

I'm going to divulge the whole thing:

> "War is just a racket. A racket is best described, I believe, as something that is not what it seems to the majority of people. Only a small inside group knows what it is about. It is conducted for the benefit of the very few at the expense of the masses.
>
> I believe in adequate defense at the coastline and nothing else. If a nation comes over here to fight, then we'll fight. The trouble with America is that when the dollar only earns 6 percent over here, then it gets restless and goes overseas to get 100 percent.
>
> I wouldn't go to war again as I have done to protect some lousy investment of the bankers. There are only two things we should fight for. One is the defense of our homes and the other is the Bill of Rights. War for any other reason is simply a racket.
>
> There isn't a trick in the racketeering bag that the military gang is blind to. It has its "finger men" to point out enemies, its "muscle men" to destroy enemies, its "brain men" to plan war preparations, and a "Big Boss" super-nationalistic-capitalism.
>
> It may seem odd for me, a military man to adopt such a comparison. Truthfulness compels me to. I spent thirty-three years and four months in the active military service as a member of this country's most agile military force, the Marine Corps. I served in all commissioned ranks from Second Lieutenant to Major General. And during that period, I spent most of my time being a high-class muscle man for Big Business, for Wall Street and for the Bankers. In short, I was a racketeer, a gangster for capitalism.
>
> I suspected I was just part of a racket at the time. Now I am sure of it. Like all the members of the military profession, I never had a thought of my own until I left the service. My mental faculties remained in suspended animation while I obeyed the orders of higher-ups. This is typical with everyone in the military service.
>
> I helped make Mexico, especially Tampico, safe for American oil interests in 1914. I helped make Haiti and Cuba a decent place for the National City Bank boys to collect revenues in. I helped in the raping of half a dozen Central American republics for the benefits of Wall Street. The record of racketeering is long. I

> helped purify Nicaragua for the international banking house of Brown Brothers in 1909-1912. I brought light to the Dominican Republic for American sugar interests in 1916. In China I helped to see to it that Standard Oil went its way unmolested. During those years, I had, as the boys in the back room would say, a swell racket. Looking back on it, I feel that I could have given Al Capone a few hints. The best he could do was to operate his racket in three districts. I operated on three continents."

War showers but a few individual men with incredible riches, while millions of soldiers, soldiers' families, and innocent civilians endure incredible misery during and after fighting. While 22 veterans commit suicide every single day,[5] with over 37,000 homeless and nearly 1.5 million former military men and women living in poverty,[6,7] the heads of the Lockheed Martins and the Dick Cheneys of the world recline back with their feet up on Carpathian elm and ebony desks whilst lighting Cuban cigars with burning $100 bills. They don't care. They are detached from and feel a sense of superiority over the general public.[8-10] The general population are expendable, faceless pawns in the grand transnational chess match for wealth and control. And unfortunately for the masses, it is America's monetary masters who, with their wallets, have the greatest influence in Washington. And of those monetary masters, it is the ones within industries (banking, weapons manufacturing) that derive the greatest financial benefit from fighting that have their fingers on the trigger, who ultimately drive decisions regarding whether to send men and women to foreign countries to kill other men and women.

Shareholders expect quarterly gains. When your job and ability to purchase survival hinges on pleasing shareholders, coupled with the idea that executives and government officials are detached from the general population and are insulated from the horrors of war, inflating threats and pulling that trigger becomes much less of a strain. Sending "strangers" overseas to shed blood is a small price to pay for a new Gulfstream G-550, a seventh mansion overlooking the Pacific Ocean, and a high-chair at the world's political roundtable. The sacrifice during war or military conflict for government officials and executives of private defense contractors is minimal while brave soldiers lay everything on the line to protect their country. Smedley Butler would go on to say in his 1935 book:

> "How many of these war millionaires shouldered a rifle? How many of them dug a trench? How many of them knew what it meant to go hungry in a rat-infested dugout? How many of them spent sleepless, frightened nights, ducking shells and shrapnel and machine gun bullets? How many of them parried a bayonet thrust of an enemy? How many of them were wounded or killed in battle?"[11]

The opulent few stuffing their pockets with green might have to make public appearances here and there, stand behind a podium, and provide hollow lip-service about how "proud they are of their heroes," but they remain mostly unaffected by the pain endured by soldiers, their families, and civilians. And there is much pain, as war is the greatest disruptor of life and harmony and exacts a heavy toll on everyone else. *Soldiers* may suffer from having to kill. Soldiers suffer from being killed. Soldiers suffer from being injured. Soldiers suffer from seeing their comrades and friends killed or injured. Soldiers suffer from mental illness after returning home, leading to struggles with employment, drug addiction, homelessness, and suicide. The *families* of soldiers suffer while their husband, wife, father, mother, son, daughter, brother, sister is away fighting as they may be in a perpetual state of stress and worry. The families of soldiers suffer when the soldier is killed or injured. The families of soldiers suffer when the soldier comes home psychologically damaged. *Civilians* suffer when their homes and cities are destroyed. Civilians suffer when they are maimed or killed or their friends and family are maimed or killed. Civilians suffer when the aftermath of war causes diseases and deformities for years after. Civilians suffer when they are left without an economy or infrastructure to sustain life.

In his 1961 farewell address to the nation, Dwight D. Eisenhower warned the American public to be wary of the "military industrial complex."[12] Our 34th president feared that business and financial interests would exploit the money-generating capabilities of war by seeking to create endless conflict. And he was right. Over the past many decades a healthy and loving marriage has formed between defense contractors, the Pentagon, politicians, lobbyists, and Congress, as billions of dollars ping-pong back and forth every year. And since the intimate union between these public and private groups, America has rarely known times of peace. Of course, standing above this crowd, eager to lend monetary assistance, are the banking money powers who benefit from extending loans to fund warring endeavors and reconstruction projects.

To net just a portion of the vast kaleidoscope of dollars fluttering about Washington, defense contractors invest millions annually on lobbying efforts – Boeing and Lockheed Martin each spent nearly $13 million in 2019 – with the intent of persuading politicians to extend military contracts, approve of military spending, and create favorable public policies.[13] Top defense contractors also focus bribing efforts toward "neutral" Washington think-tanks, whose role it is to debate and discuss foreign policy and military action, in an attempt to manipulate venal minds into voicing support for American intervention in foreign affairs; and, backed by generous donations, thinkers within such "tanks" might then be seen airing their pseudo-support on popular media outlets, which has the profound effect of convincing suggestible listeners to adopt and echo such false sentiments within their social groups. Then, after defense contractors, weapons manufacturers, and other military-related corporations have invested millions of dollars in lobbying politicians and massaging Congress, Washington scratches their backs by awarding the highest bribers with hefty military contracts. Everyone in the "Iron Triangle" wins! All negotiating parties are paid handsomely, while the American public is duped into footing the bill for military conflict, and the lives of soldiers and innocent bystanders are sacrificed.

With individual men standing to make fortunes, it should come as no surprise that defense spending in America has steadily increased over the past few decades (reaching its peak under Obama while citizens were still struggling with foreclosures and job loss due to the recession). In 2019, according to the Stockholm International Peace Research Institute (SIPRI), the United States spent $732 billion in military expenditures, an amount that topped China, Russia, Saudi Arabia, India, France, Germany, the United Kingdom, South Korea, Brazil, and Japan *combined*![14] And all of that money goes to someone, it all cycles through the same few people – government, Pentagon → private companies → lobbyists → Congress, policymakers, other officials. Wash, rinse, and repeat. Revenues earned by the top 100 defense contractors in the world in 2018 totaled over $420 billion, also according to SIPRI.[15] Of the top revenue generators that year,

Lockheed Martin, Boeing, and Northrop Grumman collected $47.3 billion, $29.2 billion, and $26.2 billion, respectively, in arms sales.[16] All of these companies derive great, great benefit from threats and fighting.

And to justify continued spending, top intelligence officials have an assembly line of villains they can inflate and then use to strike fear in the American public, whether it's the threat of terrorist groups like Al-Qaeda, the Taliban, ISIS, and Al-Qaeda again, *or* foreign leaders who our government deems as dangerous, like Bashar Al-Asad, Saddam Hussein, and Manuel Noriega, *or* entire nations, like Russia, China, or Iran. Government officials and private executives have a vast inventory of antagonists to justify many more seasons of potential conflicts, and thus, endless military contracts. In 1996, the Managing Editor of *Foreign Affairs* (a monthly journal of the Council on Foreign Relations), Fareed Zakaria, acknowledged the need for manufacturing international threats and antagonists when he stated about the threat of Saddam:

> "Yes, it's tempting to get rid of Saddam. But his bad behavior actually serves America's purposes in the region… If Saddam Hussein did not exist, we would have to invent him… The end of Saddam Hussein would be the end of the anti-Saddam coalition. Nothing destroys an alliance like the disappearance of the enemy… Maintaining a long-term American presence in the gulf would be difficult in the absence of a regional threat."[17]

In the end, it costs government officials and policymakers nothing to go to war. The money that they use to pay defense contractors does not come out of the pockets of the individual men championing war. It comes out of the government; out of the unlimited credit card they have at their disposal. The money, the debt that is generated to pay private military interests then gets deflected to the general public. The general public, you and me, we are the ones who end up financially paying for war through taxes, yet there is no lobbying money coming our way or war profits of any kind. The individuals who stand to profit bear no financial risk to war. All they have to do is send brave, yet expendable, men and women overseas to risk their lives, people they have no personal ties to – again, no financial risk to policymakers. It's all profit, baby.

But, maybe the spending is justified. Maybe the threats from around the world since the turn of the 20th century were all real and all required military intervention and human sacrifice to maintain world peace. Or, maybe in some cases our trusted and "God-loving" leaders, on the scent trail of money, have created artificial threats from time to time to justify intervention, and therefore military contracts, and therefore steady streams of cash. As I pointed out in Chapter 4, we have already seen how government officials throughout history and in every nation have been willing to lie and even attack their own people in order to justify military action or get their way. If that's the case, if we know we have been lied to in the past, what would make us think we are being told the truth about every conflict today? If it's been so easy to falsify information in the past, what would stop them from doing so now? What would stop them from, maybe not necessarily lying, but from, say, stretching the truth a bit, from maybe pointing out a foreign leader and labeling him as a tyrant, making him look scarier to the general population than he really is, and injecting enough fear or anger into the American people that they adamantly approve of military intervention? Every great nation in history has seen their leaders corrupted by power and material fortunes. Are we to believe that the very *human* leaders within our borders are the first and only to break this mold simply because they have the honorable label of being American, that those in positions of power in the United States are so benevolent that they couldn't possibly be persuaded by material gain?

In an attempt to examine our foreign activities a bit further, I have provided a couple brief summaries in Appendix A where I acknowledge the alternative, financial motives behind our involvement in select foreign countries and which individual parties sought to benefit most. I would like to provide more summaries, but I am afraid that would venture too far outside the scope of this book, so I will post them one by one on my website (bookthepit.com). Additionally, I have provided below a short list of the vast number of conflicts America has been involved in since 1900. I haven't included everything; just the ones I felt were relevant to this section.

NOTE: For those listed that do not have a Citation Reference number indicated, see References #18 and #19 in the back of the book.

1898 – Spain – America blames Spain for USS Maine explosion and goes to war with them. Acquires Cuba, Puerto Rico, Guam, and Philippines. Navy would later conclude in 1976 that the explosion was "without a doubt" internal and an accident.[20]

1903 – Honduras – US Marines intervene[21]

1903 – Colombia/Panama – US Navy enters[22]

1903 – Dominican Republic – US Troops intervene to protect US interests[23]

1906 – Cuba – Marines intervene in democratic election[24]

1911 – Honduras – Marines intervened to protect US interests (United Fruit Company & Standard Fruit Company)

1912 – Cuba – Marines landed in Havana to protect US interests

1912 – Panama – Marines intervene during election[25]

1912 – Honduras – Marines intervened to protect US interests

1914 – Dominican Republic – Fight for Santo Domingo[26]

1913-1918 – Mexico – Continued fighting versus nationalists

1914-1934 – Haiti – Occupation[27]

1917-1919 – World War I – US loans $10.35 billion to allies.[28] Cha-ching for banks. Precursor to American involvement was the sinking of the Lusitania, a British ocean liner carrying American civilians, by a German U-boat. However, Woodrow Wilson, the US government, and financial leaders knew that the Lusitania was traveling through hostile territories. Germans even tried warning the American public not to board the ship by writing a newspaper article, but most newspapers were told not to run it. The Lusitania was to be escorted by a second ship, but when it arrived to the hostile territory, the second ship was not there. It had been told to stand down. The Lusitania was also ordered to reduce its speed. After the ship sank, America had justification to enter the war.[29]

1912-1933 – Nicaragua – Occupation

1916-1924 – Dom Rep – Marine occupation

1917-1933 – Cuba – Occupation, economic protectorate

1918-1920 – Panama – Troops remain to "police" Panama after elections

1918-1922 – Soviet Russia – American forces intervene on multiple occasions

1919 – Honduras – Marines intervene in election

1922 – Turkey – Troops fight in Smyrna

1922-1927 – China – Troops intervene to stop nationalists

1927-1934 – China – Marines stationed throughout

1924-1925 – Honduras – Marines intervene in election strife

1925 – Panama – Marines intervene
1934-1945 – the Depression and World War II kept our interactions with Latin America to a minimal.
1941-1945 – WWII
1946 – Yugoslavia – Navy responds after American plane brought down
1947 – Uruguay – Bombers deployed
1947-1949 – Greece – US intervenes in elections[33]
1948 – Germany – Military intervenes due to Berlin Blockade[34]
1948-1954 – Philippines – CIA involved in Huk Rebellion[35]
1951-1953 – Korean War
1953 – Iran – CIA's Kermit Roosevelt orchestrates removal of Mossadegh. Replaces him with US-backed Shah and Zahedi[36]
1954 – Guatemala – Coup d'état involving CIA. Guatemala nationalizes land that was unused, but controlled by United Fruit Company. 200,000+ killed[37]
1954 – Vietnam – US sells weapons to French to fight Vietnamese forces
1956 – Egypt – Marines intervene. Nasser nationalizes Suez Canal.
1958 – Panama – Troops intervene in protest[38]
1958 – Lebanon – Navy intervenes during civil war
1961-1962 – Cuba – Bay of Pigs
1962 – Laos – Military occupied during civil war
1964 – Panama – Troops sent down to stop protesters protesting for the return of the canal[39]
1965 – Indonesia – CIA orchestrates military coup
1965-1966 – Dominican Republic – Troops and bombing during elections
1966-1967 – Guatemala – Green Berets stop rebels[40]
196?-197? – Vietnam War
1969-1975 – Cambodia – Military sent due to Vietnam war expanding
1970-1973 – Chile – CIA and US orchestrate removal of Allende[41]
1971-1975 – Laos – Military carpet-bombs Laos during civil war
1976-1992 – Angola – CIA supports rebels against leftist leadership[42]
1981-1992 – El Salvador – Troops intervene. 75,000 killed
1981-1990 – Nicaragua – Contra, Sandinistas. 50,000 killed
1981 – Ecuador – Jaime Roldos murdered in plain crash. Replaced with US-backed leader
1981 – Panama – Omar Torrijos murdered in plain crash. Replaced by US-backed Manuel Noriega, who was on CIA payroll

1981 – Libya – Americans shoot down Libyan fighters
1982-90 – Honduras – Troops sent down, build bases at borders
1982-1984 – Lebanon – Marines occupied Beirut
1983-1984 – Grenada – Troops and bombs sent to quell revolution
1984 – Iran – Americans shoot down two Iranian planes
1986 – Libya – Military intervenes in Tripoli
1986-1987 – Bolivia – Troops involved with cocaine raids[43]
1987 – Iran – US aids Iraq in fighting Iran
1989 – Panama – Invasion. Noriega got away from US control. 2000-3000 killed
1989 – Libya – America shoots down two more fighter jets
1989 – Virgin Island – Troops intervene during civil unrest[44]
1989 – Philippines – America provides air support during attempted coup
1990 – Liberia – Troops evacuate people
1990-1991 – Iraq – Gulf War
1992-1994 – Somalia – Troops occupy during civil war
1993-2006 – Bosnia – Military intervention
1994-1995 – Haiti – Troops intervene, replace leader with US-backed leader
1996-1997 – Zaire – Marines sent in response to Congo revolution?
1997 – Albania – Troops help foreigners evacuate
1998 – Sudan – Bombings
1998 – Afghanistan – Bombing of alleged terrorist training camps
1999-2003 – Yugoslavia – Bombings, military intervention
1999-2001 – East Timor – Military Intervention
1998-2001 – Iraq – Bombings
2000 – Sierra Leone – US C-17 aircraft delivers ammunition, Navy on standby
2000 – Yemen – US Navy deployed
2001-2014 – Afghanistan
2002 – Venezuela – Attempt to remove Hugo Chavez
2003-2011 – Iraq – WMDs
2003 – Liberia – Military personnel deployed
2004-??? – Haiti – Troops occupy Haiti
2004-Present – Pakistan – Drone strikes
2006 – Lebanon – Aircraft and troops deployed to Beirut
2007 – Somalia – Airstrikes
2009 – Honduras – Support for coup to remove Zelaya

2010-Present – Yemen – Drone strikes
2011 – Somalia – Drone strikes
2011 – Libya – Bombings
2013 – Niger – Troops deployed
2013 – Jordan – Military personnel deployed
2014-Present – Syria – Airstrikes
2014-2017 – South Korea – US Troops, artillery deployed
2014 – Central Africa – US Aircraft and personnel sent
2015 – Cameroon – Military intervenes
2016 – Yemen – Missile strikes
2017 – Syria – Tomahawk missile strike
2017 – Romania – Tanks and troops sent
2018 – Syria – Bombings
2020 – Iraq – Airstrike

Since man began colonizing territories, the wealthiest and most powerful civilizations have used their substantial strength to invade smaller nations with the intent of increasing their own country's international power and its pool of assets and resources. Unfortunately, for those with a strong sense of morals combined with national pride, America and its allies have been no different in their ambitions. Foreign countries from around the world, from South America to Africa to Asia, have consistently felt an American presence, especially over the last century or so, and it's not often been for noble reasons, though the men with their fingers on the trigger would have us believe that to be so. Aside from our involvement in the Middle East, the American population has remained relatively in the dark about our nation's activities in other non-warring nations, like Ecuador, Panama, and Chile, to name a few. And as for the few citizens who do become aware of our intervention in countries that don't seek it, the individual men who stand to reap the financial rewards justify it as the US righteously policing the world and maintaining peace. But, all one needs to do is lift the veil just slightly to reveal how our presence often accomplishes the opposite as it causes unrest and unhappiness amongst native populaces. The true motive of war is almost always resource acquisition and making that easy money. Remove money; remove the head of the snake and incentive to aggress other nations deteriorates.

Before I move on to the next section regarding Crime, I want to briefly talk about a modern tactic used to acquire control over foreign resources, a tactic that relies on the pen rather than the sword to seduce foreign leaders into accepting deals that might make them wealthy but buries their people in an abyss of debt.

## 6.4b BULLYING THE LITTLE KIDS ON THE PLAYGROUND

War is about resource acquisition. However, hostile actions are not often necessary to manipulate small countries and seize control over their wealth. Sometimes bribes, business deals, and covert tinkering accomplish the same, but with much less effort and much less financial investment. For American leaders and domestic and international business interests, this realization and subsequent shift in foreign tactics came in 1953 and involved the oil-rich nation of Iran and Teddy Roosevelt's grandson, Kermit.

During the first half of the 20th century, Great Britain, through its Anglo-Iranian Oil Company (AIOC), controlled Iran's oil. However, the Iranian people felt like they were being screwed over by Britain in a number of ways, because not only did the Middle East nation receive a small percentage of oil profits, but also the AIOC did not follow through on a number of its promises. Nevertheless, support among Iranian civilians to reacquire their resource and nationalize the oil industry intensified.

In 1951, in its first democratic election in many years, the widely popular Mohammed Mossadegh was elected as Iran's prime minister. Shortly after being appointed, Mossadegh wrested control of its oil from Britain and nationalized the oil industry – his outward aim being to give political and economic independence to Iran, while using oil revenues to reverse its struggles with poverty, diseases, and other hardships. Britain was not happy, and it took a number of measures – like sending ships to the Persian Gulf and pressuring the world market not to accept Iranian receipts – to win back control of what it had thought was stolen from them.

After unsuccessfully regaining control of Iranian oil, Britain eventually appealed to American powers for help; and, for many reasons, American powers obliged. Thus, Operation Ajax, headed by the American CIA and Kermit Roosevelt, was born. Rather than sending military forces to Iran, which would be costly and would make America look like an aggressor, they instead gave Kermit a bunch of money and allowed him to work magic within the Iranian border.

Kermit used the money to bribe politicians, Iranian civilians, and the Iranian media. He acquired control of Iranian news outlets and instructed them to generate propaganda against Mossadegh to paint the popular leader as a threat and as susceptible to Communist control. With the maelstrom of negative press in combination with buying off the right people, Kermit was able to foment civil unrest. The civil unrest soon evolved into national riots – also paid for by Roosevelt, as he gave money to both protesting sides, which is detailed in his book *Countercoup: The Struggle for the Control of Iran* – making it look to the public and the world as though Mossadegh had lost control of his country and that the Iranian people disapproved of his leadership.

Eventually, the Shah signed a decree to dismiss Mossadegh as prime minister, and Mossadegh was arrested and placed under house arrest until he died in 1967. Fazlollah Zahedi, backed by the CIA, was then installed as the new prime minister of Iran, and he, as well as the reinstalled Shah, were much more willing to play ball with western political and business interests. As a result, Britain and the US regained a controlling stake in Iran's oil, and the US proceeded to provide financial support to the Shah.

An important precedent was set during that August of 1953. With a relatively small amount of money, a single agent was able to completely change the political infrastructure of an entire nation. Military force was not needed. However, Kermit Roosevelt was a card-carrying member of the CIA. Had he been caught mingling in Iran, the country and its people would have associated him as working with the American government, and that could have led to negative consequences for Kermit and America. They knew if they were to attempt such an exercise again, an adjustment needed to be made. Thus, going forward, rather than sending government affiliates to influence foreign leaders and politicians, they would instead send ordinary citizens working as consultants for private organizations. In this way, if the individuals were discovered, there would be no ties to the American government.

John Perkins was one such consultant. In his book, *Confessions of an Economic Hitman*, he describes in detail his role as an *Economic Hitman.* The process, as Perkins explains, goes a little something like this. Business interests identify a small, resource-rich nation. Then, they hire an economic hitman, like John Perkins, arm him with contracts and cash, and send him into a country, like Indonesia, to bribe and negotiate with its leaders in hopes of coercing them into entering into large contracts and taking out huge loans to build infrastructure. Once foreign leaders do agree to such deals, the World Bank, IMF, or other organizations create a loan and lend money to complete the agreement. However, the money doesn't typically go to the small nation. Instead, it goes straight to the private entity, the private entity pays its people and they begin whatever construction project was agreed upon – Power Plants, Ports, etc.

Unfortunately for the small nation, such business exchanges are designed only to benefit the private multinational interests along with a small number of individuals within the country who were a part of the deal and who accepted bribe money. The rest of the population? They are essentially left to dry. Corrupt foreign leaders agree to give up their country's resources and their ability to profit from them in exchange for riches, and the nation's population is laced with a massive debt that is impossible to pay off. Even though the small nation's people had nothing to do with the agreement, it is deflected onto them and it becomes their responsibility, and they reap none of the rewards.

What's worse is the contractors know the debts will be too big for these countries to pay off – this is intentional. When a country inevitably falls behind on its payment obligations, the companies get to come back and ask for various cuts of meat; an Economic Hitman is once again sent to the country to negotiate concessions. He might say, as Perkins describes in an interview:

> "Listen, you lost a lot of money, can't pay your debts, so sell your oil real cheap to our oil companies. Allow us to build a military base in your country or send troops in support of us in some place in the world like Iraq, or vote with us on the next UN vote to have [your] electric utility company privatized, and [your] water and sewage system privatized, and [they're] sold to US corporations or other multinational corporations."[46]

Poorer countries, like the resource-rich nations of Latin America, are plunged into unpayable debts. They lose valuable assets to private international interests. The private international interests turn around and earn incredible profits, while the small countries lose their ability to make money, pay back their loans, and bolster their local economies.

But what happens when a country's president refuses to play ball with multinational interests and becomes "difficult"? Well, measures are taken to remove that leader and replace him with one that is friendlier to foreign business, one that is susceptible to corruption and doesn't care if his people suffer. When Mossadegh wanted to reacquire his country's oil resources, foreign interests saw to it that he was swiftly replaced with a leader that was easier to manipulate. When Guatemala's Jacobo Arbenz wanted to seize Guatemalan lands from foreign control and give it back to his people, a CIA-led campaign, which used tried-and-true Communism fears to justify intervention, led to his removal from office, and the US-backed Carlos Castillo Armas was installed in his place. Ecuador's Jaime Roldos Aguilera sought to reclaim his country's oil and other resources from foreign interests and use it for the betterment of Ecuador. John Perkins admits that he was sent down to try and "corrupt" the popular leader, and warned him that if he didn't play ball with foreign business that he might face significant consequences, but Roldos didn't budge. He ended up dying in a plane crash in 1981. A few months later in 1981, Panama's leader Omar Torrijos also wound up dying in a plane crash shortly after he took a hard stance against foreign private interests trying to take advantage of his country. Speculations of assassination surround the deaths of both leaders. To add to suspicions, Torrijos was replaced by Manuel Noriega, a man who happened to be on CIA payroll and was much easier to control – that is until he grew tired of his leash and became disobedient to his foreign masters, which led to the Panama Invasion in 1989.[46,47] Throughout the 1900s, smaller, weaker Latin American countries often found their leaders replaced by puppet leaders friendly to multinationals and willing to do as they're told in exchange for money and power. The puppeteering and exploitation of weaker nations happens all over the world, including in Asia, the Middle East, and Africa. Other wealthy countries, like China, also participate in taking advantage of smaller territories.

Sometimes, the pen is much more effective than the sword in acquiring resources, taking control of a country, and expanding global power. It's cheaper and quieter. Unfortunately, native populations always pay the dearest price when leaders sell out to foreign interests.

## 6.5 CRIME

"Poverty is the parent of revolution and crime."[1] – Aristotle

"Crime rocks," said no one ever. Fraud, robbery, violence, murder – of all the negative elements within society crime is certainly the one we are most aware of (thanks to media exposure), which makes it the most consciously unpleasant for citizens. Not only does crime cause direct and indirect harm to everyone in its periphery, but it also puts a strain on public health as people become stressed, fearful, paranoid, and distrusting of one another. It seems like just about every week now, we turn on the television only to discover another mass shooting has claimed the lives of innocent victims at some public venue. As a consequence, some Americans have become too afraid to go to malls and movie theaters. Others now find it necessary to holster firearms at all times.

I mean, is violence a problem unique to the US? No. Not at all. But it does appear to be more prevalent. According to 2017 data published by the FBI, the United States boasts a homicide rate of 5.4 reported offenses per 100,000 people.[2] This number may not seem like much on its own, but when measured against other developed countries, America stands above just about all of them. It's higher than almost all European nations; Ukraine being the lone outlier at 6.2. It's higher than most developed and underdeveloped nations in Asia. It's even higher than seemingly hostile Middle Eastern countries like Iran and Syria. For a visual comparison, I have included a table (Figure A) on the next page that displays the 2017 homicide rates of select countries.[3,4]

America is one of the most advanced and materially-wealthy countries in the world. So what the heck is going on? Where is this displaced aggression coming from? Have humans lost their morals? One could argue that the substantial population of the United States leaves it more vulnerable to murder and other crimes, but that argument doesn't seem to hold much weight since China's population is about 4 times greater, yet their homicide rate is 9 times less. So is it about skin color?

| Country | Homicides |
|---|---|
| Japan | 0.2 |
| Norway | 0.5 |
| China | 0.6 |
| Italy | 0.7 |
| Australia | 0.8 |
| Germany | 1 |
| UK | 1.2 |
| France | 1.3 |
| Canada | 1.8 |
| Syria | 2.2 |
| Iran | 2.5 |
| US | 5.4 |

*FIGURE A:* Homicide rates by country in 2017.

Some herds of men like to think Blacks and Mexicans are at the epicenter of violence and crime, but statistical analysis paints an unclear picture. In 2016, those denoted as white comprised 69.5% of Total Arrests, while those considered black comprised 26.8%. And when accounting for ethnicity, which not all agencies do, Hispanics comprised only 18% of all arrests in the US.[5] However, simply looking at overall data numbers tells an incomplete story since black people make up only 12.8% of the population and Hispanics and Latinos come in at 17.8%. If we wanted to pit race and ethnicity against each other, a better representation would be to compare groups of similar demographic and financial circumstances, like those living in low-income households. If we narrow our scope and look at data reported out of the Bureau of Justice Statistics from 2008 to 2012, we see that poor whites had a rate of violence of 46.4 offenses per 1,000 people versus 43.4 offenses for poor blacks.[6] What might surprise a few is that poor Hispanics only had a violence rate of 25.3 offenses per 1,000 people during that 4-year span. My takeaway after scouring pages and pages of criminal records is that there is a ton of data available for us to analyze, and we can twist and turn the numbers to tell any story we like; if we come preloaded with biases, we can find a way to confirm such biases. But ultimately, when it comes to producing a criminal, color doesn't matter.

Entering this world with light or dark skin does little to nothing in determining behavior. If we were really desperate to find a color to assign blame to, one would do better in looking at green instead.

Okay, so if race is a poor determinant of crime, then is the problem due to lax gun laws? Many contend that open access to firearms makes it easier for violent or mentally ill people to carry out acts of murder, and though this argument carries some truth and a positive correlation exists between guns and violence, it oversimplifies the issue. First, with or without strict gun laws, those seeking to obtain a firearm will find a way to obtain a firearm; drug laws do little to curb drug access and use. Second, crimes unrelated to guns, like rape and death from child abuse, are also quite high in the United States. For instance, 2017 FBI data concluded that there were 42.4 *reported* acts of rape per 100,000 people in America;[7] compared to the rest of the world, the US consistently ranks near the top of the list worldwide.

I couldn't care less about guns, so I have no interest in defending their existence, but it seems like America's issue of violent crime goes much deeper than the 2nd Amendment. Before a bullet can take a life, a man must decide to load a gun, point it at a human, and finally pull the trigger. For that man to be driven to such extreme actions, certain conditions must have first existed in his life to shape his thoughts and behavior. If the conditions that predictably create monsters remain unchanged, it matters little whether legislation tightens up restrictions on firearms; people will still "break" in this society, people will continue to lash out, and violence will prevail.

And we can all feel and see it – the tension building amongst the population. We can feel how *on edge* people have become. But what is causing this tension? What has been the main driver of violent crime, rape, and other harmful activities permeating throughout all corners of a nation blessed with riches beyond riches?

I often hear statements like, "Violence is simply in our nature." To what extent is this true? Well, a copious number of books have been written, studies have been conducted, and observations have been made in an attempt to dissect and understand the criminal mind and its motivations. And when it comes to the age-old question of nature versus nurture, whether we are born with violent dispositions or whether our thoughts and desires are forged from life experiences and tempered by society and culture, the topic remains contentious. Continued research throughout the last few decades, however, has unveiled that our minds are quite malleable, and environment plays a *crucial* role in sculpting a hostile man – assuming that person is born with properly working equipment, e.g., brain. The notion of violent behavior being an instinctual impulse has been challenged by many modern biologists and psychologists alike. What is "instinct" anyway, but a placeholder oftentimes used when no cause of behavior has yet been discovered. All feelings – anger, happiness, depression, sadness, guilt, shame – have a source. All violent behavior has a source. Though the source of a violent act might be difficult to identify in many cases, no man lashes out without reason or a chain of reasons – sometimes those reasons might be buried deep in his psyche and/or somewhere deep in his past. But to attribute violent behavior to simply being "human nature" is a cop out, plain and simple; it's lazy. Sure, some men are born with more aggressive tendencies than others, but predisposition does not mean predetermination.

Bottom line, crime is a complex beast, as it deals with human psychology, and it doesn't have a single cause; however, certain elements do contribute more than others. If we begin stripping back the layers, if we begin tracing the steps leading to criminal activity in America, we undoubtedly find our system of money lurking in the shadows, inducing stress, compromising morals, and turning the gears of madness. Let's explore the very complex world of crime and how it relates to money and economy.

Our scarcity-driven monetary system works on multiple levels in generating abhorrent behavior. On the first, most obvious level, crimes including but not limited to theft for survival due to material lack, a wife killing her husband for his insurance policy, or white-collar crimes (which cost organizations roughly $500 billion per year) like embezzlement, tax evasion, money laundering, insider trading, counterfeiting, and other types of fraud all link to money as a direct source.[8] Because money's involvement is so clear in cases like these, I won't waste our time going into any more depth than I already have. Instead, let's continue on down causality lane.

Mr. Aristotle astutely observed some 2,300 years ago that poverty is the parent of crime. And he's right, of course; however, we can expand upon his statement. As data has been collected and compiled throughout the years, it has been found that areas of poverty and lack typically correlate with an increase in property crime – robbery, vandalism, petty theft – but not necessarily with violent crime. When it comes to violent crime – murder, rape, assault – many behavioral experts have found *relative poverty* or *income inequality* to be of much greater influence. Now, to clarify, when I say relative poverty, I simply mean "income and wealth of individuals compared to other individuals in a specific region," as opposed to the standard definition set by many countries which is along the lines of "households with less than 60% of the median income of others in the country." If an entire population is living in poverty in a specific region, violent crime is generally less of a concern. However, if in a specific region there are some people living like kings while many are starving and struggling, violent crime can be predictably higher.

All monetary systems produce winners and losers as humans compete to acquire money from one another; a primary difference from country to country is in how big the gap is allowed to grow between its greatest winners and its greatest losers. It just so happens, the regions of the world experiencing higher levels of wealth disparity statistically experience higher rates of violent crime. It's like a rubber band – the farther apart the opposite ends are pulled, the more tension there is. For example, let's have a look at the Gini Coefficient of wealth for the United States. The Gini Coefficient or Gini Index is the most commonly used measure of income and wealth inequality, and it typically ranges from 0 to 100; 0 represents a country with completely equal distribution of wealth, and 100 represents a country where one person has all of the wealth and no one else has any. According to data gathered by Credit Suisse in 2017, the Gini Coefficient of wealth for the US sat at a staggering 85.9, indicating a very large gap; one that is higher than nearly all nations in the world, developed or otherwise.[9] As for other developed or emerging countries, South Africa, Sweden, Russia, and Ukraine join America near the top of the list – yes, Sweden, a country commonly perceived as being more equal when it comes to income and wealth. And what do these five nations have in common? They all endure high rates of violent crime (rape included).[10,11]

Money and the monetary game are at the heart of most violence and crime, and in subsets of the monetary game where the wealth gap continues to expand, crime is predictably higher – causation exists with correlation. So what is it about material inequality that fosters abhorrent behavior? Are those with less material wealth just jealous of those with more? Well, not exactly. Though our primitive, yet wonderful brains would prefer the path of least resistance by simply charging jealousy as the culprit and moving on, human behavior is quite a bit more complex than that. Let's continue drilling down and examine some of the ways in which the monetary game can stir violent ideations.

Dr. James Gilligan, a psychiatrist who spent years studying and interviewing some of the most violent criminals in the United States, discovered a deeper motive beyond jealousy shared in much of the violent crimes he evaluated.[12] He found that avoidance of *shame*, in conjunction with a need for respect, were primary components of violent behavior. Along with a need to achieve some form of justice, violence, he suggests, is ultimately an attempt to replace shame with self-esteem: "Murder represents (for the murderer) the ultimate act of self-defense, a last resort against being overwhelmed by shame and 'losing one's mind."[13]

The need for positive self-esteem – self-worth, respect from self and others, confidence, prestige, etc. – is a core driver in human behavior and motivation. We tend to take actions in life that satisfy this crucial need and to avoid its antipode. Shame, which relates to feelings of diminished self-worth, lack of control, and the feeling that one is not worthy of love and respect, causes stress and pain – both physically and emotionally. It dampens one's soul. It makes us feel less alive. And sometimes, feelings of shame and worthlessness can be so mentally debilitating that physical death feels like a more appealing alternative than living life spiritually dead. "Better to be left to rot on some high hill behind a rock, and be remembered, than to be buried alive in some stinking place [his life], and go to bed smelly like a garbage can every night," said 19-year old Charles Starkweather after he was sentenced to death for murdering 11 people in 1957.[14]

According to Gilligan, violent criminals harbor deep feelings of being ashamed, and they are ashamed of being ashamed – of course most don't often recognize it – and aggressive behavior is the language they use to express their need for respect, control, and a restored sense of self-worth. Men in many cultures are not supposed to talk about what's troubling them. It's a sign of weakness. Rather than articulating their feelings with words and admitting to pain, which risks their looking weak and further diminishing their sense of self-worth, some men instead mask their "weak" pain with "powerful" anger and violence. So again, as Gilligan has observed, much of the violent crime in his experience is about gaining respect (even if it is derived from fear and even if it is only for a moment) and saving face.[15] It's about avoiding or removing feelings of shame.

Now, relating the above abridged version of violent criminal behavior to money and our monetary system, in regions of high relative poverty, of gross wealth imbalance, where the material wealth of the game's winners is in plain sight of its losers, feelings of shame, inferiority, and inner humiliation are naturally fostered as the losers are reminded on a daily basis that they are in fact losers – that they are failures. And of course, the United States happens to be one of those regions in the world where wealth imbalance is significantly high. And as we are well aware, material wealth is highly valued in the US, probably more so than any other nation in the world; it is symbolic of social status. To be materially wealthy in our society is to be perceived as being successful, as having more value. Conversely, those who are materially poor are perceived as being less successful. They are perceived as having failed and typically don't elicit the same amount of attention, respect, and adulation garnered by their wealthy peers. Those living on the margins of society tend to be ignored and are oftentimes forgotten about; they don't really matter. And the thought of being looked down upon can call one to question his own sense of self-worth that is so crucial to a healthy life, which then spawns those feelings of shame and inferiority that can push a man to lash out so as to eradicate those "weak" feelings.

Shame and feelings of inferiority cultivate in many ways in the monetary game, not just in the form of citizens consciously and subconsciously comparing material wealth. When people become losers in society, they often must endure financial struggle and even poverty. And with financial struggle comes an inability to provide life necessities for one's family. Few things in life can bring more shame to a man than failing to put food on the table for his wife and children, as one of the hallmarks of being a man is his ability to provide for those he loves. And in the current state of the monetary game, as the wealth gap continues to expand, the pool of relative losers will inevitably increase, which means more citizens throughout society subjected to financial struggle and the feelings of shame and humiliation that accompany it. Needless to say, we shouldn't be surprised if violent crime doesn't slow down with current trends; actually, we shouldn't be surprised if it increases. If we examine the impact of the recent Great Recession, we see an uptick in suicide and crime.[16,17]

We also see a measurable rise in domestic abuse.[18,19] When the economy starts to tank, men and women start to lose their jobs and their ability to provide for their families. For people affected by economic downturns, they can start to get the sense that they have no control over their lives. That loss of control coupled with the feelings of shame and humiliation for "failing" to put food on the table can lead some men to dispense their aggression onto their spouses so as to restore pride and gain a sense of control – assuming he doesn't simply take out his frustration on himself through suicide. If a man can't control most aspects of his life, at least he can wield control over his spouse, or so he might think. Spouses and loved ones often become the victims of *displaced aggression*, where, though they might not be the source of a man's shame, they end up being the ones who absorb his pain through physical and/or emotional abuse. As an example of displaced aggression, let's say a man messes up a task at work that costs his company money. Let's say his boss then reprimands him and his colleagues scowl at him. Well, that probably wouldn't feel too good for the man, and he would probably question his value to the company; a part of him would feel ashamed for failing. Now, if tension, anger, or frustration builds inside him, he certainly cannot unleash it toward his boss or coworkers or else he risks termination. Instead, he might subconsciously suppress those negative emotions until he returns home and then release them onto subjects in a weaker position, like a spouse, child, or even a pet – subjects he has control over and who might not be able to fight back. In some cases, as we have seen in recent years in the United States, when enough anger, frustration, and tension pools in a man, his aggression is discharged onto *groups* of innocent and unrelated citizens, like when a man opens fire at a place of business or at some other public venue.

Violence and aggressive behavior can be about dominance and transferring one's negative feelings onto other individuals – indeed, such ambitions can ultimately be chiseled down to the need for acceptance, belonging, and respect, so as to avoid feelings of shame, worthlessness, and loss of self. The higher up on the social hierarchy pyramid one is, the more he is looked up to and/or revered, and the greater sense of control he has over his life. Patterns of social dominance and d*isplaced aggression*, where a man takes out frustrations on unrelated parties, are also exhibited by our primate relatives.[20] It has been found that in baboon tribes, if a superior baboon reprimands or shames a subordinate baboon, then that subordinate will find an inferior baboon and do the same, thus transferring his frustration and humiliation onto his lesser tribe member and restoring his sense of dignity. Then, the newly shamed baboon, feeling humiliated, will find a lesser baboon, and take his anger out on him. This pattern continues on down the line until there are no more baboons left to shame. All of the baboons are able to "save face," except for the baboon on the bottom of the herd's pecking order; he must swallow his negative emotions.

Crime is also often about preservation of the self; it's about salvaging one's identity and maintaining a semblance of dignity. Closely related to shame, or even a causal element, is social rejection. As I further expand upon in Chapter 9, we are social beings with a hardwired need to create meaningful relationships with others, to bond; and social alienation, to experience rejection from the herd causes literal pain in us.

In my assessments, it seems we have a distorted value system within our American culture (many other cultures are no different), where we often measure a person's worth based on the material junk he owns and not necessarily on his character. We revere men with yachts and money even if they are known scumbags, even if they are morally contemptible. And we strive to reach their social status by acquiring lifeless possessions, as we believe material excess signals success, and success earns respect. However, there are many among us within the zero-sum monetary game unable to acquire enough funds to access requisite material items to garner respect and social acceptance amongst local herds. Such material lack thus risks one's experiencing social rejection, and therefore the shame and loss of dignity that comes with it.

I bet we have all witnessed at one point in our lives, the poor kid or even an adult being ridiculed for wearing cheap or weathered clothing and subsequently being repelled by the pack. In situations like these, the target is cast aside; his confidence and self-worth diminish. So, sometimes, to elude the pain caused by social rejection and preserve the self, if a person lacks the financial means to purchase material items necessary to fit in with a social group, he might instead choose to steal from a store or assault someone for his or her possessions. Oftentimes robbery and theft are not necessarily about acquiring material goods out of avarice or lust for wealth, but it can be about elevating one's status amongst peers and gaining a greater sense of belonging. Social belonging is also part of the reason why we often observe poor citizens making purchases beyond their means; they are, in some ways, trying to fake the perception of wealth toward outsiders so as to appear more successful and preserve their self-image; conversely, they are trying to avoid appearing as failures so as to mitigate the sense of shame that arises from feeling like a failure. So, it's not always necessarily about financial ineptitude, but property crime and even living beyond one's financial means can be about boosting one's perceived social status, which can boost one's self-esteem and stave off the pain of feeling like a lesser person.

Again, we are incredibly complex creatures with core needs deeply embedded in our DNA; but, in analyzing and conferring with the works of behavioral experts, all of the inner sources of violent crime that I explained above can seemingly be reduced down to feelings of shame, humiliation, inferiority, worthlessness, etc. But, the more I think about it, those feelings, like shame, can be reduced even further to the need to fit in, to socially belong. We tend to only feel shame when comparing ourselves to others within our periphery. We feel shame when we get the sense that we are underperforming compared to others in our community and against the standards of success set by our culture as a whole. If we live in a tribe of headhunters, we would not feel shame for killing people. Rather, we would feel shame if we have acquired less heads than our fellow tribe members; we would feel like we weren't as successful, and therefore not as worthy as the top performers. If I was on a baseball team where everyone had a batting average of .200, I would feel pretty good about myself for hitting .230. I would be perceived by my baseball tribe as one of its more successful and valuable members. However, if I were on a team where everyone was batting .300, well, then suddenly my .230 batting average wouldn't feel so good. I would be one of the least valuable members of the team, and it would be hard to hold my head up with pride. I would get the sense I didn't belong, especially if teammates started sneering at me or whispering behind my back. The health-damaging belief that one does not or might not fit in produces feelings of shame.

So again, shame, self-esteem, and other negative feelings are relative, and they are almost always socially motivated; being the social creatures we are, they are almost always caused by our need for social belonging and acceptance to one degree or another. And the greater the gap in wealth and the more hierarchical separation in society, the greater the volume of people who feel detached from the "successful," materially wealthy in-groups. Feelings of failure and social rejection result.

Without spending an entire book on the subject, those, in a tiny nutshell, are but a few ways in which income and wealth inequality can foster violence and other criminal behaviors. When analyzing the global, competitive, game-like monetary system where the stakes are survival and depend on one's ability to acquire money within a finite pool, it is not difficult to see how violent paroxysms can grow and metastasize, both on small scales – a man taking out his inner anger and aggression on his family or himself or a poor teenager joining a violent gang – and on large scales – a disgruntled worker opening fire on coworkers or mass shootings. Aside from reducing a man's ability to purchase life necessities due to material lack, disproportionate wealth and relative poverty can cause social rejection and feelings of low self-worth, which breeds feelings of shame and despair, which can fuel violence and crime, as the perpetrators attempt to avoid or eliminate such painful feelings.

So, wealth and income inequality – is it right? Is it wrong? It doesn't matter. The rules of the game allow for it, and with survival at stake, right or wrong can be fed to the wolves. I am merely pointing out the positive correlation between violent crime and disproportionate wealth. If a society operates within a game-like system fueled by scarcity where life resources are distributed inequitably, then deplorable behavior is a predictable outcome and should be expected. The real question should be – do I want crime to exist? Do I enjoy its presence? If you don't want crime, then the only way we can realistically work toward reducing it is by confronting the monetary game that breeds group tension from inequality in the first place. And laws and imprisonment are wholly ineffective in curtailing criminality.

Laws have been enacted in an attempt to thwart thievery and other crimes, but if basic human needs are not met, laws are essentially useless. You can create a law that says "No Fishing in Lake Wisconsin," but if a person is starving and doesn't have access to food, he's going to fish in Lake Wisconsin (if that's the only source of food). His rational mind will effectively succumb to his survival instinct. He will weigh the risks against the rewards; the risks being whether to fish in the lake and potentially receive a fine or go to jail versus the reward, which is to fish and potentially catch dinner and avoid suffering and dying of starvation. When a man's life is threatened, he will do what he has to do to stay alive. The same goes for if his soul is threatened.

We've also tried incarcerating criminals. Compared to the rest of the world, the United States houses more prisoners than any other country. In 2019, America topped the global list by locking away 655 criminals per 100,000 people.[21] All of the nations on the list directly below the US could be considered underdeveloped or "third world," while no other industrialized nation comes even close to that rate. But, if we refer back to the high rate of violent crime that persists in America, we can conclude that its punitive system does not work. Instead, Dr. James Gilligan asserts that US prisons essentially act as graduate schools for crime; not as rehabilitation centers preparing criminals to re-enter the "civilized" world.

So, laws, imprisonment, and gun control do very little to reduce criminal behavior. We can tell the losers of the game to simply "work harder," or "play the game better," or "quit being pussies," but as history and the numbers show, such verbal "encouragement" also does nothing in preventing violence and crime. Bottom line, as long as civilians are competing against each other to obtain the scarce tool of money to access the goods to survive, gross inequality will persist, stress, tension, and anger will continue to build, and violence will live on in perpetuity. We must confront the game hiding behind the mask of *economy*.

## 6.6 TRUST: THERE'S A PILL FOR THAT

Back in 2014, fresh off of having "finished" my first book and finally allowing myself some much needed R&R, I started to feel sick. The first of the symptoms I experienced was extreme exhaustion. I was tired all the time. And no matter how much I slept, I felt like a living corpse. I paid little mind to this feeling, however, because I figured it was just a phase and that it would eventually pass as it always did.

It wasn't until I was feeling my neck one morning and felt two hard lumps that I thought, *uh oh, I better get my ass to the doctor.* I didn't want to panic since swollen lymph nodes can mean a million different things, but I couldn't help but think…cancer.

Nevertheless, I visited a local physician in Burbank. He ordered lab tests, I had my blood drawn, and the results came back showing Epstein-Barr Virus (EBV).

*Epstein-Barr Virus? What the hell does that mean*, I thought to myself.

"Mono," the doctor informed me.

"How?" I asked. "I haven't been kissin' nobody."

After he explained that the virus can be acquired through various means, he simply advised me to go home, rest, and take'er easy for a while. So I did just that.

A few months had passed, and I was curious where my EBV levels were at, so I went back to the doctor – though this time it was a clinic in Wisconsin. When I sat down with the physician, I told him the basics – that I was feeling lethargic, had swollen lymph nodes, and that my blood tests from Burbank indicated I had mono. He listened. Then, he began probing me with questions. As we talked, somehow we settled onto the topic of cancer, and I informed him of Kaitlyn's passing over a year earlier.

"That must have been tough," he said.

"Yes it was. Every aspect of it was horrible in every way. The worst moment in my life," I added.

"How has your energy level been?"

"Umm…not good. I still feel tired a lot. It's been difficult to perform physical activities."

"Have you had any…thoughts of suicide or of harming yourself," he continued.

"No, nothing like that."

"I suppose you experience swings of feeling up and down, huh?"

"Yeah, most days I feel okay, but there are certainly some days where it's like I'm reliving the situation all over again, and I feel, well, like crap," I replied. "But I suppose that's probably normal for people dealing with loss."

"Yeah. Yeah." He sat in his chair staring at his clipboard for a moment. "You know, it sounds like you might have been and may continue to be dealing with depression."

"Umm…I suppose that's possible," I said.

"Here, let me write you a prescription."

*Huh?*

"Oh, no, I think that's okay. I mean, sure there have been moments where I have felt depressed, but I don't feel depressed overall."

"Okay. But are you sure? I can just write you up a prescription really quick. I think it could help you with your down moods and energy levels."

"No, yeah, I'm good. But I'll keep it in mind just in case."

I was polite, but all I could think was, *what the F? Why is this man so damn eager to push pills on me?* All I could surmise was that maybe his office was having a slow month and he needed to drum up more business, or, that maybe he himself was receiving kickbacks from whatever drug company was supplying him with the goods; denial on my end was certainly out of the question (I say with tongue-in-cheek). Needless to say, I felt like he was trying to take advantage of me while I was in a perceived "vulnerable" state of mind, and I found myself no longer trusting him. Which is sad, because I had always seen men in white coats as the pinnacle of education, prestige, and integrity of the highest order.

But anyway, that situation, of suspecting my well-meaning doctor was trying to take advantage of me for financial gain got me to thinking. With money's seductive whispers behind the ears of every man, can we ever fully trust anybody in our global society? Can we ever be 100% confident in a product's integrity or in the sincerity of a businessman's intentions? Sadly, it seems the answer is no. With survival at stake, no man is immune to the pressures of the game; money can sniff out weakness even in the most "morally impenetrable" of us. And no industry is impervious to its influence, whether we are talking about the auto sales and repairs industry, the food industry, media, politics, or even within the sacred medical profession. When a mechanic suggests you should replace your brake pads even though you had just replaced them two months prior, because he stands to make money off of you, you cannot be certain if he actually believes your car needs new brake pads or if he is simply looking to make a quick buck off of a naïve soul. When you see a doctor and he wants to do an x-ray of your ribs because he believes that your lower ribs are abnormally disconnected from the rest of your ribcage, you cannot fully trust whether the doctor actually has your health and wellbeing in mind, or if he sees an opportunity to charge your insurance company and make a little extra dough at your physical expense.

See, not only do our scarcity-driven, competition-based monetary systems serve as a core precondition behind the detrimental, undesirable side effects I've already touched on earlier – poverty, war, ecological degradation, etc. – but public TRUST, another vital element within any society, also suffers mightily. And would you believe, the more competitive a society and the greater the socioeconomic inequality, the less trust that exists amongst its population? Data seems to support this correlation. So, it should come as no surprise that with wealth and income gaps continuing to widen in the United States, public trust has hit historical lows within its imaginary walls.[1,2] Without trust, how can any civilization expect to operate in a healthy manner? It can't. And if trust is in decay, how can a civilization expect to reverse that trend if its people are at constant odds, if they are in constant competition with one another to obtain the very thing that grants them the opportunity to survive? I'll say it again. It can't.

Money erodes the trust in everything.

And like I mentioned with crime, I think we can all feel it on a conscious and subconscious level. We don't trust each other. Sure, on a micro-level, we probably trust our friends and family to an extent (sometimes not even them), but on a macro-level, public trust has been hanging by a thread. There's a gun at every corner, and suspicion behind every handshake.

I have already talked about various countries and civilizations throughout history flat out lying to the public to incite war for material gain – barbed designs wrapped up in words of wool.

I've talked a bit about the abomination of human creation that is mainstream media with its manipulation of the public by means of propaganda, semi-truths, and outright lies at the behest of men who stand to gain considerable advantage over other men. We can't trust the very institution that is supposed to deliver us unbiased, unfiltered information, as "fake news" has become so common that it's often used as a depraved punch line in our country.

I will be talking at greater length in the next chapter about Planned Obsolescence – the engineering of products with built-in death dates or designing products to fail. We often think we can, and we ought to be able to trust that products are created to their optimum capacity and with the utmost integrity, but they are not. Every industry participates in Planned Obsolescence in some form. And they often have to if they want to stay in the game.

We already know that we cannot trust many of our elected politicians. Those venal creatures who consistently accept bribes from lobbyists of every industry while pretending to act in the best interest of the very public that elected them into office.

So, since I've already referenced trust in various ways to institutions relating to media, war, politics, etc., I am instead using this section as an excuse to focus on another institution we ought to be able to trust. One that we often place our health and wellbeing into the hands of – the medical industry. Specifically, I am going to home in on Psychiatry for a hot minute. I hate to editorialize – then again who am I kidding here, much of this book is me editorializing – but I don't hold psychiatry in very high regard, at least so far as it pertains to the administration of its "medicine" and the drugs they prescribe. "But Travis, you flagrantly misinformed, uneducated buffoon," you might say, "why should we listen to you? You're not a doctor!" I cannot refute that assertion. That is why almost everything I have written in this section in regard to psychiatry and the pharmaceutical industry has been borrowed from psychiatrists, psychologists, neurologists, and other medical professionals. And from what I have gleaned, it seems the medical, scientific, and even a healthy portion of the psychiatric community do not hold certain psychiatric methods in very high esteem either, as its disorders and diagnostic tools are not rooted in objective facts and hard science, but rather on subjective opinions and superficial symptoms.

Before I express my utter dismay for psychiatry and why it cannot be trusted, I am first going to talk about the industry that's taken the greatest advantage of mental illness and has done its best to destroy the integrity of medicine in our world – the pharmaceutical industry. Now, I shouldn't be so harsh since drug companies are partially responsible for the development, manufacturing, and distribution of modern treatments that have helped millions of people, but the industry has grown to a $1.2 trillion global market as of 2018,[3] and with such a large pool of money to compete for, many companies have shifted priorities from the health and wellbeing of individuals to capturing as much of that revenue pie as possible, no matter what it takes, even if it means exploiting some of society's most vulnerable among us – the sick.

One of the tactics used by drug companies to generate sales and compete against other companies is to use clinical trials and studies to manipulate physicians and the public. When it comes to conducting these clinical trials or reporting study information in an ethical manner, it has been discovered time and time again that drug companies have falsified data, included or excluded human subjects to skew numbers in their favor, paid doctors to sign off on studies they didn't take part in, or intentionally hidden harmful outcomes to win FDA approval or physician acceptance.

For example, I reference a well-known case involving pharmaceutical behemoth GSK (GlaxoSmithKline; SmithKline Beecham during the study) and psychiatrist Dr. Martin Keller out of Brown University. In 2001, Keller was listed as lead author for a published study "proving" that GSK's SSRI drug, Paxil (Paroxetine), was not only effective in treating children with depression, but that it was also safe: "Paroxetine is generally well tolerated and effective for major depression in adolescents."[4] Based on the report and the well-credentialed names backing the findings, doctors began prescribing Paxil to children before it was even approved by the FDA for pediatric use. Thus, in 2002 alone, roughly 2.1 million prescriptions for Paxil were written for children and adolescents in the US, equating to $55 million in sales – many of which were written by family practitioners and pediatricians.[5] Word traveled fast!

In 2004, however, the State of New York sued GSK, alleging the company issued false and misleading claims and that they intentionally concealed negative information concerning the safety and efficacy of Paxil for treating depression in children. The complaint filed by New York Attorney General, Eliot Spitzer, asserted: "GSK misled and deceived physicians and consequently the patients who relied on their professional judgment."[6]

But what possibly could they have found to warrant a lawsuit against the Paxil manufacturer?

In the words of Heath Ledger's *Joker*, "Where, do we, begin…?" First, investigators found that GSK conducted three separate studies – #329, #377, and #701 – to test the safety and efficacy of Paxil in adolescents with major depressive disorder (MDD). However, they only ended up publishing the results of Study #329. Why? Because both of the studies that went unpublished, #377 and #701, failed to demonstrate Paxil's efficacy compared to placebo. In fact, in Study #701, the placebo group actually outperformed Paxil. Even in Study #329 the results were mixed, as Paxil failed to demonstrate superiority to placebo on its two primary measures.[7]

In terms of safety, all three studies combined showed that subjects on Paxil were twice as likely to experience suicidal behavior compared to the placebo group. And in a fourth study – #716 – where there was no placebo group, suicidal behavior occurred in 12.5 percent of its adolescent subjects.[8] When the FDA performed an independent analysis of the clinical trial data, they calculated a whopping 5.9-fold increase in suicidal ideation for subjects on Paxil.[9]

However, when there's money to be made, one can expect ethics to go the way of the Dodo bird, and GSK wasn't about to let unfavorable information regarding its now-best-selling drug ruin its ability to increase revenue and please shareholders. So they made a provably conscious effort to suppress the negative findings. During the investigation, an internal email was discovered where GSK officials seem to admit their knowledge of Paxil's ineffectiveness by saying:

> "Essentially the study **did not really show Paxil was effective in treating adolescent depression**, which is not something we want to publicize. However, we should prepare a Q&A and key messages in case reporters do cover this study."

Not only did GSK make apparent their knowledge and awareness of Paxil's ineffectiveness, but also their intent on shielding that very important information from the public, including outside physicians. In an additional internal document sent to company members in 1998, GSK stated their intent to "effectively manage the dissemination of these data in order to minimize any potential negative commercial impact." Translation – 'Control information. Keep negative data away from the public. Secure the bottom line.' Hence, their decision to bury studies #377 and #701 and only publish study #329, showing Paxil in a mostly positive light.

Although GSK was spreading the word in America that Paxil was safe and effective in children, they were humming a different melody in other countries. When it came time to gain approval from European and Canadian drug-regulation agencies, the studies began to raise issues. In assessing the various Paxil studies, the United Kingdom's Medicines and Healthcare products Regulatory Agency (MHRA) not only discovered the drug was ineffective, but they also found that the risk of self-harm and suicidal behavior was 1.5 to 3.2 times greater compared to placebo.[10] The MHRA concluded that Paxil "should not be used in children and adolescents under the age of 18 years to treat depressive illness."[11]

GSK responded both to the concerned agencies and UK physicians with similar statements. In documents submitted to drug-regulatory agencies, *GSK admitted* that all of their studies "*failed* to separate paroxetine from placebo overall and so do not provide strong evidence of efficacy…"[12] And in a separate letter to UK physicians, they said, "clinical trials in children and adolescents under 18 years of age failed to demonstrate efficacy in Major Depressive Disorder and that there was a doubling of the rate of reporting of adverse events in the paroxetine group compared with placebo, including…emotional liability."[13] Suicidal behavior is included within Emotional Liability. Then, lastly, in a submission to the European Agency for the Evaluation of Medicinal Products (EMEA) GSK stated: "It must be concluded that the benefit-risk balance is in favour of not treating children and adolescents [diagnosed with MDD] with paroxetine…," and that, "…in view of a safety signal concerning a possible increase in suicidal behavior, particularly in adolescents with MDD, the use of paroxetine in children and adolescents with MDD *cannot be recommended*."[14]

Clearly, GSK knew its drug was not only ineffective, but that it was also unsafe for pediatric consumption. But would that stop them from trying to mislead and influence physicians and dispense their lucrative product within American borders? Nope. In fact, they continued to encourage their own Sales Representatives – handsomely paid pawns of industry – to tout Paxil's effectiveness to American physicians. In a memo sent out to Paxil sales reps, a GSK Paxil Product Manager stated: "Paxil demonstrates REMARKABLE efficacy and safety in the treatment of adolescent depression."[15] Among many bullet points, the memo also contained a line that said, "Paxil was significantly more effective than Placebo," even though it wasn't, before it ended with:

> "In conclusion, the findings of this study provide evidence of the efficacy and safety of Paxil in the treatment of adolescent depression. Here's another example of GlaxoSmithKline's commitment to Psychiatry by bringing forth 'cutting edge' scientific data. Paxil is truly a REMARKABLE product that continues to demonstrate efficacy, even in this understudied population."

With that pep talk, ignorant, yet galvanized sales reps – often former athletes, cheerleaders, ex-military men, etc.[16] – took to the clinics and charmed the socks off of physicians across America, using their skills in persuasion to induce prescriptions of GSK's "wonder" drug to children.

Additionally, even though GSK admitted to foreign agencies and foreign physicians of Paxil's ineffectiveness and safety liabilities, the company again failed to disclose that same info to American physicians. Instead, they carefully framed statements and bullet points to avoid lying while at the same time keeping negative information from leaking. For example, in a 2003 press release to the American public, GSK made no mention of their admissions to European and Canadian agencies, stating merely, "not a single person [who participated in the pediatric paroxetine trials] committed suicide."[17] And, they weren't wrong.

Okay, I mentioned Dr. Martin Keller several paragraphs earlier, so where exactly does he enter the fold in all of this? Well, as a recap, when Study #329 was published in 2001, Dr. Keller was credited as its Lead Author. The only thing is, he didn't actually author the article. In fact, GSK hired a third-party PR firm, Scientific Therapeutics Information (STI), to act as a "ghostwriter" for the study.[18] Now, on the surface, using the services of a company that specializes in the writing aspect of studies doesn't seem like a bad idea – I mean, doctors make their living doctorin', not writing, after all. And in the past, it was commonplace for a lead researcher of a study to have a writing assistant for improving grammar, structure, etc. within a paper; the writing assistant would then be credited in the article for his role. However, ghostwriters typically don't receive credit in medical papers they scribe – their participation remains hidden from public view – and since ghostwriters are often hired by the drug company to write the medical articles, concerns have been raised in regards to the authenticity, credibility, and transparency of the research papers.

Physicians trust and often rely on medical journals to acquire information regarding a drug's safety and efficacy in treating disease; they might even use the information within such journals to make decisions about which drugs to stock or which drugs to prescribe. Unfortunately, pharmaceutical companies are keen to this, and they use that knowledge to their advantage, as medical journals have quickly evolved from educational tools to marketing weapons with the sole intent of attracting physicians and pushing as much product off the shelf as possible. And by hiring ghostwriting firms, drug companies are granted full control over what information leaves the stable and what information is kept locked away from public vision. They can oversee every aspect of an article's creation, giving them the unique ability to exaggerate the positive aspects of their drug and underemphasize the negatives, regardless of the actual study results, and in some cases they might even go as far as falsifying data. And at the end of the process, they have the ability to slap the names of reputable doctors on the study to give it the prestige it needs when entering the marketplace. Physicians, on the other hand, have no way of knowing when they are being misled or blatantly lied to, which puts their patients' lives at risk when they prescribe drugs that carry hidden dangers.

For instance, in the early-2000s Merck began publishing articles touting the effectiveness of its drug, Vioxx, in combating pain and arthritis, catapulting it to one of their top selling drugs; it brought in $2.5 billion in 2003.[19] However, it was later revealed that the corporation hired a ghostwriting firm, Elsevier, to pen medical articles for its Vioxx studies.[20] Again, this might not seem like a big deal, but where problems start to arise is when the paying drug company begins to influence what information they want the ghostwriters to include or exclude in what are supposed to be unbiased studies. And that seemed to be the case with Merck and Vioxx. Court documents indicate that Merck officials were well aware that use of Vioxx increased the risk of heart attacks and other cardiovascular events in patients, but in exercising editorial control over the creation process of its medical articles through its ghostwriter, they intentionally withheld that information from the public for fear that it would hurt sales. They even omitted the deaths of some of the trial subjects.

What's worse (I suppose patients dying is the worst part of this all), but what is also bad is when Merck eventually published medical journals for Vioxx, they listed names of doctors who had little or zero involvement with the research.[21,22] Dr. James Bertouch was one of those doctors. When he picked up a 2003 medical journal, he was surprised as any to see his name included as one of the members of a Vioxx study's editorial board, stating, "…I didn't know anything about the journal."[23] He resigned shortly after. Then, as a consequence of Merck failing to disclose the cardiovascular risks of Vioxx, patients began experiencing heart attacks, some resulting in death. And when later studies finally proved Vioxx significantly increased the risk of cardiovascular events, Merck, feeling the pressure, decided to pull the drug from market in 2004.[24]

It has become commonplace for drug companies to not only sponsor studies and have articles written in their favor, but for them to later seek out and pay doctors to sign off as Lead Author or Contributor of the clinical trial after the research has already been conducted. In referring back to the case of Merck and Vioxx, the first author of one of their studies, Jeffrey Lisse stated:

> "Merck designed the trial, paid for the trial, ran the trial…"

and that:

> "Merck came to me after the study was completed."[25]

In 2009, a University of Wisconsin cardiologist said he was approached multiple times to put his name on drug-company-sponsored material, but declined, stating it is tantamount to "plagiarism."[26] And psychiatrist David Dunner out of the University of Washington admitted that he never saw the raw data for a 1995 Paxil study in which he signed off for as an author.[27]

Such a practice is dishonest and misleading since drug companies can make a study look like it was completed by an independent, neutral group of experts, which is an important selling point for outside physicians. When a medical professional reads a study and sees well-credentialed names attached, they assume those doctors actually conducted and wrote the study, which adds a sense of credibility and confidence in the study's findings. However, if they knew the articles were written by ghostwriters and not the doctors listed, they might be less likely to trust the article, the research, and the drug, and choose to treat their patients via a different method, which would undoubtedly hurt sales revenue.

In the 1990s, Parke-Davis (acquired by Pfizer) commissioned two companies to write articles supporting its drug, Neurontin (Gabapentin), for off-label use in treating bipolar disorder, migraines, and other conditions. Even though study data actually proved the drug to be ineffective in treating such conditions, a series of articles were, nevertheless, published concluding that the drug was effective. Pfizer then began recruiting and paying doctors to promote its benefits to outside medical professionals; one doctor reportedly received over $300,000 to promote the "blockbuster" drug to other physicians and students at medical conferences.[28] This misleading marketing campaign along with the Pfizer-produced fake articles helped launch the drug's sales performance from $97 million in 1995 to $2.7 billion in 2003;[29] through 2004, off-label use of Neurontin accounted for about 90% of the drug's sales[30] – a swing and a drive for big pharma! And sadly for the public (though happily for the drug company), once a seed is planted, it is mighty difficult to dig that thing out; well after Neurontin was exposed for being ineffective in treating migraines and other ailments, hospitals and clinics continued to prescribe it for those exact conditions.

These instances of pharmaceutical companies hiring ghostwriters and engineering articles to favor their drug, while omitting critical information, and even burying negative studies are not one-off cases. From AstraZeneca concealing multiple "cursed" studies of its antipsychotic, Seroquel, while trying to "put a positive spin" on the drug,[31] to Pfizer downplaying negative side effects of Zoloft,[32] to Wyeth covering up that its drug, Prempro, increased the risk of breast cancer in women,[33] to Eli Lilly purposely designing studies so their antipsychotic, Zyprexa, would beat out competing Haloperidol,[34] to Forest Laboratories hiding negative results of Celexa and Lexapro in treating depression in children while paying kickbacks to physicians to encourage them to prescribe their SSRI,[35] unethical behavior amongst drug companies seems to be the norm rather than an exception.

According to findings by the United Kingdom House of Commons Health Committee in 2005, roughly 75% of clinical trials printed in *The Lancet*, the *New England Journal of Medicine*, and the *Journal of the American Medical Association* were paid for by drug companies.[36] And, of those articles, it is estimated that over 50% are ghostwritten.[37] Moreover, a separate report found that roughly 56% of the published studies it assessed showed that the drug being tested was not as effective as its study claimed.[38]

And in 2008, psychologist Irving Kirsch completed a meta-analysis where he and his colleagues reviewed every single FDA study, published and unpublished, of four new-generation antidepressants: Paxil, Prozac, Effexor, Serzone.[39] In their findings, Kirsch and his team discovered that the "Meta-analyses of antidepressant medications have reported only modest benefits over placebo treatment, and when unpublished trial data are included, the benefit falls below accepted criteria for clinical significance."[40]

This is a very disconcerting trend, because medical professionals have no way of knowing whether or not they can trust clinical studies now, which, again, puts patients at risk and makes a physician's job much more difficult than it already is. As former Editor-in-Chief of the New England Journal of Medicine, Dr. Marcia Angell, sadly concludes:

> "It is simply no longer possible to believe much of the clinical research that is published, or to rely on the judgment of trusted physicians or authoritative medical guidelines. I take no pleasure in this conclusion, which I reached slowly and reluctantly over my two decades as an editor of the New England Journal of Medicine."[41]

Okay, so circling back to Martin Keller one last time, he became just another cog in the wheel of unethical behavior in the pharmaceutical industry and psychiatry. Not only were the misleading results of the Paxil Study #329 written by a ghost author, but in a 2006 sworn deposition, it seemed apparent that Dr. Keller didn't know much about the study. When asked various questions, like whether or not he reviewed the raw data or had discussions with the ghostwriter, Sally Laden, Keller's common answer was, "I don't recall…," or, "I don't remember…"[42] On top of that, it was discovered that in 1997 and 1998, GSK paid Dr. Keller roughly $1 million in consulting fees – you might consider that a conflict of interest. An investigation also revealed that some children were hospitalized during the clinical trial, and some had to be removed from the study due to severe side effects, however, they were not counted in the trial data, skewing results in favor of their drug.[43]

Nevertheless, in the case of the State of New York versus GSK, the drug company agreed to pay a measly $2.5 million in 2004[44] – a mere flick of the ear – for failure to disclose data regarding Paxil. This example just proves that the ratio of reward to risk is just too high for a drug company not to entertain the idea of printing misleading results. The staggering revenue numbers speak for themselves. In all of the cases I've mentioned briefly, drug companies have agreed to pay fines totaling amounts much less than the revenue those drugs brought in. (It must be noted, however, that GSK continued to face lawsuits regarding Paxil and a few of its other drugs, like Wellbutrin, and in 2012 they were fined a whopping $3 billion by the United States Department of Justice, the largest sum ever.)[45]

This pattern of dishonesty by drug companies does not simply end at printing misleading study results, no siree! The far-reaching tentacles of corporate psychiatry in concert with big pharma have slithered into every crevice of society. Creating the drug and manufacturing misleading or falsified studies is just the beginning. The next step is an all-out blitz of a marketing campaign, which seeks to increase visibility, persuade doctors and the public that their product is the best, and ultimately peddle as many drugs as possible. Little concern is actually paid to the health and wellbeing of the cattle, I mean people, consuming these drugs, as is illustrated in the cases where companies know of severe adverse side effects or ineffectiveness, but decide to keep that information hidden.

The indoctrination process starts by wining, dining, and seducing psychiatrists, grooming some into becoming "credible" spokesmen for their drug, and paying them handsomely to give lectures at medical conventions, conferences, etc. As the 2012 court ruling against GSK and Paxil points out: "The United States further alleges that GSK sponsored dinner programs, lunch programs, spa programs and similar activities to promote the use of Paxil in children and adolescents. GSK paid a speaker to talk to an audience of doctors and paid for the meals or spa treatment for the doctors who attended."[46]

And of course, the goal is to induce sales, so like their biased studies, the speakers recruited by drug companies aren't trained to talk about the negative aspects of a drug or its clinical trial. No! They're trained to highlight why it's so "great." Now, if we were talking about a salesman trying to sell vacuum cleaners or makeup products, having them under-report the negative aspects of their product wouldn't be as much of a big deal, because what's the worst that can happen? The vacuum doesn't pick up dirt efficiently or is programmed to mutter insults at you? In that case, you're only out a few bucks, and you can move on to another product. But with pharmaceutical drugs, we are talking about the health of individuals, and withholding information can lead to life-threatening, life-altering consequences, as I've stated. If information is not being fully disseminated, then doctors attending these lectures are not getting the complete picture they need to properly care for their patients. But again, these speaking engagements aren't about educating health professionals, they are all about marketing drugs and making sales. These lectures seek to condition and encourage other psychiatrists, physicians, and medical students to choose their drug when treating patients. And oftentimes physicians and other medical professionals are none the wiser as to a drug's sinister roots. They have no reason to be skeptical that the information they are receiving isn't entirely accurate or planted with bias. If a well-known doctor is supporting it, it must be reliable.

Additionally, because physicians are the primary channels of distribution, most of a drug company's marketing budget is spent on advertising to, charming, and manipulating physicians. Of the $26.9 billion spent on marketing in 2016, according to a Dartmouth study, roughly $20 billion of that was devoted toward advertising to and hustling physicians, which might include buying them material gifts, paying for lunches, giving out drug samples, rewarding them with lucrative speaking engagements, paid luxury vacations, etc.[47,48] And that amount doesn't include under-the-table kickbacks or "consulting fees" doctors might receive by drug companies for prescribing or promoting their product. Emory University psychiatrist, Dr. Charles Nemeroff, received $2.8 million from drug companies between 2000 and 2007, much of which went unreported, to promote antidepressants to physicians at various medical conferences and symposiums.[49,50,51] In 2013, Johnson & Johnson was fined $2.2 billion for providing kickbacks to doctors to prescribe Risperdal to elderly patients suffering from dementia and to children diagnosed with ADHD; the fine also included misleading claims and false advertising of the product.[52] The practice of psychiatrists accepting a nominal fee from drug companies to spread the word to other physicians has led psychiatrist Dr. Fuller Torrey to say, "…the present system is approaching a high-class form of professional prostitution."[53]

Dr. R. Adams Dudley, pulmonologist and professor at the University of California, San Francisco, says it's commonly known that "if you want to influence a doctor, get a meal, get a gift."[54] And thanks in part to the Open Payments initiative enacted in 2010, we are just beginning to see how true that statement is.[55,56] Using the Open Payments database, researchers discovered that out of over 900,000 doctors, about 450,000 received some form of financial gift from drug companies in 2015.[57] Most material gifts do not amount to a substantial sum of money, but for those physicians agreeing to lecture to other medical professionals at seminars and conferences on behalf of drug companies, they might be paid thousands of dollars.

Obviously, you don't need me to highlight the clear conflict of interest created by doctors receiving kickbacks from drug companies, so I'll just provide one more example, instead, of a company recruiting a doctor willing to "go the extra mile" on their behalf. It was 2003, and Chicago-based psychiatrist Dr. Michael Reinstein was approached by IVAX Pharmaceuticals (acquired by Teva) with an offer he could have refused, but chose not to. The offer was, IVAX would pay Dr. Reinstein $50,000 per year in "consulting fees," which would involve speaking engagements, and Reinstein would prescribe Clozapine, a generic form of antipsychotic, to his patients.[58] Even though Clozapine was considered a "last resort" drug due to its serious side effects, which included a potentially deadly decrease in white blood cells, seizures, inflammation of the heart muscle, and increased mortality in the elderly, Dr. Reinstein began aggressively prescribing it to his patients – 75% of his 400 patients at one nursing home received Clozapine, a lawsuit stated.[59]

Not only did Reinstein receive his $50,000 annual consulting fee, but the shrink was also showered with gifts that included tickets to sporting events, all-expense-paid trips to Miami, luxury cruises, and free medication. This was all on top of his normal salary for practicing psychiatry. The gettin' was good!

In 2012, however, his empire mostly turned to rubble when the US Attorney for the Northern District of Illinois filed a lawsuit against him, alleging that he submitted more than 140,000 claims to Medicare and Medicaid for Clozapine prescriptions and that he falsely stated providing "pharmacological management" for his patients at over 30 nursing homes and long-term care facilities in the area.[60] In 2016, Dr. Reinstein pleaded guilty and was sentenced to 9 months in prison and ordered to pay about $4.3 million in total fines, while IVAX/Teva agreed to pay the Department of Justice and State of Illinois $27.6 million for their role in bribing the doctor to induce drug prescriptions.[61,62]

Reinstein's intermingling with big pharma started even earlier in the 1990s when Novartis paid him over $200,000 to speak on behalf of Clozaril, its brand name version of clozapine, and tout the drug's efficacy to other physicians. To think, for almost two decades doctors, medical students, sales reps, and other medical professionals sat as audience members and listened to this man speak, likely absorbing the tainted information as truth. Then, I imagine many of them took the information gleaned from his lectures (and why wouldn't they) and applied it to their own practices, using their newfound "knowledge" to prescribe the drug to their patients. And their patients, having no reason to suspect any sort of foul motives, were under the impression they were being given honest and reliable care. The issue of Reinstein receiving kickbacks and acting in the best interest of IVAX and his wallet rather than his patients is just the tip of the iceberg, unfortunately.[63]

But, like I alluded, the influence of drug companies only starts with the manipulation of physicians. The other tentacles of big pharma operate simultaneously throughout normal society by infiltrating families through their television sets, planting seeds into the minds of adolescents through school initiatives, bribing government officials or institutions to act in their favor, poisoning the minds of future physicians on college campuses, and more. Due to political pressures and the financial influence of drug companies, the United States remains as one of only two countries in the world that allows for Direct-To-Consumer (DTC) advertising of prescription medications – New Zealand is the other country; DTC advertising is illegal in all other countries. And obviously the goal of DTC marketing is to make regular, uneducated people think they have a disease and encourage them to march into their doctor's office and request or even demand a certain drug. And it works. Not only is the United States the leader in per capita drug spending (also due to high drug costs), but studies have found that drugs advertised directly to consumers are prescribed at a much higher rate than drugs that are not.

Unfortunately, what the above cases illustrate is that even if a "medical expert" claims a drug to be safe and effective, we cannot actually know if that expert is telling the truth due to the amount of misleading or falsified studies. In fact, the expert himself cannot know for sure if what he is saying is truth, even if he is the most well-meaning physician in the world, and I have to think most physicians are well-meaning and want nothing more than to help their patients. And what makes the vetting process even more difficult is that pharmaceutical companies only need two positive studies comparing their drug to placebo to win FDA-approval (just one can do the trick for off-label prescribing). So, even if their drug has had negative results in 10 other studies, as long as a drug company can eke out positive data in just one or two studies, it can publish those studies alone and bury the others. And when that well-meaning physician is learning about a drug, he will only read the two published studies while remaining completely oblivious to the 10 failed ones. A 2008 report published in the New England Journal of Medicine found that of the FDA-registered antidepressant studies they assessed, roughly 31% went unpublished due largely to those studies producing unfavorable results – only the positive ones were published.[64]

Alright, so I've just spent the last many pages focusing on the deplorable behavior of the pharmaceutical industry, so where does psychiatry fit into this whole mess? Well, as I will point out, due to psychiatry's arbitrary method of labeling mental illness, where all diseases of the mind are concluded upon following subjective debate and sometimes arguments rather than on biological, empirical evidence, mental illness is ripe for pharmaceutical exploitation. And nowhere in my criticism do I imply that mental illness does not exist. Not at all! Mental illness is a very real issue. My frustration is born from the idea that individual men have identified a vulnerable and untapped demographic – including foster children, orphans, and military men and women – and they use that demographics' vulnerability for their financial gain.

The exploitation begins with the drug companies. They have product. They have supply – drugs. And it is very easy and cheap for them to create more supply. And of course, more supply means more profit potential. However, in order to move that supply off the shelf and into the bloodstream of American consumers, a company needs two things; they need a market, and they need demand. As for creating a market within psychiatry, the bible for mental illness, the DSM-5 does just the trick.

The Diagnostic and Statistical Manual of Mental Disorders, now on its 5th and largest edition (the DSM-5), not including revisions, lists and classifies nearly 300 mental disorders and is the most widely used publication in the US in helping psychiatrists swiftly diagnose and "treat" illness in patients. However, each edition has drawn heavy criticism, even by those in high positions within the psychiatric community because the mental disorders included in the manual are not decided upon based on scientific or empirical evidence. Most of the disorders, like binge-eating, premenstrual dysphoric disorder, internet addiction disorder, or anxiety are added to the text by means of subjective opinions, biased studies, and debate. Whereas cancer is detectable, measurable, and definable using various imaging tools, biopsies, blood tests, and so on, mental illness cannot be defined from a pathophysiological standpoint. It does not show up in blood tests or brains scans, as Allen Frances, psychiatrist and former Chairman in charge of developing the DSM-4, acknowledges:

> "There are no objective tests in psychiatry, no x-ray, laboratory, or exam finding that says definitively that someone does or does not have a mental disorder."[65]

Therefore, when creating the DSM, potential disorders are merely discussed amongst a committee and are literally voted on as to whether or not they should be classified as a disorder – about the most unscientific and most unreliable process of determining disease one can concoct. But, drug companies use this arbitrary and ambiguous method of classifying mental illness to their financial advantage.

Because the DSM is based on opinion and consensus, disorders are continually voted into and out of existence. For example, voted into the first edition of the DSM in 1952 as a mental disorder was Homosexuality. After years of debate, criticism, and adjustments to the definition, all forms of Homosexuality were finally voted out of existence as mental illness in 1987 with the revised version of the DSM-3.

Such a method of classifying disease is anti-science, yet psychiatrists and general physicians lean on this manual to diagnose and treat patients. Because psychiatrists and physicians are unable to observe or measure the exact mechanisms in the brain or body producing the symptoms of mental illness, their eventual diagnoses essentially boil down to a guess. Maybe a patient's depression is brought on by low serotonin levels, or maybe a person's psychotic episode was induced by an over-activity of glutamate – life circumstances are too often neglected. And based on what ultimately becomes a guess, without really knowing what is happening in the brain, and without really knowing if a person's chemical levels are out of balance, and based off of what might be unreliable or false information from drug-company-sponsored clinical studies, psychiatrists prescribe drugs that actually alter the chemical flow within arguably the most important and most delicate organ in our body. When a psychiatrist supposes his patient's depression is caused by a serotonin deficiency, though he can't know for sure if that's the case, he still might prescribe an SSRI drug that actually alters the flow of serotonin within the brain. Could you imagine if an oncologist prescribed chemotherapy and radiation to his patient for what sounds like cancer based on the symptoms she subjectively described?

All psychotropic medications target delicate processes and disrupt the natural flow of neurotransmitters in the brain, which often leads to unpredictable, sometimes hazardous, and sometimes irreversible effects. They throw drugs against the wall and hope one sticks. And if one does stick, it can only treat the symptoms – until a tolerance is built up within the patient – and does not attack the root cause of the mental illness; rather, it distracts from confronting or locating the source of a sufferer's problems.

Again, this institutionally-accepted premise of classifying mental disease and the methods of diagnosing and treating it go against the standards of science, medicine, and logic. But, since it is responsible for the mountains of cash piling into big pharma every year, this anti-scientific pig is removed from the slop, given a bath and a fresh coat of red lipstick, and rebranded as logic and science. Thus, unproven and debunked notions like, "depression is caused by a chemical imbalance," quietly and quickly go from being seen as *theory* to treated as *fact* with very little or no scientific foundation, and with the intent of legitimizing the drugs they manufactured to more effectively push them off the shelves and elevate their value on

Wall Street. It matters little if the pills lack efficacy or produce an onslaught of negative side effects including suicidal ideation; psychiatric "medicine" has made a few men very, very rich.

And whatever seems to be a cultural trend of the time and perceived as unwanted behavior opens itself up to becoming a mental disorder in the eyes of psychiatry and medicine – it's seen as an unexploited market opportunity. Heck, in the 1800s, incidents of African-American slaves attempting to escape captivity were high. Because it was happening so often, some physicians surmised that these men must be "diseased." Thus, physician Samuel Cartwright took to calling such behavior "drapetomania," and this mental illness was adopted as true by doctors of the South.[66,67] So, a trending behavior in the 1800s was runaway slaves, which medical experts decided to call a mental illness. In the 2010s we have people who love to play video games, surf the internet, and go shopping, thus, like drapetomania, doctors have decided to slap the label of disorder on those who like to do it too much – they must be "diseased."

The unscientific method of classifying mental illness has led renowned psychiatrist, Dr. William Grasser, to state at a national conference: "All of these are phony diagnostic categories…The DSM was not written to help people; it was developed to help psychiatrists – to help them make money."[68] Each addition of the DSM casts a wider net across the population, and as of 2013, it is reported that 1 in every 6 Americans receives psychotropic drugs, most of which are long-term users.[69] Assuming that trend has continued into 2020, and I would think that number has only increased, that would mean nearly 55 million Americans are receiving psychiatric medication – cha-ching! The DSM covers such a wide range of behaviors that it's reached a point where many psychiatrists fear just about every American could be considered mentally ill if they were to receive a psych evaluation. Dr. Frances warned about the DSM-5 that it includes many new diagnoses that are "at the threshold of normality," and that "These have the potential to reclassify as mentally disordered tens of millions of people currently considered normal."[70] Everyone is a potential customer now. But, with the enormous profit potential, it is hard to doubt that is the ultimate goal?

What raises even more questions regarding the reliability of the DSM is that most of the members voting on the diseases that eventually wind up in the manual just so happen to have financial ties to pharmaceutical companies. For instance, during the creation of the DSM-5, it was found that 70% of its task force members (those involved with creating the DSM) had ties to drug companies, which was a 14% increase from the DSM-4.[71] And in disorders where drugs are considered the first line of treatment, the connections between drug companies and DSM committee members were "especially strong."[72] Moreover, in the DSM-4, ALL of the members of the working groups for mood disorders and "schizophrenia and other psychotic disorders" had ties to drug companies.[73] This creates a clear conflict of interest. The late Dr. Robert Spitzer, psychiatrist and creator of the DSM-3, joined Dr. Frances in his concern over these conflicts of interest in regard to the DSM-5 by adding that there would be "…tens of millions of newly diagnosed 'patients' – the majority of whom would likely be false positives subjected to needless side effects and expense of treatment. The APA might well be accused of a conflict of interest in fashioning the new DSM-V to create new patients for psychiatrists and new customers for the pharmaceutical companies."[74] Maybe it is pride and bitterness due to being excluded from the DSM-5 and losing out on royalties, but when two of the industry's top psychiatrists speak up, it has to say something. So, how can the general public and physicians trust if a disorder was voted into existence because its voters were paid to do so, or if it was voted into the DSM because the voting members actually believe it is a mental disease? How can the general public trust the DSM and its members when what is considered diagnosable directly impacts the sales of a company's drugs?

Sadly, we cannot know for sure if a disease is being promoted due to drug company influence or because it is a legitimate issue in society. For instance, let's take a look at a case involving Dr. Joseph Biederman, superstar psychiatry professor at Harvard who has worked extensively in the fields of Pediatric Psychology and Pediatric Psychopharmacology, and who had become one of the world's biggest and most influential advocates for diagnosing Bipolar Disorder in children (as young as 2 years old) and treating them with powerful antipsychotics. Between the 1990s and 2000s, Dr. Biederman had been involved in the authoring of many studies supporting the use of atypical antipsychotics, like Risperdal (Risperidone), in treating children diagnosed with Bipolar Disorder. Thus, the rate of diagnoses of pediatric bipolar disorder skyrocketed by 4000% from 1994 to 2003, which also fueled a rapid increase in antipsychotic prescriptions, even though such drugs had not been approved by the FDA for use in children. By 2007, Medco Health Solutions reported that roughly 500,000 kids had been given at least three psychiatric drugs – 20,000 of those were under the age of 6![75] Additionally, a study out of Columbia University found that the rate of antipsychotic prescriptions doubled from 2000 to 2007 in privately insured 2- to 5-year-olds, even though only 40% received a proper mental health assessment.[76]

However, in a 2008 congressional inquiry led by Republican Senator Charles E. Grassley, it was discovered that not only was Dr. Biederman's work underwritten by 25 drug companies, but he had also failed to disclose most of $1.6 million he had received from those same companies, and lawyers believe that was just a small amount of what he actually received.[77] In addition to receiving money from drug manufacturers, the integrity of the designs of his various studies also came into question. During the senate investigation, internal documents revealed questionable meeting interactions between Dr. Biederman and several companies. In one meeting where he talked about Risperdal with Johnson & Johnson executives, the Harvard professor assured the board that his study would yield positive results, even though the study had not yet been conducted, indicating a potential bias to steer the study toward favorable outcomes.[78] Not so surprising, when a group of independent experts followed-up and researched a number of clinical studies from 2001 to 2006 involving Dr. Biederman, they found that the "studies were so small and loosely designed that they were largely inconclusive."[79]

Now, does Dr. Biederman's accepting of drug company payments to conduct drug research mean that his studies were laced with bias or misleading results? Not necessarily. But the conflict of interest does call into question the authenticity of his work. If a company is investing money in a project, it is likely they are hoping for or expecting some sort of financial benefit or return. And if a researcher expects to continue receiving such lofty payments from those companies, it is in his best interest to yield results that will help them achieve their goals. As has already been displayed, drug companies use their incredible clout to influence clinical studies and journals in the worst, yet most predictable, ways. And once a misleading article has been published, word spreads quick, and the information is cemented into the minds of physicians everywhere.

It didn't take long for pediatric bipolar disorder diagnoses to skyrocket in America once Dr. Biederman's work became publicized, and with it, physicians quickly began administering very powerful drugs for what many psychiatrists, including those involved with the creation of the DSM-5, believe are often examples of normal behavior being misclassified as disease. Dr. Jacob Azerrad, clinical psychologist out of Massachusetts, exclaimed:

> "The real scandal perpetrated by Biederman has nothing to do with his consulting fee shenanigans and everything to do with the real life (and death) consequences of the methods now used by modern pediatric psychiatry to tag normal childhood behaviors with diagnoses – like 'childhood bipolar' — and the pediatric medical profession's complicit acquiescence to such malarkey. It has been nothing short of an epic assault on our children by those who prescribe antipsychotic medications as an antidote to normal childhood behavior."[80]

Antipsychotics, also known as Major Tranquilizers, had been traditionally reserved for schizophrenic sufferers and work, in a simple sense, by inhibiting Dopamine from reaching the frontal lobes of a person's brain by blocking certain dopamine receptors (other neurotransmitters are affected, too). As one can predict, if you're blocking the "happy" neurotransmitter from reaching the part of your brain involved with personality, decision-making, cognition, and more, you're likely going to produce a dull child – hence, "major tranquilizer." Not only that, but the list of severe side effects is startling, which range from depression, mania, and metabolic dysfunction to suicidal ideation, tardive dyskinesia (tics), akathisia, and more. And in other studies conducted by several well-respected institutions, antipsychotics have been linked to brain atrophy, relapse of psychosis, and even early death.[81-89] It was the deaths of several children on antipsychotics, including a 9-year-old who died of a stroke 12 days after beginning Risperdal, that started to shine a spotlight on the use, or misuse rather, of antipsychotics in our youth.[90]

And, as one might predict after seeing how often drug companies design clinical trials to produce misleading data, Risperdal became yet another victim of such an example, as later studies showed it to be less effective and carry more adverse effects than initially reported. An FDA review of Risperdal concluded that there was no evidence that the drug was safer or more effective than older drugs. The FDA would go on to report to Janssen (Risperdal's manufacturer): "We would consider any advertisement or promotion labeling for RISPERDAL false, misleading, or lacking fair balance…if there is presentation of data that conveys the impression that risperidone is superior to haloperidol or any other marketed antipsychotic drug product with regard to safety or effectiveness."[91] Independent researchers came to similar conclusions as the FDA in studying Risperdal data, in that it was no more effective compared to older drugs, and that unethical marketing and poor scientific bases contributed to the drug's massive popularity after its approval.[92]

In his 2009 deposition, Biederman was asked what rank he held in regard to his position with Harvard. Biederman replied, "Full professor."

"What's after that?" the lawyer asked.

"God," said Biederman.

"Did you say God?"

"Yeah."[93]

With few profligate men standing to make exorbitant amounts of money, would it surprise you to know that many of the legally prescribed drugs offered by psychiatry today work similarly to drugs that have been classified as dangerous and illegal in the United States? Let's look at cocaine, for instance.

In 1884, famed neurologist and psychoanalyst Sigmund Freud published a document titled "Uber Coca"[94] in which he outlined the safety and efficacy of Cocaine in the treatment of alcohol and morphine addictions. In his paper, he would go on to say about cocaine that:

> "The psychic effect of cocai'num muriaticum…consists of exhilaration and lasting euphoria, which does not differ in any way from the normal euphoria of a healthy person. The feeling of excitement which accompanies stimulus by alcohol is completely lacking…One is simply normal, and soon finds it difficult to believe that one is under the influence of any drug at all."[95]

He would then say about its addictive properties that the use of cocaine produced "no compulsive desire to use the stimulant further; on the contrary, one feels a certain unmotivated aversion to the substance."[96]

What was hidden from public purview at the time, however, was that Merck and Parke-Davis – the two pharmaceutical companies seeking to financially capitalize on cocaine – were paying Freud to test and endorse their product.[97] Nevertheless, cocaine went on to receive praise as a miracle drug, Freud became addicted to it (ironically), and physicians began prescribing the stimulant to patients for varying ailments, including depression, at the turn of the 20th century. It wasn't until 1914, after years of addiction problems, deaths, and other side effects caused by the use of the drug that it was essentially banned in the United States. And so began a decades-long war that continues to this day of trying to keep cocaine out of our society (unless of course you work in wealthy sectors of America, like on Wall Street or in Hollywood where it is passed around like a Thanksgiving dish, and authorities look the other way).

Though cocaine is illegal in the United States, pharmaceutical companies rake in billions of dollars by prescribing legal drugs that have similar effects on the brain. Case in point, let's look at Wellbutrin out of GSK. Also known as poor man's cocaine in certain regions of North America, Wellbutrin is an atypical antidepressant and is often prescribed in combination with Selective Serotonin Reuptake Inhibitors (SSRIs) in the treatment of depression or anxiety. So, it might be common for a doctor to prescribe Wellbutrin in conjunction with an SSRI like, say, Prozac or Zoloft. Now, comprehending what I am about to write in regards to how the drugs work is unimportant. What is important is recognizing the similarity. Anyway, Wellbutrin and Prozac in combination work by inhibiting the reuptake of norepinephrine, dopamine, and serotonin into the presynaptic neurons of the brain. Now, can you guess how cocaine works? That's right, it works by inhibiting the reuptake of norepinephrine, dopamine, and serotonin into the presynaptic neurons. Sure the Wellbutrin/SSRI combination might be slower releasing since it is taken orally and in smaller doses, but the general mechanisms of action, of making those three neurotransmitters more available within the brain are there.

And of course, Ritalin (Methylphenidate), a drug commonly prescribed to children for Attention Deficit Hyperactivity Disorder also works similarly to cocaine and Wellbutrin in that it blocks the reuptake of norepinephrine and dopamine into the presynaptic neuron. The major difference in its effects, again, is in how it is administered. Whereas cocaine is commonly inhaled through the nose and can cause a high in seconds, Ritalin is ingested orally, which slows the rate of absorption within the body, causing dopamine levels to increase at a gradual rate. However, when crushed up and inhaled through the nose or injected into the veins, recreational drug users claim the high experienced from Ritalin is quite similar to that of cocaine. It is for this reason Ritalin is one of the most abused drugs on the streets.

Even though drugs like Ritalin and Concerta and amphetamines, like Adderall, have similar chemical properties and work in virtually the same ways as cocaine, they've been handed out like candy to hundreds of thousands of children and teens throughout America – some as young as 2 years old – and rates of diagnoses have consistently increased since 1997.[98] The CDC recently reported that in 2016 about 6.1 million children between the ages of 2 and 17 had been diagnosed with ADHD, and of that chunk, 62% were prescribed with ADHD drugs – nearly 70,000 between the ages of 2 and 5.[99] Dr. William Graf, pediatric neurologist at Yale, said in regard to the uptick in ADHD diagnoses that "Mild symptoms are being diagnosed so readily, which goes well beyond the disorder…to children who are otherwise healthy."[100] Though over-diagnoses and misuse of ADHD and its drugs are growing at an alarming rate, drug companies and their shareholders are making out like Pablo Escobars. Between 2007 and 2012, sales of ADHD medications shot up from $4 billion to $9 billion![101]

But it's okay! Experts claim the drugs are safe and effective (though legal drugs have been reported to cause more deaths than illegal drugs).[102,103,104] However, due to the prevalence of drug companies publishing biased and misleading medical articles, we know that even the most well-meaning medical professionals might not be getting the most complete picture of a drug. So, let's do a quick investigation of the claims that Ritalin and other ADHD medications are safe for youth consumption.

To begin with, not much is known about the long-term effects of Ritalin and other psychostimulants, but research has begun to show that it can change the way a child's brain develops. A study out of the University of Amsterdam and Johns Hopkins University compared the brains of adults who were prescribed stimulants like Ritalin in their youth to those who were not administered ADHD drugs. They discovered that adults who were given ADHD drugs at a young age had lower baseline levels of GABA – a neurotransmitter – and that their GABAergic response was altered.[105] A 2019 study concluded that Ritalin causes alterations in the White Matter of a child's brain after just four months of use.[106] In a report released out of Harvard Medical School, Susan Andersen wrote that "chronic, pre-pubertal exposure [to ADHD stimulants]…alters the expected developmental trajectory of brain structure and function and results in a different topography in adulthood."[107] In other words, exposure to Ritalin or Adderall changes the way a child's brain develops. The "sad truth," according to psychiatrist Dr. Peter Breggin who has been practicing for 60 years, is that:

> "Children raised on stimulant drugs will never know who they really were."[108]

If a child's mental development is altered in anyway, then that child and his parents may never get to know the person he was supposed to become.

And long-term effects continue. ADHD medication can damage the Basal Ganglia and Cerebellum within the brain. A study completed out of the University of Utah found that subjects who had been treated with ADHD drugs had an 8.6-fold increase in the risk for developing diseases associated with the Basal Ganglia and Cerebellum, including Parkinson's disease.[109] In a study published out of *Neuropharmacology*, researchers found that when they exposed rats to Methylphenidate (Ritalin) during early adolescence, they discovered long-lasting behavioral and molecular alterations that were consistent with dramatic changes in the function of the brain's reward systems.[110] Additionally, exposure to cocaine during the same developmental period produced some of the same behavioral effects.[111]

ADHD medication can also suppress a child's growth rate by disrupting hormone function. Researchers out of the National Institute of Mental Health found that annual growth rates were 20.3% less than expected for height and 55.2% for weight in children receiving Ritalin.[112]

Not only do ADHD drugs limit and oftentimes crush spontaneous behavior in children, but the drugs can also induce depression, apathy, and obsessive-compulsive disorder.[113] When such symptoms appear, it is not unusual for a physician to add another psychotropic drug to the child's drug regimen – polypharmacy.[114] And in terms of risk of addiction, even the Black Box Warning for Adderall says, "Amphetamines have a high potential for abuse. Administration of amphetamines for prolonged periods of time may lead to drug dependence."[115] Amphetamines can alter the way the brain functions and cause permanent heart damage. And although the drugs are popular among college students as a performance-enhancer, a study out of Brown University indicated they can actually hinder cognitive performance by impairing memory.[116]

Brain atrophy, or shrinkage, is also an area of great concern relating to psychostimulant use, though not nearly enough reliable research has been conducted to investigate this potential, devastating problem. We've already discussed Ritalin's effects on White Matter in the brain. Researchers out of the NYU Langone School of Medicine found that their subjects diagnosed with ADHD, most of whom were prescribed Ritalin between the ages of 6 and 12, had significantly decreased gray matter in various regions of the brain, including the right caudate and right thalamus, as adults.[117] The cortex in these ADHD subjects was also significantly thinner in the limbic areas.[118] A 1986 study found more than half of their young adult subjects who received psychostimulants in childhood showed atrophy of the brain.[119] Researchers concluded that "cortical atrophy may be a long-term adverse effect of this treatment."

The major limitation of the two studies above, however, and this seems to be the case in most studies comparing ADHD subjects to non-ADHD subjects, is that they fail to compare ADHD patients receiving medication versus ADHD patients not receiving medication. Failure to separate and compare these two subsets of patients is also the greatest limitation in *proving* that ADHD has biological roots. Nevertheless, the appearance of brain atrophy in ADHD subjects who happen to be receiving stimulants raises red flags, and I would think a rational action would be to err on the side of caution and discontinue use until further investigation can definitively conclude that they do not damage the brains of children. If I was a parent and I was told a medication "might" cause brain atrophy, there would be no way I would subject my child to that risk. Dr. Peter Breggin asserts that parents should avoid putting their children on psychiatric drugs in general due to the long list of detrimental side effects coupled with their lack of efficacy.[120]

Alright, so step one in moving supply off the shelves of drug companies is creating a market. The DSM-5 does that swimmingly; by having mental diseases continually voted into and out of existence, new markets are constantly being created. Because mental illness cannot be biologically detected and has no scientific basis, like cancer or coronavirus, there is no limit to how many mental health markets they can create. They are limited only by their imagination. The more disorders they can think of, the better, as more disorders means a larger market and more profit potential.

And the second step in moving supply off the shelf is in manufacturing demand. This is accomplished, as we've already seen, by publishing phony clinical studies, soliciting physicians, advertising directly to consumers, and by inducing people to fear that their normal behaviors or quirks might be a sign of disease.

So now, with an abundant supply of drugs creating the need for new markets and ever-expanding demand, we have all of these conflicting psychiatric studies "proving" that certain antipsychotics or antidepressants or ADHD medicines are safe and effective, many of which target children, yet, not only does independent research consistently contradict such conclusions, but pharmaceutical companies are constantly being exposed for tampering with trusted medical data. To think, Dr. Biederman himself has been an author or co-author in about 600 medical articles, 650 scientific abstracts, and 70 book chapters.[121] But, how many of those are tainted with drug company bias? How many of those studies have influenced practicing physicians to prescribe drugs that his studies support? We can't know for sure. And if there are hidden dangers not reported within such studies, which we have seen happens regularly, then that puts the nation's health at great risk, especially amongst children.

In 1949, Antonio Egas Moniz received the Nobel Prize for his work in studying lobotomies – an invasive procedure where connections within the prefrontal lobe of the brain are severed – in the treatment of mental illness. Thus, lobotomies were widely recognized and accepted as safe and effective in the medical community, leading thousands of mentally ill patients to go under the knife (while conscious) and experience its debilitating effects; and if non-credentialed citizens challenged such conclusions, they were immediately dismissed. It wasn't until years later, after continued research and many lives permanently ruined – including that of JFK's sister, Rosemary – that the horrible practice is now considered inhumane and has been widely discredited. Substances like cocaine and LSD were once considered healthy, miracle drugs, but are now considered dangerous and illegal. How long before Ritalin or Wellbutrin (cocaine for the poor man) are classified as dangerous drugs and thrown into the same categories as cocaine, LSD, or even lobotomies? Maybe never? I suppose as long as the streams flow rich with green, and as long as drug companies keep the pockets of lawmakers adequately stuffed, and as long as former drug company lobbyists and officials are working within the confines of the FDA, then we can safely bet that these drugs will be insulated from meaningful scrutiny for a long time.

Now, after all we've read in this section, what is the core precondition behind such deceitful, irresponsible, and dangerous behavior rampant throughout the industry? What motives would a drug company have to publish misleading clinical data? What reasons would individual men have to push dangerous drugs onto the population, especially the vulnerable, susceptible youth? Well, I can think of only one motive that makes sense to me – money. The opportunity to make money is the driver of everything listed in this section. If the life equation did not require the acquisition of money to gain access to survival, then you could bet your bottom dollar many of these psychiatric drugs would not be used in the capacity that they are used today in medicine and in the treatment of mental illness. Sure, they might still find prevalence in the recreational drug community, for people to get high or feel smoothed out, heck I could even see myself using something like Adderall if I wanted to focus more on certain projects, but on a medical level, these drugs would be used sparingly. Many of them would no longer masquerade as medicine, and there would no longer be a reason to mislead the public. Bottom line, if abhorrent behavior is rewarded in our global society, then abhorrent behavior can only be expected. No institution can fully be trusted so long as money exists as the barrier to life.

# 6.7 CHAPTER CONCLUSION

> "Money is a currency that's rank. Money topples cities to the ground, seduces men away from happy homes, corrupts the honest heart to shifty ways, makes men crooked connoisseurs of vice…Money never makes as many as it mars." – Sophocles, *Antigone*, ~441 BC

In this chapter we touched on some of the most glaring and most obvious issues plaguing our global society, and I feel like we've barely even scratched the surface. We talked about unwanted externalities like childhood poverty and how, among other negative consequences, the stresses it causes can lead to stunted development in our youth. We talked about ecological degradation and how our "throwaway" culture and habits of mass consumption have led to the rapid decay of our home. We talked about war, crime, labor exploitation, and corruption. And the point in bringing up some of the worst trends in our world is not necessarily to inform you of what is happening across the globe, because with ease of access to information these days I assume you already have a general idea at a minimum; you might even be able to illuminate me on some topics. But the ultimate point in my cynicism, in zeroing in on the negative aspects of society is to identify their source; only in identifying the source can we even begin to work toward preventing and completely eradicating such unwanted trends.

And, unbeknownst to itself, as we've pinpointed, it seems the use of money as the tool to organize society and distribute life necessities is that source. Whether it is the lack of money leading to childhood poverty and stunted development, or the allure of money driving men to exploit the most desperate among us if only to increase profit margins. Or, whether it is the lack of money that leads to homelessness, starvation, and suffering, or the temptation of money that seduces men into deceiving other men in business endeavors – money is at the heart of it all. Money is the core precondition behind just about every negative event, activity, behavior, and outcome I can think of.

And again, I've only touched upon some of the most unwanted circumstances in our society. We could continue to go down the list of negative externalities and identify money as the central culprit – from lesser examples like the seemingly harmless salesman wearing a fake smile in an attempt to persuade you to purchase a vehicle or that cousin of yours acting unusually nice because he wants you to join his pyramid scheme or Walmart taking out life insurance policies on its employees and cashing in when they die,[1] all the way up to the most severe examples like the hideous, grotesque, repulsive, sinful world of child sex trafficking. Believe it or not, the disgusting practice of abducting children and then buying and selling them for sex is a multi-billion-dollar global enterprise, and it's an issue that plagues not only the world, but every single state within the United States.[2]

And the list goes on.

Prostitution. When it comes to prostitution, I can't imagine many women subjecting themselves to its dangers, working the streets, encountering scores of hairy and sweaty men night in and night out, if not because they are desperate and need money to survive. I know psychological damage afflicts many of these women and plays a role in their circumstances, but money is the industry's bait, it's the industry's lifeblood.

We have farmers across America killing themselves at an alarming rate, as data shows that farmers, ranchers, and agricultural workers have some of the highest rates of suicide out of any other occupation in the country.[3,4] Why? Why have the men and women largely responsible for feeding the nation been driven to such extreme states of despair that they feel the only way out is by taking their own lives? Well, I can say with confidence, the source of their stress and mental anguish is money. With farmers' incomes decreasing over the years, with dairy prices dropping and the costs of operation and interest rates rising, with more people walking away from dairy and meat, with weather impacting crop yields, among other factors, many farmers are struggling to make ends meet financially. They are struggling to pay off loans, afford healthcare for their families, and provide for their loved ones. And with that financial struggle comes shame – shame from feeling like they have failed their families.

In parts of Asia, mainly India, men and women become so desperate for money that they elect to have organs, like their kidney, surgically removed and then sold on the black market.[5] Buyers come from all over the world – the UK, Russia, the United States, Sri Lanka, etc. – to an area of India known as the "Kidney Belt" in hopes of procuring one of these illegally obtained organs. And the primary reason the organ donors reluctantly choose to sell their organs? Well, it's not because they're tired of carrying excess baggage. They do it to pay off crippling debts.

We could continue this exercise ad infinitum. With any societal issue we encounter, it is likely we can find money as the core precondition, and it usually doesn't take much digging. We can talk about the illegal drug trade, suicide and domestic abuse rising during a recession, or the Homestead Strike – a deadly labor dispute in 1892 that pitted Andrew Carnegie against his striking steel workers. We can talk about endless sequels and remakes in Hollywood, corporate scandals (Enron), or about how it is the elderly who make up much a food pantry's customer-base. In just about every negative case we bring up, the wizard behind the curtain is almost always money and the pursuit of it. Money finds a way to muck up and destroy the integrity of our most trusted and beloved institutions.

The human species has accomplished many amazing things in the last hundred years and beyond. Technology has grown and continues to grow at an exponential rate, which has ushered in a standard of living the likes of which our world has never seen. But, with all of our advancements, what is it worth if society is no more or less happy than it was before this technological explosion? What does it say if our standard of living is better than ever, yet crime remains high, suicides are increasing, diseases and chronic illnesses continue to rise, a large swath of children remain hungry and homeless, and our habitats are rapidly deteriorating?

Like Sophocles wrote all the way back around 400 B.C., "Money never makes as many as it mars." I have to agree with him. It would be one thing if the good that money provided were enough to offset even a fraction of the bad; then I might be able to justify childhood poverty, homelessness, or hunger. But it doesn't. It mars much, much more than it makes. The current existence of money threatens social stability, the health of the human race, and the planet that provides us with life. Money has outgrown its purpose in today's globally connected, technologically advanced society; it is not the most efficient means to distribute resources, it is not the most accurate indicator of resources or store of wealth, its methods of tracking supply and demand are crude at best, and its use as a motivational tool is unhealthy and mostly ineffective outside of menial tasks. Therefore, since money's role in society is outdated and obsolete, meaning it no longer provides much good at all, and since money is the source of so much hardship and pain, one has to wonder why we haven't started transitioning away from it already. One has to wonder why we are so attached to it. It's like being in an abusive relationship; no matter how much money beats us down, it always knows we'll come crawling right back. I suppose indoctrination, lack of recognition, and fear of change are major reasons.

And again, it's not that money is bad, per se. It's not. It's simply a tool. But it's just that this tool is what stands between you and that loaf of bread you need to survive. It doesn't matter if there are more loaves of bread than people in a community; you need the abstract tool of money to gain access to it. You need the tool of money to gain access to that bottle of water. Or that shirt. Or that roof over your head. So that, coupled with the tool of money being limited amongst the population is what makes it so destructive. The scarce nature of money has pushed people to some pretty rotten behavior in our time, if only to capture but a piece of that cash pie so they can win their survival for yet another day. And then the game starts all over the next day. And the day after that, and the day after that, and the day after that. The game never ends. We are in a perpetual, exhausting state of competition with one another, day in and day out, just to acquire what limited money exists in the economic game. And it would also be one thing if essential resources were scarce, like if there was only one banana amongst five people; then I could understand and better accept the idea of us having to compete against each other without end. But that's not the case, either. We have produced a surfeit of essential, life resources; essential resources are abundant. And, as I've already stated, Earth, with its unique ability to grow and regenerate those resources when properly cared for, is intuitively designed to host all its passengers while we sail through this vast sea of stars.

So then the questions become – do we want to continue experiencing all of the negative externalities we've discussed in this chapter? Do we enjoy having to hear about war, crime, or environmental destruction? Does it make our hearts happy or does it make our hearts twinge to see a child suffering through poverty? Assuming most of us are capable of empathy, of feeling the pain of others, which we are hardwired to feel to varying degrees, then I assume our answers are "no" and "twinge." However, unfortunately, as long as we continue operating under our monetary systems, under the constraints of money that naturally breed insecurity and desperation, then we should expect to continue experiencing all of the negative outcomes they inevitably produce.

Or, by transitioning away from the tool of money and utilizing technology to accomplish what money is supposed to accomplish, but much more efficiently and accurately, we can quickly eradicate most negative externalities and begin to reverse the environmental destruction that has already been done – as I discuss further in Chapter 10. It's our choice, really.

# 7 EFFICIENCY: A MONETARY SYSTEM'S GREATEST ENEMY

The greatest enemy to the flow of a monetary system is *efficiency*. I know, I know. Such a statement might sound a bit radical, but allow me to explain.

An economic system that uses money needs "problems" if it wants to flourish; it needs goods to break down or exhaust if it wants a more active consumer-base, because monetary systems thrive off of constant consumption. The more we buy, the better. And more products breaking down or being used up means more products needing repair or replacement – product turnover. More product turnover translates to more sales and more economic activity; it means more money exchanging hands and more revenue for businesses.

The highest ambition of for-profit organizations in the monetary game is to maximize revenue and profit margins and continually increase shareholder value. For an organization to achieve such goals, it needs a steady stream of customers to maintain or increase sales. Higher product turnover is a way to ensure that steady stream. Conversely, lower product turnover can spell doom for a company, as it means fewer customers and fewer sales. Like the forces of supply and demand, *efficiency* and *sales* also have an inverse relationship – an increase in product efficiency equates to a decrease in sales. So, incentive to manufacture products below optimum efficiency is inherently built into the monetary game.

Not only does higher product turnover benefit a company's bottom line, but it also benefits the overall economy as it boosts national consumption, which boosts material productivity, which inflates GDP. Though GDP fails to measure the health of a nation's citizens, we rely on it, among other indicators, to measure the health of the national economy. A country can have high GDP while its people experience high levels of crime, suicide, diseases, food insecurity, lower life expectancy, etc., further supporting the notion that the game of money is completely detached from and works in opposition to the game of life and nature. Higher product turnover is wonderful for the economy, but it is a detriment to Earth – it means resources are being exhausted at a greater rate and waste is being generated at excessive and unnecessary levels. Any time a product is *not* designed and manufactured to its optimum technological capacity with the given knowledge of the time, it is a wasteful, unintelligent, and frankly, stupid use of the planet's resources.

The system of money and the system of nature have an inverse relationship, too. As an example, though a light bulb with a shorter lifespan would be great for the manufacturer of such a bulb, it would be bad for the planet as it means more waste generated and more resources used. The faster a light bulb dies, the better for a company, because that means people need to buy more light bulbs and sooner. More light bulb sales means more revenue. If a company used its resources and knowledge of the time to its maximum capacity and developed a light bulb that lasted 100 years, well, it would be wonderful for Earth, but the company would go out of business. They would mass-produce the 100-year light bulb, sell it to every household in the nation, and then barely make another sale for the next 100 years. And without a consistent stream of revenue coming in, the company would struggle to sustain itself, as it would quickly lose its ability to pay its employees and its overhead costs.

Every industry is confronted with the dilemma of needing to balance efficiency or effectiveness with the need to sustain itself with sales, because more problems equals more business. In the sphere of medicine, more sick people means more business for doctors, hospitals, and pharmaceutical companies. In the world of windows, more broken windows means more business for window and glass manufacturers. Televisions that break down faster means more people buying televisions, which means more revenue for television companies. More crime is good for a private police force and private prisons. Pantyhose that stretch and wear out faster are great for a pantyhose company. Socks that gets holes in them faster means more people buying socks. If a city is bombed, that could be good for a construction company because that means an influx in construction projects. If the tread on car tires wears out at a faster rate, the more a tire company thrives. Conversely, the more a product is designed for longevity and the longer it lasts, the worse it is for a company as it decreases overall sales. As was written in a 1928 version of Printers' Ink magazine, "the article that refuses to wear out is a tragedy of business."[1]

Arguably the most egregious example in the dilemma of efficiency versus sales, of needing steady streams of customers to maintain revenue and sustain business is in the pharmaceutical industry. In medicine, the most efficient product is the one that can completely cure a patient of her ailment. However, "the cure" can also be seen as bad for business. I once heard a pharmaceutical representative say there are two rules in the industry. First, you don't want patients to die. Second, you don't want patients cured. Now, does this motto hold any truth? I would hope not. However, since efficiency is bad for sustaining profits, it would stand to reason that a company would make more money off of repeat treatments, off of chronic therapies that maintain stable disease rather than completely curing it.

In a 2018 report issued through CNBC, Goldman Sachs analysts talked about this very issue in regard to biotech companies. One of the questions posed was: "Is curing patients a sustainable business model?"[2] Analyst Salveen Richter referred to a case involving Gilead Sciences, a firm that developed a treatment for Hepatitis C touting a 90% cure rate. 90%! How amazing for the human population! Unfortunately, Gilead quickly recognized the financial consequences of "the cure." In 2015, their Hepatitis C treatment brought in $12.5 billion. But, as more people were cured and fewer people contracted the disease, Gilead's sales began to stumble. Richter estimated in 2018 that sales from the treatment would bring in less than $4 billion – about a 70% drop-off.

In a note to investment clients, Richter went on to say, "The potential to deliver 'one-shot cures' is one of the most attractive aspects… However, such treatments offer a very different outlook with regard to recurring revenue versus chronic therapies… While this proposition carries tremendous value for patients and society, it could represent a challenge for genome medicine developers looking for sustained cash flow." And in regard to the example of Gilead's "success," Richter commented that it is "a case in point, where the success of its Hepatitis C franchise has gradually exhausted the available pool of treatable patients. In the case of infectious diseases such as Hepatitis C, curing existing patients also decreases the number of carriers able to transmit the virus to new patients, thus the incident pool also declines…"

Profits and economic growth are the holy grail of business, no matter the external costs. When faced with the choice of curing versus treating symptoms, board members and decision makers are put in a tough position as their jobs depend on increasing shareholder value. And, pharmaceutical companies bring in billions of dollars in cash each year, which is not only wonderful for the companies, but it's fantastic for the American economy. One could argue that the pharmaceutical industry is America's most important; on a global scale, the United States comprises over 48% of the pharmaceutical market – a share valued at around $514 billion.[3] The health of the American and global economy depends on unhealthy people.

In terms of tangible goods, although a product made to last as long as possible might be good for the sustainability of Earth, it is not good for the growth of a company or the financial system. And, unfortunately, the health of the monetary system comes before the health of all other systems in this world. For this reason and due to technological advancements continuously improving upon the efficiency of products, the phenomenon of Planned Obsolescence, a term attributed to Bernard London in 1932, became a commonality in our economy about a century ago. In fact, it was the light bulb industry that seemed to popularize this trend.

First, what is Planned Obsolescence, you might ask? Well, I guess the term sort of explains itself. It's when a company manufactures a product and intentionally gives it a shorter lifespan than is possible; they plan for and design a product to expire, to become obsolete before it needs to. And I understand to some that might sound like musings from within dark corners of conspiracy theory communities, but it is actually talked about somewhat openly and is a common practice in our world of money, though many companies might be hesitant to admit their participation.[4] Now, as I have stressed, I do not believe that creating a good with an artificially limited lifespan makes a company evil or immoral. The rules of the monetary game allow for and even encourage it. If a business can strike a balance between creating a product that people demand and one that lasts only long enough so as to not scare away or drive its customer base to a competing business, then that is just effective strategy. In its purest form, there are no inherent rules in the money game; you do what you need to do to secure your position and survive. The only rules that exist within the game are the ones superimposed upon and regulated by its referees. In many cases, not only is planned obsolescence clever strategy, but it is necessary for a company to remain sustainable. Companies need money to pay their employees and cover their expenses. And employees need money to buy food and other life necessities. If a company is not bringing in revenue, it won't be able to pay its employees, and the company will inevitably perish. As a result, all of its employees will lose their jobs and their ability to pay for survival. So, for the sake of self-preservation and survival, developing a product with less integrity might be necessary to keep the lights on and bellies full – even if it means putting a strain on Earth. Again, if the rules of the game allow for it, then I find it difficult to call someone unethical. It is not the individuals playing this chaotic and sometimes desperate game of survival that need to change. It's the game itself, the thing that encourages and invites such behavior that needs changing.

Anyway, back to light bulbs. The Light Bulb conspiracy is the most referenced case study on the Planned Obsolescence spectrum and the one that seemed to have kicked the tires on the trend of producing purposefully disposable products.[5] Throughout the early-1900s the quality and lifespan of incandescent light bulbs were rapidly improving as engineers continued developing stronger and stronger filaments; the goal was not only durability, but energy efficiency, too. By 1924, the common household light bulb lasted 2,500 hours or more. In fact, there is a light bulb in Livermore, California known as the Centennial Bulb that was flipped on in 1901, and it continues to burn to this day (though, the light it emits has dimmed over time).[6] The ever-increasing longevity of light bulbs started becoming a problem for manufacturers because it was diminishing sales and making it difficult to sustain business.

So, in December of 1924 a group of the world's leading light bulb companies – Osram, General Electric, Compagnie des Lampes, Philips, and many others – got together in Geneva, Switzerland to discuss this very issue. With their powers combined, they formed what would be known as the Phoebus cartel. In addition to colluding to collectively raise prices of their incandescent light bulbs, this privately organized group devised a set of rules pertaining to the production and lifespan of their lights, and they established a private *governing body* responsible for overseeing company adherence to these new standards. Within this new set of rules, manufacturers could no longer engineer and produce light bulbs that lasted longer than 1,000 hours, even if it was possible and even if engineers had ambitions to continue improving upon the efficiency of their bulbs. To ensure compliance, factories under the umbrella of the Phoebus agreement – there were hundreds – were required to submit their bulbs to a central testing lab in Switzerland. If it was found that their lights lasted longer than 1,000 hours, the company would be fined an amount commiserate with the number of hours beyond the 1,000-hour limit. So, to avoid such penalties, companies and engineers worked just as hard to create more fragile bulbs that consistently conformed to the 1000-hour standard as they did when trying to discover filaments that improved upon the product's lifespan.

And flashlights were not exempt from the influence of the Phoebus cartel, either. Prior to the 1925 agreement, GE flashlight bulbs could last three batteries and sometimes longer before wearing out. However, in the years following the Geneva collusion, engineers adjusted the amperage of their bulbs to a point where the lifespan of flashlight bulbs was reduced to one battery. The adjustment in current actually reduced the life of the battery, too.

Of course, as one would logically expect, sales for the light bulb companies under the Phoebus umbrella received a substantial boost due to the implemented restrictions – the strategy was a financial success!

The Phoebus cartel was meant to last 30 years – from 1925 to 1955; however, World War II made it difficult for companies to maintain contact with one another, among many issues, and it ended up folding in 1940.

Then, in the 1940s, the US Government began investigating and actually sued General Electric and other companies for fixing prices, creating unfair competition, and reducing the lifespan of incandescent light bulbs.[7] It took years of litigation, but when everything was completed, among the court's decisions GE was banned from intentionally limiting the longevity of its bulbs – a decision that was hardly effective.

Though the cartel dissolved well before their 30-year goal, they set an important precedent in the world of business and economics – reducing product quality and hitting the brakes on innovation was an effective strategy to increase consumption and bolster profits. In fact, it appeared to be so effective that it inspired Bernard London to encourage government and companies of all industries to adopt this method of Planned Obsolescence, and that such a process would pull America out of the Great Depression.[8] The practice of intentionally reducing product quality and stifling innovation might have been incredibly wasteful and an inefficient use of resources, but it was incredibly beneficial for business.

Examples of Planned Obsolescence are abundant and stretch across almost every industry.

In 1939, DuPont introduced Nylon to the world. Before their revolutionary synthetic material was repurposed during World War II to the production of military parachutes, tire cords, aircraft fuel tanks, and other military needs, it was used to make a new line of women's stockings. The nylon stockings were an instant hit! As soon as their product hit shelves, DuPont distributors couldn't restock them fast enough as women came in droves to purchase them.[9] Compared to their silk counterparts, nylon stockings were sturdy, long-lasting, and provided the right amount of stretch. They were so popular that after the war, when nylon stockings were reintroduced to the consumer market, riots broke out since they were in limited quantity; the craze was aptly referred to as the "Nylon Riots."[10]

Women loved that their stockings lasted forever and didn't produce "runners." However, DuPont soon realized the durability of their hosiery might be problematic for their bottom line.[11,12] In order to counter this issue, the company instructed their chemists to find a way to make the fibers of their stockings slightly weaker and more fragile so they wouldn't last so darn long.[13] Shortly after implementing the changes, the nylon stockings began to "run" again and wear out faster, and women were left having to throw away their stockings sooner and buy new sets more frequently.

In the world of technology, Apple admitted in 2017 that it deliberately slowed down the performance of older iPhones.[14,15] Of course, they told the public this was to preserve battery life and the overall life of the phone, but, come on. Are we expected to buy that? Well, I suppose our track record for believing B.S. isn't the most favorable, so I don't blame Apple for trying. As a personal anecdote, when I owned a Samsung Galaxy S5 phone, I had it for just over one year before the performance started to slow down immensely. But let's pretend for a moment that Samsung, like Apple, also admitted to slowing down old phones without the knowledge or consent of their consumers, and that they did it to preserve the life of the phone. Well, at that point in my ownership, I couldn't care less if my phone was still alive – it was so slow I could barely use the damn thing, and it was hindering my ability to do my job effectively. It might as well have been dead. And I'm no tech geek, so as an average consumer it didn't even cross my mind to fix it myself. In the end, I simply bought a new phone.

Shortly after Apple admitted to intentionally throttling the performance of its iPhones, a class action lawsuit was filed against them.[16] A court decision is still pending as of 2019.

Before Apple had legal trouble with their iPhones, a separate class action suit was filed against them regarding their iPod and issues customers were having with the battery.[17] In 2001, Apple released the iPod. Touted as the new, hip, portable way for people to listen to music, the product became extremely popular in the marketplace. However, problems arose for customers when the iPod's rechargeable battery started completely dying after about 18 months of use, much less than advertised. When customers called to complain, Apple informed them they wouldn't simply replace the cheap battery, but that the customer would instead have to buy a whole new, expensive iPod. It was the company's policy at the time. Rather than wait for a court decision, Apple settled the class action suit in 2005.[18]

In the world of printers, various computer technicians have discovered a "counter chip" in printers manufactured by companies like HP and Epson.[19] Among the many functions programmed into the chip, the software might set a pre-determined lifespan on its printers at, say, 18,000 pages or 5 years, or it might wrongly flag components as needing to be replaced after a certain amount of time even if they haven't failed.[20] The chip might even be programmed to cause the degradation of components, or to specify a date for when the printer stops allowing for the use of ink cartridges purchased by third-party retailers. The possibilities stretch as far as the human mind can reach, it would seem.

In 2016, a Dutch retailer called 123inkt fielded a number of complaints from its customers who bought non-HP ink cartridges for their HP printers.[21] On the same day of that year, September 13th, those customers received an error message from their HP printer stating, "One or more cartridges appear to be damaged. Remove them and replace them with new cartridges." Upon investigation, 123inkt found the issue "resided in the firmware" of the printer, and that HP had essentially pre-programmed a failure date for non-HP ink cartridges. They wanted people to only buy HP ink. Bear in mind, printer companies earn much more revenue from ink cartridges than from printer sales.

In other cases, chips that count the number of prints and/or have programmed expiration dates are installed directly into the ink cartridges. And rather than being programmed to fail once the ink is completely used up, it either fails once it hits its page limit or once it passes the specified expiration date. Even if a cartridge is still half full, the chip won't allow for any more prints, and the user is forced to replace the cartridge completely. The feature in such a chip also removes the ability to simply refill low cartridges, an option that would be economical, cheap, and easy.

Like with Apple, in 2017 a class action lawsuit was filed in France against printer companies like HP, Epson, Brother, and Canon for various instances of what people claim are planned obsolescence.[22] The case is still in litigation.

Unfortunately, all of the waste just in the realm of electronics has come at a significant cost in many parts of the world – namely Africa, which has essentially become the world's garbage can. In countries like Ghana, whole shipments of electronic trash arrive and are dumped into giant landfills. Maybe 10% of the secondhand products are reused, but the majority remains heaped in massive piles of computers, phones, printers, etc. And when individuals do try to salvage precious metals from the electronic goods in such technologically inferior countries, their crude methods become hazardous either to the environment or themselves. For instance, to remove metals like gold from a circuit board, individuals might bathe the circuit board in a corrosive acid and then dump the acid into streams or onto the ground. Or, in other cases, people will burn cables in an open flame in order to collect copper. The people burning the cables know the released fumes are toxic and can lead to a number of diseases, but they continue to do it because it's their way of making money so they can purchase life. Sadly though, most of the electronic waste is not salvaged and continues to grow. And the consequences? In certain regions, once beautiful landscapes with flowing rivers and green fields for kids to play soccer in have been transformed into desolate and barren wastelands of metal and plastic hills. Like cancer, how long until such sprawls of filth spread across the entire surface of the globe?

Now, it has been argued that Planned Obsolescence is necessary not only to boost sales, but also to promote continued advancement of products and technology. It's said to be beneficial for the consumer as well as the manufacturer. However, just because a product is produced with optimum efficiency for the time doesn't mean innovation ceases. And products can be designed intelligently enough to allow for easy upgrades and repairs to hardware or software. Rather than making a customer buy a whole new iPhone just to get the most advanced camera, an efficient design would allow for a customer to simply install the camera in his current phone with the required software update. For instance, Google *was* developing a type of smartphone – Project Ara – with slots that would allow a user to swap out old components for new ones – a solution introduced to help cut down on electronic waste and help the consumer save money in the long run.[23,24] Though this project has been suspended as of 2016, it illustrates the concept's capability. Unfortunately, a producer of such a concept would have to sacrifice total sales.

Planned Obsolescence isn't merely limited to manufacturing premature "death dates" into products. For decades, marketing and advertising teams have actively worked toward perfecting another branch of product obsolescence known as "Perceived Obsolescence." In cases of perceived obsolescence, consumers are psychologically persuaded to purchase newer models of a product and do away with older models, even if the older models still work perfectly fine – like with buying a new car or a new pair of shoes. And, rather than boosting sales by engineering products to break down prematurely, companies instead engineer artificial demand by focusing on the malleable mind of the consumer; they expend considerable effort into planting subconscious seeds that serve to increase a man's appetite for material junk. This strategy, introduced in the 1920s and amplified in the 1950s, saw companies bring in marketing teams and clever men, like Edward Bernays ("The Father of Spin"), to effectively manipulate consumers on a subliminal level to crave things they might not otherwise crave and *need* things they might not otherwise need. And as an intended or unintended side effect, we have descended into a throwaway, consumer culture, one of insatiable wants and needs where our minds have been so distorted that we believe the key to happiness and fulfillment is to constantly buy lifeless material goods. It was the creative minds of auto industry executives that seemingly revolutionized this approach in marketing that altered the way we view goods.

In the early-20th century, Henry Ford introduced his Model T to America.[25] Due in large part to Ford's advancements in assembly-line manufacturing, the Model T became the first affordable car for the middle-class worker in the country. By 1918, the Model T comprised half of all cars on American roads. Though it originally came in only one general design, it was robust, reliable, durable, and easy to maintain. Simply put, the Model T was engineered to last and actually lived up to its current motto of "Built Ford Tough."

By the time Alfred Sloan and General Motors entered the automobile game, it was clear Ford's machine was a force to be reckoned with when it came to performance. So instead of exhausting time and energy on competing against the reliability and longevity of the Model T, Sloan instead directed his team to focus on a different aspect of the automobile – on cosmetic design.[26] By providing the American consumer with a vehicle of varying styles, Sloan sought to capitalize on an area Ford largely ignored.

In the 1920s, General Motors employed Sloan's strategy and offered cars of differing colors, shapes, and sizes.[27] The cars were marketed with individual brand names and a hierarchy of prices so a consumer could purchase a vehicle that matched his income – a car for every man! This "ladder of success" branding and pricing model pushed the automobile to become not only a means of transportation, but also a symbol of personal status and success (or failure). And, by giving the consumer a sense of choice and the seeming ability to buy a car that matched his personality and lifestyle, GM also provided their customers with a feeling of freedom and empowerment.

Lastly, to increase demand and boost revenue, Sloan introduced the *annual line* of vehicles along with creative marketing campaigns to implant in his customers the idea that every three or four years they ought to do away with their current model and buy a newer, more up-to-date one.[28] This template for introducing an annual line of products would later be adopted by companies throughout almost every industry.

Sloan's strategy proved to be a bold one. When General Motors rolled out their new line of vehicles, they were met with instant and wild success. By the 1930s, GM was catapulted to industry leader in automobile sales, and their business model forced a reluctant Ford to adopt Sloan's strategy just to compete.

However, with the severe economic drought of the Great Depression impeding commerce in America, it wouldn't be until the 1950s when Sloan's template of annual models and hierarchy pricing and branding would take front and center. At the helm of revitalizing this revolutionary technique was a man named Brooks Stevens – an American auto and industrial designer from Milwaukee, Wisconsin. He became popular for taking the idea of Planned or Perceived Obsolescence and essentially giving it a steroid injection.[29]

As World War II and the Great Depression came to an end, the American economy slowly got back to its feet, and the middle-class worker finally had disposable income to spend in the market. Industries across the nation recognized this increase in purchasing power, and they raced to find ways to woo consumers into their stores. And Stevens? He became a cheerleader for Planned or Perceived Obsolescence, as he deemed it a necessary component of the monetary game to ensure steady sales and a healthy economy. In 1954 at an advertising conference in Milwaukee, Stevens became popular for stating that businesses need to, "Instill in the buyer the desire to own something a little newer, a little better, and a little sooner than necessary."[30] And later, that "The approach in America is one of making the American consumer unhappy with the product that he has enjoyed the use of for a period, have him pass it on to the second-hand market, and obtain the newest product with the newest possible look."[31]

Stevens' words were music to the ears of the corporate world as they were quick to embrace the designer's favorable sentiments toward business and consumerism. Companies across all industries adopted the trend of producing annual lines of products, and some industries, like the fashion industry, went as far as introducing a new line of clothes for every season. The practice of rolling out new products on a yearly basis helped ensure continued consumption and steady cash flow. And to manufacture the consumer culture Stevens alluded to, marketing and advertising firms worked tirelessly toward molding the mind of the American consumer, to condition and seduce him into mindlessly thirsting for "new."

Marketing teams essentially have one job, and it's not to inform consumers about a product's qualities or specific features. Not at all! It's about creating demand and pushing as much supply off of the shelf as possible. It's about grabbing people's attention and convincing them to purchase the product they were hired to advertise. And to penetrate our minds and hijack our desires, marketing teams employ a number of psychological tricks, including the strategic use of combinations of colors, sounds, visuals, slogans, and much more. Psychologists and behavioral researchers have spent years studying human behavior, and it hasn't taken long for them to discover the secrets to controlling our desires. Thus, marketing has become a science.

One of the most common and effective techniques involves connecting with consumers on an emotional level.[32,33] If advertising campaigns can deceive a man into associating their product with happiness, sex, togetherness, laughter, sex, fun, nobility, sex, or any other warm and fuzzy emotion, then they have a chance at creating a lifetime customer, even if a company's ethics have been called into question or their product can cause harm.[34] Rather than being told about the specs of a Ford truck in a commercial, we might instead watch it climb mountains, jump cliffs, or charge towards a burning house to insinuate fearlessness and adventure; and rather than informing consumers about all of the relevant features of a new iPhone, we are instead shown commercials of people dancing in the streets to signify fun and pleasure. Providing customers with technical information is a waste of time and money, and it's not nearly as effective as creating an emotional connection. Have you ever seen a television advertisement for pharmaceutical drugs? Of course you have. Just about all of them follow the same basic, but effective formula. Attractive males and females wear bright smiles as they walk along sunny beaches or push their children on swings, while a calm, soothing voice explains why their drug is so great over the top of upbeat music playing in the background. The ruse is obvious, but it works wonders. Drug companies (all companies) bombard every one of our senses to better guarantee that we associate their product with positive, feel-good feelings – not negative ones, obviously. That's why, near the end of every pharmaceutical commercial, the voiceover actor rapidly delivers a quiet, monotone disclaimer about a drug's long list of adverse side effects. They want us to tune out the negative and only hear and see the positive. They want emotional, irrational consumers; not practical, informed ones.

The same techniques are used by political officials to win favor of the public and secure their votes. They use flash, strategic visuals, well-timed chants and applauses, sappy music, and empty slogans to connect with voters on an emotional level. Little effort is expended into informing the public about relevant details and specific plans. They just want voters to feel love for them and hate for their competition.

If marketing campaigns aren't appealing to our emotions on a subliminal level, then it is likely they are exploiting our hardcoded *need to belong* that I keep bringing up – our fear of social exclusion. Advertisements, aimed at both adults and children, like to shine bright spotlights on our deepest insecurities and perceived inadequacies to make us feel as though we aren't good enough unless we enhance ourselves with their products. They hit us with a torrent of subliminal threats warning us that if we don't buy their newest product and get with the times that we risk becoming obsolete and outdated within our social circles. We risk being alienated from our pack.

And, as I've pointed out, material goods, like vehicles or clothing have become symbols of social status and worth in our society. If a person walks around wearing old clothes that are weathered and worn, others might perceive him as lacking money and wealth; they might perceive him as being poor. Being poor, obviously, is synonymous with being a failure in our culture. And the last thing anyone wants is to be perceived as a failure and having his societal worth called to the stand. Marketing teams have taken this existential fear of ours and successfully exploited it to their advantage. They've psychologically programmed us to believe how vitally important it is that we keep up with latest fashion trends, that we consistently buy the most popular clothes, up-to-date vehicles, or the freshest Air Jordans if we want to avoid being perceived as failures and being banished from the greater herd. We are constantly pressured into throwing away old versions of product models and making way for newer, sexier, and more socially acceptable models, even if our current one works perfectly fine.

By exploiting normal human "flaws" and threatening consumers on a subconscious level with alienation if they don't conform to the latest manufactured trends, hacking into and commandeering the human mind becomes quite simple.

The contradictory, dual nature of marketing and branding serves to not only ostracize a potential customer, but at the same time works to empower him, just as Sloan did with GM in the roaring 20s. Giving the average American a sense of choice becomes synonymous with freedom. A consumer is made to feel like he is free to choose a product that fits his preferences. He feels free to purchase what he wants, when he wants it, even if it means going into debt to acquire it.

However, especially in the earlier years of marketing and advertising, teams have had to be careful with the overflow of exposure to their potential customers. The best and most effective marketing campaigns keep its customers unaware they are being psychologically manipulated. If a commercial has properly done its job, a company's product and message become so engrained into the subconscious mind of the consumer, that he doesn't even notice his interests have been artificially molded; he doesn't know his "free" will is being controlled. The jobs of marketers have to remain stealthy, for if the consumer does suspect he is being manipulated into giving up his hard-earned cash, he might quickly become disillusioned or distrustful of that company and take his business elsewhere, to a company doing the same thing but less obviously.

From fashion, to day-to-day household items, and to automobiles, the approach of Planned and Perceived Obsolescence has been a key factor to economic growth in America throughout the 20th century and into the present. And economic growth precedes all else in Western society. When we are born today, it cannot be overstated how important our role as consumers has become for the sake of economy, hence why we are exposed to roughly 5,000 advertisements per day.[35,36] What did George W. Bush say shortly after 9/11? "We cannot let the terrorists achieve the objective of frightening our nation to the point…where people don't shop."[37] What better way to remedy grief than to buy a new fur coat. Consume, consume, consume. It's what God intended.

Now, it would be one thing if America was the only society of mindless, throwaway consumers. But, unfortunately, we are not. In our ever-connected global economy, the business model promoted heavily by men like Alfred Sloan and Brooks Stevens has spread across the world in modern times. International corporations see revenue opportunities in every corner of the planet, and their marketing tentacles have been sure to reach them all. Thus, just about every developed nation around the globe has seen their cultures reduced to one of superficial materialism, excessive wastefulness, and hypnotic consumption. Through our trend of overindulgence promoted by marketing, we have begun consuming resources at a rate greater than Earth can replenish – an indication of gross stupidity and insanity. Due to this *resource overshoot*, as I've stated, it would take more than one Earth to sustain our species, which has come at great cost. It doesn't take much common sense or logic, nor do we need a "tree hugger" to tell us that a whole world conditioned to consume, consume, consume can only spell disaster.

In the previous chapter I already discussed the problems of microplastic debris and other trash in the Great Pacific Garbage Patch along with mass deforestation in local regions of America, the Amazon rainforest, and across the planet.

Now, referring to waste, in America alone between 1980 and 2018 the total amount of solid waste generated in this country has increased by 93%, from 151 to 292 million tons per year.[38] During that same span of time, the American population has only increased by 44%. Each day, the average American generates 4.5 pounds of trash – up from 3.7 pounds in 1980. Comparing this number to other countries, the United Kingdom, Germany, and Sweden generate 2.9, 3.7, and 2.8 pounds per person each day, respectively, while the global average is 2.6 pounds.[39] Additionally, we in America comprise just over 4% of the world's population, yet we generate 12% of the world's trash and consume 17% of its energy.[40,41] Whoa! The good news is we have greatly improved upon our recycling habits since 1960. Over the last couple decades, growing concern has also mounted over electronic waste since it's generally not biodegradable and has been rapidly piling up in landfills across the globe due to high turnover – thanks in large part to Planned Obsolescence. A 2014 report showed that Asian countries, with China out in front, take the crown in total e-waste, as they generate a whopping 16 million tons of e-waste per year, while America "only" produces 10 million tons.[42] However, before we in America prematurely bow our heads in shame for not being number one at something, know that we generate 26 pounds per person per year in electronic trash compared to 8 pounds per person in Asia. They just happen to dwarf us in total population. And, as China has been vying to become a dominant power in the global economy, the environmental impact of the country housing over a billion people cannot be overstated. Like the space race in the 60s, China and America seem to be racing to see who can consume the most. It would sure help if we could start churning out more babies if we want to stay on top.

So what exactly does economy mean? What does it mean to economize? When I look up the definition on Dictionary.com, to *Economize* means to "avoid waste or extravagance" and to "conserve." And the definition of *Economy* is, "thrifty and efficient use of material resources; frugality in expenditures," and, "the management of the resources of a community, country, etc." However, if the US and the globe have adopted the spirit of Planned Obsolescence, the practice of either producing inferior goods that fail prematurely or promoting consumers to throw away products before their expiration date in order to maintain steady sales and sustain business, then it would seem the world is not running an *economy*. In fact, one could say the world has been operating an *anti-economy*. Exhausting resources as fast as we can is an extreme drain on Earth, and it's the opposite of intelligent management. But, hey, obsolescence is thought to be the very hallmark of progress. Money trumps all!

So, again, efficiency is the ultimate enemy of a monetary system. As has been illustrated, the longer a product lasts, as in the more efficient it is, the worse it is for business since it reduces the amount of overall sales, which in turn hurts the national "economy." In 1999 General Dynamics sold an armored vehicle to the Canadian Army that was built so well that when the company introduced its new-and-improved model many years later, the Canadian Department of National Defense decided to pass since they were so satisfied with the original model; consequently, General Dynamics engineered themselves out of a $2.1 billion contract.[43] Incentive to produce inferior products is naturally built into the monetary game. By removing money from the picture, we remove that incentive. A system without money doesn't need problems or products to break down for it to flourish. A system without money can simply focus on solving problems that arise in the most efficient way possible without having to worry about whether or not the solution is profitable. And contrary to what I have heard many people claim, in a monetary system not all solutions are profitable. A product that lasts forever is not as profitable as one that isn't as durable in the long run. Cleaning the oceans and rivers is not profitable. Taking care of orphans is not profitable, unless of course government funding or donations flow in and the administrators of the orphanage hoard that cash, or the children are sold to child traffickers, or people are charged fees to spend time with the neglected children. In a system without money, there would be no dilemma in the debate of whether a biotech company should develop "the cure" or, instead, treatments that only stabilize a disease but ensure repeat customers. Whereas the primary goal of producing a product in a monetary system is to make money no matter the social or environmental costs, a system without money obviously doesn't have to spend time and energy focusing on how to generate profits. So, if a creator doesn't have to concern himself with profit, then that liberates him to focus on simply building the best product possible with the given knowledge and technology of the time.

Removing money also removes the urge to hoard ideas or patents, or to protect creative properties from others. The only reason patents exist is for people or companies to maintain a differential or comparative advantage over competition; to ensure they can make money off of their creative property before others can. In a system without money, where profit motive doesn't exist, there is no need to protect ideas. Ideas can be opened up to everyone. All schematics, blueprints, and software code can be open-source. Strength in numbers; more eyes focused on a problem are usually better than fewer eyes.

Activists and critics of our waste culture have been seeking ways to change our patterns of consumption and the way we produce goods. Some people or groups want society to reject inferior goods or goods made to fail. Others urge companies to start manufacturing products that are biodegradable and can sort of mimic nature's processes by feeding the Earth after the products die and go to waste. Though I applaud anyone's efforts to promote change where change is needed, unfortunately, I fear it is all in vain. As long as money remains as the gateway to life, change will come in baby steps, if at all. By the time necessary adjustments do get made, we might have already reached our "point of no return." I guess that's okay, though. Many of us will likely be dead and gone and won't have to deal with the ramifications of our habits. It'll just be our annoying kids, and grandkids, and great grandkids having to pick up after their deceased relatives – they'll be proud of us, I'm sure.

## 7.1 SNAKE HOLES ON THE CLIMB

"See Travis, I think you're wrong about companies not wanting to be efficient in our economy. That makes no sense. They have to be efficient, otherwise a competing company can come in and do it better, and they will be able to capture that share of the market."

If only it were that simple.

Multiple barriers to market exist for budding inventors or entrepreneurs, which of course doesn't make it impossible as new companies find success every year, it just makes the process much easier said than done. For starters, an individual or company would have to come up with a new process or a better product, which is rarely a walk in the park. Then, that individual would have to secure funding to not only research and develop his idea, but then to create a prototype. Next, if he wanted to file a patent, that would require additional financial investment – anywhere from hundreds to thousands of dollars.

Then let's say an individual found a way to accomplish these initial tasks. He would then have to secure even more funding to manufacture, market, and distribute the thing. Additionally, once he enters the marketplace, his product is now competing against highly competitive corporate giants who will do whatever it takes to maintain their share of the market. As I will point out in the following paragraphs and as we've already seen with moguls like John Rockefeller, it is quite easy for corporate giants to dismantle and gobble up smaller, competing companies.

To do this, a corporate giant might offer the new competing business an attractive offer for their patent or product (sometimes this is simply to prevent from being sued). In many cases, the infant company sees dollar signs and an opportunity to cash in quick on his hard work and creative ingenuity, so he will take the corporation's offer (and I can't blame him). Because the corporation already has a brand and steady product lines, many times what will happen is they will take the patent and simply file it away, put it in a "vault" where it is never heard of again. The company *could* choose to produce the new product, but after some financial analysis they would have to decide that the cost of research and development, manufacturing, branding, marketing, and distributing would be worth the effort and investment in the long run. Unless the product is a sure thing, and such a situation rarely exists, or unless the product already has a built-in brand and audience, a company is going to continue doing whatever it is they were doing that was already bringing in consistent revenue.

However, in the event a budding entrepreneur doesn't want to sell his product or patent to a corporate giant, then the corporate giant can take other steps to crush their competition – like pushing for legislation that creates more barriers to market, or by running smear campaigns in the media, or finding bogus grounds to sue (Bill Gates went on a suing rampage to protect Microsoft in its early years), or by using various other means to bully the small business. Companies will go to great lengths to ensure newer technologies or processes aren't allowed to enter the market, unless of course they stand to reap the rewards, which led former president Woodrow Wilson to admit that America is no longer a place where:

> "…a man may choose his own calling and pursue it just as far as his abilities enable him to pursue it; because to-day, if he enters certain fields, there are organizations which will use means against him that will prevent his building up a business which they do not want to have built up; organizations that will see to it that the ground is cut from under him and the markets shut against him… We have, not one or two, but many, fields of endeavor into which it is difficult, if not impossible, for the independent man to enter."[1]

Plenty of aspiring inventors and creators have discovered potentially more efficient processes or products, from medicine to technology, but either lack of funding or pressure from outside forces have stymied such ambitions. For example, in the decades following the Phoebus cartel, dozens of light bulb patents were filed claiming their incandescent bulbs were better, more durable, and more efficient – some even touted lifespans of over 100,000 hours. However, none of them saw the light of day (pun intended) with the presence of the cartel looming over their heads.

The world of medicine, unfortunately, is far from immune to the pressures of industry sharks looking to protect their almighty dollar, too. In 1999, a pilot study was completed to test the efficacy of a nutrition-based cancer treatment, called the Kelley Treatment, against pancreatic cancer.[2] As is well known, pancreatic cancer is typically a death sentence and conventional methods do little to nothing to stop the malignancy. Once the study was published, Dr. Nicholas Gonzalez, the man responsible for taking the baton from a discouraged William Kelley, stated that his Kelley Treatment "…showed the best results for the treatment of pancreatic cancer in the history of medicine."[3] Of the 11 participants in the pilot study, 5 survived for two years, four survived for three years, and two survived for five years. To put these results into perspective, in the clinical trial that won the approval for Gemzar, a chemotherapy used to fight pancreatic cancer, out of its 126 participants not a single person lived beyond 19 months. It seemed Gonzalez potentially had something special with his Kelley Treatment.

The next step for his protocol was to run it in a larger clinical trial, since 11 participants is way too small of a sample size to form any credible conclusion. So, the National Cancer Institute (NCI) awarded Dr. Gonzalez $1.4 million to test his treatment method with a larger sample size and against the best chemo treatment at the time.

However, shortly before the clinical trial commenced, things started to change for Dr. Gonzalez and his team, and not for the better. First, new management at NCI replaced the team that had supported and believed in the Kelley Treatment. Some of the people who had initially been assigned to the study but later removed suddenly became too afraid to talk to Dr. Gonzalez for fear of being fired. One man even feared his work phone was tapped and that Dr. Gonzalez shouldn't call him there.

Next, a team from Columbia University was assigned to supervise the clinical trial. The only problem was, the principal investigator from the Columbia team, Dr. John Chabot, actually helped develop the chemo-regimen that was going up against the Kelley Treatment in the clinical trial – a clear conflict of interest. Once the Columbia team took over, Gonzalez and his constituents were barred from being a part of the admission process, citing a potential bias. This is where things became really sketchy.

Once Dr. Gonzalez was removed from the admission process, the Columbia team started accepting patients into the trial who were too sick to even eat. And since the Kelley Treatment is a nutrition-based treatment, this was a huge issue. If patients were unable to eat, then they would be unable to participate in the study. The Columbia team even accepted patients who were so sick that some died before they were able to start the nutritional therapy. However, since the Columbia team, NCI, and the National Institute of Health (NIH) insisted the study had an "intent to treat provision into protocol," the patients who died before starting the treatment or who were too sick to eat were still included in the overall data and considered as having been "treated" and were marked as failures. Dr. Gonzalez claimed that of the 39 admitted by the Columbia team, maybe 5 or 6 were actually able to do the treatment. The rest were too sick to participate. Yet, they were included in the final statistics.

Because of this, the chemotherapies used against the Kelley Treatment in the clinical trial were made to look like the clear winners. The Columbia team published the results from the study, and the NCI and NIH used that data to discredit the Kelley Treatment as ineffective.

Justifiably upset, Dr. Gonzalez filed a complaint with the Office of Human Research Protection (OHRP) in 2006. After two years of investigating, the OHRP found that almost 70% of the patients in the clinical trial were not properly admitted.[4] Unfortunately, by the time the decision was made, the misleading data had already made the rounds, the Kelley Treatment discredited, Gonzalez labeled a quack, and the $1.4 million in funding lost. And as a result, expensive and ineffective chemotherapy was protected and remains the standard for treating pancreatic cancer.

To this day, surgery, chemotherapy, and radiation remain the standard of care for treating most cancers – though immunotherapies have slowly entered the arena. And one would reasonably expect that over the last 60 years, with the advancements in science and technology, that new treatment methods have significantly improved survival rates; unfortunately, during that span of time mortality rates among cancer patients have changed very little. A meta-analysis looking at records of clinical trials for various cancers from 1990 to 2004 found that the overall contribution of cytotoxic chemotherapy to 5-year survival in adults was estimated at 2.1% in the United States.[5,6] This number supports an older study concluded in 1985 that showed chemotherapy had a mere 3% success rate in helping to avert cancer deaths.[7] Adding insult to injury, chemotherapy oftentimes reduces the quality of a patient's life, and more and more studies are showing that in many cases it is the chemo that ends up being the cause of a cancer patient's death rather than the cancer itself – not to mention, too, it can lead to other cancers.[8,9] When a chemotherapeutic agent is spilled in a hospital, it is considered a hazardous material and extreme measures are taken to clean the toxic mess, yet, we put that stuff into our bodies.[10]

So, even though chemical therapy is ineffective and dangerous, it remains as one of the primary methods of treating cancer. Why? Money, money, money. Billions and billions of dollars in revenue are generated from cancer treatments each year – Revlimid and Keytruda brought in $9.7 billion and $7.2 billion in 2018.[11] Just three doses of the immunotherapy cancer drug, Ipilimumab, given to my Kaitlyn cost around $200,000. Oodalolly! There is incentive for pharmaceutical companies to want to protect such a massive stake in the cancer market. There is incentive for companies to want to block competitors touting "natural" or "alternative" treatments from entering the fray.

"But, if natural treatments were effective in treating cancer, wouldn't a big pharmaceutical company want to buy it and sell it to the public? Couldn't they make billions, also?"

Biotech companies can patent the chemical compounds that make up their chemotherapy drugs. Therefore, once a company synthesizes a drug, spends millions on clinical trials, and gets FDA approval to sell it in the market, only that company can exploit and make money off of their product for the duration of their patent. The company that manufactures the drug is also able to set whatever price it wants on its product to recuperate its vast financial investment, and it doesn't have to worry about competitors undercutting their prices. But here's the thing. Natural substances cannot be patented. Doctors usually won't recommend and insurance companies won't insure treatment methods unless the FDA approves them. In order to get FDA approval, a treatment must be taken through clinical trials to prove its safety and efficacy. The cost just to get approval is substantial. So, let's say that a company like Pfizer spends a few million dollars to test the efficacy of Intravenous High-Dose Vitamin C in cancer patients. Then let's say it's proven to be safe and successful, and it wins approval from the FDA. Now, in order to recuperate their initial investment, Pfizer might need to charge, say, $10,000 per dose. However, since Vitamin C is a natural substance and can't be patented, any company can come in and start selling the treatment to cancer patients immediately. They don't have to wait 20 years like with patented chemotherapies. So, since Merck didn't have to invest millions of dollars in testing the Vitamin C method, it could undercut Pfizer and sell it to patients for $5,000 per dose and make an instant profit. Then, GlaxoSmithKline could enter the competition and sell the treatment for $1,000 per dose. Pfizer would be screwed, and they would almost certainly fail to see any return on their investment.

I'm going to make another bold statement here – but I predict that if money did not exist, chemotherapy would likewise fade away.

So, there is little incentive to take natural substances through clinical trials. Additionally, there is incentive for companies trying to protect their vast investments to want to push natural treatments completely out of the game. If one is approved and becomes successful, it could cause a domino effect in the industry and eat into the exorbitant revenue streams, which could also hurt the overall economy.

So, even if practitioners claim that High-Dose Vitamin C, or Resveratrol, or Hydrogen Peroxide, or the Gerson Therapy, or the Kelley Treatment, or Antineoplastons can successfully cure cancer, it is unlikely that we will ever know for sure whether these methods are actually effective. The chances that a natural treatment will get a fair, unbiased shake in the cancer market are quite slim, and sometimes measures are taken to get methods or substances banned from the United States. For instance, Laetrile was banned from the US due to its toxicity in 1963, even though chemotherapy has also been proven to be highly toxic. Until recent years, Marijuana has been illegal in America and many countries across the globe, even though it has been shown to be safe and successful in relieving symptoms of a number of ailments where conventional medicine is generally ineffective, like with epileptic seizures. The Gerson Therapy, a nutrition-based therapy like the Kelley Treatment, only practices in Mexico and Hungary because it is not allowed in the US.

These are just a couple examples of products or methods that *could* be more efficient than the current or standard, but corporate giants use their substantial resources to ward off such potential competition and protect their investments. It's not some sinister ploy, it's just business. And that's only within the medical and biopharmaceutical industry. It doesn't help, either, that some in the wealthiest sectors of society have detached themselves from the masses and carry a false sense of superiority. So, when decisions are made by wealthy members within a company's board, they may not have the health of the average citizen in their best interest. They might not even care that people could be negatively impacted by decisions they make, as is illustrated by the falsified or misleading clinical trials listed in the section on Trust and Psychiatry; the average citizen is like an expendable farm animal for many at the top of the financial pyramid. The bottom line is more important.

A number of other industries have seen aspiring innovators or innovations blocked from the market, which is perhaps most evident in the oil and auto industry. Throughout the 20th century, attempts by ambitious inventors have been made to develop more fuel-efficient vehicles or engines that run on substances other than petrol (gasoline), but with pressure from oil companies, car companies, and even government, many such developments are buried and never heard of again. To reiterate what I said about the pharma industry, it's not an evil conspiracy; it's business. Oil companies have invested billions of dollars in infrastructure and providing the research and technology to support fossil fuels. And, the companies that use fossil fuels have also poured in billions of dollars to develop and produce technologies and goods that use said fuels. So, by introducing an alternative source of fuel or energy, companies would have to undergo a massive shift and spend billions more to reinvest and rebuild infrastructure and technologies to support that new fuel source. Though cleaner energy or fuel sounds great for the environment and is possible, it simply does not make financial sense. Efficiency and the monetary game oppose one another.

One of the most brilliant minds this world has ever known had lofty ambitions to provide "free" wireless energy to the entire world. The inventor's name was Nikola Tesla, and his Wardenclyffe Tower was going to be the technology to bring his idea to fruition. To give his project legs, JP Morgan initially provided Tesla with seed money. However, and there was a confluence of factors, when investors realized Tesla's plan would have difficulty yielding any sort of return on investment, funding quickly dried up. Requests for money were sent to wealthy businessmen like JP Morgan, George Westinghouse, and John Jacob Astor, but Tesla couldn't acquire the necessary funds to continue his work, and the Wardenclyffe Tower was eventually brought down. Unfortunately, investing in the Serbian inventor's project didn't make financial sense, and to this day it seems no one fully understands Tesla's exact vision or *how* he planned on making his dream a reality.

So, even if a prospective inventor or company wants to enter certain markets and "do it better" than the rest, they face an abundance of hurdles, some of which are nearly impossible to leap. Major competitors don't care if your invention or process might be better for society or the environment; they only care that you are trying to pilfer a portion of their market share, and therefore their revenue. They will do whatever it takes to lock you out to protect shareholder value. If status quo is making them money, then status quo it is!

## 7.2 TECHNOLOGICAL UNEMPLOYMENT: BEWARE, BEWARE, BEWAAAARE

"Anything you can do, I can do better," sang Technology, "anything I can do better than you."

"No you can't," replied Human.

"Yes I can!"

"No you can't."

"Yes I can!"

"You can't build houses."

"Yes I can!"

"You can't plant crops."

"Yes I can!"

"You can't flip burgers or cook food."

"Yes I can!"

"You can't build cars."

"Yes I can, can, can!!!"

"Great," replied Human, "Since you can do everything I don't want to do, I'm going to go learn about Quantum Physics. Ooo, maybe then I can learn how to play guitar!"

Technology didn't respond. It didn't frown. It didn't smile. It just kept on folding Human's clothes.

When people talk about the future of technology, among many fears, two are most consistently brought to the foreground. The first of those fears, one which I believe has been heavily influenced by science fiction novels and cinema, is the idea that futuristic technology – robots, cyborgs, artificial intelligence – will one day become so advanced that it will develop a sort of sentience, which it will then use to take over the world, kill millions, and ultimately enslave the entire human race. Though that is an idea I will not immediately dismiss, I am reminded that all tools, which includes robots and advanced technology, are essentially extensions of us. We create them. We use them to expand our abilities beyond the limits of the human body. If ever robots or artificial intelligence do inflict harm on the human race, it will only be because humans programmed them with those capabilities. So, if anything, it is not artificial intelligence we should fear – it's us. That being said, I believe a greater concern is the escalation of advanced weaponry with increasingly devastating capabilities – nuclear devices, drones, bioweaponry, cyber-attacks – and the massive collateral damage they could cause should military or terrorist organizations decide to use them. The most sophisticated weapons of old, like a catapult used by Edward Longshanks's men in the 14$^{th}$ century, might have been capable of toppling castle walls or violently displacing groups of men, but modern nuclear weapons can decimate entire cities in an instant, while an EMP attack could knock out power to millions.

The second aspect of technology feared by humans, one that has been feared for centuries now, is the idea that machines will eventually take away our jobs and therefore, our ability to acquire money and the ability to purchase survival. Of the two fears mentioned, loss of employment due to automation has a more immediate effect on the livelihood of millions, mainly because it's actually happening. Right now. And it's been happening for decades, and at an ever-increasing rate. In the past, technological change happened so slowly that job creation could keep pace with jobs lost. However, as computing power has doubled about every two years over the past 50 years and continues to rapidly improve, job losses have been outpacing job gains; a trend that will only get worse as we march into the future, meaning it will become more and more difficult for displaced workers to keep up with having to learn new skills and find new jobs as often as might be required. In a 2017 report, analysts at the McKinsey Global Institute estimate that by 2030 roughly 30% of jobs will be lost to automation, which in America would leave some 70 million people out of work and needing to be retrained.[1] Other reports yield higher numbers. McKinsey analysts also concluded that roughly 50% of "current work activities are technically automatable by adapting currently demonstrated technologies."[2]

With today's technological advancements, there aren't many menial tasks humans can do anymore that a machine can't do better and at reduced cost. For instance, various companies have developed automated warehouse systems, like the one out of Kiva Systems (now Amazon Robotics) where fleets of mobile robots traverse under and around moveable shelves, allowing inventory to be picked, sorted, packed, and stored automatically.[3,4] On the streets, Uber has invested in the development of driverless vehicles that threaten some 5,000,000 Uber, Lyft, bus, and taxi drivers in America – Ford, Tesla, Apple, and many other companies have also begun testing and using self-driving vehicles. Autonomous freight trucks that have successfully completed cross-country shipments pose a threat to the 3.5 million truck drivers across the nation; the self-driving trucks don't need to stop for naps, potty breaks, or food.[5] In the culinary world, a company called Suzumo has created Sushi Robots that can prepare more sushi with fewer people.[6] McDonald's, Taco Bell, and a number of fast food chains have begun testing and using automated cooks that can flip burgers and dunk fries and chicken nuggets into deep fryers, along with voice-recognition systems that can take orders at the drive-thru.[7,8,9] FoldiMate developed a machine that can fold clothes, which could eventually find application in retail departments.[10,11] Amazon Go stores have eliminated the need for cashiers as its *Just Walk Out* technology allows customers to simply grab grocery items off the shelf and leave without having to scan them at a cash register; shoppers are charged once they leave.[12] Jeff Bezos, Amazon's overlord, even envisions a supermarket shopping experience completely automated by robots, where machines grab and bag items for customers and maintain inventory; these stores might only need 3 human workers to operate.[13,14]

But it isn't just menial, low-skill labor that is at risk. Even tasks requiring higher levels of skill will eventually be replaced by machines. In healthcare, robotic technology is currently used to assist in surgery, allowing for better precision and faster recovery times.[15,16] Though complete robotic autonomy in surgery is a few years away, companies continue to develop systems that reduce human involvement. Therapeutic robots are being used or tested in hospitals to facilitate rehab exercises for patients; Japanese machines are being used to assist patients in bathing, getting dressed, and preparing food.[17] Pharmacies have begun adopting robots to process and fill drug prescriptions since they can do it faster and with higher accuracy.[18] Engineers at various institutions are developing agricultural robots programmed to perform a wide range of farming activities, including driverless tractors to plant seeds, scan crops, and remove weeds, and machines to collect lettuce or pick apples.[19] And, companies around the world – America, Russia, China – have successfully built homes using 3D Printing technology.[20] In 2018, ICON constructed a 350-square-foot home in 48 hours and for $10,000 using such technology; they claim they can build a 2,000-square-foot home for about $20,000.[21]

As technology continues to progress, just about every occupation is at risk of being supplanted either now or in the very near future by more efficient automation. And that should be a good thing! Machines are tools, as I've stated. We create tools to make tasks easier, whether it is prehistoric humans using hammerstones instead of their hands to craft spears or crush nuts or Henry Ford introducing motor vehicles to make travel less exhausting and less time-consuming. We create tools so that we don't have to expend as much time and effort chopping down trees or planting crops or building houses. Tools free us from drudgery. They free us from the dangerous and the mundane, and from having to worry day in and day out about basic survival, which in turn frees us to dedicate what limited years we have on this planet to spending time with loved ones or tackling challenges that are more interesting and more fulfilling to us. Modern machines are simply the most advanced tools currently in existence – nothing more, nothing less; the progeny of human creativity and ingenuity, born out of the need to solve problems.

Unfortunately, we live in a global monetary system, which means humans need money in order to access the means to survive. Even though automation significantly cuts down on the time it takes to perform various tasks, that time saved has not trickled down to the workforce; Americans are working more than ever before – due in part to wages having stagnated over the past few decades while inflation has continued to rise.[22] Living within the constraints of a monetary system also means that technological progress is not embraced or celebrated the way it would be if we were not living in a monetary system. Rather, in many ways it is viewed as a threat; it's a threat to human employment within our market economies, which means it is a threat to the individual's ability to put food on the table and provide for himself and his family. And, a threat to employment is a threat to the health of the entire financial system.

See, if workers are displaced by machines, that means those people will not be working, obviously. If people are not working, that means they won't be making money. If they aren't making money, they can't buy goods

– food, clothing, toys. If they can't buy goods, then businesses won't receive money of any kind, which eventually forces them to close up shop. Paradoxically, if the number of displaced workers becomes too great in the future, the machines that replaced those workers will essentially be creating products for people that no longer have money to buy them. And at that point, assuming the system has remained unaltered because change terrifies us and because a few men derive substantial benefit from it, the economy screeches to a halt. The financial system would collapse; and though machines would have created an abundant supply of goods, the people would not have the money to access them. Thus, products would remain on shelves; if it's food, it would rot on shelves. Again, that is in a vacuum where the financial system continues to run as designed, technology continues to rapidly expand, and more and more workers are unable to find work after losing their jobs. Efficiency is the greatest enemy of any monetary system, and no example does a better job of highlighting this inverse relationship than automation and modern technology uprooting the global workforce. Should current technology be applied to its maximum capacity, we could achieve near optimum levels of efficiency, yet our financial systems would crumble to the Earth.

Modern machines are today's pinnacles of efficiency. At an increasing rate, technological advancements are allowing us to do more and more with less and less. Ephemeralization is what that is called – a term coined by the late R. Buckminster Fuller. With less effort, less energy, and fewer resources, we can produce more goods at a faster clip. And from the viewpoint of a CEO trying to increase shareholder value and maintain his job, the prospect of reduced costs over time and an increase in product output offered by automated systems is an attractive one. Along with an uptick in efficiency, machines can work 24 hours a day, 7 days a week. They don't require health insurance or vacation days. They don't take smoke breaks, spend half the day surfing the web, or steal from the cash register. And they don't bitch, ask for raises, get paid overtime, or protest working conditions. When it comes to increasing profit margins for companies, sometimes technology just makes financial sense. One might complain about ethics when a company installs new machines and cuts 600 jobs, but it's simply business. Companies are making logical financial decisions and doing what they are allowed to do within the game, doing what they need to do to survive and flourish. In an ever-competitive global market, companies can't afford to be "ethical" if they want to compete against other companies doing the same thing.

Using a simple abstract, let's say Roger at Advanced Medical, Inc. installs machines to manufacture syringes. The machines allow him to cut most of his labor force and greatly reduce operating expenses. By reducing costs, Roger now has the ability to decrease prices on his syringes, undercut his competitors, and attract more consumers. And consumers, always looking for the best deals, turn away from competing companies and purchase syringes from Roger. Now Dick at Progressive Syringes, Inc. has a problem. Because Roger can charge much lower prices and still churn out a profit, Dick's customer base has all but left him. If Dick wants to stay in business, he has little choice but to follow suit with Roger. So, Dick also purchases new machinery to produce his syringes; like Roger, he cuts most of his workforce, which helps reduce costs and allows Dick to decrease prices to a similar level as Roger, thus saving his company. It's not about ethics, it's about survival. It's about staying competitive with other companies and keeping the business afloat.

As a practical example, technology companies in China have begun shifting almost entirely to automation in their production facilities. For instance, after Changying Precision Technology Company introduced automated systems in its factory to produce cell phone parts, it was able to reduce its work staff from 650 employees to 60. And, to the company's benefit, production quantities nearly tripled and the defect rate was reduced from 25% to under 5%.[23]

Unfortunately, decisions to upgrade to automated systems aren't always driven by the need to survive in the marketplace. Sometimes it is about increasing profit margins and putting more money into the pockets of a very few. In my over-simplified example above, when Roger at Advanced Medical installs his new machines and lays off his employees, he no longer has to split the revenue with anyone else. All of the profits from his business can go straight into his pocket rather than having to be shared with employees – 1 man can capture the revenue of 300. Some might argue that it is *this* type of behavior that is unethical, but I continue to reiterate that it is just part of the game. If we are conditioned to compete and acquire as much as possible, and if acquiring as much as possible helps better secure our survival and comfort, then by golly that is what some people will do, even if it comes at the expense of a great many; we just have to be ready and willing to face the predictable public health consequences.

But again, therein lies the great paradox, if most of the revenue is going to but a few men and the majority of the population is unable to acquire money, then the products being produced will remain on shelves, and even the revenues of those privileged few will eventually dry up. Like the game of Monopoly, once one man acquires all of the money in circulation, the game ends; the pieces go back in the box. Only, in this manmade game of money superimposed on top of the game of life, when most of the wealth is consolidated into the hands of a few due to technological unemployment, the majority become incredibly poor and struggle to access the means to survive, suffering ensues on a grand scale, and it is easy to predict that chaos, panic, and insurrection would likely result. Additionally, once the wealth has consolidated into the hands of a very few, leaving everyone else with very little money to compete for, acquire, and then use to purchase the means to survive – like with my Thought Experiment from Chapter 4.1 – people would become so desperate that they would have no choice but to submit to the business owners, the money-holders, the Johns and the Rogers, if only to acquire a fraction of their pile of money in order to buy food. At this stage in the game, the business owners would wield more power over the greater majority than ever before. And with that leverage, with millions of people out of work and competing for scarce jobs or gigs, the business owners would be in full control when it comes to salary negotiation; they would have the ability to pay people basement level wages. If 20 hungry people are fighting for one job, emaciated Elliot might be willing to work for $3.00 per hour as long as he can buy a loaf of bread for his family. But then, gaunt Gary could come in and offer to work for $2.95 per hour before haggard Harold tries haggling with an offer of $2.50. And the bidding war to the bottom begins!

Technological advancement essentially gives us two possible roads to choose. The first road, the one unlikely to be traveled, offers a scenario where machines and automation advance to the point where basic needs are produced in surplus with very little human involvement. Down this road, rather than swimming up current, we would choose to allow our advanced tools to provide us with what tools are meant to provide us with – freedom from the mundane. Freedom to ascend the *hierarchy of needs* ladder and take on challenges that can achieve our need for self-actualization and allow us the rare opportunity to strive toward reaching our fullest potential, to fully realize our talents and skills. By providing people with access to life necessities, they would no longer be living mostly to survive. They would be living to live and experience this once-in-a-lifetime opportunity of life. Of course, I know modern society is allergic, mainly through years of social conditioning, to such an idea of citizens receiving any good or service without monetary exchange, but if the means of survival are produced in excess, what's the point of making people exchange money for them anymore? If machines can produce 20 loaves of bread with no human involvement and there are only 5 families, why not just give the families bread? Why make them first acquire artificially-valued green paper, then exchange that artificially-valued green paper for the bread? It's an unnecessary step. Of course, much of the reason why is due to the control and the power that the system of money affords few men. Using money and wages is a tactic to control humans and coerce them to produce, produce, produce. By holding money just out of reach unless people work – extortion – they can be pushed into hopeless servitude; they can be pushed to produce, produce, produce, even if it causes misery and suicidal ideation, like in Asian sweatshops or in Spanish strawberry fields. But, if humans are no longer needed as much to produce, then it would seem the use of money and wages would no longer be necessary. Money and wages would be obsolete.

So that's the first road offered by automation.

The second road, the one most likely to be traveled, follows the trend we are currently on. And that trend is, machines and automation will continue to be installed since they are more efficient, can reduce costs, and can increase profit margins. Machines and automation will continue taking jobs away from employees, the invisible hand will struggle to keep up with creating new jobs for those unemployed, the rulers will pocket the majority of the revenue, poverty will increase, and income inequality will stretch as far as it's ever been stretched before. And considering what we've already discussed in terms of the relationship between crime and income gaps, the picture that dystopian novels and films paint might not be far from reality.

And I understand my biased forecast might sound like fear-mongering, but I just see it as being the most logical outcome should the vast majority become incredibly poor. I'm not afraid of it, so maybe that means I am not fear-mongering? I also understand the argument on the other side of the coin, that if people have access to the necessities of life, if basic needs are "free," then they will become lazy and the economy will collapse and creativity will be stifled due to human inactivity. However, I will do my best to point out in Chapter 9 that this would not be the case, that humans are not the lazy creatures they are often portrayed to be. Rather, we are a creative species searching for purpose and fulfillment; sitting around all day does little to achieve those goals. Boredom and idleness hurt.

In a system where money-for-survival is eliminated, there is zero concern for profitability; rather, the primary focus is on technical efficiency. If an emerging technology is proven to be safe and more efficient than the current process, then we put it to use. We install the new tool while continuing to improve upon it and the process. However, in contrast, technical efficiency is not the primary focus within the monetary game – profitability is. So, even if technology exists that can make production faster, safer, or more efficient, if it does not help the bottom line, then it is not installed. And oftentimes in the monetary system, installing the most current, state-of-the-art, advanced tools is not profitable, because in the early years of a technology's life, it usually comes with a steep price tag. What I am implying is that the current system of money slows technical progress because financial gains come before efficiency. While the main goal of our monetary arrangement is to acquire money, the main goal of a moneyless society would be to establish a true *economy*, which means being as efficient as possible.

Whether we approve or disapprove, technology is here to stay. And if the trends of the past 50 years predict anything, it's that it will continue to improve, and it will continue replacing more human jobs than ever before. And that should be a good thing. In a society that doesn't use an arbitrary medium of exchange to distribute resources, where technological unemployment is not a concern, any technological advancement that can produce more goods or better results while cutting down on time, energy, and waste would be celebrated with open arms. In a moneyless world, if a machine came in and *relieved* a man of his mundane tasks, it would be just that, a *relief*. He would have the opportunity to progress toward different challenges without putting his daughter's life at risk. But, unfortunately, as long as we need money to access goods to survive, continued technological advancement will largely be perceived as a threat – at least as far as jobs are concerned – and new tools will be introduced to society at a much slower rate than they could be.

# 8 LAISSEZ-FAIRE CAPITALISM: A GAME WITHOUT REFS

To Govern or not to Govern, that is the question! Whether 'tis nobler in the mind to suffer the slings and arrows in the ravenous pit of the "Free" Market, or to take arms against the sea of troubles brought on by Big Brother's outrageous oversight. Damned if ye do, and damned if ye don't, 'tis my answer.

To have Government, or not to have Government; that is the question Americans have squabbled over for years. And in this chapter, my primary focus will be on one side of this contentious dilemma – *not* to have Government. That is, I will attempt to explore the philosophies of Free Market or Laissez-Faire Capitalism, the idea of completely removing or significantly reducing the role of government within a pure Capitalist system, and why such a setup would be calamitous for civilization. On a secondary level, I will also attempt to address the idea that relying on Government institutions to oversee the inner workings of society and enforce its rules is not a recipe for success, either. For the sake of simplicity and much to the chagrin of many, I'm sure, there are a number of terms and groups I am going to lump together and use interchangeably throughout this section. When I use terms such as Libertarianism, Anarcho-Capitalism, Free Market Capitalism, Neoliberalism, or Laissez-Faire Capitalism, I will simply be referring to the idea or the desire for a system where government involvement is eliminated or reduced in the marketplace, with the hope of allowing trade to flow more organically. I know definitions within each of these subgroups vary to a degree or two, but it seems the desire for no or reduced government is the unifying principle of them all. Lastly, I understand that Libertarianism is more of a movement than an actual system, and I know that it can lean left or right in its ideologies, but since Libertarianism is commonly associated with Laissez-Faire Capitalism in our country, that is how I will address it.

Now, I want to do my best in this chapter not to antagonize, insult, or demean, because at the end of the day, I believe we are all essentially seeking the same ends. We all want to live in a social setup where violence and suffering are eliminated. And we all want to live as freely and peacefully as possible. But, the trillion-dollar question has always been – how? How do we achieve such lofty goals? How do we eliminate the negative externalities plaguing our society? What system is the best system to maximize freedom and productivity while minimizing oppression? From my research, I believe those in Libertarian factions or those supporting Free Market Capitalism have the best interest of the public in mind (even if self-interest is the common theme). And though I might disagree with the feasibility of the Laissez-Faire concepts, I admire the effort, passion, and intent behind its supporters. And, just because I disagree with the workability of its concepts doesn't mean I am necessarily right. Sure I've researched and lost many nights of sleep ruminating over why I disagree with it, but like every human being, my opinions and conclusions are naturally loaded with bias and a set of values unique to me. All that being said, making statements that some might take offense to appears unavoidable when attempting to be critical of certain ideas.

Nevertheless, because the idea of Laissez-Faire Capitalism has drawn such a large number of supporters as a solution to the country's and the world's woes, I feel compelled to address this topic and do my best to show why I think it could not work. None of my gripes are anything new to the Libertarian movement; most have been addressed to some extent. However, many of the explanations and proposed solutions in regards to privatizing military, police, schools, laws, and the court system leave me unsatisfied, unconvinced, and doubtful. For instance, in talking about how military and national defense would be funded without Government financing, Murray Rothbard, one of the more highly regarded Libertarians, suggests there won't be war since citizens in an Anarcho-Capitalist society would agree to "no aggression" towards others.[1] In his book *For a New Liberty: The Libertarian Manifesto*, he also adds that it would be disadvantageous and a headache for a foreign country to attack a stateless society, so they either wouldn't attack at all or they would attack and then give up or fail.[2] Just based on the history of human civilizations across the world, I can't imagine territorial fighting would cease just because government is disbanded, especially if one territory has something the other territory wants and finds value in. Others suggest that military could be paid through private insurance. One of the problems (among many) with that proposal is that people could choose not to pay for military insurance, yet they would still receive the benefits since the military, in defending the entire country, would be defending that person who hasn't paid, too. To build and maintain an effective military, substantial investment is required, and if enough people elect not to pay, either because they can't afford it or don't want to, then pooling together enough financial resources may prove difficult. Nevertheless, when it comes to military and national defense, many Libertarians concede, including the much-respected David Friedman,[3] that government is probably needed for such an institution to work effectively. So, even though I understand that most of my objections have been addressed to some extent by very smart people within the Libertarian community, I still want to lay them out in this text because there are a number of readers who don't know much about it.

And finally, though I might be critical of Laissez-Faire ideals, I am not championing more government. The downfall of critiquing a certain philosophy or group is that it is often construed as support for its opposition. In this instance, I feel like I'm comparing Mao's reign to Hitler's (a poor analogy and a bit extreme, I know, but it gets my point across). If someone said Mao's leadership was better in every way than Hitler's leadership, I could probably find areas where I thought they were wrong, but in doing so, I might actually have to defend Hitler, which would make it seem like I supported him. I don't want to do that. I don't support Hitler, and I don't necessarily support Government. Both situations suck! Both Mao's and Hitler's regimes led to the suffering of millions. The same can be said whether we have a monetary system run by a central, governing body, or if every institution was completely privatized – millions would suffer hardships and death either way. So, just because I try to disprove certain Laissez-Faire ideas, doesn't mean I support state control, even if certain topics require me to defend the state – like with the military. In many regards I agree with a number of Libertarian philosophies and critiques, and I believe they are right when it comes to the inefficiencies and control of public institutions. However, although various institutions and consumers, speaking solely within the current monetary paradigm, would benefit from being privatized and having to face competition, abolishing government would not solve the most detrimental problems we face. On the contrary, doing so would likely exacerbate such problems.

Alright, moving on from this overly verbose exordium.

Advocates of pure Free Market Capitalism – not to be confused with the current form of Capitalism applied in the US today, which is more of a mixed economy, a hybrid of "-isms" – want government intervention removed from the marketplace to allow for the forces of competition and consumer demand to set prices and regulate the actions of business. By removing trade restrictions often imposed through government action – taxes, tariffs, legislation – it is believed that prices of products and services would naturally fall into equilibrium, and the value of a product or service would be more accurately reflected in its price. Many proponents of a Free Market system promote the idea of Voluntarism and the Non-Aggression Principle, and they view actions taken by government as being inherently coercive and forceful. For instance, taxes. For the most part, we don't have a choice of whether or not we want to pay taxes. Every week or two when we receive a paycheck, the government confiscates a portion of our income without our consent. Additionally, through pricing mechanisms and competition, Free Market Capitalists believe the market is naturally self-regulating; and to an extent, this is true. If Lights 'R Us makes a deficient light bulb, consumers will choose to buy from a competing business, signaling to Lights 'R Us that they ought to improve upon the quality of their bulbs or risk bankruptcy. Naturally, because the company wants to stay in business, it is in their best interest to make a better light bulb. Conversely, when it comes to the federal government, there are no competing governments within the country to uphold standards and keep them in check, and they don't have to worry about going bankrupt in the same way private ventures do. Because the government is essentially a monopoly, there is a natural lack of accountability and a lack of incentive, in theory, to provide goods or services of the highest quality. In a truly Free Market, where every industry is privately owned and operated – including armies, police forces, schools, and food production – the idea is that the market would hold them accountable, that the natural laws of the open market would theoretically regulate their actions, and unrestricted competition along with consumer demand would ensure high standards and incentivize proper behavior. Thus, all transactions between individuals would result in a voluntary exchange where both parties are equally benefitted. If I want a banana and George wants to sell a banana, then our exchange would be voluntary and each of us would have theoretically gotten what we wanted without force or coercion.

And the final element I want to mention within the Free Market ideology is one predicated around the idea that humans are inherently selfish, and within the market economy they will seek to appease their own self-interests. However, according to the philosophies of economists like the great Adam Smith, this is a good thing.[4] He, as well as many others after him, theorizes that when individuals strive to satisfy their own self-interests (while respecting property rights of others), that they will, perhaps unintentionally, end up making economic decisions that not only benefit themselves, but the entire economy. In a nutshell, this is part of the doctrine of the Invisible Hand.

So far, the logic and moral code of the Libertarian movement sound pretty reasonable on paper. Heck, from a moral standpoint, I think I could classify myself as Libertarian. Not only do I believe people should be free to do as they please, so long as they don't harm others, but I also believe it is immoral to initiate force onto anyone else. And that is the central principle among Libertarians. However, it is from an economic standpoint where my logic starts to diverge.

The monetary systems we have constructed to facilitate the production and distribution of resources – all shades of Capitalism and Socialism – operate as a game. At the start of this game, a pile of money is dumped onto the board. And the objective of each player within the game is to collect as much money as he can, because the stakes are life and death. The more money a man can collect, the more secure his position of survival will be. Should a player fail to collect money, he will not be able to obtain the necessities of life, like food, meaning he won't be able to eat, meaning he will suffer and potentially die. With this type of economic design, where the tool that grants us access to survival is limited amongst the game's participants, it is not difficult to see how ruthlessness can emerge. And as I have already stated, the primary difference in the Socialist rulebook compared to the Capitalist rulebook is that when one or a small handful of players obtain a vast majority of the game's money, leaving the rest of the players scrounging for what little remains, the "winning" players must give some back to the game. Nevertheless, both economic designs suffer from the same monetary constraints; both are trying to operate with the finite amount of money in this zero-sum predicament.

So, our financial system is akin to a game, and games typically need rules (laws) to maintain a semblance of order and to prevent it from getting out of hand. As culture has continued to evolve and unique situations arise that were not foreseen during the game's conception, rules are constantly updated and created as needed – like with child labor or chattel slavery. In the absence of such rules, as history has shown, there are a number of players willing to act in a way that might give them a competitive advantage in the marketplace, but that most of society deems socially unacceptable or unethical; for instance, companies have and continue to exploit children for labor because it often reduces financial costs and better helps certain individuals collect more money in their quest to win the game, but most people think this practice is reprehensible. Unfortunately, rules aren't the *end all-be all* for preventing unwanted behavior – even though labor laws exist within America, companies across the country still employ illegal workers, pay them below minimum wage, and they do it outside of the purview of the rule keepers; or, even though laundering illegal drug money is against the rules, commercial banks have been caught doing just that,[5,6] again, because the allure of collecting more money is so powerful. The competitive nature of the game and the incredible stakes are conducive to immoral behavior.

Not all games need officials to oversee its players and ensure they are following the rules. In many games, usually small-scale ones, like Pictionary or Scattergories, players do a pretty good job of regulating themselves, though it is not uncommon for bickering or cheating to occur. However, our most competitive games in society, the ones with the highest stakes, employ a neutral body of officials to uphold and enforce the rules. And when it comes to the monetary game we've developed to organize society, there is no other game in the world that is more competitive or has higher stakes. Thus, within our monetary game, like other competitive games within society, individuals (officials) are installed to uphold and enforce its rules – a governing body. The institution responsible for overseeing and maintaining this game's rules, the referees in charge of making sure participants play fairly and aren't changing the face of the dice when no one's looking, we have taken to calling it the Government.

Rather than being an entirely separate entity as many perceive it be, the governing body is simply a part of the market; it is a natural outgrowth – like an arm or a leg – of a competitive game that needs rules to make sure it's not tipped too far out of balance. The reality of it is, the more inadequacies, the more inequities discovered throughout the game's progression, the more rules are added; hence, bigger government. In a pure Free Market economy, there theoretically are no rules. There are no restrictions in competition. There are simply guidelines, principles with which we would like people to follow. Though many Laissez-Faire proponents believe "some" government is needed, the spirit of a true Free Market system is the right for players to compete unimpeded by state-imposed restrictions. Enlisting the services of a governing body to oversee <u>some</u> rules and mitigate <u>some</u> inadequacies of the game becomes a slippery slope to bigger government as more citizens fall victim and suffer due to other inadequacies within the game. Friedman and Rothbard concur that *some* or *limited* government typically leads to more government.

The great paradox, however, that separates the monetary game from other competitive games within our culture is that the officials within other games (basketball, football, etc.) are neutral; on a fundamental level, they don't have a vested interest in the players or the outcomes of the games. They are paid merely to officiate. But, in our monetary game, the referees also happen to be the players. Those individuals comprising our governing body are also competing in the game; they too are trying to collect as much money as they can to secure their comfort and survival – to win. Due to this unavoidable predicament since no one really has a choice of whether or not they want to participate in the game, our officials become susceptible to unethical behavior, such as bribery. It is not uncommon for our referees to accept money from wealthy bidders in exchange for creating or adjusting rules that benefit those bidders and help them gain an advantage over other players within the game. And even though the practice of selling legislation to the highest bidder sounds unfair and unethical, and even though it used to be viewed as corrupt and was sometimes treated as criminal activity, and even though paying the refs to bend the rules is considered cheating in every other game, it just so happens to be a legal part of the game nowadays – lobbying. So now, by using their substantial wealth, those currently winning the game have the unique ability to have rules created in their favor, which helps alleviate any worry that they could ever be knocked out of their winning positions. They are able to widen the goal posts only for themselves, essentially rigging the game and making it incredibly difficult for those losing the game to ever unseat the winning few. And the referees (Congressmen, government officials, etc.) who have accepted bribes throughout history don't do it because they are inherently bad or unethical, they do it because, well, they do it now because it's legal, but also they are simply trying to win the game for the sake of survival and the wellbeing of their families. If selling legislation helps maintain a winning position, I'd be hard-pressed to find an individual who wouldn't be tempted by that, even in the past when it was against the rules.

Because the referees double as players within the game, they are also susceptible to favoritism. Whereas referees in other games must act impartially toward other players, the referees in our monetary game often tend to give preferential treatment toward the winners while discriminating against the losers. After all, they aren't going to incriminate an individual or organization that donates to their campaigns and helps bolster their positions within the game. And they aren't about to incriminate the friends or family of such an individual either; it's in their best interest not to. Doing so would put their high positions and life security at risk.

So again, the great paradox is that rules are required within this highly competitive game of survival in order to reduce suffering and minimize repulsive behavior, but the men we assign to oversee those rules also happen to be playing the game, which naturally creates a conflict of interest and opens the game up to other forms of deplorable behavior. Because our governing body is also playing the game, it is exposed to corruption. Corporations – comprised of individuals – leverage these circumstances to their advantage, and since they have the most money, are able to offer the highest bids to the game's officials. The highest bidders, historically speaking – the Lockheed Martins, the Monsantos, and the Johnson & Johnsons – typically get their way, which means it is corporate interests largely writing the rules and hiring their own referees within our monetary game, within society. And if an individual or organization wants a rule created, it is often for the purpose of gaining or maintaining a competitive advantage within the game, which means he is going to want a rule that ideally benefits him and hinders everyone else – a situation often attributed to "Crony Capitalism."

When corporations use Government institutions to manipulate legislation and tilt the game in their favor, Libertarian supporters perceive this as Crony Capitalism, or a metamorphic abomination of Capitalism, an exception within the system derived solely from the existence of Government. And it is the assumption of Free Market advocates that if government were removed or significantly reduced from the game, that Crony Capitalism would cease to exist. But I say "nay." The natural progression of our monetary game naturally ends at Crony Capitalism, as it goes from (1) a "Free" Market system, (2) to a system with some government oversight after the realization that a governing body is needed to enforce some rules to mitigate suffering, (3) to bigger government after inadequacies continue to be discovered within the game and more rules are added, (4) to individuals and corporations using that big government to their financial advantage, (5) to corporations essentially becoming government as they place their people, their puppets, into influential government positions. Whether one calls it a Government or High Council, a governing body ends up being a natural outgrowth of the game. Crony Capitalism is simply the end game of a Free Market system – the logical progression. That's why I say it is damned if you do, damned if you don't when it comes to the debate of whether or not to employ Government and how much.

Like I stated earlier, the greatest misconception is that Government and the Private Market are separate. They are not. The market is the locus, the central body of our economy, and Government is merely a branch grown from it. It is sprouted from the seeds of Free Market inadequacies. And because the Free Market is constantly confronted with problems that private industry is not equipped or incentivized to solve, the Government branch naturally grows bigger and bigger, until it gets to the point where Government is so big that private industry and the Government feed into and off of each other. It is a cycle that repeats itself over and over again; the pendulum swings back and forth between regulation and deregulation. Throughout history, whenever government eases off the brakes or takes deregulatory measures within the market, though some private businesses do quite well in creating efficient products or services, the overall market becomes unstable, as inequities quickly arise amongst the population, wealth disparity increases, agitation and injustices grow within the greater community, and government then steps back in to try to strike a balance. For instance…

During the Industrial Revolution in America, the market was as free as it ever was. Following Andrew Jackson's abolishment of the country's central bank, Government took a more hands-off approach in other industries, as well, and allowed individuals and companies to simply compete within the market. Though high levels of material productivity were achieved in the 19th and early-20th centuries, the period was also marred by great misery and gross inequality. Workers had little to no rights, and with no standards and no regulations to protect the labor force, working conditions within factories were dangerous and unhealthy.[8] It cost money to install safeguards, so if an owner could get away with it, he would forego safety protocols for larger profit margins. As a result, accidents on the job were abundant – from 1880 to 1900 roughly 35,000 employees died each year in factory and mine accidents, the highest number in the industrial world.[9] And if a worker was badly injured or killed on the job due to safety measures being neglected, the owner faced no consequences, and he could easily find a replacement amongst the surplus of unemployed at the time. And as for the injured worker, he was basically abandoned. There was no medical assistance or workers' compensation for him or his family.

Additionally, because there were so many people desperate for wage paying labor, workers had almost no bargaining power. Therefore, workers were paid low wages that barely covered living expenses. They often worked 12 to 16 hours a day, 6 days a week, with no overtime, no vacation, and no holidays.[10] With few windows and insufficient ventilation, air quality was poor in the oppressively hot steel factories. This led to sicknesses, lung diseases, and eye problems.

And maybe worst of all, small children, as young as 4 years old, worked in the dark, smoky, and dangerous factories and mines.[11] Though they were valued because their small bodies could zip around and between unfenced, exposed machinery, kids were paid a fraction of what men were paid – they were cheap labor to the owners.[12] Many children were deprived of a decent education, proper physical activity, and nutrition, which led many to experience stunted development and health issues. In young girls, due to having to pull coal-filled carts or sledges all day, every day, they developed deformed pelvic bones, which contributed to an uptick in deaths during childbirth.

Needless to say, working conditions during the most Laissez-Faire period of America resembled the present working conditions of underdeveloped countries I mentioned earlier in this book – like those in Africa and India. With few regulations, it is now workers in those foreign countries left to endure low pay, dangerous conditions, long hours, and child labor. Awful conditions have essentially been outsourced to less regulated countries – though sweatshops are still prevalent in America.

In response to children being thrown into the factories and deprived of an education, and as a response to poor working conditions, nonexistent worker rights, an abundance of deaths and injuries on the job, and rapidly increasing wealth inequality, Big Brother inevitably stepped in; throughout the first half of the 20$^{th}$ century, Government introduced legislation to curtail child labor and give more rights to the labor force. They initiated a minimum wage, standards on work hours, overtime laws, and more. Since workers had no bargaining power in the Laissez-Faire market of the Industrial Revolution, they basically had no way out – akin to underdeveloped countries of today. Intervention by the state was one of their few bastions of hope. Like it or not, the Government's actions were induced by inadequacies in the wild, wild market.

Another of the concerns critics have with Laissez-Faire policies is that it allows for monopolies or oligopolies to form. Supporters, however, assert that this would not happen in a pure Free Market, that monopolies would not form because if a corporation raised prices above market value, then a competitor could simply enter the game and charge lower prices. And then, if the monopoly tried to undercut the new company's prices, David Friedman suggests the new company simply has to make adjustments to outlast the behemoth in a war of attrition; after all, with a greater market share, the monopolistic company will lose more money if prices are cut.[13] The new, smaller company simply has to take actions like laying off workers or shutting down parts of its plant – no problem. Or, in the scenario where the monopoly undercuts prices only in the new company's region, but charges higher prices in other regions, then the new company simply has to open up additional firms in the markets where the monopoly has raised its prices[14] – no problem once again, because opening up a new firm is super easy and doesn't take heaps of capital investment, not to mention the extreme, and sometimes violent measures powerful corporations might take and have taken throughout history to make sure competitors stay out of their business.

Once again, one only needs to look at the circumstances within the Gilded Age of the $19^{th}$ century to get a glimpse as to what happens in the game when the referees take a *more* hands-off approach. Along with abysmal working conditions, monopolistic behavior was rampant during the Industrial Revolution, most notably in the railroad industry. In an attempt to stamp out competition and control the market, one of the strategies adopted by wealthy business moguls, like JP Morgan, was to join forces with other companies and form what are known as Trusts, which came complete with their own privately-organized *governing bodies* of Trustees. With their powers combined, Trusts were able to monopolize their respective industries, which allowed them to dominate and control markets and essentially destroy competition. Without strong competitors, monopolies could use their immense power to set higher prices, discriminate against customers, and control politicians. Trusts and monopolies formed in just about every industry amidst the more Laissez-Faire period of America; they gobbled up competing businesses and helped individuals – Rockefeller, Carnegie, Morgan, Astor – to amass incredible sums of wealth and vast levels of power at the expense of the labor class. While a few opulent lived larger than kings, millions of destitute struggled to simply put a meal on the table.

Did that make them immoral men? No. The few individuals who accumulated obscene riches did what they were supposed to do, what they were raised to do. They simply played the game. And they played it masterfully. They schemed, they strategized, they built quality at times, they weren't afraid to get their hands dirty, they used every tool at their disposal, and they probably ran into some luck along the way. As a result, they won! Which is the whole point of a competition – to overcome the other players and be the last man standing. "The growth of a large business is merely survival of the fittest," said John D. Rockefeller.[7] And it was only a matter of time before America's titans began competing against each other to become the Ultimate Champion, to stand alone at the tippy top of the pyramid. Unfortunately, the game of money is not harmless like other recreational games. When someone wins and the game nears its end, people suffer, and people die. You don't get to simply put the pieces back in the box and start over. So, before we were ever able to see who would prove victorious in this real-life game of Monopoly, the officials reinserted themselves back into the game.

And once again, as a response to the economy being thrown completely out of balance, leading to unnecessary hardship amongst the population, the Government introduced new legislation, like the Interstate Commerce Commission,[15] the Hepburn Act,[16] and the Sherman Antitrust Act,[17] to break up various trusts and re-establish competition in the market.

So, during the period in time when Government was mostly on the sidelines, monopolies formed, private interests colluded with each other and they organized their own private governing bodies to control industry. Now, Anarcho-Capitalists argue that such control was only achieved through the "apparatus of the government," by private companies taking advantage of subsidies or by hijacking legislation. However, when wealthy tycoons did use government and bribe politicians to stifle competition and maintain a dominant position, it was simply because it was available and it was a cleaner method than having to resort to forceful means. Without government, the most competitive players would have found a way to win. Private interests could have acquired control of industry by purchasing their own private security forces or armies and used physical force against competitors – like with drug cartels, the mafia, or gangs; heck, even legally established private enterprises resorted to violence in an attempt to maintain control. During the infamous Homestead Strike where workers went on strike against the Carnegie Steel Company, the company hired its own private security or army in the Pinkerton Agency to forcibly end worker insurrection.[18,19] During the Ludlow Massacre, Rockefeller's Colorado Fuel & Iron Company, along with a few other mining companies, solicited the services of the Baldwin-Felts Detective Agency to break up disenfranchised and angry strikers.[20] In both instances, as well as many other instances across the country during the time, violence and death ensued. In Ludlow, the fighting didn't end until the referees, until the government intervened to break it up.

By making simple observations during the Industrial Revolution, it is easy to see how *limited* government quickly expands to *bigger* government. Gradually, as society realized that individuals working toward their own self-interests don't always produce the best outcomes, more and more rules were added. Children were exploited for labor, because men working in their own self-interest saw that they could obtain healthier profits by employing kids. However, it can be argued that monopolizing a child's time in a coal mine or a factory and depriving him of an education and the chance to be a child is not best for society. So, a new rule was created to prevent child labor. Trusts were prevalent, which threw the game out of balance. So, rules were created to limit trusts. Workers had few rights and privileges. So, rules were created to give them more rights. Wages were so insufficient in some regions that families struggled to buy meals. So, rules were created to install a minimum wage. As companies competed for market share, forests and wildlife took a beating. So, rules were created to protect the environment and wild animals. With each new flaw that could not be remedied by men working toward their own self-interests, rules continued to be added, and government power naturally grew larger and larger.

Eventually, like I mentioned earlier, problems and inefficiencies start to arise because of too much government intervention, and the pendulum swings back the other way and then government starts to deregulate within the market, which leads to a slew of previous problems and inefficiencies to reemerge – like wealth disparity and social destabilization (which contributes to higher rates of crime and suicide). As examples, after the Government took deregulatory measures during the 1970s and 1980s, which saw tax cuts given to wealthy individuals, more freedoms given to corporations, and bargaining rights limited amongst workers, wages of the middle and lower classes have basically stagnated while upper-class salaries have continued to increase, fueling an ever-widening wealth gap to this day. In 1996, after Congress passed the Federal Telecommunications Act[21] to loosen up the state's stronghold on radio stations, which gave private companies the ability to own as many radio stations as they wanted, it didn't take long before most of the stations were controlled by only a few corporations – deregulation led to monopoly/oligopoly.[22,23] The repeal of the Glass-Steagall Act in 1999, which loosened up the reins on the financial sector, was a contributing factor to the 2008 financial crisis, as commercial banks began investing in "hard-to-understand" derivatives and engaged in credit-default swaps.[24,25] Deregulation in the banking industry also played a role in the recession of 1981. In 1989 Britain privatized its water system, and since then prices have risen 40% above inflation, citizens are paying 2.3 billion pounds more per year for water, and 1 in 5 people are in debt to water companies, which impedes upon their ability to access water; and, because making repairs costs money and reduces shareholder value, many of the companies that have monopolized the industry do not take action to remedy problems, like plugging leaks; nevertheless, a vast majority of citizens want water to be renationalized.[26,27] We could go on and on with examples where loosening up regulations and letting the market run wild has often led to inauspicious results. It is nice to think that the market, left to its own devices, can achieve some sort of equilibrium and lead to social stabilization, but that is just not the case. Games are not meant to remain even. Games are meant to be won! And in a game without rules or without a "neutral" body to enforce the rules, players essentially have the freedom to compete as they see fit, which includes the freedom to limit the freedom of other players.

Moving along. While a number of advocates humbly agree that a Laissez-Faire system will still be confronted with many of the same social issues we face today, that it is simply the lesser of two evils, there are also many who seem to be under the impression that getting rid of or significantly reducing the role of Government will remedy the majority of our country's problems. That once we are released from the jaws of the state, people will suddenly agree to always respect each other's property rights, act morally, and adhere to the Non-Aggression Axiom. Logically, I cannot reconcile this ambition against the reality of the game coupled with how humans have historically behaved when backed into a corner. I struggle to accept the notion that the primary element holding us back from acting rationally and ethically is the presence of government, and the idea that removing the referees from the most competitive game in the world, where the stakes are survival and the abstract object that grants us access to that survival is limited, will encourage people to behave properly, play fairly, and not act out in an aggressive manner should their survival be threatened. Even in small-scale games, where, aside from bragging rights, the stakes are virtually nothing, people cheat to get ahead of their competition. So then how can we expect even for a moment that in the most competitive game in the world where the stakes are enormous that people will play fair? Even within the current setup of the monetary game, with refs and rules in place, people don't play fair. How can we expect for a second that by removing the refs and the rules that people will suddenly decide to become more honorable and trustworthy in their gaming, in their strategizing and scheming to obtain more money and life security? Could you imagine a professional football or basketball game without refs?

The Libertarian belief system lays its foundations on the principles of Voluntarism and the Non-Aggression Principle. In a truly Free Market economy where government is removed or substantially limited, it is their assertion that transactions would be voluntary, transactions would proceed without coercion or force, and both parties in an exchange would benefit mutually. To the Libertarian supporter, Government is inherently forceful and coercive in its authoritarian position, and Government naturally interferes with the rights of individuals in their quest to manage their own lives and property; I agree. When government intervenes in our lives, we typically have little choice but to do as they command. However, just because Government is removed doesn't mean coercion and force will disappear. The system of money is itself a system of coercion. The system of money stands above both Free Market and State-Controlled societies. Because money is scarce and because it is needed to access survival, those with the lion's share of a society's money can coerce those in dire need of it to complete tasks for them that they wouldn't otherwise want to do. And if they choose not to work for that man who has the money, then they don't get to eat. So the option becomes, either work for me or don't eat – which amounts to coercion, non-violent force, exploitation, and extortion. And when a person does end up going to work for the man with money, she essentially clocks into a totalitarian institution. The employee is monitored, she is required to be there at certain times, bathroom privileges are limited, she must dress a certain way, etc., and if she sees this as a violation of her natural freedoms and decides to express her rights in a way that breaks the dictatorship's rules, then the company can take away her ability to survive by firing her – coercive and passively forceful. The majority of the population lives in a state of coercion every single day in that they have little choice but to do things they otherwise wouldn't choose to do if it didn't risk their survival. The system of money, the monetary game, is inherently coercive with or without government.

And in referring to the idea of Voluntarism, it is envisioned by many that exchanges in the open market would happen between two equal and willing participants, and that haggling and negotiating would take place until both parties arrive at a mutually agreed upon price. Rothbard, in

*Outside, Looking In: Critiques of American Policies and Institutions*, states that: "Free-market capitalism is a network of free and voluntary exchanges in which producers work, produce, and exchange their products for the products of others through prices voluntarily arrived at."[28] Such a setup sounds nice, and in a vacuum might be how some transactions go down. However, taking into consideration the system and society as a whole, when individuals enter an agreement, one often has more leverage and bargaining power over the other. And in a society with thousands or millions of people, prices aren't negotiated by individuals, rather they are set by supply and demand within the greater market. So, if a poor family is in need of bread, the price of bread might be a bit too high for them at the grocery store, but they can't negotiate a lower price. They must pay the price that is set, even if they don't want to. Not all transactions are voluntary. Many happen out of desperation, out of the need to survive. And in those situations, the person in the position of desperation has much less bargaining power than the opposing party. For instance, consider the real situation where a father desperate to put food on the table for his family sells his child to a mining company. Or a woman whose bread-winning husband just died and can now barely afford to buy food for her children, and decides to sell her wedding ring at a price below its market value. To say such transactions are voluntary is a perversion of the word.

Thus, the ideals of Voluntarism and the Non-Aggression Principle are just that – ideals. They are merely guidelines or principles of how we would like society to operate, of how we would like individuals to interact with each other. However, the key word underlying these principles is the word SHOULD. *Should* is an idealistic word; it toils in fantasy. We can create a list of guiding principles, we can create a set of commandments. We *should* love each other. We *should* be nice to each other. We *should* not act with force or aggression toward any individual. All transactions *should* be voluntary. Thou *shall* not steal. Thou *shall* not murder. But, like with guns in America, you can create laws to limit access, but if the environment remains unchanged, an environment that sees people pushed to shame, anger, resentment, and desperation, then laws and guidelines do little to stop violence and murder. If the root causes are not removed, if we continue operating within a highly competitive game-like system that uses a scarce medium of exchange as the barrier to survival, that produces winners and losers, where the losers struggle to meet their survival needs, which leads to suffering, desperation, and panic, then people will continue to act out. Principles and guidelines become wholly irrelevant; *should* carries very little meaning. It doesn't matter if a commandment within any group states "thou shall not steal," if a person is starving, he's going to do what he needs to do to survive. If lack in a society persists, which it would especially in a pure Free Market system, then suffering and the chains of negative effects will follow; removing the referees would only exacerbate the problems we already face.

Additionally, I get the impression that Libertarians think once Government is removed that no other governing bodies will come to shape that might seek to control individuals and their rights to gain a competitive advantage. However, as I have alluded to throughout this text, governing bodies are not unique to the state. In any activity involving large groups of people, rule-creating, rule-enforcing, and decision-making groups come to form – governing bodies. Whether we are talking about a traditional Government, private institutions, or powerful crime families and organizations, it doesn't matter. When we are challenged with organizing large groups of people within complex operations, we develop structures of hierarchy and authority to better manage and delegate tasks. For instance, to control light bulb efficiency in the early-20th century, a group of private companies banded together and created the Phoebus Cartel. And in competition, humans often find it advantageous to form alliances to get the upper hand over competing interests. In 1901, JP Morgan, James Hill, and EH Harriman teamed up and created the railroad trust known as the Northern Securities Company. Even crime organizations develop hierarchical structures and form governing bodies to maintain order in the world's underbelly – like the Yakuza, the Black Mafia, or the Commission (a central governing body that oversees organized crime in America). So, within our monetary system, we can get rid of the United States Government, but rest assured other authoritative institutions will come to form and take its place. Maybe other somewhat civil governing bodies will form, or maybe a corporation will become so powerful that it becomes the central body of authority, or maybe gangs will wield control over society; I can't be certain. One thing I can be certain of, however, is that whichever groups have the most money will be the ones with the most power, the most decision-making authority, and the governing bodies will spawn from them. Competitions are meant to be won, and the winners will be in control. And, yes, I agree, that is exactly what is happening now. Only now, the controlling figures hide behind the veil of government.

In my opinion, no adult should want to be parented, so I respect that people want to feel independent and free from central decision-making institutions. However, eliminating the state will not give power back to *the people*, as is a common conception; rather, power and decision-making simply transfers to the private sector, to individually-run organizations where *the people* theoretically have zero voice. Though *the people* are supposed to be involved in decisions made by the government, they have no say in what Walmart or Apple does. Sure they can "vote with their dollar," but one's vote is only as impactful as the size of his wallet. And when a giant corporation has the ability to charge less than its competitors, consumers seem to keep coming back even if they find the company's behavior to be immoral, e.g., Walmart.

And lastly, even though I talked about it to a limited extent a few paragraphs earlier, I want to circle back and quickly address the Libertarian idea that when individuals work toward their own self-interests while respecting the property rights of others, that the results will often benefit both the individual and society as a whole. Though there are and have been circumstances where this idea rings true, there are many instances where men working to achieve their own self-interests does not benefit society as a whole and leads to detrimental consequences. For example, consider deforestation. A man who owns a lumber company cuts down trees in the interest of selling the lumber to earn money. A baseball bat manufacturer buys the lumber and produces baseball bats. Consumers then buy the baseball bats and have a hell of a good time playing baseball with their friends. In this scenario, every tier of the process benefits with individuals working toward their own self-interests. The lumber company benefits from cutting down the trees, selling the lumber, and earning money, which they can turn around and use to purchase goods or reinvest in their company. The baseball bat manufacturer benefits from purchasing the lumber, producing bats, selling them to consumers, and earning money. The consumer benefits because he wanted a bat and received a bat. And the overall economy benefits. However, the continued practice of feverishly cutting down trees to appease often-artificially-created consumer demand can end up being harmful to the environment, which ends up being harmful to the public as a whole. And obviously, this is exactly what has been happening around the world. By and large, men working towards their own self-interests often produce harmful externalities. In Bangladesh, it was in the *immediate* self-interest of the owners of a textile factory not to invest in proper building design, materials, and construction. As a result of cutting corners to save money, the building eventually collapsed and killed over 1,000 people. In many cases, it is not in anyone's immediate financial self-interest to work toward remedying potential or realized damage, and humans often seem to be unable to foresee future catastrophe, or they choose to neglect or doubt it in exchange for immediate gains.

Those subscribing to a Laissez-Faire economy envision a system where all avenues of production are owned and operated by private enterprises – this includes, but is not limited to, schools, military, the police force, fire fighters, prisons, food regulation, regulations in medicine, advanced research institutions (like NASA), and road construction. Before I conclude this chapter, I want to home in on a couple of the institutions listed and briefly illustrate how privatizing them and turning them into profit-driven enterprises would prove to be either inefficient, ineffective, or injurious to society. I would like to spend more time and break down each institution in greater detail and analyze why the complete privatization of them would be to the system's detriment, but such a task would take up too much real estate in this book and steps outside the scope of my overall thesis. I start to lose the forest for the trees; trees I am really not all that interested in exploring in the first place. Maybe in the future I will release a separate text solely about the shortcomings of a Laissez-Faire system, but for now, I don't see the value.

Anyway, let's start with technological innovation and the important role the public sector has played throughout history.

## 8.1 INVENTIONS AND INNOVATIONS

A common misconception as it pertains to technological innovation and inventions in the United States is basically, to sum it up as eloquently as I can, that the private sector rules and the public sector drools. "Ingenuity of the private sector," I've often heard extolled when new breakthroughs and discoveries in health and science are reported to the public. And when it comes to government institutions like NASA, the

DOE, the USDA, the NSF, the NIH, the DoD, or DARPA and the research they're conducting, people generally scoff. "Wasteful!" "Uncreative!" "Cuts corners!" "Lacks incentive!" "We don't need them!!!"

However, would it surprise you to know that many of the most important, many of the most influential technological advancements in American history have come from government-funded projects? Well, like it or hate it, it's true. The computer, internet, microchips, radar, microwaves, GPS, MRI technology, Google, the Human Genome Project, Vaccines (polio), Touch Screen technology, Nuclear Energy, and so much more stake their origins to the public sector.[1] Federally funded projects, especially during and after World War II, paved the way for entirely new industries and entirely new markets in the United States. And honestly, it doesn't take much critical reflection before concluding, "Well that's just common sense."

See, for better or for worse, the government doesn't really have to worry about risk. Private ventures do. And the early stages of Research and Development (R&D), like basic research, are extremely risky as costs quickly pile up while the prospects for commercial marketability are often slim. When, or if, research does end up becoming commercially viable, it might not be until 10, 20, or even 30 years (broadband and mobile) after initially breaking ground on an originally outlandish concept. Private ventures typically can't afford to take on that kind of high-risk research. They can't afford to sink millions or billions of dollars into projects that may never return a single penny of profit. Take the CERN research lab in Europe, for example. The particle-smashing Large Hadron Collider constructed at CERN took over 10 years and about $5 billion to complete. And on an annual-basis, CERN requires about another $5 billion to conduct its many experiments.[2] As of now and into the foreseeable future, there is no profit to be made on the discovery of the Higgs Boson or from the creation of miniature Black Holes. Scientists are simply conducting research to learn about our world, the universe, and our environment, and only time can tell what sort of benefits might arise from these experiments. So, since commercial marketability is nowhere to be found in the CERN experiments or many of the other publicly funded studies across the nation and the globe, it would be unwise for profit-obligated private ventures to infuse their cash into such projects. They have shareholders to please, families to feed, and jobs to maintain, so oftentimes their focus must be on products and services that provide a more immediate return on investment. Bottom line, early-stage research simply isn't profitable, though it is incredibly important since it can eventually lead to medical and scientific breakthroughs that benefit society and bring in revenue.

It is for this reason that government institutions, especially over the last 100 years, are the ones fully or partially funding basic research behind concepts previously unheard of. Currently, the US government spends around $150 billion a year on R&D, and as of 2013, universities, which are given $40 billion in federal funds annually, were responsible for 56% of basic research in the country.[3] And then, after many years, once research has turned into something that can become commercially marketable, it gets passed along to the private sector; many "spin off" companies also form from federally funded research at universities.[4,5] Private firms then take the baton into the phases of late stage development or applied research, create new products or mass produce existing technology, and then reap the tremendous financial rewards in the marketplace. It is a wonderful deal for the private companies fortunate enough to secure years of federally funded research; they get to avoid much of the riskiest parts of innovation.

The pharmaceutical industry is just one of many industries banking on government funding each year to help advance basic research (and probably to help pad the pockets of a few needy executives, if we're being honest). So, it might strike you as obvious that when the 2019 fiscal budget was released by the Trump administration, pharmaceutical companies were none too pleased when they discovered funding to the NIH was being slashed. How important is annual support from the National Institute of Health to our country and the industry of medicine, you might ask? In 2018, the Center for Integration of Science and Industry published a study analyzing financing of each of the 210 drugs approved between 2010 and 2016.[6] What they discovered was, the research behind every single drug approved during that 7-year span was associated, to varying degrees, with federal dollars. That's right. All 210 approved drugs received some sort of financial support out of the $100 billion invested by the National Institute of Health during that time period. And of course, the companies benefitting from the "free" research get to turn around, mark up drug prices, and procure magnificent profits.

Remember in Chapter 7 when I talked about Gilead Science's highly effective, but costly Hepatitis C treatment? Well, it was the NIH that invested $60.9 million into the basic research behind the drug, sofosbuvir, that touts a nearly 100% cure rate.[7] Eventually, Gilead was able to secure the rights to the patent, and they turned around and inflated the per treatment price to six figures; for a patient to complete a round of Harvoni (a sofosbuvir-based drug) it will cost them roughly $100,000, however, the cost to produce the 12-week treatment is less than $100.[8] This is just one example of many where a private company acquires the basic research supported by a taxpayer-funded state institution (NIH), significantly increases the price of treatment, and rakes in billions of dollars in earnings.

And as for the general public, you and me, we sort of get the raw end of the stick on these deals where costs are nationalized and profits are privatized. If you think about it, we provide the initial investment for the early, high-risk stages of R&D with our tax dollars, but we see none of the monetary rewards when a great product springs from that public investment. A few individuals at IBM do. Google does. Novartis does. Johnson & Johnson does. Gilead does.

During the COVID-19 pandemic, government institutions (NIH, DHHS, BARDA, etc.) have pumped billions of dollars – $6 billion was set aside for R&D through the first US stimulus package alone – into public organizations and private companies to aid and accelerate research of the disease, the manufacturing of equipment and supplies, providing infrastructure, and the development of an effective vaccine.[9,10] Through March, 2021, Pfizer, Moderna, and Novavax have received $6 billion, $5.5 billion, and $1.6 billion, respectively, for vaccine development and distribution – and that's a small percentage of the companies that have been receiving public funding.[11] If not for government subsidies, not only would research into the virus have been slowed, but when a cure or vaccine was discovered, companies would likely have had to charge more money than many families could afford just to get some sort of return on their investment. Through federal funding, families can receive the treatment either for free or at significantly reduced costs. Government investment is also the reason poor children were able to receive the Polio vaccine without crippling their families. Had a private firm alone undertaken duties to produce the vaccine, many children would not have been treated due to costs.

Now, in the past decade or so, technological innovation has stagnated a bit in the United States, and the wealthy nation lags behind other developed nations in terms of GDP spent on R&D per capita.[12] Care to hazard a guess as to why?

Well, it seems one of the reasons is that federal funding toward research has been gradually declining within the American border.[13] And, because private companies need to concern themselves with profits and more immediate returns, not as much money is being invested into basic, early-stage research. This isn't to say that private companies don't devote money toward high-risk research. Of course they do. But overall, it is much easier, less risky, and more profitable to invest in "incremental" innovation, like adding or improving upon a few features in the iPhone every year – e.g., an updated camera and a new operating system – and then repackaging and rebranding it as the next greatest product, the next "must-have-or-else" item. It is much easier and more financially reliable to pump out movie sequels and remakes with an already built-in consumer base. Funneling millions or billions of dollars into crazy ideas like Nanotechnology Invisibility Cloaks, Laser weaponry, Pigeon-Guided Missiles, Large Hadron Colliders, or Nuclear Fission is smart business only if your goal is to go bankrupt.[14-17] But, since the government doesn't really have to concern itself with bankruptcy, it can invest money, worry free, into such "radical" projects that just might end up being incredibly value to society in the future.

Technological advancement has been the ultimate catalyst for economic growth over the past 100 years. Now, it can be argued that the public sector is more important than the private sector or vice versa; however, both are integral within the monetary system we've built. For breakthroughs in research that eventually lead to futuristic technology, government institutions are vital. For that research to be used and transformed into a wide variety of useful products, the mass market can be a great place for that, since more eyes and more minds are better than fewer when it comes to looking at research and discovering different ways to use it (though patents tend to limit access to research). But, at the end of the day, it is not the public or private sector creating anything. It is us. Humans. We are infinitely creative beings, and we are responsible for any innovation that has ever been introduced into the world. We simply need access to the resources, tools, and information for our creativity to flourish.

However, since this section falls within the chapter discussing Laissez-Faire economics, this is just another example of why, within the game, getting rid of government would be adverse to socioeconomic prosperity. Like it or hate it…

## 8.2 PRIVATE SCHOOLS: PUNISHING POOR CHILDREN

Before I talk about the education arm of society and why completely privatizing schools would be a disaster for the overall health of the population, I first want to make it clear that I believe public education in present-day America and its state-mandated curriculums are doing a gross disservice to teachers and the children. The state, with its one-size-fits-all model, certainly interferes with the expertise of good teachers, and not in a good way. Rather than giving them the freedom and flexibility to impart their unique knowledge and skills onto their students, teachers are more or less teaching toward standardized tests. As a result, children are memorizing answers and learning how to take tests rather than developing problem-solving skills and acquiring practical knowledge that can be applied in adulthood. Much more can be said about the failings of America's public education system, but that's outside the scope of this section. Anyway, so just because I express my major doubts about completely privatizing education, doesn't mean I am an advocate for public schools. I am afraid the clash between public or private education is another damned if you do, damned if you don't scenario within the system of money.

Proponents of Anarcho-Capitalism call for the privatization of schools across the country. And how can a guy blame them after comparing public schools to private schools? Many private schools in America have more aesthetically appealing classrooms, smaller class sizes, more advanced equipment and tools, more teacher autonomy, among other benefits. However, the biggest difference in private schools compared to public schools is in how they are funded. Public schools are funded by local, state, and federal dollars, which allows poor families to send their children to school essentially for free, and those poor children are not punished for being born to poor parents and given a lesser education, in theory, than wealthy children. Private schools, on the other hand, earn their money primarily from tuition charged to the student and his family. Oftentimes, without government assistance, children of poor families are unable to afford private, and theoretically better, education, which puts them at a disadvantage. By privatizing the entire education system, children born to wealthy parents would have a great advantage over children born to poor parents, and we would see the social divide within our borders widen at an accelerated rate.

Let's imagine for a moment that all schools were privately funded in society, and they operated as for-profit institutions. Logically speaking, the best, brightest teachers would receive the highest salaries, meaning the best teachers would go to the schools that could offer such salaries. And, the schools that could pay the highest salaries would be the ones charging higher tuition fees. And, the students that could afford the higher tuition fees would be the ones from wealthier families. Also, logically speaking, the schools making the most money would be able to afford the best equipment.

On the flip side, let's imagine circumstances within poor, crime-ridden inner-cities. If a poor segment of society were stricken with poverty and violence, like is the case in various areas of Milwaukee, good teachers would be deterred from teaching at private schools in those areas. In order for a private school in an impoverished and unsafe neighborhood to even have a chance at luring good teachers, they would have to be willing to offer attractive salaries – salaries that are higher than competing schools in suburban areas – like, say, Brookfield, Wisconsin. However, income amongst private schools would be heavily dictated by the incomes of families in the surrounding community. If families in the surrounding communities are living in poverty, then the private schools within these communities would not be able to receive as much income as private schools in wealthier communities, meaning they wouldn't have the ability to offer the best teacher salaries that would be high enough to lure them there. So, if a private school resting in an unsafe area of Milwaukee can't offer a competitive salary, then why would a good teacher want to risk her health and wellbeing by teaching there when she can get paid more and not have to worry about her safety in Brookfield? She won't.

What this all essentially means is you would have your elite, expensive schools that have the best teachers and tools, and you would have your cheaper schools that, theoretically, have less-effective teachers and fewer resources. Naturally, it would be the children born into wealthy families who would receive the better education and best opportunities, and once again the children born into poor families who would be punished for circumstances they never had control over. This could only increase the gap between rich and poor, between the educated and uneducated, and only fuel class resentment. Children of wealthy families would have every opportunity to flourish whilst children of poor families would be left behind even more so than they already are. Though private schools in America work quite well on a smaller scale, unfortunately they only work well for a privileged few.

In a world with only privatized schools and no governing body to enforce rules, it is conceivable that some poor families might choose to not send their children to school to save money. Some might not be able to afford it. Even if the child would like to go to school, she won't be able to, and she would be deprived of a formal education; an uneducated populace is deleterious to the wealth and health of an entire community. And the child doesn't really have a choice in the matter. Some Free Market advocates might suggest that school be mandatory for children. But again, who enforces such a mandate? A governing body? It is also conceivable that poor families might find it financially advantageous to send their 9-year-old to work to help the family put food on the table, once again depriving her of an education and proper social and physical development. It wouldn't take long before society began to resemble third world countries in Africa where families send their kids to go work in the dangerous and grueling diamond mines because they are so poor and need money. You might suggest that child labor laws be enacted to protect children. But who would oversee and enforce such laws? A governing body? You might say that such a governing body, or high council, or Child Labor Board, or whatever you might want to call it could operate as a private enterprise, but then how does such an entity get paid? Does the entire town pay for it? Or only adults who have children? In any sense, payment would start to look a lot like taxes, which Libertarians regard as theft, and the private company would start to closely resemble a traditional government agency. You can dress it up and call it a private company, but if it's receiving money from the community or their fees are baked into the prices of certain goods, then it's still walking and talking like the government duck it doesn't want to be.

A Free Market society could adopt a voucher program, as has been proposed by the late Nobel-Prize-winning economist Milton Friedman, among many others, to assist all children in attending the private school of their choice. However, proposed voucher systems and voucher systems initiated in foreign countries are funded by Government entities, meaning taxpayers still foot the bill. Sure, the private schools may be operating to make a profit, but their profit essentially comes from the government, from taxpayer money. So to what degree can they actually be defined as private if they are publicly funded? And, again, if a private school system receives its income from the state, then the nation is not actually operating under a pure Free Market economy.

If a nation was operating under a pure Free Market economy, it is hard to imagine a voucher system functioning in a reliable and efficient manner. For starters, who would pay for such a program if each individual were given a choice? Would families have to rely on wealthy, altruistic donors? Such a method would be unreliable as you would never know when or from where money is coming from. Or, would you end up charging people within a community? Would you bake it into their housing expenses? Would you charge everyone a small fee within the state? Would you tack it on to product prices at local stores? In all circumstances, again, the methods start to look a lot like taxation. So, we'd end up essentially where we started. And, if it's baked into a housing expense or is mandated by the community, then it starts to violate the laws of Voluntarism and the Non-Aggression Principle. You could give citizens the option of whether or not they want to contribute to an education fund, but then you would have a large number of the population choosing to opt out, electing not to pay. Without kids or a lucrative job, I can't say for sure that I would contribute to such a fund, as it could potentially risk my immediate survival. Nevertheless, a voucher program would not work within a pure Free Market economy. Some level of public intervention would have to exist for children to be able to rely on it. And if not for some sort of voucher system or public assistance, poor children would undoubtedly be left behind. Heck, they are often left behind even with public assistance. Imagine how much worse it would be without any. Again, it wouldn't take long before we started to resemble third world countries.

Of course, another option is that wealthy private schools could offer scholarships to underprivileged children, but how many kids could a wealthy school legitimately provide tuition for before going into the red? Maybe but a few?

Issues abound when considering a privatized school system within a pure Free Market economy, like how would we ensure a minimum education standard within schools, or how would we prevent discrimination of any kind, or the implausibility of homeschooling for most families, among many others; and I could sit here and pick apart every aspect of it and solutions that have been proposed, and I could scrutinize every hypothetical, but that would easily fill up the pages of an entirely different book. So, I'm not going to do that. The bottom line, the most important drawback, is that without public assistance, a privatized education system within a pure Free Market economy would unavoidably favor the wealthy over the poor, which would be socially destructive within society. That element alone, of further discriminating against children born to poor families, renders the idea impractical. It would seem a society operating within a scarce system of money would have to adopt some form of public assistance or intervention so all children have a formal learning opportunity. In order to oversee such a system, a governing body would inevitably come to shape.

## 8.3 PRIVATIZING MILITARY: INCENTIVIZING CONFLICT

Moving along to Military and the idea of completely privatizing and turning it into a for-profit venture.

Some advocates, like Rothbard, argue that war would fade away in an Anarcho-Capitalist society, due in large part because, "a libertarian America would clearly not be a threat to anyone, not because it had no arms but because it would be dedicated to no aggression against anyone, or against any country."[1] However, I can't help but disagree with this seemingly parochial position. In an Anarcho-Capitalist society, resources would still be inequitably distributed and people would still be competing against each other for survival, so fighting would undoubtedly persist. There would still be territories lacking in resources with people struggling, that might look over to their neighbors and see that they have considerably more tangible wealth and decide it would be advantageous for their clan to invade them and try to acquire what they have. Throughout human history, tribes within certain territories have attacked tribes of other territories, with or without government, and with or without identifying with an abstract state or country.

So, taking the position that war would still exist in a pure Free Market society, as groups find incentive to attack other groups, it seems that having a military or national defense to protect citizens would still be necessary. And, as we know, building strong military infrastructure – hiring soldiers, training personnel, producing equipment, inventing new technologies – takes enormous financial investment. In a world where military is completely privatized and for-profit, who would pay for such a massive enterprise?

Some scholars within the Anarcho-Capitalist school of thought suggest that Americans who fear potential invasion by a foreign territory could choose to contribute to a military fund, or they could contribute to a fund focused on the purchase of specific defense weaponry. But again, effective, advanced weaponry takes considerable investment – the Gerald R. Ford aircraft carrier costs about $13 billion, while development and production of the F-22 fighter jet has totaled over $70 billion – and relying on individual contributions would be unreliable.[2] Not to mention, once again, people could choose not to pay but still receive the benefits of a national defense system, since national defense protects everyone.

Other advocates suggest military could be funded through private insurance companies, but we already pointed out the inefficiencies with this method at the beginning of this chapter.

So who pays to build a robust, reliable national defense system? You could require all citizens to contribute to a military fund, but again, then we are mimicking the coercive and forceful taxation practices an Anarcho-Capitalist society is trying to elude.

But why fix what isn't broken? Love it or hate it, the United States of America, in its short existence, has assembled the strongest, most well-oiled machine this world has ever known in the US Military. And its development has come entirely from public funding, from the state. Now, it has been argued, and I have no intention of expanding upon this argument here, that the US spends way, way too much money on its military every year. For instance, in 2019 the US spent $732 billion on military expenditures – an amount that topped the next 10 nations combined![3] Whether you believe the spending is reckless and unnecessary or not, the exorbitant investment has yielded the most advanced technology and equipment in existence, as well as the most well-trained personnel.

Now I ask, what private enterprise would be crazy enough or could even afford to invest that kind of cash, their own cash, in building military infrastructure strong enough to withstand an attack from a powerful adversary? Without the prospect of a return on investment or even recuperation of expenses, it would be asinine for private companies to take such great risk.

The benefit or the advantage the US Government has over private enterprises is it doesn't have to worry about profit, and it doesn't have to concern itself with risk – for better or worse. In fact, the US Government can basically print as much money as it wants to fund military endeavors. And I agree, having the ability to print money at will and taking advantage of that ability borders on fraud, but that just so happens to be the current reality and is the reason why government is better able to build the military arm of society.

And I understand private military companies are abundant in America, as the country often hires private contractors to save on costs, however, their revenue comes from the government and tax dollars, so they are basically public agencies. If not for the lucrative government contracts, if income came solely from private interests, many would either cease to exist or be significantly reduced in size. And if that were the case, they certainly wouldn't be strong enough to defend the entire country.

So who would pay? Others theorize that wealthy corporations, since they would stand to lose the most wealth in an attack, might be incentivized to finance military, or at least contribute much more, but one of the problems with that is you run the risk of having armies of men partial to the masters that feed them – to the corporations. I imagine if wealthy conglomerates paid for private military, conflicts could evolve and be less about country versus country, and be more about corporate giant versus corporate giant. I mean, that is essentially what wars already are. One giant body of humans with substantial resources attacks another giant body of humans, usually to secure control of their territory and resources. You can call that giant body a country, a corporation, an enterprise, it's all semantics. If Microsoft attacked Apple it would hardly be different than if US forces entered Nicaragua or Panama – their end goals are essentially the same in trying to secure resources and maintain a competitive advantage in the world. Maybe Microsoft simply absorbs Apple, or maybe Microsoft allows Apple to keep its name, but makes the fruity company pay them a chunk of their profits each month. Ecuador is still labeled as Ecuador, but much of its wealth is transferred north to the entities that conquered them.

And that is another concern – incentive. If a corporation or group financed its own private military, they might recognize another country has resources they would like to mine and exploit, so they might be incentivized to invade such a nation to acquire control of its resources and to build infrastructure there. Then again, who are we kidding; that already happens. The major difference in state-run societies is that private enterprises hide behind the backs of their government moms. However, when a powerful nation invades lesser nations, considerable wealth transfers into the hands of many private organizations, either through direct contracts, loans, or by acquiring access to resources, like oil.

Nevertheless, as long as access to resources remains limited and people are still competing against each other to survive – which would be the case in a Laissez-Faire society – physical conflict will undoubtedly persist. And if physical conflict remains an issue within global society, then it seems necessary to have a national defense system. The biggest issue when considering a completely privatized military is in how to properly finance it to ensure it is strong and effective; and no matter how we slice it, a purely decentralized Free Market economy would struggle in that regard. Unfortunately for those hoping for a government-less world someday, it seems even revered Laissez-Faire advocates – Friedman, Rand – agree that to build a strong military and national defense arm, a central governing body is necessary to a degree.

## 8.4 NATIONAL PARKS, POWER COMPANIES, ROADS, POLICE

I agree that in many regards privatized services and products can be more efficient, of higher quality, better maintained, and more affordable in certain cases. For instance, in referring to roads, I lived in the greater Los Angeles area, and we often wondered where all of our tax money was going. Many of its congested roadways are poorly designed and in decay, yet it seems very little is done to improve them. Rather than pledging taxpayer dollars to the improvement of inefficient roads, it feels as though city or state officials are either pocketing the money or channeling it toward other projects. And why would they consider road maintenance as a top priority? Reputation and elections are rarely won based on a candidate's track record in transportation. There is little incentive for them to improve upon the quality of LA's roads. So, in certain regions around the United States or the world, I think local inhabitants could benefit from the privatization of certain institutions, such as road building. Private companies would have greater incentive to keep roads safe, clean, and affordable, or else they run the risk of losing traffic, and therefore customers.

However, transitioning from government- to privately-operated institutions or vice versa requires trade-offs. And staying within the realm of roads, though privately-run streets and highways *might* be better maintained and designed with more intuitiveness, other issues arise that could also make it inconvenient and less efficient. For example, let's consider how private roads would be paid. One of the methods proposed and already used by some privately owned streets is the use of tolls. Private companies could charge tolls for every street you drive on, which isn't terrible, though I imagine it would end up getting pricey on a month-to-month basis. However, where the inconvenience and inefficiency could come into play is in the situation where multiple companies operate within the same city. The more companies, the more complicated it could become. Imagine a city's street grid. Imagine four different companies owning various streets throughout the city, charging various prices. Now, with modern technology, I don't imagine residents having to stop and pay at toll booths as transponders and cameras can be used to automatically charge customers, though a customer could expect multiple monthly bills, but having roads with varying prices throughout the city could make travel less efficient. A phone app could easily help drivers navigate through the cheapest routes, but I imagine the cheapest route wouldn't often take a driver straight from Point A to Point B, as some streets are going to be cheaper than others.

You might also see "wasteful construction" in cities with multiple road construction companies. Let's say Company A owns one of a city's most trafficked highways and charges people $2.00 to drive on it. People love it because it takes them straight from Burbank to Santa Monica. However, seeing the popularity and profit potential of providing such a direct path, a second company could come in, build a road right next to Company A's, but charge only $1.50 in attempt to lure in Company A's Burbank/Santa Monica travelers. Then, a third company could come in and do the same thing, but charge even less money. In the end, a region might have 2, 3, maybe 4 roads running parallel with each other, all going to the same destination – you could wind up with a mess of streets. During the Industrial Revolution when railroad companies were competing for business, 20 railroad lines existed between St. Louis and Atlanta. Such a scenario is great for the consumer as it might allow them to purchase cheaper fares, but it is an inefficient use of resources – especially if it gets to the point where one or two of the roads are no longer used because a company bows out of the competition. The road could just sit there laying to waste, because it is in nobody's financial interest to tear it down.

Of course, if companies are discouraged from building roads next to already-established roads, then that essentially gives the company with the already-established road a natural monopoly on that territory, which would partially defeat the purpose of having private companies in the first place. And if companies aren't discouraged from such a practice, I don't see why they wouldn't build a competing road next to another if they have the ability to do so and their analysts calculate that it would be profitable.

Another issue is that each road construction company would be allowed to create their own set of rules, which could become confusing, costly, and potentially even dangerous. Of course, there would be situations where companies would cooperate with each other and create a uniform set of standards, but that is not a sure thing. There would certainly be regions where competing companies don't agree to the same rules – maybe because they don't get along or maybe they feel that providing different rules of the road might better attract customers and give them a competitive advantage. In other industries, private companies that produce similar products don't always agree on uniformity. Think of iPhones compared to Androids, or Macs compared to PCs, or even similar, but competing car brands. Some accessories that work on iPhones, like phone chargers, are not compatible with Androids. And some cars require their own specific parts when you take them in for simple repairs – a strategy often used to keep customers and revenue "in house."

Other proposed methods of road funding consist of making it the responsibility of the landowner or tenants to pay for the upkeep of the roads surrounding their block; the fees would be baked into their mortgage or rent. However, if every house and every apartment had road construction fees included in their monthly mortgage or rent fees, it would hardly be any different from paying taxes.

There are plenty of other issues that could arise should a city's roads be entirely owned by private, competing businesses. For instance, what would stop a company that owns most of the roads from putting up barriers to block competing roads from passing through? It might seem like an irrational concern, but if a company found it gave them a competitive advantage, it would certainly be within their right to do so. There is also the question of perpendicular roads. What if one road passes through a competitor's road? How would a driver be charged? Would both companies charge him? Without uniformity, road standards would be on a case-by-case, company-by-company basis, which becomes unnecessarily convoluted. Too many issues and hypotheticals exist that cannot be addressed in this text, so, moving along to national parks and other public sanctuaries.

In an Anarcho-Capitalist society, nothing is sacred and nothing is off limits. Every square foot of America would be owned by private individuals, meaning absolutely anything could be exploited for profit, including national parks, rivers, lakes, and other national attractions. An altruistic proprietor might have the best intentions in mind if he were to buy a chunk of, say, Yellowstone National Park. But what happens if he loses his job or his company begins to fail, and suddenly he is struggling to pay for life necessities? It might occur to him that he could become a wealthy and comfortable man should he start digging up his resource-rich section of Yellowstone. And because he owns the land, it would be perfectly within his rights to mine and exploit any resources he finds. In the end, he might not want to disrupt the natural beauty of Yellowstone, but he might feel like he has little other choice, and there would be no rules against him bringing in bulldozers and tearing apart the majestic landscape.

In an Anarcho-Capitalist society, everything would be vulnerable to destruction-for-profit in the United States, and nothing would be protected. We would quickly realize the devastating ramifications – just look at the Amazon and other resource-rich rainforests throughout the world; they are disappearing because they lack protection, and owners – whether private or public – have financial incentive to chop and uproot them.

If a company owned a piece of the Missouri River, no one could stop the owner from dumping waste, even though the waste could flow downstream and negatively affect parts of the river that other individuals own. Rules would need to be created to prevent someone from dumping waste into a river, but then not only would we be violating someone's property rights by telling him he cannot do something on his own property, but also, who would enforce such rules? And how could you enforce such rules without resorting to some sort of "forceful" measure if the owner refuses to stop dumping waste? A society could fine him? But, if he doesn't want to pay, how could you make him pay without resorting to some form of force?

In a world with an increasing population and unlimited, irrational, and artificial consumer demands, opening up every piece of land for private exploitation can only lead to more rapid decay as companies race to beat competing companies in satisfying those insatiable consumer demands.

Speaking of creating and enforcing laws against dumping waste into rivers, that brings us to the topic of law and order and to the dilemmas of privatized forces. Advocates of an Anarcho-Capitalist society envision a society with private court systems, where each judicial firm packages together and provides its own set of laws, and citizens would get to choose which court they want to subscribe to and which set of laws they want to live by. In short, citizens within a town or city would all adhere to different sets of rules. Such a situation is just asking for confusion and trouble, and that seems obvious to me; the potential issues are too innumerable to elaborate upon.

Then when it comes to local security, if police forces were privatized and for-profit, then it would stand to reason that they would be incentivized to pull people over and issue tickets more frequently, especially if their agency was having a slow month. As a for-profit institution, some police agencies might encourage their deputies to accept bribes, as is common in some countries, like Russia. Another issue of privatizing the police is they might be more loyal to the people that pay them rather than being neutral protectors of an entire territory. If a billion-dollar business owner is paying a higher sum for the local police or has hired his own personal force, then they are most certainly going to look the other way if the wealthy man is partaking in nefarious activities. Again, much of this corruption already happens in various pockets throughout the country, but privatizing the police not only wouldn't halt the issues, but it could exacerbate them as every police force would now be incentivized by profit.

Of course, just like with every institution I've discussed so far, if every citizen is required to contribute a certain amount of dollars to a local police force or if police protection is bundled in with home mortgages or rent, then it becomes hardly any different than taxes. This method is often proposed by Anarcho-Capitalist supporters, that each citizen would pay into a fund for the police force of his choosing or they would have fees tacked onto their place of residence. In an area with high populations, citizens would have different police forces connected to different court systems adhering to different sets of laws. Ay-yi-yi!

Private security agencies are very common in the US and are contracted for numerous occasions, like when a concert venue hires security for a large concert or when Heidi Klum hires security to protect her person and her assets or even when a small business requests nighttime surveillance. But, such services often favor those most able to afford them, while those with empty wallets must forego such luxuries. There are occasions, and this is another idea in an Anarcho-Capitalist society, where large businesses, like a mall, hires private security and passes the bill to their merchants who then pass the charge to their customers in the prices of their goods. But, again, this is essentially a hidden sales tax and a service he is likely unaware he is paying for. Not voluntary, indeed.

Private firefighting companies would profit most during times of increased infernos. That's a problem as it incentivizes fire. During the many periods from 2017 to 2019 when wildfires raged across southern California, private firefighting agencies saw a rapid boost in the demand for their services, as the Golden State's wealthy went on a hiring frenzy to protect their estates. Realizing the enormous profit potential, what would stop a corrupted man from going into or paying someone to go into a wooded area and discreetly setting the forest ablaze just to boost business, just to increase profits? Morals? We all know morals are rarely a reliable deterrent when money enters the fray.

And in a situation where citizens pay "voluntary" monthly fees for firefighting services, what if a man forgets or chooses not to pay his bill one month, his house starts on fire, and firefighters arrive but watch the house burn to the ground because of the missed payment? Obviously, fault would rest on the homeowner for not paying, but to imagine capable firefighters standing and watching someone's home burn to the ground leaves one feeling unsettled. This is exactly what happened in South Fulton, Tennessee in 2011 when a couple didn't pay for the $75 yearly fee and their mobile home caught fire. The fire department watched at a distance and made sure the homes of paying residences remained safe.[1]

Lastly for this section, Electric Companies. Electric Companies have natural monopolies within a city or town, because having multiple competing firms is wasteful and ends up costing a region more money in the long run. In an Anarcho-Capitalist society that encourages competition, if a town had 3 or 4 companies providing power to the general public, that means the town would also have 3 or 4 power plants, which means they would also have 3 or 4 sets of power lines running next to and around each other. The layout would be a mess, and resources would go to waste, especially when one company already has the capacity to provide enough energy to an entire town. So, having multiple electric companies in a town is simply unnecessary. However, if only one power company existed in a given region, then the potential exists for that single company to abuse their "powers" and charge unnecessarily high prices. It is for these reasons that government regulates electric companies, for better or for worse, and why it would prove to be difficult for an Anarcho society to manage power companies.

We could talk about the privatization of other needed institutions and where issues arise that end up requiring some sort of oversight by a central, governing body, but I think we've covered enough, as half-assed as it was done to reduce the size of this book. Some of the topics not explored, but I would have liked to explore, include:

1. Who pays for those that can't take care of themselves?
    a. Disabled
    b. Cognitively Impaired
    c. Orphans
2. Who pays for research that doesn't necessarily yield profits, like much of the activities NASA does? Or cancer research? Or polio research?
3. Who pays for Food Regulation agencies to make sure food is properly served?
4. Who pays for Drug Regulation to make sure pharmaceutical companies aren't selling snake oil to the public, like they already try to do?
5. What about patents? If Company A is not able to protect its intellectual property, years of research could go down the drain from a financial point of view if Company B gets ahold of the

research and produces a product and sells it at a much lower price.
6. Who keeps track of license plates, driving records, and everything else associated with the DMV?
7. Building standards?

## 8.5 CHAPTER CONCLUSION

The further I have examined the philosophies and ideas of Laissez-Faire economics, the more apparent it has become to me that not only is such an economic setup infeasible, but it is also self-destructive. And those conclusions have led me to ask myself, why have Anarcho-Capitalist ideologies garnered so much support over the past many years? Why has the idea, which I find preposterous, that people working toward their own self-interests would benefit society been so readily accepted? Those are questions I've struggled to wrap my head around for quite some time. It just doesn't make sense to me no matter who I study within the Laissez-Faire community. But after juggling the thoughts in my subconscious mind for weeks, I have begun to suspect that one of the reasons many people support it is because of the implications it has on them as Americans.

As humans, we tend to tie our identities to abstract ideas, to intangible labels. We tie our identities to the idea of cities, states, countries, and much more. For instance, I'm not just Travis, I'm a Sauk Prairie Eagle. But I'm not just an Eagle, I'm also a Wisconsinite. But, I'm not just a Wisconsinite, I'm also an American. For many living in the United States, to be regarded as a good, strong American is just about the greatest compliment one can receive.

And of course, the idea of Capitalism goes hand-in-hand with the idea of America. And a pure Free Market system is the ultimate form of Capitalism. So, in a roundabout manner, to be an Anarcho-Capitalist or a Libertarian is to be the ultimate American. That is a great honor for many, and people take great pride in having their identities tied to the countries they live in. Conversely, to be a socialist is to be perceived as anti-American, which many receive as a piercing insult. So to support anything that has to do with government intervention can essentially be perceived as being anti-American. Being anti-American usually comes with negative feedback from peers.

So, anyway, I've begun to suspect that that is *one* of the reasons people follow this economic idea wholeheartedly. Although, I do recognize and respect that there are people who have invested years of research and theorizing, and they sincerely believe in its workability. Unfortunately, I just don't see it, just as they might not see the workability of what I am proposing. And that's okay.

Nevertheless, we can get rid of Government, but like a pernicious colony of ants, a governing body will keep coming back in some form as social issues continue to arise that the private sector is unable to remedy. And some of the most revered Libertarians in American history, including whom many consider to be the father of the Libertarian community, Adam Smith, agree that government is needed to a degree within the market economy; even though most Libertarians view tax as theft, Smith favored certain forms of taxation.[1] It is pleasant to think that abolishing government would lead to a smooth, free-flowing economy that leads to endless prosperity. It's nice to think that an Anarcho-Capitalist system, where people are "free" to hone their crafts and "freely" trade with one another, is the answer. But it's not. Anarcho-Capitalism is not the remedy we seek, nor is Government the root cause of society's problems. Neither is Government the remedy. Whether we operate under a pure Free Market or Government-run system, we would still be using a limited supply of money to distribute resources amongst the population, meaning social destabilization and suffering will always be a threat as many people inevitably become "losers" in the game and struggle to obtain the necessities of life. As long as lack persists, which it would in both economic setups, then all of the problems plaguing society now will continue to burden us.

To govern or not to govern, that was the question. Well, we're speeding into a brick wall regardless. The only difference is one scenario has the pedal to the metal while the other scenario taps the breaks from time to time, prolonging the inevitable. Either way, that brick wall is waiting for us.

# 9 HUMAN MOTIVATION: WHAT THE HECK WOULD WE DO ALL DAY WITHOUT MONEY?

"True rewards are ever in proportion to the labor and sacrifices made."[58] – Nikola Tesla

Have you ever heard of Calum (Malcolm) MacLeod? Yeah me neither. At least not until I began writing this book. And no, I'm not referring to the Scotsman who happens to be the late grandfather of Mr. Donald Trump. I'm referring to a different Scotsman. One who shares the same name, but whose extraordinary tale of incredible determination, resilience, and pure human grit drove him to accomplish an "impossible" goal that earned him the British Empire Medal, commemoration from fellow Scots, and has inspired people to write songs, books, and movies about his achievement; it catapulted him to local fame, but not fortune.[1]

So what was this grand achievement of Calum's?

It was a 1.75-mile road. That's it. Nothing more, nothing less. But the significance of this story lies not in the 'what', but rather in the 'how' of the road's inception.

In the middle of the 20th century, the small hamlet of Arnish in the northern region of the Isle of Raasay in Scotland was quickly losing residents. And as two of the last remaining inhabitants of the area, Calum MacLeod and his wife, Lexie, sought to reverse that trend and encourage new generations of Scots to move back. However, one of the problems, they recognized, was that Arnish didn't have a road connecting it to the rest of the island; it was inaccessible and isolated from everyone else. So Calum, along with the help of a few north Raasay inhabitants, lobbied Scottish officials to approve of the construction of a road connecting Arnish to other villages in the region. However, it was to no avail. Year after year they tried, and year after year their requests were denied. Finally, fed up with being ignored, Calum decided to take matters into his own hands. Literally!

Thus, at the age of 56, equipped merely with a pickaxe, a rickety wheelbarrow, a small shovel, and a road-building manual, the rugged old Scot began constructing a road entirely by himself. Day by day Calum's wife could find him outside breaking up rocks and shifting dirt away from the road. He sacrificed countless hours and litres of sweat digging up the winding path and hilly terrain. The project took Calum into his late-60s, but after 10 years of tireless dedication, he successfully completed what many considered to be an impossible task – a 1.75-mile road stretching from Arnish to the Brochel Castle; and he did it in his spare time, in between his normal wage-paying day jobs.

Soon after the project was completed, local authorities aptly named the path "Calum's Road," and in 1982 the local council adopted and surfaced it. Though the impetus of building the road was to encourage people to move back and to make access easier for his daughter when she came to visit from the Isle of Skye, Calum and his wife remained the only inhabitants of Arnish by the time of his death in 1988. However, some 30 years later the massive undertaking has etched his name into Scottish folklore, and rightfully so. I would encourage anyone to do a web search for pictures of the road. It may not be that impressive, but the blood and sweat beneath the pavement, it's a testament to man's indomitable strength and his inner drive to create, master, and achieve; such a realization leaves an indelible impression. And if nothing else, the old man's toothless grin while holding his antique of a pickaxe will put a smile on your face.[2]

So what motivated Calum MacLeod to devote a large chunk of his life toward building Calum's Road? What ultimately acted as the match that lit a fire under his fanny that drove him to achieve such an amazing feat? I think we can safely say money wasn't a driving force, since he wasn't being paid for his efforts. And I don't believe fame or recognition were contributing factors, either? So what was it? Well, it is my hope that by the end of this chapter we will have a clearer understanding not only of what motivated Mr. MacLeod, but also what motivates humans in general to pick up their metaphorical pickaxes and get to *gettin'*.

# HUMAN MOTIVATION

Whenever I talk about the idea of operating an economic system that doesn't use money or any medium of exchange, the most immediate concern people tend to have is not whether supply and demand can be accurately and efficiently calculated, nor is it about how wealth will be stored, resources distributed, or even how product variety will exist. Those issues rarely come up in conversation when I talk about removing the monetary middle man, because I think deep down people know that those functions can be accomplished with more advanced and efficient tools. No, when discussing a moneyless society, the greatest concern by far is that without the pressure or allure of money, people will become lazy. They will default to sitting on their butts chugging Sun Drop and playing Halo all day.

"What would people do," many ask.

"Nothing will get done!"

"How will people be motivated to do anything without money?"

The common conception amongst business and the greater populace has long maintained that people need extrinsic drivers – the opportunity for reward or the threat of punishment – to entice them into getting off their haunches and work. Produce! And organizational models have for decades operated under the premise that humans generally dislike work, and that "The average human being prefers to be directed, wishes to avoid responsibility, has relatively little ambition, [and] wants security above all else."[3] Because of this outmoded belief of human nature, businesses and management have clung to the idea that the average human dog "must be coerced, controlled, directed, [or] threatened with punishment to get them to put forth adequate effort toward the achievement of organizational efforts."[4] "Carrots and sticks" are necessary according to traditionalists. However, what if I told you that science, after 100 years of studying and observing human behavior, has turned that conventional wisdom on its head? What if I told you that people actually like purposeful work and will seek out responsibility to fulfill needs of self-esteem, self-actualization, social belonging, and more? And what if I told you that not only is money a weak motivational tool, but it can also have a negative effect on people's motivation and overall performance, and it can stifle creativity?

Of course, before I lay on the criticism, money and extrinsic rewards aren't completely ineffective in galvanizing personnel, in driving them to work a little harder and produce a little faster. When it comes to menial, routine, "algorithmic" tasks that have a set process and a single outcome, introducing monetary bonuses can add incentive and help employees forget about their painful boredom for a *minute* – emphasis on minute because it often only works for a short period of time. Edward Deci, a psychologist who has spent most of his career studying human motivation, asserts, "Rewards do not undermine intrinsic motivation for *dull* tasks, because there is little to no intrinsic motivation to undermine"[5] in the first place. However, any task that involves monotonous, repetitive motions can easily be automated in today's world. Machines can pull and assemble parts from the assembly line. They can flip burgers, stack boxes, swipe groceries, and drive the same routes over and over again. And it is my opinion that algorithmic jobs *should* be automated, because, like I've said, monotony and drudgery are a complete waste of the wonderful, complex phenomenon that is human consciousness.

In addition to providing some motivation for menial tasks, receiving money or a material prize *can* also be validation of a job well done; it can be a measure of success. If we get paid for a chore, it must have been because we did something good; we must have done something meaningful. And that validation can feel good. So much so that we might seek it out again, and again, and again. However, we must be careful when using money to measure success and value in modern society as perception can quickly become blurred when it's relied upon too heavily in judging what is important and what is not important. As an example, Wall Street traders are some of the most handsomely paid people in America. If we were to measure success and value based on money earned, then by all accounts, Wall Street traders would be seen as some of the most valuable members of society. However, if we simply hold a child's magnifying glass up to such a profession, if we strip away the glossy grins, slicked-back hairdos, and inflated egos, we would quickly discover that they produce absolutely nothing; and sometimes their actions can have a detrimental impact on the nation's economy. So, by measures of actual production and intrinsic value added to society, jobs involving currency speculation and gambling on stocks and so on could actually be perceived as next to worthless.

Conversely, let's home in on the farming industry. Farmers, those rough and tough, multi-skilled, tractor driving caretakers of land and livestock who bust their tails sun up to sundown producing food that keeps us alive, they get paid very little; many struggle to provide for their families, hence the rise in suicides. If we were to measure success and value to society based on income earned, then farmers could be perceived as having little value in society. However, we know this to be patently false. By using more appropriate tools to measure value in society, like common sense, we easily recognize that farmers are some of the most vital components of the system. Now let's consider stay-at-home mothers or fathers or single parents between jobs. Because this subset of people might not be participating in work that earns an income, they can also be seen and often are seen as having little value in society – wage-earning people have even been known to flip their noses at stay-at-home parents. However, we know child-rearing to be incredibly difficult work (I don't know how two parents do it, let alone one), and parents are nurturing what many economists and philosophers (like Noam Chomsky) consider as the nation's most important resource – human capital. By those standards one might consider properly raising a child in becoming a productive member of society as being much more intrinsically valuable than betting against the Saudi Riyal or speculating on Apple's stock price on a daily basis. So, receiving money *can* be validation that we did something considered valuable, which can provide short-term ego boosts, but if we lean on money too much to measure success and value, the definitions rapidly become distorted.

Now circling back to the use of money as a motivational tool for "algorithmic" tasks. As stated three paragraphs ago, when it comes to motivating people, money and extrinsic rewards *can* be effective for "algorithmic" tasks in the short-term. However, when it comes to "heuristic" tasks – that is, tasks not involving a set process, ones featuring multiple paths, choices, a certain degree of creativity, and an infinite number of outcomes, like building a financial report in Microsoft Excel or developing an ad campaign – money can have a detrimental impact on motivation, performance, and work ethic. And that can be said for artists, surgeons, engineers, scientists, children, and even monkeys. Yes, you heard me right, even performance and curiosity of our primate ancestors are dampened when extrinsic rewards are introduced to an activity.

In 1949, Harry F. Harlow and two colleagues at the University of Wisconsin ran a learning experiment on a group of rhesus monkeys.[6] To begin the study, the experimenters placed a simple mechanical puzzle into the cages of the monkeys to observe their behavior. Almost immediately, the monkeys were consumed by curiosity. They began "monkeying" with the little pin, hook, and hinge contraption with total focus and determination to discover its solution. They even seemed to be enjoying the challenge. And even though no reward was being offered, the inquisitive monkeys worked diligently toward and mastered the puzzles rather quickly. By the end of the experiment, they were often able to solve them in under a minute.

Then, in a second round of experiments, Harlow introduced external rewards (food) to the monkeys for solving puzzles, which he expected would motivate the hairy subjects to perform even better. However, to Harlow's surprise, the introduction of food reward had the opposite effect. Not only did the monkeys make more errors in trying to solve the puzzles, but they also completed the puzzles with less frequency, leading the researchers to conclude, "Introduction of food in the puzzle situation tended to disrupt, not facilitate, the learned performance of the experimental subjects."[7] It seemed in the first round of experiments the joy of the task was its own reward for the monkeys.

Money and extrinsic rewards have a way of undermining intrinsic motivation when it comes to tackling an activity. Play suddenly becomes work, and an interesting task suddenly becomes tedious when the carrot-and-stick method is introduced. In 1973 a team of three researchers (Mark Lepper, David Greene, and Roger Nisbett) at Stanford University wanted to test whether or not material rewards enhanced or diminished intrinsic motivation in children.[8] To start out, the researchers handpicked a group of preschoolers who showed a keen interest in drawing during their "free play" sessions at school. The children were then broken up into three groups. The first group was told they would receive a reward for drawing. The second group was not told that they would receive a reward, but instead were given an unexpected one after completing the drawing activity. And the third group was not given any reward at all.

Well, what the researchers discovered was that the children in the first group – the group that was told they would receive a reward – showed significantly less interest in drawing and drew less frequently during free play sessions than the children in the other two groups. Even the quality of the drawings in the expected-reward group was critiqued as worse by a panel of three "blind" judges. Lepper and Greene carried out numerous other similar studies with children, and the results were the same each time – external rewards sapped the joy and interest in otherwise intriguing activities.

And the same can be said for adults, too. The added baggage of monetary incentive tends to narrow and dull the creative mind. In 1962, psychologist Sam Glucksberg introduced the well-known "Candle Problem" to a group of participants.[9] The Candle Problem, originally envisioned by Karl Duncker and often used to test "function fixedness," involves a wax candle, a box of tacks, and a book of matches. Subjects are then seated at a small table next to a wooden wall and challenged with mounting the candle to the wall so that wax does not drip onto the table. The solution to the problem requires a bit of creativity and outside-the-box thinking, but usually after about five to ten minutes, participants are able to conquer the task. Once they overcome their "function fixedness" and see the *box* for being more than just a tack-holder, that they can empty the box, tack it to the wall, and place the candle inside it, then they've stumbled upon the solution.

In one of Glucksberg's variations of the Candle Problem, he split participants up into two groups. He told the participants in the first group that he would time them to see how long it would take them to figure out the solution; the fastest time would receive a $20 reward, and those finishing in the top 25% would receive $5. The second group was not offered any monetary reward at all; instead they were merely told they would be timed for testing purposes. Obviously the group incentivized with money would work harder and come up with the solution faster, right? Wrong! The group offered a monetary reward performed quite a bit worse than the group not offered a monetary reward. When participants in the money group were able to solve the puzzle, they did it three and a half minutes slower on average, which is significant considering it usually only takes people five to ten minutes to arrive at the answer in the first place.

Additionally, Teresa Amabile, a Harvard professor primarily known for her work in creativity, completed a study in 1993 comparing commissioned artwork versus non-commissioned artwork.[10] She had artists select ten of their commissioned pieces and ten of their non-commissioned pieces. The artwork was then given to a panel of judges who were unaware of the study and asked to score the art. In the end, the commissioned (money) works were rated "significantly less creative" compared to the non-commissioned (no money) works.

Not only are creative tasks negatively influenced by external, pay-for-production incentives, but contrary to what business and the greater populace has been led to believe, overall performance in problem-solving tasks is stifled, too. In an experiment originally reported to the Federal Reserve of Boston in 2005, a group of four researchers traveled to India to test whether or not larger incentives would enhance performance.[11] The team, which included Dan Ariely from Duke University, recruited 87 individuals whom they tasked with completing various activities that challenged motor skills, cognitive function, and creativity. The subjects were broken up into three groups. Group A was offered a measly amount of 4 rupees for completing tasks and reaching certain performance targets. Group B was offered 40 rupees. And Group C was offered a whopping 400 rupees, which equated to roughly 5-months pay for the average Indian. And can you guess what the results showed? Well, the performance of participants in Groups A and B didn't vary significantly. However, those in Group C, the cohort offered a substantial sum of money, lagged behind the other two groups in just about every category. In the final report, experimenters concluded, "Across multiple tasks, higher monetary incentives led to worse performance."[12]

Study after study after study seems to result in the same general conclusions in regards to monetary incentives and how they relate to motivation and performance – it can hinder rather than enhance. In 1999 Edward Deci and two colleagues completed a meta-analysis on 128 studies investigating extrinsic rewards and intrinsic motivation.[13] Deci and his team concluded that all types of external rewards "significantly undermined free-choice intrinsic motivation." They asserted that, "When institutions – families, schools, businesses, and athletic teams, for example – focus on the short term and opt for controlling people's behavior [using external rewards], they may be having a substantially negative long-term effect."[14]

Deci's findings apply to all industries, including science, engineering, and the financial industry. Henry Sauermann and Wesley Cohen analyzed data of over 11,000 industrial scientists and engineers, and what they discovered was that those who were motivated by money filed significantly fewer patents than those motivated by internal drivers, like the desire for intellectual challenge.[15] Additionally, the London School of Economics and Political Science published a report in 2009 examining 51 different pay-for-performance schemes within corporations.[16] Researchers found overwhelming evidence that financial incentives "reduce intrinsic motivation and diminish ethical or other reasons of complying with workplace social norms such as fairness…the provision of incentives can result in a negative impact on overall performance."[17]

So what is it about money and extrinsic rewards that cause people to lose interest in their activities and perform worse? Well, there are many reasons, including added pressure and anxiety that can narrow a person's vision and disrupt his thinking or the loss of ego that comes from feeling dependent on one's employer, but also a part of it has to do with the loss of autonomy. The loss of freedom. And as we will discover later in this chapter, autonomy is one of the key elements in motivating people to *do*. We want to feel like we are free, like we have agency. We want to feel, in a general sense, like our lives are not controlled by others. And in a situation when a person is offered a reward or compensation for completing tasks, that person might feel like he is no longer controlling his own life; he is attached to and at the mercy of the "reward-giver" or his employer, and decision-making no longer rests in his hands. And rather than choosing to take actions based on his own inner drives and free will, he is instead complying with the demands or requests of a master; he does things because his master wants him to. That has a way of toppling intrinsic motivation, creativity, and performance. In Teresa Amabile's study from earlier, the artists said they felt more constrained when doing commissioned works compared to non-commissioned works, because when they were attached to a client, they felt the need to be more careful in their creative endeavors. Play becomes work. And really, our whole system of pay-for-production operates under this principle – we are at the whims of the hand that feeds us, our behavior and actions largely dictated by an omnipotent puppet master. We do not have autonomy. We do not have the freedom we think we have, and that is part of the reason countries constantly have to remind their citizens that they are free. If you have to be repeatedly told you are free, chances are you're not.

In his comprehensive book *Drive: The Surprising Truth About What Motivates Us*, Daniel Pink describes extrinsic motivators as being on par with illegal drugs. According to scholars, he states: "cash rewards and shiny trophies can provide a delicious jolt of pleasure at first, but the feeling soon dissipates – and to keep it alive, the recipient requires ever larger and more frequent doses."[18] To back that statement up with physiological data, a neuroscientist, Brian Knutson, at the National Institute on Alcohol Abuse and Alcoholism hooked up a functional magnetic resonance imaging (fMRI) machine to the brains of a number of human subjects to measure their neural responses when told they had a chance to win or lose money.[19] When the participants anticipated potentially winning money, they experienced a surge of dopamine to the nucleus accumbens in the brain. What is significant about this finding is that the chemical process of sending dopamine, the reward/pleasure neurotransmitter, to this area of the brain mirrors the neural response of those managing addiction. When comparing the fMRI images of people expecting a cash reward to those receiving drugs like cocaine, nicotine, or amphetamines, they are almost identical. The feeling of receiving a monetary reward, "delights, then dissipates, then demands another dose," to quote Pink.

And as I've mentioned throughout this text, in our current economy money is used to incentivize people to do things they wouldn't otherwise choose to do by exploiting their fear of survival, which I've likened to extortion. It is held just out of reach unless people perform specific tasks. If they don't perform those specific tasks, they don't get money, which means they don't get to survive. No money means no food. No food means starvation and eventual death. And people don't want to starve and die, so they will take on backbreaking work if it means receiving money and the survival that comes with it. In many cases, it is not necessarily the money that coerces people into accepting unattractive, meaningless jobs; it's fear. Fear of survival. And any system whose foundations are built on fear, well, it's asking for all flavors of societal troubles.

So, contrary to popular belief, money is a weak motivational tool and can even be damaging to intrinsic motivation, performance, creativity, and ethical behavior. The "carrot-and-stick" method "fosters short-term thinking."[20] The whole idea that humans need to be bribed with reward or threatened with punishment to get them to achieve is largely armchair speculation; the arguments might sound plausible, but they are mostly incomplete and invalid.

"Okay Travis, so you're trying to establish that money is a poor motivator. But then what does motivate people? And if people don't have to be at a job every day, won't they just sit around, do nothing, and let their communities crumble to ruins?"

To address the second question, my answer is a resounding "No!"

The belief that humans are naturally lazy, and that without money we would sit around all day doing nothing is a myth. It is conditioned bologna! First of all, if that assertion were true, it would stand to reason that solitary confinement for inmates should be a vacation, yet it's not. In fact it is torturous and humans lose their minds without stimulation or interaction with others. Retirement for many folks, too, can become mind numbing and accelerate aging if they don't find meaningful activities and maintain social connections.

I also refer to sensory deprivation. Many people spend brief amounts of time in sensory deprivation tanks as a form of therapy; it can be relaxing and provide stress relief. However, depriving one of sensory stimulation over extended periods of time (hours) is not only unpleasant, but it can induce temporary psychosis and has a negative effect on cognitive function and perception as vision can become distorted – some volunteers become incapable of counting to 30.[21] Subjects in sensory deprivation studies have been reported to grow agitated, tense, anxious, and restless after various amounts of time; many experienced disturbing thoughts, panicked, and had to "tap out" and return to reality before completing the study session.[22]

If a person does lack ambition and exhibits lazy tendencies, it is oftentimes an acquired behavior; a response to life experiences and conditions that bleed a man of his innermost drives, of his inner will to achieve. Lethargy, avoidance of responsibility, and insolence can derive from a range of circumstances, like from a lack of resources or money, or from the feeling of being trapped in hopeless circumstances, or even from being micromanaged by a tyrannical boss. Such behavioral patterns derive from the deprivation of various life needs – both physiological and psychological.

And second of all, believe it or not, humans like to work – defined here as productive activity rather than perceived meaningless drudgery. In his book *The Human Side of Enterprise*, Douglas McGregor argues against conventional assumptions of man as an indolent creature needing bribes or threats in order to take responsibility within a community. He states that for humans the:

> "...expenditure of physical and mental effort in work is as natural as play or rest. The average human being does not inherently

> dislike work. Depending upon controllable conditions, work may be a source of satisfaction."

and that:

> "Man will exercise self-direction and self-control in the service of objectives to which he is committed."[23]

Being productive members of a community or an organization colors our lives with purpose and meaning; however, we want to believe that what we are submitting our valuable time and energy to is at least slightly meaningful. If a task is perceived as meaningless, sure people might choose to do nothing instead, but because we want to be busy, it doesn't take much to justify participation in an activity.

According to a recent study produced out of the University of Chicago, busy people are happier people, and we "dread idleness."[24] Stephen King wrote in his book *On Writing* that, "For me, not working is the real work."[25] Idleness is not bliss for the human mind or body, as the act of doing nothing for extended periods of time can have a negative impact on physical and mental health – boredom is a form of deprivation. The trick, like everything in life, is to strike a balance between productive activity and relaxation. Expending energy on a challenging, interesting, and meaningful task is a wonderful feeling. Then, when you come home, kick your feet up, and relax for a few hours, it feels earned; a moderate amount of idleness in this case feels great. Too much of either becomes unpleasant. It doesn't feel good to relax all day every day, nor does it improve wellbeing to work without end or perform the same activities every single day of every week of every month for the most competent portion of one's life.

Now let's move on to answering the first question above. What drives us to get out of bed in the morning?

What drove Calum MacLeod to build a road all by himself and for no monetary compensation?

What drives computer programmers to expend energy and hundreds of hours developing free software – Linux, Apache, Firefox – without the prospect of financial compensation?

What drove Nikola Tesla to devote his life to electricity and innovation, and what compelled him to turn away from a lucrative contract with George Westinghouse that would have made him one of the richest men in the world?

Why do prospective Olympic athletes spend hours, weeks, months, and years subjecting themselves to grueling exercises, punishing their bodies for the hope of representing their countries in the world games?

What drives a doctor to travel to Haiti or to a dangerous, war torn country like Syria to volunteer his services to populations in need?

Why do artists paint? Why do musicians make music? Why do writers write?

Why have I spent the last two years slaving over this book?

Why does my dad snow blow the neighbors' driveways after a snowstorm without expecting and even refusing remuneration?

What drives a parent to provide for her child without the expectation of that child ever reimbursing her for her efforts?

What is it that motivates us to take action? What sort of justifications do we need to turn meaningless work into meaningful challenges worthy of our time and effort? Well, answering that question is a tall order as many factors drive us to *do*, and what pushes one person might not push another; however, there are general principles of motivation that typically apply to the entire species. To start, as we've established in the first part of this chapter, extrinsic motivators are typically the weakest types of motivators. The use of external rewards, like money or snacks, can diminish performance, stifle creativity, create a sort of addiction problem, and it promotes shortsightedness. For a person to be fully engaged and fully immersed in an activity, motivation must come from within. Luckily, we are naturally **curious**, **creative**, **problem-solving** creatures, and we have an inherent drive to **achieve**, **master** skills, and live with a **purpose** beyond ourselves. However, sometimes there is no better justification to "work" than the idea that the activity we are participating in will make someone else happy or enhance the lives of a group of people. Our inner drive to feel connected to others not only drives us to action, but when we do achieve a sense of **connectedness**, it is one of the most gratifying feelings in the world. So, that is where I will start – on relationships as a driver.

You know, I've been pretty critical of the human species throughout this text, thus far. As a cynic who tends to focus on the negative, I can't help it; day after day I observe behavior that leaves me frustrated and disappointed, which probably isn't helped by mainstream media constantly plastering our screens with negative stories. However, though I often feel a sense of frustration toward the whole of us (I am included in this whole), I also can't help but feel proud at times as I recognize some of the amazing feats we've accomplished during our brief existence on this planet. I sometimes can't help but smile and feel inspired as I continue to discover our inner propensity for good and our inner drive to seek challenges, achieve, and help others. It gives me a glimpse of what we are capable of.

Before I started this journey shortly after Kaitlyn passed, it had always been my contention that we were born "bad."* That conflict permeated throughout our veins and those fleeting moments of selflessness had to be forcefully squeezed out of us like the last of a tube of toothpaste; goodwill was a rare exception. However, as I've continued to explore and unravel decades of research on human behavior, my position has completely flipped on the subject. I now truly believe we are born with a propensity for "good," that deep down, beneath the external strife, there is this internal yearning for peaceful connectedness not only with one another, but also with the natural world.

And what has led me to such a seemingly naïve and sappy conclusion? Well, science I guess. See, the biological machine that is our body rewards us for good behavior. Our body incentivizes positive social connections and goodwill. It electrifies with feel-good chemicals as we strive toward mastering tasks and achieving goals. Bad behavior, on the other hand? Conflict? Fighting? It hurts. The stress it causes inflicts irreparable damage to our bodies and our minds. Negative behavior wears down our biological machine and invites illness while positive behavior builds, strengthens, and promotes good health. So, because our bodies have built-in mechanisms to reward positive behavior and punish the negative, I think that is adequate reason to believe we are meant to be good. And I believe all of the nastiness we've exhibited throughout history is largely brought out by improper environmental conditions; that it is induced as a response to some sort of threat to our survival and our ability to just *be.* We prefer not to do immoral things. We prefer not to cause

***I know the notion of good and bad is subjective, and within many contexts, I don't necessarily believe in it, but in this context, I define it in the same way that our modern culture generally defines it. Peace good. Inflicting pain bad. Etc. Etc.**

harm – causing harm to others, as we will see in a few paragraphs, actually hurts us, too, assuming we are not sociopathic. It's just, this competitive game of survival we are playing against each other pushes us to look inward and focus mainly on our own individual wellbeing; the daily grind constantly pressures us into compromising our morals. And often within the game acting morally and helping others can put one at a disadvantage, while cheating and playing immorally can help one gain an advantage.

And yes, competitiveness is in our DNA, especially amongst testosterone-laden males. I revel in a hard-fought video game, board game, or basketball game, especially when I prove the victor, and I certainly admit that competing factions can push each other to accomplishing magnificent feats. We take pride in a job well done and being the best. It can earn us the respect and adulation from peers we so crave, and it can nurture our self-esteem. However, the social utility of competition has its limits and in certain environments can cause more harm than good; it can increase stress within a society and create a population of distrust and fear where citizens feel the need to constantly look over their shoulders; and it can lead to resource waste as multiple teams compete to accomplish the same goals. Competition was more useful during our primitive days of material lack.

Collectivism, on the other hand, always has been and remains one of the most dominant and beneficial inborn features of the human species. The desire to work with others toward a common goal, to create strong relationships, and to give back is baked into our being. I know that very word – collectivism – sends shivers down the spines of average Americans, as the idea of group collaboration and cooperation is generally associated with spooky words such as Socialism and Communism, which then elicits implanted images of brutal Russian or Chinese oppression, but collectivism and the need to socially belong is a hardwired, biological trait – we cannot deny nor run from that universal truth. From a purely biological standpoint, not a political one, we are born with intrinsic systems that reward *prosocial* behavior, and in the absence of human connection, healthy survival can become a struggle. And the proof? It's all around us.

For starters, life cannot be created unless two humans first come together.

Then, once that life leaves the womb, if a baby or child is not shown proper love and affection, his physical and mental development is put at risk (see Kaspar Hauser Syndrome in Chapter 6.1). Babies need human touch and are dependent on their parents or guardians for survival. Studies too many to enumerate reveal that simply holding an infant or stroking its head helps its neural and physical development. On the opposite end, children raised in institutions that are unable to develop a sense of belonging to anyone or are locked away under extreme neglect become withdrawn, frightened, and speechless. They become "pathetic creatures."[26]

Collectivism is rewarded. Think of how it feels to hug someone. Feels pretty good, doesn't it? When we bond with another person or if we are enjoying the company of friends at a party or colleagues at work, our body releases a hormone called Oxytocin. Oxytocin, also known as the "love hormone," not only rewards us by making us feel good when we are close to the ones we love, but it can also improve long-term memory, protect the brain from stress, and help shield the body from pain.[27,28] It's no wonder why it feels more gratifying to overcome challenges with a partner or a team as opposed to accomplishing tasks alone. Oh, and when you pet your dog, cat, or any other animal, both you and the animal release oxytocin, too. So shower that furry companion of yours with love and never feel guilty about it! You'll both be healthier.

Not only does our body release Oxytocin in situations of social bonding, but when we help out someone in need, the pleasure centers of our brain activate, too.[29,30] When we *give*, the ventral striatum, insula, and caudate nucleus, among other regions, fire in our brain. Helping others rewards us by making us happier, reducing stress, and boosting the immune system.[31]

And guess what? When you make someone happy, it has the reciprocal effect of making you feel happiness, as well. Have you ever heard of Mirror Neurons? When we observe someone performing an action or expressing an emotion, the same network of neurons in the emotional centers of our own brain begins to fire as though we are the ones experiencing that action or emotion – the activity of our neurons mirrors the neurons of the person we are observing.[32] So, when we give to someone and it makes him feel happy, it can have the effect of making us feel happy, too, as our brains mirror his. When we watch someone laugh, we want to laugh. When we watch someone cry, we feel a certain level of her sadness. When we watch a college basketball player pour his heart out on the court, we feel his passion. Mirror neurons play a key role in our feeling empathy for others. If we hurt someone, it hurts us, too (so long as our brain is functioning properly).

In contrast, loneliness and social exclusion are punished. Social isolation can lead to stress, anxiety, and depression, which can then bring about other adverse health effects. Likewise, social exclusion, or ostracism, is not only damaging to our health, but it's painful, too. Being rejected by an individual or a group elicits neural activity in regions of the brain associated with physical pain.[33]

Finally, common sense and studies tell us that there is power in numbers – a single human being might not be able to lift a burning, overturned car to save a man pinned underneath, but with the help of 20 others, such a magnificent feat can be achieved and a life saved. Cooperation enhances survival. Humans functioning as a collective unit are often more effective at solving problems and completing tasks than individuals acting alone. And when we come together, we wield a power feared by the most powerful (I sense the divide-and-conquer tactic is used for this very purpose; social control to protect the opulent minority against the majority).

So, though the idea of individualism sounds great and all, especially for an introvert like myself who prefers to work alone, and though we do have selfish tendencies, we must recognize our innate need to form groups, develop healthy relationships, and work as a collective unit. Our body rewards collectivism for a reason. We are meant to come together and help each other out. After decades of observing and studying the lives of Harvard graduates from the school's "Grant Study" program, professor Dr. George Vaillant was left to conclude:

> "The only thing that really matters in life are your relationships to others."[34]

At the end of the day, we are both autonomy-seeking individuals and interdependent cells within a greater whole.

In summary, relationships, the need to belong, and the positive feelings associated with giving back to the community are powerful intrinsic motivators that encourage humans to take positive action and be productive members of society.[35]

For me, accepting the notion that we are born to be good, that we are born to develop social bonds, work together, and help others is encouraging within the turbulent state of national and global affairs in recent times. It reinforces the idea that the spiral of negativity drawing us down like a black hole, causing anger, fighting, and deplorable behavior, it is not our natural state of being. In the ensuing days and weeks after the twin towers collapsed and firefighters, cops, and ordinary citizens worked feverishly, putting their lives on the line to save the lives of others, and when the entire country seemed to merge into one collective whole in response to tragedy and unfathomable pain, that to me is our most dominant and most powerful form.

Unfortunately, our environment of monetary scarcity continues drawing the worst out of us.

Observing humans from a neutral point of view, almost like a bird in a tree, I find us to be wonderfully fascinating creatures. Not only are we born with a gravitation toward connectedness, but we also come straight off the assembly line with this insatiable **curiosity**. The unknown has a way of capturing our attention; we just *have* to know what's on the other side. And that inborn curiosity functions as a powerful force in driving humans and monkeys to explore physical locations, inquire about new ideas, and develop new skills without the lure of external rewards; rather, exploring and finding answers are the rewards. We have an intense craving for new information and fresh experiences (so long as it doesn't contradict deeply rooted belief systems and cause cognitive dissonance). According to behavioral scientists, humans are "infovores."[36] We have built-in mechanisms that reward exploration and discovery, which encourages us to get off the couch and seek stimulation – part of its aim being to limit lazy behavior (though it's not always successful). In a study completed by Irving Biederman and Edward Vessel that focused on the visual systems within our brain, they found that when we acquire new information, opioid receptors associated with pleasure become active in areas like the parahippocampal cortex, where the greatest density of opioid receptors is located.[37] So, when we watch a movie for the first time, learn about an interesting subject, view beautiful scenery, or when a friend has tantalizing information for our ears, it can feel quite gratifying. It rewards with feelings of pleasure. Exposing oneself to the same stimuli over and over, on the other hand, quickly loses its enjoyable effect.

To fully grasp the intensity of our inborn passion for discovery, knowledge, and novelty, one needs only to avert his attention to mini-adults. In my opinion, children hold the key to understanding our true nature. Sure that includes some selfish behavior, but I find that children are more often sweet, kind, and caring, and the stronger their bond is with their loved ones, the stronger they become. And more importantly for the subject at hand, children are born curious. They are born with a sparkly-eyed exuberance for life that drives them to want to *do*. Children want to explore. They want to know how the world works. And sitting on their butts for even a moment is torture. They just want to *do*! Unfortunately, somewhere along the way, as we ride down the conveyor belt of society's indoctrination mills and get dumped into The Pit, that innate sense of wonder, that built-in drive to explore and discover is desaturated in us as we fasten ourselves to gear shafts and spin in the machine for 50 years; many of us gears are non-essential components of the machine. Though our inner curiosity is still there, lying mostly dormant in our bones, our daily, monotonous routines have a way of transforming us into dull automatons. We wake up, drink our coffee, go to work for 9 hours, come home, eat, watch TV, go to bed and repeat the entire process the next day, and the day after that and the day after that. By the time the workday or work week has finished, we are too exhausted to wonder. And if we do sense a spark of wonder, we are too tired to act on it.

<% Tangent!>

However, there is a ray of hope that keeps us ticking, that keeps us from completely falling into despair, at least in the beginning. As we climb the ladder of life – at least the life that modern society has carved out for us – we are promised that if we keep our noses to the ground and work hard, that each progressive rung will be bigger and better than the previous one. We are promised that if we are not satisfied, happy, or fulfilled now, that the next rung will finally make us happy. So, though we might find Middle School to be mundane, there's always High School to look forward to. And though we might eventually get tired of studying and taking tests and not having any disposable income in College, we always have the Rat Race to look forward to so that we can finally start making money and buying the things that we are told will make us happy. And so on and so on.

But then what happens when we turn 23 or 24 and we finally get that first "real" job; when we finally start making some real motherfuckin' money and acting like real adults? It's fun! It's exciting! At first…

In the first few months you wake up energized. Your aura shines bright and butterflies flutter about your tummy with the idea that you get to meet new people and learn new skills; you're treading new waters and that feeds your inner curiosity. But that feeling doesn't last long. As the months pass and you feel your life is on repeat, that excitement slowly wanes. You find that when you wake up in the morning, you feel less and less energized; your eyes droop, your feet drag across the floor, and you really don't want to have to go to work and repeat the same motions you've been repeating for the last year. You think to yourself, "Fuck. This sucks! I want out." But then you open up your spreadsheet and start adding up your expenses. You have college debt, you just bought a house, you have that car to pay off. Your stomach sinks. "Shit! I'm stuck!" Then you start thinking into the future, trying to figure out when you will be unstuck; you look down the long tunnel of your life and you realize you can't see the light. There is no end in sight. The time between now and retirement age feels like an eternity. You are trapped! And that feeling depresses you. It causes great anxiety because you know life is short, and you know you are so much more capable. You don't want to die feeling unfulfilled, like this one life you had was wasted on meaningless Sisyphus work. There is so much you want to achieve – if only you had the time. But you don't. Not right now at least. So then you eventually come to accept your circumstances. You compromise with yourself; you force yourself to believe that what you are doing matters and that the corporate climb is meaningful. You fool yourself by saying, "Once I become manager or once I become vice president, then I'll be making a ton of that sweet sweet dough, which I'm told will make me happy. I'll be able to buy what I want and have the freedom to do the things I'm actually interested in."

But then what happens? You finally reach the summit of your climb and attain that prestigious job. You upgrade your suit and you upgrade your stainless-steel gas grill. For a few months you're feeling pretty good about life. "This is living," you tell yourself. But then just like before, reality sets in. When you look beneath the superficial, material façade, you realize nothing's really changed in your life. Deep down you are no happier or more satisfied than you were before you got the promotion. You still feel a sort of emptiness inside, like something is missing. So you go to your cage, jump on your hamster wheel and take a long gaze out of your corner office window, and think to yourself, confused, "What the fuck? This sucks, too! I'm going to die soon and I've been spending my most capable years doing shit I couldn't care less about." You feel a twinge in the pit of your stomach. A few extra strands of hair fall onto your lap. For your entire adult life you were sold on this idea, the promise that if you weren't happy in your current position in the game, that the next level in this climb, in this hollowed-out race to the top, would make you happier. But it hasn't.

It's okay though, because now when you peer through the long tunnel of your life, you can finally see the light. You'll be 62 or 65 or whatever retirement age is shortly, and at that point you'll be free; you'll finally be able to do the thing you've always wanted to do your entire life. You just have to wait it out. Be patient. So you hunker down and suck it up for a few more years of your life – you're running out the clock.

But then what happens? The day finally comes when you are met with the light. You did it! Your shackles are finally unhinged and you feel a deep sense of relief and satisfaction! "YES!" You throw your hands into the air and strut into the light of retirement. You're finally free.

You go home, feeling energized, excited. You take a seat on the couch, kick your feet up, and flip on Fox News. You breathe a sigh of relief. "It's time to start living," you tell yourself through a deep yawn, "but not until tomorrow. My eyes feel heavy." Five minutes later your wife finds you crashed in your favorite chair, mouth agape and nose rattling. Tomorrow!

But then tomorrow comes. You slowly crawl out of bed and ease into your day. And why shouldn't you? You have nowhere you must be and no one you must see; what's the rush? So you take your time before beginning work on the thing you've always wanted to do. After all, the thing you've always wanted to do is going to take considerable effort, so you want to feel completely ready. But then when the time comes and you finally feel ready to pursue your goals, you realize you don't have the energy, nor do you have the passion to tackle those challenges you've always wanted to tackle. The energy and mobility you had as a 30-year-old are long gone, and you just feel so…tired now. So you finish your daily chores, meet up with a couple of friends for some coffee, come home, sit on the recliner and lull yourself back to sleep with the trusty old television.

Your inner fire has dimmed with age. You accept that you're just too old to commit to lofty goals. Plus, the thing you've always wanted to do also takes financial investment, and you don't want to be digging into your retirement funds, lest you soon find yourself broke and scrolling through the food pantry like many other senior citizens in America. You'll find some other meaningful hobby to occupy your time. You're free, after all. The world is your playground.

So then the days and weeks pass. One day in your bathroom, you look down and scan your wrinkly, sun-spotted hands. You lift your head and peer at yourself through the mirror; you take note of the fine contours tracing the curves of your aged face before an unsettling image catches your attention. In the far background through the mirror, you notice a dark, hovering figure leering at you with an expressionless gaze. Startled, you swing your head around to confront the imposter, only to realize no one is there. You must be losing your mind. So then you turn your head back around and look into the mirror once more. The dark figure has returned! It is at this point you realize the spool of your life is reaching its end. Death awaits.

Death's presence forces you to confront your own mortality and reflect upon a life that has seemingly passed you by. That familiar, uneasy feeling in your stomach returns as platitudes and banal epiphanies scroll through your mind. You think to yourself, "Each year that has passed is a year I can never have back. My entire life, committed to chasing nutrient-less carrots like a mindless rabbit. And for what? All of these talents God imbued in me. And for what I ask you, for what? To merely get by? To survive? Why must we be cursed with conscious thought if our only goal is to survive? What's the point?" Frustration overcomes you at the realization that the point of life isn't mere survival. You weren't given self-awareness or the ability to contemplate life and death only to make like cud-chewing cattle grazing in the pastures without a sense of purpose, without a sentient concern. No. That's not the point. The point of life, you realize, is to live; to laugh; to love; to connect; to play; to take on challenges that tickle the soul; to give back; to explore; to adventure; and to experience all of God's extraordinary creation. The point of life is to experience life. When the game ends, it all goes back in the box anyway, so why not pursue that which interests most? You pound your hand on the table and cry out. "Damn you! Damn you all to heck!"

After a few deep breaths, you calm yourself and stand aplomb! "My life has not been wasted," you reason with yourself, "All of my sacrifice was to make sure my children have a better life than me – that they had an opportunity to break free from the monotonous cycle of the game."

But then you stand staring into the middle ground, consciously surveying the lives of your children before realizing, "Shit, they've followed the same path as me. They were sold the same lie I was sold, and I didn't have the foresight to warn them that IT'S A TRAP!" So, after accumulating mountains of college debt and other expenses, like they were told to do by the establishment, they had little other choice than to submit to the same curiosity-killing, passion-dampening life you did. They're now trapped in the long, dark tunnel of the game, too, unable to utilize their unique talents and with no end in sight. Their childlike wonder of the world, gone. Their infinite capabilities disintegrating into thin air and floating away with the passage of time. Like you before them, they too come to accept their fate and simply try to wait it out until they reach the next rung of their life or until they are finally liberated by retirement. And also like you before them, they can at least find solace in the idea that they are raising their children to have a better life than them, that at least they will be able to break free from the chains of the vacuous game. However, as the cycle repeats, they too eventually come to realize they are no happier at the next rung of life, they no longer have sufficient energy to pursue lofty goals in retirement, and the mucous of The Pit has sucked their children into the same suffocating pattern as them. And on and on the story goes. Generations of capable and talented human beings stuck in the infinite loop of the game.

Then eventually, you die. Like tears in rain, you simply wash away, never having come close to living up to your full potential, never having been able to pursue the challenges that most interested you. Self-Actualization, according to Abraham Maslow, is the exception in our society, in that there are not many people who reach this highest-level need on his Hierarchy of Needs pyramid (which he concedes makes it difficult to study).[38] Unfortunately, most of local society and the world are swimming in the lower levels of Maslow's pyramid, simply trying to keep their heads above water, meet their most basic needs, and survive.

So then one must ask once more, if we are only here to survive, what's the point?

<kill Tangent!>

Whoa! What happened there? Ventured a little far off the reservation in talking about curiosity in children and where it goes once we become adults. What were we talking about again? Oh yeah, human motivation. What are our intrinsic motivators? What drives us? So far we've established that the need to feel a sense of connectedness and curiosity work as powerful drivers in moving us to action. But also…

Humans are ferociously **creative** beings equipped with a strong complementary drive to achieve. Everyone has the ability to create, even those who think themselves as dull and uncreative. "The capacity to exercise a relatively high degree of imagination, ingenuity, and creativity in the solution of…problems is widely, not narrowly, distributed in the population."[39] And creativity comes in all shapes and sizes, whether it's painting, developing a financial report, constructing with Legos, welding, cooking a meal, having a conversation, planting flowers around the house, coding a website, building a rocking chair, and so on, and we express this natural, almost involuntary ability every single day. For many people, not being able to create casts a gray cloud over one's head, while unshackling our inner Picassos can pull us out of depression and enhance wellbeing. When Henri Matisse was a young adult and working as a lawyer's clerk, he was often depressed and sickly. But once his mother brought home art supplies and Matisse began painting, his spirits soon lifted, his attitude shifted, and his energy increased.[40] Having a creative outlet is healthy, both physiologically and psychologically. In a 2010 analysis, researchers concluded that expressing one's artistic side can enhance mood, reduce stress, boost the immune system, and reduce the risk of chronic diseases, like those affecting the heart;[41] other studies show that taking part in creative activities can reduce the risk of dementia, as it stimulates and massages many regions of the brain.[42,43]

Playing an instrument or writing a screenplay can also help us reach that exhilarating state of *flow*. What is flow, you ask? You know that amazing feeling when you are so fully immersed in an activity that you lose track of time? That's what scientists refer to as flow. And if we've reached this state of being "in the zone," where the pre-frontal cortex in our brain relaxes and certain brain functions become "super-charged,"[44] then we know we are participating in a highly engaging and satisfying activity. When we connect with a task so deeply that we lose ourselves to it, that is when we are at our most creative, and that is when the magic happens!

Fostering one's creative side feels great and nurtures inner wellbeing and gratification, while **achievement**, on the other hand, builds self-esteem, earns adulation and acceptance from peers, and helps one reach the elusive pinnacle of Maslow's Hierarchy of Needs I briefly mentioned – that need for self-actualization or self-fulfillment.* "What a man CAN be, he MUST be!"[45] Our inherent achievement motivation drives us to significant accomplishments. Pursuing goals, especially if it gives back to the community in some way, gives us purpose and makes us feel important, like we matter in the world. A few pages earlier, I mentioned the phenomenon of software developers and open-source software projects. Have you ever heard of Linux, Apache, or Firefox? Linux is a computer operating system, like Windows; not only do 1 in 4 corporations trust Linux to support their businesses, but it also acts as the engine beneath some of the internet's most important applications and services. Then there's the web server software known as Apache. Apache comprises 67% of web servers used in the world. And lastly, there's Firefox. Firefox is the well-known web browser that serves roughly 400 million web surfers globally. And what do all three of these vitally important, widely used programs have in common? They were all open-source projects completed by unpaid developers and offered to the world at zero cost. Money was not a reward, yet scores of computer geeks devoted hours upon hours of their lives creating and coding these valuable computer tools.

Thousands of examples exist of open-source or volunteer projects that were created by enthused "hobbyists" not expecting a single dollar, but wanting a challenge, a purpose, and a chance to achieve something great and give back in some way. There are video games (Metroid II fan remakes), computer/scripting languages (PHP), cookbooks, medical research, beers, cars, and projects devoted to open-source genome analysis and protein development. From 2000 to 2001, NASA ran its "Clickworkers" experiment where volunteers were asked to perform

*** Self-Transcendence was added later in Maslow's life.**

routine science analysis normally done by scientists or graduate students.[46] Though they had no idea what to expect, during that two-year span, they had over 100,000 individuals volunteer their time, which totaled roughly 14,000 work hours. By NASA's account, the program was a "great success," and the volunteer work proved useful. In the field of mathematics, the Polymath Project sees volunteers collaborate online to solve difficult math problems, and also with great success. Open-source projects exist for law, religion, copyediting, encyclopedias, and so much more.

In his book on human motivation, Daniel Pink compares the product life of two online encyclopedia tools – Microsoft's MSN Encarta and Wikipedia.[47] Encarta was developed by a band of paid developers at one of the most powerful and wealthy companies in the world and was offered to users at a nominal fee. Wikipedia, in comparison, is free, and it's been the dedication of thousands of unpaid hobbyists that are responsible for creating and sustaining its 6 million-plus articles. Now, as Pink describes, conventional wisdom would tell us that of course a software product cooked up by a team of paid professionals within a profit-driven corporation would succeed by leaps and bounds over a free online tool patched together by a faceless army standing to gain no material reward for their work. But that's simply not the case. MSN Encarta was put to rest in 2009 while Wikipedia has rapidly blossomed into the world's largest encyclopedia; sure it can fall victim to vandals inputting false information here and there, but analysis has shown that it is reliable overall.

Why would anyone spend his or her time hacking away at computer code or contributing information to an open-source encyclopedia for nothing (monetarily speaking)? Well, because they enjoy it, and it allows them to feel like productive members of society. Researchers from Germany and Denmark examined the developers behind a number of open-source software projects throughout the world. What they discovered to be the strongest drivers was that it was "fun" for the programmers in trying to "master the challenge of a given software problem," and that it gave them an opportunity to "give a gift to the programmer community."[48] Bottom line, humans want to be useful within their social groups; it builds confidence and self-esteem and makes a person feel worthy, like he belongs. Whereas the opposite, uselessness, breaks down self-esteem, makes one feel like he holds little value within society, which can induce feelings of shame and stress; and, stress of course leads to negative effects on the mind and body – we don't want that. So, part of taking on challenges is to be useful members of a social group – be it local or global – and earn respect and acceptance from peers, which builds self-respect and self-esteem, which can add to a happier, more gratifying life.

Of the many intrinsic drivers that push us to take action and be productive, we've established that our natural curiosity and creativeness, in concert with our drive to achieve, give back, and develop relationships are some of our most powerful motivational traits. We are naturally pushed to *do* without the need for external reward. However, though we have built-in drivers, certain environmental and organizational conditions can dull our intrinsic motivation while other conditions can nurture and enhance them. Behavioral researchers, including Deci, Richard Ryan (his research partner), and Daniel Pink, allude to three elements that foster intrinsic motivation, which I will call Drive Supplements:

1. Autonomy
2. Competence or Mastery
3. Purpose

And I am going to add a fourth Drive Supplement to this list that I believe is vital in nourishing intrinsic motivation, in pushing a person from inspiration to action, and that is:

4. Access

### *AUTONOMY*

Years ago when I worked for a television show in Hollywood, I had a boss who would, at times, hover over my shoulder and watch me edit photos in Photoshop. And though I had my own process and order of doing things to help me stay organized and keep track of what I had accomplished and what remained, she would often come over and disrupt my process by moving things around on my desk so it matched her process. She would even take my completed photos and file them away, even though I needed them for reference. Needless to say, I didn't like that or the lack of autonomy afforded to me, and it was part of the reason why we did not have a good working relationship. I quickly started to feel resentful and bitter, and it reflected in my work.

In order to fully engage a person in an activity and allow him to reach a state of flow, which is crucial for maximizing performance, it is important for him to have a certain level autonomy, or freedom, over an assigned task. He must be made to feel like he is the master of his domain, and that he has control when it comes to deciding on how best to do his work. As I alluded to earlier in this chapter, when we feel like our choices and actions are dictated by or attached to someone else, we tend to lose that inner spark for a task, that inner excitement. And without passion, we become slightly disengaged and our work suffers. It's not just children that despise being told what to do – it's adults, too! Now, as Pink points out, there is a distinction between autonomy and independence. Independence has to do more with going commando on tasks, whereas autonomy simply has to do with volition and the freedom to choose. One can have autonomy whilst still being interdependent with teammates in completing a project.

Throughout the past few decades, studies have continued to show that people given autonomy exhibit higher levels of wellbeing and satisfaction, higher levels of productivity, less burnout, better grades, increased persistence toward challenges, greater innovation, and improved aptitude in understanding concepts. One study out of Cornell University examined autonomy amongst 323 small businesses. And what researchers found was that the companies that offered their employees greater autonomy grew four times faster and experienced one-third of the turnover compared to the companies adhering to a more traditional, control-oriented style of management.[49] The proof isn't limited to studies. When Pink surveyed companies that offer their employees weekly or monthly "free time" to tackle personal projects – 3M, Atlassian, Google, Georgetown University Hospital – they revealed that some of their greatest innovations have come during those moments of autonomy.

Now, as with every motivational element in this chapter, the amount of autonomy one requires can differ dramatically from person to person. I know some people who like to take direction – they feel safer under the wing of an authoritative figure. And for some people having to make decisions can be stressful, even if the decisions are seemingly trivial, e.g., "How should I end my email? Thank you? Take care? Best wishes?

Go to hell? Ahhhh, I can't do this!!!" But if someone is participating in an activity or task that he finds joy and interest in, autonomy is generally desired to enter that state of flow and extract his best work. Overall, autonomy has been shown to improve lives, and that applies to humans in every corner of the globe.

### *MASTERY*

One thing Olympic athletes, software developers, carpenters, and many others have in common when they are working on their craft, is they are gradually mastering their skills. When we expend effort into something that interests us, we get a chance to become better and better at it, and that continual improvement builds self-esteem and confidence, and it is enjoyable to varying degrees. And watching oneself improve at something is rewarding and stimulating.

Feedback is key. When an Olympic swimmer shaves seconds off of her time or a software developer compiles his code and sees his creation come to life, the observable progress is a great feeling; it's rewarding. The chance to master my basketball skills was a primary motivator for me in high school. As a pasty 5'10" Midwestern boy, I knew my chances of making the NBA and earning millions of dollars were virtually zero. However, I enjoyed playing the game, and I was relatively good at dribbling and making shots. But I wanted to be better. No matter how far my skills advanced (they didn't advance that far), I wasn't satisfied, because I felt like I could be better. And being able to observe my own gradual improvement drove me to wake up at 5:45 every morning and go to the gym before school started. The feedback wasn't instant, but over time I noticed I was making more shots, and when I dribbled behind my back I was maintaining control over the ball more often; the progress was gratifying.

Oftentimes, in pursuing one's goals, the journey toward the finish line, the work expended in mastering a skill and tackling a challenge, is more interesting and enjoyable than the actual attainment of those goals. Once a goal is achieved, then the adventure is over. And though it might feel comfortable to relax on the couch for a few days, we soon grow restless and bored and need to find new goals to occupy our time. Though all stories need an exhilarating ending, the journey throughout the middle contains the juiciest parts.

## *PURPOSE*

And as for Purpose, I've continually brought this word up along with the word "meaning" throughout this chapter. Purpose and finding a meaning beyond the self are crucial for maximizing intrinsic motivation. Without purpose, as I mentioned a few pages earlier, justifying tasks can become a struggle. If we are going to spend our limited time doing something, we want to know that it matters. The more it matters to us, the more motivated we become. It was when Kaitlyn was in the middle of her battle with cancer and we were running out of options that I found myself more driven than I had ever been in my entire life. I feverishly scoured the internet, read every piece of literature on melanoma that I could and as fast as I could, and conferred with doctors from around the country. And material reward certainly wasn't a driver. I was motivated by a purpose far beyond myself, and as futile as it seemed in retrospect, I wanted to learn everything I could in a last-ditch effort to keep Kaitlyn alive. When we care about something, when something matters to us, we get to work! We don't need external bullshit hanging in front of our faces. The fulfillment and gratification that come from pursuing and completing a purposeful task is its own reward. Attaching goals to a greater cause has a way of enriching our lives and pushing us beyond our limits.

In a 2009 study, Deci, Ryan, and Christopher Niemiec followed 246 students into the "real world" after they graduated from either the University of Rochester or a "mid-western 4-year college" (name not provided in study).[50] They wanted to compare the wellbeing of graduates who were reportedly motivated by intrinsic goals or "purpose goals" (helping others, developing skills, learning) to graduates motivated by extrinsic goals (money, fame, image). What they found was that the graduates driven by "purpose goals" had low levels of ill-being (anxiety and depression) and higher levels of satisfaction and well-being compared to when they were in college. Those motivated by goals that were meaningful to them were happier overall. However, in contrast, those driven by money and external goals were no more satisfied than they were in college and they had higher levels of stress, anxiety, and depression, even if they were successful in achieving their goals. This study again supports the notion that intrinsic, meaningful motivations promote lasting well-being, while external, profit-driven goals might provide a short-term boost but ultimately leave one feeling empty in the end.

In 2008, researchers published the results of a rather amusing set of studies associated with tasks and meaning.[51] In the first experiment, Dan Ariely, Emir Kamenica, and Drazen Prelec gave each human participant a sheet of paper with a random sequence of letters. The subjects were then told that if they could find 10 instances of two consecutive letters ('ss'), that they would receive $0.55. Upon handing their completed page in to the experimenter, they would then be asked if they wanted to complete a second sheet for $0.50. For each subsequent sheet, the payout would decrease by $0.05. Subjects were then broken out into three categories. In the first category, when a person handed in his completed work, the experimenter looked it over before filing it. In the second arm, when a subject handed in his completed sheet, the experimenter filed it without acknowledging it at all. And in the third group, when the subject handed in his work, the experimenter immediately shredded it without looking at it right in front of the subject. In the end, the participants in the first category, those whose work was acknowledged, chose to complete more sheets (9.03 on average) than the participants in the other two categories (6.77 and 6.34).

And the results were similar in the second study. Instead of using letters and sheets of paper, however, subjects were invited to construct characters out of Legos. And just like in the first experiment, participants were paid to assemble two different Lego models, and each subsequent model they completed yielded a slightly smaller monetary reward. In this study, subjects were broken out into two categories – Meaningful and Sisyphus. In the Meaningful category, when a subject submitted his Lego character to the experimenter, the experimenter simply set it aside, but kept it intact. However, in the Sisyphus category, when subjects submitted their completed models, the experimenter immediately began disassembling their work and used the pieces for the next build. In the end, not only did the subjects in the Meaningful group complete more characters on average (10.6 to 7.2), but they also completed them with greater speed.

What this shows is that if we perceive a task to be meaningless, then we are less motivated to do it, even if money is on the table. When the connection between work and purpose is severed "work becomes absurd, alienating, and demeaning."[52] However, just a simple act of acknowledging a person's work, of indicating that it is meaningful and valuable, might be all the motivation one needs to push forward and continue working on a task.

### *ACCESS*

The last Drive Supplement needed to nurture one's inner drives, the one that I've added to the list laid out by scholars far smarter than me, is Access. When the internal flames are crackling, if we don't have access to the necessary resources to keep those flames of inspiration burning, that fire quickly dims. If a man is inspired to make a film, he needs access to camera equipment. If a painter wants to paint, he needs access to paint supplies. If a child feels the music vibrating in his bones, he needs access to a guitar, a piano, or some drums. A woodworker needs access to saws and wood. Without access, people eventually lose hope, and dreams die. Unfortunately, that is exactly what happens to the children in poor regions of Africa that end up laboring in diamond mines (Chapter 6.3). They are motivated to learn; they want education. But, due to circumstances far out of their control, access to their most basic survival needs is all but cut off, so they have little other choice than submit to backbreaking labor. As time goes by their hopes for a better future fade, they dull their expectations to save from disappointment and pain, and eventually settle into and accept their life of servitude. But with access, there is no limit to what humans can learn and accomplish.

And there you have it. To maximize our inner drives, it is imperative that we have a certain level of autonomy, the chance to master a skill, a purpose, and access to the necessary tools for whatever it is we are inspired to do. If you look at some of the greatest achievements in modern history, you will find they all have these basic elements in common. For instance, let's refer back to the rugged ole Scotsman from the opening of this chapter.

Calum MacLeod was intrinsically motivated to achieve, connect with others, give back, and create, which culminated into 1.75 miles of road. If we take a closer look at his amazing accomplishment, we will find that all of the basic elements of drive nourishment were met. He had autonomy over the construction of his road. He had an opportunity to work toward mastering his craft. He certainly had purpose. And lastly, he had access to the necessary tools in his wheelbarrow, pickaxe, shovel, and manual. Those Drive Supplements coupled with his intense inner motives fueled the flames of will and self-determination for 10 years until he reached his goal.

Now let's look at Nikola Tesla. It is well known by historians that Tesla was not driven by money, which made him a poor businessman. When George Westinghouse, the investor who put his financial faith in Tesla's brilliance when no one else would, was struggling to keep his company afloat during the "Current Wars," he asked Tesla if he could restructure the terms of their contract which, at the time, paid the Serbian inventor a $2.50 royalty for every horsepower generated from his A/C motor. In response, Tesla offered to simply rip up the original contract, release Westinghouse from his contractual obligations, and save the owner's company. He didn't care about the monetary rewards, he simply loved inventing and mastering electricity. Instead of restructuring Tesla's contract or deferring payment until the Westinghouse Electric Company could weather the financial storm, Westinghouse instead paid Tesla $216,000 and acquired a number of his A/C technology patents. By accepting the investor's smaller offer, Tesla essentially saved the company. Unfortunately, however, in voiding his original contract he turned away from the chance to become one of the world's richest men. And instead, the inventor responsible for some of human history's most important inventions, including alternating-current electricity that's powered America for over 100 years, died penniless.

So what's my point in telling this tale of the man known as the "Master of Lightning?" It's to further show that humans are driven without the need for external rewards. Again, making money wasn't Tesla's prime objective, it was more of an obstacle to him, as it kept him from fully realizing his innovative ideas. And all of the money he did make he invested back into his craft. Tesla was internally driven to spend just about all of his waking hours on creating world-changing technology; by all accounts he was a workaholic. But if he wasn't motivated by external rewards, then what compelled him to dedicate so much of his time and energy to his work? Well, first of all, he was fiercely passionate about electricity – which stoked his curiosity – and he enjoyed his vocation. Additionally, he was driven to create and achieve; and, although he was eccentric and ended up becoming a recluse, he cared deeply for mankind and wanted to improve everyone's quality of life. All he needed was access to equipment and tools, which he got under George Westinghouse. Once he acquired access, he was able to work with a certain level of autonomy, he was able to participate in something that allowed him to continually improve and see results, and he had a purpose greater than himself. Unfortunately, the equipment and tools weren't cheap like those of Calum MacLeod, and funding eventually dried up for the "mad scientist."

Practical examples abound. Software and website developers, motivated by the chance to create, achieve, and give back also have autonomy over their work, an opportunity to hone their skills, a purpose in that what they are creating will ideally be used and enjoyed by the masses, and access to the tools needed to develop.

A musician certainly doesn't make music for money, because there basically is no money in music to begin with, at least not for the vast majority. And the same goes for painters, writers, and anyone in the creative arts. Most works of art never see a penny, yet musicians and artists alike spend hours working in a state of flow. Why? Well, because they are passionate about their work and the act of creating is exhilarating. And while they are creating, they typically get to work with all of the most important Drive Supplements – autonomy, mastery, purpose, and access. Of course, though it is rarely expected, if money does eventually trickle into an artist's bank account, it is simply an added bonus.

With an arbitrary medium of exchange removed from the game of life, we need not worry about whether or not man will still be productive. We need not worry that if something important needs to get done that it will be done. Every single day we can find examples of people exerting their energy toward tasks yielding no monetary rewards. They sacrifice their valuable time with a simple push from intrinsic motivators. At the most basic level, a mother bends over backwards taking care of her children, because she cares deeply about their health and wellbeing (relationships, social bonding, purpose). A man helps his buddy move into his new home because his friend needs the help and he cares enough to provide that help (social bonding, connectedness, meaning). A daughter attends to the needs of her bedridden mother. Olympic, college, and even high school athletes spend hours at the gym, weight room, or pool (passion, mastery, pride, achievement).

In the field of medicine over one million people volunteer their time in providing support to the St. Jude Children's Hospitals throughout the country and the world, totaling roughly 37,000 hours of free help each year. And, every year doctors donate their time and energy to care for patients in countries all across the globe. The organization Doctors Without Borders has a presence in nearly 80 countries where about 35,000 doctors, nurses, and other personnel volunteer their energy and skills toward helping millions of people within poor populations in dire need of medical attention.[53,54]

In 2006, Dr. Dilantha Ellegala sought reprieve from his stressful American career as a neurosurgeon. And his idea of taking a break? He joined an NGO and volunteered his skills and expertise to the Haydom Lutheran Hospital in the African country of Tanzania. When he arrived, he was shocked upon discovering that the impoverished nation had a total of only three neurosurgeons. Three! And with only six months before he was scheduled to return to America, he realized he could only help so many people.

So, Ellegala decided he would take a Tanzanian native under his wing and teach him as much and as fast as he could. The neurosurgeon ended up recruiting an enthused assistant medical officer by the name of Emmanuel Mayegga. Even though the man had no medical degree, Ellegala recognized that the Tanzanian had the necessary tools and determination to become an effective neurosurgeon – so they got to work immediately. Without monetary incentive, Ellegala worked day and night with his apprentice. After only one month of tireless training, Mayegga was performing supervised surgeries. By month three he was able to work alone, and after six months of tutelage, Mayegga was able to perform basic cranial neurosurgery, treat hydrocephalus, remove tumors, and install shunts.[55,56]

Both men, motivated by a purpose beyond themselves, accomplished in a short period of time what might typically take years. Once Ellegala left, Mayegga began passing his knowledge down to other determined individuals, who then passed it down to others, and the knowledge began to spread.

This story, detailed in the book *A Surgeon in the Village*, is yet another amazing example of what man is capable of when his mission is internally driven.

And I think the previous couple pages lead into the next concern people often have when confronted about the idea of a system without money. And that is, in the absence of monetary incentive, what will drive doctors to become doctors and surgeons to become surgeons? It is such a demanding, complex, and high-pressure job that they must be rewarded, otherwise they would choose to do something less challenging, right? I don't believe so. First of all, I always tell people that there are two types of doctors in this world. The first type of doctor is the ambitious student driven to help others in the most noble way he feels he can. The second type is the doctor that knows the medical profession can make him a lot of money. Now, of the two types of doctors, which one would you prefer to see? The one driven by money, who if he advises you to take a certain medication, you can't be sure if he is sincere in his recommendations or if he is looking to make a quick buck? Or, the one driven to help others? The answer is simple.

Second of all, as technology continues to improve, the need for surgeons and doctors will likely change; however, as long as there remains a need for doctors and surgeons in the future, people will still choose to become doctors and surgeons. Such a prestigious profession offers the opportunity to meet all of our intrinsic needs and live a fulfilling life. Community members hold doctors in the highest regard, meaning a woman who becomes a doctor can feel confident that she will earn the respect and adulation from colleagues and peers, which satisfies the needs of self-esteem. She will wake up every morning with a deep sense of feeling important and needed in the world. A surgeon also has the opportunity to *help people* and make great *achievements* almost every single day, which meets her social needs and the needs for self-actualization. Surgeons get to work with a purpose far beyond themselves when the lives of others rest in their steady hands. They also get to work within a field that isn't fully understood – the human body – which means they have an opportunity for continued learning and internal development. Lastly, doctors and surgeons have the opportunity to further master their skills and knowledge, which again adds to feelings of self-fulfillment.

You know, when I think about it, in a world where money no longer exists and our basic survival needs are met, I can actually see surgeons and doctors becoming one of the most attractive and sought-after professions. Entering the medical field would provide the ultimate path to reaching our higher-level needs – esteem, self-actualization, and self-transcendence – and it is one of the best ways to achieve life satisfaction. In my early-30s, I wanted to go back to school to become a neurologist not because of the lucrative potential, but because I found the brain to be fascinating, and I really felt like I had a knack for understanding the three-pound organ. Also, I felt it was a great way for me to do something that actually added value to the world and make a difference, rather than continuing on as an accountant where I felt devoid of purpose, like what I was doing added little to no value to society. However, I already had heaps of unpaid student loans, and the last thing I wanted to do was sink further into debt. So, I chose not to.

I've often heard that man is a wanting creature, that he has unlimited wants. Within the context of materialism and the market economy, I absolutely refute this traditional concept. When it comes to lifeless, inanimate objects, we do not have an insatiable appetite driving us to buy, buy, buy. That's why marketing has to work so hard and companies spend so much money on advertising – to convince us to want more and more things. They know that when our core human needs are satisfied – food, water, shelter, etc. – that acquiring more gadgets doesn't make us any more satisfied. Sure it might give us a hit of dopamine for a short period of time, but the novelty of a new item wears off rather quickly. Beyond our basic needs, we seek fulfillment not in cars, houses, or other dust-collecting items, but in the non-material. It is in this context that I do agree that man has unlimited wants. As he satisfies his higher priority survival needs, he doesn't simply wipe the dirt off his hands and do nothing the rest of his days. No. He becomes bored. He becomes restless and discontent, and he endeavors to fulfill other existential needs – finding love, developing relationships, building self-esteem, conquering challenges, living up to one's full potential, finding purpose, etc. Meeting such needs is just as important to a full, enriching life as the basic survival needs. Material items can add color to our lives, but they do little in creating lasting happiness and fulfillment.

So, to recap, contrary to conventional wisdom money is mostly an ineffective tool in stimulating intrinsic motivation and extracting productive behavior out of the human species; and it has little correlation with happiness in life. Beyond a certain threshold, it ceases to increase man's satisfaction. If I am making $1 million and my salary is doubled to $2 million, my happiness and satisfaction does not double with it. External rewards can be an effective prod when it comes to "autonomic" tasks, but such routine and repeatable processes can easily be automated with current knowledge and technology. When it comes to "heuristic" tasks, however, external reward systems, like money, have a negative impact on motivating people and fostering their inner talents. Money and material prizes can destroy curiosity, encourage deceitful behavior, and rip a hole in the sails of creativity.

Humans do not need money to encourage or even force productivity; in fact they better flourish without it. We are motivated by a number of internal drivers, which includes our need to feel connected with others and build relationships (which also encourages us to give back), our natural curiosity, our inherent creativity, our need to achieve, and our aversion to idleness and boredom. To best feed our internal drives, autonomy, the chance for mastery, purpose, and access are vital. Laziness is a conditioned response brought about by an amalgam of environmental factors. Conversely, people actually like work (meaningful work), and when their basic needs are met they will seek responsibility, as it helps them achieve self-esteem, a sense of connectedness, self-actualization, and self-transcendence. Psychologist Barry Schwartz sums it up wonderfully in stating:

> "We want work that is challenging and engaging, that enables us to exercise some discretion and control over what we do, and that provides us opportunities to learn and grow. We want to work with colleagues we respect and with supervisors who respect us. Most of all, we want work that is meaningful — that makes a difference to other people and thus ennobles us in at least some small way."[57]

So, without money will shit still get done? You're damn right it will! If ever we find ourselves doubting man's internal drive to achieve magnificent feats and overcome difficult challenges, we need only remind ourselves of the A/C electricity feeding our televisions or the 1.75 miles of road connecting Arnish to the Brochel Castle, among millions of other examples.

# 10 THE ANSWER

Phew! We made it! Finally! The closing segment! After 300 pages of discussing drawbacks and problems brought on by the current monetary system, it is time to refocus our energies in a more constructive manner. It is time to start talking solutions, because it's one thing to sit here and sling cow chips at the aspects of global society I disapprove of – that's easy, anyone can be a critic, and everyone is a critic, especially nowadays with the advent of social media – but nothing changes solely through finger pointing, criticism, and complaining. So let's talk about an evolved economic system that I believe can pull us away from the turbulent state of national and global affairs and ameliorate much of the world's woes.

Before we begin however, I ask that you humor me for a moment by participating in a thought exercise. I'd like you to close your eyes. Okay, you don't need to close your eyes, because then you won't be able to read what I've written. But if you will, I'd like you to imagine for a moment, your perfect world. I'd like you to envision your personal Utopia. What's your ideal world like? How do the people in your world interact with each other? Is there fighting? Is there starvation? Is the planet still in peril? If you are like most people, I would imagine you answered "No" to those last three questions. Of course you don't want war, crime, starvation, or environmental damage in your ideal world. You'd have to be insane or psychopathic to want that.

Now, unfortunately, Utopia is impossible. For one, everyone's

Utopia is different. And two, Utopia essentially means we've arrived at a perfect world, one where improvements can no longer be made. However, change is the only constant in life, and no matter how advanced our civilization becomes, we will always discover better methods of performing tasks and solving problems. We will always have goals to strive toward. So, Utopia is something we can never achieve. However, though it is not possible to build a "perfect" world, it is possible, and I would go as far as saying *much simpler* than we might think, with a few adjustments to get rid of homelessness, remove hunger, significantly reduce crime, reverse environmental decay, restore trust, and so much more. The key to reaching what many perceive as insurmountable and idealistic, mostly through years of conditioning, armchair speculation about human nature, and the like, is through EFFICIENCY. And to achieve an optimal state of efficiency, we will be focusing on, among many other aspects, TECHNOLOGY and ACCESS.

So, here I present to you *A* potential solution. It doesn't necessarily mean it's *THEE* solution, because there are infinite possibilities and the world is in constant flux, but it is the most logical one I've encountered thus far; and if nothing else, it is a step in the right direction. Also, it is not *my* solution; I can't take credit for the proposals discussed in this chapter. Many great minds before me have expended years of their lives investigating, brainstorming, analyzing, enlightening, and developing methods to permanently pull us out of The Pit. Of the scores of men and women devoted to peaceful cohabitation and world betterment, there are three names I see referenced more often than others when it comes to designing a new economic system that is actually focused on the verb "economize." R. Buckminster Fuller, the peculiar inventor and engineer behind the geodesic dome, dymaxion car, and the term "Ephemeralization" (doing more with less) discussed in Chapter 7.2, introduced his "World Game" proposal to the masses in the 1960s with the intent of tackling the world's problems through a "comprehensive, anticipatory, scientific approach." Jacque Fresco, inventor and social engineer, volunteered decades of his life to designing his Resource-Based Economy, which utilizes technology to intelligently and sustainably manage Earth's resources while providing life necessities for the entire global population; he worked tirelessly on his blueprints and designs all the way up to his death in 2017 at the age of 101. And Peter Joseph has largely taken the baton from Fresco and has continued building upon the Resource-Based Economy (not to discount the work of Fresco's associates, like Roxanne Meadows and the team volunteering its time to The Venus Project, but people are more aware of Joseph's work).

Of course, the ideas of this chapter cannot be attached to any one man or group, either, as the aforementioned would humbly admit, because knowledge is serial! Knowledge and ideas are built upon and passed down from person to person and from generation to generation to generation. No one man in the history of the world is solely responsible for inventing or discovering anything. Without prior generations first discovering how to properly harness electricity, and without the tools needed to build his motors, there would be no A/C electricity, and Nikola Tesla would not have become the man we read about and venerate today. Bill Gates would not be the Bill Gates we know about today if not for the work of scores of software developers that came before him, that developed programming languages (BASIC, Fortran) and sequences of code which they shared amongst each other and that Gates later built upon when creating Microsoft. And those coders could not have developed programming languages or been able to hack away on computers if not for the teams that worked on and built the first commercial computers. And the first computers could not have come to be without prior generations discovering how to harness electricity. And so on and so on.

Knowledge is serial! All discoveries and inventions could not have come to fruition without the work of prior generations, rendering the idea of the "self-made" man as mostly illusionary; it's a myth we tell ourselves to feed our enormous egos and to elevate our status in a group and make ourselves feel more important; it's a lie we use and a mask we wear to coddle our own personal insecurities and reassure us that we're worth a damn, because we constantly question our self-worth throughout life. Of course, there is also financial incentive in being able to proclaim "that's mine!" in society. Mankind has never ever produced a "self-made" man. Bill Gates was not self-made. Thomas Edison was not self-made. Men have worked hard to accomplish magnificent feats, sure, but all humans (including myself) owe a great deal of whatever success they achieve not only to the foundations laid by prior generations across various cultures, but also to the conditions of their upbringing, life circumstances, and the support of their parents, family members, friends, and/or mentors that helped shape them into the people they became so they could even have a chance to encounter interesting opportunities, accept them, and flourish. Einstein might have been a brilliant physicist, but do you think he would have propounded his theory of relativity had he been born in the destitute African country of Malawi where books and education become secondary to survival? It's possible, but unlikely. And if he did hypothesize about the nature of light, the chances of anyone hearing him would have been slim.

That being said, this chapter is not about deifying labels or names. It's about the logic and ideas behind developing the first truly humane, truly free, truly "economic" global system. And for those subscribing to the Libertarian mindset, it'll be the most Libertarian system ever introduced as the socioeconomic conditions will be conducive to the Non-Aggression Principle and Voluntarism. This new system will respect ownership over the most important piece of "property" – the individual. It can be argued that, though we might own material items, most of us are not the owners of our own lives as our thoughts and actions are often directed by contrived external forces. However, in our system unchained from money, we will for the first time ever have complete ownership over our own lives.

We've spent a great deal of time in this book identifying the source of many of the most unwanted and detrimental aspects of society, and what we found was that money and the need to acquire it in order to survive was at the inner core of just about every negative externality we can think of.

To recap one last time, it is not that money is evil, per se, but it is scarce. It is limited amongst the population, which means the game of money is a zero-sum game where if I want more, someone else somewhere in the world has to make do with less. And what's more is money acts as a barrier to the necessities of life. I can only access bread or underwear by first acquiring money from another player, even if those goods happen to exist in abundance. So, because money is limited within society and because it is needed to access survival, it becomes a vicious game where people are competing against each other merely to obtain money so that they can survive. And in this game of acquisition, as some of the players obtain the bulk of the money supply, other players get left in the dust, which then makes survival for those "losers" difficult. Many of the "losers" in this game, including children, end up starving and dying, even though

Earth is abundant in life sustaining, regenerative resources, and even though enough food is currently produced to feed the entire world. As money becomes scarcer in the lower tiers of society, poverty grows, along with desperation, insecurity, and what our culture defines as criminal ideation and behavior. Also, because the "winners" of the game could lose their secure and comfortable positions at any time, which would threaten their lifestyle and potentially even their ability to survive, it is in their best interest to continue acquiring money, even if they have more than enough to last multiple lifetimes. And because continual money acquisition is in their best interest, the "winners" are also prone to unethical and unwanted behavior in society. So, not only does money's scarce existence produce nasty habits amongst the "losers" of the world, but also the "winners." No one is immune to the pressures of the game. It is not hard to see how our global monetary system has created the perfect storm for all of the negative, abhorrent, life-threatening externalities we are experiencing today.

In the words of Jacque Fresco, "This shit's got to go!"[1]

So, if we want to eliminate the negative elements plaguing society and keeping us in a perpetual state of anger and frustration, the first and one of the most important features of our future economic system is the emigration from and complete removal of money. I know such an idea sounds radical, mainly due to generations of conditioning that would have us believe that money is as normal and necessary as the oxygen in the air, but it's not. Money is just a tool – an artificial and manmade one at that – but its presence has managed to muck up just about everything sacred to the life experience. I won't argue the idea that it was an important step in our social evolution, but it has most certainly outlived its value in society and now acts purely as an impediment to what I define as true progress and true prosperity, while causing way more damage than good. Its scarce existence pulls us away from our natural gravitation toward a peaceful, cooperative coexistence by pitting us all against one another in a stressful, manic, trustless competition of survival. This endless and unnecessary competition has us living in an inverted world where fear rather than compassion rules the day. Where selfish and greedy behavior is often rewarded while selfless behavior can put one's security at risk. The consequences of such an arrangement should come as no surprise then – the cancer spikes, lower life expectancy, stress-related diseases, poverty-related diseases, crime, war, civil unrest, ecological degradation, homelessness, starvation, divorce, suicides, mental illness, mass shootings, and on, and on, and on. Money is at the heart of it all. So, I understand it might sound radical to leave money in the dust, but not only is it in our best interest for a happier and more peaceful life, I would say that it is imperative if we want to reorient the planet to a healthy state and ensure the long-term survival of the human species, as well as other species, too.

That being said, with our new economic system, all forms of money, including fiat money, cryptocurrency, gold, and all other mediums of exchange will be done away with – barter can be tossed in there, too. They all serve the same purpose. More advanced technology can better calculate supply and demand. More advanced technology can better distribute resources to where they are needed. And as we've discovered, money is not needed to motivate humans, as it's been shown that we naturally seek and take on responsibility, create, and solve problems. Besides, money's disappearing act is an inevitability; whether it is 50 or 5,000 years from now, money will eventually be phased out, because it is an unnecessary and inefficient middleman in managing and distributing resources.

So, moving beyond money is the first step in climbing out of the slimy depths of The Pit. However, if money is the mob boss of negative externalities, then "fear of survival" is its loyal muscle man – its Luca Brasi. Once we get rid of money, we still need to address and eliminate fear of survival, because it will continue wreaking havoc on the population so long as it persists. It's this fear, this insecurity of being unsure of how we are going to survive day in and day out that leads us to feelings of distrust, worry, desperation, etc. which then leads to crime, scheming, warring, the coveting of material possessions, and all other forms of deplorable behavior. So, following that logic, the answer seems pretty simple if we want those negative outcomes removed from civilization. The answer seems pretty simple if we want to leave our children and grandchildren with a world of peace, prosperity, and environmental wellbeing.

We must design an economic system where every single person is secure in his or her survival. We must design a system where no one is unsure of whether or not he will eat today, or whether or not he will have a roof to protect him from a storm. By simply lifting that heavy weight off of peoples' chests, the positive ripples will touch all aspects of society.

Individuals themselves will feel significantly less stressed. The impoverished children of poor and stressed parents won't be subjected to such stress and would be given the opportunity to develop properly, both physically and mentally. Crime would be significantly reduced. As I will continue to point out, it is in the best interest of the entire population to develop an economic system where everyone's basic survival needs are met. And in a sane society, such statements would seem obvious. "Well duh, of course we should create a system so people don't have to die of starvation or live without a roof." However, in our present global society, such a statement is not obvious, and as I've alluded to, the conditions of homelessness and food insecurity are considered normal and expected. Needless to say, we do not live in a sane society.

"Okay Travis, a system where people don't have to worry about starvation or homelessness sounds great and romantic and all, but it also sounds idealistic and Utopian. How the heck do we create a system where people's basic needs are met without further destroying the planet?"

Two words. Automation and Access!

Automation, which we will go into greater depths with, is the alliterative, blanket term I'm choosing to use to represent technology, artificial intelligence, robotics, cybernetics, etc. The goal is to achieve technical efficiency by applying the most advanced knowledge and technological capabilities currently available to all areas of society, which includes the production, distribution, and management of goods and resources, public health, transportation, education, etc. Everything that can be automated will be automated.

I understand that the idea of a completely automated city might sound too futuristic, far out, and far-fetched, but it's already happening. Cities around the world – Singapore, Dubai, Tokyo, Amsterdam – are shifting to automation where they can.[59] In the "smart city" of Singapore, officials are experimenting with automated transportation (driverless taxis), delivery systems, and even police units (for better or worse).[2] They are implementing Virtual Singapore, which is an incredibly detailed 3D model of the entire city that includes data about buildings, climate, material representation of geometrical objects, terrain attributes, and much more.[3] Hotels in Singapore are even experimenting with robots that can clean rooms and deliver supplies and linen. In terms of food production, the capital city introduced the world's first commercial vertical farm so it can locally farm produce rather than having to import it from various regions.[4] Vertical farms in smart cities, as well as traditional cities, utilize robots and artificial intelligence to monitor and respond to the needs of its crops without the need for human intervention. In Dubai, self-driving "flying taxis" are being tested where passengers can simply summon a Volocopter using their phone; the driverless flying taxi comes and picks up its passengers and takes them to their destination.[5] Smart cities are implementing technology and installing sensors that can monitor and manage resources and other vital systems and institutions within the city. In Barcelona, sensors have been installed in irrigation systems to track water levels to alert crews when vegetation needs water. "Smart" buildings are being developed using automation to control lighting, ventilation, heating, etc. And as I've mentioned in the section on Technological Unemployment, automation has been extended to healthcare, housing construction, crop cultivation, grocery stores, cooking, and folding clothes, where the need for human labor is significantly reduced or completely eliminated. So, though it might sound unrealistic to have automated cities, the technology exists and it's already being implemented in every corner of the planet – however, lack of financial resources forces countries to pick and choose which technologies to implement. Without the worry of monetary obstacles in the system proposed in this chapter, we will be able to gather the most advanced technologies scattered throughout the globe and combine them into a fully automated city to achieve the highest level of technical efficiency we can. In this sense, technology will be seen for its technical value rather than its monetary value.

As we discussed in Chapter 7 and throughout this text, efficiency is the ultimate enemy of the present monetary system. It needs turnover to ensure constant consumption. The faster products turn over, the better, as it means more goods and services will be sold, which boosts the economy. However, though inefficiency and product turnover are great for the health of the economy, it is extremely wasteful from a planetary perspective as it puts a strain on the environment. By the very definition of "economy," which means to use resources carefully and avoid waste, we are not running an economy. Instead, we are running an "anti-economy." Our monetary system works in complete opposition to the natural system of Earth, which is ever apparent as we see every single life system in rapid decay.

By removing money and the need for profit to stay afloat, there will no longer be an incentive to make inefficient products. In our system of the future, there is no need to design goods to become obsolete before they need to. Instead, the sole focus will be on designing and producing the best possible product with the most advanced technology and knowledge available. Without the concern for costs of production, product turnover, or increasing profit margins the focus will be on producing a product built to last while also striving to reduce our ecological footprint. Goods will be designed so we can make upgrades when newer technology becomes available instead of having to throw it in the trash, as is the current norm, which will reduce waste and pollution.

Our future system will actually align with the immutable laws of nature, focus on careful use of resources, and work to limit waste. By definition, it will actually be economic. Technology and automation will help us achieve optimum efficiency.

And right now, companies only install new technology when it becomes financially reasonable. Even if better tech exists that can achieve "more with less," companies won't apply it unless it is profitable. And often, especially in the early stages of a new machine's life, it can be pretty expensive, so it might take a few years before the price comes down and companies actually start utilizing it. In our future system, since money is not a factor in decision making, if a piece of technology is introduced to the world and is proven to be safe and more efficient than current methods, then it gets put to use immediately. Also, some companies are hesitant to install machines because it often means employees will lose their jobs. And with job loss comes a wrench in one's ability to survive. The fear of job loss and technological unemployment will also no longer be a factor, rather, if a machine can come in and do a job better and more efficiently than a human can, it will be celebrated as a fantastic achievement. And when Bob on the assembly line is relieved of his monotonous duties, he can cheer as it means his time will be freed up to pursue other, potentially more interesting challenges in life, and he won't have to start panicking, wondering how he will feed his children, because our system will also focus on Access…

The second feature distinguishing our future system from our current model, which will help us eliminate scarcity and all of the negative outcomes that follow, is Access. People will have access to the essentials that they need to survive – and as we've pointed out, it will not cause mass laziness, since we want to have value in society, and boredom is torture. By using technology to its fullest capacity, we can easily produce an abundance of life necessities without putting a strain on Earth, which will ensure that everyone's basic needs are met. No more will a farmer have to hang his head in shame because of the debilitating feeling that he's failed his family. And no more will his family need to feel his stress or deal with the pain of loss when he takes his own life. A person only steals something he doesn't have access to. So, by giving people access to the goods they need, crime will also be significantly reduced.

The setup of our Access economy will resemble modern libraries, but with an expanded catalog of goods. In our world today, many of the items we own are used sparingly. A lawn mower gets used once a week and only for a portion of the year in some regions of the world. Recreational film equipment, like the cameras and lights that I own, are often packed away in storage for extended periods of time. The cars that we own sit idle for most of the day every day – the average American drives about 1 hour each day, or about 6% of the time.[6] As the world approaches 8 billion people, and as other nations compete to reach the American standard of living, ownership of certain items ends up being wasteful and uneconomic.

Let's home in on vehicle use for a moment. In the United States in 2019, there were 284.5 million vehicles.[7] In his book, *The New Human Rights Movement*, Peter Joseph provides a rough calculation to demonstrate how many vehicles would be needed based on the estimation that we only use our vehicles 6% of the time.[8] If we take that 6% use-time and apply it to the 284.5 million automobiles in America, we could reduce the amount of vehicles clogging our roads to about 17.1 million. Obviously, in our access economy, each region would need a cushion to ensure vehicle availability, but the actual number of vehicles needed would come nowhere near that 284.5 million figure. By simply shifting from ownership to access in the case of cars, we can significantly reduce pollution, resource use, and congestion. Think of how much easier it would be to commute through and find parking in densely populated cities like Los Angeles, where now a simple 11-mile trip can take over an hour, and when you arrive at your destination, it might take another 10 to 15 minutes to find parking on crowded streets or in parking ramps. I will dive deeper into transportation possibilities in the Transportation section, but I just wanted to quickly demonstrate the inefficiency of everyone owning one of everything.

Our new economy will have strategically placed access points where people can access the things they need, when they need them – from cars, to cameras, to film equipment, lawn mowers, and whatever society can think of. And when it comes to goods that we use all of the time, then of course those are the ones we hang on to. Most importantly, by utilizing the highest technological capabilities, which includes advanced methods of food cultivation, people will have access to food. And by taking advantage of water desalination techniques without the worry of financial cost, people will have access to water and anywhere in the world. And by employing advanced technology to build homes quickly and efficiently, and without the need for labor, people will have access to shelter.

And here's the part where I feel like I will lose some people. It will all come without a price tag. People will have *access* to it; they won't need to acquire an artificially valued piece of paper, and they won't need to exchange anything for the ability to survive.

Let's back up and reanalyze our current economic system for a minute. The more scarce an item is within our monetary paradigm, the higher its price is in the market – imagine how expensive the 2007 LEGO Millennium Falcon would be if there were only 5 in the world. However, when an item is abundant, that item's value decreases in the market, making it more affordable and accessible for a wider consumer base – now imagine if there were 300 million LEGO Millennium Falcon sets in America alone; assuming a machine produced them, meaning each additional unit cost less and less to produce, meaning it would essentially reach *zero marginal cost,* then the Star Wars starship's price would drop to almost nothing. Jacque Fresco often brought up his analogy of gold. Right now, gold is highly valuable in the world, and if people come across it, they scoop it up as quickly as they can. However, if one day it started raining gold all over the world, meaning it was abundant for everyone, it would lose its monetary value and people would start sweeping it out of their homes rather than hoarding it. The air we breathe is free, at least for the time being, because of how abundant it is. The logic behind our future system follows this same train of thought; by applying science and technology to its fullest capabilities, we can produce a surplus of available goods, rendering the whole price mechanism irrelevant. As we increase production efficiency through automation, we can reach a point of *zero marginal cost* where items can be produced without increasing production costs. If there are more than enough bananas for every single person, it makes no sense for people to have to exchange something of arbitrary value to acquire a banana, especially when the banana can largely be cultivated without the use of human labor.

I know for many people, the idea of simply providing humans with the basic necessities of life does not sit well. The word "free" carries a sort of stigma with it amongst certain groups, as though getting access to life essentials without first exchanging something of "value" will lead to the collapse of society. However, I would say, right now, the opposite is true. Our society is in rapid decay, in large part, because a vast number of inhabitants are not getting what they need to live. Also, as I consider it, the human system is the only system I can think of that requires external payment for life necessities. All organisms – humans, plants, animals – operate in a synergistic, symbiotic, give-take, cause-and-effect relationship where all things are interdependent on other life systems and processes to survive; everything is connected one way or another in the *circle of life*; life is one giant interaction of visible and invisible parts. However, unlike the human condition, no other organism in this fruitful biosphere is consciously required to make a payment or sacrifice to receive the necessary elements to survive.

Plants do not have to pay the sun or the Earth for the light they absorb or the oxygen and water they consume. Deer do not pay the Earth for the air they breathe or the grass they eat. If the Earth has it, the Earth provides it – free of charge. Children receive free care from their parents, and they don't become lazy imbeciles as a result. In fact, it's the opposite, once again. By not having to stress about survival, they are better able to develop and flourish into adulthood. And when it comes to the organs in our body, if a specific organ needs something, the body provides it – free of charge.

On that path of thought, think of our future system like the human body. First, we have the brain, which is the hub of the body, the Central Processing Unit; it's connected to, monitors, and communicates with all other systems. When an organ needs something – hormones, white blood cells – information is delivered to and from the brain in a feedback loop, and the body immediately provides the organ with what it needs so that it can function properly. And the body understands that it can only function at an optimal level when ALL other cells and organs are functioning properly. If one organ is not receiving what it needs to function properly, it begins to malfunction, and as a result the entire closed system that is the body is thrown out of balance; one organ malfunctioning can cause other organs to malfunction. So, it's in the best interest of the entire body to make sure ALL organs get what they need.

Also, the body doesn't recognize individual organs as being separate. I used to consider the brain as the most important organ in the body, until I realized that without the heart, the brain would cease to function. So then I asked myself, does that mean the heart is most important? Well no, because without arteries channeling blood to and from the heart, or without the lungs collecting oxygen, the heart would cease to pump. So, no organ or region of the body is most important. Everything, all organs, blood vessels, cells, and systems are connected to one another in a give-take synergistic relationship. They are all interdependent on other cells, organs, and systems. And because the components in this total enclosure system work in complete harmony with each other, automatically supporting the ones that need support, the body is one of the most amazing, most efficient machines in existence.

Sure we humans have assigned labels to various organs to better identify and locate them, but that doesn't mean the organs or cells are separate, per se. All is the one, and one is the all. The organs, like the countries of the world, have names and can be distinguished from other organs, but unlike our manmade countries, organs do not compete against each other. Our organs work in harmony with one another, knowing that one malfunctioning organ is a threat to the homeostasis of the entire body. Could you imagine the Lungs attacking the Liver? The body, along with all other cells and organs would suffer. The same is true of the body of Earth, its organs (countries), and its cells (people).

Now, governments throughout the history of man would have their people believe that they are the immune systems of the world, and that they only attack or conquer other regions to rid the Earthly body of invasive, malignant cells, but that has almost never been true. Attacking countries are often the malignancy – fooling the greater body into thinking they are normal cells.

In parallel to Earth's system, when an organ or cell starts to malfunction and cause harm to the rest of the body, it's usually not because it was born bad. Improper "environmental" conditions within the body are often what cause a cell or an organ to "act out." When cells and organs are not given what they need to develop and function properly, they can become destructive. Sure some cells might be predisposed to destructive tendencies, but predisposed doesn't mean predetermined.

So, in a way, I envision the future system functioning much like the human body. It will have a brain/CPU connecting the entire global body, monitoring resources, measuring supply and demand, assessing public health, etc. Countries would be the organs, but they would no longer be competing against each other. We would all recognize that we are a synergistic organism dependent on one another for optimum health and survival. We would recognize that the ideas of countries and separation are an illusion. We would realize that the division lines separating states and countries are only made up, that the lines separating Wisconsin from Illinois or the US from Canada or Russia from Finland do not actually exist. The borders we see on the map cannot be seen in the physical world. A pilot flying above Earth sees no such borders. That's because they don't exist. We made them up and now often use them in an antagonistic manner. We use these imaginary borders to form groups, by which we use to create in-groups and out-groups – "My group is better than yours!" – even though DNA tests show we are all virtually the same. An alien would have a difficult time differentiating a Scot from a Brit.

Because division lines don't actually exist, that means that countries don't actually exist. Though this notion might sound radical, like many notions in this text, the truth is there is no such thing as Mexico, Peru, or China. Those labels derive solely from our heads. Earth certainly does not differentiate one country from another.

So, in the future system, countries would operate much like organs. We can assign labels to them to better locate and distinguish the various regions of Earth, but that would be about it. All-in-all we would recognize that we are all connected in various ways, interdependent with each other, bound by the same Natural Laws of Earth, and that we all benefit from every organ functioning properly.

Lastly, we miniscule little humans roaming about the planet can be considered Earth's cells. Like the cells of the body, humans would receive from Earth, with the help of communication with the CPU, everything they need to survive and function properly. We know that when cells are healthy, the organs function better, which allows the entire body to function properly. If the cells don't receive what they need, if their environment is toxic, as we have seen throughout this text, cells can mutate into cancer, become murderers, become bullies, and many other harmful forms. When this happens, the entire organ is affected, which can affect the entire body. So, it's in everyone's best interest that all of Earth's human cells get what they need to function in a healthy manner.

In many ways, the future system, once it reaches full capacity, will mimic the human body, where all systems operate in harmony. At least, that's the goal. It might sound idealistic, but by removing the mechanism that has us divided and competing against one another – money – and by providing basic life needs to everyone, it certainly becomes attainable.

I could go on relating our future system to the human body, like how our system will have a Central Nervous System (CNS) along with a Peripheral Nervous System (PNS) connected to the various limbs of Earth; how the PNS will have nodes throughout the body, delivering and receiving information within its region, and then delivering and receiving information from the CNS. But, I will halt the analogy here and start talking specifics about how the future system can work.

So, the two components featured in our future, moneyless system, both integral in pulling us out of The Pit and away from all of the negative externalities infecting society today, are Automation and Access! The use of technology will help society function as efficiently as possible and reduce the need for human labor in the completion of monotonous, "autonomic" tasks, while access to life necessities will erase poverty, homelessness, and starvation. Access will also remove individual and group tension and reduce stress, which will reduce crime, suicides, depression, war, cancers, heart-related ailments, and more. Technology working in tandem with Access will free people up to pursue challenges that interest them without worrying whether or not they will survive. If I suddenly want to change course and become a brain surgeon, I won't have to worry if my kids or I will suffer and starve during my transition. The mundane processes, like waste management, power generation, and any other boring, autonomous task will be managed by integrated, cybernated systems. The management of one's personal life, including his preferences in style, education, activities, etc., will be left completely up to him. Humans will be the most free they have ever been! No more Asian sweatshops. No more Moroccan women slaving in strawberry fields. And no more exploited Mexicans spending their entire lives picking tomatoes in Florida. More advanced technology can and will take the place of indentured servants. The world will be better for it.

And no longer will biased politicians and businessmen seeking to make a buck be at the forefront of decision-making, where market efficiency in the form of cost savings and wider profit margins take precedence over technical efficiency and human wellbeing. Instead, by using a decentralized, interconnected, peer-to-peer network and open-source platforms, everyone will actually have a say in decisions made, unlike today in our "democratic" society where all important decisions are made by a very few, while the population as a whole has very little influence. The people will finally have a real voice, and decisions will be aided by advanced, interconnected computing systems that track resources and other vital components.

Technical decisions will be aided by verifiable *science* – conducted by engineers, technicians, physicists, etc. (which I don't want to confuse with a technocracy). Human language comes in many forms. One word can have multiple meanings depending on the context with which it is used, the background and life experiences of the conversational participants, and more, which means a person's message can fall victim to misinterpretation and misunderstanding. However, the language of science is not quite as vulnerable to misinterpretation and can be understood by people across different countries and cultures. We can give the same blueprint of an airplane to engineers in the United States and engineers in Japan and be relatively confident they will produce the same machine. When it comes to designing the technical aspects of society, our future economy will depend on the language of science to deliver the most productive outcomes rather than the biased language of business, politics, and opinion.

Whatever methods are tested and repeatedly proven to be safest and most efficient will be the methods utilized. Public debates are not needed to figure out how much less land is required per gigawatt-hour of energy for Geothermal facilities compared to Coal facilities – we can measure that. And, without monetary or profit incentive, we can better trust that the interest of the public is of greatest concern rather than whether or not it will make or save money, meaning we can better trust the motives for utilizing certain energy sources, food cultivation methods, resource extraction techniques, etc. For instance, if a town official is touting the use of solar energy and is campaigning for the installation of panels on every rooftop, the townspeople won't need to wonder if maybe a solar energy company has paid this official off to support solar energy.

Let's zoom in further to our future system.

If you and 100 of your family members and closest friends moved to an uninhabited island with no infrastructure, and it was up to you to design a system, would you design it with the expectation that a few of your family and friends will have to suffer and die? Would you accept that such an arrangement is inevitable? Probably not. I imagine with your intelligence and problem-solving prowess that you would try your best to design a system that meets the survival needs of *all* those you care about. You would want to utilize the island to its fullest capacity to ensure nobody starves and nobody suffers.

But how? What features would such a system require to meet the needs of the entire population while also giving everyone the best opportunities to contribute and flourish? Well, there are a number of elements you and your constituents must consider, which include, but are not limited to:

- Food
- Water
- Energy
- Transportation
- Construction
- Education
- Health

Additionally, whatever system and processes you install, you want to ensure they do not damage your island. After all, the island is your home, and if it sustains too much damage then its ability to produce food might be hindered, or it could become unsanitary, among many other issues, and as a result your civilization could suffer and potentially perish. So, sustainability must be emphasized in your new system, as unsustainability is completely illogical. The new system will seek to operate in accordance to Earth's natural laws and processes, and it will focus on intelligently managing resources to reduce waste.

For ease of reference, let's give our economy a name before moving forward. We can call our future system anything we want; it doesn't really matter since we're more concerned about function over titles. However, because our system of the future places a strong emphasis on the intelligent management of Earth's resources, Jacque Fresco took to calling it a Resource-Based Economy (RBE). Now, advocates like Peter Joseph have since added the prefix Natural Law to the name, since our economy adheres to the natural laws of Earth, making it a Natural Law/Resource-Based Economy (NL/RBE); however, I am simply going to call it an RBE for the rest of this text, only because it's less of a mouthful and might save me a second or two in typing.

Also, since Fresco dedicated decades of his life to designing what he called a Resource-Based Economy, I am going to be leaning heavily on his work and schematics, while taking advantage of the data and calculations compiled by Peter Joseph and his team in their extensive research. While I have tried to maintain a more informal, conversational tone with simpler language in this writing, the books written by the likes of Joseph and Jacque Fresco are much more technical, professional, and scholarly – they are better. Fresco's writings even include images of his designs if you are interested in visuals, which I imagine you will be if you've made it this far without throwing the idea in the trash.

Resource-Based Economy (RBE).

To begin with, let's talk about the physical layout of a Resource-Based Economy.

# 10.1 BASIC DESIGN

What will cities in a Resource-Based Economy look like? Well, in short, they will come in various forms and will continue to evolve as future generations discover more intuitive designs and efficient methods of organizing a city's flow and processes. However, like with any new idea or technology, there has to be a first design or a first blueprint that adequately captures all of the features envisioned by the original designer. And as for the design of Fresco's pilot city in an RBE, he has strategically elected to go with a multi-dimensional, circular shape for the purpose of efficiency, to operate with minimum energy requirements, and for ease of access to essential facilities; from overhead one might say Fresco's "test" city looks similar to a spider's web, with a central hub and concentric layers extending outward.[9]

Our modern cities traditionally take the shape of squares or rectangles, with essential stores and buildings scattered throughout, often in an unorganized, haphazard arrangement, which makes travel to and from places more time consuming and less efficient. But, in this version of an RBE, stores, facilities, and key access points would be strategically placed. More specifically, the central hub of this Resource-Based Economy would essentially act as the brains of the city. It would house the core Educational Centers, Healthcare and Child Care Facilities, the Resource Management System, and Communication and Networking Systems. Then, the first radial tier encircling the central dome would contain Access Centers where people can go to access whatever tools they require to fulfill a need. We would have the ability to either deliver tools or goods straight to a person's location, or that person would be able to travel to the access centers to pick them up himself. Extending out from there, the next three concentric layers include Research Facilities, Offices, and other Institutions. The next circular tier would be reserved for Entertainment and Cultural Activities, which includes theaters, gyms, concert halls, and more. Surrounding the entertainment center are Residential Districts, where each home would be immersed in lush gardens and trees to give one a sense of space and isolation if that's what one prefers. And if a more communal feel is what a resident desires, he would be able to live in an apartment within skyscrapers that also contains restaurants, entertainment, educational centers, and more. The Agricultural Belt follows the residential belt, which is reserved for food cultivation utilizing both indoor vertical farming and outdoor techniques. To help with irrigation and filtration, a circular waterway would encapsulate the agricultural belt. And finally, the last circular tier would contain renewable energies as well as areas for recreation. The recreational areas can include golf courses, bike paths, tennis courts, baseball diamonds, football fields, and any other facility needed to satisfy the various interests of its residents.[10]

Now, is this "spider web" layout rigid and inflexible in its design? Of course not. Cities in a Resource-Based Economy do not need to conform to any uniform design. They can and will take many different shapes. They might be linear, underground, or built as floating cities over the sea. They might be designed to strategically channel wind currents or direct sunlight. They might even be shaped like a guitar or a dinosaur. In Fresco's initial model of an RBE city, he chose the circular design because it made the most sense to him from a technical standpoint. He designed other models, as well.

I understand some people might oppose the idea of intricately planning every detail of a city. They recognize that humans are complex organisms with unpredictable behavior, and they might feel that cities need the flexibility to grow organically and expand on an as-needed basis, as humans' wants and needs constantly change. I get it and can empathize with that sentiment. Though physical design is important, I would go as far as to say it is an aspect of lesser importance in a Resource-Based Economy. The core aspects that make an RBE what it is, from my point of view, revolve around transcending the tool of money, using advanced technology to produce an abundance of life necessities, giving all people access to the means of survival, and intelligently managing Earth's resources, with the purpose of freeing people from the contrived stresses of modern life to pursue goals most interesting to them, live a full and enriched life, and reach levels of self-actualization never before seen in this world. If those core ambitions are met, then it doesn't matter to me what a city looks like. If we can meet these goals by simply renovating current cities, great! However, since the blueprint already exists for Fresco's vision of an RBE, and since it includes all of the core aspects above, I will continue approaching our future system using the circular and intricately planned framework.

In producing their own energy, food, water, and other goods, cities in an RBE are designed to be self-sustaining, self-reliable, total enclosure systems, at least as far as conditions allow. For the most part, they will not have to rely on foreign imports from other cities.

Cities in a Resource-Based Economy will essentially resemble living organisms with the ability to react to and adapt to changing environmental conditions. Sensors will be embedded throughout the entire city, which will be able to automatically measure and respond to water usage, energy consumption, food consumption, resource usage, traffic flow, the health and state of the environment, weather patterns and so much more. The information will be collected and transmitted to the Digital Node of the city, where it will be used to calculate how much energy needs to be generated, how much food to cultivate, etc., all for the purpose of intelligent resource management, maintaining dynamic equilibrium, and making sure people get what they want or need. This digital, cybernated sensory system is not about tracking and controlling citizens. Without money and needing to maintain a competitive advantage to ensure survival, there is no use for controlling people in a Resource-Based Economy. We, as a collective unit, would get more benefit from educating and liberating everyone's mind to contribute to the best of their unique abilities rather than suppressing and keeping them down.

The information that is collected within each city will be uploaded to the global "cloud" system to manage total resource levels, maintain active communication between regions, and more. In a blockchain format, the resource and decision-assisting database will be decentralized. All cities and people will contribute to it, and everyone will have access to the network "ledger" to prevent tampering and fraud. And, each "node" of the global system will be constantly updated, and they will be validated by other nodes. As is a common misconception, there is no "central" computer that corrupted individuals can manipulate, as every digital node throughout the world acts as a server and client; all networks combined make up the main server.

It might sound far-fetched to buy into the idea that embedded sensors in concert with advanced computer networks can collect, communicate, and analyze data on a 24/7 basis, but with tremendous computing power in today's world becoming more and more powerful, not only is it possible, but it is already happening. As I mentioned, cities throughout the world are currently in the process of transforming their infrastructure to become "smart," where sensors are placed in every facet of society, from buildings and streets, to clothes and farms. These advanced tools in an automated, synergistic system can process trillions and quadrillions of bits of data per hour – much, much more than an entire city of human brains combined. Artificial intelligence can then take the incredible volumes of data constantly coming in, analyze various outcomes, measure pros and cons, and offer up options and solutions that we have neither the time, nor the mental capacity to consider, which can ensure we are arriving at optimal conclusions in the most important sectors of the local and global community.

Again, these tools are meant to assist and serve, not control.

If you want to research "smart" cities on your own to comprehend the enormous potential of integrating sensors and automated technology systems with daily life to facilitate community needs, look up the self-sustaining city plans of Masdar, or the smart city designs within Singapore, Barcelona, Dubai, Toronto, and others. I am going to try and point out *some* of the potential in the next few sections, not all, since there are way too many intuitive innovations either in existence or in development to list.

You might be asking yourself, "If all of these automated tools exist, how come they haven't become more common in society? How come I have barely heard of any of these technologies?" Well, because of the limitations of money. We have the technical capacity and the necessary resources, but companies, groups, and individuals are unable to acquire enough money to produce or scale out such advancements, not to mention business entities keeping information under tight wraps so competing entities can't steal and make money off of it before they can.

## 10.2 RESOURCE MANAGEMENT

Next, let's talk about Resource Management. Within our current monetary system, we are using up resources at a rate greater than the Earth can replenish – resource overshoot. Burning through resources and throwing the planet into a state of disequilibrium is clearly not a sustainable practice, as we are witnessing the rapid degradation of all life systems, and with an ever-increasing population, it stands to reason that continuing on this path will inevitably lead to a "point of no return" (doom-and-gloom fear mongering is not needed to reach such a commonsensical conclusion). So, the goal with our Resource-Based Economy is to use resources and materials in a sustainable way, with an emphasis on maintaining Dynamic Equilibrium, which, without the pressure of needing to make sales and increase profit margins becomes a much more attainable goal. To make sure we are not depleting the Earth of vital resources, we want to make sure the usage-to-replenishment ratio is as close to 1:1 as possible. If we cut down five trees, we want to make sure we regrow five trees.

That being said, one of the initial and crucial steps in setting up our RBE is to complete a worldwide survey of the Earth's resources. To know how to best manage resources and materials, we must first know what is available and how much of each exists. We must know which resources are renewable and the time required for their regeneration and which ones are finite or take thousands of years to restore.

So, to the best of our abilities utilizing the most advanced tools available, teams of analysts will comb the planet, locate as many resources as possible, and input them into the brain, the CPU of our system. A globally connected computer network, which everyone will have access to, will contain a complete inventory of all resources and materials, as well as information about each item, e.g., renewability, durability, malleability, etc. Monitoring systems will be installed to track resource usage and availability, with automated and manual feedback loops continually updating the inventory database. Our body's "central nervous system" will be in constant communication with the "peripheral" nodes placed throughout the planet.

And if a resource or material falls below a certain availability threshold, the system will alert us, and then we can take appropriate measures to mitigate its depletion, either by transitioning to an alternative material and/or by focusing efforts on regenerating more of that material to bring it back to or above the scarcity threshold.

In addition to storing the volumes and availability of individual resources and materials, our global database will provide a wide array of other relevant information, like which regions are best for accessing Geothermal Energy, which regions are best for installing water desalination plants, where the most arable lands for food cultivation are located, etc.

A global inventory system might seem overly complex and, to some, not feasible, but once resources are input into the management system, monitoring and tracking levels and usage rates are actually quite simple. Think of modern warehouses throughout the planet. They apply comprehensive warehouse management software tools that connect warehouse facilities across multiple regions that automatically track the flow of inventory within each individual facility and store it into a central database. So, at all times, a company not only knows exactly how much of everything it has within each regional location, but also how much it has in total. Once the software is installed and inventory uploaded into the system, the process of tracking and monitoring the flow and fluctuation of goods is seamless and easy. Technology does most of the legwork.

The same concept will be applied to our Resource-Based Economy. For the management of resources and materials, we will simply take the concepts and tools used in advanced warehouses and scale out to a global level.

## 10.3 FOOD

Okay, now let's talk about food.

With the population continuing to expand – estimates put us close to 10 billion people by 2050 – it has long been feared that we will soon exceed the carrying capacity of Earth, eliciting worries of a dystopian future of mass starvation, savagery, and the "survival of the fittest" mentality on steroids. Such unsubstantiated fears and pessimism have led many individuals and groups to accept the idea that millions of people dying of starvation each year is, well, good for the world; many believe depopulation is a necessary evil for the planet and our species to prevail. However, though I recognize that perpetual growth is not a sustainable trend, I will point out that not only can Earth support 10 billion people, but it can do so without sustaining further damage as long as we manage resources intelligently.

According to data stored in the Food and Agriculture Organization of the United Nations (FAO) database, we produced over 2,900 kcal/capita/day of food worldwide in 2017.[11] That means, even without utilizing land and technology in the most efficient way we can, we already produce enough food to feed the entire global population – estimates vary, but men and women on average need 2,400 and 1,800 calories per day, respectively, to comfortably survive. And according to a separate study out of McGill University and the University of Minnesota, we currently produce enough food to feed 10 billion people.[12] Unfortunately, even though we produce enough food to feed the world, nearly 1 billion people remain undernourished; roughly 52 million children under five years old suffer from "wasting;" and approximately "45% of deaths among children under five are linked to undernutrition."[13,14]

So what gives? As I've pointed out, the tool we use to distribute essential goods – money – is crude and inefficient. Though we produce enough food, many people in poor parts of America and the world are unable to acquire money, which means food does not get channeled to them. And to add insult to injury, between 30-40% of the food we do produce gets thrown away. How stupid is that? Within our Resource-Based Economy, which emphasizes Access, food distribution will no longer be an issue, as it won't be dictated by the flow of money. Residents of the world will not be required to obtain an artificial piece of paper in order to access food. Like the body, if food exists, and it will even more abundantly in our new system, it will be intelligently distributed to where it is needed. No more sore bellies for children. No more hunger tears.

Okay, so let's talk about the potentials in food cultivation in our RBE. In our current global monetary system, the average plate of food on an American table travels about 1,500 miles before we sit down to eat it.[15] Not only is this illogical, but it's wasteful as it requires large quantities of fossil fuel to transport food to its intended destination and can lead to poorer quality of food, since it might either be processed with artificial preservatives to maintain freshness or showered with "ripening" gas after it arrives to its destination. To illustrate the inefficiencies of globalized food production, a $0.04 sugar packet that was processed in Hawaii is shipped to San Francisco for refinement, then sent to New York for packaging, and finally makes its way back to a Hawaiian café after travelling 10,000 miles.[16] Additionally, when a head of lettuce is cultivated in California and shipped 3,000 miles to D.C., it requires roughly 36 times the amount of fossil fuel energy to transport it compared to the actual amount of energy the food provides.[17] Again, this is simply an inefficient system in getting food from the fields to our mouths.

So, as much as we possibly can, our Resource-Based Economy will focus on Localization rather than Globalization when it comes to food production, which will ensure inhabitants are getting the freshest food available, will cut down on energy usage, and it will reduce the need for pesticides, preservatives, and other additives that can lead to adverse health issues.

To accomplish this, each city will be responsible for cultivating its own food, which will take place within the Agricultural Belt of the circular infrastructure. Unfortunately, and this is not intended to be a knock on farmers or farming in general, as I hold the Old McDonalds of the world in high reverence, but the reality is that traditional farming is recognized as one of the more "ecologically destructive" practices today. Of the habitable land across the globe, roughly 50% of it is dedicated to agriculture, and of that chunk, most of it is allocated to livestock.[18] In the United States, about 40% of land is used for agriculture. When we consider the millions of tons of pesticides used annually, that it consumes 70% of the world's water, and the amount of fuel required to run equipment, transport goods, and produce fertilizer, it is not difficult to see why a shift to cleaner and more efficient methods is necessary for long-term sustainability.[93]

Of the newer methods and techniques being introduced for cultivating food, vertical farming facilities utilizing soilless systems seem to hold the most potential. And for those unfamiliar with the concept, vertical farming is a method of farming and growing crops within an enclosed, vertical facility. Imagine a tall, 30-story building. Each floor within this 30-story building would be dedicated to growing various crops within controlled environments.

Not only can vertical farms output a significant amount of healthy, organic food, but they can do so while producing less waste and using less water, less energy, less pesticides (or none at all), less fertilizer, and they take up much less surface area of land. Additionally, they can be constructed anywhere, including densely populated cities, like Chicago, or even over bodies of water. And what's great is within the controlled environments any type of food can be grown inside these enclosed systems, even foods that require specific climate conditions. No longer will tomatoes need to be produced in Florida and shipped to Wisconsin. It can all be grown locally, year-round, and 24 hours a day, whether sheaths of snow blanket the ground or massive droughts parch the land.

Techniques within vertical farms vary, and they will continue to evolve as technology advances and we gain a deeper understanding of different methods, but common techniques include "hydroponic, aeroponic, and/or aquaponic water and nutrient servicing systems."[19] Before it had to close up shop due to high startup and production costs since the industry is in its infancy, a common roadblock that won't be an issue in a Resource-Based Economy, FarmedHere in Chicago utilized an "aquaponic" system where water circulated underneath the plants from large tanks of fish. The waste from the fish acted as a food source and provided nutrients to the plants. So, within our vertical farms, we can simultaneously raise fish and cultivate produce for consumption.

Crops need light. Vertical farms can be built in transparent enclosures with rotating crop systems to allow for natural light to feed the plants, and/or they can simply use artificial lighting systems, which is most common. Facilities seeking to utilize natural light whilst limiting electricity usage might consider installing parabolic mirror systems to help distribute light to plants. Again, options and techniques will continue to expand and allow for greater efficiency as knowledge and understanding grows.

The more advanced vertical farm systems currently in use across America and the world use cameras, robotics, and automated systems to care for their crops, which significantly cuts down on the need for human labor. For instance, in Jake Counne's vertical farming facility launching near Chicago, a camera monitors and analyzes the condition of each plant.[20,21] Based on data gathered in the software, the automated system adjusts the environment to meet the needs of the plant, which includes adjusting temperature, humidity, water nutrients, and more.[22] Counne's facility takes advantage of artificial intelligence and technology where it can, which includes using a roving camera that travels from level to level and automated lift systems to collect trays of plants.

And in Denmark, construction began in 2020 on what is to be Europe's largest vertical farm.[23] The facility will require minimal human supervision, as wheeled robots will perform various tasks, like delivering seeds, and sensors combined with advanced software will monitor the plants to ensure they are receiving the appropriate amount of light, nutrients, and more. And, not only will the vertical farm use considerably less water than traditional agricultural practices, but it will also operate on renewable wind power.

Like with any topic in the world, vertical farming is not free of critics. One of the criticisms directed at vertical farming facilities is that they require too much energy, which ends up costing too much money, making it more difficult to turn a profit. This will be a non-issue in an RBE since money and profit is no longer a concern. A second concern is that vertical farms cause pollution due to high fossil fuel usage. Again, this is a moot point since our RBE will transition from finite, dirty fossil fuels to renewable, abundant, cleaner sources of energy in geothermal, hydro, wind, solar power, etc. And even if we didn't shift to more environmentally friendly energy sources, vertical farming systems still leave less of an ecological footprint than conventional farming while being more productive per square foot.

We already produce enough food to feed the entire population, but with the use of vertical farms, we will be able to create an even greater abundance of all types of foods while taking up a fraction of the space. It was determined by a group at Columbia University that a 30-story vertical farm about the size of a New York City block could feed about 50,000 people.[24] In doing a quick bit of math, a New York City block is about 6.4 acres. So, if we only used 30-story vertical farms, we could theoretically feed the entire 8.275 million inhabitants of the Big Apple while taking up only about 0.5% of the land or about 1,059 acres.

Now the FAO estimates that 17 acres of land are needed to feed a single person. Other organizations calculate that between one and ten acres of land are required. If we take the more conservative estimate of needing one acre per person, that means, using conventional methods, we would need 8.275 million acres to feed the population of New York City. So, by transitioning to vertical farms, we could feed everyone while theoretically using only 0.01% of what would traditionally be required in terms of land usage – 1,059 versus 8.275 million acres.

In his book, Peter Joseph points out that if we were to build these vertical farms on the land currently used for crop production, which is about 4.4 billion acres, we could produce enough food to feed 34 trillion people.[25] Needless to say, we have the capacity to feed the population many, many times over. Hunger shouldn't be an issue today, and in our Resource-Based Economy it will never be an issue again.

## 10.4 WATER

Over 2,000,000,000 people lack access to safe drinking water around the world, mostly in developing countries,[26,27] which results in preventable diseases and deaths of adults and children – roughly 5,000 children die from diarrheal diseases every day.[28] Even in America, millions of people are exposed to unsafe water as pollution, industrial waste, and deteriorating water plants and pipes contaminate water systems. And perhaps the greatest impediment in the US to improving water systems and facilities and providing the population with safe drinking water is, as always, money. As we've pointed out, responsibly disposing of waste can be financially costly for businesses, and rebuilding and restoring deteriorating water plants is expensive, not to mention that small or poor communities typically can't afford equipment to filter out toxins. By not resolving water issues as quickly as possible, the health of a population is put at risk.

Dirty water infused with chemicals, fecal matter, and other contaminants can lead to innumerable health issues, from less severe ailments like skin rashes, hair loss, and stomach aches to more severe problems like developmental delays in children, blindness, cancer, and reproductive issues. Water is the very essence of life, as humans typically cannot survive more than a few days without it, so, and I'm stating the obvious here, providing clean, healthy water is a crucial element if we want the cells of our body to function at an optimal capacity.

Roughly 71% of the Earth's surface is covered with water.[29] And in total, if we account for the water in oceans, glaciers, lakes, rivers, the ground, and the atmosphere, Earth contains approximately 3.7 quintillion gallons of $H_20$ (that's 3,657,500,000,000,000,000 gallons).[30] Unfortunately, 97% of that seeming abundance is saline water in oceans, which means humans cannot consume it. But fortunately, water desalination technology has made it possible to separate salt from water – the most common methods being through Thermal Desalination and Reverse Osmosis. Water desalination plants have already been implemented worldwide, but due to high costs and the high amounts of energy required to separate salt from water, many water-stressed regions that could benefit from such facilities are slow or hesitant to adopt them. However, in an RBE, both of those issues become moot as financial cost will not be a concern, and with the application of the various clean, renewable energy sources to be discussed next, energy usage will also be of little to no concern. The biggest issue, then, with water desalination plants will be on how to process water without harming marine life and how to dispose of the brine that is left over from the desalination process. Many facilities currently dump the excessively salty solution back into the ocean or sea, but some experts worry such a practice could harm the marine life on the ocean- or seabed.

One potential solution to the accumulation of brine is through the experimental technique known as Capacitive Deionization, which is a process to desalinate water while minimizing brine volume.[31] Either way, as technology and knowledge continue to advance, newer and better methods will continue to be discovered that can produce potable water with greater efficiency and less waste.

In a Resource-Based Economy, without having to worry about financial costs we will install the most advanced water purification systems in each city, and where necessary, water desalination plants where freshwater is less accessible. By combining the most advanced methods and technology in producing potable water – Ultraviolet Disinfection Systems, Thermal Desalination, Reverse Osmosis Desalination, Capacitive Desalination, Atmospheric Water Generators, Gray Water Recycling Systems, and more – as well as practicing techniques to increase efficiency, which includes transitioning to vertical farms for crop production to reduce water usage by 80% and use/reuse systems for preservation, we will easily be able to produce an abundance to supply the entire population while maintaining equilibrium and reducing our ecological footprint.

## 10.5 ENERGY

The world currently uses about 0.6 zettajoules of energy each year.[32] To exceed those needs the automated cities within our Resource-Based Economy will take advantage of all forms of clean, renewable energy sources. As will be demonstrated here, by combining cleaner, renewable energies like Geothermal, Solar, Wind, Water, Hydrogen, Biomass, and even Nuclear, more than enough energy can be generated to meet the world's needs many times over, which means we can retire outdated methods utilizing finite fossil (buried) fuels, like petroleum, coal, and natural gas.

Renewable energies have been available for many years, but finite fossil fuels that pollute the environment and damage our health continue to dominate the energy market. Why? It is certainly not due to lack of knowledge or ability to harness the various energy sources that keeps us locked in to the status quo of hydrocarbons. No. It's the exorbitant amounts of money that oil and other fossil fuels bring in along with the hefty financial costs of installing new infrastructure that have us stuck in the 20th, or even 19th, century. In the context of the market, renewable energies are an emerging industry; and, with many unknown variables and substantial capital costs, the risk makes transition from traditional, established fossil fuels to renewables less attractive. For this reason, renewable energy projects – from the basic research to construction – are heavily subsidized by government institutions (like the US DOE) around the world. Then, like many other of the world's most impactful innovations, once it is established and proven to be workable, it gets passed on to the private sector.

Efficiency is the enemy of our monetary systems. And clean, renewable energy sources, once they are up and running, essentially become self-sustaining and *approach* total efficiency. This is bad for a money-based society. Whereas fossil fuels must be continuously mined, stored, distributed, and burned, with constant labor needs and capital and overhead costs, the same cannot be said for renewable energies, because once wind turbines start turning or solar panels start absorbing, very little maintenance is needed thereafter, meaning there is less "turnover" and less need for labor in the long run. And, once installation of renewable technologies is complete, each watt of energy produced becomes cheaper and cheaper over time until it reaches zero dollars – or, zero marginal cost. For instance, let's say it cost $20,000 to install a solar panel system. In this simple abstract, the first watt produced by such a system would theoretically cost $20,000. But, once two watts have been produced, the cost per watt is reduced to $10,000. At 1,000 watts, the cost drops to $20 per watt output. The more watts produced over the lifetime of the solar panels, the cheaper the energy becomes. Once the solar panels have output a total of 2,000,000 watts over their lifetime, the per unit cost of each watt drops to a single penny. And the cost continues to drop and approach zero.

So, the existence of the monetary system is essentially the sole reason why we have been so slow to graduate from fossil fuels to renewable, clean energies. Without having to acquire an artificial medium of exchange for life goods, there is no incentive to continue using oil, coal, natural gas, or any other finite material to power the world. Therefore, in an RBE, we can freely explore all renewable energy options without the intimidation of big oil or without the worry of substantial costs in research and startup. And rather than asking whether or not we have the money to transition from coal to geothermal, we will instead ask whether or not we have the resources and technical means to do so.

Okay, so to meet the world's energy needs, we would have to harvest at least 0.6 zettajoules of energy each year. Though we will utilize a combination of energy sources in our RBE, I am going to provide a quick breakdown of each source's capacity – with the help of the calculations of Peter Joseph and his team members within The Zeitgeist Movement – to illustrate the enormous potential of renewables. Let's start with Geothermal Power.

### *10.5a GEOTHERMAL*

Of the many alternative energy sources, Geothermal power seems to be the most promising – it's clean, abundant, renewable, can produce 24 hours a day, and requires considerably less land area compared with traditional methods, like with coal-burning. What is Geothermal energy, you ask? In short, it is the natural heat produced and stored within the Earth. We then capture that heat and use it to generate electricity.

Traditionally, geothermal energy has been harnessed using hydrothermal systems, which have their limitations. However, with the development of Enhanced Geothermal Systems (EGS), the energy potential of geothermal resources increases significantly. In 2006 an 18-member panel assembled by MIT performed a comprehensive evaluation of geothermal resources available in the United States. In their report, the researchers estimated that more than 13,000 zettajoules of EGS resources are present within the Earth. And of that number, they estimate that over 200 zettajoules are currently extractable, with another 2,000 zettajoules becoming available with improvements in technology.[33] In other words, considering the entire world consumes roughly 0.6 zettajoules of energy per year along with the understanding that geothermal energy can be treated as "fully renewable"[34] if properly mined, geothermal energy alone has the potential to meet the power needs of the planet for thousands of years.

And, what's better is Geothermal energy can exceed our power demands cleanly as the different types of plants produce low emissions and emit little to no carbon – the carbon footprint and emissions of *binary plants* are essentially zero.

Additionally, Geothermal plants can provide clean, renewable energy, while remaining relatively inconspicuous, and they don't require as much surface area of land compared to other methods of energy production. For instance, the Imperial Valley in California remains one of the most productive agricultural regions in the world while housing 15 geothermal power plants. And one of those power plants operates next to a wildlife refuge without disrupting the hundreds of animal species sheltered there. As for land usage, a geothermal field uses only 1 to 8 acres of land per megawatt (MW) versus 5 to 10 acres per MW for nuclear power.[35] And in a separate comparison, a geothermal facility needs about 404 square meters of land per GWh versus 3,632 square meters per GWh typically required for a coal facility.[36] To give perspective, nine geothermal facilities could fit within one coal plant with a fraction of the ecological impact.

Like with any option, Geothermal energy is not a silver bullet (not yet) in solving the world's growing energy demands, and it does come with a couple small caveats that are being worked out, which include reported cases of subsidence and minor seismic activity. However, techniques and technology continue to improve, and Geothermal energy will certainly be a major contributor as we transition from "dirty" energy to clean energy.

### *10.5b SOLAR*

The Sun, that big yellow nuclear furnace dangling in the sky, pours massive amounts of solar radiation down on us every single day and is the source of all energy on the planet. On an annual basis, it is estimated that the Earth absorbs 3,850 zettajoules of solar energy between the oceans, land, and the atmosphere.[37] And in only one hour, the sun delivers enough solar energy to power the whole world for an entire year.[38] Compared to finite fossil fuels, energy from the sun is virtually limitless, and we can count on it to be there every day – at least for the next 5 billion years or so, or unless you live near the North or South Pole. The trick, obviously, is in our ability to harness this energy.

And right now, we do have the ability to harvest and convert *some* of that solar energy reaching the Earth. The Noor Abu Dhabi solar photovoltaic plant is the world's largest solar project as of 2019; its 3.2 million solar panels covering 8 square kilometers can provide power for 90,000 people.[39] In the Mojave Desert of California, America's largest concentrated solar power plant – the Ivanpah Solar Electric Generating System – has the capacity to generate 392 MW of electricity, which can power nearly 100,000 homes.[40] Using today's solar technology, which is still in its early stages, if we only used standard 350W solar panels, we would need a field roughly the size of Arizona to meet the power needs of the entire world.[41] If we were only concerned with powering the United States, it would require about 0.5% of US land to power the nation – or a small chunk of Nevada or Texas.[42] Obviously, this is not practical, but it does put into perspective the current capabilities and potential of solar energy alone. As technology rapidly improves, solar panels and batteries are becoming increasingly more efficient, meaning the amount of land required to power the world with solar will continue to be reduced.

Between active and passive techniques multiple methods exist today for collecting solar energy and turning it into power, but I am going to focus on two of the main ones – Solar Photovoltaic (traditional solar panels) and Concentrated Solar Power (CSP).

One of the main differences in how Photovoltaics work compared to CSP systems is in how they use the sun to generate power. Traditional solar panels capture the *light* of the sun and directly convert it to electricity, whereas CSP systems collect the *energy* of the sun, convert it into heat, and then use that heat to drive an engine, which drives a generator, which produces electricity. Additionally, CSP systems are able to store the energy it collects from the sun using Thermal Energy Storage (TES) systems, while solar panels use batteries to store electricity. Of the two methods, storage methods in CSP systems are more efficient than those of Photovoltaic systems, making it a better option for large-scale power generation.

I envision both systems – along with other solar energy technologies – being utilized in a Resource-Based Economy. Photovoltaic technology can be included in the construction of buildings and integrated into homes, while CSP systems will be built for large-scale purposes. Because of storage capabilities, CSP systems can be constructed just about anywhere, meaning we can place them in scarcely populated regions of the world, like in deserts or out at sea. Most of the CSP plants operating or proposed in the United States are located in the Southwest since this region receives higher levels of direct sunlight each day. Additionally, CSP systems can be used in conjunction with other industrial applications, like food processing and water desalination; hybrid CSP-desalination systems are currently being developed.[43]

Of course, like with all energy production methods, solar energy is not without its challenges that need to be overcome, which includes intermittency, high costs, water usage, wildlife disruption, land usage, and material usage. Intermittency, in the context of solar energy, denotes the periods of time when the sun is not shining as intensely – like at night or on a cloudy day – which significantly reduces or nullifies energy collection; and it is probably the most common criticism of solar power. In our RBE, intermittent sunlight won't be an issue since we will be combining multiple energy sources for power generation; but, even if we were to solely rely on solar energy, with the development and improvement of batteries and TES systems, blackouts can almost be completely mitigated. High construction and installation costs, a major reason the world has been so slow to adopt solar energy, won't be a concern in our cities of the future, either, since money will be eliminated. And when it comes to the other challenges present, technical solutions are quickly becoming available (like transitioning from toxic substances in heat transfer to water or molten salts) while others are under development (a liquid is being worked on that can store solar energy for many years, which could reduce the need for batteries) as, again, large-scale solar power generation is still an emerging industry. Even with the current drawbacks, the ecological impact, pollution, and carbon footprint of solar energy systems are much, much lower than that of fossil fuels.

### *10.5c WIND*

As long as the sun is shining and the Earth spinning, we can count on wind, though with varying intensity, as air constantly flows from high- to low-pressure areas. Wind, like solar radiation, is generated every single day on this planet, and it doesn't require the burning of any finite resources; it's naturally produced and inexhaustible. And harnessing this abundant resource is as simple as setting up wind turbines that utilize the force of the wind to turn its blades, which then spins a generator to produce electricity. Once fully installed, wind power produces zero carbon emissions, no toxic pollution, and agricultural operations can continue in and around the wind turbines. During the construction and decommissioning of wind turbines or wind farms, there are minor emissions at present due to the use of fossil fuels to produce and transport materials, etc., but compared to fossil fuel production the emissions are miniscule. And as we completely transition away from fossil fuels, emissions even during construction will become virtually nonexistent.

So, what sort of potential does wind power wield?

A lot!

A simulation run out of the Lawrence Livermore National Laboratory in California suggests that over 400 terawatts of power could be generated by surface winds,[44] which far exceeds global usage of 18 terawatts.[45] Researchers out of Stanford University and the University of Delaware came up with a more conservative figure, however. Using a 3-D model they estimated that available wind power exceeded current global usage by five times, which, though smaller, is still significant.[46] Just to get a sense of wind's potential using a real-world example, let's say we could only use wind energy to power the world. If we mass-produced the 9,000-acre, 1,320 MW Alta Wind Energy Center in California, we would need about 13,231 of those wind farms, which would require only 0.3 percent of the Earth's surface, to power the planet.[47] And that doesn't include using offshore wind farms. Like with solar energy, this is not practical, I know, but it does give perspective on what it would take to supply wind energy to the planet's residents.

In an RBE, wind farms will be, as they currently are, strategically located in regions where winds are strongest, which includes mountaintops and even out at sea. Offshore sites are appealing since they remain out of sight from the general public and experience strong winds due to a pressure gradient created from land's ability to heat up and cool down faster than water. Just 11 miles northwest of England, the world's largest offshore wind farm in the Irish Sea – the Walney Extension – supports 87 wind turbines with the potential to generate 659 MW of power and provide electricity for 600,000 homes. The offshore wind turbines are spread out within 56 square miles of area.

Technology in wind power, like with all mediums, is rapidly improving and evolving. As I type this text, companies are in the midst of developing kite-borne turbines to access stronger winds at altitudes higher than what land-based turbines can reach. Nevertheless, like with the other renewable sources mentioned thus far, the potential and possibilities of wind power alone are substantial. Wind will always exist. The key is in developing better ways to harness its free, abundant, and renewable energy.

### *10.5d WATER*

Currently, hydropower accounts for approximately 15% of the globe's electricity production,[48] which puts it at #1 amongst all other renewables. Like with the other renewables we've touched upon thus far, the potential with water energy – whether through utilizing heat differences or harnessing energy from the movement of water to drive turbines – is exceptional. By taking advantage of traditional hydropower, wave energy, tidal energy, ocean currents, ocean thermal energy conversion (OTEC), and osmotic power, we can generate an estimated 146,720 TWh/yr (0.53 zettajoules), which almost meets the world's needs, and that's simply with current technology.[49]

With the forces of the wind and the pull of the moon, water flows and shifts every single day, making this resource essentially inexhaustible; it's all about tapping into its abundant potential energy.

### *10.5e NUCLEAR POWER*

Nuclear power is a contentiously debated topic when it comes to alternative sources of energy. Modern nuclear reactors have the ability to safely generate substantial amounts of low-emissions electricity, making it a cleaner and much more sustainable alternative to fossil fuels. However, opponents of nuclear power cite the risk of meltdowns, as can be seen from Chernobyl and Fukushima, which can leak radiation into the environment and make areas uninhabitable for years after. Though such events might be rare and though next generation power plants include greater safeguards, the risk is still present. Another concern among nuclear power critics is in regard to the high-level radioactive waste leftover from the nuclear fission process. Not only must the radioactive waste be managed and contained, but it can also remain hazardous for long periods of time – we're talking tens of thousands of years before certain materials are no longer a threat to the environment and living organisms. Nevertheless, if there are alternatives that can also produce an abundance of clean energy without the hazardous radioactive byproducts or the risk of meltdowns, however minimal, it seems logical that we utilize those while continuing to learn and improve upon nuclear power and radioactive waste management.

But again, when it comes to deciding which energy sources will be harnessed to power a city, it won't be up to politicians, businessmen, or non-experts like myself. The scientific approach of testing, gathering data, and forming evidence-based conclusions will ultimately drive our decisions.

As you can see I expedited the sections on Water and Nuclear energy. Is it because I'm lazy? No. Well, sorta. But mostly it's because when going through this section a few times over, I started getting bored reading about energy, and if I'm getting bored, then I imagine you must be getting bored, too. You get the picture at this point. Renewable sources of energy hold tremendous potential! They can provide us with abundant energy and meet global demand without the pollution, carbon footprint, ecological impact, or adverse health effects that accompany dirty fossil fuels. That being said, our Resource-Based Economy will take advantage of them all; though, not every city will have the same energy scheme, as location will determine best methods. When it comes to devising energy systems, possibilities are limitless. Manmade "energy islands" could be strategically built off of coastlines with wind turbines harnessing wind energy, solar equipment absorbing solar energy, and other technologies harnessing tidal, wave, ocean current, and thermal difference all at the same time. Or, large underwater structures could be installed that direct some of the flow of the Gulf Stream to drive turbines to produce clean power; and to prevent harm to marine species, the turbines could be built with a centrifugal separator and deflector.[50] Without the limitations of money, we will have the freedom to be creative with our energy networks, and do what is most logical, most productive, and most efficient for each city, rather than what is best for national GDP.

And when ideas and theories come along touting better, more efficient ways of generating power – scientists everywhere are working hard on revolutionary ideas right now – we will immediately invest in research to prove or disprove their efficacy. We won't have to squeeze nickels and dimes out of governments or businesses to begin researching and testing. And when a new technology or renewable energy does prove to be clean and efficient, we will not wait years for prices to go down before it is deployed.

Of course, as I said, no energy solutions are without their drawbacks that need to be worked out and improved upon. In our RBE, extensive evaluation will be conducted before employing any energy source. If some methods, technologies, or structures show to have too much of a negative environmental or social impact, then we will move on to less-damaging methods. For instance, if we are unable to develop dams that don't harm river ecosystems, then we will have to consider alternatives until we can improve upon the technology. And that's only logical, right? With many different methods at our disposal and without the mental puppetry, or rather, the influence of big energy companies polluting our minds with expensive propaganda, arriving at such logical conclusions won't be so strenuous. Whatever works best will be used, not whatever brings Company A more money or whatever brings Company B more money. The science-based approach will objectively (for the most part) determine best methods.

Energy is all around us. Life is energy. And with the expansive creative potential of the human mind, we will continue to discover innovative and efficient ways to power civilization. Possibilities are endless! I've only mentioned the most commonly known forms of renewable, clean energy. Like I stated two paragraphs above, scientists everywhere are hard at work developing innovations in energy. We have researchers at Chalmers University in Sweden working on the "liquid sunlight" I alluded to in the Solar Energy section.[51] Scientists from Washington University and Los Alamos National Lab are developing more efficient techniques for "water splitting," which isolates hydrogen from oxygen to be used as energy.[52] Engineers at Goodyear have conceptualized a tire that can generate electricity on the go for electric vehicles by harnessing the heat from friction and its rotation. New Zealand scientists are testing methods of transmitting wireless energy.[53] Researchers in various regions of the planet, including China, the US, and Israel, are working on Piezolelectric Energy Harvesting (PEH) technology to convert the mechanical energy of vehicles into electrical energy; it has been calculated that a single lane road that is one kilometer long can generate 250 kW of electric energy with traffic volumes of 500 vehicles per hour, enough to power 300 homes.[54] With PEH technology, we can essentially turn any sort of movement into electric energy, e.g., people walking along streets. And there are so many more revolutionary innovations being conceptualized and tested at this very moment. Oh, the possibilities!

But for now, simply by harnessing the potential within what we already know in the realms of Geothermal, Wind, Solar, Nuclear, Water, and/or potentially Biomass Energy (which I did not discuss), in both large-scale and small-scale systems, we will be able to power our total enclosure cities and every city in the world with minimal disruption. The key is in utilizing the most efficient combination of renewable energy systems for each city.

## 10.6 TRANSPORTATION

Transportation. Getting from Point A to Point B. Some people like driving, some people don't. I for one am of the ilk that hates it. I see it as a time waster, since I can't do anything except stare at the road and be conscientious of my driving as well as the driving of others for however long it takes to get to my destination. And when I leave work, the last thing I want to do is compete with traffic and fight congestion just to get home, make a meal, and unwind after a long day.

In our RBE, transportation and delivery systems will take on a familiar, yet entirely new look, all with a focus on efficiency in terms of energy and resource consumption and time. The transportation of passengers and freight by land, air, or sea will shift toward automation, at least as much as we possibly can, with an emphasis on access over ownership of personal vehicles. Like I mentioned a few sections earlier, every single person owning a car isn't the most intuitive practice. You might even say it's wasteful? Sure, having every adult buy a car is great for business and the monetary economy, but it is not great for our home or the responsible management of resources. Think about all of the materials that went in to manufacturing the estimated 1.3 billion cars, trucks, and buses on the road today;[55] yet, we only use our personal vehicles about 6% of the time. Yeah, not so responsible or intelligent. So, though ownership of material items is certainly permitted in our new economy, the attempt will be to shift our values from cyclical, mindless consumption (psychologically engineered through marketing) to intelligent, sustainable practices where it is most feasible. And it seems transportation is one of those areas where a transition from everyone owning a car to everyone having access to fast transportation is logical.

I know there are some people who cherish their vehicles, and that's great. Everyone has her own unique interests and hobbies that are important to living a rich life; so, far be it from me or anyone to tell a person what she can or cannot do. However, I see my vehicle simply as a tool to get me to my desired destination. Nothing more, nothing less, and I know there are many people out there who share those sentiments. So, relinquishing ownership of a vehicle and having access to automated transportation sounds more like a relief to me. And without businesses spending millions of dollars in trying to manipulate the public into tying material possessions to their personal identity, I imagine a large group of people will start to feel the same way. I imagine people will start to lose *some* interest in collecting junk to prove to everyone around them how successful she is. Once money exits the game and corporations have no incentive to make you feel inferior through advertising so that you buy their goods, I imagine junk will stop being a symbol for wealth and success. And that logic can be applied to the consumption of personal vehicles. Right now, cars are often used to signal social status to one's peers. With money removed, vehicles in the context of social status will become meaningless. Having a nice car will no longer prove to anyone how much money or wealth you have or how "superior" you might be. They will no longer compensate for inadequacies or insecurities you might have. Therefore, I believe a lot of people will lose interest in owning a personal vehicle. Access will be preferred, as it'll be more convenient and less burdensome.

Okay then, so if most people don't own a car in a Resource-Based Economy, what is the strategy for efficiently getting people to their desired locations?

In short, self-driving vehicles, flying taxis, Maglev trains, Hyperloop Transportation, and other automated transportation systems will be utilized.

Many advanced technologies are currently in operation in various countries, though to a limited extent due to financial roadblocks, while many other innovations are still in the conceptual stages. When it comes to choosing which methods to use, we will incorporate the modes that are most efficient, least energy-consuming, least wasteful, least resource-intensive, least time-consuming, and fastest – not what is best for a company's bottom line. And because transportation technology will continue to evolve and improve, meaning what is best today might not be best tomorrow, our transportation infrastructure and machines will be built in such a way to easily incorporate upgrades and enhancements.

It has been estimated that car accidents are responsible for over 1.35 million deaths worldwide each year,[56] which puts auto-related fatalities at #8 on the global cause-of-death list.[57] So, along with efficiency, the goal of transportation in our Resource-Based Economy will also be on safety, so as to significantly reduce this staggering death figure. And by utilizing automated transportation, which is safe and more reliable compared to human-guided vehicles, it is conceivable that we can bring that number to near zero.

First, let's start with personal transportation. We have already discussed driverless vehicles and flying taxis being implemented in various regions of the planet, including the United States. Such technologies will be integrated into our transportation system. If you need to be somewhere and public mass transit is not an option for you, hailing a taxi will be as easy as pulling up an app on your phone or a touch screen in your "smart" house and calling one – similar to Uber's current services, but entirely automated. In a total systems approach, imagine a driverless electric vehicle picking you up at your residence, traveling to your destination while powering itself using piezoelectric technology, Goodyear's tire-charging technology, or solar roads, dropping you off, and heading to its next customer. Or, if it is not yet capable of powering itself on the go, after it drops you off, it can automatically direct itself to the nearest charging station. Who knows, maybe with money removed from the game, innovative groups will roll out vehicles that can run on water or hydrogen.

To reduce resource consumption and congestion by reducing the number of vehicles on the road, which will also contribute to increased safety, mobility, and improved travel times, public mass transit will be an integral part of our self-sustaining cities. We have many viable options to consider, and we can't be certain which will be the best at the time of building the first test city, but here are a few choices currently in operation or in the development phase.

MagLev Trains (Magnetic Levitation), which use magnets to levitate and propel themselves forward in non-contact track systems, can be installed throughout the city and connect other cities to each other. The technology for MagLev train systems has been around for a long time, and although they are faster, quieter, require less maintenance due to less moving parts and frictionless travel, and use less energy resources compared to conventional trains, they have been scarcely implemented due to high construction costs. In terms of speed, construction is currently underway in Japan for a Maglev train that can operate at a maximum speed of 314 miles per hour.[58] Within our cities, Maglevs can be used for long distance commuting, which will get a passenger to her destination much faster than a standard vehicle. And, they can be constructed with passenger compartments that can detach from or attach to the train while it is in motion, which can significantly reduce transit times and conserve energy. Additionally, Maglev trains can be installed in vacuum tubes – Vactrains – which would allow them to reach speeds up to 5,000 miles per hour. Once this technology is refined and implemented, it will replace arduous air travel, as a trip from Los Angeles to New York in a vactrain will take only 30 minutes compared to 5 hours for a commercial flight (not including wait times, taxiing, etc.).

Hyperloop transportation is another option currently being developed by numerous companies and institutions, which includes Tesla and SpaceX, Virgin, and the US Department of Transportation.[60] Elon Musk originally opened up the concept and technology to the public so teams everywhere could lay eyes on the plans and schematics to solve technical issues or improve upon design in an open-source environment. In short, a hyperloop system consists of metal pods that travel inside low-pressure vacuum tubes at very high speeds and without friction or air-resistance. The systems being developed right now can reportedly reach speeds of about 750 miles per hour with very little to no emissions; travel from LA to New York would only take about 4 hours to complete – faster than a plane.

Other options for mass transit include Tubular Rails, Straddling Buses, and String Transport Systems. Additionally, our cities can be built with "various types of escalators, elevators, conveyors, and transveyors"[61] that move in all directions and even up the sides of buildings and can extend into homes. All systems, between personal transportation and mass transit will be seamlessly integrated to make travel faster, painless, and energy and resource efficient. And with the circular design of the city, transport systems will be able to operate without having to stop to make 90-degree turns, which, again, helps conserve energy use and cuts down on travel times.

What about delivering freight from one area of the planet to another? That, too, will be automated.

Driverless semi-trucks already exist and have made cross-country trips hauling cargo. But employing electric, self-driving 18-wheelers is just the tip of the iceberg for a Resource-Based Economy.

If we need to deliver goods across large bodies of water, we can deploy Unmanned Cargo Ships.[62] Companies all over the world are racing to develop self-sailing freighters that combine artificial intelligence and various technologies to detect obstacles in the water, plot efficient routes, observe weather conditions, and automatically navigate from one location to another.[63] And they will be able to do this without the need for humans, which means no air conditioning, water, sewage, or any other features built in to support the crew, which increases efficiency and safety. As international shipping systems evolve and advance, the vessels can be engineered as "floating plants" where they can process raw materials into finished products while in transit.

When it comes to delivering packages, takeout, medicines, and more, we can utilize Unmanned Aerial Vehicles (Drones), which can already be seen happening with companies such as Amazon and UPS and in countries across the globe, like in Singapore and Australia. These autonomous, GPS-guided flying machines can communicate with each other and maneuver around obstacles while transporting goods faster and more reliably. The utilization of drones can also reduce traffic congestion and pollution.

Our cities can also be designed to support Pneumatic Tube Transport networks, as can often be seen at banks or in hospitals, to send and receive items.

In summary, a Resource-Based Economy will utilize self-driving vehicles, automated public transit, transveyors that move in all directions, and more to transport individuals to their desired destinations, while freight will be delivered using driverless semis, unmanned cargo ships, drones, and whatever burgeoning technologies come to light. Options are limitless when it comes to the potential for future transportation methods, and I have mostly only touched on concepts already in use or in late stage development. And since vehicles will be designed more for their function rather than their marketability, it is possible they could take on an entirely new look. Only the future will tell. Either way, in our cities, fully-integrated, automatic transportation systems will make travel safer, faster, less cumbersome, and resource-efficient, and it will all happen seamlessly as the various technologies interact with each other and you.

## 10.7 HOME & BUILDING CONSTRUCTION

Traditional construction has been an historically dangerous vocation, as one in every five worker fatalities in 2018 were related to construction,[64] while non-fatal injury rates are much higher in the industry, annually, compared to other industries. And although construction practices have improved vastly in the realm of waste management, it remains as one of the largest contributors of global waste, generating hundreds of millions of tons each year; it is estimated that 30% of a building's total weight ends up becoming waste by the end of a project's completion.[65] So, to mitigate the dangers and wastefulness of traditional construction, our Resource-Based Economy will deploy various robots, 3D printing technology, and advanced materials (e.g., self-healing concrete) to automatically assemble "smart," complex, resilient buildings with very little to no need for human involvement and in a fraction of the time.

With the introduction of 3D printers in the 1980s, it was suddenly possible to manufacture solid objects in just minutes or hours and with more accuracy than ever before. And as the technology has continued to advance and improve, any Joe Schmoe now sitting at home can design and print whatever is conjured up in his mind's eye, from amorphous paperweights and tools to guns or Darth Vader helmets. Here in the 21st century, however, some engineers and companies have taken this technology to the next level and expanded it into the "printing" of homes and buildings. We've already talked briefly about how institutions around the world have successfully created small homes using multi-material 3D printers, like the 350-square-foot structure built in Austin, Texas, by ICON.

ICON's Vulcan II printer is touted to be capable of constructing a community of customizable homes up to 2,000 square feet in size.[66] Then there's the contour crafting technology (3D printing) developed by the Contour Crafting Corporation and supported by NASA; this machine is capable of automatically constructing houses, commercial and government buildings, bridges, and even lunar structures.[67] And finally there's the D-Shape 3D printer developed by an Italian engineer that uses sand to "print" solid-rock structures, including houses, artificial reefs, and home furnishings.[68] All of these machines can safely create incredible designs with unprecedented precision, while using much fewer materials, less energy, and less labor, and projects can be completed in a single day. The buildings can also be constructed to include reinforcement, plumbing, and electrical networks. The use of 3D printing technology to automatically print houses quickly, cheaply, and safely not only significantly reduces or completely eliminates risk in home construction as there is little need for human workers, but it can completely solve the problem of the millions of children and adults living without a roof over their head.

Advanced 3D printing technology might be the most promising innovation thus far for designing and constructing strong and elegant buildings, but it is certainly not the only option for the future. Many advanced tools have been developed or are in development that can be integrated into the construction process to increase accuracy and efficiency, like automatic cranes and brick-laying robots (Hadrian X).[69] The 3-D Finger Adaptive Robot Gripper is a robotic hand that can grip and use tools, and it can be used for picking items, welding, loading or unloading, and much more. Smaller, modular, all-terrain robots, like the marXbot created by the Miniature Mobile Robots Group can be used to complete low-level actions, like adding new features to a completed building.[70] And lastly, in what sounds more like sci-fi than reality, engineers at MIT are developing what they call 4D printing technology, where materials are essentially programmed to assemble themselves into specific structures based on various environmental conditions.[71] These "smart" materials can interact with one another and respond to certain stimuli, like heat, moisture, or kinetic energy, which can trigger them to fold or expand into precise shapes.

So, in utilizing existing and developing technology, home and building construction will be almost, if not entirely, automated in our

Resource-Based Economy. At its peak, the only human interaction will be in the design phase. And in this regard, architectural designers will be free to let their imaginations run wild. Utilizing machines and AI, they will be free to design structures with a complexity, flexibility, and precision that even the most skilled human laborer could not build today. And then non-experts, like myself, without a background in architecture will have the option to go online and design their own custom homes in a computer program, which can then be uploaded to and built quickly by artificial intelligence.

All homes and buildings will be built "smart" in our future cities.[72] And by "smart," I mean they will be designed to be self-sufficient, energy-efficient abodes with power generating capabilities and can respond and adapt to the environment and our personal preferences. Homes will be constructed "with their own thermal generators and heat concentrators,"[73] and photovoltaics or even solar paint can be included in "the skin of the building and in the windows" to provide electricity.[74] Buildings will know when people are home or which rooms are being occupied, and they will automatically regulate a room's temperature or power down devices when an area is unoccupied; dwellings will even be able to maintain air quality. Using advanced materials, like self-healing concrete, super concrete, graphene, and other nanomaterials, buildings will be constructed for maximum resilience, meaning they will be able to withstand severe weather and earthquakes, and they will be fireproof.

When you walk up to your home, it will be able to sense your presence and automatically unlock and open for you. If programmed to, lights will automatically power on as you walk in, and heating and cooling systems will quickly adjust to your desired room temperature. And if it is a bright, sunny day and too much light is coming in through your windows, you will have the ability to adjust the opacity of your windows to limit or completely block out sunlight. Smart devices, like our phones, will give us the ability to control all aspects of our home, e.g., lighting, temperature, window opacity, and much more.

In our homes of the future, we may no longer need dishwashers, washing machines, and other cleaning devices, as dishes and clothes can be treated with nanoparticles – nanosilver, titanium oxide, silica, etc. – that can eliminate odor-producing bacteria, prevent sunburn, remove static, and repel water and other liquids. Nanotechnology can be integrated into all areas of the house, like couches, carpets, and drapes, to keep areas clean, dry, and dust-free at all times. And speaking of the clothing we wear, fabrics can also include polymer coatings with electronic sensors that can detect one's heart rate, sleep patterns, and body temperature; they can even control the amount of heat that passes through the fabric to keep one cooler.

The furniture we relax in and the beds we sleep in will have the ability to automatically adjust to the shape of our bodies, similar to those used in hospitals, which will enhance comfort, and for sleep, it will help us achieve a better night's sleep, assist in lymphatic drainage, and more. Our beds, like our clothes, can be equipped with sensors under the mattress to monitor our sleep patterns, heart rates, and breathing.

Like we've seen in many futuristic, sci-fi movies, our homes will be able to stream computer operating systems from "the cloud" onto surfaces, like walls or mirrors, which will allow us to control various devices in the house, access the web, watch videos, play games, check the weather, and more. Corning, Inc., developed glass materials that can display images anywhere from electronic devices, meaning you can access your personal operating system on a coffee table, closet door, or room window.[75] Such technology can be integrated into exercise routines and educational modules.

And when it comes to mowing the lawn, automatic lawn mowers can be employed that have the ability to cut grass all by themselves. Of course, if you are one of the many who enjoys cutting his own grass, by all means!

Now, I understand that many of the home features I mentioned in this section might sound like a fanciful pipe dream, but it is all technology that already exists or is in late stage development – much of it has been applied in combination to "test" homes.[76] And as usual, I've barely even scratched the surface of what's possible; I didn't even talk about bathroom or kitchen features.

Automated building construction and "smart," technologically advanced buildings will provide a number of benefits within our Resource-Based Economy. It will certainly cut down on deaths and work-related injuries. It will reduce waste. And, it will reduce energy usage and time spent. Not to mention, once again, it will help us achieve the ultimate goal of providing safe and comfortable shelter for all, so that everyone will be able to not only live without the stress of worrying where they will sleep from one night to the next, but they will also be able to enjoy a high standard of living.

## 10.8 EDUCATION

It is no secret that an educated population benefits the whole of society. So, devising an educational system that meets the unique needs of ALL children will be a vital component of our Resource-Based Economy. This is not to say that education isn't considered important within our current monetary systems. It is! But the educational system and teachers, no matter how passionate or well-meaning, are handcuffed every year by strict budgetary confinements and state restrictions, meaning they have to make the most with what limited learning resources they are given. So, as a consequence, while other industries and technologies have evolved at "out-of-body-experience-inducing" speeds, the educational system has remained relatively static in the last 100 years, as emphasis on rote memorization, demotivating evaluation (grading) schemes, and mundane standardized tests remain core traits within school walls.

Then again, maybe that's by design. I suppose in order to maintain an advantage over the population and adequately protect their positions while ensuring that the majority of people happily do the bulk of the wealth producing for them without complaint, the powers that be probably don't want too many people that can "think." If people can think at their jobs, they might start to reflect on life and realize what they are doing is wasting what little time they have on Earth. They might start to consider the idea that they are being taken advantage of. And when they eventually realize they are trapped in The Pit, they might start to feel enslaved, they might start to feel claustrophobic, and those feelings could cause them to grow restless, become insubordinate, and challenge their programming. They might even begin to organize into groups, and that would be a terrible thing! "Power in numbers" is a colossal threat to the wise masters of society. So, it is up to education then to start the indoctrination process early on and mold kids into functional automatons, into mechanized computers while their brains are developing. It is up to the modern educational system to groom children and inculcate the obedient 9-to-5 mindset in them, so by the time they enter the soul-crushing workforce and eagerly become proper cogs in the wheel of society, their passion for life will have been adequately squelched, and they will have long forgotten how they used to overflow with creativity and curiosity. Like Wile E. Coyote with the Road Runner, our most fun and interesting traits are crushed with the metaphorical anvil of formal education.

However, with money removed and automation handling the repetitive and mundane tasks in our Resource-Based Economy, there is no valuable advantage gained anymore from manufacturing a "thinkless" proletariat. The educational system within our future economy will undergo a complete overhaul. A true education, not simple national indoctrination, will be afforded to all children. It will completely evolve from one of long, drawn out classroom lectures and a centralized, one-size-fits-all format (largely due to limited funding), to one that is interactive, hands-on, and tailored to fit each child's unique learning styles, needs, and abilities in a decentralized manner. We will be able to accomplish this in part because budgetary restraints will no longer limit our schools. Many schools in our current system are unable to afford updated materials as often as information is updating and changing. For instance, when science decided to reclassify Pluto and remove its label as a planet, how many schools do you think were unable to buy new textbooks with this updated information? Probably a lot. Fortunately, without money and with the utilization of technology, teachers and institutions will have the ability to provide their students with the most updated and most advanced learning resources available. And, with the assistance of AI, they will have the freedom to develop personalized curricula to give their children the best opportunities to learn, grow, and become contributing members of society in many ways.

Technology and automation have been emphasized in every area of our RBE, so far, and that continues here within the realm of education, as Artificial Intelligence, Virtual Reality, and Games will be integrated into the learning process. However, teacher-to-child and child-to-child interactions will remain vitally important to our students' development. Life is one giant interaction – we interact with an object even if we are only observing it – and as I have pointed out, all living systems are interdependent with other living systems – humans included. So, collaboration and interaction will be strongly encouraged in our future society to help develop social and group skills, which can help build confidence. Confidence and positivity, as we know, are key in fueling passion, curiosity, and creativity.

Humans are complex organisms. Everyone learns a little bit differently than others. Everyone has a slightly different style that best suits his or her needs. Some people are more visual learners, while others are better able to remember information they hear. Some people want structure, while others prefer learning at their own pace, dictating what they want to learn and when they want to learn it. With the assistance of artificial intelligence and teaching professionals, students will have the ability to design their own curriculum. Really for the first time ever, children and adults will have the freedom to follow their passions and/or explore different interests. Internet, technology, and access to information pretty much at our fingertips are what make personalized education possible.

Experiential learning (learning by doing) is a crucial element in fully understanding a subject and the environment. So, as much as we can, students will be given the opportunity to learn by physically interacting with tools and the natural world. Students will tour factories, farms, and forests to gain hands-on experience and be exposed to different fields. Fresco envisions "floating education centers" as an option for children and adult students, where they travel along networks of natural and manmade waterways, exploring and interacting with the environment in various regions of the continent, which would give them the opportunity to learn about the "real world" rather than simply reading about it in books. And when it is not possible to physically visit a location, students can take advantage of Virtual Reality (VR) to help simulate real-world experiences.

Every form of stimulation activates different regions of the brain, meaning all learning modalities provide benefit in the learning process, though to varying degrees depending on a child's neural makeup. Virtual reality technology can offer students visual, auditory, kinesthetic, and even tactile stimulation all at the same time. So now, and most definitely in our future system, virtual reality will be used in unique ways to facilitate the learning process and help students better understand many different subjects, especially subjects that are not physically accessible. For instance, children will be able to use VR systems to explore and interact with the human body, the brain, plants, planets, the center of the Earth, and so much more. Imagine a kid traveling through neural networks in the brain, making friends with and learning about Neurotransmitters along the way. To increase interest and engagement, the experience could even be turned into a game where, for instance, kids team up with, say, Calcium or Potassium ions, and together they must figure out how to open ion channels to trigger a synaptic response and help neurotransmitters reach their next destination within the brain; this could be a great way to "watch" and learn how neurons communicate and deliver information. By using virtual reality technology, children will have the opportunity to meet rare creatures, walk amongst dinosaurs, or learn about foreign terrain. Though it doesn't completely replace real-life experiences, VR can simulate any world or scenario. Like I said, if kids or adults cannot experience certain places in real life, they can at least experience *some* aspects of it in virtual reality. And as VR technology improves, the simulated environments will become more and more "real."

"We don't stop playing because we grow old, we grow old because we stop playing."[77] Through all stages of life, and that includes adulthood, play is incredibly important, and not just in the context of learning. Play, which induces laughter, happiness, the release of endorphins, and more, is crucial in living a rich and fulfilled life. So, as much as we can, we will turn learning into play and play into learning. After all, when a child is playing, he is typically engaged and having fun. And when we are engaged and having fun, not only does that activity have a grasp on our attention, but our minds are more relaxed and at ease, which is conducive to learning.

Considered by many as the world's best kindergarten, Japan's Fuji Kindergarten has taken on those very principles of turning learning into play.[78] This unique school was constructed as one large, magical playground. Trees grow in and around classrooms for kids to climb and interact with, while the roof was engineered in an oval shape and includes barriers so kids can play on and run around it; the roof even has a slide so children can slide into class. Fuji K. was strategically built to foster curiosity and creativity, and it purposely designed "small inconveniences" throughout the school grounds to encourage critical thinking and problem solving. Children have many opportunities to teach themselves through collaboration, exploration, and experiential learning. And in a unique manner, the school's classrooms are not separated by walls, allowing for noises to flow freely from one classroom to the next. The educational facility seems to encourage distraction, which happens often, like when kids look up and see fellow classmates looking down at them from the roof through a skylight. On a fundamental level, Fuji K. has successfully found a way to integrate learning and development with playtime and laughter, and it seems the young students are better for it.

In the spirit of Fuji Kindergarten, Jacque Fresco envisioned a classroom/workshop resting atop a hill, surrounded by a small body of water, where children have to work together to assemble and then row a boat across the mote. Such an arrangement would encourage collaboration, problem solving, and it would give the children a sense of achievement through persistence, which can help build confidence going into the day. It would also be a great way for students to get exercise.

Sticking with the theme of integrating play with the learning process, I see video games taking on a more prominent role in our Resource-Based Economy. Modern, mainstream video games have a unique way of capturing the attention of millions of people for hours on end. And when we play video games, we naturally want to become better at them and do well. But why? What is it about virtual games that are so captivating and mind-grabbing that they are able to monopolize much of our time when they offer no external rewards? Well, on a simple level, video games are an immersive experience that let players escape into entirely new worlds, and that alone can be exhilarating. But, on a slightly deeper level, games provide challenges that allow a player to feel a sense of Autonomy, "Purpose," and Mastery – the Drive Supplements we discussed in Chapter 9. And the evaluation/feedback systems used in games are completely opposite of those most often used in formal education. Whereas schools use decremental grading systems where a child is downgraded every time he fails to answer a question correctly, which can be demotivating, video games don't necessarily punish failure. Instead, in your attempt to complete a level or defeat a boss, your failures translate into progressive learning. Persistence is naturally encouraged in a game's design. The more you learn through failing over and over again, through trial-and-error, the better you become, and you are rewarded with self-improved skillsets and further progression into the game. And then, through persistence and self-taught skills, when you do finally succeed and beat the game or defeat a challenging level, it feels earned. It feels good! Even though rewards aren't tangible, one feels an inner sense of accomplishment from simply overcoming the challenges presented in games.

Of course, educational games do already exist, but most of them aren't nearly as engaging or fun as games produced for popular platforms, such as Nintendo or Xbox. If educational games are developed with an emphasis on simply being good games on their own merit, then they would have a better chance at getting kids to not only *choose* to play those games in their free time, but to get them to want to play them over and over again. Farming Simulator created by Giants Software comes to mind as one current example of a video game that I would consider educational and fun. When playing that game, I felt like I learned more about farming and equipment in just a few hours than I did throughout my entire life. I envision multiple ways of developing games that combine fun with learning. For instance, I am imagining a "Metroidvania" type of game where our protagonist has to travel through the human body, solving puzzles, gaining power-ups, opening up new regions of the "world," and defeating infections or tumors or whatever might be plaguing the environment. And instead of increasing your "health bar" by picking up energy tanks like in conventional games, maybe you would discover cancer fighting T-Cells; and the more T-Cells you acquire, the better your chances are of enduring and defeating tumors. It could be challenging, fun, and informative, and the player could be given the freedom to explore and discover hidden areas in the body while a memorable score plays in the background. There are so many ways mainstream gaming formats can be integrated with education.

And going back to the idea of "failure," many of us are terrified to fail. Some of this aversion is natural, and some of it is conditioned. We don't want to look incompetent or look stupid and risk ridicule and social rejection, so often we avoid challenges that might see us fail. However, failure is one of the best teachers, as arguably the greatest basketball player of all time, Michael Jordan, once said:

> "I've missed more than 9,000 shots in my career. I've lost almost 300 games. Twenty-six times I've been trusted to take the game-winning shot and missed. I've failed over and over and over again in my life. And that is why I succeed."[79]

Through continuous trial-and-error comes learning, mastery, achievement, and success. So, though I don't want to say failure will be encouraged in future education, it certainly won't be discouraged. Instead, it'll be seen as an opportunity to evaluate, learn, and grow.

To reiterate as I conclude this section, no child should ever be punished for their parents' circumstances. Therefore, in our Resource-Based Economy, every child will have an opportunity to receive an excellent education suited to his or her unique needs and interests. And every child will have access to the appropriate tools to nurture his or her talents. With money and strict budgetary limitations lifted, as well as educational resources at their disposal, teachers will have the freedom to fully utilize their knowledge and expertise in facilitating learning in students, young and old. Technology will assist teaching professionals as the educational system evolves from one of memorization and standardized tests to one of interaction, experiential learning, and collaboration. With the population's children given the best opportunity to learn and develop, society as a whole will be better for it.

## 10.9 HEALTHCARE

With money and the profit-incentive removed in our Resource-Based Economy, we can begin to restore trust in the Healthcare system. For, without the allure of financial gain, doctors no longer have any reason to push prescriptions onto patients that might not otherwise need them, and pharmaceutical companies no longer gain anything from falsifying data in clinical studies or grooming doctors to spread misinformation to other doctors. Without the seductive whispers of money behind every ear, we can better trust that our health is the only priority.

Additionally, with money removed, I predict vast changes in the landscape of medicine. For instance, as mentioned earlier, I see most psychiatric drugs being put out to pasture; and if they are used, it will be primarily as a last resort, though probably not even then. In the realm of cancer, I definitely see a shift from poisonous, yet highly profitable, chemotherapies in treating malignancies to more effective and less destructive methods. If we haven't yet cracked the code for gene therapy or stem cell treatment in fighting cancer, then I see less-toxic alternatives being utilized that don't completely destroy one's immune system, and in effect, her ability to continue fighting cancer and disease after the chemo has stopped working.

In our RBE all potential treatments will get a fair shake in the testing phase, as there would no longer be any financial incentive, and therefore no bias, to skew clinical results to discount a new, competing treatment that could undermine more profitable treatments. What this means is that non-profitable treatment techniques that use natural, healthy substances won't be sabotaged in clinical studies as they have been in the past within our current monetary system. When it comes to testing novel treatments in a moneyless society, the most important question becomes – Does the treatment work? Whereas right now, the most important question is – Is the treatment profitable? Money is placed above your health in our current economic arrangement, and that is little surprise to no one.

In that vein, with money removed from the picture, companies no longer have incentive to hoard ideas, medical patents, medical information, or any other intellectual properties in order to keep it away from competitors and maintain an advantage in the marketplace. All ideas and theories, once they are conjured up, will get tossed into the public domain so that hundreds or thousands of other brilliant minds from all regions of the planet can get their eyes on the information, study it, and build upon or off of it. With more eyes and brains devoted to solving a problem or working out a theory, the chances of it being cracked are significantly increased. Once there is no longer any incentive to keep an airtight seal on ideas or proprietary information, I will be curious to see what hidden treatments and medical findings come out of the woodwork. Who knows, maybe our trustworthy pharmaceutical companies and government-sponsored institutions have revealed everything they know about fighting cancer and other diseases. I would confidently wager that is not the case, however.

I would say right now, in our current monetary society, we don't actually have a "health" care system. I would say that a "sick" care system is a more accurate label, as medical facilities typically only give attention to those who are sick. Because most of the money gained in modern healthcare is in treating sick people and diseases, I go as far as to say sick people and diseases are wanted. If everyone took preventative measures to improve health and sicknesses significantly decreased, pharmaceutical companies and clinics would take a massive hit to their bottom lines. And that's bad. But, with money and the need for profit removed, our future system can and will focus on and genuinely encourage healthy lifestyles and disease prevention.

And that leads me to another point. Sicknesses and health issues will be significantly reduced in our Resource-Based Economy. Food will no longer be laced with preservatives since it will be locally produced. And without the need to profit, all food will be made to the highest quality and with the utmost integrity. No more will there be cheap, nutrient-less, chemical-laden "imitation" food for poor communities that can't afford quality, nutritional food. That alone will cut down on obesity, diabetes, heart diseases, cholesterol issues, and even depression. And then, aside from food, the water we drink and the air we breathe will be cleaner. There will no longer be an incentive to dump chemical waste into waterways to save a few dollars and prop up the bottom line. And as we shift away from gas, coal, and other hydrocarbons, the air will carry less pollution, meaning it'll be fresher and healthier. So, it is not hard to see how rapidly and substantially public health can improve simply by removing money and the profit incentive.

And as public health improves, the demand for pharmaceutical drugs will decrease, and peoples' drug cabinets will become barren, which would certainly be a positive trend.

Does that all sound logical and good to you so far? It sure does to me. And here's the thing, it's not Utopian or overly idealistic. I'd say it's rather simple with just a couple adjustments to the way we currently transact in life.

So then, without money, what will our healthcare system look like in the future? Well, in many ways it'll be similar, and in many ways it'll be completely different. All medical centers will be furnished with state-of-the-art equipment and the most effective medicines available; and they will have testing facilities and laboratories branching off from them. And as for the concern that humans will no longer be motivated to take on the demanding roles of doctors and surgeons without the external reward of money, I will double down on my assertion from Chapter 9 that the medical profession will become one of the most attractive fields in an RBE. Occupations in healthcare afford one respect from others, increased self-esteem, autonomy, a chance to continue mastering skills and knowledge, a great purpose, and more. They essentially offer the best opportunities for inner fulfillment and living an enriched life.

However, there might come a time where this concern becomes moot. There might, well, there likely will come a time when the demand for doctors and nurses becomes minimal, as AI and automated systems advance to the point where they can perform surgery with much more precision and less human error than surgeons, or where robots can attend to the needs of, care for, and lift heavy patients with more finesse and attentiveness than can human nurses. Depending on how advanced tools are applied, the future is bright. Scientists and engineers are developing technology once reserved only for fiction at an incredible velocity. I will attempt to discuss some of these innovations, but know that I am merely scraping the surface of what is being worked on and what is coming available. The possibilities, once again, are endless.

For instance, in our future system, if you need to pick up a prescription medication, you might have your orders fulfilled by a fully automated pharmacy, as is already happening in present-day Earth.[80] Automated pharmacies can fill prescriptions faster and with greater accuracy, which improves safety. And, you might not even need to leave your home to obtain your medication; drones, driverless vehicles, pneumatic tubes, or whatever is proven to be most efficient, could deliver it to your doorstep with video instructions on how to properly take your medicine. And if that's not convenient enough for you, 3D printing technology could give you the ability to simply "print" your pills in the comfort of your own home. In 2015 the FDA approved a 3D-printed epilepsy drug called Spritam, which is made by a machine that "prints" powder and builds the tablet layer by layer.[81]

Visits to the local doctor have been and will continue to take on a new look as we progress into the future. First of all, since there is no profit motive in our Resource-Based Economy and therefore no incentive to want sick people, prevention will be strongly emphasized. Our houses, devices, and even clothes can be embedded with sensors that can monitor heart rates, measure blood pressure, read brain waves, detect skin cancers, find eye defects, and so much more. If you happen to have high blood pressure or a skin abnormality, a "check engine" light could come on to alert you that your body needs servicing, and it'll advise you to take simple personal steps or to seek professional help. Medical companies have been inventing devices that can easily hook up to your smart phone to provide you with in-home health analysis; as one example, there exists a patch that can measure and communicate real-time heart data to your phone. Individuals can also be assigned robots to help with fitness and health; "RoboCoaches" have already been deployed in Singapore.[82]

But let's say your "check engine" light does come on. Artificial intelligence is currently being designed to analyze and diagnose ailments, and it can even devise personal treatment plans based on a patient's unique genetic makeup. They will be able to perform such tasks with more consistency and accuracy than human physicians can. Humans, no matter how brilliant, are susceptible to error, and it is not unusual for different physicians to have differing opinions regarding a single patient's health. Advanced medical tools will alleviate uncertainty and "guesswork," and it might even eliminate much of the need for in-person doctor visits. But if you need or would like human consultation, doctor visits can be conducted over the phone or through video-conferencing technology – Telemedicine – as has been the trend in our COVID dystopia. Instead of spending time traveling and sitting in the waiting room, you can describe your symptoms or take a picture of physical abnormalities, send them to your doctor, and have him chat with you remotely once he's had time to review your case.

And what if you are admitted to a hospital and require inpatient care? Well, robot nurses and other machines will be employed to assist patients and readily attend to their needs. Robear, a robot nurse with a friendly teddy bear face, has been used in Japan to help patients with their varying needs, including carrying them, helping them stand, or transferring them to their wheelchair, which can help save the backs of human nurses.[83] The TUG autonomous robot has been designed with many skills, including the ability to deliver medical supplies, pick up food orders, remove waste, keep track of schedules, supply linens, and much more, and has been hired by many medical facilities to relieve some of the heavy burden placed on medical personnel.[84] Robots now and in the future will be able to disinfect rooms, draw blood, check vitals, and analyze blood samples.

The complex role of the surgeon will also transform as we roll into the future, as robotic surgeons are being developed to assist in or perform surgeries with complete autonomy. The Smart Tissue Autonomous Robot (STAR), a robot surgeon, planned and performed an intestinal anastomosis on a pig using its own vision, tools, and intelligence, and it did it better than human surgeons given the same task.[85] The da Vinci surgical system is a machine that has been assisting surgeons for two decades now, and allows surgeons to perform surgery remotely from a console. The robotic surgical device provides surgeons with a 3D view of the surgical area, and its precise arms and hands have greater range of motion and can operate through smaller incisions, which helps improve accuracy and recovery.[86] And researchers at the University of Utah developed an automated drill that can perform certain cranial surgeries in significantly less time – down to about 3 minutes compared to 120 minutes using modern techniques.[87] Automated surgical procedures will only continue to improve and gain autonomous abilities. Other robotic surgery systems include Ion, Mako, and Navio.[88]

Now, will technology completely phase out medical professionals in the future? I don't think so. Plus, for certain procedures or operations, I think I would prefer to have human-to-human interaction. The purpose of the previous few paragraphs was merely to illustrate the enormous possibilities of technology in healthcare and to show that the demand for doctors or nurses will likely decrease, maybe significantly, in the future.

But there's more.

As of March 2020, there were over 112,000 patients waiting for an organ transplant in America; and of those filtering on and off the waiting list, 20 people, including children, die each day due to being unable to receive a donor organ in time.[89] However, we now have the ability to literally print organs using 3D Printing technology, or, in a more controversial light, we can clone organs using a patient's own DNA.[90] What this means is, a child will no longer have to desperately wait in a hospital bed for an organ as the minutes of his life tick away. Now, I know that the idea of producing manmade organs for transplantation may not sit well with you; and that's okay! Notions of life and death are complex subjects to broach. For me, I grow uncomfortable when I consider research being done to slow down or even reverse the aging process. It makes me feel uneasy knowing we will eventually have the ability to prolong human life for hundreds of years. And I certainly do not like the idea of cloning actual human beings. We all have our limits of what is personally acceptable for us based on our knowledge and life experiences. Know this – no matter how you feel about this subject, or any subject really, you're not wrong. But I won't necessarily say you are right, either, because who's to say what is truly right or what is truly wrong. The notions of right and wrong are mere personal preferences. If you feel strongly about something, it is absolutely your right to feel that way. But that doesn't mean your rights and wrongs can't change throughout your life. Mine do all the time. Plus, my concern is usually not to prove anyone right or wrong, but to learn, convey what I have come to learn, and come to a mutual understanding – not necessarily a mutual agreement, but an understanding. If we can approach subjects with that mindset, I think there would be a lot less fighting and a lot more understanding, which means less stress and a more peaceful coexistence. And when I say "we," I am included in that bundle because I certainly fall victim to my pride and ego often where I feel the need to prove myself right and my opposition wrong – that does little but create a divide in the end.

Anyway, circling back to the ethics of printing or cloning organs, I only need to imagine a young girl faced with death, where all she needs is a new liver or heart for a chance to survive and live a full life. I imagine that if it were my daughter lying in a hospital bed, I would plead for doctors to give her a cloned or 3D printed organ. Actually, if anyone I knew needed an organ transplant to continue on with life, it would be a relief for me to know that we could simply duplicate one in the lab, rather than having to needlessly sweat out waiting for a living person to sacrifice one of hers or a dead person to donate one of his. With those considerations in mind, I have no problem and even welcome the ability to generate organs in the lab. Again, you might feel differently, and that's okay.

I know there is also the controversy regarding the idea of us playing God in using manmade health advances to prolong one's life. I will keep it brief, since much can and has been said, but, one could argue that ALL human intervention in treating ailments is essentially us "playing God," whether using simple plant/herb-based remedies or more complex treatments. And you know what, if we think about it, all treatments or therapies – plant-based remedies, MRI machines, and Gene therapy alike – involve the creative arrangement of God-given elements. When we discover novel methods of approaching disease, it is only because God made it possible to do so. How are we to truly know what he intended? Maybe he scattered the potentialities across the world on purpose, like puzzle pieces, to give us the ability to explore, discover, and piece them together in order to find "improved" or simply different ways of doing things. New possibilities keep life exciting and interesting. Maybe that's part of what God intended? Who knows.

So, now and more so in the future, if a patient needs an organ transplant, she will not have to worry about whether or not an organ will come available. We will be able to "print" it using 3D printing technology. 3D printers will also be used to print prosthetics, casts, blood vessels, skin grafts, surgical tools, and much more. Again, the sky, wait no, the universe is the limit.[91,92]

In our Resource-Based, Access economy, top-notch medical care will be accessible to all residents, no matter their status in society. No longer will we come upon situations where a child is turned away from quality service because his poor family cannot afford it. A society with improved health and increased trust becomes a healthier, happier society overall, and everyone benefits because of it.

## 10.10 ADDITIONAL FEATURES

In our global monetary system, patents are used to protect ideas and inventions so companies and creators can maintain a competitive advantage over other companies and use their original ideas to make money. Simple. However, since a Resource-Based Economy no longer requires money to access the means of survival, patents no longer serve any logical purpose. Therefore, patents will no longer exist.

As I said in the previous section regarding Healthcare, all inventions, ideas, blueprints, computer codes, etc., will be in the public domain. In an open-source format, humans from all walks of life will have the opportunity to browse ideas, read about the ones that pique their interest, and expend effort in trying to solve technical challenges or simply improve upon the idea. More eyes on a problem are usually more beneficial than fewer. In an open-source, Resource-Based Economy, if someone envisions an engine that runs cleanly on water, instead of a company hoarding the idea and paying only a small group of employees to figure out how to bring the idea to fruition so they can be the first to produce the invention and make money off of it before anyone else can, every technical institution in the world will be able to provide input. There is no reason to hoard an idea anymore. And with thousands or even millions of educated people involved in solving complex issues, sharing ideas, expertise, and findings, imagine how quickly we could come up with, say, cures for various cancers.

And of course, if an individual has an idea that he would like to hang on to and figure out himself, that is his right. But he will have the option to put his ideas out into the world and seek help should he run into perplexing roadblocks.

People only steal that which they don't have access to. In a Resource-Based Economy, theft will no longer be a problem, really, since if someone needs something, they will have access to it. Crime, in general, will be reduced in a system where needs are readily met, since most crimes, as we discussed in Chapter 6.5, stem from inadequacies and competing forces in the monetary system. In this sense, the role of Law Enforcement will experience significant change. Of course, with the complexity of human behavior, it would be naïve of me to assume all crime will disappear. Though it will be substantially reduced, infractions will still occur.

Additionally, I imagine the complete removal of all laws. If we think about it, laws are only enacted when we can't figure out how or simply choose not to solve various problems. For instance, we don't want cars to go too fast in neighborhoods, so we make laws in hopes of preventing such activity. However, if we really wanted to solve the problem of speed in residential areas, instead of creating a partially effective law, we would simply design a car that couldn't go above a certain speed when it is in those areas. Or, instead of making laws that say a person can't drive while intoxicated, which does little to prevent drunk driving, a car could be designed to not operate if a man's BAC is above an acceptable threshold (I know that technology already exists). So, laws are merely created when we don't know how to solve a problem. But, our Resource-Based Economy is all about technical efficiency and finding solutions to all problems. Instead of taking the lazy, ineffective way out by creating a law for unwanted behavior, we will instead figure out how to prevent that behavior in the first place. Solutions, not laws!

So, for the most part, governmental laws will not exist in an RBE.

Without the tool of money, and as automation replaces monotonous tasks in a Resource-Based Economy, people will no longer be enslaved to their traditional jobs as they are today, where if they want to leave and try something else they risk losing their ability to survive.

Many of the occupations and industries that have rapidly

blossomed with America's shift from a manufacturing to a service economy, jobs that provide little intrinsic value outside of the monetary system, will no longer be of use in our new economy. For the most part, lawyers will no longer be needed. Say goodbye to bean-counting Accountants (that's me). No longer will we need Financial Advisors or Insurance Salesman that sell fear to support glorified, legal pyramid schemes. We will no longer need Stock Brokers, Bankers, Tellers, Legislators, Lobbyists, Wall Street Traders, Financial Analysts, Fundraising Managers, and traditional Advertisers and Marketers. And no more Legalized Drug Dealers, I mean Pharmaceutical Sales Reps, or any annoying Salespeople for that matter. All occupations related to money will become extinct. Such jobs only exist right now to serve the monetary system (some don't even do that) and simply become irrelevant in an RBE.

Alright. So, I believe the previous sections adequately cover the essential components of any society – food, water, shelter, energy, transportation, education, and healthcare. Through scientific application and by using advanced *tools* and automation in a Resource-Based Economy, we will have the ability to produce an abundance of life necessities that everyone has access to. The cities supported by a Resource-Based Economy will be self-sustaining, and with sensors embedded in every section of society that measure activity and resource usage, the cities will be able to adapt to ever-changing environmental conditions, which ensures we are maintaining dynamic equilibrium. A city that can "think" will be aware of what resources need replenishing and what resources are abundant. Such a system will help us align with the natural, immutable laws of Earth.

In a Resource-Based Economy, no one will ever have to worry about survival again. Instead, every day can be devoted to living life to the fullest; everyone will be free to spend time with and enjoy the love of family and friends, explore new ideas and challenges, master skills, or just "play." Each person will be free to carve a path best suited for him! The conditions and humane environment will make such "Utopian" goals entirely possible.

Ultimately, it is up to us, everyone to decide what path we want to follow. We can remain on the current trail of status quo, either because we enjoy the dysfunctional ride or because we are too afraid to change course, where every single life system is severely threatened, or we can chart a bold new path that seeks to remedy the figurative disease plaguing global society and bring the entire Earth system into total harmony.

The choice is yours! The choice is ours!

## 10.11 ADDRESSING RATIONAL CONCERNS

In this section, I will address just a few concerns that I anticipate people will have. I have chosen to keep my answers relatively brief and succinct, as each question could involve entire books, and I don't want to take up too much more of your time with this text since it is already bulky enough.

### *10.11a CONCERN #1 – Technology = Control*

I understand there is a large swath of people who fear that artificial intelligence and advanced technology will be used to maintain control and power over society – like using nanobots or RFID chips to track peoples' every movements and transactions, or using automation to take away jobs to make people more dependent on the state, or using large radio waves to make people ill – and such fears might incline those to dismiss the advanced technologies mentioned in this chapter and the possibilities they offer.

Now, I think the concern that technology could be used to seize control and reduce freedoms is a plausible one. Within our current economic setup, having power and control over the population and keeping the human livestock docile affords one significant advantage. Control and dependence make it easier for the winning few, the masters, to maintain a stronghold over the majority of the money supply and resources, which better ensures the survival, comfort, and security for them and their families. Because the tool that grants access to survival, comfort, and security is limited in this zero-sum game, there is incentive to take malevolent measures to maintain control over that money supply, which includes using technology for sinister purposes.

But, in defense of the Resource-Based Economy I am proposing, I recognize that tools (all tools) can be used for both good and bad. A knife can be used to open a box, or it can be used to injure a person. Nanotechnology can be used to fight diseases or it can be used to control a population or even cause physical harm. Nuclear fission can be used to decimate entire regions, or it can be used to provide energy. The environment and incentives within dictate how a tool is used.

Whether we like it or not, artificial intelligence, advanced robotics, nanotechnology, and other advanced tools are either coming or are already here. If we remain in our current monetary system where there is great incentive to get on top and then maintain control and power over the population in order to remain on top, then sure, I can see these advanced tools being used for bad.

However, in our Resource-Based Economy with money completely removed and Earth's resources declared the common heritage of all humans and with everyone having Access to life necessities, there is zero incentive to control the population. If one already has access to everything he needs to achieve a high standard of living, he gains nothing more by reaching the top and keeping society under his thumb. Therefore, in our RBE, there is no reason to use AI or advanced tools to dastardly ends.

I also want to differentiate the "cashless" society that the world is transitioning to, from the "moneyless" society promoted in our Resource-Based Economy. It seems to me that current global powers want to shift from cash to digital currency, not because it would save on resources in a logical sense, but because it will further increase their control over the masses. With digital currency, it is easier to track people, and in the wrong hands it would give people the power to "cancel" you or prevent you from making purchases if you become disobedient.

Nevertheless, a cashless society is not a moneyless society. It still uses an artificial, theoretical medium to distribute goods. It still uses money; it's just digital money.

An RBE does not use any form of money. While the current global monetary system is about consolidating and centralizing power and removing freedoms as has been the trend, especially recently as of this writing in 2020 and into 2021, a Resource-Based Economy promotes decentralization and empowering every individual to pursue her ultimate dreams (within reason, of course). An RBE is all about choice, agency, and personal freedom. By providing access to life necessities and the tools you need to pursue your goals, it is the most conducive system to free choice than any other system ever put into practice.

So, again, AI, robots, and other advanced tools are already here. Instead of using these tools to control, we only want to use them to help – famous last words. But, I understand that a happy, healthy, stress-free population benefits me and the entire Earth body, while a constrained, suffocated, stressed-out population does not. An RBE provides no incentive to use technology to dominate and control.

### *10.11b CONCERN #2 – Socialism/Communism/Marxism*

**a. "Travis, this Resource-Based Economy you are preaching about sounds a lot like Socialism/Marxism/Communism."**

It's not.

A Resource-Based Economy is not Socialism, Marxism, Communism, Capitalism, or Feudalism. It is unlike any other system ever put into practice.

All of the systems mentioned above are essentially cut from the same cloth, only designed with slight variations. They are all subsidiaries, subsystems spawned from the same monetary system. As I have mentioned a few times in this book, I don't see Capitalism and Socialism as being entirely different. Both require its citizens to compete against each other to acquire money in order to access the means of survival. Though they operate under a different set of rules, they are ultimately playing the same game. We are all essentially playing the board game Monopoly®; and just as many families tweak the rules to fit their preferences, so too do individual countries. Some nations require their competitors to return more money back into the game so that the game can last longer (Socialism – as defined in modern society). Other countries allow their competitors to acquire and keep as much money as they can (Capitalism). But make no mistake, we are all playing the same general game.

However, a Resource-Based Economy is the first system that breaks entirely free from the overarching monetary system. It is not simply a variant of Monopoly®, as it doesn't use the tool of money as the barrier between accessing food, water, and shelter, and it doesn't require citizens to compete against each other for survival. Although I love to compete and recognize the value of competition in certain situations, a competition for *survival* can get ugly really quick; it can lead to desperation, abhorrent behavior, and then all of the devastating outcomes playing out across the globe. The conditions within an RBE, on the other hand, are conducive to collaboration, as people no longer have to worry about how they are going to feed their families and survive.

### b. "Socialism DOES NOT work! It's been tried and failed!"

Socialism may not work, but I would also say that Capitalism does not work, either. For instance, America, which predominantly operates under the rules of Capitalism, is over $20 trillion in debt and is experiencing vast wealth inequality, which has led to an excess of crime and more incarcerations than many other developed nations combined. And when people point to the high standard of living of America's citizens as proof that Capitalism works, I point out that most of that high standard of living has been made possible with the introduction of automation and technology; and much of the most influential innovations in technology have been funded by the public and were also made possible by the abundance of untapped resources that Europeans settled upon when they stepped foot onto what was essentially a blank canvas. Not to mention, too, that the government has had to intervene on multiple occasions with state money to keep the system from collapsing. If America were not the super power of the world that it is, it doesn't take much deductive reasoning to see that its economy would have imploded many times over if not for Socialistic measures and legislation. The US is basically allowed to print as much money as it needs to keep itself afloat – countries of lesser power are not allowed to do that without significant repercussions.

And you know, if we wanted to, we could make an argument that the United States system is a sort of form of Communism, as we have come to define it, but rather than the government controlling resources and the population, it's a few giant corporations. They are largely responsible for telling us what to eat, how to feel, how to dress, what to think, etc. However, they don't do it through blatant force, they do it covertly. They psychologically puppeteer our thoughts by pumping billions of dollars into major news outlets and mass marketing and shoving carefully constructed narratives and suggestive advertisements down our gullets until we act how they want us to act and think how they want us to think; all while convincing us that free will is driving our decisions and that our beliefs are strictly our own. It's a genius ruse. We all proclaim ourselves to be "freethinkers," but I rarely come across people who aren't barking the same narrow talking points that everyone else in their packs are barking. Again, the people at the helm are no dummies. Societal masters have had years of honing and perfecting psychological manipulation.

Lastly, I have little interest in defending a subsystem of the monetary system, and though no country is purely Capitalistic or purely Socialistic, to say unequivocally that Socialism has been tried and failed isn't entirely accurate. Not only is Socialism a relatively young concept, but when we look at, say, the more-Socialized Scandinavian countries, we can see that they are doing quite well and are generally ranked as some of the happiest nations in the world. Additionally, the social programs introduced with the New Deal in post-World War II America gave rise to the strongest middle class this country has ever seen. So, again, to say with absolute conviction that Socialism has been tried and failed is not entirely accurate and is most certainly brought on by a flood of propaganda, especially considering that hundreds or thousands of other factors go into making a country's economy successful or unsuccessful.

Ultimately, however, all systems under the monetary game are handcuffed and limited by the imaginary tool of money. All monetary daughter systems hold the world back from reaching its full potential.

### c. "You Socialist, liberal pussy!" and other insults

First of all, it behooves me to think that such abstract insults are so confidently leveraged even to this day. What does it even mean to call someone a Socialist or a Capitalist or a Communist? Nothing really. It seems there has been a concerted effort by national and global masters to socially engineer the greater populace to shutter at and attack opposing economic ideologies in an attempt to protect their massive fortunes that have come at the expense of everyone else.

See, though our globally connected monetary system currently sees 3 billion people living in poverty, 20,000 children dying of starvation every day, etc., it has also showered a few men with great riches. Because the opulent minority are living heads and shoulders above everyone else in society, the last thing they want is an upheaval of an economic model that has rewarded them so handsomely. For fear of losing their lavish standards of living, the last thing they want is for the average and poor majority to consider alternatives. So one of the steps they take is to condition the masses – train them like dogs – to demean, ostracize, and bark at those bringing up different ideas for managing resources and organizing society. "Greedy Capitalist," they might yell in countries that favor a more equitable monetary system. Or, in countries like America you might hear people shout, "Fucking Socialist," at those opposing the every-man-for-himself attitude. Again, it baffles me that such empty insults are still used to this day – only through years of social conditioning is that made possible. And it works! And then what happens is, even if people start to consider alternative systems or ideas, they will quickly silence their own minds for fear of being shamed or alienated from the herd. Then what's worse, even if they have this gnawing suspicion that something is wrong with the current setup of society, they will convince themselves that it's good so that they can fit in with their pack – that inherent need to belong is incredibly strong. It's one of the reasons the Nazis were able to convince so many German individuals to hate the Jews.

So, the opulent minority have the rest of the population squabbling in this binary tug-of-war between what monetary system is best – Socialism or Capitalism – but America is neither. And it's both. At the same time. The pendulum has swung throughout America's history and continues to swing along the monetary continuum, with some eras leaning more toward Socialist-favoring policies and other eras leaning heavily toward Capitalistic policies.

And as much as the opulent minority have convinced most Americans to criticize and fear systems like Socialism, they benefit greatly from public welfare. The wealthiest few live in a Socialist arrangement where if they start to fail, they don't need to worry about how they will survive, because they will be bailed out to the tune of billions or trillions at the expense of the public should they begin to stumble, which we have seen over and over again in the past many decades; in a roundabout way they essentially get to print money at will and have the public pay it back. It is an interesting dichotomy where they operate in Socialism while everyone else is distracted competing against one another for leftovers in a Capitalistic state – and that's by design.

So, they want people to fear change, they want people attached to the current system, even if it is inequitable and tearing the world apart, because they themselves fear that change will cause them to lose their luxurious kingdoms. Why would anyone want to move away from a socioeconomic arrangement that has rewarded him over and over again? And that is why the masters have convinced its "lesser" populace to defend the current economic setup so fervently and attack those who question it; hence insults like "Socialist!" or "Capitalist!"

However, the opulent minority should know that in our economy of the future, everyone's standard of living will be unlike anything this world has ever seen.

### *10.11c CONCERN #3 – New World Order*

"Wait a minute, Travis, so you're talking about a One World system? You're a clueless mouthpiece for the Globalists and their New World Order!!!"

Clueless? Maybe. But it is hard to argue that anyone has a clue these days with so much lies and misinformation filling the air.

To address the above concern, though the Resource-Based Economy I envision aims to unite the global population under a single, interconnected system, similar to how the human body links every organ and cell within its interconnected, interdependent system, it is not the New World Order, the Illuminati, Russian Propaganda, or anything nefarious like that.

The ultimate goal of the New World Order's one world government is about power and control. It is about protecting resources and financial wealth from the trampling and roar of the "bewildered herd" (the majority of the population) in order for the masters to maintain elite status; it's to keep that "bewildered herd" subservient, working, and distracted so the opulent minority can reap the rewards without having to stress and labor. A globally connected Resource-Based Economy, on the other hand, is about decentralization and individual freedom. It is about declaring all of Earth's resources the common heritage of all Earth's people – just as no individual organ or cell has control over the human body's resources (unless of course cells become cancerous and hog as many resources as they can). An RBE endeavors to free the "bewildered herd" from the wage slavery so passionately opposed in the 19th century and allow individuals to rule over their own personal domain.

### *10.11d CONCERN #4 – The Bible/Revelations*

"Travis, a moneyless society? The Book of Revelation is coming true!"

In the Bible, Revelations talks about a cashless society where people are not allowed to do commerce unless they have a specific mark on their wrist or forehead. In Christianity, a cashless society might be seen and feared as a sign of the coming apocalypse, the end of times, and the deceptive rule of the Antichrist; it might also be seen and welcomed as a sign of the revelation of the Lord, the second coming of Christ.

As I write this in 2020, current global powers are expending significant effort into shifting to a cashless society. But again, what I am supporting in the "moneyless" Resource-Based Economy is completely different from the "cashless" economy in discussion today. A cashless society is about tracking and control. It still requires citizens to acquire digital money in order to access goods. A Resource-Based Economy is not that – there is no money whatsoever and citizens have access to goods without having to acquire an intermediary of arbitrary value.

While the cashless society mentioned in the Bible is about evil taking command, a Resource-Based Economy is about love and taking care of the entire population. Everyone takes care of everyone. I think such a system is one the Lord would be proud of if it ever came to fruition.

So, no, the moneyless system I talk about here is not the cashless society talked about in the Bible; therefore, it is not a sign that the Book of Revelation is coming true. No one will be "marked" in a Resource-Based Economy, and everyone will be able to transact and receive access to life necessities no matter what.

### *10.11e CONCERN #5 – Cult*

"Travis, is this whole Resource-Based-Economy thing a giant scheme of some insidious cult?"

I certainly hope not. I most definitely am not tethered to any group, nor do I worship any group leaders or anything like that. Then again, maybe I'm brainwashed and don't even know it. If any of us were brainwashed, how would we know? We wouldn't. I suppose that's the point of brainwashing. Boy, could you imagine if we as a society were all brainwashed without our knowledge? I mean, imagine a world where we have been subliminally programmed to believe that the point of our existence is to buy and consume, and that love and happiness is not experienced through deep connections with those around us but that it is gained when we acquire inanimate material objects; and that, among many oddities, if we don't have in our possession a certain amount of those material objects with specific labels on them that we are considered less successful and less worthy of love and happiness. That sure would be a bizarre world to live in, huh? Luckily our brains are strong enough to see through the thousands of hours of advertisements and media propaganda that we are immune to such psychological manipulation. Right?

Anyway, though the Resource-Based Economy is predominantly associated with The Venus Project and The Zeitgeist Movement, the ideas behind the system are universal and are not associated with any group. I support the ideas of an RBE, not necessarily the groups. And, I appreciate the amount of work Jacque Fresco put into designing a humane, resource-conscious system, and though I perceive him as incredibly smart, I don't cling to his every word. He has ideas about Love that differ from mine. He also has different ideas about God. Some people supporting an RBE are atheist, some are not – I am not. Both sides are welcomed!

From my perspective, I don't see supporters of a Resource-Based Economy as zealots. There is no chanting, meditating, ritualistic behavior, or any mind-altering practices. There is no aggressive shaming or guilt-tripping people into specific belief systems. There is no hazing or punishment for dissenting opinions. Groups supporting an RBE certainly aren't rich, they are not receiving much money, and there are no membership fees. And, though there are more-prominent figures, there is no proclaimed leader.

So, no, I don't believe the main groups supporting a Resource-Based Economy are cults, although some might be more hierarchically structured or less organized than others.

### *10.11e CONCERN #5 – Travis Making Money*

"Wait a minute, Travis. How can you be campaigning for a system without money when you yourself are still trying to make money? You hypocrite!!!"

I understand this completely logical and rational concern. If I talk the talk, I should be able to walk the walk. Right?

However, my answer to this criticism? I still live within a monetary system. The only practical way I can gain access to the necessities of life, to survive, is by acquiring money. I'm not a farmer or a boy scout, so I am not equipped with the skills to go out into the wild and survive by cultivating or catching my own food, nor would I want to. Until we collectively transition away from the tool of money, I, for better or for worse, must still participate in the game if I intend to continue on living.

If it's any consolation, I do live and have lived well below my means for all of my adult life. This isn't necessarily due to my moral stance on consumerism; it's mostly because material junk simply doesn't thrill me, and it ends up being much more burdensome than joyful.

## 10.12 THE TRANSITION

The transition. How do we get from where we are now to where we want to be? That is the trillion-dollar question likely serving as the most difficult part in implementing a Resource-Based Economy, as roadblocks and issues present themselves around every corner that need to be resolved. But that's okay. With an undertaking so massive, of course there are going to be a plethora of problems that need to be worked out. Nothing worth working toward is ever easy. The early stages of any monumental endeavor are often rife with bumps, bruises, disagreements, and unexpected obstacles; that is natural and should be encouraged.

Throughout history, great change has often come with violent clashes and heavy bloodshed. I certainly don't want that. "The road to hell is paved with good intentions," as the saying goes. Everyone has justified intentions before taking violent action. But is violence ever justified, no matter to what end? I suppose we could argue it is unavoidable in certain situations, but for the most part I would say no. It often only adds pain, stress, and suffering, even on the part of the attacker, and threatens to create lifelong enemies. So, it doesn't matter how well intended I or anyone who supports the idea of graduating to a new economy is, if violence and force are the transitional devices, then we are no better than "well-intentioned" Crusaders spilling blood in the name of Christianity, or a "well-intentioned" (in his mind) Hitler wanting to cleanse Europe and the world of "Jewry," or the Turks systematically slaughtering Armenians by the hundreds of thousands in the early-20th century. The scars of hideous action never fade. Centuries have passed and we are still talking about the genocide of Europeans against indigenous populations of North America; it's often referenced as a black mark in US history, and even though they had nothing to do with the violence, many modern Americans still feel uneasy and guilty about it, and some Native Americans still harbor resentment.

I don't want resentment, or anger, or any negative feelings that could create adversaries with violent ideations. So, if we are to transition to a Resource-Based Economy, it must only come peacefully. It must be built upon pure foundations to encourage full and peaceful participation.

On another note, people are averse to change, even if the signs of increasing decay and collapse are present. We can be like dogs in a house fire. The environment around us might be engulfed in flames and crumbling at our feet, but our fear paralyzes and prevents us from taking necessary action. What this means, unfortunately, is that even though the overwhelming signs are here that we probably need to start making adjustments very soon, as every facet of global society is experiencing rapid decay in some form, people are unlikely to be moved to change unless a major, devastating event occurs. And in this case, people will likely remain in their burning houses until the economy completely collapses or suffering swells to a massive scale (through fighting and poverty) or we've cut down our last rainforest tree. If I had to hazard a guess, complete societal collapse will likely be the catalyst for change – which is too bad, but I suppose pain and suffering are all a part of this transitory journey we call life.

However, it doesn't have to be that way. If we don't want to wait until it is too late, and if we want to avoid further global suffering, which is what I would prefer, then we can start taking steps now to transition to a humane, global economy intelligently based on the carrying capacity of Earth's resources.

The first step is Education. Since we are proposing such a drastic shift in the way we have operated for millennia, people will aggressively resist unless they are first made aware of a Resource-Based Economy and the benefits it can bring. It is important that people are first shown why a shift is necessary, which shouldn't be difficult as most of us have eyes and can see that something is fatally flawed in our world and with our current economic arrangement.

Through education – documentaries, lectures, speaking engagements, books, etc. – millions of people around the globe have already jumped on board, while thousands have volunteered their talents to various groups supporting a Resource-Based Economy. That's a great start, but it is only a start.

It is also important that the wealthiest members of the population, those who might be most resistant to change since they fear losing their luxurious kingdoms, are made aware that a transition from the monetary system to a Resource-Based Economy will allow them to maintain an extremely high standard of living, and that they will be able to live unlike they have ever lived before – in harmony amongst the greater populace and without worry about guarding their fortunes.

If people do not know why we need to transform and the benefits an RBE can bring, then they will oppose it, and the project will be dead before it even begins. So, though it is a massive undertaking, the first step is in making the population aware, of educating everyone about the possibilities and freedoms offered in the new system.

Beyond informing the public, I have to be honest, I do not know how we transition from where we are now to where we want to be. As a single human with a single brain that seems to betray me more often than I'd like to admit, I must concede that I do not have all the answers, and questions regarding the transition are so far the toughest questions by a mile. In fact, in my experiences, it is where a Resource-Based Economy receives most of its criticism. Of course, ideas have been proposed.

For instance, members of The Venus Project seek to build a test city, preferably in a cheaper, resource-rich locale. And if the first city is a success, then continue building more cities. However, though a first city will eventually need to be built, I fear if advocates are too hasty about it, then the project could be set up to fail. And if the first one fails, it could cause proponents to lose faith and consider it hopeless, while it would also give critics "proof" that such an economy could never work, which it could use to further discourage those on the fence. It seems to me, if we are to break ground on a pilot city, it must be under the proper conditions, which to me means that a large portion of the population needs to be on board and we need to already be transitioning away from the tool of money. If we begin to build a test city while still in the throes of the monetary game, then it would stand to reason that the project would be doomed, because, not only would money need to be raised to begin construction of the city, which is certainly feasible, but it is also likely, especially in the beginning stages, that those living in the city will need access to some resources outside of its "boundaries," and without money, acquiring resources from those that still require money to access survival might prove difficult. Of course, I am confident there would be those willing to part with assets for free, because they either believe in the concept, or because they are simply curious, but I don't know that it would be enough. Also, I'd be concerned those living in the first test city might feel isolated from the rest of the world, and if they did want to travel to foreign destinations, they would need money to do so, which could be a problem. So, those are but a few reasons why I feel that before a test city is built, a large number of people need to be on board first, and we would also need to be in the process of emigrating away from our monetary, trade-based system. I could be wrong.

So, after exposing the public to the ideas of a Resource-Based Economy, I believe the next step is, as I just stated, transitioning away from the tool of money – and that includes bartering and all mediums of exchange, e.g., cryptocurrency, digital currency, fiat currency. Now, we don't want people to lose their ability to survive; we don't want people to go hungry and suffer during the shift from money to access. That being said, another idea that has been proposed as a bridge between the monetary system and an RBE is the use of Universal Basic Income (UBI). The greatest concern *should* be about survival. Though the idea of UBI has many critics, it could be a workable *temporary* solution to make sure people don't starve, especially if we are planning on discontinuing the use of money anyway. I emphasize the word temporary, because I don't believe the use of UBI is a good long-term solution, as has often been considered within the monetary game over the last many decades. Throwing out more and more money into the current economy just means endless inflation. Most of the new money thrown into the game, as with the COVID stimulus packages, will just make its way up to the ruling class anyway, and with prices having risen due to an increase in the money supply, people would continue to struggle to access life necessities.

Now, the transition away from money might happen by our collective *choice* or it might start to happen *naturally*. If we *choose* to shift from money, then the process will happen a lot quicker. If we let it happen naturally, then it will take much longer, many people will have to endure incredible hardship, and we might end up pushing the environment beyond its limits. How might the transition from money happen naturally? Well, with technological advancements. As automation continues to replace more and more jobs, like in transportation with driverless vehicles, food production with automated vertical farms, automated farming equipment, automated restaurants and grocery stores, and energy production with low maintenance energy systems, a growing number of the population will lose their ability to purchase the necessities of life. When this happens, paradoxically, businesses will start to receive less money. If automated systems produce an abundance of goods, but no one has money to purchase them, then they will go to waste. Rather than wasting valuable goods, and rather than seeing people suffer through immense hardship, there might come a time where businesses simply decide to give abundant supplies away. Maybe unlikely, but I see that is a possible "natural" way that we would start to transition away from money. Once products and services reach *zero marginal cost* as automation performs monotonous tasks and humans aren't needed as much and as goods are produced in excess, money loses its utility. We might slowly realize we don't really need the artificial tool and start naturally interacting without it. Again, though, if we wait for it to happen naturally, the transition will be protracted indefinitely, whereas if we make a conscious, concerted effort to shift, it could happen rather quickly and we could avoid much of the pains that an organic transition would cause, like unnecessary casualties, an uptick in crime, insurrection, environmental abuse, etc.

So, before we break ground on a test city, it seems to me we must take two initial steps. The first is to educate everybody, and the second is to consciously transition away from money. If people know the benefits of evolving to a Resource-Based Economy and the harmful drawbacks of remaining in the global monetary game, in The Pit, then I believe they would be more likely to at least consider change. Beyond such measures, the steps in transitioning to a Resource-Based Economy still need to be worked out, as it is still in the beginning stages; and to solve this incredibly complex problem we are faced with and to develop workable plans, it will likely take a large collective of brilliant minds. I certainly cannot do it myself, and I certainly cannot think of all of the ideas myself. Nor can Peter Joseph. Nor can any single individual working within The Venus Project, The Zeitgeist Movement, or within any organization seeking to bring a Resource-Based Economy to life. Keep in mind, it took over 100,000 people just to develop the atomic bomb. It stands to reason that it would take considerably more to construct an entirely new economy.

Needless to say, in a cheesy way, we need you! That is, if you agree that change is necessary. We need your knowledge, skills, ideas, and expertise in helping us solve the trillion-dollar question!

# *11* B-YUP, B-YUP, THAT'S ALL FOLKS!

To conclude this book, an impassioned and inspiring speech is not coming from me. I think at this point, you would recognize how forced and contrived it is, and it wouldn't fit the tone I've adhered to. Hopefully with food for thought and maybe even altered perspectives, you already feel emboldened and inspired without needing phony words of wisdom. Nevertheless, I will say one or two more things before we part ways.

Ask yourself what kind of world you want to live in, and then ask yourself what steps need to be taken to get there.

Like I said, at some point in human history, people will realize money is an unnecessary part of the resource-allocation process and in human motivation, and at some point, the global community will abandon it. As long as we don't cause our own extinction, a moneyless society that leans heavily on automated systems is inevitable. And in that future system, when its inhabitants look back on this period of human existence, they will ask, "Dad, why did they let people starve when they had the means to feed them?" And dads will answer with pursed lips, "I honestly don't know sweetie. I guess it was a barbaric and primitive time."

Though money will eventually be done away with, it is my belief that such a transition is unlikely to happen in my lifetime. And though it is unfortunate as I would love to see the world a Resource-Based Economy proposes, I am at peace with whatever happens, which is part of the vicarious deathbed moment I experienced with my Kait. It is simply important to me that I throw my two cents into The Pit before I pass on to the next phase of life. This book might be buried in the rubble of forgotten books, or it might go on to help a number of people. Either way, no matter how futile my efforts might be in the end, I am left feeling lighter as all of these weighty thoughts have finally been purged from my system.

And you know, if I wanted to pretend I was a real writer, I would bring this story around full circle and wrap it up in a tight little bow by addressing that pernicious itch that started this text 400 pages ago. But I'm not going to do that because I'm not a real writer, and the itch persists.

Thank you for reading and entertaining my thoughts! I understand you might disagree with much of what I have to say, though hopefully you found some content resonated with you. If you find yourself with feathers ruffled and have some vitriol to spew my way, I look forward to hearing your thoughts. I look forward to receiving it and the healthy discourse that might follow. Remember, I am neither right, nor wrong. You are neither right, nor wrong. We are just mere mortals with tiny monkey brains trying to make sense of an infinitely complex world. None of us have all the answers, and no one can say what is best for you. We need the differing perspectives, backgrounds, and knowledge sets of everyone. Even if you disagree with my conclusions, just know that my intentions, at least in my mind, are good. This is the cheesiest thing I am going to say in this book, but, although I fall victim to my human impulses, like anger and disgust, I try to approach the world with love, understanding, and acceptance rather than hate, judgment, and intolerance, because I know that although the word and idea of love might be gooey and unmanly, it promotes good health and is the only way to truly live an enriched and fulfilled life; hate and perpetual anger damage health and leave one empty and in pain – elementary principles I have absorbed through life experience. Anyway, I genuinely care about you and your wellbeing. I don't want fame, fortune, or control. I just want to see, partly in a selfish way, a reduction in crime, poverty, war, violence, ecological degradation, exploitation, distrust, diseases, stress, suffering, and all of the negativity that money encourages. And frankly, I'm just tired of and no longer have interest in playing the game and trying to claw my way out of The Pit. A Resource-Based Economy, to me, is not the perfect answer, but it is an appropriate step in achieving my reasonable desires.

Beyond this book, do your own research, search your own inner wisdom, and come to your own conclusions. Don't believe everything I say just because my name is listed on the cover. Listen to your own inner thoughts. To do that, in order to know how you really think and feel about economic topics, the current state of affairs, and life in general, you will have to quiet the external noises (as mentioned in Chapter 2) – which includes media, friends, family, propaganda, movies, and marketing that try to get you to think the way they want you to think. Trust your own wisdom. Trust your own thoughts that derive from your own unique knowledge, observations, and life experiences. Deep down, I think we all have a strong sense of "right" and "wrong." Shut out the mind-deafening noises and trust that inherent sense!

Anyway, it's been fun. Stay safe and stay humble! Catch you on the flippity-flip! Over and out!

"Be not like dumb, driven cattle! Be a hero in the strife!" – A Psalm of Life – Henry Wadsworth Longfellow

# APPENDIX A: WAR

To give you an idea of alternative motives that push local bureaucrats that falsely label themselves as Americans to send military forces to foreign countries, I have included two brief summaries that coincide with the list of American Interventions provided in Chapter 6.4. Because this is not a book about war, I will provide the remaining summaries on my website – travolutionblog.com.

To recap, I posit that when individual men send American troops to foreign lands, it is often not for the reasons that they would lead the public to believe. Instead, the real reasons often have to do with money, resources, power, and personal gain for the ruling classes. Let's start with American involvement in Haiti in the early-20th century.

## HAITI → 1915-1934

The US Military had a consistent presence in Haiti in the late-1800s and into the early-1900s, as the Navy often intervened in local conflict. However, it wasn't until 1915 when US diplomats sent Marines down to the small country that they had a more permanent presence. Leading up to the initial invasion of Haiti, Admiral William Deville Bundy was told the reason was to "protect American and foreign" business interests; however, the American public was led to believe that noble US leaders were intent on bringing peace and order back to a country in chaos. So, what led to the US occupation of Haiti? Well, there were three main factors.

First, Haiti wasn't the most stable country at the turn of the century. The tiny nation was fraught with civil clashes, poverty, and a revolving door of leaders who usually had their careers cut short by a bloody death – much of this tumult, however, was blamed on foreign interference. Second, World War I was underway, and Woodrow Wilson and United States leaders feared Germany would invade Haiti with the intent of setting up a military base.[1]

Third, and arguably most important, the United States had private businesses established in Haiti, like the Haitian-American Sugar Company and National City Bank, and it was imperative those interests were adequately protected.[2,3] By 1911, National City Bank, controlled by the likes of Percy Avery Rockefeller and Frank Vanderlip of Federal Reserve lore, acquired control of Banque National d'Haiti, the small country's treasury and only commercial bank.[4,5] Through this maneuver, the Haitian national bank simply became another branch of National City Bank, and the giant New York firm slid in as the nation's new treasurer.

Also, in the early-20$^{th}$ century the Haitian government had been taking out many loans from American, and French, interests, consequently creating a debt that became difficult for the Haitians to manage, and they began struggling to make their payments. Thus, much of the country's national income was diverted away from building infrastructure and was instead filtered toward paying off foreign creditors, leading to resentment and unrest amongst the population. With frustrations growing in Haiti, American interests feared that if an anti-American leader were installed as President of the Caribbean nation, the banks would stop seeing payments on their loans and Haiti would halt American investments.

So, in 1915 Woodrow Wilson ordered US Marines to invade Haiti. Meeting little resistance, the Marines swiftly took hold of the National Palace and the nation's bank, where they seized $500,000 and sent it to New York.[6] For the next 20 years, American forces occupied the tiny nation, and while many Haitians lost their lives, the path was paved for National City Bank to control Haitian finances and multiple arms of its economy. The American banking firm subsequently took 40% of Haiti's wealth and channeled it toward paying off the country's debts.[7] Though the Haitian people were in gross disapproval of their country's wealth being diverted to foreign interests rather than toward developing their local economy, they were virtually powerless as US Marines squashed any sort of protests or revolts. Many Haitian dissenters were killed or abused. The American presence might have caused much anger and strife in Haiti, but it certainly made a few boys at National City Bank and other firms quite happy. Oh, and how could I forget – American citizens got to pay for their military to occupy Haiti while also receiving little to no direct benefit. Seems like an even trade. You cover the expenses, P.A. Rockefeller receives the revenues. Of course, I guess we do enjoy the benefits of lower prices at the expense of others' prosperity.

In his 1920 essay titled *Self-Determining Haiti*, published in The Nation, James Weldon Johnson would say in part, "To know the reasons for the present political situation in Haiti, to understand why the United States landed and has for five years maintained military forces in that country, why some three thousand Haitian men, women, and children have been shot down by American rifles and machine guns, it is necessary, among other things, to know that the National City Bank of New York is very much interested in Haiti. It is necessary to know that the National City Bank controls the National Bank of Haiti and is the depository for all of the Haitian national funds that are being collected by American officials…"[8]

As usual, a few people benefited financially while the majority were left to struggle. It wasn't until 1934 that Franklin D. Roosevelt ordered the removal of US Marines from Haiti, however, America controlled the country's finances until 1947. Not to make any excuses for any group's hardships, and I know other factors play a role, but I would imagine it might be somewhat difficult to pull oneself out of being a "shit hole" country if more powerful forces have continually impeded your attempts at operating autonomously.

## NICARAGUA → 1910-1933

In 1910, Smedley Butler arrived in Nicaragua with 250 marines.[9] And between 1912 and 1933, US Marines were a mainstay in the Central American country, which included reinforcements and the bombing of the Nicaraguan city of Ocotal in 1927.[10] So what led to US involvement and subsequent occupation?

American officials justified the intervention to the American public as a quest to remove Nicaragua's evil tyrant president, Jose Santos Zelaya, from office and to pacify the belligerent nation. However, the situation was a bit more complicated than that, as one would expect.

In the years leading up to US military involvement, Nicaragua had been competing with Panama in hopes of luring United States investors into their country to build a canal connecting the Pacific and Atlantic Oceans.[11] For various reasons, the United States ended up choosing Panama as its canal host. Understanding the profit potential of having an artificial waterway in their country, the Nicaraguan president, Zelaya, then began negotiating with Germany and Japan to give them the rights to build a competing canal.[12] This was no bueno for the United States. Not only would a competing canal cut into revenues, but the US was also competing against Germany for control over various Caribbean ports.

In addition to negotiating canal terms with competing countries, Zelaya also began providing aid to groups in neighboring Central American countries with ambitions of reuniting the divided, resource-rich nations.[13] Once again, this wasn't good for the United States. Zelaya's moves had the potential to lead to war between the small countries, which would threaten the Panama Canal project and threaten other US business interests, so the Nicaraguan leader had to be removed.

The US subsequently labeled Zelaya as a danger to peace in Central America, and began its maneuvering by controlling and inhibiting foreign investment into the country, which harmed Nicaragua's economy, and by supporting Zelaya's opposition. In 1909, United States officials were handed an opportunity to send forces to Nicaragua when Zelaya captured and executed two American citizens amongst a number of local rebels.[14] Thus, US military forces were sent to intervene in December of 1909, and the pressures led Zelaya to give up his position as Nicaragua's president, and he fled the country. His successor, Jose Madriz, didn't even last a year in the position as pressure from the US and rebel forces pushed him out in the summer of 1910.[15] This began a revolving door of US-backed, conservative leaders in Nicaragua, ones who were friendly to US banking and business interests.

In 1912, unrest amongst the Nicaraguan population began to mount, as its citizens were angry with the new leadership for allegedly selling out to New York bankers.[16] When opposing forces, led by conservative Luis Mena, rebelled against the US-backed regime of Adolfo Diaz, the US Secretary of State Philander Knox requested military support from President Taft; after all, they were interfering with American businesses, like those of Brown Brothers & Company and J & W Seligman & Company.[17]

Consequently, over 1,000 US Marines, including Smedley Butler, landed in Nicaragua in 1912, and they promptly secured the country for Diaz to remain as leader.[18] The victory not only protected American business interests and gave them much control over the country's economic affairs, but it also led to the ratification of the Bryan-Chamorro Treaty in 1916.[19] This act gave the US exclusive rights to build a canal in Nicaragua, and though they hadn't intended on building a waterway there, it prevented other countries from doing so, which was crucial to the US maintaining financial and political power in the region.

After fighting seized, the US withdrew a large share of Marines from the small country, but several remained throughout the next two decades. A large faction of Nicaraguans continued to feel bitter and angry toward the US and its "puppet" leaders filtering in and out of Nicaraguan office. They felt taken advantage of. Resentment toward US-supported leadership eventually culminated into a rebellion and civil war in 1927, leading to a renewed influx of US military forces. Over 2,000 US Marines intervened in the fighting, which included the Battle of Ocotal, where several bombs were dropped from American aircraft onto Nicaraguan rebels.[20] The insurgents' resolve remained strong, however, as they continued to fight until the US Marines were finally withdrawn in 1933.

Though US intervention led to US casualties, many Nicaraguan deaths, left Nicaragua in disarray and led to the brutal, 40-year long dictatorship of the Somoza regime, President Zelaya was removed from office in favor of US-friendly leaders, the safety of American business interests were protected, Brown Brothers & Co and J & W Seligman & Co were able to secure investments in the National Bank of Nicaragua and the Pacific Railway of Nicaragua, and the US procured the rights to a canal for only $3 million through the Bryan-Chamorro Treaty, which protected their project in Panama. The occupation was a win for a few individuals, as usual.

# APPENDIX B: *MASLOW & HULL - HUMAN BEHAVIOR*

I reference Abraham Maslow and his Hierarchy of Needs quite often in this text. At one point, the write-up below was included in the section discussing Human Motivation, but I later decided to remove it to help the chapter flow better. However, I feel as though some people might find this omitted section somewhat informative (although it is brief), so I decided to include parts of it here in Appendix B.

Psychologists, behavioral scientists, evolutionary biologists, scholars, and scores of other curious minds have devoted years to studying and dissecting human behavior in hopes of discovering what ultimately drives us to action. In 1943 Abraham H. Maslow, the well-known 20th century psychologist, proposed his Hierarchy of Needs theory in an attempt to explain human drives and motivation.[1] And though he certainly wasn't the first to hypothesize sources of human motivation, his five-tiered approach seems to have stuck, as it is widely referenced to this day.

Maslow's Hierarchy of Needs is a concept that places human needs in an order of priority, into a hierarchy. And though he himself admits his theory isn't an all-or-nothing, rigid concept, it provides a good baseline, a good jumping off point for analyzing behavior. The needs go in order as follows, starting with highest priority:

1. Physiological Needs
2. Safety Needs
3. Love and Sense of Belonging

4. Self-Esteem Needs
5. Self-Actualization Needs
6. Self-Transcendence Needs (introduced later by Maslow)

According to Maslow, once higher needs are satisfied, humans are able to move on to the next level of the Hierarchy and work on satisfying the next need in the chain. Anyone who has studied Maslow's theory has more than likely seen it visualized as a pyramid of needs.

At the bottom level, the most basic and foundational level, are the *Physiological Needs*, which consist of hunger, thirst, shelter, etc. The physiological needs are the first that need to be satisfied before a human feels driven to obtain anything else. For instance, in the most extreme case where a person is missing everything – food, safety, love, esteem – he will strive for food and water before all else. Sex, painting, or studying becomes secondary when a man's belly aches of hunger. In a 1950 study, Ancel Keys and his team took a group of 36 men and cut their food intake.[2] Not only did the men become listless and apathetic to conserve energy, but the men obsessed over food. Their every thought and conversation were consumed by rich feasts and delectable treats – nothing else mattered. Again, in the most extreme cases where a man is deprived of everything, he will want food first.

Next up on the pyramid are the *Safety Needs*, which is self-explanatory. It is simply our need to feel safe, to feel that the world is organized, structured, and predictable. The need for *Love and Belonging* follow the safety needs, which consist of our need to cultivate relationships – to love and be loved in return, to be socially accepted, to feel a sense of connectedness and not feel lonely. The *Self-Esteem Needs* come in at number four, which entails the need for self-respect, achievement, respect from others, prestige, etc. It includes the need to feel like one matters in the world, like he has importance. Thwarting these needs leads to harmful feelings of inferiority, helplessness, and weakness. And last on the *original* hierarchy is the *Self-Actualization Needs*, or self-fulfillment. Once all other needs are satisfied, Maslow observes, people become discontent and restless. From that restlessness emerges a need to live up to one's full, unique potential. "What a man can be, he must be." And what a person strives to be varies from individual to individual. One person might be driven to simply be a good mother. Another might be driven to study biology. Others might be driven to woodworking, sports, writing, inventing, etc.

And the need with the lowest priority, though not least in importance, is the *Self-Transcendence Need.* This final need on the totem pole, which Maslow introduced later in his life, includes man's search for a higher meaning. At the self-transcendence level, he strives to discover a purpose greater than himself.

Unfortunately, according to Maslow, it is difficult to study the levels of Self-Actualization and Self-Transcendence because most of society is constantly working to satisfy the more basic survival needs.

Again, the needs aren't fixed, per se, nor do they need to be completely satisfied before one moves on to higher-level needs. People often work toward fulfilling multiple needs at the same time. For instance, people might spend some of their time working on obtaining Love and some of their time working on Self-Esteem without satisfying one or the other first. Maslow's list merely provides a solid framework for studying human behavior and understanding what motivates us.

A second hypothesis that has stood the test of time in establishing a sturdy foundation for analyzing human motivation is Clark Hull's Drive Reduction Theory (DRT), introduced around the same time as Maslow's Hierarchy of Needs, and further expanded upon by colleague Kenneth Spence.[3] Drive Reduction Theory takes a more biological approach in attempting to explain human motivation, its primary concept being that the need to reduce various drives, or inner urges, is what causes humans to feel motivated. The theory builds upon the idea that humans have an internal need to maintain physiological homeostasis – balance – and once our bodies are thrown out of homeostasis, we are then driven to take an action that returns us to our balanced state of being. For example, if our body is deprived of nutrients, we become hungry, which activates our drive to find food and eat for the purpose of restoring nutrients to the body. Then, once we eat and the body is restored to a state of equilibrium, that drive to eat goes away. The same principle has been applied to the state of boredom, which can be considered a form of deprivation. When we feel bored, we become driven to seek out stimulation. Once we find adequate stimulation and our unique Optimal Arousal Level is reached, we no longer feel bored, and the drive to seek out stimuli is reduced – hence Drive Reduction Theory.

# APPENDIX B: MASLOW

Though both theories provide a wonderful baseline for modern researchers to analyze human motivation, and though both are widely referenced to this day, neither theory fully explains the breadth of our behavior – as Maslow concedes. Though we often act like animals, we are far more complex than every other known organism. We are more than biological machines responding to physiological stimuli. And simply reducing human behavior to biological impulses, to stimulus and response, fails to capture the full spectrum of what makes us tick, as we often take on challenges that do not meet survival needs and sometimes even put us in danger, e.g., rock climbing.

Other behavioral researchers whose works I found helpful were Mihaly Csikszentmihalyi, Edward Deci, Richard Ryan, Robert Sapolsky, Albert Bandura, B.F. Skinner, Teresa Amabile, Solomon Asch, Richard Solomon, James Gilligan, among many others.

# ENDNOTES


Chapter 1 – Seeds of Delusion (Preface)

1. G.K. Chesterton, The Everlasting Man (London: Hodder & Stoughton Limited, 1927), p. 297.

Chapter 2 – The Appetizer (Introduction)

1. "United States Hunger Facts, Poverty Facts 2016." World Hunger News. Hunger Notes, March 20, 2020. https://www.worldhunger.org/hunger-in-america-united-states-hunger-poverty-facts-2018/.
2. "Hunger Deprives Our Kids of More than Just Food." Feeding America, 2017. https://www.feedingamerica.org/hunger-in-america/child-hunger-facts.
3. "Food Waste FAQs." USDA. United States Department of Agriculture. Accessed December 14, 2020. https://www.usda.gov/foodwaste/faqs.
4. "World Child Hunger Facts - World Hunger Education." World Hunger News. Hunger Notes, July 28, 2018. https://www.worldhunger.org/world-child-hunger-facts/#:~:text=World%20Child%20Hunger%20Facts.%20Approximately%203.1%20million%20children,vulnerable%20to%20illness%20and%20exacerbate%20disease%20%28UNICEF%2C%202018a%29.
5. Friedrich Wilhelm Nietzsche and Helen Zimmern. Essay. In *Beyond Good and Evil: Prelude to a Philosophy of the Future*, p. 87. Edinburgh: T.N. Foulis, 1909.

Chapter 3 – Money's Purpose

1. Sarah Jacobs, "Just Nine of the World's Richest Men Have More Combined Wealth than the Poorest 4 Billion People," The Independent (Business Insider, January 17, 2018), https://www.independent.co.uk/news/world/richest-billionaires-combined-wealth-jeff-bezos-bill-gates-warren-buffett-mark-zuckerberg-carlos-slim-wealth-a8163621.html.
2. Andrea Tucker, "National Milk Producers Federation Class Action Lawsuit Settlement Pending," Legal Reader, September 6, 2016,

https://www.legalreader.com/national-milk-producers-federation-class-action-lawsuit-settlement-pending/.
3. Matthew Edwards v. National Milk Producers Federation (United States District Court, Northern District of California August 25, 2015), Case No. 11-cv-04766-JSW.
4. "United States Hunger Facts, Poverty Facts 2016." World Hunger News. Hunger Notes, March 20, 2020. https://www.worldhunger.org/hunger-in-america-united-states-hunger-poverty-facts-2018/.
5. "Hunger Deprives Our Kids of More than Just Food." Feeding America, 2017. https://www.feedingamerica.org/hunger-in-america/child-hunger-facts.
6. "Food Waste FAQs." USDA. United States Department of Agriculture. Accessed December 14, 2020. https://www.usda.gov/foodwaste/faqs.
7. Brad Sylvester, "FACT CHECK: Are There More Than 633,000 Homeless People And 13.9 Million Vacant Homes In The US?," Check Your Fact, December 24, 2019, https://checkyourfact.com/2019/12/24/fact-check-633000-homeless-million-vacant-homes/.

Chapter 4 – Bird's-Eye View

1. Quoted by Senator Robert L. Owen, National Economy and the Banking System of the United States, Washington D.C.: US Government Printing Office, 1939, 105, http://www.archive.org/details/NationalEconomyAndTheBankingSystemOfTheUnited- States
2. Letter to Col. Edward Mandell House (21 November 1933); Franklin D. Roosevelt and Elliott Roosevelt, "F.D.R. / His Personal Letters," in *F.D.R. / His Personal Letters* (NY: Duell, Sloan, and Pearce, 1947), p. 373.
3. "Forced Labour, Modern Slavery and Human Trafficking," International Labour Organization, 2016, https://www.ilo.org/global/topics/forced-labour/lang--en/index.htm.
4. Ann M. Simmons, "There Are More Slaves Now than Any Time in Human History ," New York Daily News, September 19, 2017, https://www.nydailynews.com/news/world/slaves-time-human-history-article-1.3506975.
5. John Kenneth Galbraith, "Money: Whence It Came, Where It Went," in *Money: Whence It Came, Where It Went* (Boston: Houghton Mifflin, 1975), p. 5.
6. Michael J. Sandel, *Democracy's Discontent: America in Search of Public Philosophy* (Cambridge, MA: The Belknap Press of Harvard University Press, 2001).
7. Frederick Douglass, Philip S. Foner, and Yuval Taylor, *Frederick Douglass: Selected Speeches and Writings* (Chicago: Lawrence Hill Books, 2000), p. 676.

Chapter 4.2 – Company Towns

1. Hardy Green, *The Company Town: the Industrial Edens and Satanic Mills That Shaped the American Economy* (New York: Basic Books, 2012).

2. Howard Zinn and Anthony Arnove, "A People's History of the United States," in *A People's History of the United States* (New York, NY: Harper, an imprint of HarperCollinsPublishers, 2017), pp. 354-357.
3. George S. McGovern and Leonard F. Guttridge, *The Great Coalfield War* (Boulder, CO: NetLibrary, Inc., 1999).

Chapter 4.3 – Lies and War

1. H.L. Mencken, Minority Report: H.L. Mencken's Notebooks (New York: Alfred A Knopf, 1956), p. 247.
2. Kenneth R. Timmerman, *The Death Lobby: How the West Armed Iraq* (London: Bantam Books, 1992).
3. Richard Sale, "Exclusive: Saddam Key in Early CIA Plot," UPI (Defense News, April 10, 2003), https://www.upi.com/Defense-News/2003/04/10/Exclusive-Saddam-key-in-early-CIA-plot/65571050017416/.
4. Roger Morris, "A Tyrant 40 Years in the Making," The New York Times, March 14, 2003, https://www.nytimes.com/2003/03/14/opinion/a-tyrant-40-years-in-the-making.html.
5. History.com Editors, "Iraq Invades Kuwait," History.com (A&E Television Networks, November 24, 2009), https://www.history.com/this-day-in-history/iraq-invades-kuwait.
6. "Nayirah Testimony," Wikipedia (Wikimedia Foundation, February 25, 2021), https://en.wikipedia.org/wiki/Nayirah_testimony#cite_note-jury-41.
7. "Deception on Capitol Hill," The New York Times, January 15, 1992, https://www.nytimes.com/1992/01/15/opinion/deception-on-capitol-hill.html.
8. "How PR Sold the War in the Persian Gulf," PR Watch, June 5, 2013, https://prwatch.org/books/tsigfy10.html#74.
9. James E. Grunig, "Public Relations and International Affairs: Effects, Ethics and Responsibility." Journal of International Affairs 47, no. 1 (1993): 137-62. Accessed March 18, 2021. http://www.jstor.org/stable/24357090.
10. Patricia Bauer, "Gulf of Tonkin incident." *Encyclopedia Britannica*, July 26, 2020. https://www.britannica.com/event/Gulf-of-Tonkin-incident.
11. Jeff Cohen and Norman Solomon, "30-Year Anniversary: Tonkin Gulf Lie Launched Vietnam War," FAIR (Fairness & Accuracy In Reporting, July 27, 1994), https://fair.org/media-beat-column/30-year-anniversary-tonkin-gulf-lie-launched-vietnam-war/#:~:text=In%201965%2C%20Lyndon%20Johnson%20commented%3A%20"For%20all%20I,American%20people%20last%20night%20with%20the%20somber%20facts.
12. San Antonio Express-News, "Release of LBJ Tapes Adds to Tonkin Debate," The Baltimore Sun, August 4, 2002, https://www.baltimoresun.com/news/bs-xpm-2002-08-04-0208040083-story.html.
13. Jim Stockdale and Sybil Stockdale, *In Love and War: The Story of a Family's Ordeal and Sacrifice During the Vietnam Years*, ed. Sybil Stockdale, 1st Edition (Harper & Row, 1984), pp. 20-21.

14. Joint Chiefs of Staff, US Department of Defense, "Justification for US Military Intervention in Cuba (TS)," March 13, 1962
15. Ibid., pg. 2.
16. Ibid., pg. 8-9.
17. Ibid., pg. 8-9.
18. Robert H. Ferrell, "The Mukden Incident: September 18-19, 1931." The Journal of Modern History 27, no. 1 (1955): 66-72. Accessed March 18, 2021. http://www.jstor.org/stable/1877701.
19. Peter Duus, John W. Hall, Marius B. Jansen, Madoka Kanai, and Denis Twitchett, *The Cambridge History of Japan: Volume 6, The Twentieth Century*, (The Cambridge University Press, 1989), pp. 290-298.
20. "The Trial of German Major War Criminals: Proceedings of the International Military Tribunal Sitting at Nuremberg Germany," Volume 4, Twenty-Fourth Day, Avalon Project - Documents in Law, History and Diplomacy, December 20, 1945, https://avalon.law.yale.edu/imt/12-20-45.asp.
21. Christopher Ailsby, The Third Reich: Day by Day, (Zenith Imprint, 2001), pp. 111-113.
22. Alfred de Zayas, (2007) "The Istanbul Pogrom of 6–7 September 1955 in the Light of International Law," Genocide Studies and Prevention: An International Journal: Vol. 2: Iss. 2: Article 4 (2007), p. 138, https://scholarcommons.usf.edu/gsp/vol2/iss2/4.
23. Tacitus, *The Annals: Book XV*. 109 AD.
24. Cassius Dio, *Roman History: Book LXII*.
25. History.com Editors, "Nero's Rome Burns," History.com (A&E Television Networks, November 13, 2009), https://www.history.com/this-day-in-history/neros-rome-burns.


Chapter 4.4 – JDR & Competition


1. Letter from J.N. Camden to J.D. Rockefeller (18 July 1876), Allan Nevins, *Allan Nevins Papers*, (Butler Library, Columbia University, New York, New York, B108 F3).
2. Ron Chernow, *Titan: the Life of John D. Rockefeller, Sr*, (New York: Vintage Books, 1998).
3. Letter from J.D. Rockefeller to J.N. Camden (4 February 1878), Allan Nevins, *Allan Nevins Papers*, (Butler Library, Columbia University, New York, New York, B108 F3).
4. Grant Segall, *John D. Rockefeller: Anointed with Oil (Oxford Portraits)*, (Oxford University Press, USA, 2001).
5. The Saturday Evening Post, October 21, 1911 – A phrase mothers would yell to their children.
6. Campbell R. McConnell and Stanley L. Brue, *Economics: Principles, Problems, and Policies* (Boston, MA: McGraw-Hill, 2005), p. 456.
7. Tobias Kretschmer, "De Beers and Beyond: The History of the International Diamond Cartel," New York University, October 15, 2003.

Chapter 4.5 – Democracy?

1. "Hylan Adds Pinchot to Presidency List; Foresees a Revolt," *New York Times*, December 10, 1922.
2. "From John Adams to Benjamin Rush (27 December 1810)," Founders Online, National Archives, https://founders.archives.gov/documents/Adams/99-02-02-5585.
3. Robert Yates, John Lansing, and Luther Martin, *Secret Proceedings and Debates of the Convention Assembled at Philadelphia, in the Year 1787, for the Purpose of Forming the Constitution of the United States of America* (Albany: Printed by Websters and Skinners, 1821), pp. 144-145.
4. Aristotle and William Lambert Newman, *The Politics of Aristotle: with an Introd., Two Prefatory Essays and Notes Critical and Explanatory, by W.L. Newman* (Oxford: Clarendon Press, 1887), p. 247.
5. Ibid., p. 499.
6. Robert Yates, *Notes of the Secret Debates of the Federal Convention of 1787, Taken by the Late Hon Robert Yates, Chief Justice of the State of New York, and One of the Delegates from That State to the Said Convention*, May 30, 1787.
7. Erin Duffin, "Total Lobbying Spending U.S. 1998-2020," Statista, March 4, 2021, https://www.statista.com/statistics/257337/total-lobbying-spending-in-the-us/.
8. Drew Griffin and David Fitzpatrick, "Politicians Live It up and Have the Lobbyists Pay," CNN Politics (Cable News Network, October 30, 2014), https://www.cnn.com/2014/10/29/politics/politicians-play-lobbyists-pay/index.html.
9. Martin Gilens and Benjamin I. Page, "Testing Theories of American Politics: Elites, Interest Groups, and Average Citizens," *Perspectives on Politics* 12, no. 3 (2014): pp. 564-581, https://doi.org/10.1017/s1537592714001595.
10. Ibid.
11. Ibid.
12. "2020 Presidential Election Results," CNN (Cable News Network, 2020), https://www.cnn.com/election/2020/results/president.
13. Albert Bandura, Dorothea Ross, and Sheila A. Ross, "Transmission of Aggression through Imitation of Aggressive Models.," *The Journal of Abnormal and Social Psychology* 63, no. 3 (1961): pp. 575-582, https://doi.org/10.1037/h0045925.

Chapter 5 – Grand Maester: The "Federal" Reserve

1. The NewsHour with Jim Lehrer, "Alan Greenspan Interview with Jim Lehrer," September 18, 2007.
2. Louis McFadden, "Congressman McFadden on the Federal Reserve Corporation, Remarks in Congress, 1934, An Astounding Exposure," (Boston, MA: Forum Publishing Company, 1934), p. 4.
3. Congressional Record, House 81:2528, March 19, 1937, Congressman Charles G. Binderup of Nebraska attributed the quote to Henry Ford during a House of Representatives session.

# ENDNOTES


4. "Board of Governors of the Federal Reserve System," Federal Reserve Board - About the Fed, March 2, 2021, https://www.federalreserve.gov/aboutthefed.htm.
5. Board of Governors of the Federal Reserve System, "The Federal Reserve System Purposes & Functions," 10th Edition, (Federal Reserve System Publication, 2016), p. 4
6. "Gold Vault: Learn about the Federal Reserve Bank of New York's Gold Vault," Federal Reserve Bank of New York, accessed January 10, 2021, https://www.newyorkfed.org/aboutthefed/goldvault.html.
7. "12 U.S. Code § 241: Creation; Membership; Compensation and Expenses," Legal Information Institute (Cornell Law School, n.d.), https://www.law.cornell.edu/uscode/text/12/241.
8. Kimberly Amadeo, "Who Really Owns the World's Most Powerful Central Bank?," The Balance, February 7, 2020, https://www.thebalance.com/who-owns-the-federal-reserve-3305974.
9. Board of Governors of the Federal Reserve System, "The Federal Reserve System Purposes & Functions," 10th Edition, (Federal Reserve System Publication, 2016), p. 1
10. "Who Owns the Federal Reserve Banks?," Making Sense of the Federal Reserve (Federal Reserve Bank of St. Louis, n.d.), https://www.stlouisfed.org/in-plain-english/who-owns-the-federal-reserve-banks.
11. Board of Governors of the Federal Reserve System, "The Federal Reserve System Purposes & Functions," 10th Edition, (Federal Reserve System Publication, 2016), p. 6
12. *Putting it Simply – The Federal Reserve*, Public Services Department, (Federal Reserve Bank of Boston, 1982).
13. "About the BEP," U.S. Bureau of Engraving and Printing (US Department of Treasury), accessed January 10, 2021, https://www.moneyfactory.gov/about.html.
14. "Coin Production," United States Mint, accessed January 10, 2021, https://www.usmint.gov/learn/history/coin-production.
15. Adam Hayes, "Open Market Operations (OMO)," Investopedia, October 9, 2020, https://www.investopedia.com/terms/o/openmarketoperations.asp#citation-1.
16. *Modern Money Mechanics* (Chicago, IL: Federal Reserve Bank of Chicago, 1971).
17. John Maynard Keynes, *The Economic Consequences of Peace* (New York, NY: Harcourt, Brace and Howe, 1920), p. 236.
18. *Putting it Simply – The Federal Reserve*, Public Services Department, (Federal Reserve Bank of Boston, 1982).
19. *Modern Money Mechanics* (Chicago, IL: Federal Reserve Bank of Chicago, 1971).
20. "Calculate the Value of $1.00 in 1960," Dollar Times, accessed January 11, 2021, https://www.dollartimes.com/inflation/inflation.php?amount=1&year=1960.
21. Drew DeSilver, "For Most Americans, Real Wages Have Barely Budged in Decades," Pew Research Center, August 7, 2018,

https://www.pewresearch.org/fact-tank/2018/08/07/for-most-us-workers-real-wages-have-barely-budged-for-decades/.

22. Elise Gould, "Why America's Workers Need Faster Wage Growth-And What We Can Do About It," Economic Policy Institute, August 27, 2014, https://www.epi.org/publication/why-americas-workers-need-faster-wage-growth/.
23. Lawrence Mishel, Elise Gould, and Josh Bivens, "Wage Stagnation in Nine Charts," Economic Policy Institute, January 6, 2015, https://www.epi.org/publication/charting-wage-stagnation/.
24. Alan Greenspan, Interviewed by David Gregory, *Meet the Press*, (NBC News, August 7, 2011).
25. Kimberly Amadeo, "Why the US Dollar is the Global Currency," The Balance, July 23, 2020, https://www.thebalance.com/world-currency-3305931.
26. Ibid.
27. William Dowell, "Foreign Exchange: Saddam Turns His Back on Greenbacks," Time (Time Inc., November 13, 2000), http://content.time.com/time/subscriber/article/0,33009,998512,00.html.
28. Charles Recknagel, "Iraq: Baghdad Moves To Euro," RadioFreeEurope/RadioLiberty, November 1, 2000, https://www.rferl.org/a/1095057.html.
29. Ron Paul, "Why the US Hates Iraq, Iran, and Venezuela," Speech, LewRockwell.com, February 17, 2006, https://www.lewrockwell.com/2006/02/ron-paul/why-the-us-hates-iraq-iran-and-venezuela/.
30. Brad Hoff, "Hillary Emails Reveal True Motive for Libya Intervention," Foreign Policy Journal, January 6, 2016, https://www.foreignpolicyjournal.com/2016/01/06/new-hillary-emails-reveal-true-motive-for-libya-intervention/.
31. Alex Newman, "Gadhafi's Gold-Money Plan Would Have Devastated Dollar," The New American, November 11, 2011, https://thenewamerican.com/gadhafi-s-gold-money-plan-would-have-devastated-dollar/.
32. J. Peter Grace, "President's Private Sector Survey on Cost Control, A Report to the President," Volume I of II, Approved by the Executive Committee, January 15, 1984.
33. "Does the Federal Reserve Ever Get Audited?," Board of Governors of the Federal Reserve System, accessed January 10, 2021, https://www.federalreserve.gov/faqs/about_12784.htm.
34. Seth Lipsky, "Why Does the Federal Reserve Fear a Real Audit?," New York Post, February 26, 2015, https://nypost.com/2015/02/26/why-does-the-federal-reserve-fear-a-real-audit/.
35. Federal Banking Agency Audit Act, Pub. L. 95-320, 95$^{th}$ Congress, 92 Stat. 391 (July 21, 1978), Amendment of Accounting and Auditing Act of 1950, https://uscode.house.gov/statutes/pl/95/320.pdf.
36. Michael O'Brien, "Report: Fed Rejects Audit by Treasury," TheHill, September 21, 2009, https://thehill.com/blogs/blog-briefing-room/news/59585-report-fed-rejects-audit-by-treasury.

37. David Harrison, "Senate Defeats 'Audit the Fed' Bill," The Wall Street Journal (Dow Jones & Company, January 12, 2016), https://www.wsj.com/articles/senate-defeats-audit-the-fed-bill-1452630386.
38. Woodrow Wilson and William E. Leuchtenburg, *The New Freedom: a Call for the Emancipation of the Generous Energies of a People* (Englewood Cliffs, NJ: Prentice-Hall, 1961), p. 24.
39. "U.S. National Debt Clock : Real Time," US Debt Clock.org, accessed January 10, 2021, https://usdebtclock.org/.
40. "United States Money Supply M2," United States Money Supply M2 - 1959-2021 Data (Trading Economics), accessed January 10, 2021, https://tradingeconomics.com/united-states/money-supply-m2.
41. Anneken Tappe, "The World Is Drowning in Debt," CNN (Cable News Network, January 14, 2020), https://www.cnn.com/2020/01/13/economy/global-debt-record/index.html.
42. Jeff Desjardins, "All of the World's Money and Markets in One Visualization," Visual Capitalist, May 27, 2020, https://www.visualcapitalist.com/all-of-the-worlds-money-and-markets-in-one-visualization-2020/.

Chapter 5.1 – A Brief History of the Fed

1. John Adams letter to John Taylor, of Caroline (12 March 1819), *The Works of John Adams, Second President of the United States*, Volume 10, (Brown Little, 1856), p. 375, https://founders.archives.gov/?q=Project%3A%22Adams%20Papers%22john%20taylor&s=1211311113&r=23
2. Theodore Roosevelt, "The Progressive Covenant with the People," Speech, August 1912, https://www.loc.gov/item/99391565/.
3. G. Edward Griffin, *The Creature from Jekyll Island: a Second Look at the Federal Reserve,* (Westlake Village, CA: American Media, 2010), p. 4.
4. Paul M. Warburg, *The Federal Reserve System, Its Origin and Growth: Reflections and Recollections*, Volume 1, (New York: The MacMillan Company, 1930), p. 40, https://fraser.stlouisfed.org/title/192/item/5441.
5. Ron Paul and Lewis Lehrman, *The Case for Gold,* (Washington, D.C.: Cato Institute, 1982), p. 22.
6. Benjamin Rush letter to James Madison (27 February 1790), *The Papers of James Madison, Vol. 13, 20 January 1790-31 March 1791*, ed. Charles F. Hobson and Robert A. Rutland, (Charlottesville: University Press of Virginia, 1981), pp. 67-70, https://founders.archives.gov/documents/Madison/01-13-02-0047.
7. Ibid., The Bank Bill (2 February 1791), pp. 372-382.
8. Pelatiah Webster, *A Plea for the Poor Soldiers, or, An Essay to Demonstrate That the Soldiers and Other Public Creditors, Who Really and Actually Supported the Burden of the Late War, Have Not Been Paid! Ought to Be Paid! Can Be Paid! and Must Be Paid!* (Philadelphia: Printed by Francis Bailey, 1790). https://oll-resources.s3.us-east-2.amazonaws.com/oll3/store/titles/2161/Webster_1366_EBk_v6.0.pdf.

9. Benjamin Rush letter to James Madison (27 February 1790), *The Papers of James Madison, Vol. 13, 20 January 1790-31 March 1791*, ed. Charles F. Hobson and Robert A. Rutland, (Charlottesville: University Press of Virginia, 1981), pp. 67-70, https://founders.archives.gov/documents/Madison/01-13-02-0047.
10. David Floyd, "Hamilton's Wall Street: What They Never Told You," Investopedia, July 16, 2018, https://www.investopedia.com/news/hamiltons-wall-street-what-musical-didnt-tell-you/.
11. Whitney K. Bates, "Northern Speculators and Southern State Debts: 1790." The William and Mary Quarterly 19, no. 1 (1962), doi:10.2307/1919956.
12. Webster, *Plea for the Soldiers*.
13. Benjamin Rush letter to James Madison (18 February 1791), *The Papers of James Madison, Vol. 13, 20 January 1790-31 March 1791*, ed. Charles F. Hobson and Robert A. Rutland, (Charlottesville: University Press of Virginia, 1981), pp. 67-70, https://founders.archives.gov/documents/Madison/01-13-02-0047.
14. X. Jefferson's Account of the Bargain on the Assumption and Residence Bills, [1792?]," *Founders Online*, National Archives, https://founders.archives.gov/documents/Jefferson/01-17-02-0018-0012
15. Alexander Hamilton letter to Robert Morris (30 April 1781), *The Papers of Alexander Hamilton, vol. 2, 1779–1781*, ed. Harold C. Syrett, (New York: Columbia University Press, 1961), pp. 604–635, https://founders.archives.gov/documents/Hamilton/01-02-02-1167
16. Thomas Jefferson letter to Samuel Kercheval (12 July 1816), *The Thomas Jefferson Papers at the Library of Congress*, (Washington DC: Library of Congress, n.d.), http://hdl.loc.gov/loc.mss/mtj.mtjbib022494.
17. Thomas Jefferson letter to Thomas Cooper (16 January 1814), *The Papers of Thomas Jefferson, Retirement Series, vol. 7, 28 November 1813 to 30 September 1814*, ed. J. Jefferson Looney, (Princeton: Princeton University Press, 2010), pp. 124-131, https://founders.archives.gov/documents/Jefferson/03-07-02-0071.
18. Thomas Jefferson, Opinion on the Constitutionality of the Bill for Establishing a National Bank (15 February 1791), *The Papers of Thomas Jefferson, vol. 19, 24 January-31 March 1791*, ed. Julian P. Boyd, (Princeton: Princeton University Press, 1974) pp. 275-282, https://founders.archives.gov/documents/Jefferson/01-19-02-0051.
19. Alexander Hamilton, The Federalist No. 33 (2 January 1788), *The Papers of Alexander Hamilton, vol. 4, January 1787–May 1788*, ed. Harold C. Syrett, (New York: Columbia University Press, 1962), pp. 465–469, https://founders.archives.gov/documents/Hamilton/01-04-02-0190.
20. Griffin, *Jekyll Island*, p. 331.
21. Gustavus Myers, *History of the Great American Fortunes* (New York: Random House, 1936), p. 556.
22. John Thom Holdsworth and Davis R. Dewey, *The First and Second Banks of the United States*, (Washington, D.C.: Government Printing Office, 1910), p. 45.
23. Joseph J. Ellis, *Passionate Sage: The Character and Legacy of John Adams*, (New York: W.W. Norton, 1994), p. 162.

24. John Adams letter to Benjamin Rush (27 December 1810), *Founders Online*, National Archives, https://founders.archives.gov/documents/Adams/99-02-02-5585.
25. Thomas Jefferson letter to John Adams (24 January 1814), *The Adams-Jefferson Letter*, vol. II, ed. Lester J. Cappon, (New York: Simon and Schuster, 1971), p. 424, https://founders.archives.gov/documents/Jefferson/03-07-02-0083.
26. Thomas Jefferson, *The Writings of Thomas Jefferson*, vol. X, ed. Paul Leicester Ford, (New York: G.P. Putnam & Sons, 1899), p. 31.
27. US Department of the Treasury, *Report of the Secretary of the Treasury for 1866*, 304: Report of Ways and Means Committee, in RD, 21-1, Appendix, April 13, 1830, p. 115.
28. Griffin, *Jekyll Island*, p. 343.
29. Sean Wilentz, *The Rise of American Democracy: Jefferson to Lincoln*, (New York: W.W. Horton and Company, 2008), pp. 206-207.
30. Andrew Jackson, "President Jackson's Veto Message Regarding the Bank of the United States; July 10, 1832," A Compilation of the Messages and Papers of the Presidents, Prepared under the direction of the Joint Committee on printing, of the House and Senate Pursuant to an Act of the Fifty-Second Congress of the United States, (New York: Bureau of National Literature, Inc., 1897).
31. Andrew Jackson, "Farewell Address," March 4, 1837. https://millercenter.org/the-presidency/presidential-speeches/march-4-1837-farewell-address.
32. Nicholas Biddle letter to William Appleton (27 January 1834), Robert V. Remini, *Andrew Jackson and the Course of American Democracy, 1833-1845*, (New York: Harper & Row, 1984), p. 111.
33. History.com Editors, "Congress Censures President Jackson," History.com (A&E Television Networks, November 16, 2009), https://www.history.com/this-day-in-history/congress-censures-jackson.
34. From the original minutes of the Philadelphia committee of citizens sent to meet with President Jackson, February 1834, according to Stan V. Henkels, Andrew Jackson and the Bank of the United States, 1928.
35. Griffin, *Jekyll Island*, p. 356
36. History.com Editors, "Andrew Jackson Narrowly Escapes Assassination," History.com (A&E Television Networks, November 16, 2009), https://www.history.com/this-day-in-history/andrew-jackson-narrowly-escapes-assassination.
37. Said to Martin Van Buren (8 July 1832), quoted in *The Autobiography of Martin Van Buren*, published in Annual Report of the American Historical Association for the Year 1918, vol. II (1920), ed. John Clement Fitzpatrick, ch. XLIII, p. 625.
38. "Deposit Act of 1836," Encyclopedia.com, January 12, 2021, https://www.encyclopedia.com/history/dictionaries-thesauruses-pictures-and-press-releases/deposit-act-1836.
39. Jeffrey Sklansky, *Sovereign of the Market: The Money Question in Early America*, (Chicago: University of Chicago Press, 2017), pp. 164-165.
40. Jackson, "Farewell Speech."
41. Ibid.

42. Ellen Hodgson Brown, *Web of Debt: the Shocking Truth about Our Money System--the Sleight of Hand That Has Trapped Us in Debt and How We Can Break Free* (Baton Rouge, LA: Third Millennium Press, 2007), p. 85.
43. Abraham Lincoln letter to Colonel E.D. Taylor (December 1864), Emanuel Hertz, *Abraham Lincoln: A New Portrait*, vol. 2, (New York: Horace Liveright, Inc., 1931), p. 957.
44. Wesley Clair Mitchell, *A History of the Greenbacks: With Special Reference to the Economic Consequences of Their Issue: 1862-65*, (Chicago: University of Chicago Press, 1903), pp. 116-130.
45. Lincoln letter to Taylor (1864), Hertz, *New Portrait*, p. 957.
46. Otto Eisenschiml, *The Hidden Face of the Civil War,* (New York: The Bobbs-Merrill Company, Inc., 1961), p. 25.
47. Frank A. Golder, "The Russian Fleet and the Civil War." The American Historical Review 20, no. 4 (1915): 801-12. Accessed March 20, 2021. doi:10.2307/1835544.
48. "The Russian Navy Visits the United States," Naval Historical Foundation Publication (Naval Historical Foundation, 1969), https://www.history.navy.mil/research/library/online-reading-room/title-list-alphabetically/r/the-russian-navy-visits-theunited-states.html.
49. Griffin, *Jekyll Island*, p. 429.
50. Abraham Lincoln letter to Col. William F. Elkins (21 November 1864), *The Lincoln Encyclopedia: The Spoken and Written Words of Abraham Lincoln Arranged for Ready Reference*, ed. Archer H. Shaw, (New York: MacMillan, 1950), p. 40.
51. W.E. Mosse, "Legacy of Alexander II," Encyclopædia Britannica (Encyclopædia Britannica, inc.), accessed January 15, 2021, https://www.britannica.com/biography/Alexander-II-emperor-of-Russia/Legacy.
52. Irwin Unger, *The Greenback Era: A Social and Political History of American Finance, 1865-1879*, (Princeton, N.J.: Princeton University Press, 1964), p. 57.
53. Ibid., p. 58.
54. Robert P. Sharkey, *Money, Class, and Party: An Economic Study of Civil War and Reconstruction*, (Baltimore: The Johns Hopkins Press, 1959), Chapter 2.
55. Unger, Greenback Era, p. 41.
56. A. Barton Hepburn, *History of Coinage and Currency in the United States and the Perennial Contest for Sound Money*, (New York: The Macmillan Company; London: Macmillan & Co, Ltd., 1903) pg. 208.
57. Nicolas Barreyre, "The Politics of Economic Crises: The Panic of 1873, the End of Reconstruction, and the Realignment of American Politics," The Journal of the Gilded Age and Progressive Era 10, no. 4 (2011): 403-23, http://www.jstor.org/stable/23045120.
58. Charles A. Lindbergh, *Banking and Currency and the Money Trust*, (National capital Press, Inc., 1913), p. 88.
59. Carter Glass, *An Adventure in Constructive Finance*, (New York: Doubleday, Page and Co., 1927).
60. Congressional Record, vol. 51, part 2, 63rd Congress, 2nd Session, December 22, 1913, p. 1446.

# ENDNOTES

61. Louis McFadden, "Congressman McFadden on the Federal Reserve Corporation, Remarks in Congress, 1934, An Astounding Exposure," (Boston, MA: Forum Publishing Company, 1934).
62. "Buell Letter," The Irish standard. [volume], Chronicling America: Historic American Newspapers, Library of Congress, (Minneapolis, MN: October 3, 1896), <https://chroniclingamerica.loc.gov/lccn/sn90059959/1896-10-03/ed-1/seq-4/>.
63. George B. Waldron, *A Handbook on Currency and Wealth with Numerous Tables and Diagrams*, "Buell Letter," (New York: Funk and Wagnalls Company, 1896), p. 43.

Chapter 5.2 – Chapter Conclusion

- None

Chapter 6 – Money: Precondition

- None

Chapter 6.1 – Childhood Poverty

1. "United States Hunger Facts, Poverty Facts 2016." World Hunger News. Hunger Notes, March 20, 2020. https://www.worldhunger.org/hunger-in-america-united-states-hunger-poverty-facts-2018/.
2. Nicole L. Hair et al., "Association of Child Poverty, Brain Development, and Academic Achievement," *JAMA Pediatrics* 169, no. 9 (September 1, 2015): pp. 822-829, https://doi.org/10.1001/jamapediatrics.2015.1475.
3. "Helping Children Succeed in School & Life: Save the Children's Literacy Programs," U.S. Programs Fact Sheet, Save the Children, Accessed April 11, 2019, https://www.savethechildren.org/content/dam/usa/reports/ed-cp/literacy-programs-fs.PDF.
4. Diana Kwon, "Poverty Disturbs Children's Brain Development and Academic Performance," Scientific American (Scientific American, July 22, 2015), https://www.scientificamerican.com/article/poverty-disturbs-children-s-brain-development-and-academic-performance/.
5. Kimberly G Noble, Suzanne M. Houston, Natalie H. Brito, et al., "Family Income, Parental Education and Brain Structure in Children and Adolescents," *Nature Neuroscience* 18, no. 5 (March 30, 2015): pp. 773-778, https://doi.org/10.1038/nn.3983.
6. Sara Reardon, "Poverty Shrinks Brains from Birth," Scientific American (Scientific American, March 31, 2015), https://www.scientificamerican.com/article/poverty-shrinks-brains-from-birth1/.
7. Joan Luby, Andy Belden, Kelly Botteron, et al., "The Effects of Poverty on Childhood Brain Development," *JAMA Pediatrics* 167, no. 12 (January 2013): pp. 1135-1142, https://doi.org/10.1001/jamapediatrics.2013.3139.

8. S Chetty, A R Friedman, K Taravosh-Lahn, et al., "Stress and Glucocorticoids Promote Oligodendrogenesis in the Adult Hippocampus," *Molecular Psychiatry* 19, no. 12 (February 11, 2014): pp. 1275-1283, https://doi.org/10.1038/mp.2013.190.
9. Christopher Bergland, "Chronic Stress Can Damage Brain Structure and Connectivity," Psychology Today (Sussex Publishers, February 12, 2014), https://www.psychologytoday.com/us/blog/the-athletes-way/201402/chronic-stress-can-damage-brain-structure-and-connectivity.
10. R. M. Thomas, G. Hotsenpiller, and D. A. Peterson, "Acute Psychosocial Stress Reduces Cell Survival in Adult Hippocampal Neurogenesis without Altering Proliferation," *Journal of Neuroscience* 27, no. 11 (March 14, 2007): pp. 2734-2743, https://doi.org/10.1523/jneurosci.3849-06.2007.
11. Karen Hughes, Mark A. Bellis, Katherine A. Hardcastle, et al., "The Effect of Multiple Adverse Childhood Experiences on Health: a Systematic Review and Meta-Analysis," *The Lancet Public Health* 2, no. 8 (August 2017): pp. 356-366, https://doi.org/10.1016/s2468-2667(17)30118-4.
12. C. Mitchell, J Hobcraft et al., "Social Disadvantage, Genetic Sensitivity, and Children's Telomere Length," *Proceedings of the National Academy of Sciences* 111, no. 16 (April 7, 2014): pp. 5944-5949, https://doi.org/10.1073/pnas.1404293111.
13. Thomas W. McDade et al., "Genome-Wide Analysis of DNA Methylation in Relation to Socioeconomic Status during Development and Early Adulthood," *American Journal of Physical Anthropology* 169, no. 1 (February 16, 2019): pp. 3-11, https://doi.org/10.1002/ajpa.23800.
14. "Studies Highlight Lasting Effects of Early Life Stress on the Genome, Gut, and Brain," Society for Neuroscience, November 4, 2018, http://www.sfn.org/Publications/Latest-News/2018/11/04/Studies-Highlight-Lasting-Effects-of-Early-Life-Stress-on-the-Genome-Gut-and-Brain.
15. Suzanne C. Segerstrom and Gregory E. Miller, "Psychological Stress and the Human Immune System: A Meta-Analytic Study of 30 Years of Inquiry.," *Psychological Bulletin* 130, no. 4 (July 2004): pp. 601-630, https://doi.org/10.1037/0033-2909.130.4.601.
16. "Stress Weakens the Immune System," American Psychological Association (American Psychological Association, February 23, 2006), https://www.apa.org/research/action/immune.
17. Chris C. Wolford et al., "Transcription Factor ATF3 Links Host Adaptive Response to Breast Cancer Metastasis," *Journal of Clinical Investigation* 123, no. 7 (June 10, 2013): pp. 2893-2906, https://doi.org/10.1172/jci64410.
18. N. D. Powell et al., "Social Stress up-Regulates Inflammatory Gene Expression in the Leukocyte Transcriptome via -Adrenergic Induction of Myelopoiesis," *Proceedings of the National Academy of Sciences* 110, no. 41 (October 8, 2013): pp. 16574-16579, https://doi.org/10.1073/pnas.1310655110.
19. Emily Caldwell, "Effects of Chronic Stress Can Be Traced to Your Genes," Ohio State News (The Ohio State University, November 5, 2013), https://news.osu.edu/effects-of-chronic-stress-can-be-traced-to-your-genes---110513/.
20. Emma Carlsson et al., "Psychological Stress in Children May Alter the Immune Response," *The Journal of Immunology* 192, no. 5 (March 1, 2014): pp. 2071-2081, https://doi.org/10.4049/jimmunol.1301713.

21. A. Sepa, A. Frodi, and J. Ludvigsson, "Mothers' Experiences of Serious Life Events Increase the Risk of Diabetes-Related Autoimmunity in Their Children," *Diabetes Care* 28, no. 10 (October 28, 2005): pp. 2394-2399, https://doi.org/10.2337/diacare.28.10.2394.
22. G. M. Thernlund et al., "Psychological Stress and the Onset of IDDM in Children: A Case-Control Study," *Diabetes Care* 18, no. 10 (October 1, 1995): pp. 1323-1329, https://doi.org/10.2337/diacare.18.10.1323.
23. A. Sepa et al., "Psychological Stress May Induce Diabetes-Related Autoimmunity in Infancy," *Diabetes Care* 28, no. 2 (February 27, 2005): pp. 290-295, https://doi.org/10.2337/diacare.28.2.290.
24. Christina Paxson and Jane Waldfogel, "Work, Welfare, and Child Maltreatment," *National Bureau of Economic Research,* Working Paper 7343, JEL 13 (September 1999), https://doi.org/10.3386/w7343.
25. "Helping Children Succeed in School & Life: Save the Children's Literacy Programs," U.S. Programs Fact Sheet, Save the Children, Accessed April 11, 2019, https://www.savethechildren.org/content/dam/usa/reports/ed-cp/literacy-programs-fs.PDF.
26. Child Welfare Information Gateway, "Child abuse and neglect fatalities 2018: Statistics and interventions," Washington, DC: U.S. Department of Health and Human Services, Children's Bureau, 2020, https://www.childwelfare.gov/pubPDFs/fatality.pdf.
27. Paxson, "Child Maltreatment."
28. Christopher Ruhm, "Are Recessions Good For Your Health?" Quarterly Journal of Economics 115(2), (2000), pp. 617-650, https://libres.uncg.edu/ir/uncg/f/C_Ruhm_Are_2000.pdf.
29. "Economic Status and Abuse," DualDiagnosis.org (Foundations Recovery Network), accessed April 20, 2019, https://www.dualdiagnosis.org/drug-addiction/economic-status/.
30. Dante Cicchetti and V. Carlson (Ed.), "Child maltreatment: Theory and research on the causes and consequences of child abuse and neglect," (Cambridge University Press, 1989).
31. American Academy of Pediatrics, "Unemployment Linked with Child Maltreatment," Science News (ScienceDaily, October 5, 2010), https://www.sciencedaily.com/releases/2010/10/101003081452.htm.
32. "Child Neglect Linked to Parental Unemployment," University of Oxford, November 2, 2017, http://www.ox.ac.uk/news/2017-11-02-child-neglect-linked-parental-unemployment.
33. Femmie Juffer, Marinus H. van IJzendoorn, and Marian J. Bakermans-Kranenburg, "Structural Neglect in Orphanages: Physical Growth, Cognition, and Daily Life of Young Institutionalized Children in India," *Child Maltreatment in Residential Care*, August 12, 2017, pp. 301-321, https://doi.org/10.1007/978-3-319-57990-0_14.
34. Rosa Monckton, "Why I'm Haunted by These Neglected Orphans That the World Has Forgotten," Daily Mail Online (Associated Newspapers, November 6, 2008), https://www.dailymail.co.uk/femail/article-1083382/Why-Im-haunted-neglected-orphans-Bulgaria-world-forgotten.html.
35. Dana E. Johnson and Megan R. Gunnar, "IV. GROWTH FAILURE IN INSTITUTIONALIZED CHILDREN," *Monographs of the Society for Research in*

*Child Development* 76, no. 4 (December 2011): pp. 92-126, https://doi.org/10.1111/j.1540-5834.2011.00629.x.

36. "Changing the Way We Care - How Many Children in Orphanages Have a Living Parent?," Changing the Way We Care – Help Orphans (CRS, Maestrol, and Lumos), accessed April 20, 2019, https://www.changingthewaywecare.org/.
37. April Shaw, James Egan, Morag Gillespie, "Drugs and poverty: A literature review," Scottish Drugs Forum, Glasgow Caledonian University, March, 2007, http://www.dldocs.stir.ac.uk/documents/drugpovertylitrev.pdf.
38. "Substance Abuse Treatment for Persons with Child Abuse and Neglect Issues," Center for Substance Abuse Treatment, Rockville (MD): Substance Abuse and Mental Health Services Administration (US); 2000. (Treatment Improvement Protocol (TIP) Series, No. 36.) Chapter 1—Working With Child Abuse and Neglect Issues. Available from: https://www.ncbi.nlm.nih.gov/books/NBK64904/.
39. Gary S. Wand et al., "Family History of Alcoholism and Hypothalamic Opioidergic Activity," *Archives of General Psychiatry* 55, no. 12 (1998): pp. 1114-1119, https://doi.org/10.1001/archpsyc.55.12.1114.
40. Izabela Milaniak and Cathy Spatz Widom, "Does Child Abuse and Neglect Increase Risk for Perpetration of Violence inside and Outside the Home?," *Psychology of Violence* 5, no. 3 (July 1, 2015): pp. 246-255, https://doi.org/10.1037/a0037956.
41. Nancy S. Weinfield, Gregory Mills et al., "Hunger in America 2014: National Report," Feeding America, (Westat and the Urban Institute, 2014), http://help.feedingamerica.org/HungerInAmerica/hunger-in-america-2014-full-report.pdf?s_src=W194DIRCT&s_subsrc=https%3A%2F%2Fwww.feedingamerica.org%2Fhunger-in-america%2Ffacts&_ga=2.71044368.1885847274.1554856284-895989055.1554856284.
42. HH Vorster and A Kruger, "Poverty, malnutrition, underdevelopment and cardiovascular disease: a South African perspective," Cardiovascular journal of Africa vol. 18,5 (2007): 321-4, https://www.ncbi.nlm.nih.gov/pmc/articles/PMC3975540/.
43. Vinicius J. Martins et al., "Long-Lasting Effects of Undernutrition," *International Journal of Environmental Research and Public Health* 8, no. 6 (May 26, 2011): pp. 1817-1846, https://doi.org/10.3390/ijerph8061817.
44. Ibid.
45. "World Hunger, Poverty Facts, Statistics 2018," Hunger Notes (World Hunger News, November 29, 2018), https://www.worldhunger.org/world-hunger-and-poverty-facts-and-statistics/.
46. Ibid.
47. Ellen L. Bassuk, Carmela J. DeCandia et al., "America's Youngest Outcasts: A Report Card on Child Homelessness," American Institutes for Research, The National Center on Family Homelessness, November, 2014, https://www.air.org/sites/default/files/downloads/report/Americas-Youngest-Outcasts-Child-Homelessness-Nov2014.pdf.
48. Mary E. Haskett, Jenna Montgomery Armstrong, and Jennifer Tisdale, "Developmental Status and Social–Emotional Functioning of Young Children Experiencing Homelessness," *Early Childhood Education Journal* 44, no. 2

(February 19, 2015): pp. 119-125, https://doi.org/10.1007/s10643-015-0691-8.

49. Staci Perlman and John Fantuzzo, "Timing and Influence of Early Experiences of Child Maltreatment and Homelessness on Children's Educational Well-Being," *Children and Youth Services Review* 32, no. 6 (June 2010): pp. 874-883, https://doi.org/10.1016/j.childyouth.2010.02.007.
50. Diana B. Cutts, Alfred M. Pheley, and Joni S. Geppert, "Hunger in Midwestern Inner-City Young Children," *Archives of Pediatrics & Adolescent Medicine* 152, no. 5 (May 1998): pp. 489-493, https://doi.org/10.1001/archpedi.152.5.489.

Chapter 6.2 – Ecological Degradation

1. David Lin et al., "Ecological Footprint Accounting for Countries: Updates and Results of the National Footprint Accounts, 2012–2018," *Resources* 7, no. 3 (September 17, 2018): p. 58, https://doi.org/10.3390/resources7030058.
2. "What Is the United States' Share of World Energy Consumption?," Frequently Asked Questions (FAQs) - U.S. Energy Information Administration (EIA), December 15, 2020, https://www.eia.gov/tools/faqs/faq.php?id=87&t=1.
3. "Oil Consumption by Country," Worldometer, accessed February 20, 2021, https://www.worldometers.info/oil/oil-consumption-by-country/.
4. "Natural Gas Consumption by Country," Worldometer, accessed February 20, 2021, https://www.worldometers.info/gas/gas-consumption-by-country/.
5. Roddy Sheer, "Use It and Lose It: The Outsize Effect of U.S. Consumption on the Environment," Scientific American (Scientific American, September 14, 2012), https://www.scientificamerican.com/article/american-consumption-habits/.
6. Center for Sustainable Systems, University of Michigan. 2020. "U.S. Environmental Footprint Factsheet." Pub. No. CSS08-08, http://css.umich.edu/factsheets/us-environmental-footprint-factsheet.
7. "World of Change: Amazon Deforestation," Earth Observatory (NASA), accessed February 20, 2021, https://earthobservatory.nasa.gov/world-of-change/Deforestation.
8. Adam Voiland, "Tracking Amazon Deforestation from Above," Earth Observatory (NASA), accessed February 21, 2021, https://earthobservatory.nasa.gov/images/145988/tracking-amazon-deforestation-from-above.
9. "Rates of Rainforest Destruction and Species Loss in the Ecuadorian Amazon," Ecuador Explorer, accessed February 21, 2021, https://www.ecuadorexplorer.com/html/regions_cities/amazon/amazon_peoples/body_rf_destuction.html.
10. Shasta Darlington, "Deforestation in Brazilian Amazon Surges to 12-Year High," CNN (Cable News Network, December 1, 2020), https://www.cnn.com/2020/12/01/americas/deforestation-brazil-amazon-bolsonaro-intl/index.html.
11. Rhett A. Butler, "Calculating Deforestation in the Amazon," Mongabay (Mongabay, January 4, 2020), https://rainforests.mongabay.com/amazon/deforestation_calculations.html.

12. "Rain Forest Threats Information and Facts," Environment (National Geographic, February 10, 2021), https://www.nationalgeographic.com/environment/article/rainforest-threats.
13. Alina Bradford, "Facts About Rainforests," LiveScience (Purch, July 28, 2018), https://www.livescience.com/63196-rainforest-facts.html.
14. "Forests," World Resources Institute, accessed February 21, 2021, https://www.wri.org/our-work/topics/forests.
15. Jahda Swanborough, "We Need to Save Africa's Forests. Here's How," World Economic Forum, November 17, 2016, https://www.weforum.org/agenda/2016/11/deforestation-africa-palm-oil/.
16. Alexandra Tyukavina et al., "Congo Basin Forest Loss Dominated by Increasing Smallholder Clearing," *Science Advances* 4, no. 11 (November 7, 2018), https://doi.org/10.1126/sciadv.aat2993.
17. "Water Facts," US Forest Service (US Department of Agriculture), accessed February 21, 2021, https://www.fs.usda.gov/managing-land/national-forests-grasslands/water-facts.
18. "Forest Habitat," WWF (World Wildlife Fund), accessed February 21, 2021, https://www.worldwildlife.org/habitats/forest-habitat.
19. Mohammad Irshad and Elizabeth Stephen, "Review: Pollination, Pollinated and Pollinators Interaction in Pakistan," *Journal of Bioresource Management* 1, no. 1 (May 5, 2014): pp. 19-25, https://doi.org/10.35691/jbm.4102.0003.
20. WWF, "Living Planet Report - 2018: Aiming Higher," M. Grooten and R.E.A. Almond (ed.), *WWF*, (Gland, Switzerland: 2018), https://c402277.ssl.cf1.rackcdn.com/publications/1187/files/original/LPR2018_Full_Report_Spreads.pdf.
21. Ibid.
22. "The IUCN Red List of Threatened Species," IUCN Red List, accessed March 3, 2021, https://www.iucnredlist.org/.
23. Arghamanyan, "Media Release: Nature's Dangerous Decline 'Unprecedented'; Species Extinction Rates 'Accelerating'," Intergovernmental Science-Policy Platform on Biodiversity and Ecosystem Services (IPBES) (IPBES, May 6, 2019), https://www.ipbes.net/news/Media-Release-Global-Assessment.
24. Frederik Saltre and Corey J.A. Bradshaw, "Are We Really in a 6th Mass Extinction? Here's The Science," ScienceAlert, November 18, 2019, https://www.sciencealert.com/here-s-how-biodiversity-experts-recognise-that-we-re-midst-a-mass-extinction.
25. Owen Mulhern, "The 6th Mass Extinction," Earth.Org - Past | Present | Future, December 8, 2020, https://earth.org/data_visualization/the-6th-mass-extinction/.
26. "How Much Water Is There on Earth?," United States Geological Survey, accessed February 21, 2021, https://www.usgs.gov/special-topic/water-science-school/science/how-much-water-there-earth?qt-science_center_objects=0#qt-science_center_objects.
27. "Where Is Earth's Water?," United States Geological Survey, accessed February 21, 2021, https://www.usgs.gov/special-topic/water-science-school/science/where-earths-water?qt-science_center_objects=0#qt-science_center_objects.
28. Jeff Inglis, Tony Dutzik, and John Rumpler, "Wasting Our Waterways: Toxic Industrial Pollution and Restoring the Promise of the Clean Water Act,"

Environment America Research & Policy Center, June 2014, https://environmentamericacenter.org/sites/environment/files/reports/US_wastingwaterways_scrn%20061814_0.pdf.

29. Ibid.
30. Ibid.
31. Associated Press, "Study: Unsafe Toxins Found in Drinking Water at Thousands of U.S. Schools," Fox News (FOX News Network, September 25, 2009), https://www.foxnews.com/story/study-unsafe-toxins-found-in-drinking-water-at-thousands-of-u-s-schools.
32. Rebecca Sutton, PhD, "Chromium-6 in U.S. Tap Water," Environmental Working Group, December 20, 2010, https://static.ewg.org/reports/2010/chrome6/chrome6_report_2.pdf?_ga=2.264228751.268267.1556752290-1941027165.1556752290.
33. Inglis, "Wasting Our Waterways."
34. "National Summary of State Information," EPA (United States Environmental Protection Agency), accessed February 21, 2021, https://iaspub.epa.gov/waters10/attains_nation_cy.control.
35. Walter G. Wright, "TOXIC RELEASE INVENTORY/OIL AND GAS EXTRACTION INDUSTRY: ENVIRONMENTAL GROUPS SUPPLEMENT PETITION TO EPA TO ADD CERTAIN INDUSTRY SECTORS," Mitchell Williams Law FIrm, February 4, 2014, https://www.mitchellwilliamslaw.com/toxic-release-inventoryoil-and-gas-extraction-industry-environmental-groups-supplement-petition-to-epa-to-add-certain-industry-sectors.
36. Caryl Sue, "Great Pacific Garbage Patch," National Geographic Society, July 5, 2019, https://www.nationalgeographic.org/encyclopedia/great-pacific-garbage-patch/.
37. Charles J. Moore, "Trashed Across the Pacific Ocean, Plastics, Plastics Everywhere...," Natural History, v. 112, n...9, Nov. 2003.
38. L. Lebreton et al., "Evidence That the Great Pacific Garbage Patch Is Rapidly Accumulating Plastic," *Scientific Reports* 8, no. 1 (March 22, 2018), https://doi.org/10.1038/s41598-018-22939-w.
39. Caryl Sue, "Great Pacific Garbage Patch," National Geographic Society, July 5, 2019, https://www.nationalgeographic.org/encyclopedia/great-pacific-garbage-patch/.
40. Ibid.
41. "The Great Pacific Garbage Patch," The Ocean Cleanup, February 11, 2020, https://theoceancleanup.com/great-pacific-garbage-patch/.

Chapter 6.3

1. Oxfam, "No Relief: Denial of Bathroom Breaks in the Poultry Industry," Oxfam America (Oxfam, May 9, 2016), https://www.oxfamamerica.org/explore/research-publications/no-relief/.
2. GMWC Organizing Committee, "Striving for a Just and Safer Workplace: Central Minnesota's Poultry Industry and its Disposable Workers," Greater Minnesota Worker Center, (April 1, 2016), http://www.mygmwc.org/wp-

content/uploads/2016/04/Striving-for-a-Just-and-Safer-Workplace-Final-04262016.pdf.

3. "Unsafe at These Speeds: Alabama's Poultry Industry and Its Disposable Workers," Southern Poverty Law Center (The Southern Poverty Law Center & Alabama Appleseed, March 1, 2013), https://www.splcenter.org/20130228/unsafe-these-speeds.
4. GMWC, "Safer Workplace."
5. "Injuries, Illnesses, and Fatalities," U.S. Bureau of Labor Statistics (Bureau of Labor Statistics, U.S. Department of Labor, Survey of Occupational Injuries and Illnesses, in cooperation with participating state agencies., November 8, 2018), https://www.bls.gov/iif/oshwc/osh/os/summ1_00_2017.htm.
6. "Anti-Slavery Program," Coalition of Immokalee Workers, October 24, 2018, https://ciw-online.org/slavery/.
7. Eve Turow Paul, "You Need to Know: The Slavery Conditions on Tomato Farms," HuffPost (HuffPost, April 27, 2015), https://www.huffpost.com/entry/you-need-to-know-the-slavery-conditions-on-tomato-farms_b_6735842.
8. Oxfam America and Dina Mesbah, "Like Machines in the Fields: Workers without Rights in American Agriculture," Oxfam America, March 15, 2004, https://s3.amazonaws.com/oxfam-us/www/static/oa3/files/like-machines-in-the-fields.pdf.
9. Pat Gillespie, "Press Release: Sixth Immokalee Slavery Case Suspect Arrested: Group Accused of Keeping, Beating, Stealing from Immokalee Laborers," Coalition of Immokalee Workers, January 18, 2008, https://ciw-online.org/blog/2008/01/slavery_plain_and_simple/.
10. "Anti-Slavery Program," Coalition of Immokalee Workers, October 24, 2018, https://ciw-online.org/slavery/.
11. Turow Paul, "You Need to Know."
12. "Migrant Tomato Workers Face Chronic Abuses," Southern Poverty Law Center, April 15, 2008, https://www.splcenter.org/news/2008/04/15/migrant-tomato-workers-face-chronic-abuses.
13. Alexi C. Cardona, "Slavery in the Shadows: Survivor Tells Her Painful Story for Human Trafficking Awareness Month," Naples Daily News (Naples, January 20, 2019), https://www.naplesnews.com/story/news/crime/2019/01/20/survivor-tells-her-story-national-human-trafficking-awareness-month/2550631002/.
14. Human Trafficking, "Are There Sweatshops in the United States?," The Dunken Law Firm, April 29, 2020, https://www.thedunkenlawfirm.com/sweatshops-in-the-united-states/.
15. "7. Forced Labour," International Labour Organization, accessed February 23, 2021, https://www.ilo.org/global/topics/dw4sd/themes/forced-labour/lang--en/index.htm.
16. "Poultry Workers," National Center for Farmworker Health, Inc., 2014. http://www.ncfh.org/uploads/3/8/6/8/38685499/fs-poultryworkers.pdf.
17. Lisa Cohen, "How America's 'Ground-Zero' for Modern Slavery Was Cleaned up by Workers' Group," CNN (Cable News Network, September 28, 2018), https://www.cnn.com/2017/05/30/world/ciw-fair-food-program-freedom-project/index.html.

18. "Forced Labour, Modern Slavery and Human Trafficking," International Labour Organization, accessed February 23, 2021, http://www.ilo.org/global/topics/forced-labour/lang--en/index.htm.
19. Aida Alami, "Workers in Spain's Strawberry Fields Speak Out on Abuse," The New York Times (The New York Times, July 20, 2019), https://www.nytimes.com/2019/07/20/world/europe/spain-strawberry-fields-abuse.html.
20. "Rape and Abuse: the Price of a Job in Spain's Strawberry Industry?," The Guardian (Guardian News and Media, April 14, 2019), https://www.theguardian.com/global-development/2019/apr/14/rape-abuse-claims-spains-strawberry-industry.
21. Tobias Jones and Ayo Awokoya, "Are Your Tinned Tomatoes Picked by Slave Labour?," The Guardian (Guardian News and Media, June 20, 2019), https://www.theguardian.com/world/2019/jun/20/tomatoes-italy-mafia-migrant-labour-modern-slavery.
22. "Digging in the Dirt: Child Miners in Sierra Leone's Diamond Industry," International Human Rights Clinic, Harvard Law School, 2009, http://hrp.law.harvard.edu/wp-content/uploads/2014/07/Digging_In_The_DirtLR.pdf.
23. "Global estimates of child labour: Results and trends, 2012-2016," Alliance 8.7, International Labour Organization (Geneva: 2017), http://www.ilo.org/wcmsp5/groups/public/---dgreports/---dcomm/documents/publication/wcms_575499.pdf.
24. "Child Labour in Africa," International Labour Organization, accessed February 23, 2021, https://www.ilo.org/africa/areas-of-work/child-labour/lang--en/index.htm.
25. "Labor & Community," Brilliant Earth, accessed February 23, 2021, https://www.brilliantearth.com/conflict-diamond-child-labor/.
26. "Tanzania: Hazardous Life of Child Gold Miners," Human Rights Watch, October 28, 2020, https://www.hrw.org/news/2013/08/28/tanzania-hazardous-life-child-gold-miners.
27. "Labor & Community," Brilliant Earth.
28. "Child Labor," Diamonds for Peace, June 25, 2020, https://eng.diamondsforpeace.org/child-labor/#_edn1.
29. "Child Labour and Exploitation," UNICEF India (UNICEF), accessed February 23, 2021, https://www.unicef.org/india/what-we-do/child-labour-exploitation.
30. Manit Rastogi, "For Thousands of Diamond Traders, a New Bourse in Surat Promises to Add to the Shine," The Economic Times - Rise (Economic Times, March 29, 2019), https://economictimes.indiatimes.com/small-biz/sme-sector/for-thousands-of-diamond-traders-a-new-bourse-in-surat-promises-to-add-to-the-shine/articleshow/68626309.cms?from=mdr.
31. Rumani Saikia Phukan, "Child Labour in Diamond Industry Continues in India Despite Abolition," MyIndia, February 8, 2015, https://www.mapsofindia.com/my-india/government/child-labour-in-diamond-industry-in-india-it-will-continue-why.
32. "Life and Death in Apple's Forbidden City," The Guardian (Guardian News and Media, June 18, 2017), https://www.theguardian.com/technology/2017/jun/18/foxconn-life-death-

forbidden-city-longhua-suicide-apple-iphone-brian-merchant-one-device-extract.

33. "Leading Article: The Gruesome Reality of Sweatshops," The Independent (Independent Digital News and Media, October 22, 2011), https://www.independent.co.uk/voices/editorials/leading-article-gruesome-reality-sweatshops-2094318.html.
34. Associated Press, "Death Toll Tops 1,000 in Bangladesh Factory Collapse," CBS News (CBS Interactive, May 10, 2013), https://www.cbsnews.com/news/death-toll-tops-1000-in-bangladesh-factory-collapse/.
35. China Daily, "Lung Disease Claims Far More Lives than Accidents," Ecns.cn, February 9, 2015, http://www.ecns.cn/2015/02-09/154133.shtml.

Chapter 6.4 – War: Trading Red for Green

1. Smedley D. Butler, *War Is a Racket* (New York: Round table Press, Inc., 1935), p. 5.
2. R. McNair Wilson, *Monarchy or Money Power* (London: Eyre and Spottiswoode, Ltd., 1933), pp. 68,72.
3. Aaron Gregg, "Defense Stocks Spike after Airstrike against Iranian Commander," The Washington Post (WP Company, January 3, 2020), https://www.washingtonpost.com/business/2020/01/03/defense-stocks-spike-following-airstrike-against-iranian-commander/.
4. Hans Schmidt, *Maverick Marine: General Smedley D. Butler and the Contradictions of American Military History* (Lexington: University Press of Kentucky, 1998).
5. Gregg Zoroya, "VA Study: 22 Vets Commit Suicide Every Day," USA Today (Gannett Satellite Information Network, February 1, 2013), https://www.usatoday.com/story/news/nation/2013/02/01/veterans-suicide/1883329/.
6. "Veterans Experiencing Homelessness," United States Department of Veterans Affairs, November 18, 2019, https://www.va.gov/HOMELESS/pit_count.asp.
7. National Center for Veterans Analysis and Statistics, "Veteran Poverty Trends," United States Department of Veterans Affairs, May, 2015, https://www.va.gov/vetdata/docs/SpecialReports/Veteran_Poverty_Trends.pdf.
8. Peter Belmi et al., "The Social Advantage of Miscalibrated Individuals: The Relationship between Social Class and Overconfidence and Its Implications for Class-Based Inequality.," *Journal of Personality and Social Psychology* 118, no. 2 (2020): pp. 254-282, https://doi.org/10.1037/pspi0000187.
9. Michael W. Kraus, Stéphane Côté, and Dacher Keltner, "Social Class, Contextualism, and Empathic Accuracy," *Psychological Science* 21, no. 11 (October 25, 2010): pp. 1716-1723, https://doi.org/10.1177/0956797610387613.
10. Joshua Holland and Bill Moyers, "Why the Wealthy Tend to Think They're Better Than Everybody Else," Alternet.org, January 22, 2014,

https://www.alternet.org/2014/01/why-wealthy-tend-think-theyre-better-everybody-else/.

11. Butler, *Racket*, p. 6.
12. Farewell address by President Dwight D. Eisenhower, January 17, 1961; Final TV Talk 1/17/61 (1), Box 38, Speech Series, Papers of Dwight D. Eisenhower as President, 1953-61, Eisenhower Library; National Archives and Records Administration.
13. Bryan Bender and Sarah Cammarata, "Defense Lobby Spending Totals for 2020," POLITICO, January 29, 2021, https://www.politico.com/newsletters/morning-defense/2021/01/29/defense-lobby-spending-totals-for-2020-793059.
14. "U.S. Defense Spending Compared to Other Countries," Peter G. Peterson Foundation, May 13, 2020, https://www.pgpf.org/chart-archive/0053_defense-comparison.
15. Aude Fleurant, Alexandra Kuimova, et al., "The SIPRI Top 100 Arms-Producing and Military Services Companies, 2018," SIPRI Fact Sheet (Stockholm International Peace Research Institute, December 2019), https://www.sipri.org/sites/default/files/2019-12/1912_fs_top_100_2018.pdf.
16. Ibid.
17. Fareed Zakaria, "Thank Goodness for a Villain," Newsweek, September 15, 1996, p. 43.
18. 91st Congressional Record, 1st Session, Vol. 115, Part 13 (Bound Edition, June 23, 1969), pp. 16840-16843.
19. Barbara Salazar Torreon & Sofia Plagakis, "Instances of Use of United States Armed Forces Abroad, 1798-2020." Congressional Research Services, July 20, 2020, https://crsreports.congress.gov/product/pdf/R/R42738.
20. Louis Fisher, "Destruction of the Maine (1898)." The Law Library of Congress, August 4, 2009.
21. "The Banana Wars – 10 Quick Facts About America's Military Interventions in the Caribbean & Latin America," Military History Now, September 20, 2020, https://militaryhistorynow.com/2020/09/20/the-banana-wars-10-quick-facts-about-americas-early-military-interventions-in-the-caribbean-latin-america/.
22. Lester D. Langley (1983). *The Banana Wars: An Inner History of American Empire, 1900-1934* (Lexington, KY: University Press of Kentucky, 1983), pp. 22-27.
23. Ibid., pp. 27-33.
24. Ibid., pp. 34-42.
25. Salazar Torreon, *Instances of Use.*
26. Langley, *Banana Wars*, pp. 141-148.
27. Salazar Torreon, *Instances of Use.*
28. "World War I War Debts," Encyclopedia.com, accessed February 27, 2021, https://www.encyclopedia.com/history/dictionaries-thesauruses-pictures-and-press-releases/world-war-i-war-debts.
29. Griffin, *Jekyll Island*, pp. 247-260.
30. Ben Aris and Duncan Campbell, "How Bush's Grandfather Helped Hitler's Rise to Power," The Guardian (Guardian News and Media, September 25, 2004), https://www.theguardian.com/world/2004/sep/25/usa.secondworldwar.

31. Edmund L. Andrews, "I.G. Farben: A Lingering Relic of the Nazi Years," *The New York Times*, May 2, 1999, https://www.nytimes.com/1999/05/02/business/the-business-world-ig-farben-a-lingering-relic-of-the-nazi-years.html.
32. Diarmuid Jeffreys, *Hell's Cartel: IG Farben and the Making of Hitler's War Machine* (Metropolitan Books, January 5, 2010).
33. Paul T. Calbos, "Cold War Conflict: American Intervention in Greece," Indiana University, May 1993, https://apps.dtic.mil/dtic/tr/fulltext/u2/a274662.pdf.
34. History.com Editors, "Berlin Blockade," History.com (A&E Television Networks, June 1, 2010), https://www.history.com/topics/cold-war/berlin-blockade.
35. Rhodri Jeffreys-Jones, *The CIA and American Democracy* (Yale University Press, July 1, 2014), pp. 88–89.
36. Kermit Roosevelt, *Countercoup: the Struggle for the Control of Iran* (New York: McGraw-Hill Book Company, 1981).
37. Gerald K. Haines, "CIA and Guatemala Assassination Proposals 1952-1954," Declassified, CIA History Staff Analysis, June 1995, https://nsarchive2.gwu.edu/NSAEBB/NSAEBB4/docs/doc01.pdf.
38. Lawrence A. Yates, The US Military Intervention in Panama: Origins, Planning, and Crisis Management, June 1987-December 1989, Contingency Operation Series (Washington D.C.: Center of Military History, United States Army, 2008), https://history.army.mil/html/books/just_cause/CMH_55-1-1_Just_%20Cause_opt.pdf.
39. Ibid.
40. Ian Beckett and John Pimlott, *Counter-Insurgency: Lessons from History* (Barnsley, South Yorkshire: Pen & Sword Military, 2011), p. 240.
41. Peter Kornbluh, "Chile and the United States: Declassified Documents Relating to the Military Coup, September 11, 1973," The National Security Archive, accessed March 1, 2021, https://nsarchive2.gwu.edu/NSAEBB/NSAEBB8/nsaebb8i.htm.
42. Howard W. French, "From Old Files, a New Story of US Role in Angolan War," *The New York Times*, March 31, 2002, https://www.nytimes.com/2002/03/31/world/from-old-files-a-new-story-of-us-role-in-angolan-war.html.
43. Joel Brinkley, "US Sends Troops to Aid Bolivians in Cocaine Raids," *The New York Times,* July 16, 1986, https://www.nytimes.com/1986/07/16/world/us-sends-troops-to-aid-bolivians-in-cocaine-raids.html#:~:text=The%20Reagan%20Administration%20has%20sent%20United%20States%20Army,the%20world's%20cocaine%20is%20produced%20in%20the%20area.
44. Michael York, "Troops Ordered to Calm Virgin Islands," *Washington Post*, September 21, 1989, https://www.washingtonpost.com/archive/politics/1989/09/21/troops-ordered-to-calm-virgin-islands/e8dc2f2d-bcc7-49cf-835d-6d672d73102b/.
45. John Perkins, "Zeitgeist: Addendum," interview by Peter Joseph, Video (Gentle Machine Productions, 2008).
46. Bobby Ghosh, "A Brief History of CIA Assets," *TIME Magazine*, October 28, 2009, http://content.time.com/time/specials/packages/article/0,28804,1933053_1933052_1933042,00.html.

# ENDNOTES


47. Elida Moreno, "Panama's Noriega: CIA spy turned drug-running dictator," *Reuters*, May 30, 2017, https://www.reuters.com/article/us-panama-noriega-obituary-idUSKBN18Q0NW.


Chapter 6.5 – Crime


1. Aristotle and Benjamin Jowett (translated by), *The Politics of Aristotle* (Oxford: Clarendon, 1885).
2. "Table 16 - Rate: Number of Crimes per 100,000 Inhabitants," 2017 Crime in the United States, Criminal Justice Information Services Division (FBI, September 10, 2018), https://ucr.fbi.gov/crime-in-the-u.s/2017/crime-in-the-u.s.-2017/tables/table-16.
3. "Homicide Rate - Victims of Intentional Homicide, 1990-2018," United Nations Office of Drugs and Crime (United Nations), accessed March 2, 2021, https://dataunodc.un.org/content/data/homicide/homicide-rate.
4. "Intentional Homicide Victims," United Nations Office on Drugs and Crime (United Nations), accessed March 2, 2021, https://dataunodc.un.org/crime/intentional-homicide-victims.
5. "Table 21 - Arrests," 2016 Crime in the United States, Criminal Justice Information Services Division (FBI, September 18, 2017), https://ucr.fbi.gov/crime-in-the-u.s/2016/crime-in-the-u.s.-2016/topic-pages/tables/table-21.
6. Erika Harrell, Ph.D., Lynn Langton, et al., "Household Poverty and Nonfatal Violent Victimization, 2008-2012," NCJ 248384, Bureau of Justice Statistics, November 18, 2014, https://www.bjs.gov/index.cfm?ty=pbdetail&iid=5137.
7. "Table 16," FBI.
8. Roomy Khan, "White-Collar Crimes -- Motivations and Triggers," *Forbes Magazine,* February 22, 2018, https://www.forbes.com/sites/roomykhan/2018/02/22/white-collar-crimes-motivations-and-triggers/#765168271219.
9. "Global Wealth Databook 2017," Credit Suisse, Research Institute, November 2017, global-wealth-databook-2017-en.pdf.
10. "Rape Statistics by Country 2021," World Population Review, accessed March 2, 2021, https://worldpopulationreview.com/country-rankings/rape-statistics-by-country.
11. "Crime Index by Country 2018," Numbeo, accessed March 2, 2021, https://www.numbeo.com/crime/rankings_by_country.jsp?title=2018#:~:text=Crime%20Index%20by%20Country%202018%20%20%20,%20%2024.29%20%2078%20more%20rows.
12. James Gilligan, *Violence: Reflections on a National Epidemic*, First Edition (New York: Vintage Books, May 1997).
13. Ibid., p. 76
14. James M. Reinhardt, *The Murderous Trail of Charles Starkweather* (Springfield, IL: Charles C. Thomas, 1960), p. 51.
15. Gilligan, *Violence*, p. 109.

16. Brian Bell, "Do Recessions Increase Crime?," World Economic Forum, March 4, 2015, https://www.weforum.org/agenda/2015/03/do-recessions-increase-crime/.
17. Aaron Reeves, Martin McKee, and David Stuckler, "Economic Suicides in the Great Recession in Europe and North America," *British Journal of Psychiatry* 205, no. 3 (June 12, 2014): pp. 246-247, https://doi.org/10.1192/bjp.bp.114.144766.
18. Karen Nikos-Rose, "Domestic Violence Increased in the Great Recession," UC Davis, July 13, 2020, https://www.ucdavis.edu/news/domestic-violence-increased-great-recession.
19. Princeton University, "The Rise of Intimate Partner Violence during the Great Recession," Phys.org (Phys.org, June 6, 2016), https://phys.org/news/2016-06-intimate-partner-violence-great-recession.html.
20. Robert M. Sapolsky, *Why Zebras Don't Get Ulcers: the Acclaimed Guide to Stress, Stress-Related Diseases, and Coping* (New York: Henry Holt and Co., 2004), pp. 255-263.
21. "Countries with the Largest Number of Prisoners per 100,000 of the National Population, as of June 2020," Statista (Statista Research Department, June 2020), https://www.statista.com/statistics/262962/countries-with-the-most-prisoners-per-100-000-inhabitants/.
22. Child Welfare Information Gateway, "Child abuse and neglect fatalities 2018: Statistics and interventions" (Washington, DC: U.S. Department of Health and Human Services, Children's Bureau, 2020), https://www.childwelfare.gov/pubPDFs/fatality.pdf#page=2&view=How%20many%20children%20die%20each%20year%20from%20child%20abuse%20and%20neglect?.

Chapter 6.6 – Trust: There's a Pill for that

1. Esteban Ortiz-Ospina and Max Roser, "Trust," Our World in Data, July 22, 2016, https://ourworldindata.org/trust.
2. Uri Friedman, "Trust is Collapsing in America," *The Atlantic*, January 21, 2018, https://www.theatlantic.com/international/archive/2018/01/trust-trump-america-world/550964/.
3. Matej Mikulic, "Global Pharmaceutical Market Size 2001-2019," Statista, May 25, 2020, https://www.statista.com/statistics/263102/pharmaceutical-market-worldwide-revenue-since-2001/.
4. Martin B. Keller et al., "Efficacy of Paroxetine in the Treatment of Adolescent Major Depression: A Randomized, Controlled Trial," *Journal of the American Academy of Child & Adolescent Psychiatry* 40, no. 7 (July 2001): pp. 762-772, https://doi.org/10.1097/00004583-200107000-00010.
5. The People of the State of New York by Eliot Spitzer vs. GlaxoSmithKline, plc. & SmithKline Beecham Corporation (2004), Supreme Court of the State of New York, June 2, 2004.
6. Ibid., p. 17.

7. Ibid., p. 6.
8. Ibid., p. 7.
9. "Volume 1 Video Deposition of Martin Keller," Transcript, State of Minnesota District Court, County of Hennepin, Fourth Judicial Circuit, Court File No. PI-04-012879, September 6, 2006, http://psychrights.org/States/Minnesota/martin-keller-depo-329.pdf.
10. New York vs GSK, p. 12.
11. Ibid.
12. Ibid.
13. Ibid.
14. Ibid., p. 13.
15. Ibid., p. 9.
16. Shahram Ahari, "Under the Influence: Can We Provide Doctors an Alternative to Biased Drug Reviews?," Senate Committee on Aging, United States Senate, Senate Hearing 110-624, 110th Cong., 2nd sess., (Washington D.C.: March 12, 2008), https://www.govinfo.gov/content/pkg/CHRG-110shrg45474/html/CHRG-110shrg45474.htm.
17. New York vs GSK, p. 16.
18. "Video Deposition of Martin Keller."
19. Val Brickates Kennedy, "Merck Crushed on Vioxx Withdrawal," MarketWatch (CBS, September 30, 2004), https://www.marketwatch.com/story/merck-at-eight-year-low-on-withdrawal-of-vioxx-drug#:~:text=Vioxx%20produced%20sales%20of%20%242.5%20billion%20for%20Merck,the%20company%20expects%20to%20meet%202004%20dividend%20estimates.
20. Ray Moynihan, "Merck Defends Vioxx in Court, as Publisher Apologises for Fake Journal," *BMJ* 338, no. may11 1 (May 11, 2009), https://doi.org/10.1136/bmj.b1914.
21. Jim Edwards, "Docs Say Merck Placed Their Names on Ghostwritten Vioxx Articles," Moneywatch, *CBS News*, May 12, 2009, https://www.cbsnews.com/news/docs-say-merck-placed-their-names-on-ghostwritten-vioxx-articles/.
22. Kate Hagan, "Merck Accused of 'Ghost Writing' Medical Article," *The Age*, April 23, 2009, https://www.theage.com.au/national/merck-accused-of-ghost-writing-medical-article-20090422-afdk.html?page=-1.
23. Kate Hagan, "Name in Merck journal surprised doctor," WAtoday, May 8, 2009, https://www.watoday.com.au/national/name-in-merck-journal-surprised-doctor-20090508-ay0v.html.
24. Kennedy, "Merck Crushed."
25. Leemon McHenry, "Of Sophists and Spin-Doctors: Industry-Sponsored Ghostwriting and the Crisis of Academic Medicine," *Mens Sana Monographs* 8, no. 1 (January 2010): pp. 129-145, https://doi.org/10.4103/0973-1229.58824.
26. John Fauber and Meg Kissinger, "UW linked to ghostwriting," *Milwaukee Journal Sentinel*, August 15, 2009, http://archive.jsonline.com/features/health/53315032.html.

27. Sarah Boseley, "Scientists take money for ghostwritten papers," *The Guardian*, February 7, 2002, https://www.theguardian.com/uk/2002/feb/07/research.health1.
28. Bernadette Tansey, "Huge Penalty in Drug Fraud / Pfizer Settles Felony Case in Neurontin off-Label Promotion," SFGATE (San Francisco Chronicle, January 27, 2012), https://www.sfgate.com/business/article/Huge-penalty-in-drug-fraud-Pfizer-settles-2759293.php.
29. Ibid.
30. Rachel V. Smith, Jennifer R. Havens, and Sharon L. Walsh, "Gabapentin Misuse, Abuse and Diversion: a Systematic Review," *Addiction* 111, no. 7 (March 18, 2016): pp. 1160-1174, https://doi.org/10.1111/add.13324.
31. Jim Edwards, "Exec Warned AZ on Negative Seroquel Results: 'We Cannot Hide Them'; Info Later 'Buried,'" *CBS News* (CBS Interactive, February 27, 2009), https://www.cbsnews.com/news/exec-warned-az-on-negative-seroquel-results-we-cannot-hide-them-info-later-buried/.
32. McHenry, "Of Sophists."
33. Adriane J. Fugh-Berman, "The Haunting of Medical Journals: How Ghostwriting Sold 'HRT,'" *PLoS Medicine* 7, no. 9 (September 7, 2010), https://doi.org/10.1371/journal.pmed.1000335.
34. Robert Whitaker, *Mad in America: Bad Science, Bad Medicine, and the Enduring Mistreatment of the Mentally Ill* (Cambridge, MA: Perseus, 2002), pp. 279-281.
35. "United States Files Complain Against Forest Laboratories for Allegedly Violating the False Claims Act: Pharmaceutical Company Allegedly Marketed Drugs for Unapproved Pediatric Use and Paid Kickbacks," United States Department of Justice, Office of Public Affairs, February 25, 2009, https://www.justice.gov/opa/pr/united-states-files-complaint-against-forest-laboratories-allegedly-violating-false-claims.
36. "The Influence of the Pharmaceutical Industry," House of Commons Health Committee, HC 42-I, 4th Report of Sess. 2004-05, Vol. 1 (House of Commons London: The Stationery Office Limited, April 5, 2005), https://publications.parliament.uk/pa/cm200405/cmselect/cmhealth/42/42.pdf.
37. Ibid.
38. "Are Ghost Authors Affecting the Authenticity of Clinical Trials?," Enago Academy, February 6, 2019, https://www.enago.com/academy/are-ghost-authors-affecting-the-authenticity-of-clinical-trials/.
39. Irving Kirsch et al., "Initial Severity and Antidepressant Benefits: A Meta-Analysis of Data Submitted to the Food and Drug Administration," *PLoS Medicine* 5, no. 2 (February 26, 2008), https://doi.org/10.1371/journal.pmed.0050045.
40. Ibid.
41. Marcia Angell, "Drug Companies & Doctors: A Story of Corruption," *The New York Review*, January 15, 2009, https://www.ncbi.nlm.nih.gov/pmc/articles/PMC4572812/#b1-cvj_10_1011.
42. "Video Deposition of Martin Keller."
43. List of original Paxil court documents – Jon Jureidini, "Paxil Study 329: Paroxetine vs Imipramine vs Placebo in Adolescents," Healthy Skepticism,

January, 2010, http://www.healthyskepticism.org/global/news/int/hsin2010-01.

44. Reuters, "GlaxoSmithKline Settles Paxil – Related Suit," *Fox News*, August 26, 2004, https://www.foxnews.com/story/glaxosmithkline-settles-paxil-related-suit.
45. "GlaxoSmithKline to Plead Guilty and Pay $3 Billion to Resolve Fraud Allegations and Failure to Report Safety Data: Largest Health Care Fraud Settlement in US History," United States Department of Justice, Office of Public Affairs, July 2, 2012, https://www.justice.gov/opa/pr/glaxosmithkline-plead-guilty-and-pay-3-billion-resolve-fraud-allegations-and-failure-report.
46. Ibid.
47. Lisa M. Schwartz and Steven Woloshin, "Medical Marketing in the United States, 1997-2016," *JAMA* 321, no. 1 (January 1, 2019): pp. 80-96, https://doi.org/10.1001/jama.2018.19320.
48. Katherine Ellen Foley, "Big Pharma spent an additional $9.8 billion on marketing in the past 20 years. It worked," *Quartz*, January 9, 2019, https://qz.com/1517909/big-pharma-spent-an-additional-9-8-billion-on-marketing-in-the-past-20-years-it-worked/.
49. "Shrinks for Sale: Psychiatry's Conflicted Alliance, The Corrupt Alliance of the Psychiatric-Pharmaceutical Industry," Citizens Commission on Human Rights International, Accessed March 4, 2021, https://www.cchrint.org/issues/the-corrupt-alliance-of-the-psychiatric-pharmaceutical-industry/.
50. John Dorschner, "Senator tells University of Miami he's 'troubled' over hiring," The Miami Herald, PsychSearch.net, June, 10, 2010, Senator tells University of Miami he's `troubled' over hiring.
51. Gardiner Harris, "Top Psychiatrist Didn't Report Drug Makers' Pay," *The New York Times*, October 3, 2008, https://www.nytimes.com/2008/10/04/health/policy/04drug.html.
52. "Johnson & Johnson to Pay More Than $2.2 Billion to Resolve Criminal and Civil Investigations: Allegations Include Off-label Marketing and Kickbacks to Doctors and Pharmacists," United States Department of Justice, Office of Public Affairs, November 4, 2013, https://www.justice.gov/opa/pr/johnson-johnson-pay-more-22-billion-resolve-criminal-and-civil-investigations.
53. Sarah Boseley, "Scandal of scientists who take money for papers ghostwritten by drug companies," *The Guardian*, February 7, 2002, https://www.theguardian.com/uk/2002/feb/07/research.health1.
54. Dennis Thompson, "Survey reveals how many doctors receive money, gifts from drugmakers," *CBS News*, May 3, 2017, https://www.cbsnews.com/news/doctors-receive-money-gifts-from-drugmakers-pharmaceutical-companies/.
55. Deborah C. Marshall, Madeleine E. Jackson, and Jona A. Hattangadi-Gluth, "Disclosure of Industry Payments to Physicians," *Mayo Clinic Proceedings* 91, no. 1 (January 1, 2016): pp. 84-96, https://doi.org/10.1016/j.mayocp.2015.10.016.
56. "CMS' Open Payments Program Posts 2015 Financial Data," CMS.gov, Centers for Medicare & Medicaid Services, June 30, 2016,

https://www.cms.gov/newsroom/press-releases/cms-open-payments-program-posts-2015-financial-data#:~:text=For%20Open%20Payments%20program%20year%202015%2C%20health%20care,attributable%20to%20618%2C931%20physicians%20and%201%2C116%20teaching%20hospitals.

57. Thompson, "Survey."
58. Nancy A. Melville, "Psychiatrist Accused in Alleged Prescription Kickback Scandal," *Medscape*, March 25, 2021, https://www.medscape.com/viewarticle/776265.
59. Ibid.
60. Ibid.
61. Jason Meisner, "Doctor given prison for taking kickbacks to prescribe risky drug," *Chicago Tribune*, March 11, 2016, https://www.chicagotribune.com/news/breaking/ct-medicare-fraud-kickbacks-sentencing-met-20160311-story.html.
62. "Pharmaceutical Company to Pay $27.6 Million to Settle Allegations Involving False Billings to Federal Health Care Programs," United States Department of Justice, Office of Public Affairs, March 11, 2014, https://www.justice.gov/opa/pr/pharmaceutical-company-pay-276-million-settle-allegations-involving-false-billings-federal.
63. "What is a Pharmaceutical Kickback?" Meds Lawsuit, Accessed March 4, 2021, https://medslawsuit.com/frauds/what-is-a-pharmaceutical-kickback/.
64. Erick H. Turner et al., "Selective Publication of Antidepressant Trials and Its Influence on Apparent Efficacy," *New England Journal of Medicine* 358, no. 3 (January 17, 2008): pp. 252-260, https://doi.org/10.1056/nejmsa065779.
65. Allen J. Francis, M.D., "Psychiatric Fads and Overdiagnosis: Normality is an Endangered Species," *Psychology Today*, June 2, 2010, https://www.psychologytoday.com/us/blog/dsm5-in-distress/201006/psychiatric-fads-and-overdiagnosis.
66. Kevin White, *An Introduction to the Sociology of Health and Illness* (Los Angeles, CA: SAGE Publications Ltd, 2017), pp. 42-42.
67. Samuel A. Cartwright, *Report on the disease and physical peculiarities of the negro race* (Washington, D.C.: Georgetown University Press, 2004), pp. 28-39.
68. James Bradshaw, "Glasser headlines psychotherapy conference," *The National Psychologist*, November 1, 2006, https://nationalpsychologist.com/2006/11/glasser-headlines-psychotherapy-conference/10879.html.
69. Thomas J. Moore and Donald R. Mattison, "Adult Utilization of Psychiatric Drugs and Differences by Sex, Age, and Race," *JAMA Internal Medicine* 177, no. 2 (February 2017): pp. 274-275, https://doi.org/10.1001/jamainternmed.2016.7507.
70. Allen J. Frances, M.D., "The DSM 5 Field Trials, Part 2: Asking the Wrong Question Will Lead to Irrelevant Answers: A waste of talent, time, and money," *Psychology Today*, November 23, 2010, https://www.psychologytoday.com/us/blog/dsm5-in-

distress/201011/the-dsm-5-field-trials-part-2-asking-the-wrong-question-will-lead.

71. R. Collier, "DSM Revision Surrounded by Controversy," *Canadian Medical Association Journal* 182, no. 1 (January 12, 2010): pp. 16-17, https://doi.org/10.1503/cmaj.109-3108.
72. Lisa Cosgrove et al., "Financial Ties between DSM-IV Panel Members and the Pharmaceutical Industry," *Psychotherapy and Psychosomatics* 75, no. 3 (April 2006): pp. 154-160, https://doi.org/10.1159/000091772.
73. Collier, "DSM Revision."
74. Allen Frances and Robert Spitzer, "Letter to APA Board of Trustees July 7 2009 from Allen Frances and Robert Spitzer," Accessed March 4, 2021, https://www.scribd.com/document/17172432/Letter-to-APA-Board-of-Trustees-July-7-2009-From-Allen-Frances-and-Robert-Spitzer.
75. Gardiner Harris and Benedict Carey, "Researchers Fail to Reveal Full Drug Pay," *The New York Times*, June 8, 2008, https://www.nytimes.com/2008/06/08/us/08conflict.html.
76. Mark Olfson et al., "Trends in Antipsychotic Drug Use by Very Young, Privately Insured Children," *Journal of the American Academy of Child & Adolescent Psychiatry* 49, no. 1 (January 2010): pp. 13-23, https://doi.org/10.1097/00004583-201001000-00005.
77. Harris and Carey, "Researchers Fail."
78. Senator Chuck Grassley letter to Dr. Drew Gilpin Faust and Dr. Peter L. Slavin (20 March 2009), United States Senate, Committee on Finance (Washington, D.C.: March 20, 2009), http://s.wsj.net/public/resources/documents/WSJ-Major_Protocol_Violation_Letters032009.pdf.
79. Harris and Carey, "Researchers Fail."
80. Jacob Azerrad, PhD, "The Real Biederman Scandal," Alliance for Human Research Protection, July 22, 2011, https://ahrp.org/the-real-biederman-scandal/.
81. Maria G Morgan et al., "Prospective Analysis of Premature Mortality in Schizophrenia in Relation to Health Service Engagement: a 7.5-Year Study within an Epidemiologically Complete, Homogeneous Population in Rural Ireland," *Psychiatry Research* 117, no. 2 (February 15, 2003): pp. 127-135, https://doi.org/10.1016/s0165-1781(03)00002-7.
82. John L. Waddington, Hanafy A. Youssef, and Anthony Kinsella, "Mortality in Schizophrenia," *British Journal of Psychiatry* 173, no. 4 (October 1998): pp. 325-329, https://doi.org/10.1192/bjp.173.4.325.
83. O.-P. Mehtonen et al., "A Survey of Sudden Death Associated with the Use of Antipsychotic or Antidepressant Drugs: 49 Cases in Finland," *Acta Psychiatrica Scandinavica* 84, no. 1 (July 1991): pp. 58-64, https://doi.org/10.1111/j.1600-0447.1991.tb01421.x.
84. Morgan, "Premature Mortality."
85. T. Gerhard et al., "Comparative Mortality Risks of Antipsychotic Medications in Community-Dwelling Older Adults," *British Journal of Psychiatry* 205, no. 1 (July 2014): pp. 44-51, https://doi.org/10.1192/bjp.bp.112.122499.

86. Lon S. Schneider, Karen S. Dagerman, and Philip Insel, "Risk of Death With Atypical Antipsychotic Drug Treatment for Dementia," *JAMA* 294, no. 15 (October 19, 2005): p. 1934, https://doi.org/10.1001/jama.294.15.1934.
87. Philip S. Wang et al., "Risk of Death in Elderly Users of Conventional vs. Atypical Antipsychotic Medications," *New England Journal of Medicine* 353, no. 22 (December 1, 2005): pp. 2335-2341, https://doi.org/10.1056/nejmoa052827.
88. Sudeep S. Gill et al., "Antipsychotic Drug Use and Mortality in Older Adults with Dementia," *Annals of Internal Medicine* 146, no. 11 (June 5, 2007): pp. 775-786, https://doi.org/10.7326/0003-4819-146-11-200706050-00006.
89. Helen C. Kales et al., "Mortality Risk in Patients With Dementia Treated With Antipsychotics Versus Other Psychiatric Medications," *American Journal of Psychiatry* 164, no. 10 (October 2007): pp. 1568-1576, https://doi.org/10.1176/appi.ajp.2007.06101710.
90. Azerrad, PhD, "Biederman."
91. FDA approval letter from Robert Temple to Ms. Wasserman of Janssen Research Foundation, US Department of Health and Human Services, Food and Drug Administration, NDA 20-272, December 29, 1993, http://psychrights.org/Research/Digest/NLPs/TempleRisperdal(1993).pdf .
92. Paula J. Caplan, Ph.D., "Diagnosisgate: Conflict of Interest at the Top of the Psychiatric Apparatus,"*Aporia*, Vol. 7, Issue 1, March 5, 2015, https://www.madinamerica.com/wp-content/uploads/2020/12/Diagnosisgate.pdf.
93. "Video Deposition of Joseph Biederman, M.D.," Transcript, Superior Court of New Jersey Law Division, Middlesex County, Civil Action Docket Number L-6661-06, February 26, 2009, http://psychrights.org/Drugs/Biederman/090226JBiedermanDepoTranscript.pdf.
94. Sigmund Freud, "Uber Coca," Secundararzt im k.k, All- gemeinen Kronkenhause in Wien, Centralblatt fiir die ges, Therapie, 2, 289-314, 1884. Can be retrieved from the following Journal: Howard Shaffer, "Uber Coca: Freud's Cocaine Discoveries," *Journal of Substance Abuse Treatment* 1, no. 3 (1984): pp. 205-217, https://doi.org/10.1016/0740-5472(84)90023-0.
95. Ibid.
96. Ibid.
97. Steven B. Karch, *A Brief History of Cocaine: from Inca Monarchs to Cali Cartels: 500 Years of Cocaine Dealing* (Boca Raton, FL: CRC Press, 2017).
98. Sarah Harris, "Number of children given drugs for ADHD up ninefold with patients as young as THREE being prescribed Ritalin," *Daily Mail*, June 28, 2013, https://www.dailymail.co.uk/health/article-2351427/Number-children-given-drugs-ADHD-ninefold-patients-young-THREE-prescribed-Ritalin.html.
99. "Data and Statistics About ADHD," Centers for Disease Control and Prevention, November 16, 2020, https://www.cdc.gov/ncbddd/adhd/data.html.

100. Garth Kant, "Radical increase in kids prescribed Ritalin," *WND*, April 1, 2013, https://www.wnd.com/2013/04/radical-increase-in-kids-prescribed-ritalin/.
101. Ibid.
102. "Vital Signs: Overdoses of Prescription Opioid Pain Relievers --- United States, 1999--2008," Centers for Disease Control and Prevention, Morbidity and Mortality Weekly Report, 60(43); 1487-1492 (Centers for Disease Control and Prevention, November 4, 2011), https://www.cdc.gov/mmwr/preview/mmwrhtml/mm6043a4.htm.
103. Scott A. Bonn, Ph.D., "Prescription Drugs Are Far More Deadly Than Street Drugs: Unethical doctors enable their drug-addicted patients," *Psychology Today*, April 28, 2014, https://www.psychologytoday.com/us/blog/wicked-deeds/201404/prescription-drugs-are-far-more-deadly-street-drugs.
104. Brian Shilhavy, "Legal Drugs vs. Illegal Drugs: Are we fighting the Right War?," *Health Impact News*, January 5, 2012, https://healthimpactnews.com/2012/legal-drugs-vs-illegal-drugs-are-we-fighting-the-right-war/.
105. Michelle M. Solleveld et al., "Age-Dependent, Lasting Effects of Methylphenidate on the GABAergic System of ADHD Patients," *NeuroImage: Clinical* 15 (June 2017): pp. 812-818, https://doi.org/10.1016/j.nicl.2017.06.003.
106. Cheima Bouziane et al., "White Matter by Diffusion MRI Following Methylphenidate Treatment: A Randomized Control Trial in Males with Attention-Deficit/Hyperactivity Disorder," *Radiology* 293, no. 1 (August 13, 2019): pp. 186-192, https://doi.org/10.1148/radiol.2019182528.
107. Susan L. Andersen, "Stimulants and the Developing Brain," *Trends in Pharmacological Sciences* 26, no. 5 (May 2005): pp. 237-243, https://doi.org/10.1016/j.tips.2005.03.009.
108. Peter Breggin, M.D., "Simple Truth 7: Stimulant Drugs Crush the Life out of Children," *Simple Truths About Psychiatry*, Video Series, https://breggin.com/video-series/.
109. Karen Curtin et al., "Increased Risk of Diseases of the Basal Ganglia and Cerebellum in Patients with a History of Attention-Deficit/Hyperactivity Disorder," *Neuropsychopharmacology* 43, no. 13 (September 12, 2018): pp. 2548-2555, https://doi.org/10.1038/s41386-018-0207-5.
110. William A. Carlezon and Christine Konradi, "Understanding the Neurobiological Consequences of Early Exposure to Psychotropic Drugs: Linking Behavior with Molecules," *Neuropharmacology* 47 (October 21, 2004): pp. 47-60, https://doi.org/10.1016/j.neuropharm.2004.06.021.
111. Ibid.
112. James Swanson et al., "Stimulant-Related Reductions of Growth Rates in the PATS," *Journal of the American Academy of Child & Adolescent Psychiatry* 45, no. 11 (November 2006): pp. 1304-1313, https://doi.org/10.1097/01.chi.0000235075.25038.5a.
113. Peter R. Breggin, "The Rights of Children and Parents In Regard to Children Receiving Psychiatric Diagnoses and Drugs," *Children & Society* 28, no. 3 (June 17, 2014): pp. 231-241, https://doi.org/10.1111/chso.12049.

114. Peter R. Breggin, "Psychostimulants in the treatment of children diagnosed with ADHD: Risks and mechanism of action," *The International Journal of Risk & Safety in Medicine*, 12.1 (January 1, 1999): pp. 3-35, https://www.deepdyve.com/lp/ios-press/psychostimulants-in-the-treatment-of-children-diagnosed-with-adhd-YWXbsyteZF#:~:text=R.%20Breggin%20/%20Psychostimulants%20in%20the%20treatment%20of,or%20novelty%20(e.g.,%20listening%20to%20classroom%20teachers.
115. "Adderall XR Capsules," Black Box Warning, US Food and Drug Administration, Accessed March 4, 2021, https://www.accessdata.fda.gov/drugsatfda_docs/label/2004/021303s005lbl.pdf.
116. Lisa Weyandt et al., "Neurocognitive, Autonomic, and Mood Effects of Adderall: A Pilot Study of Healthy College Students," *Pharmacy* 6, no. 3 (June 27, 2018): p. 58, https://doi.org/10.3390/pharmacy6030058.
117. Erika Proal et al., "Brain Gray Matter Deficits at 33-Year Follow-up in Adults With Attention-Deficit/Hyperactivity Disorder Established in Childhood," *Archives of General Psychiatry* 68, no. 11 (November 2011): pp. 1122-1134, https:/doi.org/10.1001/archgenpsychiatry.2011.117.
118. Ibid.
119. Henry A. Nasrallah et al., "Cortical Atrophy in Young Adults with a History of Hyperactivity in Childhood," *Psychiatry Research* 17, no. 3 (March 1986): pp. 241-246, https:/doi.org/10.1016/0165-1781(86)90052-1.
120. Breggin, "Rights of Children."
121. Vera Sharav, "Biederman Scandal," https://ahrp.org/the-real-biederman-scandal/.

Chapter 6.7 – Chapter Conclusion

1. James Call, "Walmart Sued for Collecting Life Insurance on Employees," *WFSU Public Media,* May 7, 2010, https://news.wfsu.org/wfsu-local-news/2010-05-07/walmart-sued-for-collecting-life-insurance-on-employees.
2. Jaclyn Gallucci, "Human Trafficking Is an Epidemic in the U.S. It's Also Big Business," Fortune, April 14, 2019, https://fortune.com/2019/04/14/human-sex-trafficking-us-slavery/.
3. Wendy Jeannette Ringgenberg, "Trends and Characteristics of Occupational Suicide and Homicide in Farmers and Agriculture Workers, 1992-2010," *University of Iowa*, 2014, https://doi.org/10.17077/etd.3k25y6k2.
4. Matt Perdue, "A Deeper Look at the CDC Findings on Farm Suicides," National Farmers Union, November 27, 2018, https://nfu.org/2018/11/27/cdc-study-clarifies-data-on-farm-stress/.
5. Mathew Abraham, "Trafficking of Human Organs in India," The Pontifical Academy of Social Sciences, Human Trafficking: Issues Beyond Criminalization, *End Slavery* (Vatican City: April 17-21, 2015),

http://www.endslavery.va/content/endslavery/en/publications/acta_20/abraham.html.

Chapter 7 – Efficiency

1. *Printers' Ink*, Magazine, vol. CXLIII, no. 6 (New York: May 10, 1928).
2. Tae Kim, "Goldman Sachs asks in biotech research report: 'Is curing patients a sustainable business model?'," *CNBC*, April 11, 2018, https://www.cnbc.com/2018/04/11/goldman-asks-is-curing-patients-a-sustainable-business-model.html.
3. Matej Mikulic, "Global pharmaceutical sales from 2017 to 2020, by region," Statista, March 9, 2021, https://www.statista.com/statistics/272181/world-pharmaceutical-sales-by-region/.
4. Chun-Hui Miao, "Planned Obsolescence and Monopoly Undersupply," *Information Economics and Policy* 23, no. 1 (March 2011): pp. 51-58, https://doi.org/10.1016/j.infoecopol.2010.03.003.
5. Markus Krajewski, "The Great Lightbulb Conspiracy: The Phoebus cartel engineered a shorter-lived lightbulb and gave birth to planned obsolescence," IEEE Spectrum, September 24, 2014, https://spectrum.ieee.org/tech-history/dawn-of-electronics/the-great-lightbulb-conspiracy.
6. Entergy Team, "A Lighting Legend: The Centennial Bulb," Circuit by Entergy (Questline Inc., March 1, 2018), http://circuit.entergy.com/home/a-lighting-legend-the-centennial-bulb.
7. "United States v. General Electric Co.," United States District Court D. New Jersey, Civ. A. No. 1364, 82 F. Supp. 753, January 19, 1949, https://www.leagle.com/decision/194983582fsupp7531667.
8. Bernard London, "Ending the Depression through Planned Obsolescence," *Revue Du Mauss*, vol. 44, issue 2, 2014, pp. 47-50, https://doi.org/10.3917/rdm.044.0047.
9. Giles Slade, *Made to Break: Technology and Obsolescence in America* (Cambridge, MA: Harvard University Press, 2007), pp. 123-128.
10. Emily Spivack, "Stocking Series, Part 1: Wartime Rationing and Nylon Riots," *Smithsonian Magazine*, September 4, 2012, https://www.smithsonianmag.com/arts-culture/stocking-series-part-1-wartime-rationing-and-nylon-riots-25391066/.
11. Baris Batuhan Gecit, "Planned Obsolescence: a Keyword Analysis," *Pressacademia* 7, no. 4 (December 31, 2020): pp. 227-233, https://doi.org/10.17261/pressacademia.2020.1335.
12. Viviane Monteiro, "Does the Planned Obsolescence Influence Consumer Purchase Decisions? The Effects of Cognitive Biases: Bandwagon Effect, Optimism Bias and Present Bias on Consumer Behavior," Escola de Administração do Estado de São Paulo, 2018.
13. Cosima Dannoritzer, dir., *The Light Bulb Conspiracy*, Documentary, ARTE, August 8, 2016.
14. Tripp Mickle and Kirsten Grind, "Apple Faces Multiple Lawsuits Over Slowed-Down iPhones," *The Wall Street Journal*, March 28, 2018,

https://www.wsj.com/articles/apple-faces-multiple-lawsuits-over-throttled-iphones-1522229400.
15. Gecit, "Planned Obsolescence."
16. "Naylor, et al. v. Apple Inc.," US District Court for the Northern District of California, Case No. 5:19-cv-04421-SVK, August 5, 2019.
17. Peter Cohen, "Apple settles iPod battery class action suit," *Macworld*, June 1, 2005, https://www.macworld.com/article/1045105/ipodsuit.html.
18. "Apple iPod Battery Class Action: Consumers prevail in false advertising lawsuit," Gibbs Law Group LLP, Accessed March 5, 2021, https://www.classlawgroup.com/apple-ipod/#:~:text=Apple%20iPod%20Battery%20Class%20Action%20Gibbs%20Law%20Group%E2%80%99,about%20iPod%E2%80%99s%20battery%20life%20was%20false%20and%20misleading.
19. Michael Engel, "Sustainable Software Design," *Green Information Technology*, 2015, pp. 111-127, https://doi.org/10.1016/b978-0-12-801379-3.00007-3.
20. Dannoritzer, *Light Bulb Conspiracy*.
21. Jan Willem Aldershoff, "HP pre-programmed failure date of unofficial/non-HP ink cartridges in its printers," *MYCE*, September 16, 2016, http://www.myce.com/news/hp-pre-programmed-failure-date-unofficial-non-hp-ink-cartridges-printers-80457/.
22. Patrick Nelson, "France goes after companies for deliberately shortening life of hardware," *Network World*, January 5, 2018, https://www.networkworld.com/article/3245765/france-goes-after-companies-for-deliberately-shortening-life-of-hardware.html.
23. Sam Byford, "Google reportedly cancels Project Ara modular smartphone plans," *The Verge*, Circuit Breaker, September 1, 2016, https://www.theverge.com/circuitbreaker/2016/9/1/12762236/google-project-ara-suspended-modular-phone-report.
24. Luke Pensworth, "What Happened to Project Ara?," *DailyWireless*, March 7, 2020, https://dailywireless.org/mobile/what-happened-to-project-ara/.
25. History.com Editors, "Model T," History.com (A&E Television Networks, April 26, 2010), https://www.history.com/topics/inventions/model-t.
26. Slade, *Made to Break*, pp. 35-50.
27. Jim Donnelly, "Alfred Sloan: The man who made General Motors great," *Hemmings*, January 2015, https://www.hemmings.com/blog/article/alfred-sloan/.
28. David Hounshel, *From the American System to Mass Production, 1800-1932: The Development of Manufacturing Technology in the United States* (Baltimore, MD: Johns Hopkins University Press, 1984), pp. 260-267.
29. Richard Heseltine, "Hero: Brooks Stevens, the greatest visionary of all?," *Auto Classics*, March 1, 2018, https://www.autoclassics.com/posts/reviews/brooks-stevens-car-excalibur-hero.
30. Stephanie Buck, "GM invented planned obsolescence during the Great Depression, and we've been buying it ever since," Timeline, March 2, 2017, https://timeline.com/gm-invented-planned-obsolescence-cc19f207e842.
31. Dannoritzer, *Light Bulb Conspiracy*.
32. Amanda Bowman, "Emotional Marketing: Scientifically Proven Ways to Increase Sales and Reduce Churn," *Crowdspring*, October 22, 2018, https://www.crowdspring.com/blog/emotional-marketing/

# ENDNOTES

33. Omar Jenblat, "Council Post: Let's Get Emotional: The Future Of Online Marketing," Forbes (Forbes Magazine, February 26, 2018), https://www.forbes.com/sites/forbesagencycouncil/2018/02/26/lets-get-emotional-the-future-of-online-marketing/?sh=5bf43c3d4d0c.
34. "Leveraging the Value of Emotional Connection for Retailers," Motista, 2018, https://www.motista.com/sites/www.motista.com/files/download_link/Leveraging%20Emotional%20Connection%20for%20Retailers.pdf.
35. Caitlin Johnson, "Cutting Through Advertising Clutter," CBS News, Sunday Morning, September 17, 2006, https://www.cbsnews.com/news/cutting-through-advertising-clutter/.
36. Jon Simpson, "Finding Brand Success In The Digital World," Forbes (Forbes Magazine, April 25, 2017), https://www.forbes.com/sites/forbesagencycouncil/2017/08/25/finding-brand-success-in-the-digital-world/?sh=6ab04dda626e.
37. George W. Bush, "President Holds Primetime News Conference," The White House, Office of the Press Secretary, October 11, 2001, https://georgewbush-whitehouse.archives.gov/news/releases/2001/10/20011011-7.html.
38. "Advancing Sustainable Materials Management: 2018 Fact Sheet," United States Environmental Protection Agency, December, 2020, https://www.epa.gov/sites/production/files/2020-11/documents/2018_ff_fact_sheet.pdf.
39. "Municipal Solid Waste Factsheet," Center for Sustainable Systems, Pub. No. CSS04-15 (University of Michigan, October, 2020), http://css.umich.edu/factsheets/municipal-solid-waste-factsheet.
40. Ian Tiseo, "Global Waste Generation – Statistics & Facts," Statista, November 26, 2020, https://www.statista.com/topics/4983/waste-generation-worldwide/.
41. "Frequently Asked Questions (FAQs)," U.S. Energy Information Administration (EIA), December 15, 2020, https://www.eia.gov/tools/faqs/faq.php?id=87&t=1.
42. C.P. Baldé, F. Wang, R. Kuehr, J. Huisman, "The global e-waste monitor – 2014, United Nations University," IAS – SCYCLE, Bonn, Germany, 2015, https://i.unu.edu/media/unu.edu/news/52624/UNU-1stGlobal-E-Waste-Monitor-2014-small.pdf.
43. Rich Smith, "When Making a Great Product Actually Hurts a Company: Enter General Dynamics Corporation," *The Motley Fool*, December 24, 2013, https://web.archive.org/web/20170716171708/https:/www.fool.com/investing/general/2013/12/24/when-making-a-great-product-actually-hurts-a-compa.aspx.

Chapter 7.1 – SNAKE HOLES

1. Wilson, *The New Freedom*.
2. Nicholas J. Gonzalez and Linda L. Isaacs, *What Went Wrong: the Truth behind the Clinical Trial of the Enzyme Treatment of Cancer* (New York, NY: New Spring Press, 2012).

3. Dr. Joseph Mercola, "Kelley Treatment: The Cancer Treatment so Successful – Traditional Doctors SHUT It Down," *Mercola*, April 23, 2011, https://articles.mercola.com/sites/articles/archive/2011/04/23/dr-nicholas-gonzalez-on-alternative-cancer-treatments.aspx.
4. "Letter to Steven Shea," U.S. Department of Health and Human Services, Office for Human Research Protections (Columbia University Health Sciences, June 2, 2008), http://www.hhs.gov/ohrp/detrm_letrs/YR08/jun08a.pdf.
5. Graeme Morgan, Robyn Ward, and Michael Barton, "The Contribution of Cytotoxic Chemotherapy to 5-Year Survival in Adult Malignancies," *Clinical Oncology* 16, no. 8 (December 2004): pp. 549-560, https://doi.org/10.1016/j.clon.2004.06.007.
6. Martin L. Ashdown et al., "Chemotherapy for Late-Stage Cancer Patients: Meta-Analysis of Complete Response Rates," *F1000Research* 4 (July 13, 2015): p. 232, https://doi.org/10.12688/f1000research.6760.1.
7. John Cairns, "The Treatment of Diseases and the War against Cancer," Scientific American 253, no. 5, November, 1985, pp. 51-59, https://www.jstor.org/stable/24967842?seq=1#metadata_info_tab_contents.
8. Carly Fraser, "Chemotherapy Kills: Doctor Claims More People Die From Chemo Than Cancer Itself," *LiveLoveFruit*, February 7, 2018, https://livelovefruit.com/chemotherapy-kills/.
9. Michael Wallington et al., "30-Day Mortality after Systemic Anticancer Treatment for Breast and Lung Cancer in England: a Population-Based, Observational Study," *The Lancet Oncology* 17, no. 9 (September 1, 2016): pp. 1203-1216, https://doi.org/10.1016/s1470-2045(16)30383-7.
10. "Hazardous Material Spill Procedures," University of Toledo, Procedure No. HM-08-013, February 14, 2020, https://www.utoledo.edu/depts/safety/docs/HM-08-013.pdf.
11. Kathlyn Stone, "Top 20 Blockbuster Cancer Drugs," The Balance, November 20, 2019, https://www.thebalance.com/top-cancer-drugs-2663234.

Chapter 7.2 – Technological Unemployment

1. McKinsey Global Institute, "Jobs Lost, Jobs Gained: Workforce Transitions in a Time of Automation," McKinsey & Company, December, 2017, https://www.mckinsey.com/~/media/mckinsey/industries/public%20and%20social%20sector/our%20insights/what%20the%20future%20of%20work%20will%20mean%20for%20jobs%20skills%20and%20wages/mgi%20jobs%20lost-jobs%20gained_report_december%202017.pdf.
2. Ibid.
3. David Edwards, "Amazon now has 200,000 robots working in its warehouses," *Robotics & Automation News*, January 21, 2020, https://roboticsandautomationnews.com/2020/01/21/amazon-now-has-200000-robots-working-in-its-warehouses/28840/.
4. Nick Statt, "Amazon says full automated shipping warehouses are at least a decade away," *The Verge*, May 1, 2019, https://www.theverge.com/2019/5/1/18526092/amazon-warehouse-robotics-automation-ai-10-years-away.

5. Sebastian Blanco, "An Autonomous Semi-Truck Just Drove Across America To Deliver Butter," Forbes (Forbes Magazine, December 12, 2019), https://www.forbes.com/sites/sebastianblanco/2019/12/12/an-autonomous-semi-truck-just-drove-across-america-to-deliver-butter/?sh=40341dc813c5.
6. Andrew Webster, "Suzumo's sushi robots can make almost 1,000 rolls an hour," The Verge, April 8, 2012, https://www.theverge.com/2012/4/8/2932743/suzumo-sushi-robot.
7. Rachel Premack, "Robots are already working in fast-food restaurants – here's exactly what they're doing right now," Business Insider, June 26, 2018, https://www.businessinsider.com/mcdonalds-kfc-panera-robot-employees-2018-6.
8. Alicia Kelso, "White Castle Is Adding Flippy, The Automated Robot, To Help Cook Sliders And Fries," Forbes (Forbes Magazine, July 14, 2020), https://www.forbes.com/sites/aliciakelso/2020/07/14/white-castle-is-adding-flippy-the--automated-robot-to-help-cook-sliders-and-fries/?sh=17d8b78a2487.
9. Rich Duprey, "Now McDonald's Is Testing Robots in Its Kitchens," *The Motley Fool*, July 9, 2019, https://www.fool.com/investing/2019/07/09/now-mcdonalds-is-testing-robots-in-its-kitchens.aspx.
10. "Take the Work Out of Laundry Folding," FoldiMate, accessed March 4, 2021, https://foldimate.com/.
11. Karissa Bell, "The $1,000 laundry-folding robot is back and it's fine, I guess," Mashable, January 6, 2019, https://mashable.com/article/foldimate-laundry-robot-demo/.
12. Amazon Go, https://www.amazon.com/b?node=16008589011.
13. Josh Kosman, "Inside Amazon's robot-run supermarket that needs just 3 humans workers," New York Post, February 5, 2017, https://nypost.com/2017/02/05/inside-amazons-robot-run-supermarket-that-needs-just-3-human-workers/.
14. Noah Manskar and Josh Kosman, "Amazon opens full-size grocery store with no cashiers," Fox News, February 26, 2020, https://www.foxnews.com/tech/amazon-opens-full-size-grocery-store-with-no-cashiers.
15. "About da Vinci Systems," Intuitive, Accessed March 4, 2021, https://www.davincisurgery.com/da-vinci-systems/about-da-vinci-systems.
16. Jack Carfagno, "Top 5 Robotic Surgery Systems," DocWire News, May 15, 2019, https://www.docwirenews.com/future-of-medicine/top-5-robotic-surgery-systems/.
17. Noel Maalouf et al., "Robotics in Nursing: A Scoping Review," *Journal of Nursing Scholarship* 50, no. 6 (September 27, 2018): pp. 590-600, https://doi.org/10.1111/jnu.12424.
18. Meghann Chilcott, "The Growing Trend Of Pharmacy Automation," Forbes (Forbes Magazine, November 7, 2018), https://www.forbes.com/sites/forbestechcouncil/2018/11/07/the-growing-trend-of-pharmacy-automation/?sh=52f7e0ac67ca.
19. Stephen Gossett, "Farming & Agriculture Robots," *Built-In*, July 30, 2019, https://builtin.com/robotics/farming-agricultural-robots.

20. Brian Obudho, "7 Biggest Companies Building 3D Printed Houses," All3DP.com, Accessed March 4, 2021, https://all3dp.com/2/2019-best-companies-building-3d-printed-houses/.
21. Icon 3-D House Printing, Accessed March 4, 2021, https://www.iconbuild.com/.
22. Madison Hoff, "The coronavirus shutdown is revealing America's troubling obsession with work," Business Insider, March 31, 2020, https://www.businessinsider.com/us-work-more-than-other-countries-even-with-coronavirus-shutdowns-2020-3.
23. Abhijit Roy, "Robots replacing workers, cutting cost, raising productivity," National Herald India, May 10, 2017, https://www.nationalheraldindia.com/news/rise-of-the-robots-china-takes-a-powerful-lead-artificial-intelligence-robotics-rpa.

Chapter 8 – Laissez-Faire

1. Murray N. Rothbard, *For a New Liberty: The Libertarian Manifesto* (Auburn, Alabama: Ludwig von Mises Institute, 2006), pp. 295-299.
2. Ibid.
3. David D. Friedman, *The Machinery of Freedom: Guide to a Radical Capitalism* (New York: s. n., 2015).
4. Adam Smith, *The Wealth of Nations* (Random House USA, 2020).
5. Matt Taibbi, "Outrageous HSBC Settlement Proves the Drug War is a Joke," *Rolling Stone*, December 13, 2012, https://www.rollingstone.com/politics/politics-news/outrageous-hsbc-settlement-proves-the-drug-war-is-a-joke-230696/?sub_action=logged_in.
6. Spencer Woodman, "HSBC moved vast sums of dirty money after paying record laundering fine," International Consortium of Investigative Journalists, September 21, 2020, https://www.icij.org/investigations/fincen-files/hsbc-moved-vast-sums-of-dirty-money-after-paying-record-laundering-fine/.
7. William J. Ghent, *Our Benevolent Feudalism* (New York: The Macmillan Company, 1902), p. 29.
8. Howard Cincotta, "The Struggles of Labor," in *An Outline of American History* (Washington, D.C.: Office of International Information Programs, United States Department of State, 1994), https://usa.usembassy.de/etexts/history/ch8.htm#struggles.
9. Eric Foner, *Give Me Liberty!: An American History* (New York, NY: W. W. Norton & Company, 2020).
10. "Industrial Revolution Working Conditions," History on the Net (Salem Media), accessed March 5, 2021, https://www.historyonthenet.com/industrial-revolution-working-conditions.
11. Elias Brck, "Child Labor in the Industrial Revolution," History Crunch, October 5, 2016, https://www.historycrunch.com/child-labor-in-the-industrial-revolution.html#/.
12. History.com Editors, "Child Labor," History.com (A&E Television Networks, October 27, 2009), https://www.history.com/topics/industrial-revolution/child-labor.

13. Friedman, *Machinery of Freedom*, pp. 19-23.
14. Ibid.
15. Interstate Commerce Commission, US Congress, 49th Cong., sess. II, chs. 103, 104, February 4, 1887, https://www.loc.gov/law/help/statutes-at-large/49th-congress/session-2/c49s2ch104.pdf.
16. "Hepburn Act," 34, stat. 584 (1906), Accessed March 5, 2021, https://legislation.lawi.us/hepburn-act/.
17. "Act of July 2, 1890 (Sherman Anti-Trust Act)," Enrolled Acts and Resolutions of Congress, 1789-1992, General Records of the United States Government, Record Group 11, National Archives, July 2, 1890, https://www.ourdocuments.gov/doc.php?flash=false&doc=51.
18. Zinn, *People's History*, pp. 276-277.
19. Joseph Adamczyk, "Homestead Strike," *Encyclopedia Britannica*, March 4, 2020, https://www.britannica.com/event/Homestead-Strike.
20. Zinn, *People's History*, pp. 354-357.
21. "Telecommunications Act of 1996," US Congress, 104th Cong., sess. 652, 110 stat. 56, Public Law 104-104, February 8, 1996, https://www.congress.gov/104/plaws/publ104/PLAW-104publ104.pdf.
22. Zinn, *People's History*, p. 671.
23. Joseph Tiller, "How the Telecom Act of 1996 impacted Hip-Hop," *A3C*, July 25, 2019, http://blog.a3cfestival.com/how-the-telecom-act-of-1996-impacted-hip-hop.
24. History.com Editors, "Glass-Steagall Act," History.com (A&E Television Networks, March 15, 2018), https://www.history.com/topics/great-depression/glass-steagall-act.
25. Arthur E. Wilmarth, "To Restore Financial Stability, Bring Back Glass-Steagall," The Hill, September 30, 2020, https://thehill.com/opinion/finance/518803-to-restore-financial-stability-bring-back-glass-steagall#:~:text=The%20undermining%20and%20repeal%20of%20Glass-Steagall's%20prudential%20buffers,to%20finance%20speculative%20trading%20in%20the%20capital%20markets.
26. Sondhya Gupta, "England's running out of water – and privatization is to blame," *The Guardian*, March 21, 2019, https://www.theguardian.com/commentisfree/2019/mar/21/englands-running-out-of-water-and-privatisation-is-to-blame.
27. "A warning: Water privatization in England and Wales," in *The battle against water privatization*, The Socialist Democracy, February, 2005, http://www.socialistdemocracy.org/WaterChargesPamphlet/AWarningWaterPrivatisationInEnglandAndWales.html.
28. Murray Rothbard, *Outside Looking In: Critiques of American Policies and Institutions, Left and Right* (New York: Harper and Row, 1972), pp. 60-74.

Chapter 8.1 – Inventions and Innovations

1. Peter L. Singer, "Federally Supported Innovations: 22 Examples of Major Technology Advances That Stem From Federal Research Support," The

Information Technology & Innovation Foundation, February 14, http://www2.itif.org/2014-federally-supported-innovations.pdf.

2. Alex Knapp, "How Much Does It Cost To Find A Higgs Boson?," Forbes (Forbes Magazine, July 11, 2012), https://www.forbes.com/sites/alexknapp/2012/07/05/how-much-does-it-cost-to-find-a-higgs-boson/?sh=14dc54913948.
3. Singer, "Federally Supported Innovations."
4. "American-Made Innovation: Sparking Economic Growth," The Science Coalition, vol. 3, April, 2017, http://www.sciencecoalition.org/successstories/reports#reports.
5. NASA Spinoff, NASA Technology Transfer Program, *NASA*, Accessed March 4, 2021, https://spinoff.nasa.gov/.
6. Ekaterina Galkina Cleary et al., "Contribution of NIH Funding to New Drug Approvals 2010–2016," *Proceedings of the National Academy of Sciences* 115, no. 10 (February 12, 2018): pp. 2329-2334, https://doi.org/10.1073/pnas.1715368115.
7. Rachel E. Barenie et al., "Public Funding for Transformative Drugs: the Case of Sofosbuvir," *Drug Discovery Today* 26, no. 1 (January 2021): pp. 273-281, https://doi.org/10.1016/j.drudis.2020.09.024.
8. Raymond A. Miller, Hilary S. Cairnie, Aparna Nemlekar, Megan E. Bowers, "NIH May Own Gilead's Blockbuster Hepatitis Drug Due to Misstep," *Troutman Pepper*, March 23, 2018, https://www.troutman.com/insights/nih-may-own-gileads-blockbuster-hepatitis-drug-due-to-misstep.html.
9. Tony Stamp, Steven R. Phillips, Nathaniel J. Bell, "US $2T stimulus COVID-19 package includes significant R&D funding," *DLA Piper Publications*, April 10, 2020, https://www.dlapiper.com/en/us/insights/publications/2020/04/us-2t-stimulus-covid-19-package-includes-significant-randd-funding/.
10. Karen Weintraub and Elizabeth Weise, "Federal spending on COVID-19 vaccine candidates tops $9 billion, spread among 7 companies," *USA Today*, August 10, 2020, https://www.usatoday.com/story/news/health/2020/08/08/feds-spending-more-than-9-billion-covid-19-vaccine-candidates/5575206002/.
11. "COVID-19 Medical Countermeasure Portfolio," Biomedical Advanced Research and Development Authority, US Department of Health & Human Services, Accessed March 5, 2021, https://www.medicalcountermeasures.gov/app/barda/coronavirus/COVID19.aspx.
12. "Gross Domestic Spending on R&D," *Research and Development (R&D)*, OECD iLibrary, Accessed March 5, 2021, https://doi.org/10.1787/d8b068b4-en.
13. "Federal R&D as a Percent of GDP," American Association for the Advancement of Science, 2020, https://www.aaas.org/sites/default/files/2020-10/RDGDP.png.
14. Owen Bowcott and Alice Ross, "Military 'invisibility cloaks' could breach Geneva conventions," *The Guardian*, March 14, 2016, https://www.theguardian.com/science/2016/mar/14/military-invisibility-cloaks-stealth-could-breach-geneva-conventions.
15. "Advancing National Security Through Fundamental Research," Defense Advanced Research Projects Agency, Accessed March 5, 2021, https://www.darpa.mil/about-us/advancing-national-security-through-fundamental-research.

16. Harm Venhuizen, "I weird DARPA projects that make science fiction seem like real life," *Military Times*, September 4, 2020, https://www.militarytimes.com/off-duty/military-culture/2020/09/04/8-weird-darpa-projects-make-science-fiction-seem-like-real-life/#:~:text=%208%20weird%20DARPA%20projects%20that%20make%20science,Lab-grown%20blood.%20Blood%20pharming%20successfully%20decreased...%20More%20.
17. Heather Fishel, "Strange: In WWII Pigeons Were Trained To Guide Missiles," *War History Online*, February 10, 2018, https://www.warhistoryonline.com/world-war-ii/pigeon-guided-missiles-wwii.html.
18. Kimberly Amadeo, "US Military Budget, Its Components, Challenges, and Growth," The Balance, September 3, 2020, https://www.thebalance.com/u-s-military-budget-components-challenges-growth-3306320.

Chapter 8.2 – Private Schools

- None

Chapter 8.3 – Privatizing Military

1. Rothbard, *For a New Liberty*, p. 238.
2. Our Bureau, "Meet the US Navy's $13 billion aircraft carrier: USS Gerald Ford, most expensive warship ever built," USA Defense News, November 13, 2020, https://usadefensenews.com/2020/11/13/meet-the-us-navys-13-billion-aircraft-carrier-uss-gerald-ford/.
3. "U.S. Defense Spending Compared to Other Countries," Peter G. Peterson Foundation, May 13, 2020, https://www.pgpf.org/chart-archive/0053_defense-comparison.

Chapter 8.4 – National Parks, etc.

1. Associated Press, "Firefighters watch home burn; Owner didn't pay," CBS News, December 7, 2011, https://www.cbsnews.com/news/firefighters-watch-home-burn-owners-didnt-pay/.

Chapter 8.5 – Chapter Conclusion

1. Smith, *Wealth of Nations*, Book V, Ch. II, p. 691.

Chapter 9 – Human Motivation

1. Roger Hutchinson, *Calum's Road* (Edinburgh: Birlinn, 2008).

2. George Martin, "He took the high road! How Scottish islander gave up waiting for an access route to his remote village... so picked up his tools and built one himself (and they even named it after him)," Daily Mail, May 16, 2018, https://www.dailymail.co.uk/news/article-5736785/Scottish-islander-gave-waiting-road-remote-village-built-one-himself.html.
3. Douglas McGregor, *The Human Side of Enterprise* (New York, NY: McGraw-Hill Book Company, Inc, 1960), p. 34.
4. Ibid.
5. Daniel Pink, Drive: The Surprising Truth About What Motivates Us (New York, NY: Riverhead Books, 2009), p. 60.
6. Harry F. Harlow, Margaret Kuenne Harlow, and Donald R. Meyer, "Learning Motivated by a Manipulation Drive.," *Journal of Experimental Psychology* 40, no. 2 (1950): pp. 228-234, https://doi.org/10.1037/h0056906.
7. Ibid.
8. Mark R. Lepper, David Greene, and Richard E. Nisbett, "Undermining Children's Intrinsic Interest with Extrinsic Reward: A Test of the 'Overjustification' Hypothesis.," *Journal of Personality and Social Psychology* 28, no. 1 (1973): pp. 129-137, https://doi.org/10.1037/h0035519.
9. Sam Glucksberg, "The Influence of Strength of Drive on Functional Fixedness and Perceptual Recognition.," *Journal of Experimental Psychology* 63, no. 1 (1962): pp. 36-41, https://doi.org/10.1037/h0044683.
10. Teresa M. Amabile, E. Phillips, and M.A. Collins, "Person and Environment in Talent Development: The Case of Creativity," in *Talent Development: Proceedings of the 1993 Henry B. and Jocelyn Wallace National Research Symposium on Talent Development*, edited by Nicholas Colangelo, Susan G. Assouline, and DeAnn L. Ambroson (Unionville, NY: Trillium Press, 1994).
11. Dan Ariely et al., "Large Stakes and Big Mistakes," *Review of Economic Studies* 76, no. 2 (April 1, 2009): pp. 451-469, https://doi.org/10.1111/j.1467-937x.2009.00534.x.
12. Ibid.
13. Edward L. Deci, Richard Koestner, and Richard M. Ryan, "A Meta-Analytic Review of Experiments Examining the Effects of Extrinsic Rewards on Intrinsic Motivation.," *Psychological Bulletin* 125, no. 6 (November 1999): pp. 627-668, https://doi.org/10.1037/0033-2909.125.6.627.
14. Ibid.
15. Henry Sauermann and Wesley Cohen, "What Makes Them Tick? Employee Motives and Firm Innovation," *National Bureau of Economic Research*, October 2008, https://doi.org/10.3386/w14443.
16. Nic Paton, "Performance-related pay doesn't encourage performance," *Management Issues*, June 25, 2009, https://www.management-issues.com/news/5640/performance-related-pay-doesnt-encourage-performance/.
17. Ibid.
18. Pink, *Drive*, p. 52.
19. Brian Knutson et al., "Anticipation of Increasing Monetary Reward Selectively Recruits Nucleus Accumbens," *The Journal of Neuroscience* 21, no. 16 (August 15, 2001), https://doi.org/10.1523/jneurosci.21-16-j0002.2001.
20. Pink, *Drive*.

21. "Sensory Deprivation and its Frightening Effects," *Exploring Your Mind*, June 17, 2020, https://exploringyourmind.com/sensory-deprivation-and-its-frightening-effects/.
22. GF Reed, "Preparatory set as a factor in the production of sensory deprivation phenomena," Proc R Soc Med, 55(12) (December, 1962), pp. 1010-4, PMID: 13973544; PMCID: PMC1897523.
23. McGregor, *Enterprise*, p. 47.
24. Christopher K. Hsee, Adelle X. Yang, and Liangyan Wang, "Idleness Aversion and the Need for Justifiable Busyness," *Psychological Science* 21, no. 7 (June 14, 2010): pp. 926-930, https://doi.org/10.1177/0956797610374738.
25. Stephen King, *On Writing: A Memoir of the Craft* (New York, NY: Scribner, July, 2010), p. 153.
26. David G. Myers, *Psychology: Tenth Edition in Modules*, 10th ed. (New York, NY: Worth Publishers, 2012), p. 451.
27. Jade Wu, Ph.D., "The Power of Oxytocin," *Psychology Today*, February 11, 2020, https://www.psychologytoday.com/us/blog/the-savvy-psychologist/202002/the-power-oxytocin.
28. Allison M. Anacker and Annaliese K. Beery, "Life in Groups: the Roles of Oxytocin in Mammalian Sociality," *Frontiers in Behavioral Neuroscience* 7 (December 11, 2013), https://doi.org/10.3389/fnbeh.2013.00185.
29. W. T. Harbaugh, U. Mayr, and D. R. Burghart, "Neural Responses to Taxation and Voluntary Giving Reveal Motives for Charitable Donations," *Science* 316, no. 5831 (2007): pp. 1622-1625, https://doi.org/10.1126/science.1140738.
30. Lizette Borreli, "How Helping Others Effects Your Brain," *Brain & Life*, September 20, 2018, https://www.brainandlife.org/the-magazine/online-exclusives/neurology-news-how-helping-others-affects-your-brain/.
31. E. W. Dunn, L. B. Aknin, and M. I. Norton, "Spending Money on Others Promotes Happiness," *Science* 319, no. 5870 (March 21, 2008): pp. 1687-1688, https://doi.org/10.1126/science.1150952.
32. Tania Singer et al., "Empathy for Pain Involves the Affective but Not Sensory Components of Pain," *Science* 303, no. 5661 (February 20, 2004): pp. 1157-1162, https://doi.org/10.1126/science.1093535.
33. Karen Gonsalkorale and Kipling D. Williams, "The KKK Won't Let Me Play: Ostracism Even by a Despised Outgroup Hurts," *European Journal of Social Psychology* 37, no. 6 (September 21, 2006): pp. 1176-1186, https://doi.org/10.1002/ejsp.392.
34. Alexander Green, "The Only Thing That Really Matters," *The Oxford Club*, February 3, 2017, https://oxfordclub.com/2017/02/the-only-thing-that-really-matters-2/.
35. Roy F. Baumeister and Mark R. Leary, "The Need to Belong: Desire for Interpersonal Attachments as a Fundamental Human Motivation.," *Psychological Bulletin* 117, no. 3 (1995): pp. 497-529, https://doi.org/10.1037/0033-2909.117.3.497.
36. Irving Biederman and Edward Vessel, "Perceptual Pleasure and the Brain," American Scientist, September 26, 2019, https://www.americanscientist.org/article/perceptual-pleasure-and-the-brain.
37. Ibid.
38. Abraham H. Maslow, *A Theory of Human Motivation* (Mansfield Centre, CT: Martino Publishing, 2013).

39. McGregor, *Enterprise*, p. 48.
40. Myers, *Psychology*, p. 459.
41. Heather L. Stuckey and Jeremy Nobel, "The Connection Between Art, Healing, and Public Health: A Review of Current Literature," *American Journal of Public Health* 100, no. 2 (February 2010): pp. 254-263, https://doi.org/10.2105/ajph.2008.156497.
42. Beat Ted Hannemann, "Creativity with Dementia Patients," *Gerontology* 52, no. 1 (2006): pp. 59-65, https://doi.org/10.1159/000089827.
43. Steven L. Bressler and Vinod Menon, "Large-Scale Brain Networks in Cognition: Emerging Methods and Principles," *Trends in Cognitive Sciences* 14, no. 6 (2010): pp. 277-290, https://doi.org/10.1016/j.tics.2010.04.004.
44. "How Creativity Works in the Brain," National Endowment for the Arts, Art Works, July 2015, https://www.arts.gov/sites/default/files/how-creativity-works-in-the-brain-report.pdf.
45. Maslow, *Motivation*.
46. ClickWorkers, NASA, Accessed March 6, 2021, http://nasaclickworkers.com/classic.php.
47. Pink, *Drive*, pp. 14-15.
48. Jürgen Bitzer, Wolfram Schrettl, and Philipp J.H. Schröder, "Intrinsic Motivation in Open Source Software Development," *Journal of Comparative Economics* 35, no. 1 (March 2007): pp. 160-169, https://doi.org/10.1016/j.jce.2006.10.001.
49. Dr. Christopher Collins and Matthew Allen, "Research Report on Phase 4 of Cornell University/Gevity Institute Study Human Resource Management Practices and Firm Performance In Small Businesses: A Look at the Effects of HR Practices on Financial Performance and Turnover," Cornell University, Paper 06 – 10, March, 2006, https://ecommons.cornell.edu/bitstream/handle/1813/77287/WP06_10_Research_Report_on_Phase_4_.pdf?sequence=1&isAllowed=y.
50. Christopher P. Niemiec, Richard M. Ryan, and Edward L. Deci, "The Path Taken: Consequences of Attaining Intrinsic and Extrinsic Aspirations in Post-College Life," *Journal of Research in Personality* 43, no. 3 (June 2009): pp. 291-306, https://doi.org/10.1016/j.jrp.2008.09.001.
51. Dan Ariely, Emir Kamenica, and Dražen Prelec, "Man's Search for Meaning: The Case of Legos," *Journal of Economic Behavior & Organization* 67, no. 3-4 (September 1, 2008): pp. 671-677, https://doi.org/10.1016/j.jebo.2008.01.004.
52. Ibid.
53. Karen Mingst, "International Organization," Encyclopædia Britannica (Encyclopædia Britannica, Inc., May 21, 2020), https://www.britannica.com/topic/international-organization.
54. Doctors Without Borders, https://www.doctorswithoutborders.org/.
55. Vicky Hallett, "Why A Surgeon Taught A Non-Doctor To Do Brain Surgery," NPR, May 21, 2017, https://www.npr.org/sections/goatsandsoda/2017/05/21/523969459/why-a-surgeon-taught-a-non-doctor-to-do-brain-surgery.
56. Tony Bartelme and Catharina Hoek-Ellegala, *A Surgeon in the Village: an American Doctor Teaches Brain Surgery in Africa* (Boston, MA: Beacon Press, 2017).

57. Barry Schwartz, "Rethinking Work," *New York Times*, August 28, 2015, https://www.nytimes.com/2015/08/30/opinion/sunday/rethinking-work.html.
58. Nikola Tesla, ed. Samantha Hunt, *My Inventions and Other Writings* (Penguin Classics, 2011).

Chapter 10 – The Answer

1. Peter Joseph, "Zeigeist: Moving Forward," Video (Gentle Machine Productions, 2011).
2. Evan Ackerman, "After Mastering Singapore's Streets, NuTonomy's Robo-taxis Are Poised to Take on New Cities," *IEEE Spectrum*, December 29, 2016, https://spectrum.ieee.org/transportation/self-driving/after-mastering-singapores-streets-nutonomys-robotaxis-are-poised-to-take-on-new-cities.
3. "Virtual Singapore," Singapore Government, National Research Foundation, Prime Minister's Office, 2020, https://www.nrf.gov.sg/programmes/virtual-singapore.
4. Lori Zimmer, "The World's First Commercial Vertical Farm Opens in Singapore," *Inhabitat*, October 26, 2012, https://inhabitat.com/the-worlds-first-commercial-vertical-farm-opens-in-singapore/#:~:text=The%20dense%20metropolis%20of%20Singapore%20is%20now%20home,other%20day,%20which%20are%20sold%20in%20local%20supermarkets.
5. Ben Flanagan, "The maker of Dubai's flying taxi aims to set flight within the next three years," *Wired*, September 9, 2019, https://wired.me/science/transportation/dubai-drone-flying-taxis-volocopter/.
6. "How Much Time Do Americans Spend Behind the Wheel," US Department of Transportation, Volpe Center, December 11, 2017, https://www.volpe.dot.gov/news/how-much-time-do-americans-spend-behind-wheel.
7. "US Vehicle Registration Statistics," Hedges & Company, January 28, 2021, https://hedgescompany.com/automotive-market-research-statistics/auto-mailing-lists-and-marketing/.
8. Peter Joseph, *The New Human Rights Movement: Reinventing the Economy to End Oppression* (BenBella Books, March 21, 2017).
9. "Circular Cities," The Venus Project, Accessed March 6, 2021, https://www.thevenusproject.com/resource-based-economy/environment/circular-city/.
10. Ibid.
11. "New Food Balances," Food and Agriculture Organization of the United Nations, Accessed March 6, 2021, http://www.fao.org/faostat/en/?#data/FBS.
12. Eric Holt-Giménez et al., "We Already Grow Enough Food for 10 Billion People … and Still Can't End Hunger," *Journal of Sustainable Agriculture* 36, no. 6 (July 2012): pp. 595-598, https://doi.org/10.1080/10440046.2012.695331.
13. "Undernourished people in the world," Worldometer, Accessed March 6, 2021, https://www.worldometers.info/undernourishment/.

14. Dr. Francesco Branca, "Malnutrition is a world health crisis," World Health Organization, September 26, 2019, https://www.who.int/nutrition/topics/world-food-day-2019-malnutrition-world-health-crisis/en/.
15. Worldwatch Institute, "Globetrotting food will travel farther than ever this Thanksgiving," CropChoice, November 26, 2002, http://cropchoice.com/leadstry4fe2.html.
16. "How Far Does Your Food Travel to Get to Your Plate?," CUESA, February 5, 2018, https://cuesa.org/learn/how-far-does-your-food-travel-get-your-plate.
17. Mike Barrett, "How Far Does Your Food Travel? 4 Reasons to Choose Local," *Natural Society*, December 17, 2013, https://naturalsociety.com/how-far-food-travel-food-miles-1500-average/.
18. Hannah Ritchie, "Half of the world's habitable land is used for agriculture," Our World in Data, November 11, 2019, https://ourworldindata.org/global-land-for-agriculture.
19. Joseph, *New Human Rights*, p. 303.
20. Alexia Elejalde-Ruiz, "Many have tried and failed to make vertical indoor farming work. One Chicago entrepreneur thinks he can do it," *Chicago Tribune*, August 7, 2019, https://www.chicagotribune.com/business/ct-biz-backyard-fresh-farms-vertical-indoor-farm-20190807-j7bzv2axi5cfrfuvspqyht7xku-story.html.
21. David Roeder, "Vertical farm planned for former big-box store in Calumet City," *Chicago Sun Times*, July 15, 2020, https://chicago.suntimes.com/business/2020/7/15/21326440/vertical-farm-planned-for-former-big-box-store-in-calumet-city.
22. Ibid.
23. Vanessa Bates Ramirez, "Europe's Biggest Vertical Farm Will Be Powered by Wind and Planted by Robots," *Singularity Hub*, December 11, 2020, https://singularityhub.com/2020/12/11/europes-biggest-vertical-farm-will-be-powered-by-wind-and-planted-by-robots/?fbclid=IwAR1L24flSyfgEnkJGnOLrdYG2xjMFG_w0sRPStgnYFGVL8N524bFYSAxsH4.
24. Bina Venkataraman, "Country, the City Version: Farms in the Sky Gain New Interest," *The New York Times*, July 15, 2008, http://www.nytimes.com/2008/07/15/science/15farm.html?_r=0.
25. Joseph, *New Human Rights*, p. 306.
26. Alexandra Witze, "More than 2 billion people lack safe drinking water. That number will only grow," *Science News*, August 16, 2018, https://www.sciencenews.org/article/future-will-people-have-enough-water-live.
27. "2.1 billion people lack safe drinking water at home, more than twice as many lack safe sanitation," World Health Organization, UNICEF, July 12, 2017, https://www.who.int/news/item/12-07-2017-2-1-billion-people-lack-safe-drinking-water-at-home-more-than-twice-as-many-lack-safe-sanitation#:~:text=Some%203%20in%2010%20people%20worldwide%2C%20or%202.1,to%20a%20new%20report%20by%20WHO%20and%20UNICEF.
28. "Global Water Use," Worldometer, Accessed March 6, 2021, https://www.worldometers.info/water/.

# ENDNOTES


29. "How Much Water is There on Earth?," United States Geological Survey, Accessed March 6, 2021, https://www.usgs.gov/special-topic/water-science-school/science/how-much-water-there-earth?qt-science_center_objects=0#qt-science_center_objects.
30. Ibid.
31. M. E. Suss et al., "Water Desalination via Capacitive Deionization: What Is It and What Can We Expect from It?," *Energy & Environmental Science* 8, no. 8 (May 5, 2015): pp. 2296-2319, https://doi.org/10.1039/c5ee00519a.
32. "Terajoules of energy used," The World Counts, Accessed March 6, 2021, https://www.theworldcounts.com/challenges/climate-change/energy/global-energy-consumption.
33. Jefferson W. Tester et al., "The Future of Geothermal Energy: Impact of Enhanced Geothermal Systems (EGS) on the United States in the 21st Century," Massachusetts Institute of Technology, 2006, https://wayback.archive-it.org/all/20110310030646/http://geothermal.inel.gov/publications/future_of_geothermal_energy.pdf.
34. Ibid.
35. "Geothermal Power Plants – Minimizing Land Use and Impact," Office of Energy Efficiency & Renewable Energy, Energy.gov, Accessed March 6, 2021, https://www.energy.gov/eere/geothermal/geothermal-power-plants-minimizing-land-use-and-impact.
36. John W. Lund, "Characteristics, Development and Utilization of Geothermal Resources," Geo-Heat Center, Oregon Institute of Technology, 2007, https://oregontechsfstatic.azureedge.net/sitefinity-production/docs/default-source/geoheat-center-documents/publications/geothermal-resources/tp126.pdf?sfvrsn=7a078d60_2.
37. "Science & Climate Definitions: What is Solar Power?," University of California-Davis, Accessed March 6, 2021, https://climatechange.ucdavis.edu/climate-change-definitions/how-is-solar-power-generated/#:~:text=The%2070%20percent%20of%20solar%20energy%20the%20Earth,however%2C%20is%20where%20things%20get%20even%20more%20interesting.
38. "Solar Energy Basics," National Renewable Energy Laboratory, Accessed March 6, 2021, https://www.nrel.gov/research/re-solar.html.
39. Humza Aamir, "UAE powers on Noor Abu Dhabi, the world's largest solar project," *TechSpot*, July 1, 2019, https://www.techspot.com/news/80740-uae-powers-noor-abu-dhabi-world-largest-solar.html.
40. Peter W. Davidson, "Celebrating the Completion of the World's Largest Concentrating Solar Power Plant," US Department of Energy, Energy.gov, February 13, 2014, https://www.energy.gov/articles/celebrating-completion-worlds-largest-concentrating-solar-power-plant#:~:text=As%20the%20largest%20concentrating%20solar%20power%20%28CSP%29%20plant,Gas%20%26%20Electric%20and%20Southern%20California%20Edison%20Company.
41. Anikat, "How Many Solar Panels Would Be Needed to Power the World?," Ecotality, March 16, 2021, https://ecotality.com/how-many-solar-panels-to-power-the-

world/#:~:text=A%20total%20of%2051.42%20billion%20solar%20panels%20would,the%20calculated%20size%20of%2018TW%20of%20solar%20plants.

42. Bill Nussey, “How much solar would it take to power the U.S.?,” The Freeing Energy Project, July 6, 2018, https://www.freeingenergy.com/how-much-solar-would-it-take-to-power-the-u-s/.
43. Kasra Mohammadi et al., “Hybrid Concentrated Solar Power (CSP)-Desalination Systems: A Review,” *Desalination* 468 (October 15, 2019): p. 114083, https://doi.org/10.1016/j.desal.2019.114083.
44. Charles Q. Choi, “Studies Show Wind Power’s Massive Potential,” *Inside Science*, September 10, 2012, https://www.insidescience.org/news/studies-show-wind-powers-massive-potential.
45. “These are hot topics these days...,” The World Counts, Accessed March 6, 2021, https://www.theworldcounts.com/stories/current_world_energy_consumption.
46. M. Z. Jacobson and C. L. Archer, “Saturation Wind Power Potential and Its Implications for Wind Energy,” *Proceedings of the National Academy of Sciences* 109, no. 39 (September 10, 2012): pp. 15679-15684, https://doi.org/10.1073/pnas.1208993109.
47. Joseph, *New Human Rights*, p. 317.
48. “World Energy Resources: Hydro,” World Energy Council, 2013, https://www.worldenergy.org/assets/images/imported/2013/10/WER_2013_5_Hydro.pdf.
49. Joseph, *New Human Rights*, p. 323.
50. Jacque Fresco, *Designing the Future* (Venus, FL: The Venus Project, Inc., 2007), http://www.files.thevenusproject.com/hotlink-ok/designing_the_future_ebook/Jacque%20Fresco%20-%20Designing%20the%20Future.pdf.
51. Ambra Dreos et al., “Exploring the Potential of a Hybrid Device Combining Solar Water Heating and Molecular Solar Thermal Energy Storage,” *Energy & Environmental Science* 10, no. 3 (November 18, 2016): pp. 728-734, https://doi.org/10.1039/c6ee01952h.
52. Washington State University, "Water splitting advance holds promise for affordable renewable energy," *ScienceDaily*, March 9, 2020, www.sciencedaily.com/releases/2020/03/200309130034.htm.
53. Caroline Delbert, “The Dawn of Wireless Electricity Is Finally Upon Us. Here’s How New Zealand Will Do It,” *Popular Mechanics*, March 31, 2021, https://www.popularmechanics.com/science/a33522699/wireless-electricity-new-zealand/.
54. Hailu Yang et al., “A Preliminary Study on the Highway Piezoelectric Power Supply System,” International Journal of Pavement Research and Technology 11, no. 2 (March 2018): pp. 168-175, https://doi.org/10.1016/j.ijprt.2017.08.006.
55. Andrew Chesterton, “How Many Cars are there in the world?,” CarsGuide, August 6, 2018, https://www.carsguide.com.au/car-advice/how-many-cars-are-there-in-the-world-70629.
56. Alex Kopestinsky, “How Many People Die in Car Accidents?,” PolicyAdvice, February 27, 2021, https://policyadvice.net/car-insurance/insights/how-many-people-die-in-car-accidents/.

57. "Road Safety," World Health Organization, The Global Health Observatory, Accessed March 7, 2021, https://www.who.int/gho/road_safety/mortality/traffic_deaths_number/en/.
58. "All You Need To Know About the World's Fastest Train – L0 Series Maglev," Maglev.net, April 2, 2018, https://www.maglev.net/worlds-fastest-train-l0-series.
59. Mateja Kovacic, "What Will the Automated City of the Future Look Like?," *Smithsonian Magazine*, April 10, 2018, https://www.smithsonianmag.com/innovation/what-will-automated-city-future-look-like-180968760/#:~:text=%20What%20Will%20the%20Automated%20City%20of%20the,prototype%20of%20a%20state-controlled%20smart%20city.%20More%20.
60. Ed Blazina, "U.S. Department of Transportation Posts Hyperloop Framework," Government Technology, July 27, 2020, https://www.govtech.com/transportation/US-Department-of-Transportation-Posts-Hyperloop-Framework.html.
61. Fresco, *Designing*, p. 35.
62. "Unmanned Cargo Ship Development Alliance," Adimar Shipping, Inc., September 26, 2017, https://www.adimarships.com/unmanned-cargo-ship-development-alliance/#:~:text=The%20Houston%2C%20Texas-based%20rating%20company%20called%20the%20American,making%2C%20autonomous%20navigation%2C%20environmental%20perception%20and%20remote%20control.
63. "The Good, the Bad and the Ugly: Unmanned Ships," Hellenic Shipping News Worldwide, January 28, 2020, https://www.hellenicshippingnews.com/the-good-the-bad-and-the-ugly-unmanned-ships/.
64. "OSHA Data & Statistics: Commonly Used Statistics," United States Department of Labor, Occupational Safety and Health Administration, Accessed March 7, 2021, https://www.osha.gov/data/commonstats.
65. Mohamed Osmani, "Construction Waste," in Waste, *ScienceDirect*, 2011, https://www.sciencedirect.com/topics/earth-and-planetary-sciences/construction-waste.
66. Icon 3-D House Printing, Accessed March 4, 2021, https://www.iconbuild.com/.
67. Contour Crafting Technology, Accessed March 4, 2021, https://contourcrafting.com/.
68. D-Shape Project, Accessed March 4, 2021, https://d-shape.com/company/.
69. Caroline Delbert, "Watch a Bricklaying Robot Set a New Lay Speed Record," *Popular Mechanics*, June 5, 2020, https://www.popularmechanics.com/technology/robots/a32772384/bricklaying-robot-record-video/.
70. Michael Bonani et al., "marXbot," Biorobotics Laboratory, Miniature Mobile Robots Group, Accessed March 4, 2021, http://mobots.epfl.ch/marxbot.html.
71. SJET 4-D Printing Technology, Massachusetts Institute of Technology, Accessed March 4, 2021, http://www.sjet.us/MIT_4D PRINTING.html.
72. "Home of the Future," Videoneat, 2012, https://www.videoneat.com/documentaries/3432/home-future/.
73. Fresco, *Designing*, p. 46.

74. Ibid.
75. Corning Display Glass, Accessed March 4, 2021, https://www.corning.com/worldwide/en/products/display-glass.html.
76. "Home of the Future," Videoneat.
77. "We don't stop playing because we grow old, we grow old because we stop playing," has been attributed to a number of historical figures, including Benjamin Franklin and George Bernard Shaw.
78. Fuji Kindergarten, Accessed March 4, 2021, https://fujikids.jp/en/.
79. Jamie Barret and Michael Jordan, "Failure," Commercial (Nike, 1997), https://www.chicagotribune.com/news/ct-xpm-1997-05-19-9705190096-story.html.
80. Pharmacy, "The Rise of Digital Pharmacies—How Will This Shape the Future of Pharmacy?," Infowerks, July 21, 2020, https://infowerks.com/rise-digital-pharmacies/.
81. Mike Murphy, "The FDA has approved the first drug made by a 3D printer," Quartz, August 3, 2015, https://qz.com/471030/the-fda-has-approved-the-first-drug-made-by-a-3d-printer/.
82. Steven Millward, "In Singapore, robots are now leading workouts for the elderly," *Tech in Asia*, October 5, 2015, https://www.techinasia.com/singapore-robot-instructor-for-elderly-people-robocoach.
83. David Szondy, "Robear robot care bear designed to serve Japan's aging population," New Atlas, February 26, 2015, https://newatlas.com/robear-riken/36219/#:~:text=Robear%20is%20based%20on%20Riken%27s%20Robot%20for%20Interactive,It%20was%20developed%20by%20the%20RIKEN-SRK%20Collaboration%20.
84. TUG Autonomous Robot, Aethon, Accessed March 7, 2021, https://aethon.com/mobile-robots-for-healthcare/.
85. Eliza Strickland, "Autonomous Robot Surgeon Bests Humans in World First," *IEEE Spectrum*, May 4, 2016, https://spectrum.ieee.org/the-human-os/robotics/medical-robots/autonomous-robot-surgeon-bests-human-surgeons-in-world-first.
86. "About da Vinci Systems," Intuitive, Accessed March 4, 2021, https://www.davincisurgery.com/da-vinci-systems/about-da-vinci-systems.
87. Stacy Kish, "Get Ready: Your Future Surgery May Use An Automated Robotic Drill," University of Utah, May 1, 2017, https://unews.utah.edu/get-ready-your-future-surgery-may-use-an-automated-robotic-drill/.
88. Jack Carfagno, "Top 5 Robotic Surgery Systems," DocWire News, May 15, 2019, https://www.docwirenews.com/future-of-medicine/top-5-robotic-surgery-systems/.
89. "Organ Donation Statistics," Organdonor.gov, Health Resources & Services Administration, US Department of Health and Human Services, Accessed March 7, 2021, https://www.organdonor.gov/statistics-stories/statistics.html.
90. Dr. Francis Collins, "Progress Toward 3D Printed Human Organs," NIH Director's Blog, June 20, 2019, https://directorsblog.nih.gov/2019/06/20/progress-toward-3d-printed-human-organs/.

# ENDNOTES


91. "3D Printing In Healthcare: Where Are We In 2021? (Updated)," AMFG, August 30, 2019, https://amfg.ai/2019/08/30/3d-printing-in-healthcare-where-are-we-in-2019/#.
92. "The Ultimate List of What We Can 3D Print in Medicine And Healthcare!," The Medical Futurist, April 11, 2017, https://medicalfuturist.com/3d-printing-in-medicine-and-healthcare/.
93. "Global Water Use," Worldometer, Accessed March 7, 2021, https://www.worldometers.info/water/#:~:text=The%20data%20on%20water%20consumption%20in%20the%20world,20%25%20for%20industry%20and%2010%25%20for%20domestic%20use.


APPENDIX A


1. "U.S. Invasion and Occupation of Haiti, 1915-34," US Department of State, The Office of Electronic Information, Bureau of Public Affairs, Accessed March 8, 2021, https://2001-2009.state.gov/r/pa/ho/time/wwi/88275.htm.
2. P. J. Hudson, "The National City Bank of New York and Haiti, 1909 - 1922," *Radical History Review* 2013, no. 115 (January 1, 2013): pp. 91-114, https://doi.org/10.1215/01636545-1724733.
3. Westenley Alcenat, "The Case for Haitian Reparations," Jacobin Magazine, January 14, 2017, https://www.jacobinmag.com/2017/01/haiti-reparations-france-slavery-colonialism-debt/.
4. Peter James Hudson, "Where Does Haiti Fit in Citigroup's Corporate History," *Bloomberg*, June 13, 2012, https://www.bloomberg.com/opinion/articles/2012-06-13/on-citigroup-s-anniversary-don-t-forget-its-brutal-past.
5. Michael L. Krenn, Ph.D., "National City Bank in Haiti," Florida International University, Accessed March 7, 2021, http://islandluminous.fiu.edu/part07-slide12.html.
6. "U.S. Invasion and Occupation of Haiti, 1915-34," US Department of State, The Office of Electronic Information, Bureau of Public Affairs, Accessed March 8, 2021, https://2001-2009.state.gov/r/pa/ho/time/wwi/88275.htm.
7. Brian Weinstein and Aaron Segal, *Haiti: Political Failures, Cultural Successes* (Praeger Publishers, February 15, 1984), p. 29.
8. James Weldon Johnson, "Self-Determining Haiti," *The Nation*, August 28, 1920, https://www.thenation.com/article/self-determining-haiti/.
9. Langley, *Banana Wars*, pp. 61-62.
10. Ivan Musicant, *The Banana Wars: A History of United States Military Intervention in Latin America from the Spanish-American War to the Invasion of Panama* (New York: MacMillan Publishing Co., 1990), pp. 309-315.
11. Ibid., pp. 137-156.
12. Tim Merrill, "Nicaragua: A Country Study," US Library of Congress, Federal Research Division (Washington D.C.: 1994), pp. 19-24, https://tile.loc.gov/storage-services/master/frd/frdcstdy/ni/nicaraguacountry00merr_0/nicaraguacountry00merr_0.pdf.

13. The Editors of Encyclopaedia Britannica, "José Santos Zelaya: president of Nicaruaga," Encyclopaedia Britannica, Accessed March 7, 2021, https://www.britannica.com/biography/Jose-Santos-Zelaya.
14. "Zelaya Broke Fait to Kill Americans," *The New York Times*, November 23, 1909, https://www.nytimes.com/1909/11/23/archives/zelaya-broke-faith-to-kill-americans-gs-holland-says-his-forces.html.
15. Langley, *Banana Wars*, pp. 63-64.
16. Ibid., p. 67.
17. Benjamin T. Harrison, "Woodrow Wilson and Nicaragua," Caribbean Quarterly, vol. 51, no. 1 (Taylor & Francis, Ltd., March, 2005), pp. 25–36, https://www.jstor.org/stable/40654491.
18. Langley, *Banana Wars*, pp. 68-74.
19. "Interoceanic Canal (Bryan-Chamorro Treaty)," US Library of Congress, 39 Stat. 1661, Treaty Series 624, June 19, 1916, https://www.loc.gov/law/help/us-treaties/bevans/b-ni-ust000010-0379.pdf.
20. Musicant, *Banana Wars*, pp. 309-315.

APPENDIX B

1. Maslow, *Motivation*.
2. Ancel Keys, Josef Brožek, Austin Henschel, Olaf Mickelsen, and Henry Longstreet Taylor, "The Biology of Human Starvation," Vol. 1. pp. xxxii + 764, Vol. 2, pp. viii + 765-1386. (St. Paul, MN: University of Minnesota Press; London: Oxford University Press, 1950.).
3. Clark L. Hull, *A behavior system: An introduction to behavior theory concerning the individual organism* (Greenwood Press, January 1, 1974).

# ABOUT THE AUTHOR

I mean, what more is there to say about Travis that hasn't already been said in this text. He's an asshole. A delusional asshole. Plain and simple. Let's just hope he never punishes us with his hack writing or paper-thin thoughts ever again.

**bookthepit.com**
**thepitbook2021@gmail.com**

Made in the USA
Monee, IL
24 March 2025

14510954R00262